CONTEMPORARY VISIONS IN TIBETAN STUDIES

CONTEMPORARY VISIONS IN TIBETAN STUDIES

Proceedings of the
FIRST INTERNATIONAL SEMINAR OF YOUNG TIBETOLOGISTS

EDITED BY

Brandon Dotson
Kalsang Norbu Gurung
Georgios Halkias
Tim Myatt

With the Assistance of Paddy Booz

Published by Serindia Publications, Inc.

First edition, 2009

Serindia Publications, Inc.
PO Box 10335
Chicago, Illinois 60610 USA
info@serindia.com
www.serindia.com

ISBN: 978-1-932476-45-3

Typeset by Toby Matthews, toby.matthews@ntlworld.com
Printed and bound in Hong Kong

Library of Congress Cataloging-in-Publication Data

International Seminar of Young Tibetologists (1st : 2007 : University of London)
Contemporary visions in Tibetan studies : proceedings of the First International Seminar of Young Tibetologists / edited by Brandon Dotson ... [et al.]. -- 1st ed.
p. cm.
Selection of papers from seminar convened by Tim Myatt and Brandon Dotson at School of Oriental and African Studies, University of London, Aug. 9-13, 2007.
Includes bibliographical references and index.
ISBN 978-1-932476-45-3 (hardcover)
1. Tibet (China)--Civilization--Congresses. 2. Tibet (China)--History--Congresses. 3. Tibet (China)--Religion--Congresses. 4. Tibetologists--Congresses. 5. Tibet (China)--Study and teaching (Higher)--Congresses. I. Dotson, Brandon, 1978- II. Title.

DS785.A1I59 2007
951'.5--dc22

2009027683

The International Seminar of Young Tibetologists is supported by

Arts & Humanities
Research Council

Contents

PART TWO
HISTORY, CULTURE AND RELIGION

Acknowledgements

The time and energy of a great many people has gone into the founding of the International Seminar of Young Tibetologists (ISYT), the convening of the first ISYT conference, and the publication of this volume of conference proceedings. The editors and conveners would like to extend their thanks to Dibyesh Anand, Chelsie Anttila, Anthony Aris, Robert Beer, Peter D'Sena, Clare Davies, Yangdon Dhondup, Heidi Fjeld, Tsering Dhundup Gonkatsang, Clare Harris, Tina Harris, John Harrison, Michel Hockx, Michael Hutt, Lama Jabb, Christian Jahoda, the Rev. Father David Johnson, Thomas Kauffmann, Rob Mayer, Martin Mills, Saul Mullard, Ulrich Pagel, Tsering Passang, Charles Ramble, Joona Repo, Mary Rodeghier, Alexey Smirnov, the Tibet Foundation, Pema Tsho, Ben Walker, Kalsang Yeshe, Ronit Yoeli-Tlalim and Zinta Zommers.

The ISYT is thankful for the generous financial support it has received from the Aris Trust Centre for Tibetan and Himalayan Studies, the Sub-Faculties of East Asia Area Studies and South and Inner Asia Area Studies of the Oriental Institute, University of Oxford and from His Grace the Duke of Marlborough. None of this would have been possible without the financial backing of the Arts and Humanities Research Council of Great Britain, which supported the ISYT with a Research Networks and Workshops Grant that allowed, among other things, for the participation at the conference of a dozen scholars from Tibet, China, India and Nepal.

We are also grateful to Shane Suvikapakornkul at Serindia Publications, to Toby Matthews for his excellent work typesetting the book, and in particular to Paddy Booz for his proofreading and indexing work and for shepherding the book through the publication process.

Preface

The present volume is a selection of papers presented at the first International Seminar of Young Tibetologists, convened by Tim Myatt and Brandon Dotson at the School of Oriental and African Studies, University of London, 9–13 August 2007. The International Seminar of Young Tibetologists (ISYT) is in many ways an attempt to return to the origins of the international Tibetan studies community, its intimacy and broad spectrum of interests. In this respect the ISYT consciously adapts in its name the title of one of the early, highly successful Tibetan studies conferences, the Seminar of Young Tibetologists, convened by Martin Brauen and Per Kværne in Zürich in 1977.

That seminar was followed by another meeting in Oxford in 1979, convened by Michael Aris and Nobel Peace Prize laureate Aung San Suu Kyi, which marked the formal beginning of the International Association for Tibetan Studies (IATS). The IATS seminar has since been held every three to five years, and, with the end of the Csöma de Kőrös conferences, it became the premier conference in the field of Tibetan studies. With its success came sustained growth, and by the time of the fifth seminar (the 1977 Seminar of Young Tibetologists has been awarded—wrongly, some contend—status as the first IATS seminar) in Narita, it was impractical for participants to attend every paper, a state of affairs that is still bemoaned today.

One natural consequence of the success of Tibetan studies has been a tendency to fragment into sub-fields. Smaller meetings now proliferate, taking as their focus increasingly specific topics that are defined temporally, spatially or by their problem-oriented approach. This is also replicated at the IATS seminars through the organization of the conference into panels that serve essentially the same purpose as small conferences. On the one hand, this is a matter of practicality and convenience, and on the other hand, it is driven by a fundamental question facing Tibetan studies as an area-studies discipline. As Chris Vasantkumar discusses in his contribution to the present volume, one of the dominant discourses within area studies over the past several years has been a movement towards problem-oriented approaches and away from an older ideal of wide-ranging knowledge of a geographically defined area. In the case of Tibetan studies, a strong imperative for preservation and documentation has fed into the tendency to assert a sort of Tibetan exceptionalism, but there is little doubt, as Janet Gyatso remarked in her presidential address at the 10th IATS seminar in Oxford, that "the pendulum is swinging back the other way."[1] While this trend is part of the creative growth of the field, one side effect has been a compartmentalization into sub-fields that risks a loss of any overarching perspective. Again, lest we fall once more into the old trap of Tibetan exceptionalism, let us assert from the outset that this soul-searching pervades all of area studies, and that we have in many ways arrived late in the game, since similar issues have been debated for decades in the field of social and cultural anthropology.[2]

In concert with the growth of Tibetan studies as an academic field, the shape of the field has changed as China, in the 1980s, opened Tibet to foreign researchers. This development transformed the field, and ushered in a new wave of Tibetan studies researchers who tend to value dialogue and field research over traditional philological studies. The result can be described as a generation gap in Tibetan studies. The younger researchers nearly all speak Tibetan and have contacts in Tibet, Nepal, India or Bhutan, and many of them treat contemporary issues ranging from development studies to modern art. The older generation, due in large part to the circumstances prevailing in past decades, is less likely to speak Tibetan, and its work tends to be text-based. The new wave of Tibetan studies still attends to traditional concerns such as philology, linguistics, historical research and religious studies, but there is a distinct shift towards the study of contemporary Tibet, its identity and its future.[3] While this is an oversimplification of the situation, and can be easily exploded with a few well-chosen counterexamples, I doubt that many within the field would dispute that this characterization holds within it some truth.

By harnessing the creative energy of this new generation of scholars who have been produced in dialogue with Tibetans, Chinese, Indians, Nepalese, Bhutanese and so on, the ISYT is perhaps able to lend some perspective to the field as a whole at a time when Tibetan studies finds itself increasingly compartmentalized. Beyond being a simple pulse-taking exercise, there is also the potential to create here a space in which contemporary, creative approaches to the overall field can be articulated and tested. This is an ongoing process, but it is evident already in many of the contributions to this volume.

The generalist orientation of the ISYT allows participants to attend a wide variety of papers and to reflect both on their unity and on their dissonance. This lends itself to self-reflection on the discipline of Tibetan studies itself and the viability of the area-studies model upon which it is predicated, as can be seen in Chris Vasantkumar's chapter. Problem-oriented research that pursues topics outside of the confines of the Tibetan cultural area can also be found here, particularly in Anne-Sophie Bentz's discussion of the "Tibetan example" of diaspora alongside other diasporas and the relevance of the Tibetan example to diaspora theory, and in George FitzHerbert's study on the (in)applicability of oral-formulaic theory to recitations of the Gesar Epic. We also find differing methodological approaches to Tibetan material culture in Diana Altner's chapter on Tibetan fishermen and in the respective chapters by Emilia Róża Sułek and Michelle Olsgard Stewart on caterpillar fungus, its social transformative effects and its management.

Elsewhere, Tibetan tradition is scrutinized, sometimes upheld and sometimes revised. Such is the case in Elijah Ary's analysis of the invented tradition of Tsongkhapa's two main disciples, Tsering Dawa's fascinating and far-ranging discussion of the origins of polo, Marc-Henri Deroche's presentation of a 16th-century source of the *ris med* movement, Beri Jigme Wangyal's discussion of the tradition of Tibet's prehistoric rulers, Kadri Raudsepp's reflections on the Tibetan polemical tradition and the authorship of the *sNgags log sun 'byin*, traditionally attributed to Chag lo tsā ba Chos rje dpal, and in Kalsang Norbu Gurung's analysis of the various ways in which Bonpo tradition has deployed the figure of Kong tse (Confucius) and how this has developed over time.

Another prevailing theme in many of the papers is the intimate connection between Tibetans within and outside of Tibet, and the various conflicting elements that go into the creation of modern identities. This is evident in Joona Repo's discussion of Tibetan religious architecture in India, which has generally tended towards cultural conservatism. Similarly, Georgios Halkias explores historical threads in Himalayan material culture and finds a continuity of transnational identity in Tibetan Buddhist–Hindu murals executed in present-day Kinnaur, in lieu of murals once depicting the 1679 trading treaty between Tibet and the Himalayan Hindu principality of Bashahr.

While political and cultural history is present in most of the chapters, it is the central focus in Brandon Dotson's considerations of the implicit and explicit power dynamics of Tibetan dynastic marriage during the imperial period, Dobis Tsering Gyal's presentation of the roles of the main state oracles under the dGa' ldan pho brang government of the Dalai Lamas (1642–1959), Alice Travers' analysis of risk management in the demotion and dismissals of officials towards the end of the same period (1885–1952) and Tsering Choekyi's precis of the problematic relationship between Taiwan, the PRC and the Tibetan government in exile.

Taken together, these chapters, as the first fruits of the ISYT, bear witness to a diversity and vitality of scholarship that will continue to characterize the field as we put forward new agendas and come to terms with new interdisciplinary developments.

In a sense, however, there is nothing particularly "*nouvelle*" about this *nouvelle vague* of Tibetan studies: each generation, faced with a new set of circumstances, generates new creative responses, and so it has always been. By the time that the next ISYT conference is convened, some of its members will no longer qualify as "young": per admittedly arbitrary ISYT guidelines, members shall be no more than six years out of a PhD or no more than six years into an academic post. Like the mythic Tibetan kings, who, according to tradition, were succeeded by their sons upon their reaching maturity, ISYT members shall be replaced by a new generation of scholars. So, just as we cry "The king is dead! Long live the king!" so the institution of the ISYT shall remain as a venue constantly on the crest of the Tibetan studies zeitgeist.

NOTES

1 Janet Gyatso, "Presidential Address, Tenth Seminar of the International Association for Tibetan Studies, Oxford, 2003," *Journal of the International Association for Tibetan Studies* 1 (2005), 5.

2 For an engaging take on the situation facing Himalayan ethnography, and a call for a comparative approach, see Michael Oppitz, "Close-Up and Wide-Angle. On Comparative Ethnography in the Himalayas – and Beyond. The Mahesh Chandra Regmi Lecture, Dec. 15th 2006," *European Bulletin of Himalayan Research* 31 (2007), 155–71.

3 These trends, including the growing numbers of modern Tibetan studies researchers at the IATS conferences, are discussed in Robert Barnett, "Preface." In *Tibetan Modernities: Notes from the Field on Cultural and Social Change. Proceedings of the Tenth Seminar of the International Association for Tibetan Studies, Oxford, 2003*, ed. Robert Barnett and Ronald Schwartz (managing editor: Charles Ramble) (Leiden: Brill, 2008), xi–xxi.

PART ONE

Engagements with Modernities: Tibet, China and Diaspora

1

Tibet Incidental to Tibetan Studies?

Views from Various Margins

CHRIS VASANTKUMAR

In this essay, I propose to critically explore the issue of the centrality of Tibet to Tibetan studies. This may seem like a strange turn of phrase, but I will explain what I mean presently. Let me begin by recounting two moments from the 2006 meeting of the International Association of Tibetan Studies (IATS) in Königswinter, Germany, which provided inspiration for the ideas below. First, the original impetus for this paper was born at the meeting of Tibet anthropologists at IATS, where much time was devoted to bemoaning the inability of our sub-field to keep up with the theoretical and topical advances of more mainstream anthropology. One insight to emerge from the discussion was that a key factor in the lack of give and take between Tibet anthropology and the rest of the discipline was the general trend over the last two decades in mainstream anthropology to replace area studies based paradigms with more problem-oriented or theoretically inclined work. Tibet anthropology, intent on remaining primarily "about" Tibet, has for better or worse remained wedded to the study of its particular area.

To assist Tibet anthropology into a richer articulation with broader disciplinary trends, and to help open up received notions of precisely what "we" are "about" to question, I want to explore the political and intellectual stakes of anthropological inquiries that deal with "Tibetan" topics or peoples but which are not primarily about Tibet. Specifically, I want to explore the issue of what a marginal project – studying Tibetan populations of Amdo/northwest China and their trans-Himalayan peregrinations – can teach us about the essentializing assumptions that underlie many, though not all, Tibetological approaches.

While one would be hard pressed to argue that Amdo is marginal to Tibetan studies, the Amdowas who move between China and India negotiate marginal terrain on multiple levels, moving between nation-states, navigating the boundaries of language, dialect group, religious belief and regional culture. Such migrations can be undertaken for many reasons, from a commitment to Tibetan freedom, to a drive to acquire marketable skills such as English proficiency, to a desire to relieve the tedium and alienation of daily life in a context where economic and cultural opportunities are in short supply. In all of these cases, migration to India can impart critical perspective, not only with regard to fictions of Chinese nationalism, but also concerning the limits and difficulties of Tibetanness in exile. Such perspective can supplement perceptions of China as generally repressive of Tibetan language and culture (even if this repression is highly variable by region) and as imposing uniform Han-centric educational schema on its diverse minority populations, with an awareness of the limits of life in exile communities in India. In such a light, the latter can be seen as alternately too tied to the preservation of Buddhist monasticism at the expense of modernizing Tibet's education system, or as places in which religious practice and Tibetan culture more generally have become a realm of surfaces that can match neither the "sincerity" nor "humility" of such practices of Tibetan communities "in China."

Over the course of my fieldwork in Amdo and Dharamsala, I have encountered Tibetans who feel marginal in both places, at home in neither China nor India. How to figure these betweennesses without reducing them to some sort of unitary, essentialized marginality in the context of a Tibetan studies that remains emphatically, if multiply, centered on something called Tibet is one of the pressing challenges of the field, a challenge that recent trends in anthropology may help to resolve. The potential of anthropology to contribute to this endeavor may be somewhat limited by the ambivalent reception of anthropologists (especially theoretically inclined ones) among certain sectors of the Tibetanist community.

The second moment from the IATS meeting, related below, should make clear that anthropologists of Tibet write from multiple margins themselves, margins both of their discipline and of Tibetan studies itself.

Soon after my arrival in Königswinter, I was chatting about the relationship between anthropology and Tibetan studies with one of the hosts of the conference. This individual, who shall remain nameless, was rather more resigned than sanguine about the growing numbers of anthropologists in the Tibetan studies field. In fact, in an unguarded moment, this person likened their increasing presence at recent IATS meetings to the increasing presence of Muslim migrants in Germany. "We don't know where they come from but every time there are more and more of them." The most charitable reading of this analogy is that it was a poorly executed attempt at humor. Less charitable and more interesting readings would highlight the uncomfortable parallels between anthropologists at the IATS gathering and Muslims in Germany as alien presences with inscrutable cultural practices of their own that cause problems for traditional assumptions about the nature of the polities to which they have migrated and, more troublingly for purists, show no signs of going away. While, in principle, both groups of migrants are supposed to be welcome in their new domiciles, in practice, the condition of Muslims in Europe and of anthropologists in Tibetan studies is fraught with the sorts of tensions that accompany perceived impingements on what is thought to be the proper terrain of longer-term residents. In subtitling this paper "views from *various* margins," I seek to highlight the multiplicity and incommensurability of both the Tibetan margins that we seek to inscribe and the disciplinary margins that we must negotiate within the academy.

In my own work, I have felt a sense of poaching on the terrain of Tibetanists rather acutely, given that I initially positioned myself as an anthropologist of China, that I conducted my dissertation research mostly in Chinese and English and that my Amdo-ge remains a work in progress. Still, I think coming at things from this angle has given me some critical perspective on what studying Tibet might mean in a multi-disciplinary context. Anthropology these days is devoted not simply to recording cultural diversity but to opening up the terms of the debate themselves to critical interrogation. In this light, I suggest a way to convert the threat anthropology seems to pose to the purity of Tibetan studies into something more promising. This would be to reconcile recent movements away from area-focused research in anthropological practice with more religiously, philologically or literarily oriented modes of studying something called Tibet.[1] This in turn involves paying attention to what we think we are referring to when we talk about studying "Tibet."

To do so I want to return to the issue of area-based versus problem-oriented research I raised earlier. Tibetan studies did not precisely emerge out of the Cold War area studies paradigm that developed in the American academy in the aftermath of World War II. For one thing, America itself has until recently arguably remained firmly on the periphery of the Tibet field. For another, Tibetanists in America have always operated on the margins of more geopolitically "relevant" areas. One could argue, though, that Tibetan studies' pulling together of multiple disciplines in an attempt to amass knowledge about a culturally or territorially defined subject has given it something of an area studies cast. Certainly some of the problems that Tibetanists are currently confronted with will be familiar to others who are trying to rethink (or, alternatively, preserve) what are by now traditional assumptions about the relationship between culture, territory and academic inquiry.

Early essays in an area studies vein, such as Ruth Benedict's wartime appraisal of Japanese culture, *The Chrysanthemum and the Sword*,[2] were themselves built upon preexisting notions of the intimate relationship between culture and territory as encapsulated in Wissler's notion of the culture area. Moves towards the consolidation of an area studies framework were furthered by early Cold War era initiatives that provided military funding for "producing knowledge on areas of the world important to the United States Security."[3] While the official links to national defense soon fell by the wayside, the particular paradigm of approaching and funding research through the lens of "politically defined geographic areas"[4] has persisted until the present. It has become commonplace to use the phrase area studies to denote scholarly approaches based on a particular conflation of territory, culture and geopolitics. While initially conceived as part of an interdisciplinary assault on "the compartmentalized learning"[5] that characterized the mid-century American academy, the association of a place, a culture and a representative polity (or set of polities) has ossified into a compartmentalism that is just as tenacious, if not more so, as previous academic divisions of labor.

When it comes to area studies, Tibet is in some respects the exception that proves the rule – since the loss of self-rule in 1951, it has been an area without or, rather, with more than one geographical referent. While the focus of Tibetan studies has been split between the lands of historic Tibetan political control (however amorphous and shifting these may have been) and the new spatial contours of the Tibetan diaspora in India, Nepal and the West, the discipline, despite these territorial complications, has not been immune to area studies paradigms that conflate territory, culture and polity. The degree to which this is true is illustrated by the fact that most scholars of Tibet think that when we refer to Tibet and Tibetanness there is some sort of central underlying logic of territory, language, culture or history that draws together the manifold beliefs and practices that are swept together under these unifying rubrics. An illustration of this thought in practice is Matthew Kapstein's suggestion that "... though local, tribal, and sectarian identities often play a divisive role in the Tibetan world, they presuppose, and in some respects also maintain, the very fabric of that world."[6]

In his concluding reflections on his co-edited volume on religious revival in contemporary Tibet, Kapstein attempts to outline the factors that both contribute to senses of pan-Tibetan identity and reassure scholars at Tibetan studies conferences that they are all on some level speaking about the same "thing." "Besides the Tibetan folkloric notion that Tibetans are those who speak the Tibetan language and eat tsampa (parched barley flour) as their staple food," he writes,

> one can point to the geographic coherence of the Tibetan world ..., the sense of a shared history among the Tibetan people, and their use of a common literary language ... as well as to aspects of genealogy, myth and folklore, in addition to Tibetan religion per se.

> And Tibetan religion, it must be stressed, reinforces the Tibetan sense of identity in part by engendering a shared culture in many areas of life that in postindustrial, secularized societies are no longer treated as religious.[7]

While this is a seductive vision of a culturally unified, uniformly believing, preindustrial Tibetan people, on closer inspection it rapidly starts to break down. Formal geographic coherence of the so-called Tibetan world is small consolation to Tibetan migrants who cross highly policed and topographically perilous national borders. The notion of geographic coherence is also a poor match for the 'scale and scatter'[8] of the Tibetan diaspora in the West and elsewhere. While the events of the last half century have done much to forge a sense of shared history among diverse Tibetan populations, it would be difficult, except in retrospect, to construct a unified historical narrative that would encompass all communities that today self-identify as Tibetan.

Kapstein's appeal to the centering function of Tibetan religion is also problematic. Non-believers and arguably even Bon practitioners are incidental[9] to this implicitly Buddhist formulation. Further, religion for Tibetans is posed as an alternative to the disenchanted, postindustrial world that we inhabit. We need to acknowledge that the fabric of the so-called Tibetan world is inextricably entangled with the fibers of multiple symbolic and political universes, including "our" own. Further, notions of a unitary or simple Tibetan sense of identity need to be pluralized. This means acknowledging difference within Tibetan communities as something generative rather than attempting to conceal it or explain it away like some sort of family shame. By getting beyond these orientalizing formulations, we can begin to find a place for less narrowly constrained visions of Tibetanness and move from essentializing visions of the Tibetan world to Tibetans in the world.

Three brief conversations from my research can make this point more concretely. In June 2006, I had dinner with a monk friend in his quarters within the precincts of Labrang Monastery in Gansu Province, China. After we finished eating, we started talking about a trip he had taken to central Tibet in the preceding months. As he showed me pictures of himself and his classmates from the provincial Buddhist Studies Institute (*foxueyuan*) grinning in People's Liberation Army (PLA) overcoats at the top of the Tanggu pass and posing in front of the Potala Palace, Tashilhunpo, Sera, and Sakya monasteries and other eminent edifices of Ü-Tsang, I commented on his calling these landmarks by their Chinese names (*budala gong, zhashilunbu si, sela si, sajia si*). Realizing what he had been doing, he became self-conscious, and our conversation quickly veered into a discussion of dialectical differences between Amdo and Lhasa Tibetan as a complicating factor in attempts to standardize terms.

My monk friend began this portion of the conversation, conducted entirely in Chinese, by contrasting the role of *Putonghua* ("common language") in standardizing Chinese with the lack of such a standard in Tibetan. "Yes, this is a problem for us," he began. "Which one should we speak? You could make the case for *Lasa hua*; after all, Lhasa is the capital." Yet amongst Tibetan speakers in China, no figure or institution has enough power to get people to speak a single standard language. Despite the inability of Tibetan populations in China (*Zhongguo*) to agree on a single, standard language accessible to all, my friend still stressed that when it comes to Tibetan ethnicity, linguistic competence is even more important than religion. Even as he acknowledged the existence of non-Buddhist, even atheist Tibetans, he doubted whether Tibetans who are unable to speak Tibetan are Tibetan at all. After all, he remarked, "neither religious belief nor Buddhism are fundamentally linked to ethnic (*minzu*) identity." To rephrase Melville, what my friend was saying is that one can be Buddhist in any kind of skin. Being a good person is not tied to ethnic identity. Language, by contrast, was for him central to *minzu* identity. If the language changes, he argued, the *minzu* will certainly change as well, with the ultimate possible result of a loss of distinctiveness (*minzu tezheng*). As an example, he cited the present condition of the *Man*, or Manchu, who went, in his words, from a minority nationality turned emperor (*guowang*) to a people who no longer know their language or their script and have suffered accordingly. Of course not every monk would suggest that religion is not integral to Tibetanness, but the fact that my friend did just that should not be ignored because it does not fit with essentialized notions of what Tibetan culture should be.

The second conversation I relate took place in July 2007 in Dharamsala. I was talking over dinner at Nick's Italian Café with Dorje, an Amdowa poet who I had first met in Labrang in the winter of 2003. Since last seeing him in the summer of 2006, he had grown increasingly frustrated at life in exile. The substance of Dorje's critique of the current situation has to do with the conservatism of the Tibetan exile community. Specifically, while he praises the Dalai Lama, he reserves nothing but contempt for the leader's staff and for the officials he has had to deal with at the library, who forced him to give up his researches into Tibetan history. Further, he is frustrated by the focus of the educational system. He laments its excessive emphasis on Buddhism, which he says is good for the heart but isn't useful "in society," and for emphasizing tradition at the expense of modernization. He has, he says, basically given up on traditional Tibetan culture. As far as he is concerned, it is on its last legs in China and is, anyway, not an adequate basis for real Tibetan self-determination.

While acknowledging the potential spiritual benefits of Buddhism and repeatedly professing his respect for the Dalai Lama, he suggests that Tibetans need other things – jobs, freedom of expression, technical expertise, modernization – before they need salvation. He reserves special contempt for monks. While acknowledging that there are some sincere, humble ones out there, he suggests that many more are motivated by money, prestige and the good life rather than by religious motives. He laments all the money that has been lavished on Tibetan Buddhist study centers in Europe and America, arguing that that money could be put to better use in improving the material conditions of Tibetans living in the People's Republic of China (PRC).

Some unguarded comments reveal the depth of his anti-clericalism. "The Cultural Revolution was a good idea. I like the ideas behind it,"[10] he began. The problem with it, he explained, was that it was conducted by the Chinese, not by the Tibetans themselves. Seeing my surprise at this remark, he elaborated:

> ... during the last Kalachakra, the Dalai Lama said that accidents are important to people's lives. Without accidents there can be no change and without change there can be no progress. One thousand years ago in Tibetan history, there was a king named Langdarma. At that time, Buddhist monks had easy lives, they had patrons in every home and they had lots of money. But the Tibetan people were very poor, didn't know about education, didn't know about any other countries.

The monks benefited at the people's expense. But Langdarma changed that, he took care of the monks (here Dorje makes slashing motions across his wrists) and helped the people. "I think he was a great man." In Dorje's vision, traditional Tibetan culture stultifies rather than sustains Tibetans in exile. In its place he is trying to piece together a synthesis of an exile-based anti-Chinese sentiment and the pro-modernization thinking of a group of Xining-based Tibetan-Chinese intellectuals. He seeks not the reinvigoration of traditional culture but modernization on Tibetan terms.

My third example dates from early March 2004, when over the remains of dinner in another monk friend's new quarters, just outside the precincts of the monastery in Xiahe, Gansu Province, I heard a most remarkable story. Hualdan, a wiry twenty-six-year-old monk, described in excellent Mandarin his abortive attempt to cross illicitly from China to Nepal, from where he had hoped to proceed to the Tibetan refugee communities of north India for religious and practical training. The previous January, he had traveled from Xiahe to Lhasa in central Tibet. Once there, he purchased binoculars and high-quality maps of the area. After a fortnight of planning and research he set off with five other Tibetans from his home village. By day he would scan the terrain ahead with his binoculars, consult his map, plot a route around any potential obstacles, and proceed by night.

This system worked well initially; they had made it past Sakya and their goal seemed to be within reach. But their luck ran out at 10 pm on the group's sixteenth night out of Lhasa when they came to a village near the Nepalese border. There they were spotted by a local Tibetan woman; hearing her shouts, more villagers came out to see what was going on. Despite Hualdan's protestations to the contrary, the villagers soon surmised his party's ultimate destination and intervened to prevent them from crossing to Nepal. They said, "This area is our responsibility (*women de zeren*) and what you are doing is wrong." Hualdan and his friends tried to bribe them, offering them six hundred Chinese yuan (approximately US $75), but the villagers would not be dissuaded. "No," they said. "We support the Communist Party. Before the Communists came we didn't have noodles to eat (*meiyou mian keyi chi*) or water to drink (*meiyou shui keyi he*) or clothes to wear (*meiyou yifu keyi chuan*); now we do, and this is all because of the Communist Party." So they seized Hualdan and his companions and turned them in to the Public Security Bureau (PSB).

In disbelief, I had to ask twice to confirm that Tibetan villagers foiled his bid for freedom. For his troubles, Hualdan was sentenced to three months and two weeks of hard labor in Shigatse. Yet as remarkable as this account is, it is only half the story. Within almost the same breath, the conversation shifted to Shanghai where he had lived for seven months studying Mandarin. When I asked him about his time there, his response shocked me: *Shanghai shi women Zhongguo zui fada, zui xiandai de diqu* ("Shanghai is *our China's* most developed, most modern place"). Hualdan's story is remarkable on at least two counts. First, his experience of being turned over to the authorities by communist Tibetans shatters received Western notions of Chinese repression and Tibetan flight, and displays internal cleavages within the Tibetan population that most Tibetans would rather not talk about. Second, even after all he has been through, Hualdan is still an assiduous student of Mandarin who sees fit to frame a discussion of development and modernity in terms of an imagined Chinese national collectivity within which he includes himself (*women Zhongguo*). The juxtaposition of Chineseness and Tibetanness in Hualdan's story illustrates the complexity of the position of subaltern individuals and collectivities within the contemporary Chinese nation-state, even as they may look beyond its bounds and the co-implication of at least some projects of Tibetan identity with those of PRC nation-building.

Like many other conversations, the three recounted above took place in contexts where "local" understandings of Tibetanness are informed by a sense that multiple modes of being Tibetan, some more morally desirable than others, exist in the world. My friends in Labrang are well aware of the attractions and drawbacks of Tibetan life in India, whether they have been there or not. Similarly, my contacts in Dharamsala live their lives cognizant of the vicissitudes of the loved ones that they, their friends or their relatives have left behind in China, or of the lives of reputed ease that emigrant friends have made for themselves in Europe or America. They are also aware that their own modes of being Tibetan are simultaneously divergent and convergent with these alternative models. They are aware that there is something both familiar and strange about Tibetan life elsewhere.

This may sound like a slight modification of Kapstein's assertion that local identities presuppose and maintain the "fabric of the Tibetan world,"[11] but what I intend is something different. Instead of assuming that the relationship between part and whole is obvious and unproblematic, I think we need to look at the ways in which pan-Tibetan visions of community are not simply manifested or reflected in local instances, but are constructed by them (and through them) in interested, partial ways. In this light, the articulation of unitary Tibetan identities that actively seek to elide intra-Tibetan difference comes to be seen as a political act.

In coming to terms with this realization, it may be beneficial to unseal the sutures that bind ethnicity to interests and races to places. In the process, visions of Tibetanness (in the plural) come out of the garden and into history. With regard to this loss of innocence, Tibet scholars might be able to learn something from work on the representation of ethnic identity among minority communities more generally. In his essay "New Ethnicities," Stuart Hall, the doyen of British Cultural Studies, writes of two overlapping phases in the politics of antiracism in Britain. In the first phase of antiracism, a generalized Black Experience gained hegemony as a unifying framework that temporarily subsumed other axes of difference in the context of a struggle to become subjects rather than objects of representation. One could argue that a comparable process has taken place in Tibet, where the Fall of Tibet itself seems to have fostered a struggle over the relations of representation, out of which a somewhat phantasmic yet remarkably durable, transnational, imagined Tibet as moral destination and Tibetanness as moral identity has been fashioned. This has emerged out of a situation which, Michael Aris suggested, previously had been characterized by diversity, divisiveness and a marked lack of trans-local imaginings in national terms.[12] In this light, the construction of a pan-Tibetan sensibility that transcends differences of region, dialect and religion should in fact be seen as one of the central achievements of the exile government in India.[13]

According to Hall, once the struggle for the relations of representation has been won – once the marginality, stereotypic quality and fetishized nature of images of blacks have been contested by the "counter-position of a 'positive' black imagery—the struggle has shifted to one over the politics of representation itself."[14] For Hall, a central feature of this shift is "the end of the innocent notion of the essential black subject."[15] The cacophony of myriad histories, traditions and ethnic identities that were elided in the oppositional cast(e) of the first moment come roaring back in the "recognition of the extraordinary diversity of subject positions, social experiences and cultural identities which compose the category 'black'...."[16] Blackness, here, is cut loose from mythic anchors of essential content and becomes an ethnicity with "no guarantees in nature." An ethnicity without guarantees also "inevitably entails a weakening or fading of the notion that 'race' or some composite notion of race around the term black [or, for our purposes, Tibetan] will guarantee the effectivity of any cultural practice or determine in any final sense its aesthetic value."[17]

Hall's account is suggestive in that on some levels the end of "innocent" notions of the essential *Tibetan* subject seems overdue. And yet the ethics of such an intervention are troubling. With this potential loss of innocence, in which the plurality of legitimately "Tibetan" subject positions could reemerge, scholars are confronted by a second fall of Tibet – a realization that Tibetans need not be independence partisans or devout Buddhists devoted to world peace, but instead may just as likely be broad persons, pragmatic participants in Chinese and Indian nation-states, rather than piners for a return to moral destinations.[18] The lesson learned is that attention needs to be paid to where and when pan-Tibetan oppositional ethnic identities are or are not articulated and what roles the differential marginalities of Tibetans in the Chinese and Indian (trans)national civic orders of ethnicity play in shaping these articulations and silences. In doing so one must be careful that a scholarly focus on the constructedness of Tibetan unity is not used to disempower Tibetans who might seek to mobilize tactical essentialisms for praiseworthy ends.

In applying these insights, I want to return to the operating assumption of Tibetan studies, indeed the assumption that makes it possible: that it is centered on, or, to adapt Hall's language, is "guaranteed" by something called Tibet. This assumption has become so deeply ingrained that it has taken on the performative power to reproduce Tibetan studies as centered on a particular melding of religion, culture and politics, and as to generally (but not completely) foreclose the discussion of certain topics such as Tibetan atheists, contemporary Tibetan modernists and Tibetans who have prospered in contemporary China. Things have begun to change, of course, but it is unclear whether these changes are viewed as salutary or as the contamination of the pure soil of the motherland by unwelcome squatters.

Putting this question aside for the moment, I propose that we do something radical here and stop thinking, briefly, about Tibet. Or at least try to think of this unifying meta-narrative of Tibet as momentarily incidental to our intellectual projects. What would our studies speak to if we removed the crutch of a unifying meta-narrative and gave some thought to the actual linking work that renders studies of *lurol* (ritual) in Rebgong, traditional medicine as practiced in north India, the popularization of Tibetan spiritual practices in Colorado, and the innovative aesthetics of contemporary artists in Lhasa, as somehow referring magically to the same thing?

I'm certainly not advocating throwing the baby out with the bathwater, I'm just asking that we think about what we're bathing in the first place. What can these and other researches tell us not simply about Tibet, but about similar processes in the wider world? Is there room for thinking about a sort of trans-Tibetan studies where we strive not to highlight the uniqueness, exceptionalism or individuality of Tibetan regional cultures but to foreground the "middle grounds"[19] of transcultural give and take on which such practices occur?

In my own work, I focus not on the unique cultural specificities of Amdowas, but instead seek to understand their place in contemporary *colonial* (n.b.: not post-colonial) modes of organizing social difference within the PRC. In studying Tibetans not (necessarily) for their uniqueness but for their comparability with other first peoples in settler societies (the Navajo in the US, the Maori in New Zealand, various aboriginal populations of Australia), I want to try to shift the frame of inquiry, if only slightly, away from Tibetan exceptionalism and towards an attention to the complex social matrices in which Tibetans are caught up. In this enterprise I ask not just what the movements of Amdowas can teach us about transnational Tibet, but also what they can teach us about such topics as new modalities of Chinese nationalism and the ambivalent position of subaltern populations within multiethnic nation-states. In this sense, while I have worked closely with Tibetans in various places, "Tibetan" and otherwise, my own work is not primarily "about" Tibet.

To conclude, I would like to suggest the desirability of fostering a Tibetan studies that looks both inward and *outward,* one that deals seriously and critically with Tibetanness as a historical, literary, religious or anthropological object, as well as with Tibetans as compelling subjects, *and* seeks to cultivate a comparative sensibility that supplements a Tibet-centric focus with an eye towards the sort of contribution our projects can make to knowledge more generally. A useful way of proceeding here may be to attempt to transcend the dichotomy between area- and problem-oriented approaches and begin to think of the concept of area as itself a problem that can serve to orient one's research. Tibet, here, can be simultaneously integral and incidental to academic projects that seek to understand the problem of Tibet as an "area" of study as itself "the object, site and ultimately the substance" of our intellectual endevors.[20]

NOTES

1 I draw here on Axel's discussion of the attempts on the part of the nation-state to convert diasporic populations from threat to promise. Brian Keith Axel, *The Nation's Tortured Body: Violence, Representation and the Formation of a Sikh "Diaspora"* (Durham, NC: Duke University Press, 2001).

2 Ruth Benedict, *The Chrysanthemum and the Sword: Patterns of Japanese Culture* (New York: Houghton Mifflin, 1989).

3 Pál Nyírí and Johanna Breidenbach, *China Inside Out: Contemporary Chinese Nationalism and Transnationalism* (Budapest: Central European University Press, 2005), ix.

4 Ibid.

5 Marshall K. Powers, "Area Studies," *The Journal of Higher Education* 26. 2 (1955), 87.

6 Matthew Kapstein, "Concluding Remarks." In *Buddhism in Contemporary Tibet – Religious Revival and Cultural Identity*, Melvyn Goldstein and Matthew Kapstein (eds), (Berkeley: University of California Press, 1998), 145.

7 Kapstein, 140.

8 Maurice Freedman, *The Study of Chinese Society: Essays by Maurice Freedman* (Stanford: Stanford University Press, 1979), 383.

9 This claim only makes sense if one assumes that the Tibetan "religion" to which Kapstein is appealing here is a cohesive whole.

10 In this section, direct quotes are in inverted commas, otherwise reported speech is paraphrased.

11 Kapstein, 145.

12 Michael Aris, *Hidden Treasures and Secret Lives* (London: Kegan Paul, 1989), 8.

13 c.f. Kapstein, 144.

14 Stuart Hall, "New Ethnicities." In *'Race' Culture and Difference*, D. James and A. Rattansi (eds), (London: Sage, 1989), 253.

15 Hall, 254.

16 Ibid.

17 Ibid.

18 In these suggestions, I draw on the influential work of Liisa Malkki on the "routes" of belonging. Liisa Malkki, "National Geographic: The Rooting of Peoples and the Territorialization of National Identity among Scholars and Refugees." In *Culture, Power, Place: Explorations in Critical Anthropology*A. Gupta and J. Ferguson (eds), (Durham: Duke University Press, 1997), 52–74.

19 Richard White, *The Middle Ground: Indians, Empires, and Republics in the Great Lakes Region, 1650–1815* (Cambridge: Cambridge University Press, 1991).

20 Paul Rabinow, *Anthropos Today: Reflections on Modern Equipment* (Princeton: Princeton University Press, 2003), 19.

2

In the Land of Checkpoints

Yartsa gunbu Business in Golok 2007, a Preliminary Report from the Field

EMILIA RÓŻA SUŁEK

For Richard Hoggart

Introduction

The growing popularity of Asian medicinal systems has reached Central Europe.[1] At a post office in Warsaw, Poland, people can have a look at a little stall, a mini-pharmacy, selling herbal remedies from the Far East. They will find there a little flyer that advertises a product called *Cordyceps Mycelium Capsules*. Imported from China, it is an extract of a fungus called *kordiseps* (original spelling). The author of the flyer introduces a few interesting details about this unknown fungus' place of origin and its life cycle: "[*k*]*ordiseps* belongs to the kingdoms of plants and animals at the same time. It grows in the highlands of China and Tibet. In summer it is a fungus, in winter it lives in the ground as a parasite with a moth larva (…) In spring it begins the life-cycle of an organic fungus again thus reproducing its biological cycle." This obscure and exotic information about a Tibetan medicinal fungus refers to something that really does exist in Tibet. It is *Cordyceps sinensis*, known in Tibetan language as *yartsa gunbu* (*dbyar rtswa dgun 'bu*)[2] and for English speakers as caterpillar fungus, native to the Qinghai-Tibetan Plateau and adjoining mountain valleys.

Caterpillar fungus collected by local populations has become an important economic factor in many parts of Tibet.[3] Its importance is highlighted by worrying news appearing from time to time on Tibet-related websites. In July 2007, for example, World Tibetan Network News (WTNN) reported that fighting broke out between people from Kardze (dKar mdzes) Tibetan Autonomous Prefecture (hereafter

TAP) in Sichuan Province when residents of two neighboring townships took up arms and hand grenades to dispute the border line between their *yartsa* grasslands.[4] Six people were killed and over one hundred injured. In June unrest broke out in Nagchu (Nag chu) Prefecture of the Tibet Autonomous Region. A group of Tibetans in Sog (Sog) county protested against Hui Muslims and their arrogant behavior at the market.[5] A simple quarrel over a *yartsa* transaction turned into a bigger conflict when a growing number of agitated Tibetans got involved. As a result, up to thirty Tibetans were arrested, and the Huis kept their shops closed for the next few days. These two examples come from two parts of Tibet that still keep their pastoral character, but unconfirmed rumors of clashes between the nomads competing over *yartsa* resources are heard of in other areas of pastoral Tibet as well.[6]

Yartsa gunbu at the post office in Poland, or any other country where so-called alternative therapies are in vogue, is a distant link in a long lasting and far flung process. Collected by people in Tibet, bought up by local middlemen, sold to pharmaceutical companies in mainland China, processed and widely distributed in China and the world outside – *yartsa* has to travel long distances to reach the hands of its customers. A dietary supplement, aphrodisiac, ingredient of expensive dishes in upscale restaurants in Chinese metropolises, *yartsa* is priced for its strongly marketed universal qualities. The surge in its price and consumption in the past two decades reflects economic reforms and availability of disposable income in China. The high demand for herbal medicines in China and abroad has an indirect and complicated impact on the situation in Tibet, where the flow of *yartsa* begins. It impacts the lives of people such as those described in the post office flyer: "[t]he healing qualities of *kordiseps* were discovered first by Himalayan cattle and sheep herders – they observed that their animals became more vigorous after eating the fungus." While the healing qualities of *cordyceps* were long known by medical practitioners, in the last decades developments in the market for alternative therapies enabled Golok nomads to discover the market value of *yartsa gunbu*.[7]

Research Outline

This chapter is based on research conducted in Golok (mGo log) TAP, Qinghai Province, China, throughout the *yartsa* harvesting season of 2007. Out of the six counties that comprise Golok, the main fieldwork area covered parts of two – Machen (rMa chen) and Gabde (dGa' bde) – known for *yartsa* resources and recent rapid economic changes. The research consisted of participant observation and interviews (in Tibetan) within communities of pastoral nomads collecting *yartsa* on the grasslands, local Tibetan traders and their trading partners in Golok marketplaces, towns and villages. It reports first-hand observations from the lives of *yartsa gunbu* collectors and traders.

The study focuses on the new developments in the *yartsa* business in Golok TAP in 2007. It introduces historical background and general setting of the *yartsa* trade, and the present day social and economic life in Golok during the *yartsa* cropping season, when people's activities and concerns center around the fungus harvesting, buying and selling. In addition, it discusses the place of *yartsa* digging in the nomads' cultural codes of behavior and their attitudes to the environment, and it reports opinions expressed by influential locals in Golok on the phenomenon of the *yartsa* trade and its importance for the area. Finally, it touches upon the intra-ethnic cooperation networks, and competition on the *yartsa* market in Golok TAP, and signals the development of the new entrepreneurial class in the local Golok society resulting from the boom in *yartsa* trade. Tibetan traders' own narratives of their careers and motives that made them quit the herder's life and enter business punctuate this report.

Research Parameters

The Golok TAP lies in the southeast corner of Qinghai. It covers an area of over 78,000 sq km, though this is not the entire land area labeled in early 20th-century writing as Golok; parts of the former Golok territory are now incorporated into other provinces and prefectures.[8] Golok is famous for the Amnyemachen Mountain Range (A myes rma chen), one peak of which, Machen Gangri (rMa chen gang ri), at 6,282 m, was once thought to be even higher than Mt Everest.[9] More importantly, Amnyemachen is a popular pilgrimage site, and the abode of the chief of all territorial deities of northeast Tibet/Amdo. Its impact is widely recognized in and around Golok. The Amnyemachen circumambulation route might become a popular trekking route, as the Golok tourist bureau officials hope.[10] The source of the Machu River (rMa chu/Yellow River) is located in the west of Golok. The Golok territory can be roughly described as stretching from the sources of the Machu along its upper part through the mountain grasslands that merge into forest farming villages of south Banma (Pad ma) county. The Machu source area is a part of the so-called Three Rivers Area (Mandrydzagsum; rMa 'Bri Dza gsum)[11] in Golok and Yushu (Yul shul) Prefectures, and has been designated a natural heritage site by the Chinese authorities. It is a popular theme of Chinese postcards, which show the natural treasures of the Qinghai-Tibetan Plateau, and is a recurring theme in the Chinese environmentalist rhetoric.

The terrain of Golok rises from the southeast to the northwest, shaping the climate and ways of life of its inhabitants. While the average annual temperature is around 0°C, in winter the temperature can drop to as low as –30°C (the lowest temperature in Dawu/rTa bo[12] in 2007), and in summer it can rise to about +25°C during the day, but still fall close to freezing at night. Snow and hail are common at all times of year. In 2007 there was snow on the ground in Dawu in July, and the hills around the town were covered in snow as late as 28 July. The annual amount of precipitation decreases from east to west. The high humidity in the "lower Golok" – Jigdril (gCig sgril) and Banma counties to the southeast – makes the climate milder, and allows small-scale field cultivation. When the land rises up with the Qinghai-Tibetan Plateau, Golok gets drier, and the "upper Golok" of Martod (rMa stod) county in the northwest consists of grasslands over 4,000 and up to 5,000 m high above sea level; this area has been subject to rapid desertification of the pasturelands in recent decades.[13] In the public political discourse in China the blame for that is often falsely placed on the local residents and the "traditional" pasture system that supposedly runs contrary to environmental protection. This is generally recognized as a pretext for the state-imposed program of mass resettlement of a large part of its rural population. The counties studied, Machen and Gabde (along with Darlag/Dar lag, which is not covered in the present study) form the central core of the whole Golok TAP. This "middle Golok," which stretches between Amnyemachen to the north and Bayankara mountain range to the south, is characterized by treeless rolling hills of grassland up to over 4,000 m above sea level. It is a home for nomadic pastoralists who depend for their subsistence on their large herds of yaks and sheep. The sale of livestock and livestock products is a major source of income for the mainly rural population of Golok, which is the third least populated of the Qinghai prefectures.

20th-Century Historical Overview

In the first half of the 20th century, before the Chinese government was established in Golok, the Goloks were organized on a tribal basis, still recognizable in contemporary local society. They formed loose polities that comprised a confederacy, and most of the Golok tribes retained political power and varying degrees of independence from the centers of authority outside of Golok. The advent of the Communist era in Tibet brought the incorporation of Golok tribes into the modern state of the People's Republic of China, and the founding of Golok Tibetan Autonomous Region in 1954, which was renamed Golok Tibetan Autonomous Prefecture the following year. Communist attempts at building a uniform socialist society backed by a strong central authority emanating from Beijing were more difficult to resist than the Hui warlords (principally Ma Qi and Ma Bufang), who had *de facto* power over a large part of Qinghai and tried to bring Golok tribes under their direct control by arms during the period of the Chinese Republic (1911–49). Many Chinese would probably agree with the statement by Sun Shuyun in her book on the Long March: "[t]he warlords' internecine wars, their lack of any moral values and ideals except for keeping their power and territory, and the damage they inflicted on the nation, were among the curses of the 20th-century China."[14]

When the Communists replaced the warlords on the political stage, the new "altruist" justification for political actions was introduced to replace the criticized warlords' "egoist" one. However, from the perspective of Golok and other Tibetan parts of Qinghai, the situation did not change objectively. Golok and the whole of Qinghai is remembered for persecutions and mass killings of the local populations, mentioned in the late Panchen Lama's famous critique of the crimes of the Cultural Revolution.[15] Leaving aside the extremities of Chinese politics in Tibet, the new communist authorities instituted a whole panorama of political and economic reforms on Marxist-Leninist lines with Soviet assistance.

The introduction of the commune (*nyamli*; *mnyam las*) system by the end of the 1950s and early 1960s opened the list of changes in state-planned livestock management: the herds changed their ownership from individual households to collectives that were the only permitted production and day-to-day management units. In the early and mid-1980s, when economic reforms swept across China, the state communes were disbanded and the livestock was returned to the private ownership of nomad families according to family size. However, this re-privatization did not affect the rangelands ownership and the pastures were still used communally. In 1985 the government formulated the Grassland Law of the People's Republic of China (*Zhonghua renmin gongheguo caoyuanfa*) and land contracts were granted to individual households as long-term leases.[16] The Goloks have the right to manage the land and use the profits, but the land is still owned by the state. Big infrastructure developments in Tibet, which started in the 1990s, were speeded up in the Jiang Zemin era with the announcement of the "Great Opening of the West," or *Xibu da kaifa* campaign, in 1999 designed to bridge the economic gap between the poor "Wild West" of China and the rapidly developing East. The campaign has resulted in major material improvements, primarily affecting county towns and to a lesser extent villages. This has included health care and education facilities, electric power plants and investments in transportation infrastructure.

The construction of a network of roads brought markets within easier reach of most Golok families, thus facilitating both the selling of livestock products and the purchasing of food and necessary household commodities. Roads in Golok were a kind of Achilles' heel of the region and this, taken together with the Goloks' reputation as notorious brigands, robbing caravans and strangers who tresspassed on their land, no doubt discouraged many outside traders from coming to the area.[17] Thus the locals traveled long distances to the outside markets of Labrang (bLa brang), Kumbum (sKu 'bum) or Ngaba (rNga ba) to trade their products for barley, tea and other supplies unobtainable from their land. With the recent Chinese road construction projects the appearance of Golok towns has visibly changed. And even though two decades ago a main town like Dawu had just one road and not much more than two lines of buildings along it, today the town is busy with life and has all sorts of shops, with vegetables trucked from Sichuan, boutiques selling trendy urban clothes and photograph studios where one can have pictures taken of oneself in an elegant Western wedding dress or a Chinese princess' outfit. There still are many areas in Golok that one can reach only on horseback or on a motorbike negotiating floods, ice sheets and the destruction caused by summer rains. Hospitals in county towns and smaller villages show little trace of recent financial input, and there are no petrol stations other than a shed with drums of petrol in smaller settlements. There are not many facilities that could be enjoyed by tourists whom the local tourist agencies want to bring to the area in order to increase the prefecture's income. Whatever the situation in smaller counties looks like, the recent economic changes in Golok have been considerable, and this is partly the outcome of the new road construction projects.

Contemporary Golok society faces similar economic problems as other parts of Tibet and pastoral minority areas in China. Declining productivity of the grasslands is probably the most significant problem, and to reverse pasture degradation the program of relocating pastoralists from the endangered areas to new, mostly urban housing was announced. Resettling nomads in Golok TAP covers not only the most degraded parts of the prefecture and areas around the Machu river sources that are under the Three Rivers Area protection plan. On the contrary, the program stretches through the whole of Golok, and in every county one easily finds concrete resettlement quarters for the nomads built within or in vicinity of towns and villages. It is difficult to collect accurate information about the program. The nomads generally receive free housing and financial and material (coal, wheat) support from the government. However, the amount of money they receive and the length of time they will be aided differ even within one resettlement site, where households from various localities are placed. Moreover, rules about whether a family can retain its livestock and keep the animals on the grassland or or be forced to sell them vary as well, though it is no secret that many families skip this rule and entrust the animals to their relatives, hoping for better times to come back to the highlands, or simply rejecting the mass killing of their whole herds. A local official from Darlag county was quoted by the Xinhua news agency: "... due to erosion and desertification, more and more people are realizing the benefits of resettling... The government has done a lot to persuade those who are truly reluctant to move."[18] While it remains true that a number of resettled nomads declare their satisfaction with their new life (especially elderly people whose children migrated to the towns long ago, or ones from the margins of economic sustainability), the "traditional" leaders of local communities express their concern with the state's resettlement program, seeing it rather as aiming at the nomads' cultural *status quo* than at improving their life and the environmental conditions.[19]

Cutting the size of herds and dividing and fencing off pasturelands are further strategies for developing rural regions and making herd management more "scientific" and economically predictable.[20] However, the implementation of these policies differs from place to place, and in Machen and Gabde counties fenced pastures are found in some parts, while not in others. Fencing is expensive and carries a potential for exacerbating local conflicts over boundary demarcation, the size and quality of the allocated rangelands, transfer from summer to winter pastures and access to water or *yartsa* resources.[21]

All these policies, as well as the establishment of roads, have complex implications for the structure of pastoral communities in Golok. They affect the way nomads shape their community life and the way they interact with urban centers. It brings them closer to the sphere of state-promoted consumerism. Collecting medicinal plants for their own consumption and occasional sale was a part of economic life in Golok before, but the development of the *yartsa* trade on the scale that is now observed in the area was possible only thanks to contemporary developments aimed at opening Golok to the state-promoted socialist market economy.[22] In the new history of Golok that started with its incorporation into the People's Republic of China, the area has been known as one of the poorest parts of Qinghai, with 80 percent of the prefectural budget still financed through subsidies from the provincial or central government in the early 1990s.[23] Golok is still one of the smallest economies in Qinghai, but the boom in *yartsa* trading has opened a new chapter in the economic life of the Golok highlands.

Yartsa Rush

In the beginning of May when the time of *yartsa* harvesting approaches, a genuine *yartsa* rush breaks out in Golok. Harvests are one of the most common topics to talk about behind the wheel and at the table. Everybody seems to talk about *yartsa* – nomads, townspeople, Tibetans, strangers, men and women, lay people and monks. The importance of *yartsa* harvests is reflected in the everyday language: the usual *Cho demo?* or *Cho erka?* (*How are you?*; *Khyod bde mo? Khyod e dka'?*) is often replaced by phrases: *Yartsa e yo ka?* (*Have you got* yartsa*?*; *dByar rtswa e yod ka?*) or *Yartsa mang nga e yo ka?* (*Have you got many* yartsa*?*; *dByar rtswa mang nga e yod ka?*). After such greetings, a reply should come: *Yartsa mang nga me ka* (*I haven't got many* yartsa; *dByar rtswa mang nga med ka*). This standard complaint does not represent the real state of a person's business or *yartsa*-hunting results, and is a routine question to start any conversation. The harvests are the topic people talk about, a reason for personal pride and a subject of dreams for some and fears for others. In a photograph studio, a Hui trader, Mr. Ma, was taking photos of his newly bought *yartsa* pieces, proud to be the owner of such splendid specimens. And a monk from Ragya (Ra rgya) Monastery admitted that he dreamt of many *yartsa*. Although many monks search for *yartsa*, he never did. Neither was he one of those monks to whom people come for divination concerning when and where to go to get good harvests. But he took his dream as a bad omen for the Golok grasslands. "The extinction of *yartsa* may happen soon," he said.

The fear of the forthcoming over-exploitation of *yartsa* resources was one of the ways the local authorities explained a regulation banning entry to Golok to all people who have neither land of their own in the prefecture, nor relatives who do. One inescapable feature of the landscape for anybody visiting Golok in the spring 2007 was the checkpoints (*rtartog bziesa*; *lta rtogs byed sa*). A traveler to Golok had to pass many control posts, set by the local administration or by the nomads themselves. At the checkpoints all those who wanted to enter the prefecture had to show identity cards, or in any other way prove their right to be there during the *yartsa* cropping season. On the road between Ragya and Dawu (76 km), a three-hour journey on motorbike that crosses a 4234 m mountain pass, there were four checkpoints. From Dawu to Jigdril, the usual eight-hour bus journey was extended by two more hours due to the stops at five control posts, with the biggest one in Mendrin (sMan 'brin) where the old track to Jigdril runs over the mountain pass above the village crossroads. However, the biggest checkpoints were set on local dirt roads, leading nowhere but to the grassland, and among the strictest in Machen was the one that led to Domkhok (sDom khog), an area famous for rich *yartsa* fields. A barrier, a few tents and a queue of cars, nomads on motorcycles and groups of people sitting at the roadside, all waiting for somebody to lift the barrier closing the way to the pasturelands, clarified the picture of how highly sought after the local *yartsa* resources are, and how important it is to guard them.

This is supplemented by the stories of unsuccessful gatherers who did not manage to get through the control posts, and of those successful ones who had good luck and got to the grasslands to live the dreamt-of life of a *yartsa* gatherer. These constituted the hope, luck and despair that came with the new spring and the new *yartsa* harvesting season.

A *Yartsa* Gatherer's Day

The *yartsa* gatherer's working day can last up to ten hours. Having drunk a few bowls of milk tea, everybody who is able sets off in groups for the mountains. A long march up the hills of the family land leads through ice-covered streams, between herds of yaks and up the stony slopes. The path rises up steeply, and on the way to the alpine *yartsa* meadows the gathering teams stop several times to rest. Having arrived up there, to the heights of the family land, the gatherers proceed slowly, on their knees or crawling, or bending the body and leaning on a small hoe with the eyes fixed on the patch of dry grass in front. Each gatherer carefully "scans" every square centimeter of land. "Look first in front of you, then look further ahead" (*rNgun na rngun du ti, de ni thag rang nga ti*; *sNgun na sngun du bltas, de nas thag ring nga bltas*) was the simpest advice on how to search for *yartsa*. Skillful gatherers do not need to put their nose in the grass to find the fungus – some are able to see it from two or three meters distance. But if nothing is found, the gatherer takes a few steps more and continues his search elsewhere.

The gatherer's equipment is simple and does not include anything special for *yartsa* harvesting. The basic tool is a 25 cm or longer iron hoe (*kakle*; *kag le* or *zhur*; *gzhor*) with a blacksmith-made blade and a metal or wooden handle; this is used in every rural household to chop dry dung. Once the *yartsa* gatherer finds a tiny brownish "head" (*go*; *mgo*) of the fungus sticking out from the ground, the whole bulk of topsoil is lifted out with the hoe. The fungus is skillfully extracted and the soil should be replaced and compacted. The fungus goes into the pocket of the happy gatherer where, wrapped in a plastic bag like those for instant noodle soup, it will travel for a few hours before everybody gets home. The gatherers do not wear any special clothing either, and only ladies take care to wear gloves to protect the hands, dust masks (*khayol; kha yol* or *khadym*; *kha thum*) against strong sun and dusty air, colorful cloth sleeve-protectors (*purhyb; phur shubs* or *lakhyb*; *lag shubs*) and hats.

A long working day in the mountains ends in the evening, when the whole team runs down the slopes of their pasturelands jumping between dry bushes and

Figure 1: Yartsa *gathering requires a certain degree of fitness. (Photograph: ES)*

pica holes from one mound of earth to the other, whistling to the yaks to bring them home on the way. At home the *yartsa* is counted, and each piece is cleaned of its layer of earth with a toothbrush (*sochy*; *so 'khru* or *sobshi*; *so bshi*), and left to dry. Everybody agrees that it is best to dry it the sun, but it takes a shorter time to dry the fungus on the stove. The cleaned and dried fungus will wait now for somebody to take it to town for sale; if the town is close to the settlement, or instant money is needed, one may carry fresh *yartsa* to the market for on-the-spot sale.

The work of *yartsa* gathering is strenuous; it might even be described as boring. It requires a certain degree of fitness but at the same time gives a chance for social bonding. During the day, the settlements of the gatherers' families are almost empty. Only the oldest and youngest members of the household stay at home. Everybody who is fit enough to walk up to the mountains takes a chance to earn money from *yartsa*. In four-generation families, the elderly take on the task of house-keeping when the others are away – no need to hide the key under a stone in the yard and the stove will be pleasantly warm when the gathering team, hungry and worn out, finally returns. Neighboring households can share the cost

Figure 2: *A small hoe is used to replace the dug out earth. In her left hand the lady holds a piece of* yartsa. *(Photograph: ES)*

of renting a babysitter to look after the kids and keep an eye on the household when the people are away.[24]

The cropping season is an occasion to have the whole family in one place. Children who attend boarding schools away from home enjoy a special holiday so they can help their families with the harvesting. The Golok Prefecture High School (mGo log khul bod yig mtho rim slob 'bring) has a break over twenty days long, Snowland Nomad Girls' School (Gangs ljongs rtswa thang bu mo'i slob grwa) near Ragya enjoys a five-week break and Dr Dargye's Snowland Charitable Medical College (Gangs ljongs dar rgyas kun phan sman rtsis slob gling) in Dawu is closed for over a month from late April until the end of May. Relatives who have quit the life of a herder in hopes of "catching up" with modern life in a big town outside of Golok come back home. Monks leave their monasteries to look for additional income through *yartsa*, even though the codes of Buddhist monastic discipline prevent them from digging. As ever, reality runs counter to prescribed behavior. Singing and breaks for lunch make the working time pass pleasantly and gives the *yartsa* harvests their social dimension.

MARKET VALUE

Yartsa is the most sought after natural commodity in Golok. However, the trade is often seen as a new phenomenon, introduced to Golok in the last decades. As a sixty-year-old Gabde trader puts it: "when I was a little boy, there were no Chinese, and the grass belonged to yaks, sheep and horses. There was no other use for it." It is hard to locate the beginnings of the trade exactly, but the 1970s are recollected by the nomads and traders as the first time that news spread of the *yartsa* trade with mainland China. "When I was herding around Nyenpoyurtse (gNyan po g.yu rtse) in 1975, I heard that somewhere in Golok and Gabde people trade with bags of *yartsa*," another trader says. Individual reports mention ten-to-twelve *gyama* / *jin*[25] quotas that the nomads in Gabde had to meet in a month of a cropping season under the commune system. However, before the communes were dissolved and official restrictions on private business removed, the business could not develop.

The Golok highlands are known for their abundance of medicinal plants used in the traditional Tibetan and Chinese medicine. Some of these had been collected as part of a profitable business in previous decades.[26] However, with the rise of *yartsa*, the price for other medicinal plants found in the Golok uplands has appeared unsatisfactory to the gatherers, and the number of suppliers has declined. Even *pimo* (*pas mo*; *Fritillaria*), formerly collected by Golok nomads as a supplementary source of income, seems to have been slowly abandoned since the *yartsa* boom started. No middleman was prepared to pay as much for it as for the caterpillar fungus. One *gyama* (500 g) of *pimo* sold for between 500 to 600 yuan in 2007. The same amount (one *gyama*) of *yartsa* sold for 40,000 to 50,000 yuan (spring 2007) depending on the quality of the fungus. High prices paid for *yartsa* make the effort worthwhile for the middlemen to travel to the nomads' settlements to buy *yartsa* directly on the grassland.

The great popularity of the *yartsa* trade is understandable when the number of *yartsa* pieces that one person can collect in a season is considered. Thirty to forty pieces a day sounds moderate, but it gives over one thousand pieces for a four-to-five-week-long season per gatherer. This result is not uncommon, and is by no means the smallest figure. The price paid at the Golok markets for a single piece of caterpillar fungus in spring 2007 averaged from 15 to 20 yuan depending on the fungus' quality and size, although the nomads reported that for a particularly good *yartsa* the price could rise up to 30 yuan or more.

In a good harvesting season, income from *yartsa* is unparalleled with anything else in the area. For a household that fully engages in *yartsa* hunting these days, the income, supplemented with livestock products from a middle sized seventy-yak herd, can easily provide a comfortable living, bank savings, investments in the winter house, children's higher education (primary and middle schools in Golok were free in 2007), etc. At the grassroots level of everyday expenses, the mathematics is simple: for the price of one middle sized caterpillar fungus one could buy 10 kg of roasted barley *tsampa* (*rtsam pa*) flour or over 2.5 kg of mutton or yak meat or 1.5 kg of butter (prices for May/June 2007; Dawu).

The range of goods and services that one could spend *yartsa* money on is broad, and luxury expenditures, such as whitening creams and mobile phones, sell well in the *yartsa* harvesting season. The red-light district of Dawu is also busy with life in the season.

It is common for families to keep a record of the total income from *yartsa* gathering, though clearly some of the proceeds are retained for private use and are not recorded. Reliable figures are thus not easy to calculate. Being easily convertible into cash, *yartsa* is a good way of keeping one's savings. On the one hand, caterpillar fungus connects such places as Golok to the market economy, but on the other hand, it retains its "barter" value. Some fungus does not need to be converted into cash, and transactions involving binoculars, wristwatches and

Figure 3: *Door-to-door sellers of calculators and other simple goods in a restaurant. The nomad at the table wants to pay for his shopping in yartsa. Traders are estimating the fungus' value; the one standing at the door holds yartsa. (Photograph: ES)*

leather belts changing hands in exchange for a few pieces of *yartsa* are not unknown. However, it is not barter in the sense of exchanging goods without referring to money. Current "conversion rates" for *yartsa* are widely known, and the fungus will not circulate as an object of use, but will be sold at the *yartsa* market soon after.[27] Nomadic communities in Golok have historically lived with low supplies of cash. Transactions are often credited and accounts settled after the *yartsa* season. Dried *yartsa* is easy to store without the risk of deterioration. Therefore, it gives its owner a chance to enhance its market value over time. It may well be imagined that it serves as an alternative currency for the locals.

Market Life

The *yartsa* market space in a Golok town or village has a "spontaneous" street character. The transactions happen on the street, away from the township's official market precincts, which are too small to house a large number of *yartsa* sellers and buyers. During the day, but also late in the evening, groups of people sit on the pavements discussing *yartsa* prices: the sellers with backpacks or suitcases full of *yartsa* brought straight from the mountains; the buyers with cardboard boxes for newly bought fungus; chairs and a folding table for those traders who need more comfort; and noisy spectators, eager to sneak a look over somebody's arm to watch the transactions, or to back up one or another of the other business parties. Only rarely do traders rent a shop that becomes a fixed point on a town map where one can conduct business. Alternatively, general stores selling boots, horse tack and expensive coral beads can be used as seasonal storehouses for *yartsa*.

For nomads coming down from the hills to put *yartsa* on the market, this is a rare opportunity to take a break in town, so discussions over *yartsa* drift along and nobody is in a hurry to hop on his horse or motorbike to go home. The traders count and weigh the fungus with metal scales (*gyama*; *rgya ma* – the same term used as a unit of measure). Haggling lasts a long time and transactions are discussed individually, between buyer and seller, and depend on the quality of collected fungus and personal connection between the two parties: *yartsa* can be traded either per *gyama* (500 g) or per piece. Mobile phones ring every now and then; those without a telephone cannot be realistically imagined to do business in Golok. Detailed notes are taken in a notebook that a professional trader carries with him. Calculators are in play in the traders' hands, but many transactions are discussed secretly. The secrecy of the business is the key to success and the prices are voicelessly negotiated in the language of gestures in the folds of the overlong sleeves of Tibetan robes. *Yartsa* is not an exception here, and the price of sheep or horses is discussed similarly. Selling yak hides and sheep skins in autumn and winter also takes place everywhere, showing that the *modus operandi* of *yartsa* trading does not differ significantly from common trading patterns.

Among the middlemen buying *yartsa* are Tibetans, Hui Muslims and Han Chinese. They form a hub of a true "commodity ecumene," with a network of relationships crossing trans-cultural borders.[28] Han traders are clearly visible in the prefectural capital and the peripheries of Golok, such as Ragya township, but their numbers shrink noticeably within the Golok highlands. Public discourse in Golok holds the Muslims in low esteem, and they are blamed for many misfortunes by the local population. Ma Bufang's atrocities are well remembered by the elderly and these memories are transmitted to the young generations. Reliable informants say that in 2005 the Dawu government initially granted, and then withdrew permission for the building of a mosque in the town. The summer horse festival in 2007 brought inter-ethnic unrest; it started with an infamous incident in a Hui restaurant when a Tibetan nomad found something resembling human tooth in a dish of food.[29] "The police said it wasn't human," a Tibetan *yartsa* trader said,

Figure 4: *At a* yartsa *market, the prices are voicelessly negotiated in the language of gestures in the sleeves of Tibetan robes. (Photograph: ES)*

suggesting that the restaurant owner bribed the policemen in charge of investigating the incident. It reveals the widespread belief that the Huis are influential and cooperative with the Chinese. Also, most Tibetans believe that Hui traders are the most powerful players in the *yartsa* business.[30]

However, the laws of the market seem to prevail over prejudice. When the spirit of commerce comes on the stage, economic interests win over ethnic differences, even if only temporarily. "I sell to the one that pays me more," most Tibetan middlemen claimed. Tibetan traders today open cooperatives with the Muslims; while the Tibetan partner has a better social standing in the area, the Hui partner ensures that Chinese documents are properly filled in and tax regulations duly followed. The capital and imagined personal connections of the Muslim traders might inspire Tibetan traders to open a business with the Huis. Andrew Fischer observes that Tibetans ought to have a "natural advantage" in the *yartsa* business.[31] However, an impression shared by outside observers that Tibetan middlemen are rising in power and gaining control over a growing part of the *yartsa* business in the area is contradicted by the complaints of the Tibetan traders themselves: "I sell to you, you sell to me, and *yartsa* can circulate endlessly between Tibetan hands with a very small profit." The lack of capital, experience, intra-ethnic solidarity and entrepreneurial spirit is blamed for the still low position of the Tibetan middlemen in the *yartsa* business.

Yartsa Quality

The story of Tibetan–Muslim cooperation must be supplemented by narratives of supposed swindles played by competitors at the market, especially the Huis: "It would be good if the Chinese big bosses came directly to us, otherwise Huis paint the *yartsa* yellow so that it has a better color and insert pins in them so that the *yartsa* gains weight. These are not honest tricks," many informants complained. This narrative briefly describes important quality markers: the yellowish color and large, firm larval body of the *yartsa* are the two main attributes impacting its price. The fact that *yartsa* is normally bought in *gyama*s tempts sellers to increase its weight fraudulently. Traders say the harvesters soak the fungus before bringing it to the market and inject it with salt water. The extreme of reported *yartsa* tricks is represented by circulating stories of a "fake *yartsa*" produced somewhere outside Golok. This *yartsa*, made of dough, has been seen by purchasers of the end product at markets in Sichuan and elsewhere in China.

Caterpillar fungus harvested at the beginning of the cropping season has a short "head" or fruiting body. This kind of *yartsa* is in particular demand on the market. The short "head," sticking 1–2 cm out of the ground, is a reason for the harvester's pride in finding the fungus even though it is hardly visible. It will raise the fungus' market price, too. Larger specimens are always in demand as well. Some traders say they keep the biggest *yartsa* for their own use. Put into a bottle of good *baijiu* (spirit alcohol) with deer antlers, *pimo* and medicinal herbs, it makes *menchang* (*sman chang*), a medicinal drink that helps to restore health and is the main way the locals use *yartsa* at home. Hot water can be used instead of alcohol. Another factor influencing fungus quality is the altitude at which it grows. "Very rarely do the traders pay attention to this," a village doctor says, but the price list for using another person's pastures for *yartsa* gathering mentions the highest fees for gathering in the uppermost parts of the valleys. This suggests that altitude is sometimes taken into account in *yartsa* price negotiations.

Roadblocks and the Black Market

In previous years, researchers working in Golok Prefecture reported attempts by local authorities to control the amount of *yartsa* digging.[32] Similar attempts were reported from other areas of Tibet.[33] Roadblocks were set up in the Golok TAP to control the seasonal influx of people in the cropping season and to collect the user's fee that *yartsa* collectors from outside of Golok had to pay to enter the Golok highlands. Part of the money was meant to go to the herders who owned the rights to the plot of *yartsa* land the newcomer was going to use. Otherwise the money should "return" to nomads through county and prefecture programs aimed at patching up the environmental consequences of the grassland exploitation. That tension over the final use of prefectural and county money has been a hot issue was shown by international reports over the past years highlighting social unrest in several areas of Tibet, where inhabitants protested against misappropriation of the fee money by local officials.[34]

The informal leaders of local communities in Golok express concern with the overexploitation of *yartsa* fields and pollution of the local environment: "the Chinese and Huis they come here, cut the trees, leave rubbish everywhere, and throw their socks on the mountains and in the rivers." Religious leaders show concern with the danger of offending the mountain gods, *zhibdag* (*gzhi bdag*) or *yulha* (*yul lha*), with careless digging of *yartsa* in the mountains, and the profaning of a sacred land by those who are unaware of its sanctity.[35] There is a danger that the gods will leave their mountain abodes in Golok. Digging of *yartsa* is also blamed for worsening quality of the pasturelands, along with fishing, building hydroelectric power plants and gold digging. *Yartsa* and gold mining are often mentioned simultaneously as examples of environmentally destructive and economically exploitable politics of today's China, which running counter to the long term interests of the Tibetan population.[36] Herders comment on the worsening state of the grassland: "I was born here, I live here, and will die here, and through my life I could see that since *yartsa* digging started the horses, yaks, and sheep are getting weaker and weaker. Gold, *yartsa*, *pimo* – all of that should stay in the ground for the benefit of animals, and all people." *Yartsa* is eaten by herds, the herders say, and it influences the whole grassland ecosystem. Eliminating it from the grassland not only drains grassland resources. Digging *yartsa* by careless gatherers leaves holes in the ground that contribute to the on-going deterioration of the pasturelands.[37]

It is important to stress, however, that whereas researchers to Golok TAP a decade ago reported only a small percentage of nomads engaged in *yartsa* harvesting,[38] today's situation is different. The herders criticize the gatherers for destroying their land, but a growing number of nomads either gather *yartsa* on their land by themselves or lease the land to outside gatherers. Given the regulation banning entry to Golok TAP to outside gatherers, leasing the land under *yartsa* gathering was illegal in spring 2007. The *yartsa* "underground" had (and one can

Figure 5: *Evening at the checkpoint. On such dirt road checkpoints like this one everybody knows everybody else, and checking identity cards is not necessary. (Photograph: ES)*

expect that it will still have) a vital life in local society. Complaining of the gatherers' poaching of the nomads' resources is more a figure of speech in a situation where the nomads themselves benefit highly from the *yartsa* gathering.

The official argument behind the new policy of limiting the number of *yartsa* gatherers in Golok speaks of environmental protection. The same concern, although less grounded in the modern scientific discourse on environmental protection, is repeatedly expressed in everyday discourse in Golok. However, the new policy finds its critics also among those who speak of the environment. "If they want to preserve the environment, they should start by closing the gold mines in Martod," a local doctor said. Among the *yartsa* traders who come from a nomadic background, the closing of Golok TAP to outside *yartsa* collectors was welcomed with mixed feelings: gratitude by some, discontent by others. "For us traders, it's pretty bad that they banned entry to Golok for other gatherers, as it simply causes less *yartsa* to reach the market. But for herders it's better – nobody walks through their pastures and destroys the delicate and scanty grass," Dube (gDu bhe),[39] a middle-aged middleman, commented on the recent policies.

However, the strictness of control procedures varied. So did the consequences of breaking the ban on entry to Golok grasslands. New employees coming to Golok to take their job in a restaurant or at a building site were asked for papers and guarantees from the employer. People caught on the way to the pasturelands, and having no identity cards and no way to explain their presence in a given county, could expect to be sent back from whence they came. And the "illegal" hunter caught on the way back from the grassland would be fined, the harvest could be confiscated, or the driving license taken. Yet the varying degrees of control procedures and the help of well paid intermediaries made evading control possible, and there were people who managed to pass through control posts. "Money can buy everything," a local community leader says, suggesting that the checkpoint workers and owners of the land have an informal deal on charging outsiders for coming to Golok.

The formal closing of Golok did not entirely exclude people from other areas from hunting *yartsa* in the prefecture. Nomads gathering *yartsa* on their land sometimes see a few silhouettes far away on the mountains. And although their first comment is: "Thieves! Must be some Chinese" (*Rkunma! Gya chazyg yin kha zyh re*; *rKun ma! rGya cha tshig yin kha zig red*), not only Chinese and Huis travel to Golok for the *yartsa* cropping season. Nomads with abundant pastures sell the right to harvest fungus on their land to other diggers. "I am the owner of the land and I decide how much the fee is," a seventy-two-year-old nomad says, and mentions sums ranging from 2,000 to 4,000 yuan per gatherer who will set up a tent in "his" mountains and hunt for *yartsa* for the whole season. "I have people from Guinan, Guide, Hualong ..."[40] the nomad goes on, saying how far the fame of his *yartsa* resources extends.

Being unable to estimate the possible income from *yartsa* hunting, a collector from outside the prefecture might be put in a difficult situation, like Amchok (A mchog) and his two relatives, who arrived from Drango (Brag 'go) in Sichuan, and found a Golok nomad who sold him the right to collect *yartsa* on his land for 1,800 yuan. After several days in the mountains, it turned out that either the gatherers had no luck or *yartsa* didn't grow there. Amchok's wish to cancel the unwritten contract with the nomad met with a claim for 6,000 yuan compensation for all three members of the unsuccessful team. The nomad took Amchok as a hostage, and let the others return home to fetch money, threatening their families with phone calls and warnings that the hostage would be carried away, to a place where nobody could find him.[41]

The Nomads and Traders

Tibetan nomads and traders are the first link that opens a flow of *yartsa* from Tibet via mainland China to the outside world. The *yartsa* trade allows nearly everybody with modest capital to invest and do business. Among the Golok middlemen there are many life stories told. Some traders, such as Lhundup (lHun sgrub), owned a herd of eighty yaks just a decade ago, but decided to sell the animals and move to town to look for a better future for his family. Others, like Yadon (Yar dung), continue their herders' life, saving money from selling animal products to invest in the *yartsa* business. Yadon moves to the town for every *yartsa* season and hires seasonal workers to herd his sheep and yaks when he is away. Last year he hired the herders for a longer period and went on holiday to Malaysia with his business partner. Riga (Rig dga'), a fifty-year-old trader, the only son of his elderly mother, lacking the hands in his household to do the herding jobs, entrusted his animals to his cousins and opened a clothing shop, doing *yartsa* business on the side. For the owner of just a tiny herd, unable to save money from trading livestock products, or having no animals at all, like Sherten (Sher bstan), an ex-monk, there is only one solution: borrow money. Sherten borrowed 3,000 yuan at 5 percent interest and for the first time in his life bought *yartsa* to sell later at a profit. Bank loans are not the most common source of capital to invest in the business. Most traders claim to have other sources of money, and Hui Muslim friends are much sought after when a loan is needed.

For many Tibetan middlemen, entering the *yartsa* trade was the first step into business other than the occasional selling of animal hides, meat or milk products.

Becoming a professional trader is a long process. Geleg (dGe legs) says he started his business when he was twenty. He drove a motorbike to nearby nomad settlements to buy *yartsa*. Having just 2,000 yuan to invest, he had to sell the fungus on the same day he bought it, and his profit was no more than 2 jiao[42] on a piece of fungus. Now, seven years later, he has an elegant jeep and two houses, and usually buys and sells 30–35 *gyama* of *yartsa* in a year, getting 6,000 yuan of profit on every *gyama* of fungus that goes through his hands. But this is nothing compared to the profits of Muslim traders, he says. Tibetans just do not have enough money to keep *yartsa* for a long time and to buy large quantities. In Geleg's estimation, Muslims are much more commercially minded than Tibetans; although 6,000 yuan of profit is enough for Geleg, he knows that his Muslim partner will get a 100 percent larger profit on every *gyama* of the same fungus.

Temdrin's adventure with the trade started soon after de-collectivization. Being a child of a large family, he decided to take a business challenge and left his share of state-allocated animals to his brothers. Today he is a prominent local figure, and his life story has been published in a local newspaper:

> "From 1982 I was going all over Golok and buying medicinal plants, mainly *yartsa*. In the beginning the profit was good, so I invested heavily in the business. In more than 15 years there were many ups and downs in managing the business, and sometimes I even had to worry about my food and clothing. Then I came to Machen County and borrowed 200 yuan from somebody. In the morning I was buying hides and wool from nomads and selling them to others in the evening, and I tried to enjoy life even though I earned very little money. In five years of making small profits, I saved up 20,000 yuan. The profit from livestock products wasn't bad, but was changeable, and it was hard to make any prediction (…), so I was afraid it would go like that *yartsa* business before. I told myself I needed to open a shop that would give me more stability in business. I imagined that opening a Tibetan products shop would be the right idea, and from 1993 I invested 20,000 and opened a shop. The shop soon became very popular, and in one year I got a profit that doubled the invested money. The array of products was slowly getting bigger, I became rich and got a position in the county. In 2001 I got a good opportunity to invest in property development in Dawu, invested 200,000 yuan, and built a three-storey hotel. (…) I am a happy man.'"[43]

Unlike many Tibetan middlemen, Temdrin (rTa mdrin) is a full-time trader. He buys and sells *yartsa* all year round. In winter, when the fungus runs scarce at the market, its price rises, and anyone who does not need an immediate income and can take a risk in business may get a much higher price for his spring harvests: in December 2007 the price rose to 77,800 yuan per *gyama* of the best quality fungus. "I lost my money not once but twice as the prices can change between morning and evening several times," the traders often boast about the risky nature of their business. The future prices of *yartsa* are hard to foretell. They rose as rumors circulated that the Chinese swimmers who won gold in the diving contest in May 2007 did so as a result of their intake of *yartsa* dietary supplements. One may expect that the successes of Chinese athletes at the 2008 Olympic Games in Beijing will offer another proof of the marvelous effects that *yartsa* products can have on the human body's condition. Therefore, Temdrin cannot realistically foresee the end of the *yartsa* business, and he says that the fungus prices will rocket from the Games year onwards as demand rises. Yet contrary to expectations, 2008 brought a worsening of the yarsta market. Steady growth was cut short by travel restrictions and the general economic downturn.

Why *Yartsa*?

For the discussion on the economic processes in contemporary Golok and the other *yartsa* cropping parts of Tibet, medicinal qualities of caterpillar fungus are relatively unimportant. The medicinal reputation of *yartsa* is reflected in its price. The principal value of the fungus for its collectors and traders is its money-generating power. The economic processes that dictate *yartsa* prices are hard to follow for an average *yartsa* gatherer at the local level. It is common knowledge that guests at expensive restaurants in Shanghai can order a special meal with *yartsa* that – seen in the context of prices and salaries in Golok TAP – costs astronomic sums of money. But hardly any of the gatherers are aware that in the Tibet Hotel in Beijing, for example, *Pure Yartsa Capsules* by Tianzhi cost up to 9,000 yuan for 50 g, and 2,800 yuan for the 12 g set.[44] In a stylish hotel hall they are sold among elegant shirts, shoes, cigarettes and many Tibet-related souvenirs from China. Exposed in glass display cases, on red or gold velvet, *yartsa* triumphs in this collection of products recommended as a visiting-card of today's China. In Poland, to buy *Kordiseps Mycelium Capsules*, advertised on the post office flyer quoted in the introduction, one should be ready to pay 160 PLN (around one-tenth of a teacher's average monthly net salary) for a forty-day package.[45] The price would increase if the product were officially approved – not having state approval, it circulates in the time-honored communist tradition of selling on the black market.

In the common discourse in Golok, there are several examples of *yartsa* usage. It is usually claimed to be a good medicine against cancer and aging; as the Golok nomad says: "I don't know what the Chinese use *yartsa* for. I've heard its good for cancer, and when hair goes gray it helps to restore the color." However, it is difficult to explain why *yartsa* is in such demand in mainland China. One explanation is that people there have much spare money and can spend it on perhaps useful but not absolutely necessary products, like *yartsa*, to show their prestige and financial status. Doctors of traditional Tibetan medicine can comment more extensively on the trade and the reasons of its fast growth. They, too, albeit admitting historical usage of *yartsa* by Tibetans, see the fast growing demand for *yartsa* as a phenomenon more of social and economic, rather than "medicinal," character. "The quality of *yartsa* will never match its price," a Tibetan doctor from Golok says, explaining the reasons why demand for *yartsa* seems to grow endlessly. "Nowadays people have lots of money and think of having a good life. Men, especially businessmen, want to retain their sexual potency, and *yartsa* has a good influence on sexual enthusiasm. They want to stay forever young, as if they were always thirty. Epidemics like SARS in 2003 also remind people of the need to take care of their health. And eating *yartsa* helps to build up the immune system and prevents illness," the doctor says. But in his own medical practice, *yartsa* is not much used. "It has mostly nutritional value, and not any specific medicinal one," he says. "But this is its power, that it can be used for everything, even put in expensive meals in Chinese restaurants in Shanghai. The Chinese pharmaceutical companies will use it more and more, people will buy more *yartsa* products. The demand will rise, and the number of *yartsa* at the market will drop, so the prices will go up, and the market will not collapse soon. Especially since attempts to make synthetic *yartsa* have not brought satisfactory results so far," the Golok doctor explains.[46] The *yartsa* gatherers in Golok might be unfamiliar with the product markups in Beijing or other commercial centers in China, but the buyers from distant metropolises also have very limited knowledge of the processes that go on in the Golok economic context, thus they have to go through middlemen in making business with the faraway land of Tibetan nomads.

Conclusion

When the next *yartsa* season is over, the situation returns to normal. The price of everyday goods goes down, and dozens of beggars from other parts of Tibet and China who migrate to Golok to earn money by begging during the *yartsa* season go back home. But the long-lasting effect of the *yartsa* boom will be visible longer. Czesław Miłosz, a Polish poet and 1980 winner of the Nobel Prize for Literature, wrote about life under a state-planned economy: "[i]n the countries of the New Faith [...] the liquidation of small private enterprises gives the streets a stiff and institutional look. The chronic lack of consumer goods renders the crowds uniformly grey and uniformly indigent.'"[47] *Yartsa* collecting and trade has contributed to the economic development of Golok, and the prestige consumer goods, shining motorbikes and Buddhist temples that have mushroomed in the last decade are *signum temporis*, a sign of the more prosperous times.

Yartsa is a cash crop of Golok and as such its importance for the area is hard to overstate. In the last fifty years the Golok highlands were affected both by economic engineering administered on pastoral communities by the Chinese state authorities and by the declining productivity of the land resulting from the gradual drying of the Qinghai-Tibetan Plateau, increasing population pressure and the debacles of central planning.[48] In a modern China that tries to successfully combine its socialist heart with the capitalist call to get rich, and to start business and build the welfare of the nation by taking up commercial initiatives, there are not many possibilities to step on the path of a semi-capitalist life, especially in such "Wild West" lands as Tibet. *Yartsa* hunting is a relatively easy and popularly available means of supplementing household income, and it easily finds its place in a timetable of pastoral activities in Golok. The increasing involvement in the "commodity economy" pushes the Golok pastoralists into cash-earning activities, among which *yartsa* gathering is relatively accessible. Being a reserve for an individual's or household's savings – in cash or in kind – *yartsa* serves as cash for a rainy day, an insurance that people can turn to when animal epidemics, natural disasters, economic failures or political disturbances – of the kind that were frequent in Golok in the last century – occur. The seasonal *yartsa* rush that breaks out in the area annually shows the newly gained importance of *yartsa* in the economic and social life of Golok.

While on a general level the *yartsa* outflow to China awakens patriotic sentiments and a feeling of regret that the main benefactors of *yartsa* business are outside Tibet,[49] on the individual level the *yartsa* trade seems to offer a chance to change one's life for the better. For those that have decided or been forced not to continue their lives as nomads, the *yartsa* business is a chance to start a new life in town. The same holds true for all sorts of people displaced from their customary lifestyles and places of origin. Golok towns are slowly getting crowded with resettled nomads being relocated and urbanized according to the state's directives on the environmental protection of pasturelands. For them – deprived of their conventional livelihood, having no herds and no "urban" job – to dig *yartsa* is a question of economic survival. Resettlement policies are explained by the nomads as a tool to protect the grassland. According to this logic, a ban on digging *yartsa* would be a natural consequence of new environmental directives issued by the state and prefectural authorities.[50] However, the resettled nomads can still come back to their pasturelands in spring and collect the fungus that grows on their land. "If they ban digging altogether, we'll be hit hard," says one of many resettled nomads whose family yearly income depends to a large extent on *yartsa* collecting. The nomads resettled into Golok towns can still benefit from the *yartsa* trade, albeit by being shifted into a changed set of social relationships and networks, sometimes far from their home area. In any case, the formation of a new entrepreneurial class in Tibetan societies in China is of crucial importance for these people's economic, cultural and political survival.

The commercial activity around caterpillar fungus digging and selling in the last two decades far exceeds any of the previous stages in this species' history in the area. The increasing demand for *yartsa* raises the competition for its resources. Prices paid for *yartsa*, and prefectural and township strategies for controlling the flow of fungus out of Golok, reflect this situation. With the tightening of control over the number of gatherers entering Golok each season, individual creativity and local arrangements functioning beyond the control of the state flourish. Future *yartsa* scenarios may vary. The available material is obviously too scanty to permit political speculation as to what shape future *yartsa* policies will take.

One may wonder though: did the Golok authorities listen to the local voices of dissent about large numbers of fungus diggers flooding the prefecture, which Susan Costello reported?[51] This sensitivity to civil disobedience would be a big achievement, not only in China. Closing access to pasturelands to non-residents and instead allowing the locals to benefit from their land, letting them employ harvesters working on "their behalf," seems to be the solution that many nomads in Golok would favor today. To devise a policy that benefits everybody is undoubtedly a hard task, and experiments take time to work. To see if this experiment will bring more failures or more successes, one needs to monitor future outcomes in the region.

Notes

1 This paper was envisioned as a field research report. It was my priority to make it a vivid "flesh and blood" description of the cultural and social milieu of everyday life in Golok, as dominated by *yartsa* harvesting and trade. "It's now or never," as Elvis Presley sang, to try to describe the field and the people with this down-to-earth approach; I also tried to capture some of the atmosphere of the place – in a way that Richard Hoggart did so bravely in his book on British working-class life. Great thanks go to my friends from Xining and Golok TAP, to AC, AL, G and his family, TsL and Ch, as well as Agata Bareja-Starzyńska, Adam Kozieł, Bianca Horlemann, Andreas Gruschke, Emily T. Yeh, Roman Frąckowski and Tina Niermann. I am grateful to Brandon Dotson for going through my paper so carefully, and to my anonymous reviewer whose comments helped me improve the text. Special thanks go to Mona Schrempf, Toni Huber and Melvyn C. Goldstein for their constructive criticism and never-ending encouragement in my

studies. Finally, my warm thoughts go to RAS and LJ. The research was conducted under the auspices of the Shanghai Academy of Social Sciences, China.

2 In this paper, Tibetan words are transcribed according to local pronunciation. The Wylie transcription in brackets indicates the Tibetan spelling. When two names for one thing are in use, both are given: the first one used in *gorked (mGo skad)*, Golok dialect, and the other one in a dialect used by the Wanah (sBra nag) part of the population of Golok TAP.

3 "Tibet" means one thing for the government of China, and another for the Tibetan Government in Exile. While the former claims that "Tibet" stands only for the area within the borders of the Tibet Autonomous Region, the latter says that this name could be applied also to the ethnically Tibetan areas that form so-called Tibetan Autonomous Prefectures within today's Qinghai, Gansu, Yunnan and Sichuan Provinces of China. Whatever the intricacies of local politics in Golok in the pre-PRC past might have been, there is no doubt today that Goloks and Wanahs in Golok TAP declare themselves to be Tibetans, and their land part of Tibet. In this paper, "Tibet" will be used to identify both the TAR and the TAPs in those four Chinese provinces.

4 *World Tibetan Network News (WTNN)*, "Gun Battle between Rival Tibetan Groups in Kardze leaves 6 Dead." http://www.tibet.ca/en/wtnarchive/2007/7/20_6.html, accessed 29 August 2007.

5 Tibetan Center for Human Rights and Democracy (TCHRD), "Commotion between two Communities lead to Arrest of 30 Tibetans" (July 2007), 4.

6 Conflicts over *yartsa* were highlighted during the horse racing festival in Lithang (*Li thang*), Sichuan, in August 2007, when a nomad, Rongye Adrak, stepped on to the stage, grabbed a microphone and gave a speech to the thousands of nomads who had gathered to watch the horse racing. He demanded the Dalai Lama's return to Tibet, and the release of the Eleventh Panchen Lama. But he started his speech by calling the nomads to stop getting into petty fights among themselves for land and gathering caterpillar fungus. See Maria Kruczkowska, "Setki aresztowanych po awanturze o Dalajlamę," *Gazeta Wyborcza* 181 (04.08.2007-05.08.2007), 9. For more examples of conflicts over harvesting of *yartsa*, see also Kunga Lama, "Crowded Mountains, Empty Towns: Commodification and Contestation in Cordyceps Harvesting in Eastern Tibet" (MA Thesis: University of Colorado at Boulder, 2007), 96–99. One informant told me that in 2007 in one of the mountain "villages" in Machen (rMa chen) County, a Hui *yartsa* gatherer trespassing the local nomads' *yartsa* fields was killed in a fight (personal communication, 1 June 2007).

7 It is difficult to decide when exactly *yartsa gunbu* found its way into Tibetan *materia medica*. The doctors in Golok point out that *yarsta*, under the name *dabshid* (*da byid*), was mentioned already in the *rGyud bzhi*, the fundamental treatise of Tibetan Medicine: g.Yu thog yon tan mgon po, *bDud rtsis snying po yan lag brgyad pa gsang ba mang ngag gi rgyud* (Ziling: mTsho sngon mi rigs dpe skrun khang, 2002), 74. Other historical sources of information about *yartsa* used by medical practitioners in Golok are 18th-century writings of De'u dmar bstan 'dzin phun tshogs, *gSo rig gces btus rin chen phreng ba* (Ziling: mTsho sngon mi rigs dpe skrun khang, 1993).

8 Steven D. Marshall and Susette Ternent Cooke, *Tibet outside the TAR. Control, Exploitation and Assimilation. Development with Chinese Characteristics* (CD-Rom, 1997), 2207; Don grub dbang rgyal and Nor sde, "mGo log lo rgyus deb ther." In *mGo log rig gnas lo* rgyus, vol. 1 (Zi ling: Srid gros mgo khul rig gnas lo rgyus rgyu cha zhib 'jug u yon ltan khang, 1991), 6.

9 Joseph F. Rock, "Seeking the Mountains of Mystery. An Expedition on the China-Tibet Frontier to the Unexplored Amnyi Machen Range, One of Whose Peaks Rival Everest," *National Geographic Magazine* 57.2 (1930), 131.

10 Personal communication, Jigdril, 18 May 2007.

11 The three rivers are Machu (Yellow River, Huanghe), Drichu ('Bri chu; Yangtze) and Dzachu (Dza chu; Mekong).

12 With reference to the prefectural capital of Golok, the primary name used in this discussion will be Dawu because that is the most widely known name for the place. Locals refer to it simply as "Golok" too.

13 Among the other purported reasons for the desertification of Martod grassland, digging medicinal plants reaches 31.8 percent in statistics published in "Bod kyi skye khams lta ba dang 'brel ba'i bklag deb." In *rMa rgyal gangs thigs* (rMa yul skyes khams khor yug srung skyob tsogs pa, nd.), 11. "Unchecked digging up of herbs" is one of the main causes of land degradation in China according to state officials; see Dee Mack Williams, "The Desert Discourse of Modern China," *Modern China* 23.3 (1997), 335.

14 Shuyun Sun, *The Long March* (London: Harper Perennial, 2007), 44.

15 Panczenlama (10th Panchen Lama, Chos kyi rgyal mtshan). "Wystąpienie na forum Stałego Komitetu TRA Ogólnochińskiego Zgromadzenia Przedstawicieli Ludowych, Pekin 1987." In *Tybet. Zamiast nadziei i błogosławieństw*, ed. Adam Kozieł (Warszawa: Stowarzyszenie Studenci dla Wolnego Tybetu, 2008), 146.

16 Melvyn C. Goldstein, *Nomads of Golok: a Report* (1996), http://www.cwru.edu/affil/tibet/nomads.htm, accessed 29 August 2007, 19. Only since 1982 was the grassland declared state property in China, which is "best understood in relation to the low priority the Chinese government accorded to grassland as compared with forests and other natural resources"; see Peter Ho, *Institutions in Transition. Land Ownership, Property Rights and Social Conflict in China* (Oxford: Oxford University Press, 2005), 83. On the Grassland Law and Golok, see Bianca Horlemann, "Tibetische Viehzüchter in der VR China: neue Chancen – neue Konflikte." In *Asien heute: Konflikte ohne Ende ...*, ed. Stephan Conermann (Hamburg: EB-Verlag, 2006), 42–44.

17 For descriptions of the dangers awaiting travelers to Golok, see for example Joseph F. Rock, *The Amnye Ma-chhen Range and Adjacent Regions: A Monographic Study* (Rome: IsMEO, 1956), 126–28; Andre Guibaut, *Tibetan Venture* (Hong Kong: Oxford University Press, 1987), 18 ff; and Bianca Horlemann, "The Goloks through Western Eyes: Fascination and Horror." In *Tibet in 1938–1939. Photographs from the Ernst Schäfer Expedition to Tibet*, ed. Isrun Engelhardt (Chicago: Serindia, 2007), 91 ff.

18 This quotation from a Darlag county official, see "100,000 Tibetan Nomads Ordered to settle in Towns," http://www.sinodaily.com/reports/100000_Tibetan_nomads_ordered_to_settle_in_towns_999.html (accessed 1 May 2007).

19 Personal communication, Machen, 21 May 2007.

20 "Scientific planning" was also a postulate to be employed by herders in Inner Mongolia. This, as well as other ideological conceptions revealing the state's view that the pastoralists' way of managing herds is economically irrational, is described by Williams: Dee Mack Williams, *Beyond Great Walls: Environment, Identity, and Development on the Chinese Grasslands of Inner Mongolia* (Stanford: Stanford University Press, 2002), 31, and has many parallels in Tibet. See for example Daniel J. Miller, "Tough times for Tibetan Nomads in Western China: Snowstorms, Settling down, Fences, and the Demise of Traditional Nomadic Pastoralism," *Nomadic Peoples* 4.1 (2000), 83–109. Contemporary China's concern with employing science in herd management has its roots in the 1920s Soviet Union: "its belief in scientific planning of an economy and the state ownership of industry, and its obsession with heavy industrial and military development as the keys to state power," see W.C. Kirby, "China's Internationalization in the Early People's Republic: Dreams of a Socialist World Economy." In *The History of the PRC (1949–1976)*, ed. Julia Strauss (Cambridge: Cambridge University Press, 2007), 22. It has been elaborated by contemporary authorities of the PRC that have widened the spectrum of applicability of centrally administered science to the realm of the Tibetans' herd management. On the other hand, calls for "development" are often a key phrase used by modern states to execute policies running contrary to the citizen's benefit. This can be observed in many countries of the West, too. Pro-development

and pro-environmental rhetoric in contemporary China can be observed in state pronouncements in Qinghai, where the two change places easily depending upon often temporary priorities.

21 Emily T. Yeh, "Tibetan Range Wars: Spatial Politics and Authority on the Grasslands of Amdo," *Development and Change* 34.3 (2003), 500. However, my own informants from Golok often say that fencing resulted in decrease in conflicts over land in the area. They tend to agree with conclusions of Fernanda Pirie: "Feuding, Mediation and the Negotiation of Authority among the Nomads of Eastern Tibet," *Max Planck Institute for Social Anthropology. Working Papers* 72 (2005), 22.

22 Medicinal plants were one of the export "products" of Tibet in the first half of the 20th century: Robert B. Ekvall, *Cultural Relations on the Kansu-Tibetan Border* (Chicago: University of Chicago Press, 1977), 6. In those days, as Ekvall writes: "in a sense, the Chinese and Moslems of the region [were] the intermediaries in the trade between the Tibetan country and the outside world." The situation as he describes has parallels with today's business relations in Golok (see further in this paper).

23 Bianca Horlemann, "Modernization Efforts in Mgo Log: a Chronicle, 1970–2000." In *Amdo Tibetans in Transition: Society and Culture during the Post-Mao Era*, ed. Toni Huber (Leiden: Brill, 2002), 244.

24 It is hard to verify the stories of specialized *yartsa* season bands that roam the land and rob the *yartsa* gatherers' houses/tents when the owners are away. However, *yartsa* season babysitters have not only to look after the family's children but also the property; the neighboring household being sometimes in the next mountain valley. It is not surprising, therefore, that the salary of a male babysitter can reach up to 3,000 yuan. This indicates the size of the income coming from *yartsa* harvesting in nomad households that can afford such a salary within its monthly budget.

25 A weight measure used for *yartsa* is *gyama* (*rgya ma*) or *jin* (Chin.), an equivalent of 500 g.

26 Plants that grow in the Golok highlands and are used in traditional Tibetan medicine include: *ranye* (*ra mnye*; *Polygonatum cirrhifolium*, *nyehing* (*mnye shing*; *Asparagus sp.*), *wa chy* (*ba spru*; *Mirabilis himalaica*), *hcholamar* (*sro lo dmar po*; *Rhodiola sp.*). See Christa Kletter and Monica Kriechbaum, *Tibetan Medicinal Plants* (Stuttgart: Medpharm Scientific Publishers, 2001); Tsewang J. Tsarong, *Tibetan Medicinal Plants* (Kalimpong: Tibetan Medical Publications, 1994).

27 Caroline Humphrey, "Barter and Economic Disintegration," *Man* 20.1 (1985), 60.

28 Arjun Appadurai, "Introduction: Commodities and the Politics of Value." In *The Social Life of Things. Commodities in Cultural Perspective*, ed. Arjun Appadurai (Cambridge: Cambridge University Press, 2001), 27.

29 The common belief among Golok Tibetans says that Muslim cooks put human ashes, bath water or the urine of an imam into meals served to the Tibetan guests in order to convert them to Islam. For more on tales about the Muslims told in Golok and other areas of Amdo, see Andrew M. Fischer, "Close Encounters of an Inner Asian Kind. Tibetan-Muslim Coexistence and Conflict in Tibet, Past and Present," *Crisis State Programme Working Papers*, 68 (2005), 19.

30 The Huis' entrepreneurial talents were recognized as an aspect of their ethnic identity and a part of their minority culture during the period of the *minzu*/ethnic minorities identification; see: Dru Gladney, *Dislocating China: Reflections on Muslims, Minorities, and Other Subaltern Subjects* (London: Hurst, 2004), 87. This interesting example of ascribing to an ethnic group such a "secular" ethnicity marker as being gifted businessmen suggests there might be similar state-recognized assumptions concerning other ethnic groups' business abilities or disabilities. These assumptions might be reflected in people's self-image. Tibetans often complain of Muslim businessmen's dominance in the market. The number of souvenir shops run by Huis in tourist sites such as Kumbum, small scale "catering" business for Tibetan monks at lunch time in monasteries and the lack of similar petty businesses run by Tibetans is explained as a result of the Tibetans'

supposed bad luck in business and their disinterest in earning money. Such opinions expressed by Tibetans themselves would be surprising for authors who travelled to Tibet in the past and praised the Tibetans' trading skills; see for example Bell's accounts: "[a]s with the Arabs from of old, so with the Tibetans. Many are devoted to robbery, all to trade, while religion overshadows everything," Charles Bell, *The Religion of Tibet* (1931; reprint, Delhi: Motilal Banarsidas, 2000), 7.

31 Andrew M. Fischer, *State Growth and Social Exclusion in Tibet. Challenges of Recent Economic Growth* (Copenhagen: NIAS Press, 2005), 166.

32 Goldstein, 10; Susan Costello, "The Flow of Wealth in Golok Pastoralist Society: Toward an Assessment of Local Financial Resources for Economic Development." In *Tibetan Modernities. Notes from the Field on Cultural and Social Change*, ed. Robert Barnett and Ronald Schwartz (Leiden: Brill, 2008), 94; Horlemann 2002, 262.

33 Not only from Qinghai (Yushu, for example), but also from Yunnan Province and the Tibet Autonomous Region; see Daniel Winkler, "Yartsa Gunbu – *Cordyceps Sinensis.* Economy, Ecology and Ethno-mycology of a Fungus Endemic to the Tibetan Plateau," www://ourworld.cs.com/danwink/id_m.htm, accessed 1 May 2007), 13. Such *yartsa* digging was also mentioned to me in personal communication from Andreas Gruschke (1 December 2007), Michelle L. Olsgard (12 August 2007) and local informants (May-June 2007).

34 *Tibetans, Chinese Battle Over Access to Medicinal Fungus*; http://www.ens-newswire.com/ens/jun2005/2005-06-02-01.asp, accessed 29 August 2007.

35 Toni Huber writes of the practice of "sealing of territory" to protect the local resources, plants included, and to guard against disturbing the local territorial deities in Amdo. Angering them might result in "bringing various kinds of misfortune to the community who lived within their sphere of influence": see Toni Huber "Territorial Control by 'Sealing' (*rgya sdom pa*). A Religio-political Practice in Tibet," *Zentralasiatische Studien* 33 (2004), 142. Some informants from Golok say that if disturbed by members of neighboring non-Buddhist populations, the mountain gods do not turn their anger onto Tibetans unless the outsiders were helped by the Tibetans themselves.

36 The Golok highlands were known for their gold deposits for much longer than the existence of the People's Republic of China. The Ma clan, which is remembered as so oppressive of the Tibetans in Golok in the first half of the 20th century, was also gold-fever driven. The 1980s saw a minor gold rush in the area. In 2002, there was a ban on all alluvial gold mining in Qinghai, see Tibet Information Network (TIN), *Mining Tibet: Mineral Exploitation in Tibetan Areas of the PRC* (London: 2002), 26, but local witnesses say that private gold washing is still met at a few sites in Banma.

37 A television advertisement on Qinghai TV, Amdo dialect service, broadcast in spring 2007, showed Tibetans climbing the mountain slopes. They dug *yartsa*, but did not replace the soil in the resulting hole. The next shot of the short movie showed the desert encroaching on the mountain grassland, and the fertile alpine meadow turned into a barren field of sand. In everyday discussions about the problems arising from *yartsa* exploitation, it is always the "others" – Han Chinese or Huis – who are blamed for not replacing the soil after digging out the fungus.

38 Bianca Horlemann, personal communication, Berlin, 17 April 2008.

39 The people whose stories and opinions are quoted here hide behind pseudonyms taken from the names of popular singers of spring 2007 in Golok. Their music accompanied every interview, and kept its influence on the research and writing process.

40 Guide (*Trika;* Khri ka) and Guinan (*Mangra*; Mang ra) are counties in Tsolho (mTsho lho)/Hainan TAP, Qinghai, approximately 293 and 238 km to Dawu (from the county seats). Hualong (Bayan; Ba yan) Hui Autonomous County in Tsoshar (mTsho shar)/Haidong TAP, Qinghai.

41 To read more, see Emilia Sułek, "Tseren's Last Gold Rush. Tales of *yartsa* hunting in Tibet," *International Institute for Asian Studies Newsletter* 46 (2008), 20–21.

42 One jiao is one-tenth of one yuan; ten fen make one jiao.

43 dPal chen rDo rje, *Kha char bu yug khrod nas 'tshar long byung ba'i khros po* (Newspaper article, source and year unknown), 1.

44 The official exchange rate was approximately 8.00 yuan for 1.00 American dollar at that time, data from 22 April 2007.

45 Janusz Czapiński and Tomasz Panek, eds., *Diagnoza społeczna 2007. Warunki i jakość życia Polaków* (Warszawa: Rada Monitoringu Społecznego, 2007), 162.

46 In fact, some foreign pharmaceutical companies claim that they have cultivated a *Cordyceps* that even exceeds the potency of wild *yartsa*. See for example "Heilpilze: *Cordyceps*." (Institut für Ernährungs und Pilzheilkunde, available online: http://www.mykotroph.de/pdf/MykoTroph_Factsheet_Cordyceps.pdf, accessed 25 August 2007), 3.

47 Czesław Miłosz. *The Captive Mind* (London: Penguin Books, 2001), 66.

48 The situation is far more complicated than that, and the "campaigns of destruction" – the Great Leap Forward (1958–1961) and the Cultural Revolution (1966–1976) – under Mao Zedong, who explicitly called for the conquest and harnessing of nature on the way to achieving China's "greatness," highlight many examples of centrally administered mismanagement being a simple failure of imagination. Reservoirs, dams and irrigation projects proceeded from the Soviet school of thinking on the environment. The damage wrought by these often disastrous large-scale projects was exacerbated by deep plowing, fertilizers, eliminating pests and implementing such ideas as described by Becker: "[i]n Qinghai, for example, prison inmates tried to make iron-hard soil suitable for plating by digging little holes and filling them with straw and grass which were set on fire;" Jasper Becker, *Hungry Ghosts: Mao's Secret Famine* (New York: Free Press, 1996), 70–82; see also Elisabeth Economy, *The River Runs Black: The Environmental Challenge to China's Future* (London: Cornell University Press, 2007), 50 ff. According to some writers, pressure from the central government to increase production is to be blamed for the "four decades of overstocking;" Dillard H. Gates, quoted in Sylvie Dideron and Marie-Louise Beerling, "The Socio-economic Situation of the Herders in Guoluo Prefecture. A Review of Research Conducted under the QLDP." In *Living Plateau: Changing Lives of Herders in Qinghai. Concluding Seminar of the Qinghai Livestock Development Project*, ed. Nico van Wageningen and Sa Wenjun (Kathmandu: ICIMOD, 2001), 36. The elderly herders in Golok remember similar examples as those given by Becker from the commune era, when they were ordered to plough the grassland and try to cultivate crops, with no results.

49 A Chinese-English-Japanese language coffee-table book, *Qinghai. A Remote Province of China*, is not likely to reach the hands of nomads in Golok, but if so, some of them would be outraged to read what follows: "[w]ith the pollution-free ecological environment the highland Qinghai has been planned as the treasure house of the Traditional Chinese Medicines and Tibetan Medicines, including *Chinese* caterpillar fungus" (emphasis added). *Qinghai. A Remote Province of China* (Xining: China Travel-Tourism Press, 2004), 82.

50 Human Rights Watch (HRW), "'*No One Has the Liberty to Refuse*'. Tibetan Herders Forcibly Relocated in Gansu, Qinghai, Sichuan, and the Tibet Autonomous Region," *Human Rights Watch* 19.8 (June 2007), 49.

51 Costello, 94.

3

Fishery in Southern and Central Tibet

An Economic Niche is Going to Disappear

DIANA ALTNER

Introduction

This chapter will discuss the business of Tibetan fishermen in the past and the present, and will give an outlook for the future.[1] It starts with an overview of the basic natural and cultural conditions for fishery in Tibet, which has generally been limited by the lack of a real fishing and fish-eating tradition among local populations. Markets for fish have traditionally been small. Although the rivers and lakes of Tibet abound with fish, fishing is not in favor nor does it constitute an appreciable resource for the population. Most Tibetans are agriculturalists and pastoralists, and the few Tibetan communities who have depended upon fishing have done so due to lack of land. Their economic and social status has always been low in Tibetan societies. A short introduction on the status of fishermen in traditional Tibetan society will be given before considering the sole remaining village community where the inhabitants live as fishermen. Although prior to the 1990s the urban population in Tibet gradually changed due to immigration from Chinese provinces where fishery traditions are well established, there was no strong stimulus for fishery development. However, due to a continuing influx of Chinese migrants over the past decade, fishery in that single village experienced a sudden boom as the demand for fish increased, and the formerly poor economic status of these Tibetan fishermen improved greatly. Local subsistence fishing has developed into a commercial fishery. This chapter will research the economic upturn of the village and its consequences, and also look at recent changes and the reasons for abandoning fishing.

Basic Conditions for Fishery in Tibet

The natural and cultural conditions for fishing in Tibet vary greatly. While the natural landscape of the Tibetan plateau offers potential for fishery, the cultural conditions tend to contradict the exploitation of that resource. In that connection there are three facts to be considerated: the natural fish population as a source for fishery in contrast to the attitude of the Tibetans towards fish as food, and the position of the Tibetan fishermen in Tibetan society.

The Natural Fish Population

Western China has fishery potential that is small by world standards, but significant nonetheless. Although the region is cold and arid, there are many lakes and rivers fed by runoff from nearby mountains. Fisheries have been established for more than forty years, but contribute less than 0.2 percent of agricultural production.[2] Western China has a comparatively small fish fauna of 190 species. In Tibet there are only fifty-six species, of which ten species are economically valuable.[3] Zhang Chunguang even mentioned seventy-one species and subspecies.[4] There exist mainly three classes of fish: trout (Salmonidae), carp (Cyprinidae) and catfish[5] (Siluriformes).

The lakes and rivers with the highest abundance of fish are Namtso (gNam mtsho) Lake, Yamdroktso (Yar 'brog g.yu mtsho) Lake and Yarlung Tsangpo (Yar klung gtsang po) River. Yamdroktso contains between approximately 200,000 and 300,000 tons of fish.[6] Namtso is also said to contain abundant fish supplies.[7] The Food and Agriculture Organization (FAO) estimates the fish population there at 49.2 kg per hectare.[8]

Many early travel accounts on Tibet also mention an abundance of fish and sometimes even of single fish species in Tibetan rivers and lakes. One of the most important trading routes from Gyantse (rGyal rtse) to Lhasa led along the western and northern shores of the Yamdroktso. Waddell described fish population close to the village of Yarsig (Yar gzigs)[9] at the beginning of the twentieth century as follows: "[f]ish were so abundant in this stream below the bridge that they seemed literally to jostle one another, so that some of the Indian followers, wading in, scooped them out on the bank, and in a short time caught in this way over three hundred lbs. weight." (…) "... all like carp in general appearance, and almost scaleless; though some of them are different in size and arrangement of their spots."[10] Further on, Waddell writes, "Fish were extremely abundant everywhere and were good eating. Many were large, from one to three pounds or more. Most of them had very minute scales, and a moustache of a pair of bearded feelers."[11]

Fish as Food?

Fishery in Tibet has generally been limited by the lack of a real fishing and fish-eating tradition among local populations. Dietary and related cultural factors have in part contributed to this situation. Tibetans prefer consumption of products from the pastoral economy, such as mutton, beef, and dairy foods, and animals associated with water tend to be culturally categorized as dangerous or ambivalent, and thus best avoided as food. There exist many prejudices against fish as food in Tibet, and popular accounts still maintain the "myth" that Tibetans don't eat fish at all. Tibetan Buddhists believe that taking the lives of fish is a sin; each one is a life, or soul. "Still, Tibetans do not eat the meat of small animals. Since a life is life, no matter what size, people consider it better to take just one life, of a single large animal. It would take the lives of many small animals to produce as much meat."[12]

Another reason for avoiding fish as food is the supposition that fish feed on human corpses that are disposed of in lakes or rivers as a form of burial. Macdonald described an experience he had after the consumption of fish: "[o]ne day we landed some tasty specimens, and after they had been fried and eaten I happened to wander along the bank looking down into the water, and came upon hundreds of similar fish feeding on a human corpse, which had been thrown into the river as a form of burial.[13] We never ate local fish again!"[14] Duncan also mentioned this reason for the dislike of fish as food: "... fish eat human corpses thrown in the river which makes them odious; but the fundamental motive seems to be that of transmigration and cannibalism. Human beings may be reborn into fish who may eat corpses and when caught furnish food for other people; all this makes a circle of cannibalism which is repugnant to the Tibetan. If fish is eaten one is cautioned to avoid the fish ears which are said to be actual human flesh."[15]

The attitude towards fish as food has changed in the last decades. Tibetans have the popular belief that spring fish is very healthy, and the fact that it is sought after is often emphasized by the following proverb: *dpyid nya rgyal por ma rag, ston ka khyi yis za* ("The spring fish is hard to get even for the king, the autumn fish is eaten by dogs"). Generally fish is also regarded as a very good medicine for several diseases. Dried fish is said to be an excellent drug for pregnant women — not only during their pregnancy but also while they give birth. Fish from holy lakes are said to be of a very special quality. Sherring described the medical meaning of fish from Lake Manasarovar in Western Tibet: "So great is the sanctity of these waters that fishing is forbidden, and whatever fish are cast up by the violence of the waves are considered peculiarly efficacious for the exorcism of evil spirits and the cure of all kinds of cattle disease. The fish, after being cleaned, should be carefully dried in the sun and kept until the time that a cure has to be

Dried fish from Lake Manasarovar in Byi'u dgon pa[17] *(Pu rangs county in Western Tibet).*

Fish being sold to tourists. (Photos by Andreas Gruschke, 1999.)

wrought. A portion should then be cut off and allowed to burn on hot coals, and the noisome smoke and odour emitted should be conveyed into the nose of the patient by close application, when the resultant effects are wonderful, a fact which is easily credible."[16] Also nowadays dried fish from the lake plays an important role and is sold by the local residents.

Although the attitude towards fish as food has changed in the last decades for Tibetans, today fish does not play an important role in their nutrition — compared to other food. Therefore, Tibetan markets for fish have traditionally been small. Fishing is not in favor nor does it constitute an appreciable resource for the population.

The Status of Fishermen in Tibetan Society

The pre-modern central Tibetan state, the Ganden Phodrang (dGa' ldan pho brang), was ruled and administered by a tiny elite of Buddhist clerics and hereditary nobility. From the time of its founding in the mid-17th century, both social and religious criteria were used by the elite to define social ranking. The regent to the Fifth Dalai Lama,[18] Desi Sangye Gyatso (sDe srid Sangs rgyas rgya mtsho), allocated the fishermen the lowest level in his presentation of the organization of Tibetan society. According to him, the first, highest level — the ruler and leaders (*rgyal rigs*) — who served Buddhism, were followed by the nobility (*rje rigs*). People who lived on agriculture, trade and carpentry formed the third level. Butchers, ferrymen, ragyepa (*rags rgyab pa),*[19] beggars and fishermen belonged to the final and lowest level.[20] According to Veronika Ronge,[21] until 1959 fishermen were classed as tradesmen (*lag shes bdag po*: "owner of a handicraft") who were also regarded as low level. Among the different trades there again existed social ranks, but even there the fishermen, butchers, ferrymen, and ragyepa as occupational groups who benefited directly from the deaths of living beings ranked on the lowest level. They mostly lived in poverty and economic uncertainty, were sometimes forced to beg, and were regarded as "impure." Sangye Gyatso also alluded to the fact that fishermen and butchers who violate the Buddhist moral code of not killing living beings have no hope of a higher rebirth. Fishermen who kill fish live at the cost of these animals.[22] Tibetan Buddhists seem to regard the killing of fish as a very special sin. Duncan reported of Tibetans that: "[a]mong nature's creatures the killing of fish is the greatest of sins. For this a variety of reasons are given — such as a fish can make no outcry for help and plea for mercy; and set forth in 'To kill the tongueless fish is an unforgivable sin'..."[23]

In Tibetan literature, fishermen are often mentioned in so-called "*delog* stories" (*'das log*). *Delog* refers to one who has crossed the threshold of death and returned to tell about that experience and the sufferings that await anyone with a morally negative life, according to Buddhism. Often it is fishermen who are reborn into and suffer in the different hell realms.[24] "In the dramatic plays of the harvest festivals and the New Year Religious dances these four classes [butcher, hunter, fishermen, and heretic] are the villains. They must all spend considerable time in Hell after death to overcome the sins of taking life. People, therefore, avoid eating with a butcher or even talking to him very much lest the sins of the butcher descend upon them."[25] In theatre and opera performances, fishermen often play the role of the outcastes, although they are also often depicted as converting to a morally correct life according to Buddhism.

In pre-modern Tibet, social contact with those occupational groups who were "professional sinners," such as fishermen, was generally avoided. When unable to fish, many fishermen in fact depended upon begging and thus only amplified their already despised social status. The custom of intermarriage between different fishing families became long-standing since there was no chance to find partners from another social level. Low social level was a heritage that became virtually impossible for Tibetan fishermen to overcome. Fishermen were regarded as "dirty" and for this reason the development of a real fishery tradition was hindered and nobody seemed to go fishing voluntarily.

The Significance of Fishery in the Tibetan Economic System

Ri dwags ma sngon/ nya ma bshor bde bar sdod
"Don't hunt wild animals, don't catch fish, keep them in peace!"[26]

The dominant economic systems in Tibet are agriculture and nomadism. In larger cities the significance of the industrial and service sectors increased in the last decades. In this connection, trade, transport, handicrafts, tourism and the restaurant and hotel business should be emphasized. Compared to the predominating agricultural and nomadism culture, fishery can be described as an "economic niche" in the Tibetan economic system. Although rivers and lakes abound in fish, that source of food was obviously not sufficiently used. The topographic conditions did not offer ideal preconditions for fishery but at many places fishing would have been possible.

The social sanctions against fishermen — based on Buddhism — and the attitude of the Tibetans towards fish as food had a hindering effect on the development of a real fishery tradition. Restrictions concerning the catching of fish also supported the effect. Because certain lakes were considered to be of great religious significance, fishing activities were often regulated at the highest levels of government in the pre-modern central Tibetan state in Lhasa. For instance, the *kashag* (*kha shags*), or cabinet, regulated the size of holes in fishing nets so that young fish and other non-edible creatures were protected,[27] while various Dalai Lamas and regents issued proclamations banning fishing. McGovern mentioned the consequences of such a practice at Yamdroktso: "[o]nce or twice we saw where formerly there had been villages of moderate size which had now become deserted.... In this particular instance the downfall of these villages was due, so my companions told me, to the abolition of fishing. Although fish is considered a dirty food, the Tibetan peasants not infrequently eat it, and Yamdrok Lake is well known for the size and excellence of fish; but the present Dalai-lama, who is more than usually strict in his observance of religious injunctions, issued strict orders that the catching of fish should be stopped ..."[28]

The northern and western shore of Yamdroktso was one of the regions where fishery in the past played an important role for the local economy. Since many foreign travellers crossed the lake on their way to Lhasa, fishery was more or less well documented (or at least mentioned) by most of them. During my fieldwork in that region I was also told that fishing activities in the area were stopped in the 1930s and 1940s due to the restrictions of the central government. Before that time, a remarkable number of local dried fish was exported to Bhutan. Actually, there were two main reasons for the reduction of fishing activities at the lake. During the reign of the Fifth Dalai Lama the so-called *nya 'bru* ("fish barley") was introduced as compensation for the restrictions of fishing. The central government took the *nya 'bru* from two sources: interest for barley lent during the fallow period and taxes from the farmers (both in the form of barley). The main reason for giving up fishing activities in the 1930s and 1940s was the so-called *nya dmar* ("fish profit"). *Nya dmar* is the term for additional land given after the death of the Thirteenth Dalai Lama (1933) to villages that depended on fishing due to a lack of land. Most of the residents living at the lake are nowadays ashamed of the fishing tradition of their ancestors. Only a few people at the lake still go fishing to get some additional income in springtime.

Nevertheless, a fishing culture simply developed at places in central and southern Tibet where the local residents depended on that source of income or food due to geographical circumstances, such as the lack of fertile land. The example of the end of the fishery at Yamdroktso emphasizes that the Tibetans stopped fishing activities as soon as enough fertile land was available for their subsistence.

Tibetan Terms for Fishermen

Several Tibetan terms for fisherman are derived from the word fish (*nya*): *nya pa* (fisherman), *nya lto pa* (fish eater), *nya 'dzin* (fish catcher) and *nya zan* (fish eater). The term *nya dol pa* also belongs to that category; *nya dol* means "fishing net" and a *nya dol pa* is somebody who uses a fishing net — a fisherman. Sarat Chandra Das translated *nya dol pa* as "a fisherman; such as those living on the southern shores of Yamdok Tsho,"[29] and emphasizes with that example the local presence of fishermen in that region that he documented at the end of the 19th century. The term *dol pa* is no longer used today for fishermen. The most common word for fishermen is *nya pa*, which also means fish seller. In Lhasa fishermen are also called Chunpa (*'jun pa*). That name is a local characteristic since it is derived from the name of the fishing village Chun ('Jun) — the last fishing village in the region.

The Last Fishing Village in Central Tibet

According to available historical evidence, it appears that few Tibetans ever depended predominantly upon fishing for their livelihoods. Nowadays, in central

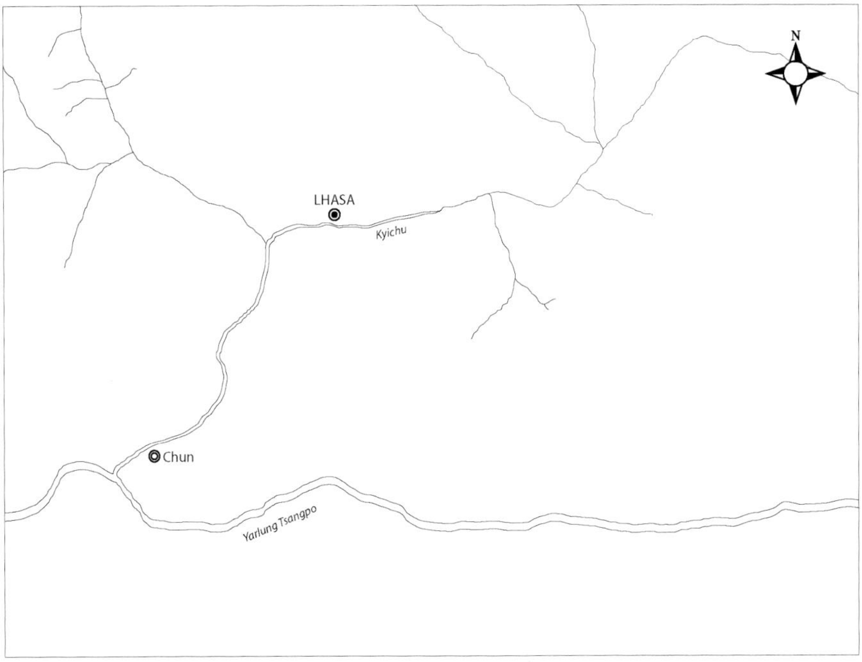

A map with the location of Chun. (Design by Norma Schulz and Diana Altner.)

Tibet there is only one remaining village community where the inhabitants still live as fishermen. The village of Chun, situated on the east bank of the southern part of the Kyichu (sKyid chu) River, belongs to Chushur county and Tsarpanang Shang (mTshar pa nang shang).[30]

The village borders directly on the Kyichu River to the west, and mountains surround it to the south and east. In literature Chun is also called Chunpa ('jun pa.)[31] The Tibetan word *'jun* means "to subdue, to tame, to discipline."[32] An older name for the village was lJon,[33] and the Tibetan term *ljon pa* means "forest, trees." It cannot be clearly explained what aspect was "disciplined" by the people of Chun — it could have been the river, but also the forest (there area still many trees in the region).

The location of Chun can be compared with an island. Until 2004, it was only possible to reach Chun by water transport, principally the traditional yak-hide boat or coracle. No bridge or road existed at all. Chun's proximity to the river was only one reason for the development of a fishing tradition there; a shortage of arable land was another. Due to these two circumstances, the people of Chun have long depended significantly upon fishing. Until 1959, they lived largely by providing ferry transport services on both the Kyichu and Yarlung Tsangpo rivers. They also paid their taxes to the Ganden Phodrang state and local monasteries in the form

Overview of Chun. (Photo: Diana Altner, 2004.)

of these services. An important water transport route served by the Chunpa went from Lhasa to Samye (bSam yas) Monastery.

Today, eighty families live in Chun; these number around 400 people. The village has its own monastery, which is situated on the mountain to the south. The monastery has different names: Chunpa Gonpa ('Jun pa dgon pa) but also Gongkar Gonpa (Gong dkar dgon pa).[34] In Western literature there is only one comment about the village Chun, found in the diaries of Heinrich Harrer for the year 1950. He mentions a village (Djum) that he visited on his way from Lhasa to Samye that has not a single piece of land and whose inhabitants are the only ones in Tibet who have the right to go fishing, to deal with fish, and who pay their tax in the form of fish.[35] The Chunpa estimate that their village was founded around 1,000 years ago. The first mention of Chun in Tibetan literature was made in the 17th century.[36]

Today, with modern roads and bridges rendering the traditional water transportation services of the Chunpa redundant, the economic life of Chun is based upon a mix of fishery, agriculture, seasonal pastoralism and handicrafts. In addition to the lack of arable land in Chun, a large part of the available land is damaged regularly by flooding of the Kyichu River. Chun's economic fortunes have improved greatly with the influx of Chinese migrants to the Lhasa area over the past decade or so, with the result that local subsistence fishing has now developed into a commercial enterprise.

In his book *Malay Fishermen: Their Peasant Economy,* Raymond Firth classified a group of Malay fishermen as belonging to a peasant economic society[37] and described them with the following characterization: they use a simple, non-mechanised technique, small units of production, production for subsistence as well as for the market, and have no dependence on the world market.[38] While the harvests from the fields are seasonal, within the bounds of fishery the yields can be made every day. Fishing offers the opportunity to get an additional win everyday in the form of food or money.[39] Fishermen who belong to a peasant society are often forced to sell their haul, to exchange it and to be involved in agriculture alongside fishing. Concerning Firth's definition of peasant fishermen the Tibetan fishermen can also be classified as belonging to that group. The fishing technique that they use is relatively simple and unmechanized, the units of production are very small and they use their haul for subsistence and for selling it to the market. Besides fishing they depend on the yields of their fields, but these yields are not sufficient for their families. The fishermen of Chun are also peasant fishermen.

The Economic Upturn of Fishery and its Consequences

Economic and social transformations resulting from the reforms implemented under Deng Xiaoping have fundamentally changed life in central Tibet. The new post-1980 policies allowed for a renaissance of traditional Tibetan culture. Restrictions on religious activities were loosened, and traditional customs enjoyed a revival.[40] Accordingly, activities such as slaughtering once again became openly regarded as a Buddhist sin, and stigmatized. The introduction of a free market economy had consequences for the living standard of the Tibetans and their social organization. The development of infrastructure led to an expansion of different economic fields. Individual trading activities were permitted once again. In relation to all of these factors, the life of the fishermen in Chun has also changed dramatically since the early 1980s.

The inhabitants of Chun regard the year 1982 as the second major turning point in the history of their village. What is regarded as the first progressive change occurred in 1959, with the collapse of the feudal system, when the village ceased to be a dependency[41] of Drepung ('Bras spungs dgon pa) Monastery near Lhasa. For the residents of Chun, the 1980s mark the beginning of an improvement in their economic conditions due to three main factors: the strong increase

Two Chunpa fishing on the Kyichu River. (Photo: Diana Altner, 2004.)

in Chinese demand for fish; improvement of fishing technology; and changes in work relations — the beginning of working for Chinese middlemen.

Since the early 1980s, the demand for fish has increased steadily in central and southern Tibet. For the fishermen of Chun, the late 1980s and early 1990s were the most productive in terms of their actual catch.[42] The increased demand for fish could only be satisfied by using modern nets. During the first years (early 1980s) the increase of the quota and the income were the consequences of that "run for fish." Prior to 1959, fish were usually caught using dragnets in summer, and with spears through holes in the ice during winter. Today, gillnetting is the main method used. The introduction of gill nets had consequences for the division of labor. When using the old nets, six people and two boats were necessary for fishing: two people were responsible for rowing the boats, with two people for the upper and two more for the lower part of the net. Nowadays, there are only two people required for fishing, one rowing and the other using the net.

At that time — in the 1980s — the rivers still had an abundance of fish and thus the price was rather low. The price of fish has a wide seasonal fluctuation, with spring fish very popular throughout central and southern Tibet and therefore very expensive, while autumn fish is comparably cheap. The high-valued fish is even exchanged against barley one to one by weight during springtime, and fishermen of Chun generally get 3 *jin*[43] barley for 1 *jin* fish in neighboring villages. The price difference between spring and autumn is further increased because the fish population in spring is lower than in autumn.

During the late 1980s, the Tibetan fishermen began working to order for Chinese bosses. These organizational changes had consequences for the division of labor, for relations and organization between the fishermen themselves, and for the marketing of the catch. Before the fishermen started working for middlemen they sold their fish themselves in Nyemo, Lhasa, and in various villages. Nowadays, the catch is generally collected by the middlemen at different places and paid for immediately. These middlemen sell the fish to fish markets in Lhasa or export them to other parts of China. The Chinese middlemen are only interested in live fish. The fishermen keep their catch alive in special nets in the river. The middlemen transport the fish later in thick plastic bags that are filled with water and additional oxygen, thus ensuring the fish arrive safely alive at the market. Nowadays, there are several fish markets in Lhasa city. The most important market for imported fish from mainland China is situated closed to the Potala and offers a wide range of many kinds of fish and seafood. The most important market for local fish can be found close to the Tibet Museum in the east of Lhasa. Fish and seafood are offered fresh, often still alive, but also frozen. At the Lhasa night market there is also a big range of different kinds of fish.

Prices for fish in October 2004

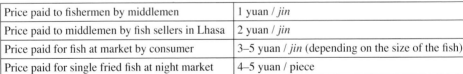

Price paid to fishermen by middlemen	1 yuan / *jin*
Price paid to middlemen by fish sellers in Lhasa	2 yuan / *jin*
Price paid for fish at market by consumer	3–5 yuan / *jin* (depending on the size of the fish)
Price paid for single fried fish at night market	4–5 yuan / piece

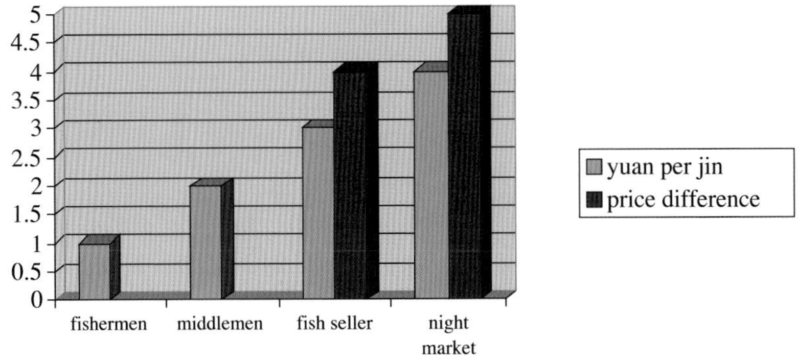

Source: own research in October 2004.

In October 2004 the middlemen paid 1 yuan for 1 *jin* of fish to the Tibetan fishermen; in Lhasa the fish was sold for 3 yuan per *jin* by the fish sellers. Bigger fish were even sold for 5 yuan. According to the Lhasa fish seller, they paid 2 yuan for 1 *jin* of fish to the middlemen. At the night market, individual local fish are offered for 4 to 5 yuan per piece.

The price differences are remarkable. The reason why the fishermen do not sell their fish by themselves to get a higher profit is because of lack of transport and market stalls. The low prices that the fishermen are paid by the middlemen — compared to the prices for fish in Lhasa — are accepted. With these price differences, the costs for transport, for distribution and for the marketplace are not included. For that reason the real profit for the current fish sellers is hard to compare.

Today, the fishermen from Chun work for several middlemen. Since the middlemen have an agreement with them concerning fish prices, the fishermen themselves do not have much influence on pricing. The fishermen say that they do not sell their fish by themselves directly to consumers since they lack transport possibilities and market stalls. The fishermen regard the delivery of live fish to middlemen as the most comfortable way of conducting the fish trade. This way they avoid the act of killing the fish. The fish that are caught for subsistence have

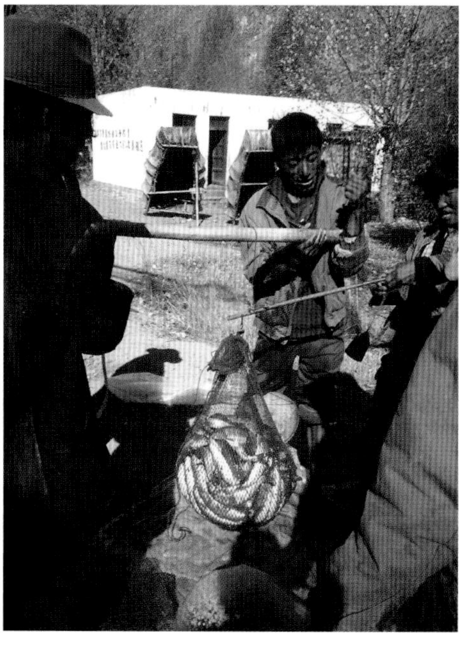

The fish is sold to the middlemen.

Market for local fish in Lhasa.
(Photos: Diana Altner, 2004.)

to be killed, of course, but that normally happens in a "passive" manner: the fish suffocate in the bottom of the boats or later on the grass where they are spread after being caught. By delivering the still-living fish to other people, the fishermen avoid the direct act of killing (at least "passively"), but they pass on the fish with the certainty that they will be killed. The knowledge that the death of the fish is a result of the activity of the fishermen is as sinful as the killing act itself from the Buddhist religious point of view. The ideal proximity between catching the fish and the act of killing them should be as attenuated as possible, perhaps in order to keep the religious "pollution" as limited as possible.

As a result of the rising demand for fish, rivers are becoming gradually over-fished. Another reason for the decrease of the fish population in the Kyichu and Yarlung Tsangpo is the increasing level of pollution entering these rivers. Although there is not much industry in the region, the wastewater from Lhasa city is polluting the rivers. Another factor to negatively affect the ecology of the rivers has been the introduction of foreign fish species from China. One foreign species[44] in particular, introduced in the beginning of the 1990s, increased dramatically in local rivers and is competing against local fish species for food. The fact that fish in Tibet grow much slower due to the climatic conditions and are more sensitive to environmental changes than in other areas is another reason why the fish population won't recover fast. A fish needs four to five years to reach a weight of 200g and ten years for 500g. The weight of the fish that are caught today is seldom more than 250g. To give young fish a chance to survive, the government of the Tibet Autonomous Region (TAR) has fixed the minimum size for the holes in fishnets at 50mm.[45] Previous methods used by Chinese fishermen, including poison, electricity and dynamite, are now forbidden. Unfortunately, these rules are violated from time to time and many young fish are killed in this way. According to Zhang Chunguang, a first step towards the protection and recovery of fish populations has been taken by the declaration of "no fishing areas" and "non-fishing seasons" in the counties of Medrogongkar (Mal gro gung kar) and Taktse (sTag rtse), where fishing is forbidden between March and May for up to five years.[46]

Before 1980, the fish quota was easily increased by increasing the number of boats and nets. Due to recent over-fishing other alternatives must be found to satisfy the demand for fish. One possibility that is already used is the introduction of aqua culture close to bigger cities.[47] Due to over-fishing the fishermen of Chun have been forced to widen the radius of their fishing activities. Although they formerly used to find fish in Chushur county throughout nearly the whole season, since 2000 they have sometimes had to travel far to find enough fish. Nowadays, fishing activity takes place throughout the whole year, with the exception of the Saga Dawa (*sa ga zla ba)* Festival (during the fourth month of the lunar calendar).

The seasonal organization of the Chun fishery is strongly connected with seasonal temperature variation. In summer and autumn, fishing activities take place mostly in nearby regions, but the cold temperature in winter offers the chance to go fishing further away and transport the fish back fresh to Lhasa. In autumn, there is much more fish available than in spring, and the natural result is that during that time the catch is much higher. In September and October, fish is caught exclusively in the Kyichu and Yarlung Tsangpo rivers in Chushur County, with October said to be the month with the greatest abundance of fish. At this time, the water level of the rivers is lower than usual, which makes it easier to go fishing. In November and December, the fishermen increase their radius of activity as far as Nyemo County to fish along the Yarlung Tsangpo. Usually they stay for several days in the same places, where they often spend the night on the shore of the river in tents. During the springtime, the fishermen can often travel as far as Shigatse (gZhis ka rtse), sometimes even to Ngari (mNga' ris). The fishermen are sometimes absent from home for one to two months. In most cases they are filling orders placed by Chinese middlemen. The fish dealers coordinate with the fishermen and pick up their catch regularly at whatever site they use. Since around 2000, the fishermen have been increasingly acquiring mobile phones as a new means of communication. This has improved contact between the middlemen and the fishermen, since the latter previously had to go in person to Lhasa for every business matter, which can now be dealt with cheaply within minutes. The fishermen can now sell their catch while still on the river, while the Chinese middlemen are able to reach their suppliers everywhere. In this way the communication and transport networks of the fishing industry, and indeed others as well, have been greatly improved by the use of mobile phones.

Recent Changes and Reasons for Abandoning Fishing

The most significant recent changes in Chun were introduced by the construction of the new shortcut road between Lhasa and Gongkar Airport, with two new bridges crossing the Kyichu and the Yarlung Tsangpo and one tunnel in between. Within the context of this project[48] the village was connected to the local road network, and the former "island" location is now a thing of the past. Nowadays the village can be easily reached by car. A trip by taxi from Lhasa to Chun takes around one hour.

The consequences of the road are various. The construction of the new tunnel also produced an interesting by-product: stone. Since the land on the shore of the Kyichu where the tunnel was built belongs to Chun, the inhabitants are allowed

Walking to Chun by foot in 2003.

The same place one year later.

Climbing to Chun in 2003.

The same place in 2004.

to collect stone there for free. This offered a new source of income: selling stone. There is now a tendency to give up fishing for this new business opportunity. This is the first time that there has been a real alternative to fishing and the Chun fishermen want to use it. Not only does the stone offer a new source of income, the new road also offers a way to transport the stone to the main road. Constructing new houses of stone has become popular throughout the whole region, even in Chun, and the demand for stone is high. Next to the stone business, the inhabitants of Chun established another new source of income: a transport business between Chushur and Lhasa. In additon to the transportation of stone, the Chunpa also carry all kinds of products between these two places. Although breaking stone is a hard job, and the income is lower than that from fishing, more and more fishermen prefer the stone business since it offers the possibility to stay with their families instead of going far afield on fishing trips. Additionally, the people in Chun have found a further source of income; they have started building model boats for the growing tourist market in Lhasa.[49]

The Case of Lungpa

Close to Chun there is another place that depended for a long time on fishing: Lungpa[50] (Lung pa). That village is located in Gongkar county on the northern shore of the Yarlung Tsangpo. Lungpa is situated on the other side of the tunnel that was constructed as a part of the shortcut to Gongkar airport.

Many parallels exist between these two villages. The geographical location of the village was the same as in Chun and could be compared with an island. There

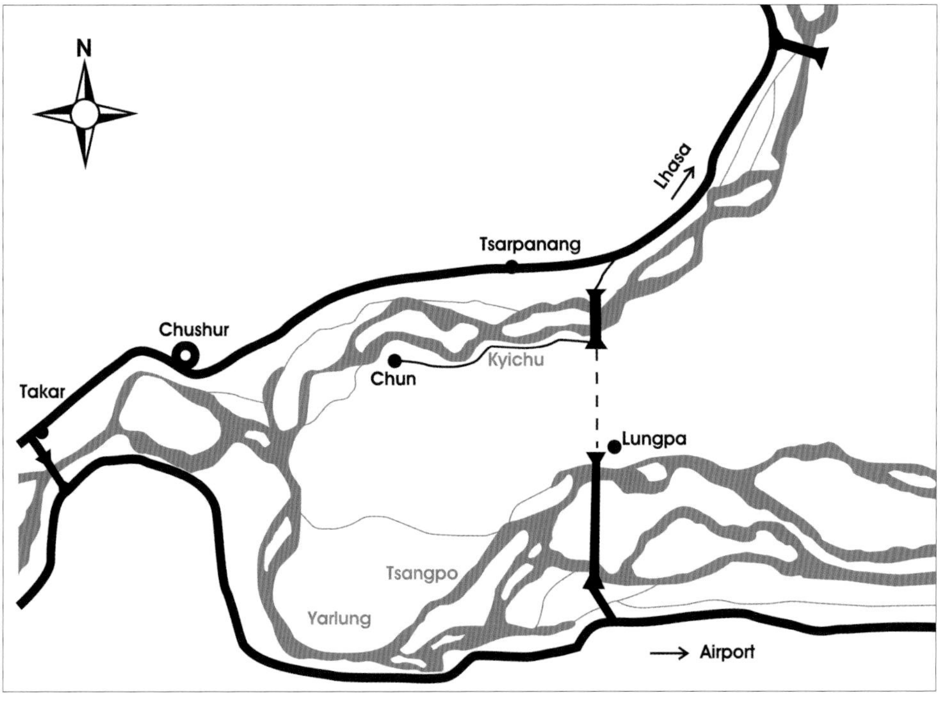

Map showing Chun ('Jun) and Lungpa.
(Design by Jenny Julius)

The newly constructed village of Lungpa. On the right-hand side in the background is the bridge. (Photo: Diana Altner, 2004.)

was no chance to get to Lungpa by crossing a bridge; the inhabitants depended on water transport by boats. But there existed another interesting parallel: the lack of fertile land and the dependency on fishing and ferry services. When the new bridge over the Yarlung Tsangpo was constructed in 2001 the whole village was resettled. The new Lungpa is now located around three km to the west of its old location, close to the bridge. Every family was presented 25,000 yuan by the local government to build new houses. The new village now has around 200 people. Most of them lived as fishermen before the village was connected to the local network. But all of them gave up that business and started collecting and selling stone, or they got jobs in the companies that were responsible for the construction of the bridge and tunnel project.

Whether or not the inhabitants of Chun will also give up their fishing activities, as did the people in Lungpa, depends on different factors. How fast will the fish population decrease in future, and how difficult will it become to get enough fish for the growing market? In any case, the Chunpa have already started looking for alternatives for their income, and their dependence on fishing will decrease.

Conclusion

Will fishery disappear in southern and central Tibet? To answer that question different positions should be considered: the natural conditions for fishery in Tibet and its changes, the cultural conditions for that business and the general changes in Tibetan economy, society and infrastructure over the last decades.

The prospect for the fishery business was never positive in Tibetan society. While the natural conditions — especially the fish population — offered good chances for using that resource for subsistence or additional income, these resources were exploited too much in the last decades. As a consequence the rivers are over-fished and polluted. Although the government started reacting to these problems, the ecological balance is highly endangered and partly destroyed due to several factors. The peak of the fishery business in Tibet has already been reached, and the global problem of over-fishing has also touched the roof of the world.

As already explained, fishing cultures developed naturally at places in central and southern Tibet where the local residents depended on that business due to geographical circumstances. If we look at places where fishery played an important role for the local economy in the past such as the Yamdroktso region and Lungpa village we detect that the fishing activities were given up as soon as there a real alternative for income arose. The social status of fishermen within Tibetan society has not really changed, despite the fact that now many of them have become wealthy during the past two decades. In the eyes of outsiders (non-fishermen) they still live as sinners since they take the lives of many living creatures. What are the arguments of the fishermen for commercial fishery? Most of them answer the question using the story of the Buddha's ink, which goes like this: "[o]nce upon a time, there were many fish on the earth. All these fish could fly and they were flying around the whole day teasing mankind by darkening the sunlight. One day, the Buddha decided to take the fish to his home. But they also teased the Buddha by drinking all his ink. The Buddha became angry, and he took one Tibetan and told him that he and his descendants would have to go fishing. So, if fishermen were told by Buddha to go fishing, it can't be a sin!"

In fact, fishermen consider their occupation, at least superficially, with composure. Former fishermen at the Yamdroktso suggested that they don't regard fish as real living beings with a soul; rather they can be compared with water bubbles. In spite of these explanations, Tibetan fishermen do believe that sin is involved in their occupation, and their maintaining distance from the act of killing the fish is clear evidence of this. Fish that are caught for subsistence are usually put on the bottom of the boats or kept in fishnets on the land, and thus slowly suffocate. Fish that are sold are handled in two different ways. Fish that are to be dried are placed on the grass where they also slowly suffocate.[51] The majority of the catch is sold live to buyers. Thus, direct killing by the fishermen is always either avoided completely or left to other people. Fishermen also make a distinction between catching fish for subsistence and for profit, the latter being considered far more negative. Most of them cease fishing at an age of around fifty-five to sixty years. Older, former fishermen intensively engage in religious practices in order to try and compensate for their sins. This pattern is also usual in other occupation groups who take life, such as hunters and soldiers.[52] Fishermen who consider they were morally polluted when they were young expect cleansing of their sins by strengthening their religious activity when they become older.

The demand for fish has not stopped, rather it continues to increase. However, the social expressions of the values that are derived from Buddhism seem to form a kind of balance to the law of the market. Although fishing has become a lucrative business during the last twenty years, more and more fishermen now look for alternatives. The consequences of over-fishing and the decreasing of the fish population make it more and more difficult to catch enough fish. But this is only one reason for giving up that business. For the inhabitants of Chun there is for the first time a real alternative of doing another business instead of fishing. The infrastructural improvement was only the first step on the way to a decreasing dependency on fishery. It was maybe also the first step on the way to giving up fishing entirely. The revival of Tibetan Buddhism and its values in modern Tibetan society supports of course the wish of the fishermen to stop doing their business and offers their descendants a chance to perhaps live without the "pollution" of fishing.

Notes

1 This chapter draws on my doctoral thesis, "Die Verkleinerung der Yakhautboote. Fischereikulturen in Süd- und Zentraltibet im ökonomischen und soziokulturellen Wandel des modernen China" ("The Reduction of the Coracles. Fishing Cultures in southern and central Tibet and their Economic and Sociocultural Change in Modern China"). I undertook fieldwork in southern and central Tibet during 2003 and 2004 in southern Tibet in Lhasa, Nangkartse (sNa dkar rtse rdzong), Gongkar (dGong kar rdzong), Chushur (Chu shur rdzong) and Nyemo (sNye mo rdzong). In 2003 I had the possibility to cooperate officially with the Tibetan Academy of Social Sciences (TASS). Pema Gyatso and Ngodrub Tsering assisted me during my interviews and accompanied me to the field. I thank them very much, and also Beimatsho who helped me to organize my fieldwork. In 2004 I undertook my fieldwork and Tibetans accompanied me too. All interviews were done in Tibetan, English or Chinese; I saved my information by making notes or taping cassettes (for instance fishermen songs). Several working processes (such as the construction of a yak hide boat) I documented by filming and taking pictures.

I thank Toni Huber, Brandon Dotson and an unknown reviewer for giving comments to an earlier version of this chapter.

2 Keith F. Walker and H. Zhang Yang, "Fish and Fisheries in Western China." In *FAO Fisheries Technical Papers* 385, ed. T. Petr (Rome: FAO, 1999), 237.

3 Ibid., 247.

4 Zhang Chunguang, "Xizang de yulei ziyuan" ("Fish Resources of Tibet"). In *Zhongguo Xizang (China's Tibet)* (Beijing, 1997), 54.

5 Tibetan: *nya kha leb,* also *dpa' kha leb.*

6 Duojie Caidan and Jiangcun Luobu, *Xizang jingji jian shi. shang/xia (A Short History of the Economy of Tibet)* (Beijing: Zhongguo Xizang chubanshe, 2002), 222.

7 "A Xinhua news item recently stated that Tibet is rich in fish. This was the conclusion of a survey conducted by the Aquatic Department of Tibet. The survey was confined to the huge lake in central Tibet, Nam Tso, or the Sky Lake which is several days' journey from Lhasa. According to the Aquatic Department, fishing in the Nam Tso lake during the five-month-long freezing season alone could produce about 300 tons of fish and according to the same survey the annual fishing potential of the lake, which is 4,700 metres above sea-level, is 14,000 tons. The Autonomous Region alone has about 1,500 lakes totalling 23,800 square kilometres and here the annual fish resources have been estimated at 820,000 tons." See "Tibet Rich in Fish," *Tibetan Bulletin* 14.1 (March/April, 1983), 19f.

8 Walker and Yang, 247.

9 Also known as Baldi (dBal di). The same place name is also found north of Yarsig, being the former Baldi dzong (dBal di rdzong).

10 L. Austine Waddell, *Lhasa and its Mysteries. With a Record of the Expedition of 1903–1904* (London: J. Muray, 1905), 301. The carp species described here is named *Gymnocypris waddelli.*

11 Waddell, 182.

12 Rinjing Dorje, *Food in Tibetan Life* (London: Prospect Books Place, 1985), 18.

13 Next to sky burial water burial is quite common in Tibet. At Yamdroktso corpses are bound in cotton cloth and disposed of in different parts of the lake. Sometimes they can be seen from the shore. During my fieldwork in 2003 I observed such burials of both human corpses and animal carcasses in the region. Also see the description of water burial at the Nyang River: Wen Zhida. "*Niyang he shuizang*" (Water burial at the Nyang River), *Xizang Minsu* (Tibetan Folklore) 3 (1998), 59.

14 David MacDonald, *Twenty Years in Tibet. Intimate & Personal Experiences of the Closed Land Among All Classes of its People from the Highest to the Lowest* (1932; reprint, New Delhi: Cosmo Publications, 1996), 151.

15 Marion H. Duncan, *Customs and Superstitions of Tibetans.* London (1964; reprint, New Delhi: Book Faith India, 1998), 243.

16 Charles A. Sherring, *Western Tibet and the British Borderland. The Sacred country of Hindus and Buddhists with an Account of the Government, Religion and Customs of its People* (London: E. Arnold, 1906), 273.

17 Chinese: Jiwu si. I thank to Andreas Gruschke for this information.

18 Ngag dbang blo bzang rgya mtsho (1617–1682).

19 The *ragyepa* were responsible for carrying the corpse out of the town in traditional Tibet.

20 Kristina Lange, *Die Werke des Regenten Sans Rgyas Rgya mc'o (1653–1705): eine philologisch-historische Studie zum tibetischsprachigen Schrifttum.* Veröffentlichungen des Museums für Völkerkunde zu Leipzig. Heft 27 (Berlin: Akademie Verlag, 1976), 111.

21 See Veronika Ronge, *Das tibetische Handwerkertum vor 1959.* Beiträge zur Südasienforschung Bd. 43 (Wiesbaden: F. Steiner, 1978), 31.

22 Lange, 111.
23 Duncan, 243.
24 See also Delog Dawa Drolma, *Delog. Journey to Realms beyond Death* (Varanasi and Kathmandu: Pilgrims Publishing, 2001).
25 Duncan, 66f.
26 That request can be found in the edict of Zhwa lu, that was published by Kun dga' blo gros rgyal mtshan dpal bzang po ti shri (1310–1358) in 1340 or 1352 and was dircted at the people in central and western Tibet. (See Giuseppe Tucci, *Tibetan Painted Scrolls,* vol. 2 (Roma: La Libreria Dello Stato, 1949), 750, V). I thank Toni Huber for the advice of this source.
27 "The fishing activity around Yar 'brog g.yu mtsho in southern Tibet was regulated by the central government in Lhasa as the lake is of great spiritual significance. The Kashag (Cabinet of the Tibetan Government) regulated the size of fishing net holes so that young fish and other non-edible creatures were protected." That quotation I found at the homepage: http://www.tew.org/tibet2000/t2.ch2.water.html, accessed 29 March 2008. A source — "Tsering 1996" — was mentioned. Unfortunately I could not find out any further information concerning that source or even the original Tibetan document.
28 William Montgomery McGovern, *To Lhasa in Disguise. A Secret Expedition through Mysterious Tibet* (1924; reprint, New Delhi: Book Faith India 1992), 306–7.
29 Sarat Chandra Das, *Tibetan-English Dictionary* (1902; reprint, Delhi: Book Faith India, 1995), 473.
30 During my fieldwork in 2003 and 2004 the village Chun was the focus of my research. I visited the place several times and lived there with a familiy. I did interviews (single, groups) with many Chunpas (different sex and age).
31 The Chinese name of the village is Junpa.
32 See Melvyn C. Goldstein, ed., *The New Tibetan-English Dictionary of Modern Tibetan* (Berkeley: University of California Press, 2001), 398 and Heinrich A. Jäschke, *Handwörterbuch der Tibetischen Sprache* (1871; reprint, Bad Honnef am Rhein: Biblio Verlag, 1971), 183.
33 See Tshe ring, "Nya grong ljon zhes pai ming 'thob tshul skor gyi dmangs khrod shod srol" ("Oral Tradition on the naming of the fishing village lJon"). In *Lhasa sKyid chu* (*Lhasa River*) (Lhasa, 1999), 37–39.
34 Another name for the monastery is Chunpa Khang ('Jun pa khang). The monk who is responsible for the monastery and who also lives in Chun thinks that Gongkar Gonpa is the right name of the building. Unfortunately there exist no historical documents about the history of the village or the monastery in Chun. The monastery was destroyed during the Cultural Revolution and rebuilt in the 1990s. The founder is said be Sonam Gyatso (bSod nams rgya mtsho) from India.
35 Found in an unpublished diary by Heinrich Harrer (dated 1 October 1950); I thank Isrun Engelhardt for this advice.
36 See Ngag dbang blo bzang rgya mtsho, *gSung 'bum* (*Collected works of the 5th Dalai Lama*), Vol. 17, 239. The place Chun on the Lower Kyichu River (*skyid smad 'jun*) was mentioned. I thank Prof. Per K. Sørensen for this advice.
37 Raymond Firth, *Malay Fishermen. Their Peasant Economy* (London: Routledge & Kegan Paul, 1966).
38 Firth, 5–6.
39 "Fishing can be used like casual day labour, to give an agriculturist a little extra food or cash immediately, or to fill a gap in another task." See Firth, 2.
40 See also Melvyn C. Goldstein and Matthew T. Kapstein, "Introduction." In *Buddhism in Contemporary Tibet. Religious Revival and Cultural Identity*, ed. Melvyn C. Goldstein and Matthew T. Kapstein (Berkeley, Los Angeles and London: University of California Press, 1998), 10.

41 Chun was subordinated to Drepung Gonpa until 1959. Villagers between eighteen and sixty were liable to pay taxes to the monastery and the central Government.

42 The years between 1983 and 1993 were called the "fat" years.

43 One *jin* (Tibetan: *rgya ma*) is 1/2 Kilo.

44 The Chinese name of that species is *yi yu* ("shining fish"), the Tibetan name is *ci nya*. Compared to the local fish that have a oblong form that new species looks rather strange since it has a round form.

45 Zhang Chunguang, 55.

46 Ibid.

47 In the neighborhood of Lhasa there are several fish farms; they are exclusively Chinese-run.

48 Chinese: *liang qiao yi sui* ("two bridges, one tunnel"), see map.

49 I bought such a model boat for 150 yuan. I was told that that the same price is also paid by the middlemen, but I suppose they may actually pay much less.

50 Chinese: Longba. In the publication of Guandong Sheng (1994) Lungpa is still mentioned as a fishing community (next to Chun) in the Tibet Autonmous Region. See Guandong sheng, ed., *Zhongguo minzu wenhua daguan. Zangzu, Menbazu, Luobazu* (*The impressive cultures of China's nationalities. Tibetans, Menba, Luoba*) (Beijing, 1994), 44.

51 Nomads also kill domestic animals by suffocation — see, for instance, Angela Manderscheid, *Lebens- und Wirtschaftsformen von Nomaden im Osten des tibetischen Hochlandes* (Abhandlungen -Anthropogeographie, Institut für Geographische Wissenschaften, Freie Universität Berlin, Band 61, Berlin: Dietrich Reimer Verlag, 1999), 61 — but not exclusively. Goldstein and Beall describe how yaks are killed with a sword. See Melvyn C. Goldstein, and Cynthia M. Beall, *Die Nomaden Westtibets. Der Überlebenskampf der tibetischen Hirtennomaden* (Nürnberg: DA Verlag, 1991), 98.

52 See Toni Huber, "Gewalt in tibetisch-buddhistischen Gesellschaften," *Mitteilungen des Museums für Völkerkunde Hamburg* 36 (2005), 458.

4

Exploring the Rush for "Himalayan Gold"

Tibetan Yartsa gunbu *Harvesting in Northwest Yunnan and Considerations for Management*

MICHELLE OLSGARD STEWART

Introduction

Yartsa gunbu, or *Cordyceps sinensis,* a rare fungus endemic to the Tibetan Plateau, is highly valued in traditional Chinese medicine (TCM) and international biomedical research.[1] Within TCM, *yartsa gunbu* (known as *dongchong xiacao* in Chinese) is categorized as a "warm" medicinal substance, and is commonly administered in tonic form to replenish kidney, liver and immune function, and to help against respiratory disease, fatigue, night sweating, arrhythmias and other heart diseases, hyposexuality, hyperglycemia, hyperlipidemia and renal failure.[2] Recent biomedical research has revealed that its polysaccharide fractions modulate immune activity and inhibit tumor growth.[3] The latter characteristics are of growing interest in international cancer research for exploring novel agents for radiation mitigation to improve the outcome of current radiation treatment. Petrova et al. reveal that *C. sinensis* modulates nuclear transcription factor NF-kB, which demonstrates promise for both radiation mitigation and anti-cancer;[4] Xun et al. revealed that mice trials of CorImmune, a cultured strain of *C. sinensis*, accelerated leukocyte recovery and stimulated lymphocyte proliferation;[5] and Yoshikawa et al. indicate that *C. sinensis* and one of its active ingredients, cordycepin, function as human tumor cell suppressors.[6]

While the recent rise in demand for *yartsa gunbu* (hereafter referred to as *yartsa)* is attributed to TCM and biomedical research markets, its medicinal use originates in traditional Tibetan medicine (TTM). Tibetan use of *yartsa* was initially documented by Nyamnyi Dorje, a Tibetan physician and lama who lived from 1439 to 1475,[7] while the first Chinese documentation of *dongchong xiacao* was reportedly in Wang Ang's medicinal reference, *Ben Cao Bei Yao*, in 1694;[8] the Tibetan use of *yartsa* predated its Chinese integration by over 200 years. Some recent publications have claimed that *yartsa* was discovered by a Tibetan yak herder approximately 1,500 years ago, who noticed that his yak herd grew exceptionally energetic after grazing upon a certain kind of mushroom;[9] these claims are not verified, however, and it is not known exactly how or when it was first integrated into TTM.[10]

Though TTM demand for *yartsa* does not significantly drive the larger economy of the resource, most Tibetans maintain that it is a powerful medicinal: one young girl who reportedly had very bad vision and had to wear thick prescription glasses, drank two grams of *yartsa* per day for one week and never had to wear glasses again.[11] Likewise, a traditional Tibetan doctor near Zhongdian detailed a case of a female patient who had a serious liver-related illness; after failing to improve after various treatments, he prescribed her two grams of *yartsa* per day for two weeks and she convalesced by the end of the treatment.[12] The same Tibetan doctor also noted that it is often administered to women during childbirth to give them energy. Within TTM, it is generally used for enhancing immune system function, virility and is prescribed, often paired with other medicines, for Hepatitis B, kidney, lung and heart function.[13] If the price for and potential income from *yartsa* were not so high, many Tibetans would likely use it much more regularly. In the past, harvesters often collected and kept *yartsa* for the household; currently, however, they keep very little for personal consumption, if any at all. Harvesters in northwest Yunnan generally only keep *yartsa* for the household's elderly or sick, and in these cases they generally keep later-season *yartsa,* which is of the lowest market value, as later discussions will explain.

Over the past decade, *yartsa,* or "Himalayan gold,"[14] has become arguably the single most important constituent of rural Tibetan economies of the Tibetan Plateau. During this time, prices for *yartsa* have increased by a factor of ten[15] and the cash profits earned during the six-week harvesting season account for 50–80 percent of Tibetan annual cash income across the Tibet Autonomous Region (TAR), Qinghai, Gansu, Sichuan and Yunnan provinces.[16] This income is critical as China's economy becomes increasingly more cash-reliant.

China's current economic development initiatives[17] directed at the Tibetan Plateau underline the importance of securing current livelihood strategies because the promises of economic development are not fulfilled equally for all. Yeh discusses the politics of economic development in Lhasa and how often times its touted benefits, such as education and increased employment opportunity, do not reach many rural populations, which leaves them marginalized by many of the emergent labor opportunities due to language or skill-based barriers.[18] The mountainous terrain that semi-pastoral Tibetans utilize for subsistence also hinders development projects, such as infrastructure and roads. It is likely that the current campaign to "Develop the West" will directly develop the urban areas of the west,[19] highlighting the need for research investigating the current social and ecological underpinnings of livelihood systems in order to better understand ensuing transitions.

While region-specific developmental campaigns may not directly reach the rural populations of these areas, paradoxically, large-scale political economic transitions within China are dramatically influencing local-level processes across the Tibetan Plateau through marketization of its resources.[20] Tibetan *yartsa* harvesting is driven entirely by TCM demand, which continues to rise due to China's burgeoning middle class and increased consumption of such high-value commodities. Rising market demand for *yartsa* is dramatically shifting Tibetan subsistence patterns as thousands of Tibetans migrate to *yartsa* areas to access this increasingly lucrative resource. Response to market demand is also influencing Tibetan cultural practices and belief systems; Kunga Lama discusses some of the moral quandaries arising for harvesters who choose to collect *yartsa* on sacred mountains, capitalizing on economic opportunity at the cost of their traditional reverence for these spaces.[21] Social conflicts mount as the stakes for *yartsa* increase: a feud erupted in Sichuan in July 2007 due to conflicts over access to fuel wood and *yartsa*, which resulted in eight fatalities,[22] and a similar conflict occurred in Qinghai in 2006.[23] Local-level responses to rising market demands vary significantly across regions due to highly heterogeneous social and ecological systems and histories. The need for management, however, is uniform across regions.

Despite its critical importance to contemporary livelihoods, increasing demand for the resource and escalating social conflicts, the sustainability of *yartsa* harvesting remains unknown. Harvesters are currently concerned that resource yields are threatened and are potentially decreasing. Informal interviews with harvesters in Yunnan during July 2007 revealed that across each of three sites, *yartsa* yields per harvester were noticeably less in 2006 than in 2007. Similar reports have been noted elsewhere.[24] Sustained *yartsa* resources and harvesting depends on both resource life-history patterns and how harvesting practices potentially impede resource viability. In order to co-create (with the community) management guidelines for sustainable harvests, baseline measures of resource abundance and harvesting impediment to resource viability are needed; both of these measures are currently lacking and are aims of future research.[25]

In addition to continued research, there is a need to shift this resource into the community-based resource management (CBRM) arena both in theory and practice. While several studies have underlined the importance of *yartsa* to local economies and livelihoods, there has to date been little mention of its management considerations. The recent social uprisings and harvesters' concern for diminished resources suggest that strategies for management are in need of exploration. Lacking ecological understanding of the resource system has discouraged attempts to postulate management options. While it is critical to accurately account for ecological complexity and limitations in resource management, it is also important to make way towards management in the face of ecological uncertainty. This chapter suggests that exploring current harvesting practices through participant observation will be a productive way to move towards management in relation to what is currently known about *yartsa*. As will be shown, harvesting practices are complex negotiations between the underlying ecological characteristics of the resource viability and its broader political economy, specifically market demand and preferences for certain qualities. Moreover, this chapter underlines the importance of localized explorations of harvesting practices because all *yartsa* social landscapes are not the same; different geographic spaces have unique social, economic and environmental histories that underpin how current practices emerge.

In order to contextualize *yartsa* with its general ecological and political economic influences, the following discussion begins with an overview on *yartsa*'s life history parameters, followed by a discussion of its transitioning market demand. With these broader parameters in mind, I shift to a local-level exploration of two harvesting practices that have emerged in northwest Yunnan and demonstrate that both early season and live caterpillar harvesting intimately relate to broader political economic and ecological characteristics of the system. Lastly, I relate these practices to their considerations for community-based resource management.

The following discussion is based on a preliminary study conducted in northwest Yunnan during the summer of 2007. Informal and semi-structured interviews were conducted with harvesters, government officials and nature-reserve staff across three ethnically Tibetan villages, Adong, Dongwa, and Xusong — these are well-known *yartsa* regions in northwest Yunnan and most interviewees told me that approximately one-half of their households generally participated in the spring harvest. I also conducted informal interviews at TCM shops in Deqin, Zhongdian, Kunming and Beijing. The discussion based on these findings aims to foster future research on *yartsa* and continue discussions of its implications for management. It does not intend to serve as an outline for management strategies.

Origins of a Commodity: *Yartsa Gunbu* Ecology

The term *Cordyceps* is derived from the Latin roots *cord* and *ceps*, meaning "club" and "head," respectively, referring to the physical characteristics of its reproductive fungal fruiting body, which emerges from the head of its host (see Figure 1). The literal translation of its name in Tibetan and Chinese, "winter-worm summer-grass," reveals the indigenous understanding of its life cycle. *C. sinensis* parasitizes the root-boring larva of ghost moth *Thitarodes* (*Hepialus*), using it both as a means of nutrient supply and substrate for growth during its year-long growth cycle.[26] *C. sinensis* spores attach to the larva in late summer and slowly ingest its vital organs and tissues throughout the winter (winter worm). In the early spring, the fungus develops a horn-like fruiting body from the head of the larva. The fruiting body, which facilitates wind dispersal of spores to new host species, protrudes above the soil and appears to harvesters as a 5–10 cm-long, brown blade of "summer grass." Of the nearly forty species of *Thitarodes* on the Tibetan Plateau, thirty can reportedly be infected by *C. sinensis*.[27]

The life cycle of the *Thitarodes* ghost moths consists of a larval stage that spans from one to three years, depending on its origin, and a reproductive moth-stage that lasts for only three to seven days. During its larval stage, it feeds on grassland vegetation roots and is noted to prefer the young roots of plant species of

Figure 1. *A harvest: the fruiting body is visible above and the larva is still below ground, the harvester has revealed the portion of the fruiting body that was below-ground (whitish coloring); harvesters often spot yartsa when only 2–3 cm of the fruiting body are exposed.*

the families Polygonaceae, Fabaceae, Cyperaceae (including *Kobresia*), Poaceae and Liliaceae.[28] During the summer months, the larva is generally located at approximately 10 cm depth in the soil, which is the primary root zone for most grassland sedges and shrubs, and during the winter it burrows deeper in the soil, to approximately 30 cm depth, to avoid the deep frost zone of the Himalayan winter.[29] Larvae distribution and relative abundance across the Tibetan Plateau remain unknown. During its reproductive moth stage, *Thitarodes* are not able to eat and only aim to reproduce. Adult female moths reportedly lay approximately 600 eggs, and it is presently unknown whether or not they preferentially lay eggs on a particular species of grassland vegetation.[30]

The exact mechanisms of how *C. sinensis* spores attach to *Thitarodes* larvae are not known, but spores likely penetrate host species without having to be ingested, which has been observed in other similar entomopathic fungi.[31] Once fungal spores attach to the larva and begin to develop throughout the late autumn, the parasitized larva exhibits a behavioral change and migrates to the upper 5–6 cm of the soil and vertically orients with its head towards the surface. Such behavior can possibly be explained by what Roy et al. have discussed as common host responses in other fungal parasitisms, including: (1) behavioral fever; (2) community evasion tactic; and (3) neurological effect. Parasitized insects can onset behavioral fever, or increased body temperature, by seeking out environmental locations that are at a higher temperature than normal living conditions. Though this behavior is energetically costly to the infected host it can in some cases suppress the pathogen or delay death. Community evasion refers to infected-host retreat from its surrounding community to prevent fungal infection of other individuals. Lastly, vertical migration may be a neurological side effect of secondary metabolites, which are often produced by the parasitic fungus to reduce bacterial breakdown of the host body, which in turn secures its nutritional components, lipids and organs, which will provide forage throughout the Himalayan winter. When the fungus has extracted all of the nutrition from the larva, thus ready for spore release, it stops producing the secondary metabolites and the larval body begins to "soften," or decay.[32]

In early spring, when snowmelt exposes the high alpine grasslands and the fungal fruiting body is visible above the soil, the fruiting body is short, elongating as the approximate six-week growth period elapses. It eventually develops *sporacia*, or spore-releasing nodules, at the top-most portion of the fruiting body. It is not presently known how soon after the development of *sporacia* actual spore release occurs.[33] Spores are potentially released when environmental conditions reach humidity levels in excess of 95 percent, as is observed in other entomopathic fungi reproduction patterns,[34] which might indicate that the commencement of the rainy season triggers the release of spores.[35] More biological research investigating specific timing and environmental parameters of spore release would be beneficial.

The Making of "Gold": Rising Market Demand

Wild-harvest *yartsa* is one of the most expensive products within TCM (see Figure 2). On average, in 2005, one kilogram was 20,000 yuan (approx. 2,500 USD), in 2006 it was 40,000 yuan (5,000 USD), and in 2007, 60–80,000 yuan (7,500–10,000 USD).[36] A general medical treatment often prescribes two grams per day for two weeks: using 2006 market prices, a treatment would cost 1,120 yuan (140 USD) — approximately one-fifth of the per capita disposable income of urban households in China for 2006 (5,997 yuan/yr, or 750 USD).[37]

The rapidly increasing market demand for *yartsa* is a culmination of many factors, including China's rising middle class, which results in increased consumerism; greater "openness" of the "West" (western regions of China) and consonant increases in tourism; attention to regional resources; and greater publicity of its medical efficacy. The first two reasons are intimately related. In his recent anthropological commodity chain analysis of *yartsa*, Kunga Lama notes that "Tibet sells," and that Tibetan commodities are novel to consumers because the "myth of Tibet" captures consumer interest.[38] For many of China's urbanites, Tibet and the "West" conjure associations of wildness and expanse, which cater to a consumer

Figure 2. *A TCM store owner in Zhongdian sorting a pile of* yartsa; *she was selling it for 100 yuan/gram (approx. 2–3 pieces). 1 July 2007.*

appeal for products from distant and exotic places. For example, two *yartsa* companies recently announced that they would merge in order to market the "Potala Palace" brand *C. sinensis* as the "No. 1 brand in the Mainland China;"[39] the Potala labeling leverages both cultural and regional associations of *yartsa*'s origin for increased consumer appeal.

While the "Tibetanness" of *yartsa* likely explains some consumer motivations for purchasing it, it is distinct from other "fetish" resources because, as detailed earlier, its medicinal use is noteworthy and increasingly being explored. *Yartsa* initially began gaining attention after two major events, the World Games in 1993 and the Severe Acute Respiratory Syndrome (SARS) epidemic of 2003.[40] In 1993, three Chinese female runners broke records in the 1,500 m, 3,000 m and 10,000 m events; their coach attributed their successes to the integration of *C. sinensis* into their training diets. This "testimony" sparked interest in *yartsa*'s capacity to improve endurance and athletic performance, and has since spurred several studies exploring its influences on athletic performance.[41] In 2003, the SARS outbreak sparked an increase in demand for Tibetan medicine in general, and the price for *yartsa* doubled from 4,000 yuan per *jin* (500 g) to 8,000–10,000 yuan per *jin* in the TAR.[42] Claims about *yartsa*'s effectiveness propelled it into the public interest and its consumption rates increased significantly.

Yartsa's association with the SARS epidemic critically engages it with China's current increases in respiratory illnesses due to its economic development and associated environmental trade-offs. China is currently the world's largest producer and consumer of coal, the emissions of which are environmentally destructive and cause an array of respiratory illnesses; currently 30–40 percent of China's territory, especially the southwest, is suffering from acid rain and respiratory diseases caused by poor air quality.[43] Asthma is but one of many secondary effects of poor air quality, and the number of asthmatic children and adults is increasing. It has been estimated that from 2001 to 2006, the number of asthma cases in China increased by 40 percent and incidents rates are more acute in larger cities and among children.[44] As China continues to pursue economic development at the cost of its environment, its residents are likely to continue to bear the burden of poor air quality and its related health impacts. A TCM store employee in Beijing noted that *yartsa* is often purchased to treat respiratory illnesses such as asthma.[45] As traffic congestion and economic development continue to worsen air quality, demand for *yartsa* will likely continue to escalate in the coming years.

A final facet of *yartsa*'s market demand is its prestigious role in the contemporary Chinese gift economy of the wealthy. China's gift economy, part of what is known as *guanxi* ("connection," "relation"), refers to the standard practice of gift exchange in order to cement social bonds or gesture wishes to establish them, including bonds that might secure business or political affiliations or favors. Yang has recently discussed the resilient nature of *guanxi* practices, and claims that they are constantly adapting to new institutional arrangements as capitalism proliferates throughout China.[46] For instance, in the past, household items might have been preferred *guanxi* exchanges; however, in China's contemporary context of consumerism, they are no longer sought after; in these cases, those who can afford them opt for more rare and unique *guanxi* exchanges. Due to its rarity and expense, *yartsa* is an appealing choice. Most TCM stores that sell *yartsa* have ornamental packages and gift boxes, ranging from approximately 200–4,000 USD, which are purchased by wealthy Chinese as respectful gifts for persons of high rank, friends or family members with illnesses.[47] Yang further notes that China's transitioning political and economic relations make *guanxi* flourish among businesses and the urban-industrial sphere; arrangements among private entrepreneurs, between private entrepreneurs and state managers, or between entrepreneurs and officials — especially local officials — are secured through gift exchange. [48] This trend is observed in Deqin, where a government official noted that nearly 25 percent of the locally harvested *yartsa* was purchased within Deqin for gifts to government officials or other persons of rank visiting the area.[49] China's business ventures and increasing interest in the West will likely continue to position *yartsa* in *guanxi* practices and exchanges for social currency.

China's rising middle class, the "Develop the West" campaign and environmental pollution all contribute to a continued rise in *yartsa* demand, underlining the need to understand its supply. There have been several attempts and successes to artificially cultivate its mycelia on various substrates, such as liquid amino mixes or legumes,[50] but successful cultivation of the paired complex of caterpillar larvae and fungus has not yet been achieved. In TCM, *yartsa* value is defined by the size of the caterpillar, which reveals that demand for wild-harvested resource will remain even while cultivated forms develop. Cultivated *yartsa* may satisfy the demand of less wealthy consumers, who in other cases might not be able to afford this medical treatment or have had to opt for another herbal remedy in its place.[51]

Harvesting Practices: Negotiating Market Demand and *Yartsa* Ecology

Recognizing that *yartsa* demand will likely continue to rise, it is necessary to explore common responses in other resource systems to increase the supply of a natural resource. In theory, increased supply can be achieved by artificial cultivation; mechanization of harvesting to improve efficiency and yield; extensive harvesting, or harvesting across a larger spatial scale or longer time frame; and intensive harvesting, or more harvesting within a specific harvesting area.[52] The first two responses are not as relevant to *yartsa*. Artificial cultivation has not successfully created the caterpillar and fungus complex, and increased mechanization is not possible due to rigorous terrain and difficulty in locating the resource.[53] Extensive and intensive harvesting is thus utilized to increase supply, which places additional tensions on the social institutions at work on these landscapes and the biological provision of the resource. Whether harvesters are more inclined to opt for harvesting intensification or extensification hinges on availability of non-harvested *yartsa* areas. There are cases of extensification where harvesters opt to collect on sacred mountains, though recent social conflicts and harvester claims that more harvesters are collecting in traditional areas indicate that harvest intensification is the more prevalent pathway. This pathway is especially vulnerable to negative harvesting externalities, such as trampling and holes, because more of them accrue over time and space.

Yartsa ecology suggests that harvesting practices impact resource viability if they reduce spore availability, reduce host abundance or distribution, or negatively impact environmental conditions that directly impact the host, such as reduce host forage or habitat. These parameters are best explored by analyzing harvest timing and soil impact, namely, whether harvesting occurs before or after spores are released, and how harvesting methods interfere with either host or *yartsa* viability. The following discussion explores these parameters in current harvesting practices in northwest Yunnan, where timing and "live caterpillar" harvests emerge as two potential interactions with resource viability. These practices are each influenced by broader political economic factors through market demand, preference and regional history. The following will begin with an overview of each of these practices and how they potentially interact with resource ecology, and then shift to a discussion of considerations for management.

Timing of Harvests: Early Versus Late Season

Early versus late season harvesting refers to *yartsa* harvesting that occurs prior to or after reproductive spores have been released. The rigidity of the larval body likely indicates whether spores have been released: a "hard" larval body likely indicates that spores have not been released and a "soft" larval body likely indicates that they have been. Another visual cue of early or later season *yartsa* is whether *sporacia*, the textured nodules that release spores, are visible on the fruiting body. Harvesters will often squeeze the body of the larva as a measure of its quality: firm bodies are the best quality while soft indicates lesser quality and thus lesser market value.

The greatest *yartsa* harvesting intensity in northwest Yunnan occurs in the early season, ranging from 1 May to 26 June across Adong, Dongwa and Xusong. This is the standard harvesting season across much of the Tibetan Plateau, so it is accurate to conclude that most *yartsa* harvesting occurs before spores are released.

Harvesters collect *yartsa* during the early season for three main reasons. First, it is the "best quality" by market standards, thus harvesters earn the most income for *yartsa* of this form. Early season *yartsa* is visually distinguishable from other forms: it has a short fruiting body;[54] a large, firm larval body; and, in several cases, a yellowish body color. Late-season *yartsa* sharply contrasts with this form, where the larval body has begun to shrink, decompose and *sporacia* are visible on its longish fruiting body. Market value, as evidenced by retail prices for varying *yartsa* grades in Zhongdian and Deqin, prefers early season collections and sells "highest quality" (early season) *yartsa* for 80–100 yuan per gram ($10–12 USD/gram), while "lesser quality" (later season) collections sell for 50–60 yuan per gram. Harvesters claim that they can sometimes earn up to 200 yuan ($26 USD) for one pair of "highest quality" *yartsa*. It is not currently known how, or if, early verses late season *yartsa* differ in their medicinal efficacy. It would be important to know whether this visual grading stems from a fundamental variation in medicinal function, or whether this preference has emerged for other reasons alone.

Second, harvesters prefer early season harvesting for opportunistic reasons; harvesters wish to secure as much of the resource as possible before others find it. This rush for "Himalayan Gold" is commonly seen across other common-property resource systems, where resource extractability, or when one person's takings of the resource diminishes its availability to other harvesters,[55] is linearly related with the harvesters' desire to collect as much of the resource as possible when it becomes available. *Yartsa* fruits once annually, and thus creates high incentive for harvesters to migrate to harvesting areas early in the season to collect.

Third, while the market value and opportunism are likely the key factors driving early season harvests, low opportunity costs for early season harvesting also afford Tibetans the prospect to engage in practices during this time. Opportunity costs, meaning the other activities that must be foregone during that time, are lower during this season because other household or livelihood activities are not as pressing. Household activities during the early season, namely the feeding of domesticated animals, can often be satisfied by few members of the household. Kunga Lama describes village demographics during this time of "crowded mountains, empty towns," where only the very young and old remain in the village, often maintaining minor household chores, while other household members harvest.[56] As the spring progresses and agricultural needs escalate, opportunity costs increase and some harvesters need to return home. Interviews revealed that harvesters generally return home from the high mountain harvesting camps one-to-four times during a season, whereas other harvesters might remain in the mountains for the duration of the season. Opportunity costs lessen if households can divide them between their members: one woman from a polyandrous marriage (the wife of two brothers) informed me that she was able to remain in the mountains for the duration of the season because one of her husbands went to the mountains to harvest while the other remained in the village to attend to planting needs. Integral to opportunity cost measuring is the fact that profits earned per unit effort are highest at the start of the season when the resources are most abundant. Though *yartsa* is always difficult to locate, the difficulty increases as the season progresses because its annual supply diminishes.

Early season *yartsa* harvesting can potentially impact resource viability if it diminishes the number of spores needed to secure future resources. It is currently not known how sensitive *yartsa* resources are to spore abundance. Some scholars claim that spores are so prolific and in such abundance that they will never be a limiting factor in fungal reproduction. However, *yartsa*'s sensitivity to spore abundance has not been purposively examined and thus more research is needed before assumptions of endless spore availability are integrated into resource management schemes. Precautionary measures should be taken because the costs of misstep are high: if a sufficient number of spores are not released, the number of hosts being parasitized may decline, which could diminish harvests in the future.

"Live *Yartsa Gunbu*" Harvesting

How Tibetans extract *yartsa* from the grasslands can have multiplicative effects on host forage and substrate because its larval hosts live below ground and forage on roots (see Figure 3). The extent to which extraction methods physically damage grassland habitats is a useful measure for gauging how they potentially impact resource viability. For example, larger, deeper holes in the grassland can presumably harm *yartsa* viability more than small, shallow invasions.

Harvesters in northwest Yunnan generally use a standardized tool to harvest (see Figure 4). Hoe-like in shape and function, the metal tool is approximately 3 cm wide at its digging tip, 18 cm long and 6 cm wide where it joins the wooden

Figure 3. Yartsa gunbu (Cordyceps sinensis), *showing fungal fruiting body emerging from the larval head.*

Figure 4. *The standard* yartsa *harvesting tool in NW Yunnan.*

handle, which is angled at 45 degrees to the working end. This tool has reportedly been used traditionally across these areas for generations. One elderly harvester, around fifty-five years old, reminisced that when he was young, the only tool he carried to the mountains was one that had a *yartsa* hoe at one end, and an axe to fell timber at the other. Its historical use and the continued persistence of *yartsa* suggest that impact from this tool might not be severe, but how increased harvesting rates might interact with the current system remains unclear.

Harvesters in northwest Yunnan do not believe their harvesting practices negatively impact the grassland. Several respondents justified their beliefs by illustrating that the hole they make (to extract *yartsa*) is small, and that they always fill the hole back in with the soil or grass after they are done. One respondent claimed that he even fills in harvest-related holes he comes across, indicating that not all harvesters exercise the same care. Many respondents claim to fill in holes because it allows *yartsa* to come back the following year in the same location. For this reason, some harvesters mark the grasslands with small stones so that they can find their harvest location the following spring.

An intriguing aspect of current *yartsa* harvesting practices in northwest Yunnan is live caterpillar harvesting, or harvesting of larvae that have not yet been parasitized. Prior to interviews, I had never heard of this practice, and scholars working in other *yartsa* areas[57] have not encountered this practice. I have since encountered one documentation of harvest-interaction with live caterpillars in Dolpa District in Western Nepal. Its author notes that harvester encounters with live larvae generally yields three responses: two where harvesters will conserve the live larvae and one where they consume the larvae after roasting them, which they believe cures joint aches.[58] In the Dolpa conservation responses, harvesters cover the encountered larvae with soil in the belief that it will produce *yartsa* the following year, and some believe that encountering a live larva at the beginning of the season is good fortune, thus they leave the live larvae in the soil. The article does not detail how extensive live larvae harvesting is in this area, nor does it explore the origins of this practice, both of which are meaningful lacunae to examine. *Yartsa* harvesting was new to Dolpa district in general, established only in the past twenty years, which also underlines the need to investigate when and why this practice emerged.

In northwest Yunnan, live caterpillar harvesting occurs on a much smaller scale than *yartsa* harvesting. Harvesters in Adong and Xusong generally reported harvesting between zero to seven live caterpillars in 2007, with a similar range in preceding years. Collecting live caterpillars is seen as an opportunistic addition to *yartsa* collections: harvesters occasionally encounter live caterpillars in the neighboring soil when extracting *yartsa*, collecting them as they encounter them. One harvester explained that this trend is the "man and woman," that if they dig in the immediate area around their *yartsa*, they often find the "other" one (meaning the live larvae).[59]

There are reportedly two reasons why harvesters collect live caterpillars. First, the economic stakes are incredibly high if harvesters can find a willing buyer. A single live caterpillar is in some cases sold for 100–200 yuan ($13–26 USD), as compared to the highest price harvesters might earn for a good quality pair of *yartsa,* which was 40 yuan in 2007 (on average they earned 25–30 yuan). "Live *yartsa*" seems to target a fetish market demand for consumers, mainly Han tourists or wealthy high-ranking officials, who find it appealing, novel and almost *machisimo* to eat. One harvester said he sold a pair of "live *yartsa gunbu*" to tourists for 100 yuan each, who proceeded to eat them immediately. Many harvesters noted, however, that it is not always possible to find a willing tourist or middle man interested in purchasing their collected live caterpillars, which makes this revenue unreliable.

Second, as in Dolpa, some harvesters collect the live larvae for household consumption. Many interviewees reportedly fried the live larvae they collected and ate them as a family, or occasionally they were put in wine. Some Tibetans claim that "live *yartsa gunbu*" is the strongest form of *yartsa*, while others simply claim that it is good for their health. It is highly unlikely, however, that the non-parasitized larvae offer any other benefit than additional dietary protein. One exceptional claim underlines the degree to which some harvesters maintain this practice, where a young harvester reportedly ate a live caterpillar immediately after he found it to make him "very strong." Notably, some harvesters chose to conserve the live caterpillars they encountered — one man said that he found ten live caterpillars in 2007 but that he did not keep any of them because of his Buddhist beliefs.

It is presently unknown how extensively live caterpillar harvesting occurs across a broader spatial area. If this practice only exists in northwest Yunnan and Dolpa district, perhaps unique or similar historical events engendered these practices. Some interviews suggest that live caterpillar harvesting in northwest Yunnan might be an artifact of a previous biological experiment in the area that was attempting to artificially cultivate *yartsa*. In 1997, several researchers built a research station near Deqin to investigate how to artificially cultivate *yartsa*. At the time of its operation, researchers of the "Cordyceps Station" reportedly paid local harvesters to collect live larvae specimens for their experiments. It is not known how many larvae were collected during its time of operation, but the project continued for approximately eight years, suggesting that a significant number of live larvae were extracted. Cordyceps Station was never able to successfully cultivate the parasitic complex of larva and fungus. Spores were repeatedly placed on live caterpillars in various ways, but researchers were unable to achieve fungal germination and development.[60] Eventually the operation was stopped, though the building remains and is now used for other research projects in the surrounding nature reserve, Baimaxueshan. It is still referred to as Cordyceps Station by researchers in Yunnan.

Live larvae harvesting practices have the potential to critically impact the grassland environments and thus future *yartsa* viability. If these practices are escalating or have recently developed, they are critical to integrate into management strategies in the near future.

Moving Towards Management: Considering Linkages

Both early season and live caterpillar harvesting provide meaningful illustrations of how to begin shifting *yartsa* towards the realm of community-based management based on what is currently known about the resource system. As discussed, these practices potentially impact resource viability by interacting with spore release and larval populations, indicating that precautionary measures could be taken to lessen potential impact on future resources.

While the majority of harvesting intensity occurs before spores are released, an equally important angle to examine is how much *yartsa* remains in the grasslands after the harvesting season, and whether it is enough to sporolate future hosts to ensure viable harvests. To examine this view, it is necessary to explore what "triggers" the end of the *yartsa* harvesting season and which factors contribute to harvesters' decisions to stop harvesting at a particular time. If harvesters return home from harvesting areas because they can no longer find any *yartsa*, it suggests that resource exhaustion or barren *yartsa* mountains might be causing them to return. However, if harvesters return home due to the fact that market prices for late season *yartsa* are significantly diminished, it is possible that some *yartsa* remains on the grasslands to secure future populations. The latter scenario suggests that market value for early season harvests could, rather paradoxically, serve as a means to sustain it.

Interviews suggest that both major "triggers" cause Tibetans to stop harvesting. Many respondents claimed that *yartsa* becomes so increasingly difficult to find that it is no longer worth their time or effort to continue searching for it. On 26 June in Dongwa, when nearly all harvesters had returned home, an interviewee told me that he would return home the following day because in the prior three days of searching he had only found one. Moreover, his wife awaited him and he was eager to get back. At the same harvesting camp that day, another harvester showed me three small, shriveled *yartsa* that he pulled from his pocket, all of them wrapped in a handkerchief: the fruits of his labor after two days of harvesting.

Both harvesters relayed how few remained at that point in the season, and how it wasn't worth the cold or effort.

Other respondents, however, claim that they stop harvesting when the larval body becomes too "soft," referring to the fact that its economic value is minor. Late season harvests are worth very little profit: often harvesters will only earn 2–5 yuan per piece which, as previously noted, they often keep for family consumption by the elders or the infirm. One interviewee from Adong reported that when the price is so low, it is no longer worth her time because she had to return home for household labor.

These observations have several implications for management. The "triggers" behind the end of the harvesting season have dichotomous implications on resource viability which to date has not been brought to attention. The former trigger of barren harvesting grounds suggests that no *yartsa* remains in the grasslands after the harvesting season, which can be problematic for future resource viability if the resource is limited by spore abundance. The latter trigger of decreased market value for soft *yartsa,* however, indicates that decreased profit causes harvesters to stop harvesting; in this case there may be a sufficient number of *yartsa* to secure future resources. This latter scenario is a promising one to explore for management. *Yartsa* "softness" likely emerges evenly and at the same time across grassland ecosystems along similar elevation gradients; once this signal of reduced market value emerges, harvesters could stop collecting in that zone and leave the remaining *yartsa* for resource viability measures. Harvesters currently demonstrate standardized measures of "soft" versus "hard" *yartsa*, which suggests that this "trigger" might be easily assessed and agreed upon by harvesters. This management strategy is obviously meaningless if all *yartsa* have been collected in an area by the time "softness" occurs.

Using softness as a natural bound to the harvesting season would be a minor shift in current harvesting practices because, as noted, there are several motivations for early season harvests; trying to change harvesting practices at the beginning of the season would likely meet many more challenges. Exploring ways to secure remaining *yartsa* on the grasslands after the harvesting season, namely by formally bounding the end of the season while some *yartsa* remain to sporolate future hosts, will be a productive avenue to explore for management.

Live caterpillar harvesting practices potentially interact with host viability by disturbing both population abundance and soil habitat; the extent of this practice is unknown, therefore management may pertain only to certain communities or may not dramatically threaten resource viability. However, due to its potential impact, it is meaningful to explore potential management implications in case the practice is more broadly at work and, up to now, has been unobserved across other systems.

Live larvae harvesting in northwest Yunnan is sustained by occasional market demand. If market demand for "live *yartsa gunbu*" increases in any way similar to the booming demand for *yartsa* in recent years, the negative impacts on the environmental and resource viability would be dramatic. First, *yartsa*'s fruiting body provides a visual cue to harvesters at the soil surface where the underground resource is located. Live larvae, however, reside below ground and do not have an above-ground cue to harvesters where they are located; therefore collections would be obtained only after extensive, haphazard searching and digging, which would be highly destructive to the grasslands. Second, and related to this, if live larvae harvesting practices escalate significantly, physical impact to the grasslands would at least double. Live caterpillars are found in the soil at 10 to 30 cm below the surface, tending towards 10 cm in the summer and 30 cm in the winter to avoid the Himalayan frost zone. *Yartsa*, however, is found in the upper 5 to 6 cm of the soil; in addition to the haphazard nature of live larvae harvesting, each extraction would yield more than two times the current level of *yartsa*-related soil disturbance. Third, a "live caterpillar harvesting season" would not be temporally constrained in the same way the *yartsa* season is. Live caterpillars are available in the grasslands at any point during the year when its habitat is accessible to harvesters. Therefore, if harvesters could collect this lucrative resource at any point in time, grassland degradation would invariably be of concern.

Relating live larvae harvesting to management is a localized process because it is unclear how extensively it occurs. Due to its potential for extensive damage to the grassland ecosystems, it should be critically examined across *yartsa*-harvesting regions. In areas where this practice emerges, the extent to which it occurs and the motivations underlying should be critically examined. If harvesters are collecting live larvae for household consumption only, sharing knowledge with harvesters about the potential impacts the practice has on future *yartsa* viability will foster community-based decisions to either reduce or cease these practices. If occasional profit motivates harvesters to collect live larvae, sharing knowledge of the potential impacts of this practice with both consumers and harvesters will be necessary.

Conclusion

Yartsa harvesting practices are complex negotiations between the broader Chinese political economy of the resource through increased demand and the preferences for "high quality" (early season forms). They also involve unique social histories in relation to the ecology of the resource, which both spatially and temporally limits resource provision. The supply of *yartsa* interacts with social and environmental characteristics of the resource system, which can produce social and environmental costs such as social conflicts and resource depletion. As *yartsa* demand continues to escalate, a nuanced understanding of the local-level processes and negotiations underlying its supply will be critical in transitioning this resource system towards management. The recent social conflicts and fears of declines in *yartsa* abundance highlight the importance of initiating the move towards sustained resource management.

Community-based natural resource management (CBNRM) is a meaningful way to manage common-property resources like *yartsa* because it is subtractable and renewable; in addition, remote factors make centralized monitoring expensive and provide harvesters with a vested interest in its conservation and sustained harvesting.[61] CBNRM has served as a productive turn away from a bimodal state or market-based resource management approach, and has more effectively navigated socio-ecologically complex territories by securing a place for local communities to participate and influence resource decisions. There is still considerable work to be done in mainstreaming CBNRM pathways, which scholars and practitioners actively pursue.[62]

While a limited ecological understanding of the resource has precluded conclusive management recommendations, this chapter suggests that certain management considerations can be made based on current observations of harvesting practices. Early season harvesting may hinder future *yartsa* viability if it reduces its capacity to sporolate future hosts. Likewise, live caterpillar harvesting can diminish future *yartsa* viability if it is extensively practiced because it impacts both host populations and habitat. In response to these harvesting practices, management considerations can be made in relation to the end of the harvesting season, and whether it can be curtailed using the measure of resource "softness." Moreover, by first investigating how extensively and intensively live larvae are harvested, considerations can be made in relation to knowledge sharing between about its potential impacts.

To date, *yartsa* management has not been a topic of conversation among practitioners and scholars working in *yartsa* areas for several reasons. During 2007, an employee of Conservation International informed me that the organization and others were hesitant to approach *yartsa* resource management out of fear of making inaccurate suggestions based on incomplete or inaccurate understanding of the ecological parameters of the resource.[63] While ecological uncertainty of the resource certainly exists, this chapter has illustrated that certain precautionary measures of sustaining the resource can be explored through close examination of local harvesting practices. As emphasized, harvesting practices are complex negotiations with both market demand and local ecologies. Some management strategies might prove more effective if targeting consumer demand, while others may benefit from targeting certain harvesting practices. Complex ecology of the resource should not impede future discussions of management, but rather foster greater conversation and integrated investigation.

Lastly, while this chapter has promoted the consideration of community-based resource management strategies for *yartsa*, it is necessary to approach community-based assignments with caution. While the social and environmental context of the Tibetan Plateau is far from static and homogenous, interviews in northwest Yunnan suggest that informal rules of access and ownership of *yartsa* harvesting rest on a complex web of historical ties to geographic areas and other communities. As *yartsa* management takes shape in the coming years, it will be critical to recognize that community-based assignment of access to or exclusion from harvesting areas is a political process — how a community is defined, who is included and what types of power relations emerge from its definition will be essential to explore. There may be instances where some communities dominate in resource decisions due to historical standing, political appointment or, more recently, due to alignments with conservation initiatives in the region. These inquiries engage with similar works underway by contemporary scholars across other common-property resource systems.[64]

Notes

1 The research for this paper was made possible through support from the Biodiversity Conservation and Sustainable Development Program of Southwest Yunnan, University of Wisconsin-Madison, with funding from the Integrative Graduate Education and Research Traineeship program (DGE-0549369) of the National Science Foundation (NSF); the NSF East Asian Pacific Summer Institute (EAPSI) Award (OISE-0714319); the Association for Asian Studies Small Grant; the University of California Pacific Rim Mini-Grant; and the University of California-Santa Cruz Environmental Studies Department Award. I would like to thank Alan Richards, Jeff Bury, Emily Yeh, Sean Gillon, Brian Petersen, Georgios Halkias and Brandon Dotson for their valuable suggestions on earlier drafts of this paper; Yang Yongping and his colleagues at the Kunming Institute of Botany for their assistance and logistical support within China; and the many people in northwest Yunnan who generously shared their homes, time and insights with me.

2 J.S. Zhu, G.M. Halpern and K. Jones, "The Scientific Rediscovery of an Ancient Chinese Herbal Medicine: Cordyceps Sinensis Part I," *Journal of Alternative and Complementary Medicine* 4.3 (1998), 291.

3 E.J. Buenz, B.A. Bauer and T.W. Osmundson et al., "The Traditional Chinese Medicine Cordyceps Sinensis and its Effects on Apoptotic Homeostasis," *Journal of Ethnopharmacology* 96.1–2 (2005), 19–29; W.Y. Zhang, J.Y. Yang, and J.P. Chen et al., "Immunomodulatory and Antitumour Effects of an Exopolysaccharide Fraction from Cultivated Cordyceps Sinensis (Chinese Caterpillar Fungus) on Tumour-Bearing Mice," *Biotechnology and Applied Biochemistry* 42 (2005), 9–15.

4 R.D. Petrova and A.Z. Reznick et al, "Fungal Metabolites Modulating NF-kappa B Activity: An Approach to Cancer Therapy and Chemoprevention (Review)," *Oncology Reports* 19.2 (2008), 299–308.

5 C. Xun and N. Shen et al., "Radiation Mitigation Effect of Cultured Mushroom Fungus Hirsutella Sinensis (CorImmune) Isolated from a Chinese/Tibetan Herbal Preparation — Cordyceps Sinensis," *International Journal of Radiation Biology* 84.2 (2008), 139–49.

6 N. Yoshikawa and K. Nakamura et al., "Cordycepin and Cordyceps Sinensis Reduce the Growth of Human Promyelocytic Leukaemia Cells through the Wnt Signalling Pathway," *Clinical and Experimental Pharmacology and Physiology* 34 (2007), S61–S63; N. Yoshikawa and K. Nakamura et al., "Cordycepin, an Active Ingredient of Cordyceps Sinensis, Inhibits Tumor Growth by Stimulating Adenosine A3 Receptor," *Acta Pharmacologica Sinica* 27 (2006), 65–69.

7 Daniel Winkler, "Yartsa Gunbu (Cordyceps Sinensis) and the Fungal Commodification of the Rural Economy in Tibet AR," *Economic Botany — Special on Fungi* (forthcoming).

8 Zhu et al., 289.

9 See S. Sharma, "Trade of Cordyceps Sinensis from High Altitudes of the Indian Himalaya: Conservation and Biotechnological Priorities," *Current Science* 86.12 (2004), 1614–19; and S. Devkota, "Yarsagumba [Cordyceps sinensis (Berk.) Sacc.]; Traditional Utilization in Dolpa District, Western Nepal," *Our Nature* 4 (2006), 48–52.

10 These claims are based on a natural medicine website: http://www.personalhealthfacts.com.

11 Personal field notes, Adong, Yunnan, July 2007.

12 Personal field notes, Zhongdian, Yunnan, June 2007.

13 Winkler forthcoming.

14 A term used in Bhutanese *yartsa gunbu* arenas; see Rachelle Gould, "Himalayan Viagra, Himalayan Gold? Cordyceps Sinensis Brings New Forces to the Bhutanese Himalaya," *The Bulletin of the Yale Tropical Resources Institute* 26 (2007), 63–68.

15 Kunga Lama, "Crowded Mountains, Empty Towns: Commodification and Contestation in Cordyceps Harvesting in Eastern Tibet" (MA Thesis: University of Colorado, 2007), iii.

16 Daniel Winkler, "Yartsa Gunbu — Cordyceps Sinensis: Economy, Ecology & Ethno-Mycology of a Fungus Endemic to the Tibetan Plateau." In *Wildlife and Plants in Traditional and Modern Tibet: Conceptions, Exploitation and Conservation*, ed. A. Boesi and F. Cardi (Milan: Memorie della Società Italiana di Scienze Naturali e del Museo Civico di Storia Naturale di Milano, 2004), 69.

17 Initiated in 2000, China's "Develop the West" campaign (*xibu da kaifa* in Chinese) aims to bring economic prosperity to China's interior to lessen the economic gap between the "west" and its wealthy eastern seaboard; see David Goodman, "The Campaign to 'Open Up the West': National, Provincial-level and Local Perspectives," *The China Quarterly* 178 (2004), 317–34.

18 Emily Yeh, "Tropes of Indolence and the Cultural Politics of Development in Lhasa, Tibet," *Annals of the Association of American Geographers* 97.3 (2007), 597.

19 Goodman, 317–21.

20 For a similar discussion in relation to Yunnan forestry, see Nicholas Menzies, *Our Forest, Your Ecosystem, Their Timber: Communities, Conservation, and the State in Community-Based Forest Management* (New York: Columbia University Press, 2007).

21 Lama, 77.

22 *The Australian,* 19 July 2007, "Eight Die in Gun-Battle Over Fungus." http://www.theaustralian.news.com.au/story/0,25197,22098182-1702,00.html, accessed 25 July 2007.

23 *Radio Free Asia*, 1 June 2005, "Tibetans, Chinese Forces Clash in Qinghai Province over Alleged Graft."

24 Winkler forthcoming.

25 My proposed dissertation research will explore the relationship between *yartsa gunbu* life cycles and harvesting practices in northwest Yunnan, China.

26 Winkler 2004, 71.

27 S.J. Chen and D.H. Yin et al., "Resources and Distribution of Cordyceps Sinensis in Naqu Tibet," *Zhong Yaocai* 23.11 (2000), 673–75; as cited in Winkler forthcoming.

28 Winkler forthcoming.

29 Zhang Canming, interview in Zhongdian, June 2007; Dr. Zhang is a biologist based out of Zhongdian who has been investigating artificial cultivation of *yartsa* for over twenty years; to date he has not succeeded but continues to work on it.

30 Ibid.

31 H.E. Roy, D.C. Steinkraus and J. Eilenberg et al., "Bizarre Interactions and Endgames: Entomopathogenic Fungi and Their Arthropod Hosts," *Annua. Rev. Entomol.* 51 (2006), 332–36.

32 Harvesters are intimately familiar with these secondary metabolites, as "softness" is often a measure for quality of *C. sinensis.* Harvesters will often squeeze the body of a caterpillar to determine how "firm" or "soft" it is, the former characteristic of which increases its market value. Thus, the early season (pre-spore releasal) form of *C. sinensis* is more "firm" (secondary metabolites being released) and more valuable, whereas later season (nearing or after spore releasal) is more "soft" (secondary metabolites no longer released) and less valuable.

33 Zhang Canming, personal communication, June 2007, Zhongdian.

34 Roy et al., 334.

35 Matsutake harvesting season begins after *yartsa* ends and just as the rainy season begins.

36 Zhang Canming; personal field notes from interviews at TCM stores in Zhongdian and Deqin; 2006 figure corroborated by Lama, 69.

37 NBS. "Fast Growth on Urban Household Income and Expenditure in Past Half Year," ed. China Statistical Information Network: National Bureau of Statistics of China, 2006.

38 Lama, 49.

39 *Sinocast*, 15 June 2007, "Along Tibet, Meibong Cordyceps to build up No. 1 Aweto Brand." http://findarticles.com/p/articles/mi_hb5562/is_200706/ai_n22745370, accessed 20 July 2007.

40 Lama, 47–49.

41 See Conrad Earnest, Gina M. Morss and Frank Wyatt et al., "Effects of a Commercial Herbal-Based Formula on Exercise Performance in Cyclists," *Medicine & Science in Sports & Exercise* (2004), 504–09. Melvin Williams, "Dietary Supplements and Sports Performance: Herbals," *Journal of the International Society of Sports Nutrition* 3.1 (2006), 1–6.

42 Lama, 47.

43 Hengwei Liu, Weidou Ni and Zheng Li et al., "Strategic thinking on IGCC development in China," *Energy Policy* 36 (2008), 1–2.

44 Jonathan Watts, "Doctors Blame Air Pollution for China's Asthma Increases," *The Lancet* (August 2006), 719–20.

45 Personal interview, Beijing, June 2007.

46 Yang Mayfair, "The Resilience of Guanxi and its New Deployments: A Critique of Some New Guanxi Scholarship," *The China Quarterly* (2002), 459.

47 Reports of this in TCM shops in Deqin, Zhongdian and Beijing.

48 Yang, 463.

49 Personal interview, Baima Xueshan park manager, Deqin, Yunnan, July 2007.

50 See John Holliday and Matt Cleaver, "On the Trail of the Yak: Ancient Cordyceps in the Modern World," *Aloha Medicinals Project Report 2004* (2004), 1–63.

51 Personal interview with TCM practitioner in Beijing during August 2007. When patients are not able to afford *yartsa* for treatment, she would recommend other herbal remedies that have similar effects, but which are not as powerful as *yartsa*.

52 B. Belcher and K. Schreckenberg, "Commercialisation of Non-Timber Forest Products: A Reality Check," *Development Policy Review* 25.3 (2007), 364–70.

53 Harvesters often walk bent over, lie on the ground or crawl on their knees looking for the small blade of "brown grass."

54 Some descriptions of this stage of *yartsa* is that the fungus is "still inside" the caterpillar, a perception that the "grass" is perhaps a given length, and as the season progresses, the "grass" grows out of the caterpillar, which makes it less potent.

55 Elinor Ostrom, *Governing the Commons.* In *The Political Economy of Institutions and Decisions,* ed. James Alt and Douglass North (Cambridge: Cambridge University Press, 1990); Elinor Ostrom, "Revisiting the Commons: Local Lessons, Global Challenges," *Science* 284 (1999), 278–84.

56 Lama, 5.

57 Daniel Winkler has not encountered this in Sichuan or Qinghai, and Emilia Sulek (see this volume) has not encountered this in Qinghai.

58 Devkota, 48.

59 This trend of pairs was also commonly reported for *yartsa gunbu* pairs; one harvester said the "law of harvesting" was that if you found one, there would be another. The "man and woman" metaphor was used a few times to explain this trend as well, suggesting that this metaphor is not specific to just live caterpillar harvesting.

60 Personal interview with Zhang Canming, who was familiar with Cordyceps Station during its time of operation, July 2007 in Zhongdian.

61 For further discussion of common-property resources, see Ostrom 1999; also Robert Wade, *Village Republics: Economic Conditions for Collective Action in South India, South Asian Studies.* (Cambridge: Cambridge University Press, 1988).

62 Menzies 2007.

63 Personal interview, June 2007, Kunming, Yunnan.

64 See Menzies 2007.

5

Tibetan Refugees in India, or How Diaspora Politics Can Be Influenced by an Omnipresent Host Country

ANNE-SOPHIE BENTZ

Introduction

It is strange that, despite the obvious place that Tibet occupies between India and China, the Tibet question should be overlooked in the study of Sino-Indian relations. Dawa Norbu comments upon the lack of scholarly attention devoted to the Tibet question in "Tibet in Sino-Indian Relations: the Centrality of Marginality," where he contends: "Both imperial historians and post-colonial area specialists have failed to observe the interconnected web of politics of Sino-Indian relations within which the Tibet Question is interwoven." For him, this neglect is all the more regrettable, since, as we shall see, "Tibet has had an integral role in the modern history of Sino-Indian relations."[1] I wish to focus here on the impact that the Tibet question further had on Tibetan nationalism, as it developed in India, or, more generally on Tibetan politics in India,[2] and on how Tibetan nationalism became a factor in Sino-Indian relations.

I will, to that effect, rely on the findings of diaspora scholars in order to shed new light on the Tibetan diaspora.[3] It is undeniable that, over the years, the Tibetan diaspora has established a particular relationship with India, which has had an impact on Tibetan diaspora politics. And this particular relationship is but one aspect of a larger triangular relationship formed by the diaspora, the host country and the home country — a triangular relationship that has been thoroughly researched by diaspora scholars such as Kim Butler, Robin Cohen, William Safran, Gabriel

Sheffer, Khachig Tölölyan and Steven Vertovec, who have been trying for more than a decade to bring new theoretical thinking into the diaspora debate.

I will briefly look at the current state of Tibetan diaspora studies before commenting on diaspora theories and on which theoretical tools can be most useful to cast new (theoretical) light on the Tibetan diaspora. I will then analyze the context of Tibetan politics in India, that is, I will look at India–China relations and the way those relations tend to affect Tibetan politics in order to try to determine whether India is sustaining or constraining Tibetan nationalism in exile. This will require my drawing a further distinction between official India and unofficial India, between the government and the people. I will conclude with a series of considerations of the way Tibetan refugees feel about India with regard to the various expressions of Tibetan nationalism.

I. The Current State of Tibetan Diaspora Studies[4]

In his 1997 review of Frank Korom's two collections of essays, *Constructing Tibetan Culture: Contemporary Perspectives* and *Tibetan Culture in the Diaspora*, Martin Baumann offers an overview of the state of Tibetan diaspora studies at the time when these were published.[5] He contends that, despite the relative lack of theoretical attention devoted to most Tibetan diaspora studies, the case studies edited by Frank Korom would be interesting for other diaspora scholars to take into account.

He cannot help but observe that "until now relatively few studies have been published on the scattered communities and settlements of Tibetan refugees in exile,"[6] which he accounts for by the assertion that diaspora studies are looked down upon in Tibetology. The first use of the term diaspora in Tibetology dates back to Margaret Nowak (1984).[7] There then followed what Martin Baumann calls the ten-year adoption gap, until the disciplinary adoption of the diaspora term (in 1995 Axel Christian Ström used the term diaspora again and a whole panel, "Tibetan Culture in the Diaspora," was dedicated to the Tibetan diaspora during the 1995 IATS conference): "Since then, the term seems to have taken off, forming a sub-branch in Tibetology called Tibetan diaspora studies."[8]

If he sees a new trend in the two volumes under review, as well as an effort to catch up with diaspora studies at large, he also acknowledges a continuing peripheral importance of diaspora studies within Tibetology. It is true that there has been a new interest in the Tibetan diaspora, but, considering the limited number of Tibetologists who dedicate their work to this subject and the limited number and small size of the panels that have dealt with this sub-branch in the last two

IATS conferences (2003 in Oxford; 2006 in Königswinter), this new interest appears now to be over. In retrospect, Martin Baumann seems to have been on the whole overly optimistic.

Besides, as he rightly observes, most studies devoted to the Tibetan diaspora, as well as studies devoted to other diasporas,[9] fail to provide a clear understanding of the very concept of the term, which substantiates the need to draw on diaspora theory in order to design useful tools to approach the Tibetan situation.[10] This remark, made more than ten years ago, is still valid today. Even if a number of publications on the Tibetan diaspora have come out since then, such studies do not rely much on diaspora theories, thus preventing any further theoretical input in Tibetan diaspora studies.[11]

This is something that I now intend to do; I will look at what diaspora scholars have to offer, with the aim of providing theoretical tools to study the Tibetan diaspora. In doing so, I raise a number of questions, such as: Does the theoretical approach of these diaspora scholars apply to the Tibetan diaspora?

II. What Does the Theory Say?

Modern diaspora studies, which I would date back to the launch of the journal *Diaspora* in 1991, begin with acknowledging a problem, i.e., the fact that the rapid takeover and widespread use of the very word diaspora threatens this word's descriptive usefulness. This problem has rendered even more acute the need for a new definition, as Khachig Tölölyan observes in the introductory statement of *Diaspora*.[12] Since then, several scholars have tried to come up with their own definition of a diaspora, which usually turns out to be not so much a definition as a list of constitutive criteria. I will retain here William Safran's list of criteria. The criteria, in their summarized version, read: 1. dispersion or dispersal; 2. a collective memory about the homeland, also known as the homeland myth; 3. a troubled relationship with the host society, or, alternatively, with host societies; 4. an idealization of the homeland, which eventually induces a return movement; 5. a commitment to the maintenance or restoration of the homeland; 6. a continuous relation to the homeland, which is important in the definition of the diaspora's identity.[13] This list of criteria has been debated and reconsidered by other diaspora scholars, who have offered a number of adaptations, especially regarding dispersion or dispersal and the troubled relationship with the host society, and who have even suggested additional criteria.[14] It seems that, judging from this list, and even from the above-mentioned adaptations and additions, Tibetan refugees qualify quite well to the status of diaspora. Even though the Tibetan diaspora is never mentioned by the diaspora scholars considered here, there should be no doubt as to whether Tibetan refugees actually constitute a diaspora.

In a later article, William Safran speaks of evolving degrees of "diasporaness" or "diasporacity" based on a continuum of attitudes and forms of behavior towards the homeland. These degrees go from a vague family tradition of origins, eclipsed by full social, cultural, and political integration into the host nation, to an acute awareness of origins, to an active interest in the general fate — and in important specific events — of the homeland, to influencing a hostland government to pursue policies favorable to the homeland, to going off to fight for the homeland, and to preparing to return to the homeland.[15] The question for William Safran is: How many of these characteristics must be found among an ethnic or religious minority in order for this minority to qualify as a diaspora? He gives no theoretical answer to that question, yet, in that perspective too, there is little doubt that Tibetan refugees exhibit a (very) high degree of "diasporaness" or "diasporacity," which again is proof enough that there actually is a Tibetan diaspora.

The next questions reads: To which type of diaspora do Tibetan refugees belong? Robin Cohen and Kim Butler have offered alternative typologies, which are drawn at least partly on the origin of the dispersion. Robin Cohen's typology is made up of five different categories, i.e., victim, labor, trade, imperial and cultural diasporas, while Kim Butler's typology is made up of six categories, i.e., captivity, state-eradication exile, forced and voluntary exile, emigration, migration and imperial diaspora. And to the question, "To which category does the Tibetan diaspora belong?" the answer is quite obvious: Robin Cohen's victim category and Kim Butler's state-eradication exile category. Although these diaspora scholars never use the Tibetan diaspora as an example, it is easy to see in both typologies which category the Tibetan diaspora belongs to, especially as the closest analogy, the Palestinian diaspora, is often used as a case in point by the same diaspora scholars.

The triangular relationship mentioned in the introduction is the important work to be considered by diaspora scholars. Kim Butler identifies three agents in the formation and development of diasporas, that is, the homeland, the hostlands and the diasporan group itself.[16] Steven Vertovec speaks of "'a triadic relationship' among (a) globally dispersed yet collectively self-identified ethnic groups, (b) the territorial states and contexts where such groups reside, and (c) the homeland states and contexts whence they or their forebears came,"[17] and Gabriel Sheffer mentions "the inseparable links between diasporas and their entire nation, and their real or imagined national-states and host national-states."[18] In all cases, the three aspects of the triangular relationship remain the same, i.e., the diaspora, the host country and the home country, yet the different wording used by these diaspora scholars is clearly indicative of different ways of envisioning the relationship, which can be better understood by looking specifically at aspects that are of interest to these diaspora scholars.

First, diasporas can be seen as challenges to nation-states, that is, to the various nation-states involved, the host country, but also, when the homeland does not exist strictly speaking, the nation-state that has power over the homeland, though the emphasis usually is on the host country. The diaspora is thus often presented as a challenge to the host country, that is, the host country as a nation-state, by which diaspora scholars mean that the diaspora is a challenge to the identity, or to the homogeneity of the nation-state. For William Safran, "[d]iaspora communities pose a more serious challenge to host societies than do other minority communities."[19] A closely linked idea, put forward by Robin Cohen, is that there is an instrumental use of the nation-state, or even of nation-states, as this involves both the host country and the home country, on the part of diasporas.[20] Two questions read: Is that the case for the Tibetan diaspora? Is the Tibetan diaspora a challenge to India? It is difficult to see how a handful of Tibetan refugees could threaten the identity of India, which is not homogeneous to start with. This does not mean, however, that the Tibetan diaspora does not constitute a challenge to India, but it is of a different kind, as the Tibetan diaspora's mere existence can be seen as a challenge to India's relationship with China.

Second, diasporas can be seen as instruments in the hands of both the home country and the host country. William Safran, notably, presents diaspora politics as being caught up between a homeland and a hostland, which, in their own different ways, put pressure on the diaspora, usually for politically motivated reasons.[21] In this respect, the Tibetan diaspora is a special case because the home country does not exist as an independent state. If there is pressure from the nation-state that has power over the home country, i.e. China, there is no obvious pressure from the actual home country, so William Safran's formulation would have to be slightly rephrased. The use of the Tibetan diaspora by the host country, which is what matters here, will be discussed in the course of this article.

Third, there is a relationship between the overall political context in the host country and the diaspora's identity or consciousness. The proposition here is that the more open, the more democratic, the more pluralistic and the more tolerant the hostland is, the less *raison d'être* does a diaspora have; in other words, diaspora consciousness weakens, or is bound to do so, if the hostland presents all the above-mentioned characteristics. It is true that India may be said to present all of these, yet, as we shall see, competing factors may explain why the Tibetan diaspora's identity, though perhaps weakened, remains quite strong.

Thus, diaspora scholars, when considering the triangular relationship, generally emphasize two aspects: the relationship of the diaspora with the host country and the relationship of the diaspora with the home country, which is only logical, as their purpose is to explain the reasons behind the diaspora's dual or divided loyalty between the host country and the home country.

I would like to work here on an aspect of the triangular relationship that has suffered from theoretical neglect – the relationship between the host country and the home country – or, in this particular case, the country that has power over the home country. I consider this relationship of the utmost importance, not least because of the impact on another aspect of the triangular relationship, which is the relation between the host country and the diaspora. Indeed, in my view, the relationship between India (the host country) and China (the country which has power over the home country) has an impact on Tibetan diaspora politics (an impact that clearly is a consequence of the relations between India [the host country] and the Tibetan diaspora [the diaspora]). I thus intend to go back to the context of Sino-Indian relations over the last fifty to sixty years, the better to understand its impact on India's attitude towards Tibetan refugees.

III. India–China Relations, or the Context of Tibetan Politics in India

I do not plan to detail the evolution of Sino-Indian relations over the past fifty to sixty years, but I will retain a number of key events that have had an impact on India's attitude either towards the Tibet issue or towards Tibetan refugees. This historical review is carried out with a view to underlining the place of Tibet within the triangular relationship that defines the conceptual framework of diaspora studies. It draws on Pal Singh Sidhu and Jing-dong Yuan's analysis of Sino-Indian relations and falls into four phases: Cooperation (1947/1949–1962), Cold War (1962–1976), Détente (1979–1998) and Re-Normalization (1998–today).[22]

1. Cooperation? (1947/1949–1962)

The tone of India–China relations was set with Jawaharlal Nehru's vision of what India's role in the world should be – a catalytic role in establishing a moral world order based on peace and cooperation. J. N. Dixit explains the Indian viewpoint: "[Jawaharlal] Nehru was animated by a vision of Asian resurgence, and of Asia emerging as a significant force in international relations on the basis of Sino-Indian friendship and cooperation."[23] In keeping with Jawaharlal Nehru's vision, India and China ought to work towards cooperation and even friendship.

Despite this envisioned friendship, a number of incidents, all more or less closely linked to the Tibet issue, plagued India–China relations almost from the outset. The first notable incident is China's invasion of Tibet in 1951, which prompted an exchange of diplomatic notes between India and China. But China's conclusion was: "As long as our two sides adhere strictly to the principles of mutual respect for territory, sovereignty, equality and mutual benefits, we are convinced that the friendship between China and India should be developed in a normal way, and that the problems relating to Sino-Indian diplomatic, commercial and cultural relations with respect to Tibet may be solved properly to our mutual benefit through normal diplomatic channels."[24] This diplomatic note, which is totally in keeping with Jawaharlal Nehru's vision of what these relations ought to be, sets the tone of India–China relations. The incident is thus overcome and the climax of cooperation is attained with the "Agreement Between the Republic of India and the People's Republic of China on Trade and Intercourse Between Tibet Region of China and India," signed on 29 April 1954, but which is better known as the Panch Sheel Agreement.[25] The slogan "Hindi Chini, Bhai Bhai" (India and China are brothers) becomes popular. This period is often seen as "the hype of Sino-Indian brotherhood."[26]

A second incident, which I am not going to develop here, occurs in 1956 with India's invitation of the Dalai Lama to attend the 2500 Buddha Jayanti, the birth anniversary of the Buddha. (B.R. Deepak notes this as "Tibet Resurfaces in New Delhi.")[27] The third incident is the 1959 Tibetan rebellion in Lhasa and the Dalai Lama's subsequent flight into exile. In the words of Dawa Norbu, "[This event] placed a strain on Sino-Indian relations from which, some argue, they never recovered."[28] The exile of the Dalai Lama thus placed Jawaharlal Nehru in a dilemma: On the one hand, he was inclined to extend his support and sympathy to the Tibetans, but on the other hand, he was not in favor of giving the Tibetans unrestricted freedom in India for pro-independence activities. He was doing all that he could to avoid political questions and to focus on purely economic or social questions. His advice to the Dalai Lama was to do nothing – adopt a wait and see strategy – because he (Nehru) was not going to recognize a government in exile.

Thus, in spite of a willingness on the parts of both India and China to discard the Tibet issue in order to sustain incipient Sino-Indian friendship, India and China had, in the end, no choice but to take the Tibet issue into account, as shown by the three above-mentioned incidents. As for India's impact on Tibetan politics, several occasions arose when India's attitude made a difference. India not only refused to support, but in the end sabotaged Tibet's first appeal to the United Nations, on 7 November 1950. When this appeal was eventually sponsored by El Salvador, the Indian representative to the United Nations, Jam Saheb of Nawanagar, made a convincing speech, after which all other states decided to withdraw their support for the resolution. During the Dalai Lama's first India visit for the 2500 Buddha Jayanti, Jawaharlal Nehru's influence was decisive; the Dalai Lama decided not to remain in India only because strongly advised by Nehru himself to go back to Tibet to reach an agreement with the Chinese.[29] When the Dalai Lama eventually reached India in March 1959, there was no hope of any recognition of the government in exile by India, and this was reflected in the formal name adopted by the government in exile, the Central Tibetan Administration.

True, this lack of proactive political support on India's part is compensated for, or thought to be compensated for, by strong social and economic support to Tibetan refugees and by a kind of passive *laissez faire* attitude on India's part. Still, these examples clearly show that the Tibetan diaspora is seen as a challenge, that is, as a strain on India's relationship with China. Hence there is a typical reaction in terms of diaspora theories: first, pressure from the host country to avoid having a diaspora, to avoid becoming a host country at all, and then, when this turns out to be impossible, to prevent the diaspora from becoming politically active.

2. Cold War (1962–1976)

"India had reconciled itself to China claiming suzerainty over Tibet and eroding the authority of the Dalai Lama in the hope that this stand would stabilize Sino-Indian relations."[30] The logic behind such a trade-off was that Tibet had been sacrificed on the altar of Sino-Indian friendship. After the outbreak of the 1962 war between India and China, however, it came to be thought that the sacrifice had been, after all, useless.[31]

The 1962 war is a crucial landmark that radically changed the course of Sino-Indian relations. For Mira Sinha Bhattacharjea, for example: "There seemed little possibility that India and China would once again establish, or want to establish, a beyond-the-ordinary relationship, or that they would share a compelling strategic commonality."[32] It can also be said that the India–China war had an impact on India's attitude towards Tibetan nationalism, as a new sympathy, or a new solidarity, developed in India for the Tibetan cause.

This new solidarity first took the form of covert military help, with the Chakrata project, that is, the creation of a Tibetan unit within the Indian army, General Uban's Unit 22, also known as Establishment 22, which is part of the Special Frontier Force. India was also included by the United States in the Tibetan guerrilla operations with the creation in New Delhi of a Special Service Centre from which all guerrilla operations would be jointly conducted. If there is no denying that India, and the United States as well, were instrumentalizing the Tibet issue to pursue other more national goals, such as, for India, securing the Himalayan border, the military help provided for the Tibetans was nonetheless real. As Kenneth Knaus recalls "[t]he Tibetans had little choice but to accept the support of both countries in the hope of using it for their own more immediate objective of re-establishing an independent Tibet."[33] For the Tibetans, whatever India's underlying motives, such help could be used to further Tibetan nationalism, so that the instrumentalization can be said to have come from both sides.

India then offered political help, with R. Zakaria, the Indian delegate to the United Nations, sponsoring the Tibet resolution of 18 December 1965, which can be seen as a complete turnaround on India's part. He made sure to deny any instrumentalization on India's part of the Tibet issue – "We have refused to use the Tibetan refugees as pawns in our conflict with China. We do not believe that the sufferings of one people should be made a weapon in the armoury of another."[34] – but, no matter what, this new help was warmly welcomed by Tibetan refugees.

Yet this spirit of solidarity did not last, and the rupture came with the 1971 Bangladesh war, when India had to play the Tibet card to prevent China from siding with Pakistan. The use of the Tibet card meant that India was then in no position to give any more political support to the Tibetan cause. And with India's absorption of Sikkim in 1975, the idea became quite popular in India that Tibet was traded for Sikkim. This reaffirmed that Tibet belonged to China, in exchange for China's recognition of Sikkim as an integral part of India.

As the Tibetan diaspora became more and more settled, and taking into account new international developments, India came to the realization that Tibetan refugees could be useful, and so started instrumentalizing the Tibetan diaspora. In other words, the nature of the relationship between the host country and the diaspora was substantially changed during this period of Sino-Indian relations.

3. Détente (1979–1998)

A number of important changes then occurred, particularly the new post-Mao leadership in China and the Desai-led government in India, which led to a process of normalization. The key events of this process were the visit to China by India's foreign minister, Atal Bihari Vajpayee, in February 1979, followed by Deng Xiaoping's offer in June 1980 to settle the border conflict between India and China. As always, though, India–China relations were still dependent on the larger Cold War context. The Soviet Union's interest in Tibet took the form, notably, of a declaration on 1 May 1980 by which the Soviet Union was prepared to support the Tibetan cause if asked to do so by the Dalai Lama; this had serious consequences.

For Dawa Norbu, "This period of Soviet interest in Tibet coincided with one of excellent Indo-Soviet relations, and it enhanced India's deterrence posture against China, thereby compelling Beijing to engage in a serious dialogue with the Dalai Lama."[35] The Soviet Union's new attitude towards Tibet thus benefited the Tibet issue. To avoid a strain on Sino-Indian relations emanating from this valorization of the Tibet issue, Deng Xiaoping started negotiating with the Dalai Lama. In the end, the global Cold War context, and Sino-Indian relations therein, can be said to have had an indirect consequence on Tibetan nationalism, in the form of an incentive for China to engage in a dialogue with the Dalai Lama.

With the end of the Cold War in view, India and China reached the climax of the normalization process, as epitomized in Rajiv Gandhi's ice-breaking visit to Beijing in 1988. This visit was very much commented upon, and, for many, the mood was reminiscent of the whole Panch Sheel atmosphere. This translated into a number of official visits (Rajiv Gandhi's visit was followed by Li Peng's visit to India in December 1991) and also into the institutionalization of confidence-building measures through the signature of the Agreement on the Maintenance of Peace and Tranquility and the Agreement on Confidence-Building Measures, in 1993 and 1996 respectively.

India's attitude towards Tibetan nationalism evolved in this new context of India–China relations to come back to a total lack of political support, which is still meant to be compensated for by strong social and economic support to Tibetan refugees. The answer to the question, "Is India still instrumentalizing the Tibetan diaspora?" is no longer straightforward during this phase, because the global Cold War context seems to have been playing a more significant role, thus impeding any direct instrumentalization of the Tibet issue.

4. Re-Normalization (1998–today)

The current phase of India–China relations was triggered by a crisis, namely, India's 1998 nuclear tests, though it was not so much the nuclear tests per se as the justifications that India (Prime Minister Atal Vajpayee and Defense Minister George Fernandes) gave, i.e., the China threat, which put an end to the détente phase of India–China relations. The process of normalization, which started during the détente phase, slowed but did not come to a standstill. In fact, dialogue still prevailed and India and China managed to work through the tension created around the nuclear tests. In effect, there was a crisis, but it was quickly overcome and no real change affected India–China relations, except that the rapidity with which the crisis was resolved testified to a new cordiality in India–China relations. India's attitude towards the Tibet issue did not change fundamentally compared to the previous phase of India–China relations, and it is now hardly possible for India to play the Tibet card against China.

Thus, the Tibetan diaspora started out as constituting a challenge, but both India and China seem to have learned to live with it,[36] so that the Tibetan diaspora is not much of a challenge anymore except on rare occasions. I would thus say that, with time, a *modus vivendi* developed between the host country and the diaspora, as well as between the host country and the country which has power over the home country – a balance seems to have been reached in the very specific triangular relationship that applies in this instance.

IV. Is India Sustaining or Constraining Tibetan Nationalism?

As the preceding brief overview of India–China relations has hoped to make clear, India's sustaining or constraining impact on Tibetan politics in exile varies according to the evolution of the bilateral, and even multilateral, context.

Indeed, during the first phase of India–China relations, India does not want to have anything to do with the Tibet issue, as the issue hampers India–China relations, which are India's top priority. Yet, as the Tibet issue keeps coming back, India eventually takes the Tibet question into consideration and so curtails Tibetan nationalism as much as possible. This lack of political support for the Tibetan cause seems to be compensated for by a strong economic/social support for Tibetan refugees.

Then, with the outbreak of the 1962 war, which starts the second phase of India–China relations, India begins to use the Tibet issue against China and provides covert military support as well as political support. It may be argued that India is then sustaining Tibetan nationalism, but the evolution of the international context translates into a number of trade-offs (the Bangladesh war, Sikkim for Tibet), which eventually leads India to drop all political support to Tibetan refugees.

India–China relations then enter a third phase, the phase of normalization, but the Tibet issue does not benefit from this change, which brings India's Tibet policy back to its initial configuration. At the same time, however, another development linked to the growing Sino-Soviet drift allowed for an improvement of the Tibetans' nationalist agenda until the end of the Cold War, in the form of China's dialogue with the Dalai Lama.

A crisis triggers the fourth phase of India–China relations, but in the end there is little change, which implies not much change for the Tibet issue. Tibetan exile politics are constrained by India, with still no political support, but rather social and economic, support.

If such a summary perspective accurately gives the impression that India's policy regarding Tibetan nationalism wavers between support and constraint, I now intend to qualify that statement by distinguishing between official India and unofficial India. Indeed, I wish to contend that there are a plurality of perspectives that hide under 'India.' Official India is the state, that is, state policy as conducted by India's prime ministers, whereas unofficial India is constituted by a variety of other actors whose role also has an impact on the way Tibetan politics are conducted in India. Those other actors are made up of the Indian people at large (public opinion, organizations, individuals), as well as a special category of politicians: members of parliament, opposition leaders, even Congress Party members who disagreed with Jawaharlal Nehru's handling of the situation, and others. Their vision of the Tibet issue may not be in keeping with the state's handling of the question, and so their attitude does not necessarily follow the pattern of Sino-Indian relations. This will be made clearer by an analysis of examples of their attitude towards the Tibet issue over the last fifty to sixty years of Sino-Indian relations.

The Dalai Lama's two autobiographies are quite revealing of the Indian people's general attitude, if not towards the Tibet issue, at least towards Tibetans in India. He recalls that when he made the trip from Tezpur to Mussoorie, many Indians were there to greet him, with cries such as "Dalai Lama Ki Jai!" (victory to the Dalai Lama) and "Dalai Lama Zindabad!" (long live the Dalai Lama). He felt as if in a dream, and repeatedly said that he would never forget this enthusiastic welcome from the Indian people. "It was a journey of several days, and a memorable experience, because everywhere the train stopped enormous crowds had gathered to cheer us. [...] It warmed my heart. [...] Clearly they had not just come to look at me – they had come to show their sympathy for Tibet."[37] He has the overwhelming impression that he can count on the Indian people. Yet no matter how right he was, it is important to distinguish between the spontaneous welcome of the people and the cordial but cold welcome of the government. This sympathy is clearly not matched by the state or its representatives, starting with Jawaharlal Nehru.

In time this sympathy became organized, as a number of Indian support groups were created to sponsor the Tibet issue. One example is the India–Tibet Friendship Society, an organization composed of friends of Tibet whose declared objective is to make Tibet free of Chinese occupation. The Bharat Tibet Sahyog Munch (BTSM), an association gathering Indians and Tibetans all over India, similarly follows a two-fold objective that consists in fostering good relations between Indians and Tibetans in India and in supporting the Tibetan cause. These are but two examples of Indian support groups.[38]

Mahesh Yadav, an Ayurvedic doctor from Bhopal who has been fighting for the Tibet issue since 1994 and who is the founder of the Mahatma Gandhi Tibet Freedom Movement, is the epitome of individual support for the Tibetan cause.[39] He has written over 3,000 letters with his own blood to various leaders and organizations in India and abroad, urging them to break their silence on the Tibet issue and to come forward to support the Tibetan freedom struggle. He has organized blood donation camps for the Tibet cause in Mumbai, Delhi and other towns and cities, and on 10 December 2005 he launched a campaign, "Save Tibet – Save India, Save Tibet – Save Humanity." He has most recently written a blood letter to the Indian president, A.P.J. Abdul Kalam, where he sought support for the Free Tibet issue, and where he urged him to take up a strong foreign policy towards China. He also sent a blood letter to Prime Minister Manmohan Singh, urging him to take up the Tibet issue with his Chinese counterpart, Hu Jintao.[40]

Nancy Jetly, in her book *India China Relations, 1947–1977: A Study of Parliament's Role in the Making of Foreign Policy*, deals specifically with parliamentary opposition to Jawaharlal Nehru's handling of India's foreign policy.[41] In her analysis, it is evident from a number of debates at the Lok Sabha that many opposition leaders, such as S.P. Mookerjee and V.G. Deshpande from Hindu Mahasabha and J.B. Kripalani from the Praja Socialist Party (but a former Congress Party member), but also Congress Party members such as Sardar Patel, spoke up against Jawaharlal Nehru's policy regarding the Tibet issue.[42] Although the focus was more on the border question than on the Tibet issue itself, it can be argued that those members of parliament were either directly or indirectly opposing Nehru on the Tibet issue, as these two problems were in effect intrinsically linked.

As a conclusion, I would like to borrow the remarks of Anand Kumar, National Secretary of the India–Tibet Friendship Society, on the Indian people's attitude towards the Tibet issue. He believes that there was at first a great interest in the Tibet question, an interest that grew even stronger in the years following the India–China war, and that, as a consequence, there was hardly any resistance, not to speak of hostility, against Tibetan nationalism on the part of India's people. But this sympathy turned into a growing passivity over time, and this, according to him, is where we stand now.

Over time the Tibetan community has also become more active to sensitize Indian people, as the All-Party Parliament for a Free Tibet, Students for a Free Tibet, the India–Tibet Friendship Society and the India–Tibet Coordination Forum, to name some of the organizations working for the Tibetan cause, have had special programs and conferences on the Tibet issue and have dedicated much time to newsletters, websites, etc. This, in diaspora theories, could actually be regarded as a case when the diaspora is instrumentalizing, or trying to instrumentalize, the host country.

It thus seems that while official India has been trying to restrain Tibetan nationalism, though such constraints very much depended on the different phases of India–China relations, unofficial India has been more supportive of Tibetan nationalism. Yet, to retain Anand Kumar's conclusion, the Indian people's sympathy for the Tibet issue has been turning into a growing passivity over time, a few exceptions notwithstanding.

The relationship between the diaspora and the host country is further complicated by the host country being a kaleidoscopic entity, so that there is not one single relationship to speak of, but several. It should be noted, however, that the kaleidoscopic nature of the host country suffers from a lack of theorization in diaspora theories, as most authors tend to consider the host country as a unified entity. I wish to contend that India's varied nature must be taken into account in order to assess properly the complex relationship between India and the Tibetan diaspora, and thus also the overall impact of India on Tibetan politics in exile.

V. What Do Tibetan Refugees Think of India?

To be fair, the Tibetan refugees' vision of India must also be taken into consideration. I thus wish to turn my attention to the reaction of the Tibetan diaspora as regards the role played by India in the definition, or control, of diaspora politics, because this vision of India may also affect the way Tibetan refugees define the content or form of Tibetan nationalism. The questions here are: What do Tibetan refugees think of India? Do they feel supported or do they feel restrained by India's handling of Tibetan politics? How much autonomy do they have? And how do they feel about it?

The Dalai Lama's answer to India's help is made up of both thankfulness and understanding. He never loses an opportunity to thank India for what it has done for Tibetan refugees, and though he is slightly bitter because India is not supporting the Tibet issue politically, which he had expected initially, he has come to terms with India's overall attitude with respect to the Tibetan cause.

I would like to argue here that almost all Tibetans refugees in India share this perspective; I base my argument on a number of interviews that I conducted among refugees in various Tibetan settlements all over India.[43] Though the formulation of questions is never neutral, in this set of questions, I was even less neutral than I could have been; I was leading the interviewees to specific answers, and so I was surprised when their answers differed from my expectations.

The questions read:

> "1. Would you say that the Indian government has done a lot to help Tibetan refugees in the past fifty years? 2. And if you do not think so, what else do you think could have been done? 3. Do you think that the Indian government should more openly support the Tibetan cause? 4. Would you say that the Indian government is impeding the political expression (e.g. by censuring Tibetan media or by prohibiting demonstrations) of Tibetan refugees or of the Tibetan Government in Exile (e.g. by preventing the Dalai Lama to meet other political leaders in India or by prohibiting any political activity of the Tibetan Government in Exile)? Please specify. 5. Do you think that the Indian government is still doing a lot to help Tibetan refugees and to support the Tibetan cause? 6. Would you say that the Indian government's attitude towards Tibetan refugees is dictated by the Chinese government (totally, partly, not at all)?"

I thought that the interviewees would first want to display an unambiguous enthusiasm with possible details on the Indian government's actual realizations for Tibetan refugees, before qualifying the Indian government's support for the Tibetan cause. I was expecting then, as a possible qualification, a distinction between political and social/economic support, with an emphasis on the lack of political support on India's part. I was also, more specifically, looking for a possible qualification regarding an evolution over time of the Indian government's attitude towards the Tibetan cause and, consequently, towards Tibetan refugees. I wanted eventually to enable the interviewees to put the burden on China, should they want to.

It turned out that the answers to these questions did not always meet the above-mentioned expectations. The interviewees would all agree that India had done a lot for Tibetan refugees, or even that India had done all that could be done for Tibetan refugees. But the expected qualifications, i.e., an evolution over time, implying that India is now doing less for Tibetan refugees, and a distinction between political and social/economic support, were not as obvious or as spontaneous as I had expected, despite the fact that the formulation of the questions, in my view, explicitly invited the interviewees to take such qualifications into account.

Very few interviewees would indeed accept the idea that India is doing less now for Tibetan refugees than at the beginning of exile. On the contrary, whenever I tried to imply such a thing, they would simply deny it, except for one interviewee, Thubten D. from New Delhi. He admitted: "Now there are signs of restricting Tibetans to engage in political activities, it was not like that before!" Only when forced to consider the distinction between political and social/economic support, half of the interviewees would agree that there has always been a lack of political support for the Tibetan cause on India's part, but then again, quite a few of these interviewees would then try to find excuses for India, which was something that I had not expected at all. There were some regrets, notably about the right to demonstrate and the legal status of Tibetan refugees in India, but many of these regrets also came with excuses for India's behavior. Tsewang C., from Dharamsala, thus explained: "India could have done more on the political level, but we have to understand the position of the Indian government." Tenzin C., also from Dharamsala, added: "We cannot blame India for what it has not been able to do." While Karma C., from Dharamsala, further explained: "They have been very generous, but they have their own laws, duties and responsibilities, so it is right that they should stop us from time to time."[44] These reactions show a consciousness and an acceptance on the interviewees' part of the implications of refugee status, as well as a consideration for India's own interests, which are close to the understanding towards India expressed by the Dalai Lama.

I would like to follow on with a few quotations that, in my view, represent the way Tibetan refugees feel about India, about India's past and present support for Tibetan refugees and, more generally, for Tibet. Dolma Y., from New Delhi, explains: "They have done a lot for us, I do not know if they could have done more, we are just thankful for what they have done. It would, of course, be nice if they decided to support more openly our cause." Rinchen S., from Dharamsala, adds: "They have always supported us inwardly." For Tseten R., from Gangtok: "They are helping the people of Tibet but not the cause of Tibet!" They are convinced of India's willingness to support the Tibetan cause, but at the same time they are aware of India's own limitations, which is the reason why they try to find excuses for India rather then blaming the host country.

Conclusion

In the course of this article, my intention has been to use diaspora theories to shed new light on the Tibetan diaspora in India. I wanted, more specifically, to take a political perspective while looking at the triangular relationship between the diaspora, the host country and the home country. In addition, my aim has been to include the country that has power over the home country; this leads me to suggest that in this case and other similar cases, a quadrangular relationship, instead of the usual triangular arrangement, be addressed. Within this quadrangular relationship, the explicit focus lies on the relationship between the diaspora and the host country, which can be considered to derive, in this case, from the relation between the host country and the country that has power over the diaspora's home country.

Two conclusions, which could prove useful for diaspora scholars working in a comparative perspective, can be drawn from this analysis. First, the Tibetan diaspora in India is a case where the diaspora has a strong respect for the host country, induced by a sentiment of thankfulness, despite the fact that the host country's behavior towards the diaspora has been, and still is, somewhat negatively influenced by the relationship with the country which has power over the diaspora's home country. Second, in the case of the Tibetan diaspora in India, the host country is a kaleidoscopic entity, something which could also be said, though to a lesser extent, of the diaspora, so that what might be seen as a one-dimensional factor is indeed a multi-dimensional factor in the quadrangular relationship, thus complicating even further the relation between the host country and the diaspora.

This said, I think that further studies of the Tibetan diaspora are needed in order to better understand the quadrangular relationship that is at stake, but also for diaspora scholars to have enough rough material to include the Tibetan case in their comparative studies of diasporas. A renewed interest in Tibetan diaspora studies, which would take up from where Frank Korom and others left off, would be more than welcome.

Notes

1 Dawa Norbu, "Tibet in Sino-Indian Relations: The Centrality of Marginality," *Asian Survey* 37.11 (November 1997), 1094.

2 It is to be understood that Tibetan nationalism develops mostly in India, as even if the Tibetan diaspora is now more widely spread than at the beginning of the dispersion, most Tibetan refugees still live in India; also, it can be argued that Tibetan politics are conducted from India, for a number of reasons, including, of course, the fact that the government in exile headquarters are in Dharamsala.

3 I am making an assumption here, namely, that Tibetan refugees living in exile, and particularly in India, do constitute a diaspora. It is true that this assumption can be discussed — and deserves to be discussed, something to which I will turn in the course of this study — even if Tibetologists themselves use the term diaspora, not to mention that there seems to be something called Tibetan diaspora studies.

4 Martin Baumann is the only scholar to have actually looked at Tibetan diaspora studies – other Tibetologists have been concerned with this sub-branch of Tibetology, insofar as they have worked on the Tibetan diaspora, but they have not tried to discuss Tibetan diaspora studies at large. I will therefore mostly rely on his findings, up to 1997, and on my own experience of the more recent work on the Tibetan diaspora, from 2003 onwards, to try and give an idea of the current state of Tibetan diaspora studies.

5 Martin Baumann, "Shangri-La in Exile: Portraying Tibetan Diaspora Studies and Reconsidering Diaspora(s)," *Diaspora* 6.3 (winter 1997), 377–404; Frank. J. Korom, ed., *Tibetan Culture in the Diaspora. Proceedings of the Seventh Seminar of the International Association for Tibetan*

Studies, Graz 1995 (Vienna: Verlag der Österreichischen Akademie der Wissenschaften, 1997); Frank Korom, ed., *Constructing Tibetan Culture: Contemporary Perspective* (St-Hyacinthe: World Heritage Press, 1997). *Tibetan Culture in the Diaspora* is the collective volume of the panel led by Frank Korom himself at the 1995 IATS conference in Graz.

6 Baumann, 378.

7 Margaret Nowak, *Tibetan Refugees: Youth and the Generation of Meaning* (New Brunswick, N. J.: Rutgers University Press, 1984).

8 Baumann, 390.

9 His idea is that the lack of theoretical framing found in Tibetan diaspora studies has nothing special about it since the same neglect can be found in other diaspora studies.

10 Baumann, 390–91.

11 A possible exception being Dibyesh Anand, "A Contemporary Story of 'Diaspora': The Tibetan Version," *Diaspora* 12.2 (Summer 2003), 211–29.

12 Khachig Tölölyan, "The Nation-State and Its Others: In Lieu of a Preface," *Diaspora* 1.1 (Spring 1991), 4.

13 For the full text, see William Safran, "Diasporas in Modern Societies: Myths of Homeland and Return," *Diaspora* 1.1 (Spring 1991), 83–84.

14 See in particular Robin Cohen, *Global Diasporas: An Introduction* (London: University College London Press, 1997) and Kim D. Butler, "Defining Diaspora, Refining a Discourse," *Diaspora* 10.2 (Fall 2001), 189–219. Regarding 1. dispersion or dispersal, Robin Cohen comes up with two additional ideas, i.e. the idea that the origin of the dispersion is often traumatic and the idea that instead of a dispersion there could be an expansion from a homeland, for trade or colonial purposes, while Kim Butler insists on the fact that the dispersion is more a scattering than a transfer, as there should be a minimum of two destinations. Regarding 3, a troubled relationship with the host society, Robin Cohen considers the possibility of a distinctive creative and enriching life in tolerant host countries. Kim Butler would add another distinguishing criterion involving the temporal-historical dimension, that is, a diaspora should be at least two generations old. What is unsure, however, is whether all criteria are needed for a given ethnic group to be considered a diaspora, or if some of these criteria are indeed sufficient for a diaspora to exist as such.

15 I am leaving some of these degrees out. For the full text, see William Safran, "Comparing Diasporas: A Review Essay," *Diaspora* 8.3 (Winter 1999), 255–91.

16 Butler, 206.

17 Steven Vertovec, "Three Meanings of 'Diaspora', Exemplified among South Asian Religions," *Diaspora* 6.3 (Winter 1997), 279.

18 Gabriel Sheffer, *Modern Diasporas in International Politics* (London: Croom Helm, 1986), 3.

19 Safran 1991, 97.

20 Robin Cohen, "Diasporas and the Nation-State: From Victims to Challengers," *International Affairs* 72.3 (1996), 518–19.

21 Safran 1999, 258.

22 Waheguru Pal Singh Sidhu and Jing-dong Yuan (eds), *China and India: Cooperation or Conflict?* (Boulder, CO.: Lynne Rienner Publishers, 2003). I am borrowing their division, but not necessarily their terminology.

23 J. N. Dixit, *Across Borders: Fifty Years of India's Foreign Policy* (New Delhi: Picus Books, 1998), 35.

24 Quoted in B. R. Deepak, *India and China 1904–2004: A Century of Peace and Conflict* (New Delhi: Manak, 2005), 134–35.

25 The full name of the agreement, with its reference to "Tibet Region of China," implicitly establishes India's recognition of China's sovereignty over Tibet. The name Panch Sheel refers to the additional five principles of peaceful coexistence contained in the agreement: "1. mutual

respect for each other's territorial integrity and sovereignty; 2. mutual non-aggression; 3. mutual non-interference in each other's internal affairs; 4. equality and mutual benefit; and 5. peaceful co-existence."

26 Deepak, 157.

27 Deepak, 167.

28 Norbu, 1086.

29 Tenzin Gyatso (Fourteenth Dalai Lama), *My Land and My People* (1977; reprint, New Delhi: Srishti Publishers and Distributors, 1999), 153.

30 Dixit, 52.

31 This is notably Dawa Norbu's stance in "Tibet in Sino-Indian Relations."

32 Mira Sinha Bhattacharjea, "1962 Revisited." In *Crossing a Bridge of Dreams: Fifty Years of India China*, eds. G.P. Deshpande and Alka Acharya (New Delhi: Tulika, 2001), 445.

33 John Kenneth Knaus, *Orphans and the Cold War: America and the Tibetan Struggle for Survival* (New York: Public Affairs, 1999), 266.

34 *Indian Leaders on Tibet* (Dharamsala: Department of Information and International Relations, Central Tibetan Administration, 1998), 88–89.

35 Norbu, 1092.

36 In the Declaration on Principles for Relations and Comprehensive Cooperation between India and China, signed on 23 June 2003, India reasserted its recognition of China's sovereignty over Tibet, something that China had been expecting. One paragraph stipulates that: "The Indian side recognizes that the Tibet autonomous region is part of the territory of the People's Republic of China and reiterates that it does not allow Tibetans to engage in anti-China political activities in India. The Chinese side expressed its appreciation for the Indian position and reiterated that it is firmly opposed to any attempt and action aimed at splitting China and bringing about 'independence of Tibet.'"

37 Gyatso (Fourteenth Dalai Lama) 1999, 219.

38 This information comes from the two interviews that I conducted with Anand Kumar, National Secretary of the India–Tibet Friendship Society (28/09/2005), and Chemey Yungdrung, in charge of the Kangra district chapter of the Bharat Tibet Sahyog Munch (BTSM) (07/09/2005). A number of other support groups were recently created, such as Friends of Tibet (1999) and Students for a Free Tibet (1994, 2000 for Students for a Free Tibet–India, whose objectives are very similar, see: http://www.friendsoftibet.org/, http://www.studentsforafreetibet.org/ and http://sftindia.org/).

39 Mahesh Yadav is but one example of strong individual support for the Tibetan cause, and I would not want to use it to over-generalise about the Indian public's general attitude towards the Tibet issue. I am saying more about this later drawing on Anand Kumar's analysis.

40 See http://www.bloodmovementforpeace.org/.

41 Nancy Jetly, *India China Relations, 1947–1977: A Study of Parliament's Role in the Making of Foreign Policy* (New Delhi: Radiant Publishers, 1979).

42 The Constituent Assembly of India functioned as the Provisional Parliament until the first Lok Sabha, then known as the House of People, was constituted following General Elections in 1952. So, technically, Sardar Patel did not participate in any debates at the Lok Sabha, but only at the Constituent Assembly.

43 Note that the questions that I asked are extracted from one section entitled 'Host Country' of a questionnaire which was devised for a larger purpose than just figuring out what Tibetan refugees think of India. I used this questionnaire, which I designed myself, at various times between February 2004 and July 2006 in various places throughout India: Mundgod, Bylakuppe, New Delhi, Dharamsala, Gangtok, Ravangla, Kalimpong, Darjeeling and Choglamsar. It includes the following sections: 'Personal Data,' 'Contact,' 'Mobility,' 'Religion,' 'Nationality,' 'Political

Engagement,' 'Host Country' and 'Return.' It was meant to lead to more in-depth interviews, depending on the willingness of the interviewees. Especially, it was not meant to produce any usable quantitative data, as the number of interviewees (around 50) is clearly not high enough for such an undertaking, but instead was meant to provide for a set of qualitative data from the different places mentioned here.

44 Other examples of such reactions include Tenzin D., from Bylakuppe, who said: "They are not helping us politically, but they have their own national interest to think of!" Sonam T., from Dharamsala, admitted: "It could have done more on the political level but it has to take its interests into consideration." Dawa C., from Darjeeling, added: "But India has its own interests which cannot be compromised by a handful of refugees."

6

Adhering to Tradition

Maintaining the Canon of Tibetan Architecture in India

JOONA REPO

Today, Tibetan Buddhist architecture is a global phenomenon due to the widespread distribution of Tibetan refugees throughout the world. The first Tibetan refugees fled to India, Nepal and Bhutan following the 1959 Lhasa Uprising, which marked a drastic shift in China's policy in Tibet, although new refugees continue to arrive from Tibet every year. Many made their way to countries such as the United States and Switzerland, both of which maintain sizeable Tibetan refugee communities to this day.

One of the most physically apparent indicators of the presence of Tibetans in their host countries is the Tibetan style architecture they build, which is almost always religious. Although Tibetan refugee architecture has received little attention, the research that has been conducted in this field has mainly focused on Tibetan architecture in Europe, with few words devoted to South Asia, and particularly India.[1] The overall lack of written material is somewhat surprising because Tibetan refugees have been actively constructing religious buildings in India at least since the early 1970s, and there are now hundreds, if not thousands, of Tibetan Buddhist buildings that have been built within the country, with India no doubt having the highest concentration of Tibetan Buddhist refugee architecture in the world. These buildings, especially those more recently constructed, are often extremely elaborate. The new assembly hall, or *tsogkhang* (*tshogs khang*), of the Loseling College of Drepung Monastery (Fig. 1) is the newest large-scale building project in Dhoeguling Settlement in Mundgod, India. The new hall is impressive and costly, and is perhaps the largest Tibetan Buddhist assembly hall in India, if not the world. This building will now be the third

Loseling assembly hall, as the previous two became successively too small for the growing monk population.

Figure 1. *The new assembly hall of Drepung Loseling in Mundgod, India at various stages of construction. Top, a picture of the building in December 2005 (photograph by the author); below, in August 2007. (Photograph by Alan D. Turner)*

Compared to most other refugee communities in the world, the Tibetans are perhaps unique in the way that they recreate the architecture of their homeland on such a large scale, and in such large numbers, in their host countries. In many ways Tibetan Buddhist architecture in India avidly attempts to look "Tibetan," whereas the constructions themselves, as well as the building materials used, are usually a striking departure from traditional Tibetan architecture. Although there a number of issues to consider when trying to understand why the Tibetans construct these types of buildings, in this paper I will address one of these: the role of Buddhism and Tibetan Buddhist tradition in the construction of 'Tibetan style' architecture in exile. Are these types of buildings ritually necessary or not, and why is there this need to replicate previously existing architecture?

These questions are necessary in order to answer an even more vital, long-term question: Are the religious buildings that the Tibetan refugees construct actually preserving Tibetan Buddhist culture, or are they instead nostalgically clinging to an image of Tibet that is not only redundant and impractical in India, but also harmful to the long-term evolution of Tibetan art and architecture? Perhaps for an artistic tradition to remain alive and sustain itself, change is inevitable and necessary. This was true in Tibet itself, where gradual changes can clearly be observed in Tibetan art and architecture throughout recorded history.[2] In this paper I will present the various physical and theoretical religious elements of Tibetan refugee architecture and their interpretations, to come to an understanding of the true potential of Tibetan Buddhist architecture in a contemporary context.

THE BUILDINGS

When looking at Tibetan refugee architecture in India, it is apparent that religious buildings are the most elaborate, and the ones which are constructed in a Tibetan style. Domestic refugee houses do occasionally incorporate Tibetan elements into their structures, though this is rare.

The majority of Tibetan Buddhist refugee buildings in India are relatively similar, particularly in terms of ornamentation. These features include the red *penbe* (*span bad*) parapet and its various medallion ornaments and decorative beam ends, trapezoidal window frames, roof ornaments such as the *gyeltsen* (*rgyal mtshan*) or victory banners, *gajira* (*ga dznyi ra*), deer and wheel, Chinese ornamental roofs, a verandah at the entrance and decorated pillars (Figs. 2 and 3). The walls of Tibetan Buddhist assembly halls in India, if colored, are almost always white, with few exceptions.

Figure 2. *The assembly hall of Purang Shenpen Ling Monastery, Mundgod, India. The roof is adorned with multiple gyeltsen, two sets of Dharma wheels and deer as well as a gajira, which can be seen in the middle of the elevated section of the roof. Also seen here is the penbe parapet decorated with yellow medallions, decorative protruding beam ends and rows of white dots. (Photograph by the author, 2005)*

The form and layout of most assembly halls in India is also homogeneous. The standard layout includes the main hall, containing an altar with its holy objects and seating for the monastic community. At the far end of the hall, next to the altar, one can often find one or two attached rooms that function as protector shrines. The section of the building above the altar is often crowned by an ornamental Chinese roof, and is generally higher than the rest of the building (Fig. 3). This height is almost always achieved by adding one or more extra floors to the back section of the building, with the resultant space being used to house abbots and high-ranking resident or visiting lamas.

The building materials, however, vary throughout India, with the use of red brick, cement and reinforced concrete being overwhelmingly the most popular. In North India, one can occasionally find materials that are somewhat closer to those originally used in Tibet, such as stone and wood being used in buildings such as the assembly hall of Nechung Monastery in Gangchen Kyishong (Fig. 4), or the Norbulingka Institute's main temple in Sidhpur, which will be discussed later.

Figure 3. *Drepung Gomang assembly hall, Mundgod, India. This building displays all the commonly seen decorative and visual elements of monastic Tibetan refugee architecture, including the Chinese style roof, decorated pillars in the entrance way, white walls and a red benma frieze. (Photograph by the author, 2005)*

Figure 4. *Nechung Monastery assembly hall, Dharamsala, India. (Photograph by the author, 2008)*

Figure 5. *Drepung Loseling assembly hall near Lhasa, Tibet. (Photograph by the author, 2007)*

Figure 6. *A cement-carved gyeltsen on the roof of Drepung Gomang assembly hall, Mundgod, India. (Photograph by the author, 2005)*

When comparing the assembly halls of Drepung Monastery near Lhasa (Fig. 5) with their re-established versions in Mundgod (Fig. 1), India, one can easily see the similarities between the two, and why many Tibetans would consider the latter as traditional. These refugee buildings are, after all, clearly based on actual Tibetan prototypes. However, when looking more closely at the buildings, they differ greatly from those in Tibet. Firstly, the inward slanting walls, which one can see in almost every building constructed in Tibet before the 1950s, are not present on the vast majority of refugee built buildings in India. In terms of materials, most religious buildings in Tibet were constructed from stone, wood and/or stamped earth, which is hardly ever the case in exile. A similar situation can be seen in the detail used on religious buildings, with roof ornaments, such as *gyeltsen*, often made of brick or concrete and decorated with carved cement (Fig. 6). The use of these traditionally non-Tibetan materials can even be seen in South India on what would have been textile hangings on the outside of Tibetan monasteries, which have now been transformed into cast concrete 'sun-breakers,' as they are often called, yet decorated to look the same as their original cloth versions (Fig. 7). Although it is highly possible that traditional Tibetan materials such as gilt copper *gyeltsen* or textile hangings would be preferred, it is clear from the

Figure 7. *Jangchub Choeling Nunnery in Mundgod, India, with its roof ornaments: gyeltsen, gajira, Dharma wheels and deer. Above the windows and entrance are the painted sun-breakers. (Photograph by the author, 2005)*

widespread use of concrete and cement that the Tibetans are quite happy using them in the production of their architecture and that the use of traditional materials is in no way a religious necessity.

These decorative elements are clearly perceived as important in some way in the practice of Tibetan Buddhism because they are being reproduced on almost every newly constructed Tibetan religious building. Even elements such as the trapezoidal window frames and decorative beam ends, which traditionally feature in all vernacular domestic architecture in Tibet, are usually today used in exile only for buildings associated with a religious establishment. This Tibetan style, based on actual prototypes in Tibet, is thus perhaps seen as encapsulating a tradition which is necessary for the continued survival and practice of Tibetan Buddhism, both because of the Buddhist themes that its stylistic details are seen to represent, which will be explored below, and because these elements directly invest Tibetan identity in Buddhism.

Buddhist Concepts

One of the most convincing prototypes for the Tibetan assembly hall is the so-called '*vihara* plan,' which can still be seen today at Ajanta or Nalanda; it is of course Indian in origin, not Tibetan. Traditionally the *vihara* consisted of a central space, surrounded by cells to accommodate monks, with a small temple or shrine located at the opposite end of the complex in a separate room, directly across the courtyard from the main entrance. The Jokhang, the first and most sacred Buddhist building in Tibet, is an example of the early application of the *vihara* plan in Tibetan architecture, as its common name *tsuglagkhang* (*gtsug lag khang*) suggests.[3] Although today the rooms that would have been occupied by monks are shrine rooms, one can hardly mistake the original layout (Fig. 8), which has been compared to the *vihara* caves of Ajanta.[4]

The application of the *vihara* plan is evident in later Tibetan temples and assembly halls as well, although in a modified form. An example of this can be seen at the Pelkor Chöde Tsuglagkhang in Gyantse, whose construction was commenced 1418 by the Sakyapa prince Rabten Kunzang Phag. The pillared assembly hall is highly reminiscent of a *vihara*, with rooms attached to a main central space that acts as the principal assembly hall. The attached rooms function as smaller chapels with the room at the far end of the central space, opposite the entrance, being the main shrine.

However, by at least the mid-17th century – if not earlier – during the rise to power of the Gelug sect, the plan of the assembly hall began to transform, and

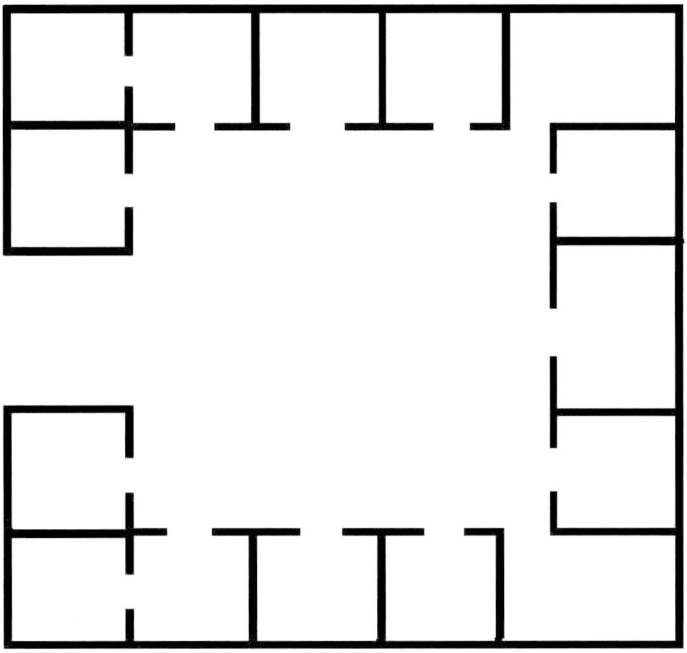

Figure 8. *A basic and generic example of the vihara plan, based on the main assembly hall of the Jokhang in Lhasa. (Drawing by the author)*

one will often find that these and later monastic assembly halls have few or no adjacent rooms, departing in many ways from the traditional *vihara* form.[5] The same can be seen in refugee assembly halls, such as the new assembly hall of Ganden Jangtse in Mundgod. Although this specific hall has no attached chapels, it is not unusual to find a *gonkhang* (*mgon khang*), or protector chapel, attached to a refugee *tsogkhang* on the right side of the hall, near the altar, as has been noted.[6] One can sometimes also find more than one or two attached rooms, although this is extremely rare in India. It is, however, considered appropriate practice, as noted by the late Chogye Trichen Rinpoche in his building manual.[7] In fact, when reading the manual, one realizes that the description that he gives of assembly halls is almost identical to that of the *vihara* plan, and is based on the Vinaya, which he cites as an authentic reference for the building of these religious buildings.[8]

Another important concept incorporated into Tibetan assembly halls is the mandala, although this is not usually immediately apparent from the physical form of a *tsogkhang*. The concept of the mandala is essentially Indian, and is today mainly employed in Hindu and Buddhist architecture. The term itself refers to a circular plan (although this often includes the form of a square as well) with a center, as the Tibetan term *kyilkor* (*dkyil 'khor*) suggests.[9] Thus the mandala concept can be imposed on almost any imaginable phenomenon ranging from the division of countries and kingdoms, human bodies, buildings, the universe and divine palaces. In terms of Tibetan Buddhist architecture, it is the last two types that are traditionally employed, and particularly the latter one in the case of the *tsogkhang*. Clear examples of the use of these two types of mandalas in Tibetan architecture can be seen in Samye, where the layout of the monastic complex closely follows the Abhidharma exposition of the universe, and the Tholing Dukhang, which presents the visitor with the divine mansion of the Buddha Vairocana.

Chogye Trichen Rinpoche himself notes that "Tibet's own pure tradition of temple architecture is a system that incorporates the good and harmonious from amongst various architectural features of the celestial palaces described in the tantric divisions of architecture."[10] The same is echoed by various sources, including Geshe Gendun Samdrup, the designer of a recently built assembly hall at Ganden Jangtse Monastery in Mundgod, who, when asked about the matter, also agreed on the importance of these textual materials in relation to architecture. These types of statements elucidate two things that appear to be extremely important for Tibetans and Tibetan Buddhists in general. First, the Tibetan religious building tradition is "pure," and second, the reason for this is that it is based on authentic texts and correctly constructed, "pure" precedents. However, the Tibetan assembly hall of today is highly unreminiscent of a mandala, and perhaps the only physical features that hint at the building being based on a mandala plan are some if its ornamentation, including the fact that there is an ornate Chinese roof located above the altar.

Although Tibetan assembly halls appear very different from the original *viharas* in India as well as the layout of a mandala, the important thing to note here is how the prototype and the idea originated in India. Furthermore, one can also see how this concept has been passed down in a type of visual transmission lineage to the present day, whether or not the actual concepts can be seen correctly applied in the physical structures. This concept of an uninterrupted continuation of a tradition is a form of validation and plays a central role in Tibetan art and Buddhism.

It is clear from conversations with designers of Tibetan Buddhist refugee architecture that most believe that their buildings fall in line with the Vinaya, and are ultimately based on the *vihara* and mandala concepts, derived from various sutric and tantric literature. Despite this, instead of going directly to the relevant religious scriptures, Geshe Gendun Samdrup and most other architects use previous Tibetan assembly halls in India and Tibet as prototypes for their buildings. This raises a number of questions. First, if one is continually copying a traditional architecture, an architecture that has shown signs of change and evolution throughout its history, and is still changing, how can the Tibetans claim that the reason for building Tibetan style assembly halls is because of the religious importance and significance of the form of the present buildings? Surely, if this was the reason for building Tibetan style assembly halls, then the Tibetans would endeavor to move closer to the layouts and designs described in the original Buddhist root texts that they so often mention, instead of copying buildings which fall so far afield from the types described in the Indian texts.

Second, how can one justify or claim that one is actually basing these assembly halls on various sacred texts and traditional Indian plans if they are not directly employed in the actual practice of designing and building? After all, other Tibetan Buddhist peoples have been successfully applying the mandala plan to their religious architecture and continue to do so today. The Kalmyk temple (Fig. 9), or *khurul*, is an excellent example of the actual architectural application of the specifications and details of the tantric mandalas described in the textual tradition. These buildings are square, with a central Chinese roof, and are often decorated with the iconographically correct ornamental garlands and gates as described in various tantric works.

Figure 9. *An outtake from a photograph of the now-destroyed Tsagan Aman Khurul, Kalmykia, Russia.*

Despite the importance of textual tradition, Tibetan Buddhism places extreme importance on the concept of religious lineages that can be traced back to an enlightened being, such as Buddha Shakyamuni. The teachings that Buddha Shakyamuni gave are thus believed to have been passed down by successive teachers and practitioners up to today, creating an unbroken transmission lineage which ensures the correctness and purity of the teachings. The same rule can easily be applied to the arts, where successive masters have received instructions on painting, sculpture or architecture, in an unbroken lineage that is traditionally traced to a transcendental Buddha, tantric deity or even a Hindu god.[11] In the Menri tradition of painting, the creation of the style is attributed to Menla Döndrub, who is believed to be an incarnation of the Bodhisattva Manjushri.[12] His painting style still flourishes today in a form that has been passed down through a lineage of painters.

Statues and paintings of religious figures must also follow strict iconographic and iconometric rules that have been expounded in various religious texts, such as the *Kalachakra Tantra*.[13] This does not mean, however, that stylistic changes have not taken place, and that all images of Buddha Shakyamuni have the same proportions; in fact the situation is quite the contrary. A number of different personal interpretations of Menla Döndrub's style exist, not to mention that Menla Döndrub's own iconometric rules differ from those that existed before him.[14] As Philip Denwood notes in relation to architecture, there is little evidence of the types of specifications mentioned by Trichen Rinpoche seen in Tibetan architecture, particularly today.[15] However, he does go on to say that "there is nearly always something in a Tibetan religious building which is only there to refer to the prototype," particularly in the terminology used for specific parts of the building.[16] Thus, although buildings may vary a great deal from their prototypes, whether due to reasons of personal creativity or practical necessity, there is always an ideal which is maintained. Therefore, it seems that it is this ideal which is passed from one generation to the next, although the actual physical form of the building may evolve a great deal. The same appears to have also been true in India, before these rules ever arrived in Tibet.

Although Denwood is speaking specifically about Tibetan architecture in relation to Indian prototypes, the same can be applied to Tibetan refugee architecture based on original Tibetan prototypes in Tibet. Again, in relation to the concept of lineage in Tibetan Buddhist teaching, the most correct and reliable source, even more so than written texts or manuals, is always one's own teacher who is considered superior to even the Buddha Shakyamuni.[17] Simply going back to the original written teachings of the Buddha is not seen as sufficient and could lead to misinterpretation of the teachings.

I would again like to apply this concept to architecture. As the religious architecture in Tibet is seen as "pure," the best prototypes are thus the most recent religious buildings which have been built correctly in keeping with an architectural lineage. If a monastery today were to build a new hall, the monks would most definitely follow the architectural tradition that has been passed down to them by their teachers or master architects instead of attempting to copy the architectural style of Nalanda Monastery in Bihar. This new hall would be subjected to change due to personal creative modifications by the architects, whether due to necessity or taste. In the same way, the new prayer hall of Drepung Loseling is different in materials and form in many ways from any traditional building in Tibet. Yet when looking at its elements, which are strongly traditionally inspired, there can be no doubt that there is a concerted attempt to stick to an ideal: the traditional Gelugpa assembly hall.

Figure 10. *Photocopy of a drawing demonstrating how the Norbulingka Institute complex correlates with the iconometry of the Thousand-Armed Avalokiteshvara as designed by Kazuhiro Nakahara. (Photograph by the author, 2008)*

In the Norbulingka Institute, on the other hand, the form of the complex of structures has been laid out according to the bodily proportions of the Thousand-Armed Avalokiteshvara (Fig. 10), something never before seen in Tibetan architecture, at least to my knowledge. Here the ideal is still there as the collection of buildings continues to use an "authentic" concept, that of iconometry, albeit in a new way. The main temple in the complex (Fig. 11), which must be counted among the finest examples of Tibetan architecture built by refugees in India, although containing non-traditional elements, appears traditional and conservative in many ways and is clearly carrying on an ideal which is reinforced by it being based on "pure" Tibetan prototypes, despite having been designed by the Japanese architect Kazuhiro Nakahara. Notwithstanding its impressive temple, the Norbulingka Institute, named after the Dalai Lama's summer palace in Lhasa, is not a monastery. The large complex, located in Sidhpur, near Dharamsala, instead functions primarily as a site dedicated to the preservation, at a high standard, of a variety of Tibetan visual arts ranging from the religious, such as thangka painting and sculpture, to the more mundane, such as furniture-carving and clothes-making. The temple was thus a joint project undertaken by the various departments housed

Figure 11. *The Norbulingka Institute's main temple, Sidhpur, Dharamsala. The building uses traditional materials such as stone and wood, has inward slanting walls and is decorated with actual textiles, a gilt Chinese roof and ornaments. (Photograph by the author, 2008)*

in the institute, which explains the high quality of the craftsmanship displayed in its form.

The layout of the Norbulingka according to the proportions of a deity highlights an extremely important aspect of Tibetan art, whether it is architecture, painting, sculpture or any other media. When creating an outline for a painting of a deity, apart from the iconography, the proportions and scale are vital for the image to become an appropriate object for *rabne* (*rab gnas*), or consecration, and subsequent veneration.[18] It is no surprise that in Trichen Rinpoche's manual the sections on *The Origin of the Art of Painting and Sculpting Images* and *Body Proportions of the Sacred Figures* immediately follow the section on architecture as the two are related, for temples and assembly halls must also follow sacred proportions.[19]

However, the use of these architectural and iconometric proportions, derived from the tantras or the Vinaya, which are rarely precisely adhered to in any case, are only one aspect of the "purity" of a complete building. Before a religious building can be established, a foundation ritual must take place, preceded by the selection of an appropriate site. Not doing so, and failing to appease various earth spirits and deities, would cause problems in the future for the monastic community.

The selection and appropriation of a building site is a complex matter. First of all, a suitable site for the construction of a religious building must be selected through a geomantic process. A number of manuals which list various auspicious and unfavorable geographical features are consulted before the site is chosen.[20] Examples of desirable geographical characteristics include "a tall mountain behind and many hills in front, two rivers converging in from the right and left, a central valley of rocks and meadows resembling heaps of grain, and a lower part which is like two hands crossed at the wrists." Examples of unfavorable features include "a ravine in the shape of a spear's point" and a place where "the earth and sky meet in a sharply pointed curved shape like the fangs of Yama."[21] If one is unable to find a location with all the favorable characteristics, a number of steps, such as the erection of stupas, can be taken to avert the negative characteristics that are present. Following this, rituals and offerings must be performed on the site, followed by a number of tests that must be conducted to ensure that the soil and surroundings are appropriate.[22] Following the selection of the site, a foundation ritual must take place. The foundation not only allows one to take possession of the site from various human and non-human beings, such as the earth goddess and earth owning deity (*sa bdag*), but also removes all negative and interfering influences from the site.

The selection of appropriate sites, however, may not be so simple in exile. In Tibet, founders of monasteries had more choice over where they could build, and many monasteries were indeed built in front of mountains or large hills. This is certainly not the case with many Tibetan refugee monasteries, and instead they are forced to make the best out of the land that they are given or are able to acquire. Although this does not prevent the performance of the foundation rituals, it demonstrates the situation in which these buildings are constructed. Even before construction begins, rules that are dictated in various texts are followed as closely as possible, yet these are clearly bent. Here again, it is the motivation of attempting to follow the texts which counts.

It could easily be argued that these various rituals and the physical details of Tibetan style Buddhist architecture constitute a vital element of Tibetan Buddhist architecture in general, which allow the religious buildings to embody the symbolism and teachings of this spiritual tradition. Tcheuky Sèngué lists a number of the distinctive features of Tibetan architecture and shows how they are not just decorative or sentimental, but have a symbolic function in a Buddhist context.[23] The reddish-purple *penbe* frieze represents the Dharma as a cause for sentient beings to be born in pure lands, the decorative beam ends symbolize rays of the light of Dharma and enlightenment, the roof symbolizes the end of suffering, and the entrance's protruding veranda (either two- or single-storied) represents the importance of the spiritual over the mundane.[24] As these parts have significant meaning, it is not surprising that their incorporation into Buddhist refugee architecture is preferred.

The visual aspects of religion are clearly an essential part of Tibetan Buddhism, perhaps even more so than in any other religion or tradition of Buddhism. The reasons for this stress on the visual are largely due to Tibetan Buddhism's overwhelming emphasis on the practice of the Vajrayana. The Vajrayana places great value on the correct and continual use of visual imagery in its practice. All of these are strictly prescribed in tantric texts, and their use in the practice of the Vajrayana is considered essential. In relation to this, the Vajrayana also emphasizes visualization practices. Although visualization of figures such as the Buddha Shakyamuni is shared in common with non-Vajrayana Mahayana and Hinayana traditions, it is in the tantric tradition where the visualisation of various Buddha-figures and mandalas becomes of prime importance in meditation. These visualisation practices are thus directly linked with the physical world, as can be seen, for example, in the use of the mandala plan in Tibetan Buddhist architecture. Thus, buildings that bear little physical resemblance to painted mandalas can and are conceptually conceived of as mandalas.[25]

Buddhism and style

It must be remembered that to the average Tibetan refugee, the Tibetan style religious building may well be an essential part of the way that they personally and collectively experience and conceive of their religion and identity. It is of course not the fact that the building is simply a Buddhist temple or hall which makes the Tibetans relate and identify with these buildings, but that they are *Tibetan* Buddhist. One way in which this "Tibetan*ness*" is reflected in these buildings is not only through the form of Buddhism that is practiced in them, and by the practitioners, but also by the form and appearance of the buildings themselves.[26] Also, as demonstrated above, a number of architectural and decorative elements carry significant symbolism in the Tibetan Buddhist world and thus one could argue that they have enough spiritual value to justify their continued use in Tibetan architecture in India.

Although one could easily come to the conclusion that the Tibetan style is always necessary for a building to function as a Tibetan Buddhist ritual space, in reality I would argue that it is not. The Tsuglagkhang in Mcleod Ganj is a perfect example of this (Fig. 12). The temple, "designed by the Dalai Lama himself in a modern idiom," could not be further from a traditional Tibetan temple in appearance.[27] Despite its appearance and form, the temple is perfectly capable of functioning as a correct setting for Buddhist ritual and practice, as can be seen

Figure 12. *The central section of the Tsuglagkhang in Dharamsala, photographed from the front. The space behind the yellow doors on the ground floor, below the large Tibetan national flag, contains a throne of the Dalai Lama. The two temples halls are housed on the first floor. (Photograph by the author, 2008)*

on the inside. The Dalai Lama himself noted in his autobiography that the completion of the Tsuglagkhang meant that he "now had the opportunity to take part in the various ceremonies of the traditional Tibetan calendar in an appropriate setting."[28] If this temple, used and commissioned by the most widely recognized spiritual authority in Tibetan Buddhism, is considered an "appropriate setting," this already clearly indicates that a building need not be constructed in Tibetan style for it to function correctly in a spiritual sense. It is possible, however, that the construction of the Tsuglagkhang was an early attempt at cultural integration in India, as can be seen at the Tibet-Institut in Rikon, Switzerland (Fig. 13), although at the Tsuglagkhang we see hardly any Tibetan architectural elements.[29] It is also possible that the Tibetans, and the Dalai Lama, did not wish to take the risk of provoking a negative reaction from the local Indian population at this early stage by building a temple in a completely foreign style right in the middle of McLeod Ganj.[30] One also needs to remember that in the late 1960s, when construction began on the Tsuglagkhang, the Tibetans were still in the early days of the diaspora and perhaps lacked the organization, collective skill and finances to build a Tibetan style temple.[31] Although the Tsuglagkhang may function as a

Figure 13. *Tibet-Institut, Rikon, Switzerland. The building appears highly modernist yet clearly contains Tibetan influenced elements. These include the dark colored frieze at the top, mimicking a penbe parapet, the gajira, as well as the white color and apparent thickness of the walls. (Photograph by the author, 2002)*

correct setting for Buddhist ritual and practice, one could just as well argue that the Tibetans may personally have preferred if the temple were Tibetan in style, and since the vast majority of religious buildings from the 1970s onwards are built in a Tibetan style, this seems to be the case.

This is also apparent when looking at Tibetan Buddhist architecture built outside of Tibet before the 1950s, where one can clearly see the use of Tibetan prototypes. This is evident in Chengde, China, where the Qianlong Emperor (r. 1736–1795) constructed a complex of buildings modelled on Tibetan ones, in the Forbidden City, where the Yuhuage pavilion is modelled on the Tholing Serkhang, in the Kalachakra temple in St. Petersburg, and in Mongolian Buddhist architecture, to list a few examples. The same is true today in Europe and North and South America. New buildings like the temple at Deer Park in Wisconsin and the Lerab Ling Temple in Roqueredonde, France, clearly attempt to look as traditionally Tibetan as possible, although the majority of Buddhists using these buildings are non-Tibetan. Even in buildings such as the Tibet-Institut, which is largely used by Tibetan refugees, and which was purposely built by Swiss architects *not* to replicate Tibetan architecture, a *penbe* frieze along with painted squares made to look like decorative beam ends, have been added, along with a *gajira*, Dharma Wheel and deer.[32] The Tibetan style can even be seen at Nalanda Monastery

Figure 14. *New assembly hall building at Nalanda Monastery, Lavaur, France. (Photograph by the author, 2007)*

(Fig. 14) in Lavaur, France, where a new assembly hall has visibly Tibetan elements incorporated into its exterior, yet is self-confessedly not based on Vinaya or tantric texts. Instead, the building is based on the Chinese tradition of Feng Shui, as was ordered by the monastery's spiritual guide, Lama Zopa Rinpoche, who also wanted it to appear Tibetan. This building, like the temple at Deer Park and the Tibet-Institut, was designed by a Westerner; in this case a French monk living at the monastery.

The importance of famous or high-ranking religious personalities, such as Lama Zopa, in connection with the construction of Tibetan style religious architecture cannot be overlooked, not only because they are often the patrons of such buildings, but also often contribute to their design. I would even argue that the Tsuglagkhang is seen as an "appropriate setting" by Tibetans simply because it has the blessings of the Dalai Lama, who is seen by the vast majority of refugees as the highest-ranking figure and lineage holder of Tibetan Buddhism, and thus whatever he says, goes, at least officially.

There can be no underestimating the personality cult that surrounds the Dalai Lama, whom the vast majority of Tibetans and Tibetan Buddhists consider a human incarnation of Avalokitesvara. Despite this, how much influence he has over the day to day life of Tibetans is questionable. The same applies for monastery life in general, and for the construction of assembly halls. Although the Dalai Lama is often requested to endorse the building of new assembly halls, as this almost guarantees a successful fundraising campaign, he often criticizes elements of the buildings which he inaugurates or previously endorsed. These include overly elaborate decoration, lavish murals and unnecessarily large size.

Despite the example set by the Dalai Lama's construction of his simple main temple and private residence, monasteries continue to spend large sums of money on the construction of their assembly halls, many of which have various unnecessary and unused auxiliary rooms or spaces on their higher floors. Although it is believed by most Tibetan refugees that the Dalai Lama is infallible, the communal effort and will to implement changes and advice given by the Dalai Lama is often lacking. The Tibetan refugee community is frequently, not surprisingly, highly conservative, particularly with regard to monasteries. Change to the pre-existing way of doing things is often unwelcome, whether in the case of religious matters, visual arts or architecture, as is discussed, particularly in relation to painting, by Clare Harris in *In the Image of Tibet.*[33]

Finally, especially in the case of the buildings in India, one must consider the presence of the outsider in the design process, especially that of the foreign donor. For example, in the case of the large Gelug monasteries in Mundgod, most building projects today depend heavily on donations from abroad, particularly from foreign Tibetan Buddhists. The Tibetan refugees living in the so-called camps around the monastic compounds (also called "camps") in Mundgod, would never be able to support these monasteries which house thousands of monks, let alone pay for vast building projects. Westerners, Taiwanese and overseas Chinese communities play an important role in the finances of the monasteries by sponsoring individual monks, the monastery as a whole or particular buildings. The new Drepung Loseling building relies heavily on funding from countries such as the United States and Japan.[34] The act of sponsoring or helping with the construction of a monastery or temple is believed by Buddhists to be a highly meritorious act, perhaps helping to explain why these large building projects receive funding relatively easily when compared to many humanitarian projects in the settlements.[35]

Aside from the act of offering money, the actual role of the outsiders in the design process in India is unclear, apart from cases where the actual designer was a foreigner (for example in the case of the Norbulingka). Despite this I have heard in various discussions that it is often not only the general monastic community who insists on a "traditional" Tibetan assembly hall, but foreign donors as well.[36]

Conclusion

Buildings in Tibet were built in a specific way for a number of reasons. An obvious example is the flat roofs of Tibetan assembly halls. Today in India all assembly halls, such as those in Mundgod, continue to have flat roofs. This is in strong contrast to the houses of the lay Tibetans who live in settlements around the monasteries, in houses that mostly have pitched roofs, a logical solution in a region that has a long and wet monsoon season every year. This adjustment can even be seen in other Tibetan Buddhist regions, such as Bhutan, where pitched roofs have become an element of their traditional architecture. However, the thought of making this or other adjustments, or at least experimenting with them, has not occurred to the conservative monastic authorities who seem to prefer an almost nostalgic copying to a practical and more contemporary Tibetan Buddhist architecture.

Even if certain symbolic elements are deemed necessary for a religious building, there is still a window for creativity and change, as has been seen with buildings like the Tibet-Institut, which, although not perfect in its design, demonstrates the potential of contemporary Tibetan architecture.

Despite the popularity of the type of Tibetan Buddhist refugee architecture that is prevalent today, I do believe it should be possible to redefine what Tibetan Buddhist architecture is in a refugee context without having to sacrifice its "Tibetan*ness*." As is suggested in the title of a work by Mary Van Dyke, *Constructing Tradition: Tibetan Architecture in Europe*, tradition is not something concrete or inherent, rather it is constructed and interpreted. Thus what Tibetan refugees see as traditional Buddhist architecture is constructed through a multitude of factors from their refugee experience, not only a strict adherence to Buddhist principles. The definition of styles, in this case Tibetan style architecture, is also subjective, with the process of labeling based on selecting a number of outstanding features and elements which, when combined together in one building, are labeled as "Tibetan style." With the concepts of tradition and style both being so fluid, the designers and patrons of Tibetan Buddhist refugee buildings could easily incorporate the essential Buddhist elements of their architecture, including foundation rituals, layouts and architectural details, with newly inspired design. As I have shown, what is preserved in artistic lineages is not really a strict adherence to a particular form or style, as these are constantly subject to change. Instead, the essential element is the concept of being able to relate one's present creations with those of the past in some way, so as to validate them, not necessarily to produce exact copies. A contemporary Tibetan building following the Buddhist textual tradition, as well as incorporating any architectural elements or ornamentation deemed as essential to the religious functioning of the building, should thus logically be acceptable. In my opinion this would be highly preferable to the act of simply attempting to copy old buildings and labeling the results as "traditional."

Ernesto Noriega noted that without change: "A nostalgic approach, limited to the strict reproduction of old models, ignoring the new environmental conditions and rejecting the introduction of appropriate materials and technologies would render the tradition inflexible and non-adaptive. And the indiscriminate use of forms and symbols inappropriately and out of context, turning distinctive elements into mere decorative clichés, could finally reduce Tibetan architecture to a caricature of itself"... and thus "unwillingly accelerating its death..."[37]

Notes

1 See Mary Van Dyke, "Constructing Tradition: Tibetan Architecture in Europe," 2 vols, (PhD Dissertation, London: School of Oriental and African Studies, 1996); Mary Van Dyke, "Grids and Serpents: A Tibetan Foundation Ritual in Switzerland." In *Constructing Tibetan Culture: Contemporary Perspectives*, ed. Frank J. Korom (Quebec: World Heritage Press, 1997), 178–227; and Peter Chevetzoff, "L'Architecture Tibétaine en Occident: Mutations et Continuité," (DEA Dissertation: Université de Paris X Nanterre), 1991. A brief account of the status of Tibetan refugee architecture in India can be found in Ernesto Noriega, "Tradition and Innovation in the Tibetan Diaspora." In *Managing Change; Sustainable Approaches to the Conservation of the*

Built Environment, ed. Jean Marie Teutonico and Frank Matero (Getty Trust Publications: Getty Conservation Institute, 2003) 161–79.

2 See Paola Mortari Vergara and Gilles Béguin, eds., *Dimore Umane, Santuari Divini: Origini, sviluppo e diffusione dell'architettura tibetana/Demeures des Hommes, Sanctuaires des Dieux: Sources, développement et rayonnement de l'architecture tibétaine* (Rome: Universita de Roma, 1987).

3 According to Philip Denwood, originally the term *vihara* probably meant "monastery" but in Tibet the term, translated as *tsuglagkhang*, has come to mean "temple." This is indeed true in the large Gelug monasteries, including those in South India, where the main *tsogkhang* (also commonly known as *dukhang* (*'du khang*) of a monastic college is commonly referred to as the *tsuglagkhang*. Denwood further notes how the term *vihara* also seems to have become the label for a particular type of architectural layout. Philip Denwood, "Uses of Indian Technical Literature in Tibetan Architecture," *South Asian Studies 6* (London: Society of South Asian Studies, 1990), 95.

4 Andre Alexander, *The Temples of Lhasa: Tibetan Buddhist Architecture from the 7th to the 21st Centuries* (Chicago: Serindia Publications, 2005), 114.

5 An assembly hall "should be square in shape" according to Thubten Legshay Gyatsho, *Gateway to the Temple: Manual of Tibetan Monastic Customs, Art, Building and Celebrations* (Kathmandu: Ratna Pustak Bhandar, 1979), 35.

6 The protector chapel is also noted by Chogye Trichen Rinpoche, Thubten Legshay Gyatsho, 39. The protector chapel of Ganden Shartse, for example, is a separate room, located in the same building but not attached to the hall. It is accessible via a balcony and some stairs to the right of the hall. The protector hall should be on the right, as is noted by Chogye Trichen Rinpoche, and although this is usually the case, I have seen examples, such as the new assembly hall of Jangchub Choeling Nunnery, where the protector hall is located on the left.

7 The manual states that "to the left and right of the assembly halls are different sanctuaries." See Gyatsho, 39.

8 Gyatsho, 35.

9 The term *kyil* suggesting centre and *khor* referring to a circle or surroundings.

10 Gyatsho, 35

11 The Hindu deities Vishvakarman and Brahma are attributed with having taught the use of proportions, iconometry and all other essential elements of the graphic arts to an Indian king, who became the first human proponent of these artistic "sciences." Gega Lama, *Principles of Tibetan Art*, vol.1 (Darjeeling: Jamyang Singe, 1983), 35.

12 Gyatsho, 59.

13 Gyatsho, 59.

14 As Gega Lama, a painter of the Karma Gadri tradition, notes: "Menla Döndrup revised the standard of proportion for the various religious motifs, composition and design." Gega Lama, 46.

15 Denwood, 101.

16 Denwood, 101.

17 This fact is stated in a vast number of Tibetan Buddhist texts. As Pabongka Rinpoche, perhaps the most famous Gelug teacher of the 20th century, stated: "Some people think they can know the path by reading books and not have a guru, but this is not good enough – you must rely on a qualified guru." Pabongkapa Jampa Tenzin Trinley Gyatso, *Liberation in the Palm of Your Hand: A Concise Discourse on the Path to Enlightenment* (Somerville, MA: Wisdom Publications, 1997), 252.

18 *Rabne* literally means "superior abiding" and is a ceremony by which an enlightened being is asked to bless and abide with an object, such as a statue.

19 Gyatsho, 55–75. The iconometry of deity figures is also, like architectural specifications, based on various texts such as tantras.
20 Such as Gyatsho, *Gateway to the Temple.*
21 Gyatsho, 29
22 This is called the "testing of the directions." For example, according to Chogye Trichen Rinpoche, a hole must be dug into the ground and filled with water. One then takes one hundred paces away from the hole and then returns. If the hole is still full of water, then that is a good sign; if the water has been absorbed, it is unfavorable.
23 This symbolism may well vary depending on sect and lineage, and it is unclear which tradition this explanation follows.
24 Tcheuky Sèngué, *Le Temple Tibétaine et son Symbolisme* (Vernègues: Claire Lumière, 1998), 30–31.
25 Denwood, 101.
26 The term "Tibetan*ness*" is used by Frank J. Korom in "Introduction: Place, Space and Identity: The Cultural, Economic and Aesthetic Politics of Tibetan Diaspora." In *Tibetan Culture in the Diaspora: Papers Presented at a Panel of the 7th Seminar of the International Association for Tibetan Studies,* Graz, 1995 ed. Frank J. Korom, (Vienna: Verlag der Österreichischen Akademie der Wissenschaften, 1997), 1–8.
27 John F. Avedon, *In Exile from the Land of Snows* (London: Michael Joseph, 1984), 103.
28 Tenzin Gyatso (Fourteenth Dalai Lama), *Freedom in Exile: The Autobiography of the Dalai Lama* (London: Hodder & Stoughton, 1990), 201.
29 The Tibet-Institut is a Tibetan Buddhist monastery located in Rikon, Switzerland, which is built in a Swiss modernist style but with some external Tibetan architectural details. The aim in its design was to create a building that consciously would not stand out and appear foreign in comparison to Swiss architecture, yet would also attempt to incorporate certain Tibetan features. See Peter Lindegger-Stauffer, "Das Klösterliche Tibet-Institut in Rikon/Zurich," *Asiatische Studien* 25 (1971), 377–88.
30 Indians are generally quite tolerant and even encouraging of Tibetans and their efforts to maintain their culture, as noted by Dawa Norbu, for example. See Dawa Norbu, "The Settlements: Participation and Integration." In *Exile as Challenge: The Tibetan Diaspora*, ed. Dagmar Bernstoff and Hebertus Von Welck (Hyderabad: Orient Longman Private Ltd, 2004), 186–212. There have been problems, particularly recently, in Karnataka for example, where Indians have heatedly demonstrated against, amongst other things, the economic inequality around Tibetan settlements, where the refugees and their monasteries are generally far wealthier than the local Indians (Phayul, *Bhagat Singh Samithi Asks Tibetans to 'Quit India'*, http://www.phayul.com/News/article.aspx?article=Bhagat+Singh+Samithi+Asks+Tibetans+to+'Quit+India'&id=9771&c=1&t=1, accessed 28/07/2006).
31 A large majority of the refugee Tibetan religious buildings depend on foreign funds for their construction. Needless to say, today there are many more foreign donors and sponsors than there were in the 1960s.
32 The architects of the Tibet-Institut were the Swiss architects Ulrich Flück and Robi Vock; see Van Dyke 1997, 181.
33 Clare Harris, *In the Image of Tibet: Tibetan Painting after 1959* (London, Reaktion Books, 1999).
34 Personal communication, Konchok Sithar, lecturer and vice-president at the Potala College, Tokyo, 14/11/2007.
35 The merits of constructing monasteries can be seen, for example, in Lama Zopa Rinpoche, *The Benefits of Building a Monastery*, http://www.lamayeshe.com/lamazopa/build.shtml, accessed 23/7/2008.

36 Personal communication, Geshe Gendun Samdrup, designer of the Ganden Jangtse Tsogchung, 13/3/2008.

37 Noriega, 162

7

Loss of Memory and Continuity of Praxis in Rampur-Bashahr

An Itinerant Study of 17th-Century Tibetan Murals

GEORGIOS T. HALKIAS

1. Till the Sutlej Goes Dry and Horses Get Horns

I arrived at the Shish Mahal Palace in Rampur-Bashahr on 17 July 2007 intent on locating a unique set of murals said to have honored a trading treaty between the Hindu raja of Bashahr, Kehri Singh (1639–1696), and the government of Lhasa (dGa' ldan pho brang) headed by Blo bzang rgya mtsho, the Fifth Dalai Lama (1617–1682).[1] Identifying the historical frescoes was of no small importance, as they are the only art-historical relic of this kind in northwest India, and unique to the culturally Tibetan world.[2] Furthermore, in the absence of any Tibetan and Bashahari official documents, the murals were expected to reaffirm Bashahr's military cooperation with the Tibetans during the Tibet–Ladakh–Mughal war of 1679–1684.

The Moravian missionary and explorer, August Hermann Francke (1870–1930), who visited the former capital of Bashahr in the summer of 1909, photographed the murals in the raja's garden house (Fig. 1). He reported that Rampur was the first place up the Sutlej River where one encounters Tibetan Buddhist architecture and art.[3] Historical ties between Tibet and Bashahr go back to at least the 17th century,[4] when the princely ruler of Bashahr, Kehri Singh, sided in 1679 with the Mongol commander dGa' ldan tshe dbang on a Tibetan–Mongol punitive expedition against the kingdom of Ladakh. The result of their mutual cooperation during the war was a sworn agreement stipulating that no taxes be levied on Bashahari and Tibetan merchants when trading on each others' territories, while

a. Fresco in the palace, Rampur.

Figure 1: *Murals depicting the Tibet-Bashahr treaty (after Francke, 1914).*

an official delegation from Bashahr should be sent tri-annually to the towns of Tsaparang, Purang, Dawa, Ruthog and Gartok in western Tibet.[5]

For the small Himalayan state of Bashahr, the Tibet–Bashahr treaty of 1679–1684 was undoubtedly of great economic importance. Historical documents, in all likelihood contemporary to their discovery by Francke and his assistant at Namgya (upper Kinnaur) and Tsaparang in 1909,[6] testify that tax-free commerce between Tibetans and Bashaharis should be observed in perpetuity. Similarly, the Kinnauri oral tradition preserves the formulaic expression that the treaty was meant to last until the "Sutlej goes dry, crows become white, horses get horns, and stones – stated to be at the borders of both the States and on which [the] treaty was written – produce hair or wool."[7]

Although the crows did not turn white and the stones marking the borders have yet to produce wool, commercial relations between Bashahr and Tibet did not last past the 20th century. Neither did the art-historical frescoes from the Raja's palace that recall an age-old trafficking of traders, cultures and goods. In the Shish Mahal, where once stood the Tibetan frescoes, I discovered paintings of popular Tibetan Buddhist and Hindu deities executed in Tibetan style. They were inaugurated in 1966 according to their Tibetan inscription. The dedication reads that they were decorated for the commemoration of the royal patron of religious arts and present-day Dharmaraja of Bashahr, Virbhadra Singh (b. 1934). In the following discussion it will become clear that the murals symbolize an alliance of faiths and cultures in the western Himalayas which, according to oral histories and written records, has long been forged between the kingdom of Bashahr and the borderlands of Tibetan civilization.

2. The Raja and the Lama

The principality of Bashahr (also known as Bashahar, Bushahar, Bushahr) was once among the largest of the twenty-eight Shimla Hill States; these were under the administration of the British Raj, which was keen to invest in regional and transcontinental trade and to exploit Himalayan resources. Bashahr bordered on the north with Spiti, on the east with Tibet, on the south with Garhwal and on the west with Jubbal, Kotkhai, Kumharsain, Kotgarh and Kulu. Caught in the machinations of the British imperial enterprise,[8] it was subjected to political-cum-economic

Figure 2: *Map of Bashahr, Shimla Gazetteer; unknown year and binding.*

vicissitudes, acceding to the Indian Union in 1947. On the 8 March 1948, along with twenty other princely hill states of Punjab and Shimla, Bashahr signed an agreement that resulted in its inclusion in the Indian state of Himachal Pradesh[9] (Fig. 2).

Rampur, a small township situated at 1,005 meters on the left bank of the Sutlej, served as Bashahr's winter capital. Being well connected with major trading routes that joined Indian markets with Central Asia and Tibet, it buzzed with mercantile activity, especially in November during the Lavi fair, the largest trading event in the north Himalayas, which attracted traders from Kashmir, Ladakh, Yarkand and the Indian mainland.[10] Concerning the origins of the Rampuri fair, the *Census of India* (1961) reports:

> "About three hundred years ago during the regime of Raja Kehar Singh of Bushahr, a trade treaty was signed between the Bushahr State and Tibet ... Horses from Tibet and swords from Bushahr were exchanged in token of this friendship. It was written in the treaty that their friendly relations would continue till this time ... Since then, it is presumed that trade relations increased and eventually [the] Lavi fair was held.'"[11]

Figure 3: *Shipki pass, Namgya village.*

Rampur was also located along major pilgrimage routes to sacred sites in western Tibet worshipped by Hindus, Bon and Buddhists alike, i.e., Mount Kailash and Lake Mansarovar. Missionary and pilgrimage activities were intensified by trading opportunities, creating the conditions for Tibetan Buddhist monasticism to take eventually a firm stronghold in these borderland regions. Twenty-two km from the village of Namgya in upper Kinnaur[12] lay the trans-Himalayan mountain pass of Shipki, accommodating crossings to and from western Tibet (Fig. 3). This treacherous transcontinental passage must have been in use from ancient times, for among the ruined castles reported by Francke at Shipki village, there were no living memories of the origins of mKar gog, the oldest castle, built above the village in cyclopean style. A second castle, known as Seng ge mkhar, is said to have received its crooked ground plan "through a race round its base executed in opposite directions by a poisonous snake and a scorpion," and was built, in all probability, during the Ladakhi occupation of mNga' ris by orders of King Seng ge rnam rgyal (1570–1642), and named after him.[13]

In Bashahr, encounters between Buddhists and Hindus go back to the first millennium. Traditional and historical sources concur that the Raja of Bashahr

Figure 4: *Devtā procession, Rampur-Bashahr.*

was revered as semi-divine by his subjects, ruling through a ritual superstructure termed "government by deity" (*devtā kā rāj*),[14] while three appointed *vazirs* (ministers) held both "judicial and revenue powers" in the areas under their jurisdiction and were rewarded by the raja with a *jagir* (estate) for their services to the state.[15] Based on ancient legends, the ruling family descended from the Hindu god Krishna, who, through his grandson Parduman, came to Sarahan in order to marry the daughter of Raja Bavasa Deo. Another story relates a Brahmanic origin to the ruling family.[16]

Buddhist missionary activities in the area seem to go back to the reign of King Kanishka (78–101 CE), for according to the *Shan Chien Pi Po Sha*, penal provisions existed for Buddhist monks who indulged in sex with Kinnauri women.[17] If the actuality of these naughty monks is not enough proof for early Buddhist activity in the region, later influences readily point to the prevalence of the cult of tantric master Padmasambhava, while at least eleven villages in upper Kinnaur claim temples founded by the renowned Tibetan translator of Buddhist scriptures, Rin chen bzang po (958–1055).[18]

Cross-religious narratives played their part in the legitimation of the treaty between the Hindu principality and the Buddhist government of Lhasa. To recapitulate the event: in 1679, having crossed the Tibetan border at Shipki pass, the Raja Kehri Singh and his entourage proceeded to make ablutions and offerings at Lake Mansarovar on their way to Puling in western Tibet to meet dGa' ldan tshe dbang dpal bzang, the Mongol military commander and ex-resident Buddhist monk of Tashilhunpo Monastery in central Tibet. During what may have been an initial encounter by emissaries prompted by the pretext of pilgrimage to the sacred lake, Kehri Singh met dGa' ldan tshe dbang, the Jungar prince of the Hongtaiji family, and "swearing by the Great Saint Buddha," they entered into a trading agreement in order "to pave the way of the golden way of friendly relations."[19]

Just as pilgrimage to the holy places of western Tibet served as a pretext for a clandestine meeting between the two leaders, the legacy of Buddha Śākyamuni forged a common cultural ground between the Hindu born and raised raja and the Mongol representative of the Buddhist theocracy in Lhasa. Inspired by Tibetan religious-cum-political (*chos srid*) narratives of incarnating Bodhisattvas, Kinnauris maintained the belief that each raja of Bashahr, at his death, "re-incarnated as the Gurú Láma or Gurú of the Lámas, who is understood to be the Dalai Láma of Tibet."[20]

3. The Murals During the Reign of Raja Shamser Singh (1839–1914)

During his sojourn to the capital of Bashahr in 1909, Francke reports seeing a Tibetan Buddhist temple with a sloping roof that was stylistically similar to other buildings in the area and appeared to have been only "twelve or thirteen years old" containing "modern frescoes" and "a huge prayer wheel." More striking, however, is his discovery of art-historical murals at the Shish Mahal Palace. Concerning these he writes:

> In one of the Rāja's garden houses, we found more Lamaist frescoes. One of them interested me in particular, for it evidently represents a historical scene ... The fresco evidently represents the treaty between Tibet and Bashahr concluded about 1650 AD, when Bashahr was supported by the Mughal emperor. The figure in the middle is apparently the Mughal emperor, surrounded by his soldiers. The elephant procession which approaches from the left is either the retinue of the Mughal, or the Bashahr king, Keharī Singh. A party of Bashahr people, distinguished by their black round hats, are placed in front of the Mughal, while the embassy from Tibet is shown on the right side of the painting.[21]

Nowadays, the only visible Buddhist structure can be seen in Rampur's main bazaar. This recently constructed temple was inaugurated by the present Dalai Lama in 2006 and is clearly of Tibetan architectural style with yellow painted pagoda-like roofs. The Tibetan attendant of the temple had no knowledge whether this temple was built upon an older edifice, or whether there were any murals in the area commemorating the treaty. To my further disappointment, the curator of the Shish Mahal, Mr. Thakur, an advocate by profession and long-term resident of Rampur, claimed to have never seen any Tibetan-style murals, and this was confirmed by other inhabitants I interviewed during my visit.

In retrospect, this should not have come as a complete surprise. During an interview with the chief minister of Himachal Pradesh and heir to the palaces of Rampur and Sarahan, Raja Virbhadra Singh assured me that he had never seen or heard about any Tibetan paintings in the area.[22] This was particularly vexing, for in 1931 an Indian civil servant named French was so impressed by the Tibetan-style frescoes at the Shish Mahal to remark that "in Rampur-Bashahar the art of the Himalayas and the art of the land beyond the Himalayas, of Tibet and the Far East, meet with a crash." French, familiar with Francke's publication of twenty-two years earlier, further remarked on the luck of resemblance between the Hindu and Tibetan paintings at the raja's residence:

> Near the Shish Mahal is a Hindu temple with a fresco painted in Tibetan style. There is a similar picture in the Potala, the Dalai Lama's palace at Lhasa. The subject is a treaty between Bashahar State and Tibet in the days of the Mogul Emperor. It is interesting to find it side by side with the Shish Mahal frescoes. Neither shows the slightest sign of any influence from each other. [23]

It would indeed be instructive if a copy of the art-historical paintings were to surface in the chambers of the Potala Palace,[24] for it would point to the import of the Tibet–Bashahr treaty beyond the glory and welfare of Bashahr, which had to pay tribute to the Mughals in the 17th century.

The disappearance of the treaty-murals in Rampur-Bashahr coincided with their erasure from traditional sources of memory. It is symptomatic of many marginal histories the world over, neglected for recollections of history better served by states and individuals. It is also a loss due to drastic changes brought upon many Himalayan borderlands ever since they had to discontinue cultural and economic exchanges with Tibet and succumb to Indian and Chinese militarization.[25]

4. Concluding Remarks: Loss and Continuity in Rampur-Bashahr

During my visit to the Shish Mahal Palace, I was granted access to all buildings except the old palace quarters and a garden house made into an office by the Indian National Congress Party. Adjacent to the Congress Party office and near the main road stood a smaller summer house with a pagoda-style roof that matched Francke's and French's descriptions of a "garden house" and a "Hindu temple" (Fig. 5). In this wooden house I was expecting to locate the murals commemorating the 1679–1684 Tibet-Bashahr treaty. What I discovered instead were 20th-century Tibetan Buddhist and Hindu murals, accompanied by a short inscription in Tibetan; the murals are clearly visible to anyone looking through the windows and entrance to the house made of wooden frame and glass.

In this one-room structure, consciously staged as a Hindu reception hall for the meeting of dignitaries, there was a sofa, with a kitsch golden-color cover, and two small tables, one of which, dressed in a similar glistening cover, served as the base for a framed printed image of the Hindu god Śiva. On the right and front walls there were paintings of popular deities from the Buddhist and Hindu pantheon executed in colourful Tibetan style and framed by Tibetan ornamental symbols (Fig. 6). With the exception of Mañjuśrī ('Jam dpal dbyangs), Vajrapāṇi (Phyag na rdo rje), Kubera Jhambala and a semi-visible wrathful deity covered by the printed-image of Śiva, painted at the edges of the right wall, the

Figure 5: *Garden house, Shish Mahal Palace.*

Figure 6: *Buddhist-Hindu murals, Shish Mahal Palace.*

remaining Buddhist deities occupied the front wall with Padmasambhava in the center with two consorts, framed on both sides by the Medicine Buddha (Sangs rgyas sman bla), Śākyamuni, Amitāyus (Tshe dpag med), Samantabhadra (Kun tu bzang po), Vajradhara (rDo rje 'chang) and Vajrasattva (rDo rje sems pa). With the same colors and artistry, the right wall depicted Hanuman, Śiva, Gaṇeśa, Kṛṣṇa, and Sītā and Rāma. On the crown of the Hindu goddess Durga, depicted with many arms and riding on a tiger, we find an image of the famous original sandstone sculpted *Lion Capital of Aśoka* preserved at Sarnath Museum. The Aśoka Chakra (wheel), adopted in the national flag of India, is represented at the base of the image, on which Indian lions stand back to back facing the four directions.

The painted inscription on a golden background, twelve lines written in black *dbu chen* script, reads that the murals were inaugurated on the 15th of the third month in the spring of 1966 (Fig. 7). The painter of the murals and author of the inscription, Ca ras Shes rab senge, possibly a rNying ma monk from Nesang village,[26] records Buddhist prayers of refuge to the divinities of the Old School, meritorious dedications, eulogies and a meeting between Raja Virbhadra Singh,

Figure 7: *Tibetan inscription, Shish Mahal Palace.*

the present heir of Bashahr, his mother and two guests, one of whom may have been a Sikh with some importance in the region. Typical of many Tibetan prayers aiming to secure birth to Buddha Amitābha's pure land, the author concludes the inscription with an aspiration prayer (*bde smon*) and dedication of merit for birth in Sukhāvatī (*bde ba can*).[27]

Elsewhere, the language of the inscription appears outdated, addressing the patron of the religious paintings in royal terms as *rgyal po* (raja), and it is quite puzzling that, apart from the painter, none of the members present would have been able to read it. For an outsider, these designations may appear simply honorific, but given the old tradition of rajas ruling the area for generations, it may account for one of Virbhadra Singh's early political campaigns before becoming

Figure 8: *Vajrapāṇi and Hunaman. Tibetan Buddhist temple, Kamru, Sangla.*

chief minister of Himachal Pradesh in 1983, an office he held on and off for fifteen years until December 2007.

The suspension of commercial and pilgrimage links between Tibet and Kinnaur did not detract from enriching interactions between Himalayan Buddhists, Tibetan refugees and tribal communities. In Kamru, the ancient capital of Bashahr in the valley of Sangla, regional Tibetan-style inventions of art preserve the coexistence of Tibetan and Hindu worlds. Similar to the 1966 Tibetan-style exemplars in Rampur-Bashahr, below the ancient fort of Kamru-Bashahr on the external wall of a Buddhist temple erected in 2005, there is a depiction of Hanuman, the simian companion of Rāma, next to a wrathful form of Buddha Vajrapāṇi (Fig. 8). This joint proselytism is executed in contemporary Tibetan temples and religious art.[28]

In the aftermath of Tibet's occupation by the People's Republic of China, Tibetan refugees and their patrons have been prompt to re-establish religious ties with the borderland regions through the erection of Buddhist temples across the old kingdom of Bashahr: in Rampur (2006); Sarahan (date?); Kamru (2005); Rekong Peo (1992); and, at the time of this investigation, in Nako to accommodate the Fourteenth Dalai Lama's (b. 1935) teachings in 2007. More research should be done, however, before speculating on a revitalization of Tibetan Buddhism in Bashahr as part of the Tibetan diaspora movement in the state of Himachal Pradesh.[29]

To conclude, the 17th-century murals depicting the Tibet-Bashahr treaty were not visible, and yet not gone. Throughout my journey, and in the sources I visited, the murals persisted as stereotypes of multi-layered political, economic and religious interactions that have transpired since ancient times between Himalayan polities and Tibet. The Tibetan-style murals of 1966 belonged to a world of different political divisions. Designed to promote a symbiotic fusion of Indian nationalism with two prevailing religions in Kinnaur, they served as venues for regional *realpolitik*; not failing in the process to introduce novel styles of Indo-Tibetan religious syncretism indebted to the impact and currency of Tibetan civilization in the border-lands of India.

5. The Tibetan Inscription

Location: Shish Mahal Palace, garden house, Rampur-Bashahr

[±#] number of illegible syllables
fn. footnote readings indicate suggested spelling
( ) parenthetical explanations

Transliteration

1. [±2] na mo // thog ma'i sangs rgyas mgon po 'od mi 'gyur / rigs lnga'i sangs rgyas
2. [±2] rdo'i 'chang / rig 'dzin brgyud pa mkha' 'gro bka' bsrung[30] bcas / thams cad ma lus
3. bdag la dgongs su gsol / bdag gis dge bcu chos la spyod pa yis / mtho rigs[31]
4. thar pa'i go 'phang thob par shog / brgyu[32] 'byor spyin[33] pa'i bdag po dge ba'i chos la dgyes zhing /
5. sangs rgyas kyis bstan pa rin po che dar zhing rgyas la yun ring du gnas par gyur cig /
6. dge bdun[34] lun[35] cing[36] sbyin bdag la sogs pa'i sems can thams cad bde skyid phun sum tshogs
7. pa dam pa'i chos la spyod pa dang / rten 'di la yang mchod pa rgya chen po rgyun mi 'chad pa
8. 'byung bar mdzad du gsol // / 'di chos rgyal don rgyud kyis 'khris don kyi bzhugs
9. pa khang phun tshogs dga' khyil si tang spyid[37] zla pa[38]3 tshes 15 spyi lo 1966 la rgyal po bhil bha
10. dhru sing dang rgyal yum byas de dus sig tri ri dhur dga' sing byas / / sban tra ri dhur bha nan byas
11. lha bris ne sang ca ras shes reb[39] senge nas bris pas
sems can rnams la phan pa myur thob shog //
12. 'chi[40] ma bde ba can du bskye[41] bar shog /

Translation

(Homage and Prayer)

1. [±2] namo. Primordial Buddha, Protector Unchanging Light (*Kun tu bzang po*), Buddhas of the Five Families,
2. [±2] Dorje'i 'Chang (Vajradhara), lineage of Vidyadharas (Awareness Holders), Sky-Goers, and Dharma Protectors,
Everywhere (wherever you may reside) without exception
3. Please pay heed to me.

(Dedication of Merit)

Having practiced the ten Buddhist virtues

4. May I attain the highest level of liberation.

Delighting in the virtuous qualities of a lord offering his wealth for alms

5. May the precious teachings of the Buddha spread, increase and abide for a long time.

(Eulogies and Purpose of Inscription)

6. May the present *sangha*, the benefactor, and all sentient beings experience joy

7–8. in the practice of the supreme doctrine, and
May there be sublime and uninterrupted offerings towards these murals (*'di rten*).
This dharma-king, (arrived) for this purpose (the inauguration of images) residing at the

9. House Phun tshogs dga' khyil si tang, on the 15th day of the third month of spring[42] of 1966, during which King Bhil bha

10. dhru sing and his mother (*rgyal yum*) officiated, then the Sikh Tri ri dhur dga' sing and (then) sBan tra ri dhur bha nan.[43]

(Colophon)

11. (This inscription) has been composed by the painter of the sacred images, Ne sang Ca Ras Sherab Senge.
May we swiftly encounter benefit and

12. In the next life (after death),
Take birth in Sukhāvatī (the Land of Bliss).

Notes

1 For a study of the Tibet-Bashahr treaty, see Luciano Petech, "The Tibetan-Ladakhi Moghul War of 1681–83," *The Indian Historical Quarterly* 23.3 (1947), 195–99. Research in Kinnaur has been conducted as part of the project "Islam and Tibet: Cultural Interactions (8th–17th centuries)" sponsored by the Arts and Humanities Research Council based at the Warburg Institute, University of London. Interested readers may browse through visual material gathered on-site at the University of London's E-repository: http://sas-space.sas.ac.uk/dspace/handle/10065/580. I wish to thank Charles Burnett, Brandon Dotson, Arik Moran and Sebastien Boret for reviewing this chapter and offering their suggestions.

2 There is precedence to this custom in the establishment of the Temple of the Treaty (*gtsigs kyi gtsug lag khang*) and its murals in De ga g.Yu tshal during the reign of the Tibetan emperor Khri gTsug lde brtsan (815–841) to commemorate the council and subsequent peace treaty between Tibet, China the Uighurs and possibly Nanzhao; see Matthew Kapstein, "The Treaty Temple of De-ga g.yu-tshal: Identification and Iconography." In *Essays on the International Conference on Tibetan Art and Archaeology and Art* (Chengdu: Sichuan ren min chu ban she, 2004), 98–126.

3 August Hermann Francke, *Antiquities of Indian Tibet* (1914; reprint, Delhi: Low Price Publications, 1999), 6.

4 The Bon claim historical precedence in the region from ancient times. This was challenged for the first time in the 7th century when Zhang zhung had to acknowledge Tibetan suzerainty. Up until the early 20th century, songs of the Kinnauri Shar rgan festival differentiated between the "religion of the gods" (*lha chos*) and the "religion of Bon" (*bon chos*); Francke 1914, 21. For a contemporary Bon account to the area of Kinnaur by scholar-adept (*mkhas grub*) 'Jigs med nam mkha'i rdo rje (1897–1955), see his biography, *Khyab bdag 'khor lo'i mgon po mkhas grub 'jigs med nam mkha'i rnam thar dad brgya'i rma bya rnam par rtse ba* (vol I, Chapter 9; reproduced by Sonam Dakpa, Tibetan Bonpo Monastic Centre, 1972), 426–73; for research based on this text, see Brenda Li, "A Phyogs med Pilgrimage by a Ris med Bonpo Monk, 1924–1925: as Illustrated in the Biography of Khyung sprul 'Jigs med nam mkha'i rdo rje" (MPhil Dissertation: University of Oxford, 2007).

5 Translation of the Tibet-Bashahr treaty according to the *Tibetan Memorandum* (December 1943). British Library Archives. Punjab Hill States, Residency Files – G-29-60/43. Ref. IOR/R/2/361/8. Our historical sources are not in agreement concerning the names of these towns; see Petech, 198. For a translation of the Tibet-Bashahr treaty and a survey of sources, see Georgios T. Halkias, "Until the Feathers of the Winged Black Raven Will Turn White: Perspectives and Sources for the Tibet-Bashahr treaty of 1679–1684," Proceedings of the 13th IALS conference, Rome, September 2008. To be published as a supplementary volume in *Rivisti degli Studi Orientali*.

6 Halkias forthcoming.

7 *Census of India* 1961, 192. According to the Namgya document studied by Francke and Petech, the agreement between the two parties was said to last "till the Kailāsa of the white snows, palace of the Lord of the three times, navel of the Jambudvīpa, will melt; till the great lake Mānasarovar will empty itself; till the feathers of the winged black raven will become white; till the Kalpa will change;" see Petech, 198–99. The earliest historical reference to the invocation of Kailash and Manasarovar to bear witness to treaties between parties appears to have occurred in the 12th century during the reign of lHa chen Utpala, and is most likely of western Tibetan origin; see August Hermann Francke, *A History of Western Tibet* (1907; reprint, Delhi: Pilgrims Book, 1999), 65.

8 For a recent study of Bashahr's colonial history, see Arik Moran, "From Mountain trade to jungle politics: The transformation of kingship in Bashahr, 1815–1914," *The Indian Economic and Social History Review* 44.2 (2007), 147–77.

9 M. R. Thakur, *Myths, Rituals and Beliefs in Himachal Pradesh* (Delhi: Indus Publishing Company, 1997), 21.

10 Poonam Minhas, *Traditional Trade and Trading Centres in Himachal Pradesh* (Delhi: Indus Publishing Company, 1998), 77. This three-day fair is still held annually in Rampur on 25 November. According to the *Census of India* 1961, 192, in that year the participants were "estimated to be six to eight thousand persons on the peak days of the Lavi fair i.e., on the 11th and 12th November; whereas this [sic] used to be about twenty-five thousands persons or even more during the previous fairs on the third day of the fair."

11 *Census of India* 1961, 189. Moran, 151, remarks that the Tibet–Bashahr treaty laid "the foundations for Bashahr's economic advantage as a viable trade centre in the region."

12 In Namgya (spelt sNam rgya in a historical document consulted by Francke), Tibetan is still spoken and according to the village lama, the eighty families that comprise the residents of this community are Himalayan Buddhists. There is also evidence for the pre-Buddhist worship of the Himalayan ibex (*Capra ibex*), typical in these border regions, exemplified by the horns of the animal offered to the local deities, along with pinned paper Bon mantras protecting the entrance to some village houses.

13 Francke 1914, 26. In 1684, at the end of the Tibet–Ladakh–Mughal war, upper Kinnaur was lost by the Ladhakis and was granted to the Raja Kehri Singh as compensation for assisting the Tibetan–Mongol army during the war.

14 For a discussion of Bashahr's politico-religious administration, see Peter Sutherland, "Travelling Gods and Government by Deity: an Ethnohistory of Power, Representation and Agency in West Himalayan Polity" (DPhil Thesis: University of Oxford, 1998); Thakur, 130–43. The Kinnauri worship of *devtā*s continues to this day, and during my visit I witnessed two processions of the local deity, one on 17 July 2007 outside the Hotel Bushahar Regency in Rampur and one at Kamru village (Sangla valley) on 20 July 2007 (Fig. 4).

15 R. Rahul, "The System of Administration in the Himalayas," *Asian Survey* 9.9 (1969), 699.

16 *Gazetteer of the Simla Hill States, 1910,* Punjab States Gazetteer, Volume VIII (New Delhi: Indus Publishing Company, 1910), 5. In his government report, Captain Charles Pratt Kennedy, Superintendent of Shimla Hill States, submits that Bashahr "was founded by an emigrant Rajput from the Daccan in *Samvat* 472 A.D. (412 A.D.) by one named Dunber Singh"; Poonam Minhas, 47–48.

17 O.C. Handa, *Buddhist Monasteries of Himachal* (Delhi: Indus, 2004), 179. The Kinnauri, locally known as Kanauras, cover a large tract of tribal areas of Himachal Pradesh, especially the areas comprising Kinnaur district and Kanawar Kothi or Kulu district. Similarly to other tribes in the Himalayas, their name implies a class of mythical beings between humans and gods which, along with Gandharvas (the later people of Gandhara), were known as heavenly musicians and singers; see Thakur, 28.

18 Ibid., 184. David Seyfort Ruegg observes that: "In the geographical area covering the northwest Himalayas of the Indian subcontinent (Gandhāra), the western Himalaya, Kaśmīr, present-day Afghanistan (Bactria), and part of the Iranian world, there evidently existed at the turn of the second millennium, a remarkable religious and cultural symbiosis in which Buddhism and Śivaism had some share"; *The Symbiosis of Buddhism/Hinduism in South Asia and of Buddhism with 'local cults' in Tibet and the Himalayan Region,* (Vienna: Österreichische Akademie der Wissenschaften, 2007), 126.

19 *Tibetan Memorandum.* According to some traditions of local folklore, there may have been more pedestrian reasons for the agreement reached between the two leaders and their armies: "The prevailing folk tradition states that one time Kinnaur's Raja Kehrī Singh (1639–1696) crossed the Shipkī Pass with a band of armed followers (*dalbal*) and entered Tibet. He there had a hand to hand combat with Tibet's military commander, Gyālden Chevang. As a consequence (*phalsvarūp*) of this unexpected (*ākasmik*) encounter the two promised (*pratijnā kī*) that henceforth neither of them will loot and attack the others country. [They also agreed that] arrangements will be made for transaction of business in each other's countries free (*unmukt*) of restrictions [i.e., free trade agreement]. Furthermore, this union (*sandhi*) was to remain intact until there will be no more snow on Mt. Kailash, no water in the Manasoravar Lake, and when the black crow turns white. It is thus said that after this incident the ancient mutual (*pārasparik*) looting and fighting that used to take place between the two countries was put to an end and that their friendship grew and expanded"; P. N. Semvāl, "Tibbat aur Buśaihr kī cir-maitrī" (Tibet and Bashahr's Long Lasting Friendship), *Somsī*, 4.2, (April 1978), 37–38, translation by Arik Moran.

20 This Kinnauri belief is reiterated in H.A. Rose, *A Glossary of the Tribes and Castes of the Punjab and North-West Frontier Province: Based on the census report for the Punjab* (Punjab: Government printing, 1911–1919), 98.

21 Francke 1914, 7. In *Antiquities of Indian Tibet,* Francke provides a black and white image of the fresco (Plate IV, a,). He is mistaken in dating the treaty to 1650. For problems concerning Francke's dates, see Petech, 175, fn. 8.

22 Personal interview, 13 July 2007, Oakover, Shimla.

23 J. C. French, *Himalayan Art* (London: Oxford University Press, 1931), 95.

24 Mural illustrations of the 821–822 treaty between Tibet and China can be seen today at the Potala Palace; see Kapstein, 101–02.

25 After China invaded and captured part of Ladakh in 1962, trans-Himalayan commerce in upper Kinnaur has come to a halt with Indian military posts stationed along the old caravan routes, while travel restrictions are observed from Rekong Peo onwards, regulated by frequent police check-posts along the Hindustan–Tibet Highway.

26 Nesang (Tukpa) is located in Kinnaur District near the Tibetan border where dialects of Tibetan are spoken.

27 Although the earliest canonical strands of Pure Land views in Tibet derive from 9th-century Sanskrit manuscripts, translations of the Chinese *Sukhāvatīvyūha* sūtras alongside Tibetan pure land compositions were also common. Nowadays, a fair number of aspiration prayers (*bde mon*) and commentarial works (*'grel ba*) derive from two Indian Sukhāvatī sūtras, accompanied by innovative tantric practices and Pure Land ritual texts represented in all major schools of Tibetan Buddhism; see Georgios T. Halkias, "Transferring to the Land of Bliss: Among Texts and Practices of Sukhāvatī in Tibet" (DPhil Thesis: University of Oxford, 2006).

28 For a discussion of the collocation of Buddhism and Hinduism with reference to the existence of earlier syncretistic movements in the vicinity of and in western Tibet (mNga' ris skor gsum; Zhang zhung; Pu rangs, and Gu ge), see Ruegg, 127–29.

29 For a list of contemporary Tibetan Buddhist monasteries in Kullu, Mandi, Kangra, Shimla and Sirmaur districts, see Handa, 330–31 and 218–28.

30 *srung.*

31 *ris.*

32 *rgyu.*

33 *sbyin.*

34 *dge 'dun.*

35 *lus.*

36 *can.*

37 *dpyid.*

38 *ba.*

39 *rab.*

40 *phyi.*

41 *skye.*

42 I suggest in my translation that the term *spyid* [line 9] is a corruption of *dpyid* (spring). An alternative reading would give *spyi* instead of *spyid.*

43 During the ceremony, Raja Virbhadra Singh (b. 1934) presided along with his mother and two dignitaries, who might have been the raja of Baghat Durga Singh (1901–1977) and the ex-minister of Punjab, Darbara Singh (1927–1998).

8

Tibetans in Taiwan: 1949–2006

Tsering Choekyi

I. Introduction

This paper will examine the changing political relationship between the Tibetan government-in-exile and the Republic of China (ROC), as well as the controversial role and influence of the Mongolian & Tibetan Affairs Commission (MTAC) in this relationship. I begin with the first Tibetans to arrive in Taiwan and the changes in attitude and policy of the Kuomintang (KMT) and the Democratic Progressive Party (DPP) towards Tibet and Tibetans. Then I examine how the two visits to Taiwan by HH the Dalai Lama have affected that relationship and undermined the role and status of the MTAC after the establishment of the Taiwan–Tibetan Exchange Foundation.

Early Contacts

The first Tibetan ever to visit Taiwan seems to have been Changkya Hutuktu, a lama from Amdo.[1] He was said to have had a close relationship with Chiang Kai-shek and the KMT government; he also served as the head of the Buddhist organizations in Taiwan. He was warmly welcomed in Taiwan, preached there until his death in 1957 and is credited for bringing an important Buddhist relic to Taiwan. His former residence was turned into the newly established Mongolian & Tibetan Cultural Center in Taipei, and one of the floors houses a small exhibition about his life.

Gyalo Thondup, elder brother of the Dalai Lama, was the first officially acknowledged Tibetan to visit Taiwan since 1949. Taipei Radio announced the meeting between Gyalo Thondup and President Chiang Kai-shek on 21 May

1950.[2] It was Gyalo Thondup who later facilitated semi-official contacts between the Tibetan government-in-exile and the Republic of China (ROC) as well as with the People's Republic of China (PRC) government in 1979. He had good personal relations with President Chiang and his successors in Taiwan. When he was a student in Nanjing in the mid-1940s, it is said that Chiang and his family took personal care of him. They kept in touch and after 1959 he visited Taiwan several times. Despite their close personal ties, they failed to reach any understanding on the legal status of Tibet. In fact, Gyalo Thondup was and continues to be a main critic of KMT policy on Tibet.

After 1959, some 85,000 Tibetans fled to India, Nepal and Bhutan.[3] In the early days of exile, very few Tibetans came to Taiwan, mainly because of the distance between India and Taiwan, as well as Taiwan's lack of official contacts with the Indian government and the absence of asylum policies in Taiwan.[4]

Among the few Tibetans who moved to Taiwan early on is Chamatsang from Lithang, a former trader and member of the Tibetan resistance movement, the Chushi Gangdruk (Four Rivers, Six Ranges).[5] Chamatsang arrived in Taipei on 18 September 1959. The KMT government gave him a red-carpet welcome and conferred upon him the position of Lieutenant General in the Republic of China army. This was said to be in recognition of his role in fighting the Communist forces in Tibet and with the intention to make him lead a guerrilla unit to be air-dropped into Tibet at an opportune time in the future. The KMT government raised NT$550,000 in the name of the "Support Committee for the Liberation of the International Minorities."[6] The proceeds went to the purchase of two buildings in Tienmu in suburban Taipei, to be used as the headquarters of the "Taiwan Branch of the Tibetan Resistance Movement" and residence of the exiled "Tibetan General."

He was followed by some twenty to thirty Tibetans, mainly from Amdo and Kham, who were initially trained to be air-dropped into their home districts for intelligence gathering.[7] Some of these so-called "Amdowas" were actually Hui or Chinese Muslims from the Kachu area who had escaped the Communist invaders. When the Communists took total control of Tibet in 1959, the Taiwanese authorities saw no point in air-dropping this trained group of "Tibetans." This small group of Tibetans and their families formed the nucleus of the Tibetan community in Taiwan until the late 1990s, when more Tibetans arrived for religious or economic reasons.

Archival documents show that the Taiwan government had established a training centre in Tamsui, a beach town about 20 km from Taipei, for Tibetan fighters, nearly thirty of whom had been flown into Taiwan from India.[8] There are still about ten of them living in Taipei. Some have returned to India and many others have returned to Tibet.[9] Around that time, the US Central Intelligence Agency (CIA) also flew Tibetan fighters to the United States and Saipan Islands for training in subsequent missions inside Tibet.

Two prominent early exiles to Taiwan were the ex-Tibetan cabinet ministers (kalon; *bka' blon*) Zurkhang and Yuthok. Because of some personal differences and rivalry with Tsipon Shakabpa, who later authored the book *A Political History of Tibet*,[10] these two *kalon* seem to have been deceived into seeking asylum and protection in Taiwan. They were used by the MTAC to set up an alternative Tibetan government-in-exile in Taiwan, to discredit the Tibetan government-in-exile set up by HH the Fourteenth Dalai Lama in India. Later on when they realized that Tsepak Dorjee, an Amdowa who was an officer of the MTAC, was actually running the show on their behalf, they refused to cooperate. They tried in vain to persuade the Kuomintang authorities to change their policy and support the Dalai Lama's position for recognizing Tibetan independence. Since they refused to cooperate, the alternative *kashag* (Tibetan cabinet) in Taiwan ceased to function. Later, Yuthok managed to escape from Taiwan on the pretext of a medical check-up and sought political asylum in Canada. Zurkhang remained and met a tragic death from opium overdose in old age. Both men are reported to have been extremely regretful of their decision to seek asylum in Taiwan.[11]

II. Taiwan's Policy Towards Tibet

The first contact between Tibetans and the ROC government took place soon after the Tibetan revolt against Communist Chinese rule over Tibet failed (1959).[12] Earlier, by 1949, the KMT party left the mainland, took control of the island of Taiwan and formed the ROC gvernment, declaring itself the legitimate government of China representing its entire people, including the Tibetans. This assertion that Tibet was a part of China has never been accepted by the Tibetan government-in-exile or the Tibetan people, and therefore remained a major stumbling block for improving relations while the KMT was in power.

Prior to 1949, there was limited interaction between Tibet and the KMT government in the eastern parts of Tibet called Kham and Amdo, which refer to culturally Tibetan areas in the provinces of Yunnan, Sichuan, Qinghai and Gansu, when the KMT was the legitimate ruling party in China. During the last year of KMT rule, an official representative was sent to the Tibetan capital of Lhasa on the occasion of the young Fourteenth Dalai Lama's formal enthronement ceremony. When the KMT re-established itself in Taiwan, it continued its old policy of regarding Tibet as part of China, as represented by the formation of the Mongolian & Tibetan Affairs Commission (MTAC). This office was set up in 1912 after the formation of the Republic of China as a strategy to pursue and implement its minority nationalities policies to include regions like Tibet and Mongolia, among others, as part of the Chinese motherland.

In the 1950s, the ROC was able to have some contact with Tibetans in the Indian town of Kalimpong near the borders of Sikkim and Bhutan, where a sizeable community of prominent Tibetans, including businessmen, former government officials and resistance leaders were found. The ROC considered Tibet as a common ally against the Chinese Communist Party.[13] The Tibetans, however, were not as enthusiastic about this position despite President Chiang Kai-shek showing considerable concern over the 1959 Tibetan national uprising and the exile of His Holiness the Dalai Lama to India.[14]

Lee Teng-hui, the serving President of Taiwan, had publicly expressed his admiration for the Tibetan leader and was instrumental in inviting HH the Dalai Lama to Taiwan in 1997. This official visit raised hopes for a special, closer relationship to develop between the two governments and their peoples; as a gesture of the improving relationship, more than 140 Tibetans living in Taiwan illegally were granted asylum. It is estimated that there are about 500,000 practicing Tibetan Buddhists in Taiwan and that about 1,000 Tibetan lamas from India and Nepal visit Taiwan annually, according to the MTAC.[15] A second visit planned in 1998 was called off due to strong opposition from Beijing. HH the Dalai Lama also turned down an invitation to attend President Chen Shui-bian's inauguration on 20 May 2004, apparently to avoid causing trouble during the sensitive transition of power in Taiwan.

The main reason why the Tibetan government-in-exile[16] was and is still opposed to the MTAC is because it symbolizes the ideological and official position that Tibet and Mongolia are and will always remain a part of China, whether under communist Chinese rule or the more democratic rule of the KMT.[17] Whereas the Tibetan government-in-exile has been seeking Taiwan's acknowledgment for the Tibetan people's right to self-determination and support against communist rule, the official policy of the former KMT government has been that only after the liberation and unification of the two Chinas would a national assembly discuss and consider granting the right of self-determination to the Tibetan people. Chiang Kai-shek and subsequent leaders have clearly stated this policy to officials of the Tibetan government-in-exile, including Gyalo Thondup, elder brother of HH the Dalai Lama, and Phuntsog Tashi Takla, a former minister in the Tibetan assembly (*kashag*), during his numerous visits to Taiwan.[18]

Pro-Tibet Policy of the Democratic Progressive Party (DPP)

After the Democratic Progressive Party (DPP) defeated the Kuomintang party (KMT) and came to power in May 2000, President Chen Shui-bian advanced a pro-Tibetan policy. During the inaugural ceremony to open the Taiwan–Tibet Exchange Foundation in January 2003, he said that the Republic of China would no longer regard the Tibetans as "people from mainland China." Chen's speech thus indirectly recognized Tibet as an independent state. The ceremony was attended by representatives from the Tibetan government-in-exile.[19]

Recent shifts in the relationship between Taiwan and Tibetan exiles reflect changes in geopolitical strategy on both sides. The Tibetan exiles have sought to move beyond the tense acrimony that previously characterized the relationship, while the Taiwanese have sought to use their policy on Tibet to assert their growing sense of a separate nationhood apart from China. These shifts have been reflected in the changing role and status of Taiwan's Mongolian & Tibetan Affairs Commission. The controversial MTAC, which has been a thorn in the side of the Tibetan exile community for a long time by fostering intra-Tibetan strife, now finds itself increasingly marginalized in light of the Taiwan–Tibet rapprochement.[20]

III. The MTAC's Role and its Effect on the Tibetan Community

During the 1960s and 1970s, the MTAC made considerable efforts to win over Tibetans in exile to acknowledge the legitimacy of the KMT government and its sovereignty over China. In the pursuit of this policy, it generated a negative view of Taiwan among the majority of Tibetan people and their government-in-exile. However, the Dalai Lama's visit to Taiwan in 1997 changed the situation and the relations started to improve. Visiting Taiwan used to be considered an act of disloyalty to the Dalai Lama and of treachery to the Tibetan national cause, until Tibetan–Taiwanese relations improved in the mid-1990s. The MTAC brought many Tibetans to Taiwan with the hidden aim of using them as political pawns and of sending them on potential covert missions inside Tibet. It is estimated that more than 500 Tibetan people have received direct financial help and assistance from the MTAC.[21] This caused considerable problems for the Tibetan government-in-exile in India, which did not want to see the financing and support of activities among disgruntled elements in Tibetan society.

A main task of the MTAC in the 1970s was to invite Tibetans and Mongolians to visit Taiwan during the National Day celebrations and thus continue to lend legitimacy to their policy of regarding Tibet and Mongolia as a part of China.[22] In 1994, for example, members of the MTAC signed a joint agreement with a group of people from Chushi Gangdruk, the Tibetan guerrilla organization that had fought the communists. The agreement said that after the reunification of China, Taiwan would declare Tibet as an autonomous region and recognize the Dalai Lama as its leader. This declaration between the MTAC and a section of the Tibetan people angered the Tibetan community in exile and caused considerable misunderstanding.[23] The contents of the agreement did not call for a major change in the policy of the Tibetan government-in-exile, but the fact that the MTAC, as an official Taiwanese body, had engaged in such negotiations by side-stepping the Tibetan government-in-exile was interpreted as a direct challenge to the position of the Dalai Lama and the sovereignty of Tibet. Therefore, the signatories to that declaration were criticized and seen as enemies of Tibetan national interests. The signing of the agreement led to a major split within the guerrilla organization Chushi Gangdruk. A new Chushi Gangdruk was formed by members loyal to the Dalai Lama and the Tibetan government-in-exile later that year. On 15 October 1994, the newly formed Chushi Gangdruk met in Dharamsala and sent a letter to Lee Teng-hui condemning Taiwan's nefarious activities among the Tibetan community:

> We are keenly aware that the so-called Mongolian and Tibetan Affairs Commission of your Government has been engaged in covert activities in [the] Tibetan community since our exile in 1959. It has been creating sectarian discord, regional disunity, tension amongst the Tibetan community of three provinces of Tibet. More than that, it has been inciting misunderstanding and mistrust between Tibetan government under the leadership of His Holiness the Dalai Lama and sections of Tibetan community with the sole aim of weakening the Tibetan struggle for independence from the People's Republic of China. The Tibetan government has withstood all these devious schemes and sinister plots.[24]

The letter went on:

> We thought that your Government understood the uselessness of spending every year millions of dollars of the taxpayers of your country on such criminal activities, which only helped fill the coffers of a few people in the MTAC and a handful of disgruntled Tibetans. We took encouragement from your own invitation last year to His Holiness the Dalai Lama to visit Taiwan and your positive statement on Tibet. There were also signs of improvement in relations between governments of your country and ours. But your Government showed its true color this year when some people of your country, mainly from the MTAC, and a few disgruntled members of our association entered into

a so-called Agreement on the basic issue relating to Tibetan sovereignty. ... our loyalty to His Holiness the Dalai Lama and our government is unshakable. [25]

Taiwanese have long questioned the role of MTAC. The Democratic Progressive Party (DPP), Taiwan's largest opposition party and a supporter of independence for the island, had for many years advocated the abolition of MTAC and vowed to do away with it should the party come to power. On that first visit in 1997, the Dalai Lama met with key DPP leaders and told them that the MTAC had "spoiled your [Taiwan's] reputation among the Tibetans." When the Dalai Lama said, "This is quite a long and complicated problem — even the previous KMT government knows that the Tibetans are quite troubled by the MTAC," President Chen responded, "...But it is quite difficult to solve the problem overnight. The DPP government also fully understands the situation and is very interested in resolving the predicament."[26]

IV. Changes After the Dalai Lama's Two Trips to Taiwan: After 1997

His Holiness the Dalai Lama's first visit to Taiwan in 1997 and his second in 2001 have been important milestones in the history of the propagation of Tibetan Buddhism in Taiwan and of Tibetan–Taiwanese ties. The first visit was made possible through a tremendous effort and work shared by both Tibetan and Taiwanese officials and private citizens. The ROC government approved the Chinese Buddhist Association of ROC's invitation to the Dalai Lama, and the visit was a tremendous success. His Holiness's first visit served as a major turning point for the two sides. Within a few months after this visit, "His Holiness the Dalai Lama Religious and Cultural Foundation" was established in Taipei. On 20 January 2003, the Taiwan government made a long-overdue decision to abolish the cabinet-level Mongolian & Tibetan Affairs Commission, subject to the majority approval of the parliament

The Dalai Lama's second visit in 2001 helped cemented ties of friendship between Taipei and Dharamsala. The Dalai Lama's relations with Taiwan, however, have not been smooth, as the Tibetan leader has tried to balance his concerns for Taiwan with his negotiations with Beijing (for the welfare of Tibetans in Tibet), in the hope of achieving a negotiated settlement with the communist government along the lines of his "middle path" policy.

The Taiwanese government, first in 1997 under Lee Teng-hui of the KMT and then in 2001 under Chen Shui-bian of the DPP, invited HH the Dalai Lama mainly to demonstrate their alliance against the communist-led government in Beijing. In following "the enemy of my enemy is my friend" policy, all three parties were trying to forge closer links to achieve their respective strategic political objectives. Yet each had its own agendas to pursue. The KMT wished to use the Dalai Lama's visit to demonstrate that the Tibetan government-in-exile, representing a major minority nationality of China, was willing and ready to cooperate with a KMT-led future democratic and unified China free of communist tyranny. On the other hand, the DPP wished to demonstrate that Taiwan, like the Tibetans in exile, has the right and will to declare their independence from mainland China.

As for HH the Dalai Lama, the visits to Taiwan were undertaken with the hope of demonstrating his "middle path" approach, that is, he and the Tibetan government-in-exile were ready to cooperate with the Chinese people to achieve their common aspirations for personal and national freedom under a genuinely democratic constitution of China, similar to that of Taiwan. In doing so, the Dalai Lama was taking a risky step because his Taiwan visits were severely denounced by Beijing and his call for a negotiated settlement was criticized as hypocritical. In April 2001 during the second ten-day visit to Taiwan, HH the Dalai was welcomed by President Chen Shui-bian. He spent most of the time giving religious teachings in different parts of Taiwan. After the people of Taiwan elected their native-born Chen Shui-bian as president in March 2000, ending the KMT's fifty-year rule over the country, the democratic government of Taiwan invited the Dalai Lama to visit Taiwan. The Tibetan spiritual leader postponed his visit many times, because, it was alleged, he did not want to provoke Beijing. The Dalai Lama's concerns and precautions, however, were totally ignored by Beijing. Before heading for Taiwan in 2001, the Dalai Lama told the press that Beijing had shut the door for dialogue and negotiations and denied permission for his delegation to visit Beijing. This was interpreted as a show of his disappointment towards Beijing.[27]

As a gesture of support for Tibetan independence, for example, the DPP ordered its offices all over the world to hoist the Tibetan national flag throughout the Dalai Lama's stay in Taiwan. A large Tibetan flag flew over Taipei city headquarters during the Tibetan leader's visit.[28] A commentary by the PRC's official Xinhua news agency on 1 April 2001 said the Dalai Lama's tour was "a political visit" driven by separatist motives he shares with officials in Taipei. Xinhua further added, "The Dalai's second Taiwan trip will certainly be a political visit for collaborating with Taiwan independence forces to separate the motherland." The Dalai Lama called on China to send a representative to the island to "watch my movements and investigate whether I'm involved in anti-Chinese activities," as Beijing claimed.[29] HH the Dalai Lama was also genuinely interested in meeting

Buddhists and spreading the Dharma in Taiwan; these are among his fundamental duties as a Buddhist leader and teacher.

V. Future Prospects

It is clear from this brief history of Tibetan–Taiwanese relations that KMT policies towards the Tibetan people were neither accepted nor favored by the Tibetans, despite changes in the controversial role of the MTAC and its questionable activities among exiled Tibetans. As the new ruling party of Taiwan, the DPP has taken a different approach relative to previous KMT rule. President Chen Shui-bian made it clear in a speech that the point of the fanfare was to signal the normalization of relations between Taiwan and the Tibetan government-in-exile. While the Dalai Lama has maintained an office of representatives in Taiwan since his historic visit in 1997, tensions between the KMT and DPP have surfaced periodically on the issue of Tibet.

President Chen attributed this tension to the ROC government's rhetoric of regarding Tibetans as *dalu renshi* or "people of the mainland." By taking a different view from China's erstwhile claim of sovereignty over Tibet, President Chen also undermined Taiwan's cabinet-level Mongolian & Tibetan Affairs Commission, which has been the cause of prickly relations with Tibetans in exile for a long time.

An alternative channel for direct interaction was made through the establishment of the Taiwan–Tibet Exchange Foundation, which is expected to serve as the key institutional mechanism for the future development of Taiwan–Tibet relations. The Foundation consists of government think-tank members, DPP members and private entrepreneurs familiar with Tibetan affairs. Understandably, the DPP and the Tibetan government-in-exile have long shared mutual sympathies. Kelsang Gyaltsen, one of two special envoys of HH the Dalai Lama, reckoned that the DPP was interested in resolving the Tibetan issue, particularly the controversial status of the MTAC.

VI. Conclusion

For the last fifty years, Taiwan's national government has held Tibet to be part of China, a position that has been a big stumbling block for Tibetan–Taiwanese rapprochement. On the other hand, the Democratic Progressive Party (DPP) — under the leadership of Chen Shui-bian — declared in a radical party position paper in

1997 that, "[t]he DPP will continue to support the Tibetan people's struggle for freedom." And with respect to the Mongolian & Tibetan Affairs Commission, which has been another major deterrent to improved Tibetan-Taiwanese ties, the DPP has called for the "immediate abolition" of this commission.[30]

The fact that Beijing reopened a fresh round of talks with representatives of the Dalai Lama in June 2007 and again in 2008 might seem to point to the complete irrelevance of the diplomatic breakthrough across the strait. One might well wonder about the actual significance of Taiwan–Tibetan relations at present. Can this normalization have any meaningful political effects, and if so, in what ways might they prove to be factors in the larger dynamics of the region? Beijing is definitely alarmed and taking notice and continues to assert that the Tibet issue is an internal matter.

President Chen's declaration that Tibetans — and Mongolians — are not "people of the mainland" puts Beijing in a decidedly awkward position.[31] The normalization of Taiwan–Tibetan relations might aggravate cross-strait tension in another way as well. It promotes grassroots support for the Tibet issue, so that for the first time in its history the Tibet movement will have found an effective voice in the Chinese-speaking world.

While the pro-Tibetan stance of President Chen may sound encouraging to the Tibetans, the Beijing leadership has all along maintained the hard line that unless the Dalai Lama acknowledges that Tibet is an inseparable part of China and that Taiwan is an inseparable part of China, then any meaningful dialogue for negotiating the status of Tibet cannot be broached. The linking of issues related to Taiwanese and Tibetan sovereignty by Beijing makes it harder rather than easier for Tibetans in their struggle for a peaceful settlement of the issue of Tibet. So far, six rounds of talks have been made between representatives of HH the Dalai Lama and the United Front Office that deals with affairs relating to the minority nationalities of the PRC. In order not to infuriate Beijing any further, and with the hope of achieving conclusive negotiations in the future, HH the Dalai Lama has refrained from visiting Taiwan again.

Notes

1 Tenzin N. Tethong, "Tibet and Taiwan: Past History and Future Prospects." Paper delivered at Stanford University, 27 December 2005, 8.

2 Tsering Shakya, *The Dragon in the Land of Snows: A Modern History of Tibet since 1949* (London: Pimlico, 1999) 40.

3 For a detailed understanding of the modern history of Tibet, see Melvyn C. Goldstein, *A History of Modern Tibet: the Demise of the Lamaist State 1913–1951* (Berkeley: University of

California Press, 1989), and idem, *A History of Modern Tibet: 1951–1959* (Berkeley: University of California Press, 2007).

4 Tethong, 3.

5 Four Rivers Six Ranges (*chu bzhi sgang drug*): a people's resistance movement against China that began in eastern Tibet.

6 Tsering Namgyal, "The twisting saga of Tibet–Taiwan relations," *Asia Times online,* 23 May, 2003, http://www.atimes.com/atimes/China/EE23Ad02.html, accessed 20 June 2007.

7 Of forty-nine men air-dropped into Tibetan areas between 1954–57, only twelve managed to escape alive. P. T. Takla interview, *Zla gsar* (New Moon), an occasional Tibetan magazine published from Delhi, issue 3–4 (1991), 120–167.

8 Ibid.

9 Peggy Chen, "Tibetans in Taiwan" (M.A. Dissertation: National Taiwan University, 2002), 33–36.

10 W. D. Shakabpa, *Tibet: A Political History* (New York: Potala Publications, 1984).

11 P. T. Takla interview, *Zla gsar.*

12 Jung Chang and Jon Halliday, *Mao: the Untold Story* (London: Jonathan Cape, 2005), 473–77.

13 岩口敬子, 從蒙藏委員會的角色看台灣對中國的想像 — 以西藏為主 (國立政治大學, 台史所, 2007).

14 President Chiang Kai-shek Speech in *The Lama Killing: the tragedy of Tibetan 40-year exile* 喇嘛剎人 林照著, 324.

15 http://www.taipeitimes.com/News/local/archives/2001/01/07/68758, accessed 15 June 2007.

16 The Tibetan government-in-exile started calling itself the Central Tibetan Administration of HH the Dalai Lama (CTA) after it started seeking autonomy for Tibet rather than full independence.

17 Warren Smith, *Tibetan Nation: A History of Tibetan Nationalism and Sino-Tibetan Relations* (Boulder, CO: Westview Press, 1996), 223–86.

18 P. T. Takla interview, *Zla gsar.*

19 http://www.atimes.com/atimes/China/EE23Ad02.html, accessed 5 July 2007.

20 See Abraham Zablocki, **"**Taiwan's Shifting Tibet Policy: The Changing Role of the Mongolian and Tibetan Affairs Commission." Paper delivered at the China and Inner Asia session of the AAS Annual Meeting, 31 March–3 April 2005, Chicago.

21 Interview with Chueh-An-Tsering , MTAC, 19 July 2007.

22 Tethong, 14.

23 Interview with Chueh-An-Tsering, MTAC, Taipei, 19 July 2007

24 Tsering Namgyal, "The Twisting Saga of Tibet–Taiwan Relations," *Asia Times Online,* 23 May 2003, http://www.atimes.com/atimes/China/EE23Ad02.html, accessed 20 June 2007.

25 Ibid.

26 Ibid.

27 Cao Chang-Ching (曹長青), "Tibetan tragedy began with a farce," *Taipei Times*, Wednesday, 25 April 2001.

28 Tsering Namgyal, "The twisting saga of Tibet–Taiwan relations," *Asia Times Online,* 23 May 2003, http://www.atimes.com/atimes/China/EE23Ad02.html, accessed 20 July 2007.

29 Yang Hsu-Tung, *Letter to Bush* (President of Taiwan Tati Cultural and Educational Foundation, Tuesday, 17 Oct 2000), 2, accessed from http://taiwantt.org.tw/fortaiwan/fortaiwan11/new_page_12.htm.

30 *Tibetan Bulletin* — The Official Journal of the Tibetan Administration, May–June 2000, Volume 4, Issue 2.

31 Tashi Rabgey, "Normalizing Taiwan–Tibetan Relations" (PhD Dissertation: Harvard University, 2003), 45–55.

PART TWO

History, Culture and Religion

9

The Tibetan Gesar Epic as Oral Literature

SOLOMON GEORGE FITZHERBERT

When considered simply in its textual form, the Tibetan Gesar epic — which tells of the birth, youth, marriage, adventures and conquests of the warrior-king Ling Gesar and his loyal kinsmen — is a vast literary corpus. It is often described as the longest epic in the world, and correctly so, when we consider the scores of volumes of non-duplicating Gesar texts published in China and Tibet since the 1980s.[1] However, as a fluid genre of traditional storytelling, the Gesar epic is primarily, to this day, a performative, rather than a literary tradition. As such it is better compared to other living traditions of inspired epic recitation, such as the Kyrgyz Manas, than to the classical textual epics of ancient India or Greece. Gesar singers (*sgrung mkhan*) are rated first and foremost not for their ability to recall and repeat a fixed text, but as inspired individual singers who have mastered the distinctive rhapsodic style of Gesar performance and have a thorough devotion to and knowledge of the stories, nuances and the characters that audiences (within distinct regional traditions)[2] expect to encounter. For although there is no fixed narrative, the Gesar genre is far from entirely freewheeling, and is constrained by a necessary traditionality in style, form and content. The Gesar epic is in this regard a prime example of a living oral epic tradition in which singers find authenticity in inspiration, while still depending on the traditionality of their tales for their authority. It is the purpose of this chapter to probe, with reference to existing scholarship on traditional oral poetry, the bounds between this traditionality and innovation in the tellings of Gesar.

Dating the Gesar Tradition

The basic plot-frame of the Gesar epic owes a good deal to Tibetan conceptions of divine kingship, heavenly descent and the elemental cults of earth, sky and mountain which pre-date Buddhism in Tibet, and on these grounds many scholars have been inclined to assume that the Gesar narrative tradition likewise predates Buddhism in Tibet.[3] Certainly, both the *form* and the *content* of the *gling sgrung* ("Tales of Ling") suggest an ancient provenance. With regard to form, we know for example from the *Old Tibetan Chronicle* found at Dunhuang (described by some as the "first Tibetan epic") that the memorialization of the past by means of narrative interspersed with songs sung in the first person by its protagonists was already active during the Tibetan imperial period. With regard to content, the frames of reference found in the Gesar tradition — the emphasis on clan and kinship; on local mountain deities, divination and protective spirits of the land, the elements and the individual; and on the culture of "the fort" (*mkhar*), and the horse-back warrior/huntsman's life — certainly resonate with what we know of the imperial and pre-imperial period.[4] Also suggestive of ancient origins are the resonances in the epic tradition of a high-god associated with the sky. This connects the Gesar tradition with the mythic complex that ties together pre-Buddhist deities such as gNam the, Pe dkar, Tshangs pa and Srid pa'i rgyal po.[5]

In additon, the salience of the goddess Ma ne ne, who has associations with Bonpo cosmogonic myths,[6] as Gesar's protector and celestial "aunt" who plays a role analogous to that of Athenae in the Iliad, even in Buddhist versions of the epic, also adds credence to the argument that the Gesar tradition has ancient and perhaps pre-Buddhist origins.

If the narrative tradition does indeed conceal an ancient core, then the most pervasive layer of accretion in the eastern Tibetan tradition has been the incorporation of tantric religious narrative tropes. In addition to the elaborate Buddhist pantheons invoked, shape-shifting through magical manifestation (*sprul pa*), treasure-doors, crystal caves and hidden lands are all central narrative tropes in the modern Gesar tradition which appear to have been borrowed from mainstream Vajrayana Buddhism.[7]

As narrative, therefore, the tradition gives expression to themes from a wide range of sources, some more ancient than others, but as R.A. Stein argued with such scholarly rigor, since all these themes continued to be current in late pre-modern Tibetan culture, and continue to this day to have resonance with living Buddhist, Bonpo and other "secular" belief traditions, their presence in a Gesaric context cannot prove anything about the priority or the age of the Gesar tradition itself. In other words, since Bon is a living religious tradition, and mountain cults an ongoing part of Tibetan culture, the inclusion of such elements in the Gesar tradition could have taken place at any stage, even in recent centuries. As Stein also pointed out, there are no definite mentions of Ling Gesar in any independent Tibetan sources before the (probably) 14th to 15th century[8] *Rlangs po ti bse ru*, and this suggests that the Gesar epic tradition may, on the contrary, be quite young. In his analysis of the Gesar myth, Stein was always inclined to give priority to textual sources for its development, and as a result saw it developing in its current form only in the 15th and 16th centuries and drawing on the mythologized history of "treasure" texts "discovered" in the 14th century, such as the *bKa' thang sde lnga* and even the *Rlangs po ti bse ru* itself. Even late in his career,[9] Stein appeared to retain a belief in the possibility of an *ur text* for the epic, and in the fragmentary nature of our contemporary oral-derived sources.

Such an approach, I believe, must be laid to rest. Although textual influence continues to be important in the Gesar storytelling tradition (as we shall see below), its core "orality" as a vernacular tradition, carried on largely in highland (*'brog pa*) communities with low rates of literacy, should now be acknowledged. Today, we are not witness to fragments of an epic in a state of decomposition, but to the expressions of an ongoing and mobile narrative tradition. This core "orality" of the tradition can explain its long absence from the literary record while still allowing for the possibility of its preservation of ancient continuities.

Living Narrative and Inspired Innovation

As a narrative tradition, the Tibetan Gesar epic therefore presents us with a problem of the "is the glass half full or half empty?" variety. Are we to be surprised by its narrative *stability* — the wealth of shared narrative features retained by a predominantly oral tradition, which find expression in versions whose compositions are radically separated in time and space? Or should the emphasis be placed on its *instability* — its variability in the hands of different tellers, and the general absence of verbal congruence across versions?

Finding a consistent narrative core to any given section of the Gesar epic, which is shared across Tibetan textual versions, is almost impossible, and telling the story of Gesar is a task that is rightly left to the artistry of storytellers, not the analysis of academics. Everything from the name of the hero to the structure of his father's family, from the age of his mother to the place of his birth, is subject to variation. Characters appear then disappear, characters are merged and substituted for one another to such an extent that it becomes hard to distinguish them (particularly the women and the lesser heroes). Narrative features — journeys, magic tricks, heroic raids, competitions for brides, festive tribal assemblies, conflicts with Hor, Khro thung's devious ploys and the slaying of evil ogres and beasts — recur with such frequency and circularity that it is often easy to forget where in the story you are.

The narrative instability and flexibility of the tradition, even in its "core" episodes such as the birth, the defeat of the great Demon and war with Hor, are subject to such wide narrative divergence that it often seems more appropriate to depict the Gesar narrative tradition as a *genre* of storytelling and song, like the lighter traditions surrounding A khu ston pa or 'Brug pa kun legs, rather than as an "epic," with all of that term's Aristotelian connotations of unity of plot[10] and its association with the classical epics of Greece or India. Gesar is a magical figure, a figure of fairytale, subject to endless invention and reinvention according to the religious orientation, education (oral and literate), regional origin and verbal artistry of singers and authors. It is an acknowledged aspect of the Tibetan tradition that telling the Tales of Ling (*gling sgrung*) is as much about inspiration as it is about memorization. In Tibetan idiom the tales are said to "fall" or "cascade" (*'bab*) through the inspired, entranced or sometimes 'possessed' medium from an extra-mundane source. The transmission of the epic is therefore not just about memorization and oral transmission passed down from generation to generation, but is crucially, and explicitly, in the hands of the spirits.[11] Sometimes the tradition is described as being "part of the landscape" — it is conceived as an intangible organic entity living in the land and in the people.[12]

As a result of this conceived salience of inspiration to the recitation of the epic, the same narrative, even the same song, unless it is read from a book, will rarely be sung twice. Indeed, in the eastern Tibetan Gesar tradition nearly every song within any given recitation will typically end with some formulaic refrain to the effect:

> If you have understood [this song], keep it in mind,
> If you have not understood, there will be no repetition.[13]

Therefore the narrative instability I highlight in this article is not to be explained in terms of deviation from an established traditional core,[14] but is itself a central characteristic of the tradition. Recent work on both the Mongolian Geser tradition[15] and the Ladakhi Kesar tradition,[16] which have compared recent tellings to older versions, have highlighted this essential narrative flexibility in both of these areas of its dissemination, and both Heissig and Herrmann have explained it in terms of the core orality of the tradition. Research on the eastern Tibetan tradition yields the same conclusion; the search for an authoritative and complete literary version (a search that R.A. Stein never fully relinquished) must be laid to rest. Adaptation and innovation are central and vital characteristics of this living narrative genre.

Oral Literature

Several scholars deconstruct the "orality" of oral literature as having three dimensions: orality of *composition*, *performance* and *transmission*.[17] However, the (by now) classic methodology pioneered by Milman Parry and Albert Lord on the compositional technique of traditional oral poetry is based on the inseparability of these dimensions. Parry and Lord depict the "oral poet" as at once a performer, composer and transmitter of traditional literature, all three of which are part of the same synchronic process. The Lord-Parry theory has been hugely influential in the study of epic traditions and has developed into a major field of literary study in its own right, described by some of its practitioners with significant capitals as Oral-Formulaic theory.[18] The foundation of the theory is that performers of "oral-traditional poetry" draw on a great stock of verbal and story elements that they inherit from tradition and which are shared between performers. Oral poets use these traditional building blocks — epithets, verbal phrases known as *formulas*, their smaller components known as *formulaic expressions*, and wider narrative *themes* — to compose their poems *while* they perform.

The persuasiveness of oral theory in deconstructing the structural and linguistic features of the world's important epics has had the effect of taking the "authorship" of these epics (most conspicuously the Homeric epics, but also Beowulf and others) away from notions of supremely talented and literate individual poets and putting it instead in the hands of pre-literate performative traditions,[19] akin in many ways to the living oral tradition of recitation concerning Gesar in large parts of northern and eastern Tibet. Indeed, when reading Lord's descriptions of illiterate epic singers in the Balkans in the *Singer of Tales*, their apprenticeship and the development of their proficiency in navigating and utilizing the traditional narrative and performative elements of the tradition, it takes very little imagination to think that he might be describing the similar tradition of bardic performance in Tibet.

The fundamental insight of Lord's work on the poesis of oral composers is sound with regard to the Gesar tradition; Gesar performers do not tend to reproduce identical narrations at different tellings, but are driven, not least by the rapidity and length of their narrations, to rely on stores of verbal formulas and epithets which they adapt, combine and recombine to fit their chosen meter or rhythm.[20] Their narratives also tend to display a repetitive circularity illustrative of their recurrent use of story *themes*. For example: a prophecy is received in a dream; an assembly of heroes is held; a smoke-offering is made; an amazing bird is described; a message is sent; a journey is embarked upon; a mounted hero is described with all his weaponry and finery; Khro thung hatches a plan; a sling-shot is fired; a battle is fought; an animal is hunted; a wife is obtained; a divination is made; a traders' caravan is met — these are just some examples of typical Gesaric "themes" which recur again and again and may crop up anywhere within the grand narrative of any given version.

Lord's theory of oral-traditional poetry also helps to account for many of the specific formal characteristics of the narrations of "inspired bards" (*babs sgrung gi sgrung mkhan*) such as Grags pa.[21] "Composition in performance" helps to account for the high incidence of repetition and the recurrent use of epithets even when they are out of context (Achilles is still "swift-footed" when seated; Joru is still *ma ngan* "not bad" even when addressed by adversaries); it also helps to account for inconsistencies, omissions and narrative conflations. Furthermore, Walter Ong's work on the kind of "literature" one can expect in the absence of writing and in the absence of the psychologies that the written word engenders, is also instructive. Ong suggests that the kind of narrative forms you would find in a society without writing are likely to be:

additive: with simple grammar and many lists.

conservative and *aggregative* rather than analytic: it will not try to "make you look at something in a different way." In Ong's example, "the oak is sturdy and will remain that way"; in a Gesaric context, sTag gzig is associated with wealth, Tsa ri with medicine, Gru gu with weapons etc.

situational and *homeostatic*: the situations and the actions depicted will be close to the human life-world; analogies will draw on familiar things — a Gesaric example would be the frequency of allusion to everyday objects in *'brog pa* life: hearth stones, sling shots, cattle and horses.

agonistic: "heavy," psychologically unelaborated heroic characters will be presented as vying with each other, as we find in Gesar in the exchange of first-person songs between adversaries, and so on.[22]

Of course Tibet is by no means a society without writing — on the contrary, it is a society which greatly venerates the written word — but as a lay tradition, the Tibetan Gesar phenomenon has tended to flourish in a largely illiterate or only partially-literate milieu. When applied to the repertoire of the bard Grags pa for instance, both Lord and Ong's observations are highly pertinent. There is no doubt that Grags pa's narrations were highly formulaic — the same phrases and verbal constructions are found again and again throughout the text with only minor variation — an adjective changed here, a verb substituted there, and this is particularly true of the opening invocatory sections of his songs in which the characters call upon their deities to help them and "guide" their song.[23] bSam grub's narrations present a somewhat more complicated picture; despite his illiteracy,[24] bSam grub's language is elaborate, and he uses a sophisticated verbal and narrative style that is less obviously oral-formulaic than Grags pa's. Thematic repetition may be just as frequent in bSam grub, but formulaic constructions are less evident at the level of individual lines and phrases.

However, beyond these insights about the structural features that non-literate composition in performance will typically generate, Lord's theory about the specific bounds of the oral *tradition*, which furnishes the singer with the building blocks of his art, starts to appear more culturally specific to the Balkan traditions of recital that he used as his template. On a general level his theory works; Gesar singers draw on a wealth of narrative motifs that are common to the tradition at large, and it is a bard's inclusion of these motifs which ensures that their narration has authority with the audience. However, Lord argued for more than this; he argued that the tradition furnishes not just general narrative motifs, but a large stock of *verbally specific* lines (*formulas*), phrases (*formulaic expressions*) and even long, *verbally specific* narrative sections, which was his definition of *themes*,[25] and it was from these traditional (i.e. shared across singers) building blocks that the songs were made. This claim is only partially supported by the evidence with regard to Gesar. While *individual* bards may build up a great store of verbal phrases, and even longer descriptive passages (Lord's *themes*) which they use in their "composition in performance," these verbally specific building blocks often tend, in the Tibetan context, to be *their own*, and only a few epithets and formulaic phrases find expression across different versions of the tales.[26] In his attempt to make his insights a general or universal theory of oral composition, Lord tried to have it both ways: on one side he constantly stressed the compositional freedom of the bard as the explanation for the rhetorical inconsistency of oral-derived texts such as the Homeric epics, but on the other side, he defined formulas, formulaic expressions and also themes, very narrowly as *verbally specific* building blocks that were *furnished by tradition*, and learnt over a long period of apprenticeship. Therefore the bard's compositional freedom, in Lord's theory, is actually no more than a freedom of "combination and separation and recombination"[27] of traditional elements. Lord also claimed to be able to discern the written (as opposed to oral) phrases, lines and themes in a poem by their use of images and so on which have "no traditional resonances." For Lord, oral literature was traditional, while written literature was individualistic.[28]

In the case of Gesar, my research indicates that the verbal congruence which Lord's theory suggests we should find across different versions of the same tale is in fact minimal. Even versions that come from the same regional narrative tradition and share a wide range of narrative features — for example, Grags pa and bSam grub both come from Kham and their narrations share the same core genealogy of Ling (which I describe elsewhere as the "Chos 'phen nag po tradition"[29]) and the same cast of characters — still only display minimal verbal congruence with each other beyond names and titles, and even these are variable. For example, while Grags pa favors *gling dkar stod* as the name for Ling, bSam grub makes more frequent use of *rma khams gling*, and while Grags pa uses *ja ma* and *bza'* for "wife," bSam grub favors *ga ma*. Their verbal, grammatical and rhetorical styles are completely distinctive from one another, and will not be mistaken by anyone with any familiarity with their work. However, both bSam grub and Grags pa are traditional singers, and the verbal dissimilarity between their versions surely does not mean only one of them can be classed traditional and the other as an innovator.

If we are to give Lord's model the benefit of doubt, this absence of substantial verbal correspondence between the repertoires of two traditional singers from broadly the same regional narrative tradition could be explained in two ways: on the one hand, as an indication that they are not really singers from within the same tradition, but give expression to *different*, discreet local traditions of which there might be very many; or on the other hand as an indication that the "tradition" is so rich and broad that different bards can draw on *different* traditional elements — they can both, therefore, be traditional, but without necessarily overlapping in their traditional details. Both of these arguments are feasible, but neither is very persuasive. With regard to the first, it is certainly possible that some bardic repertoires may indeed resemble (in verbally specific, formulaic terms) those of other bards who have developed their skills steeped in the same local tradition and listening to the same master-storytellers of the elder generation (either live or on cassette or radio, or even in books). However, I suspect that the kind of verbal similarity described by Lord would only be found in Tibetan bards who have literally learnt their songs from each other or from the same third party,[30] and the repertoires of such singers whose recitations are learnt, and who do not expand beyond what they have learnt, tend to be limited. Indeed the modern bards with the largest repertoires (such as Grags pa and bSam grub) tend to emphasize how widely traveled they are in Tibet, and how they have developed their styles over many years of practice and in interaction with audiences and storytellers from all over Tibet — rather than just by listening to one particular singer.

To give Lord his due, he emphasized that the degree to which a bard expanded and improvised beyond what he had learnt from others was a mark of his talent and his maturity as a singer who had mastered the traditional elements, and this accords with what I understand of Tibetan bards. However, the degree of rhetorical idiosyncrasy that Tibetan bards display suggests the Gesar epic, even within regional traditions, is considerably more narratively and verbally fluid than the Balkan performative traditions he examined.

As regards the second argument: to say the tradition is so broad that it furnishes the verbal building blocks for two singers (such as Grags pa and bSam grub) whose individual repertoires stretch together to over 3,000 hours without ever overlapping, starts to sound absurd. If the stock of "traditional elements" can be so broad, it is hard to see what can be excluded from that stock, at which point the relevance of a theory that distinguishes between oral-traditional poetry and any other kind of "individualistic" poetry starts to look weak.

Having said this, although extended verbal congruence between specific textual versions of the Gesar epic is unusual, it is not unknown. Indeed, in my readings I have come across a few very interesting sections of almost verbatim duplication between the transcribed narrations of a modern illiterate "inspired" bard (bSam grub) and an older literary version. This raises important issues about the relative importance of memorization and innovation, and the applicability of Lord's theory of oral-traditional poetry to the Tibetan Gesar tradition.

bSam grub's Verbatim Replication of the "Lingtsang Woodblock"

These duplicated sections are from the narrations of bSam grub, in which passages from both his *lHa gling* (bSam grub vol. 1) and his *'Khrungs gling* (bSam grub vol. 6) duplicate, almost verbatim, sections from the "Lingtsang woodblock"[31] *lHa gling gab tse dgu skor*. In a particular instance of such replication (there are probably more that I have not seen), sPyi dpon (the wise old uncle of Ling) has a prophetic dream which augurs the coming of the hero. In this dream, sPyi dpon sees the sun rising from the peak of rMa rgyal spom ra and a series of other auspicious events, then he sees a lama (depicted in a way suggestive of Padmasambhava) approach him riding on a snow-lion, and the lama sings him a prophetic song about the impending arrival of Gesar in the world. Then sPyi dpon awakes and rouses his household from slumber — his servants wake and stretch; the old goat bleats (*ra rgan 'bar 'bar*); the old dog barks (*khyi rgan zug zug*); and the servants make their morning devotions (*kha thod jo bo mjal mjal*) and so on. In bSam grub's published narrations we find this passage repeated, almost word for word, on two (and maybe more) different occasions: the prophetic dream (SI, 14b–16a/ LWLL, 27–30) is found almost verbatim in his *lHa gling* (bSam grub vol. 1, 143–46) and in his *'Khrungs gling* (bSam grub vol. 6, 8–9). The prophetic song within the dream is only replicated in vol. 1, while the passage after his awakening and the rousing of the household is only found in vol. 6. The meaning of the replicated passage is, however, somewhat garbled in the transcripts of bSam grub's narrations (particularly the vol. 6 repetition) and this suggests the duplication is not simply the work of a transcriber cutting corners by copying out a published text, but suggests that bSam grub's narrations were really very close to the older text. The replicated passages are too long to reproduce here in full, but to give just a short taste, opposite is one passage as it is found in three variants — one the "Lingtsang woodblock," and two the narrations of bSam grub, the second of which is somewhat abbreviated.

After this section, bSam grub vol. 6 (*'Khrungs gling* — variant 3 above) leaves the narrative as found in the woodblock, but bSam grub vol. 1 (*lHa gling* — variant 2 above) continues to follow it, reproducing the lama's prophetic song in a similarly verbatim manner, with only minor deviations that Lord's theory would lead us to expect. After the song, the text of bSam grub vol. 6 (variant 3 above) then takes up the thread again, in the description of sPyi dpon and his household awakening, and of the servants' "tea-making song."

This prophetic dream is an important event in the woodblock narrative and it is even found in gCod pa don grub's influential resumé of the epic story.[32] This prophecy asserts Gesar's relevance for the entire Land of Snows, and is the basis on which much of the ensuing action takes place — the convening of a tribal assembly and so on. So bSam grub's replication of it, as an illiterate singer, could justify a range of conclusions.

On one hand, we could argue that this constitutes a proof of Lord's theory that verbally specific, though minorly adjusted, extended descriptive passages (his definition of *themes*) are furnished by the oral tradition at large and find expression in tellings by different singers. On this understanding the author of the "Lingtsang woodblock" in ca 1910[33] was drawing on the same unbroken oral tradition as bSam grub in the 1990s. This is not impossible, given the centrality of this prophetic dream to the plot of the heroic birth-narrative.

Alternatively, we could describe it as a minor miracle, as "unexplainable,"[34] or as support for the extra-mundane inspiration of "inspired bards" (*babs sgrung pa*).

Finally (and this I find the most persuasive because of the specificity of these replicated passages which are not found in other versions), we could conclude that somehow bSam grub has learnt this passage from direct exposure to the "Lingtsang

1. "Lingtsang woodblock" Stein 1956: I (SI): 14bff; LWLL 1999: 27–28:	**2. bSam grub vol. 1, *lHa gling*: 143ff:**	**3. bSam grub vol. 6, *'Khrungs gling*: 8ff:**
De'i dus su bar mi yi yul lho 'dzam bu gling gi byang phyogs kha ba can gyi rgyal khams su gtogs pa mdo khams g.yang gi ra ba gling ru mthong ba kun smon rma g.yas lung khra phug bco brgyad / khra phug 'dzam lung la kha / khra stod gnam rdzong g.yon lag / mkhar chen po shar ri'i 'brug rdzong gzims chung padma nyi shar nas / grub chen ku ku ri pa'i skye ba'i cha shas dpa' thul sum cu'i skye mgo thod pa sum cu'i dang po/ dbang thang sum cu'i rtse mo / spyi dpon rong tsha khra rgan de nyid 'od gsal gzims kyi/gyi srang lam la/ rmi ltas khyad par can zhig rmis te/ de yang shar rma rgyal spom ra'i rtse mo nas gser gyi nyi ma gcig/zhig shar/ nyi zer bod la ngoms/ de'i dkyil nas gser gyi rdo rje zhig byung te/ bar gling gi zo dor skyid rgyal stag ri'i rtse la bab/ brda lung thang na bod kyi mgul lha rnams 'tshogs/ smon lam la nas dngul gyi zla ba tshes/ gser gyi la nas skar tshogs bkrag/ ger mdzo ri la 'ja yi srang thag sbrel/ ma pham mtsho la 'od kyi zer thag brkyangs/ nu bo seng blon rgyal po'i phyag na dar dkar po'i klad phor/ dmar ljang gis 'ja' sprin 'khrigs/ dar ser gyi sham bu can gyi gdugs gser gyi yu ba can zhig bskor ba /nub stag gzig spang hol phyin chad/ shar rgya nag tan thing ri yan chad/ lho rgya gar ri mam gi tshun chad/ byang hor yul yung khri wan tshun chad khyab bdar/ yang lho nub kyi nam mkha' nas 'ja' sprin dkar po zhig gi steng/ bla ma pad zhu can seng ge dkar mo chibs shin/ g.yas rdo rje/ g.yon kha(Tam/ 'dzin pa zhig gi sna bud med dmar mo rus rgyan can zhig gi khrid de/ chabs gcig tu 'di skad zer/ dpon chen po ma nyal yar la lang/	*De yi dus su bar mi yi yul lho 'dzam bu gling gi byang phyogs kha ba can gyi rgyal khams su gtogs pa'i mdo khams g.yang gi ra ba/ gling sa mthong ba kun smon/ rma g.yas lung khra khug bco brgyad/ khra khug 'dza lung la kha/ khra stod gnam rdzong phyug mo'i g.yon lag gzim chung padma nyi shar nang/ grub chen ku ku ri pa'i skye ba'i cha shas/ dpa' thul sum cu'i rtse mo/ thod pa sum cu'i dang po/ dbang thang sum cu'i rtse mo spyi dpon rong tsha khra rgan des smon lam sgrub sbyor gyi phrin las rgya cher mdzad skabs/ 'od gsal gzim gyi srang lam na rmi ltas khyad par can zhig byung ba de yang shar rma rgyal spom ra'i rtse mo nas gser gyi nyi ma gcig shar nas nyi zer bod la ngom zhing de'i gzhi dkyil nas gser gyi rdo rje zhig byung te/ bar gling gi zo dor skyid rgyal stag ri'i rtse la bab/ brda lung thang na bod kyi mgul lha rnams smon lam 'tshogs/ smon lam la nas dn-gul gyi zla ba tshes/ gser gyi skar tshogs bkra/ ger 'dzo ri la 'ja' yi srang thag khyab/ ma pham mtsho la 'od kyi zer thag brkyangs/ nu bo seng blon rgyal po'i phyag na dar dkar dmar ljang gi 'ja' sprin 'khrigs/ dar ser gyi* [144] *sham bu can gyi gdugs gser gyi yu ba can zhig bskor/ nub stag gzig gi spang ho la tshun chad/ shar rgya nag kring thing ri yan chod/ lho rgya gar ri mam tshun chad/ byang hor yul yung khri la tshun chad khyab/ yang lho nub kyi phyogs nas 'ja' tshon steng nas bla ma pad zhu can seng ge dkar mo dregs pa can la 'chibs/ g.yas rdo rje/ g.yon kha Tw'om bsnams pa zhig gi sna bud med dmar mo rus rgyan can zhig gis khrid de 'di skad cig zer/ dpon chen po ma nyal yar la long/*	*De'i dus su/ bar mi yi yul lho 'dzam bu gling gi byang phyogs kha ba can gyi yul/ mdo khams g.yang gi rwa ba gling sa mthong ba kun smon/ rma dil yag lha lung* [9] *bco brgyad khra spung se/ 'dzam gling la mkhar gnam rdzong g.yang chen po lha tshogs kyi gzim chung padma nyi shar gyi rje btsun ston pa shar/ grub chen dbang po rigs kyi skye ba/ dpa' brtul sum cu'i dang po/ dbang thang sum cu'i gtso bo/ pha spyi dpon rong tsha khra rgan de nyin mo 'od gsal zil gyi gsal/ rmi lam khyad par can zhig rmis/ de yang shar rma rgyal spom ra'i rtse mo nas gser gyi nyi ma shar/ nyi zer dkyil nas gser gyi rdo rje zhig byung te/ ger mdzo'i ri la 'ja' yis gzung thag 'then/ 'og la 'od kyi bkang phu bo seng blon gyi phyag nang dar dkar dmar 'ja' yi sprin 'khrigs/ dar ser gyi sham bu can mdung ser gyi yu ba can zhig gis bskor/ shar rgya nag thing ri'i rtse/ lho rgya gar ri dmar mtsho chen/ byang hor yul yang khrig se tshun chad khyab pa/ lho nub kyi nam mkha' nas 'ja' sprin dkar po zhig gi steng bla ma pad ma 'byung gnas kyi phyag g.yas rdo rje bsnams/ g.yon kha Tam'dzin nas dpon chen ma nyal yar la longs/*

woodblock" text, which we know is a widely available textual version. That this text was in fact a primary source for bSam grub's apprenticeship as a singer is also given sidelong allusion in bSam grub's biography (abridged translation):

> [when he was eleven years old bSam grub went through a transformative crisis after his grandfather died. Fearful that his son's soul had "gone wandering," his father took him to the local monastery where the *tulku* took care of the child.] While he was in the care of the *tulku*, bSam grub had a dream one night in which *he dreamt that like the tulku, he could read and recite every episode of the Tales of Ling* (italics mine), and that after waking from that dream it was as if those texts had been etched onto his mind. From that day forward a great yearning to tell the stories of Gesar was aroused in him, and gradually he began to recite, and what he recited, "inexplicably" (*ci yin 'di yin ma shes par*) was the episode called *'Khrungs gling me tog ra ba*.[35]

Well, *'Khrungs gling me tog ra ba* is the title of vol. 2 of the "Lingtsang woodblock," and I have not come across other versions of the birth using the same title.

It seems to me that bSam grub has at some point aurally learnt major parts of the textual Lingtsang version, perhaps from the very *tulku* mentioned in his biography. From what I have read of bSam grub's narrations on the lead-up to the birth of the hero (which is admittedly only a fraction of the total — the hero is born towards the end of vol. 6 of his version), it seems that bSam grub extrapolates at length using the Lingtsang text as one of his narrative bases or kernels. This method of extrapolation is also hinted at in bSam grub's biography. When describing his method, it says:

> from that time his ability to recite the tales has expanded — from one he tells one hundred, from a hundred he tells a thousand.[36]

So if bSam grub has learnt from the Lingtsang text, then even this — the only example I have found of anything like a traditional *theme*, as Lord conceived of them — also plays against Lord's conception of oral-traditional poesis, since these passages have been transmitted and very possibly composed through *writing*.

Textual Transmission in Oral Tradition

If it is the case that bSam grub learnt this version from a textual source (by listening to it recited), it highlights the main weakness of the Lord-Parry Oral-Formulaic theory, namely what some critics have called the "Great Divide"[37] that the theory postulates between oral and written poetry. What the bSam grub example most clearly illustrates is that oral and literary transmission overlap. Lord was reluctant to admit the influence of texts on oral transmissions. He saw oral literature[38] as historically and creatively prior to written literature. With regard to traditional literature, he described written texts as "the last degenerative stages of a tradition, when texts have been fixed by being written down."[39] He also denied the possibility (with regard to Homer) of their being "transitional texts" that make use of both literary and oral techniques "because the two techniques are, I submit, contradictory and mutually exclusive."[40]

This is clearly not the case with Gesar. As we have seen with regard to bSam grub, written texts, rather than ossifying or degenerating an oral tradition, can feed and enrich it. This is true not only of Gesar, but of other genres of Tibetan traditional literature, in which oral and written forms continue to overlap and support one another. To take one example from my own experience — a learned Ladakhi monk from Matho Gonpa, near Leh, whom I met at the Sakya Ngor pa monastery near Dehra Dun in India, recently told me a story that, he said, he had been told by his Lama. The story was about Srong bstan sgam po and how he sent an "emanation monk" to southern India to find a sacred sandalwood statue (*yi dam*) buried in the sand under a "place where elephants sleep." This is a story familiar from the well-known 14th-century religious history the *rGyal rabs gsal ba'i me long* by Sakyapa bSod nams rgyal mtshan (1312–75). The story the Ladakhi monk (also Sakyapa) told me, however, had interesting embellishments when compared to the story as it is found in that text; the monk's story was told as an explanation of "how Glang Dar ma[41] came to be," which is given no allusion in the *rGyal rabs gsal ba'i me long*. The literary account runs like this: an "emanation monk" born from the mind of the Tibetan emperor Srong btsan sgam po flies to southern India and there he meets the king of Magadha and impresses him with his levitation. He then explains to the king how a very special sandalwood tree is buried under the sand on the shore beneath the place where the elephants sleep. The amazing tree is then unearthed and 108 sacred images are obtained.[42] However, the "oral" version from the Ladakhi lama had more. His narrative followed the textual one very closely up to the point where the tree is disinterred, at which point his oral version elaborates: when they go to fetch the sandalwood, *they disturb the elephants and drive them away. One fearless elephant kicks the earth in anger and vows that after seven generations, he will disturb the Buddhist teachings* (this narrative is not found in the *rGyal rabs gsal ba'i me long*). Seven generations later, he continued, Glang Dar ma (the rebirth of this angry elephant) succeeds to the throne of Tibet, and upsets the Buddhist teachings. This, according to the monk, is the story of "how Glang dar ma came to be." Clearly, in this example, the story-embellishment revolves around a play on the name Glang (as *glang po che* means "elephant"), but it also clearly illustrates how traditional (and well-known) textual narratives in Tibet can coexist with ongoing oral traditions concerning the same stories. Even if the story of the angry elephant does have a textual source (of which I am unaware), the point I am trying to make with this example is clear enough: oral traditions continue, even when stories are given textual expression, and often these texts serve as supports for an ongoing oral tradition, not as a sign of their degeneration. We can see a similar survival of oral traditions beyond the consignment to text with regard to many mythical narratives from most cultures, ancient and modern — to take one obvious example, Valmiki's Rāmāyana omits many of the most well-known narrative features preserved by local traditions in India.

Much of traditional Tibetan literature, often transmitted orally/aurally, exists within a similar ongoing interplay between written and oral forms. The vast corpus of traditional Tibetan literature in general — scriptures, "treasure texts" *(gter)*, religious histories (*chos 'byung*) and even saintly biographies (*rnam thar*) — all typically display features suggestive of this culturally enshrined and ongoing interplay.[43]

The "Great Divide"

So much for the difficulties in separating oral and literary *transmission* in a Gesaric and a wider Tibetan context. But even the divide between oral and literary *composition* is not nearly as clear cut as the Lord-Parry theory would like to suggest. After all, on a purely empirical subjective level, isn't it true that we compose phrases and sentences before we write them down? At what level, then, is our composition "literary?" As critics such as Ruth Finnegan[44] and Jack Goody[45] have suggested, the postulation of a clear rupture between oral and written composition in most cultural contexts where oral traditions co-exist with literacy is in practice untenable.

If we look, for instance, at the written texts produced by the contemporary literate bard Guru rgyal mtshan, who writes his versions (and whom I interviewed and observed at work in mGo log in 2005), they are just as formulaic, repetitive and so on as the transcribed narrations of an illiterate bard such as Grags pa. Should we therefore conclude that Guru rgyal mtshan is *imitating* oral composition? Perhaps. But on reflection, is his method of composition really so different from Grags pa's or bSam grub's? Guru rgyal mtshan writes his work by pen, and he does not make corrections or amendments to the cursive texts he produces, which he describes as "revealed treasure tales" (*gter sgrung*). His *literary* composition may therefore be described as an analogous form of "inspired" performative composition, only in the absence of an immediate audience.[46] As a recording device, is the pen really so different from the tape recorder?

Therefore, while the general corpus of Tibetan traditional literature raises plenty of questions for oral theory, the Gesar tradition offers more particular insights into the influence of texts on oral traditions in the Tibetan context: bSam grub's replication of text found in the "Lingtsang woodblock" is a clear example of the *direct* role of a textual transmission in an oral composer's art. And the illiterate Grags pa's initiatory dream, in which he dreamt that manuscripts covered with written Tales of Ling were stuffed into his insides,[47] illustrates further the indirect or *conceived* role of textual transmission, even to an illiterate bard like Grags pa whose work appears to lack any replication of known texts. These examples together illustrate both the *real* and *conceived* influence of written texts on oral composition and performance in the Gesar tradition.

While Lord was reluctant to acknowledge the important influence of texts on oral traditions (he regarded such influences as contaminations), he was keenly aware of its converse: the influence of orality on textual traditions, which is also certainly true of the Gesar corpus. Lord was keen to emphasize how many aspects of literary poetics are in fact "derived from the world of orality,"[48] and certainly with regard to Gesar literary compositions, this is corroborated — the written Gesar texts are still designed to be orally performed, and this has an important influence on their style.

From Structure to Meaning: Oral Theory Beyond Lord

In an attempt to get around the problem of this "Great Divide" between orality and literacy which is at the center of Lord and Ong's work, J. M. Foley, as the main successor and propagator of the Oral-Formulaic theory, has moved away from the mechanistic language of Lord and Parry, which stressed the distinctive mechanical *necessity* of formulas and so on to oral-traditional composition, and instead coins the notion of "traditional referentiality."

In his works *Immanent Art* (1991) and *Homer's Traditional Art* (1999), Foley tries to move the focus of Oral-Formulaic theory away from an explanation of the *structural* features of oral literature, and towards a consideration of *meaning* in oral-formulaic poetry. He does this by means of a receptionalist theory,[49] which considers how formulas and epithets in oral poetry conjure a whole gamut of meaning that extends beyond the narrow information encoded in the brief epithet itself, and refers to a wider range of signification furnished by the tradition at large. For example, any reference to "grey-eyed Athena" conjures Athena in her totality. The greyness of her eyes may be irrelevant within the context of the particular passage, but is a shorthand indication that we are talking of the same Athena, about whom many stories and associations would be known by an audience versed in the tradition. It is this "traditional referentiality" that gives traditional literature its depth, and is what Foley calls "immanent art":

A process of composition and reception in which a simple, concrete part stands for a complete, intangible reality. *Pars pro toto*, the part standing for the whole, as it were.[50] "Grey-eyed Athena" and "wise Penelope" are thus neither brilliant attributions in unrelated situations nor mindless metrical fillers of last resort. Rather they index the characters they name, in all their complexity, not merely in one given situation or even poem, but against an enormously larger traditional backdrop.[51]

Thus, argues Foley, traditional oral poetry operates "like a language, but moreso" (his favored catchphrase), a language in which traditional formulas, epithets and so on as described by Lord and Parry, operate as the basic semantic units, and the building blocks of the poetry.

With regard to the Gesar tradition, this theory's dependence on "traditional" (i.e. shared rather than idiosyncratic) epithets and formulas and so on means it is only really applicable to that store of names and formulaic elements shared across versions of the Gesar epic, which, as has already been stated, is smaller than might be imagined, but it also has relevance for the large stock of broader (verbally nonspecific) narrative or imagistic motifs, which are at the core of the Gesar epic's traditionality.

A good example of such a motif in the Gesar tradition with which to consider the suitability of this theory is that of "metallic birds" who come to attack the infant soon after his birth, which the infant-hero fells with his arrows. This motif is elaborated differently in many different versions, but metallic birds, in one form or another, are found in nearly all: the screeching metal-beaked birds of Baldano's Buryat version, the Raven-General Xiala of the recent Monguor version, the "seven iron birds" of Grags pa's version, the "three birds of ill-intent" in the "Lingtsang woodblock" and so on.[52] So if each individual treatment of this motif is the *pars*, what is the *totus*? What is the "complete intangible reality" that all these expressions signify? Is each instantiation of this motif somehow referring to the same entity or event? Foley's theory suggests that at the level of reception, they do. Foley distinguishes between "inherent" and "conferred" meaning and between "connotative" and "denotative" meaning. The meaning of traditional poetic formulas, at the level of reception, he says, involves an inherent and connotative meaning that a non-traditional poetic line lacks. It has this extra layer of signification, furnished not by the intention of the author/narrator (Husserlian phenomenalism), nor by the words themselves, but by its invocation of a wider traditional context already understood by the listener. To understand the meaning of such poetry is like learning a language.

Foley's is an excellent explanation of the enduring appeal of traditional oral literature as an imaginative experience, which is expressively enriched as one becomes more familiar with it. This model suits the Gesar tradition well. That the birds sent to kill the infant Gesar, for example, despite the wide narrative and rhetorical differences (i.e differing conferred and denotative meanings) with which this motif is treated, do also have shared meaning at the level of reception — they all somehow refer to the same epic event, the same birds. However, if they all do refer at the level of reception to the same core idea, how to model that idea remains a problem. To my mind the signified should not here be modeled in terms of its *completeness*, as Foley does (with regard to the signified of the fixed Homeric epithet), but in terms of its *openness* — open not just in its expression, but also in its *meaning*. It is this openness, this possibility of supplementation which in a very flexible narrative tradition like that of Gesar makes any new telling interesting. Moreover, at the level of interpretation, a step removed from simple cognition, the meaning of any given image or motif can remain far from fixed, so that while some might understand the malign birds as real creatures in a distant past, others might understand them as symbols of religious heresy, while still others might see them as symbolic of negative psychological or physiological forces, and so on.

Conclusions on Oral Theory and Gesar

Lord's insights into the nature of bardic composition remain a persuasive explanation of the structural or formal features of many of the Gesar narratives, and particularly of Grags pa's published narrations. However, the formulas, epithets and narrative themes that Grags pa uses, when we compare them to other versions, are by and large his own. They have "traditional referentiality," but in their verbally specific form they are particular to his rhetorical style, and by and large are not shared by other bardic transcriptions or texts. His work is formulaic, and makes repetitive use of narrative *themes* (in both of Lord's senses — wide and narrow), but these again, particularly the *themes* in the narrow sense, are his own.

What this indicates is that there is just as much scope for individualism in oral composition as there is in literate composition, and this constitutes a revision of Lord's theory. Lord romanticized the oral poet as being the voice of the collective, the voice of tradition. The evidence from Gesar, however, suggests that the tags "oral" and "traditional" are not necessarily as mutually supportive as he supposed. The extent of a composer's "traditionality" — the extent to which he or she replicates inherited structures, phrases, passages — has little to do with whether he/she is literate or not, and oral composers can be just as creative as their literary counterparts, while literary composers can be just as traditional as their oral counterparts.

To give him his due credit, the primary targets of Lord's work were the Homeric epics, concerning which scholars had long privileged the notion of a literate author, so in that context Lord was at pains to stress the possibility of a rich verbal and poetic stock which does not require literacy for the generation of a great and rich art. He was also at pains to emphasize the compositional *freedom* of the oral-traditional poet as he works within this rich traditional stock. For emphasizing the inherent flexibility of oral-traditional literature, and for emphasizing the possibility of a rich and evolved literature that stands behind traditional textual works, Lord's work is both applicable and supportive of the living Tibetan Gesar tradition.

However, the degree of compositional freedom exercised by a bard in Lord's theory is more culturally specific. His theory has been criticized by others on the grounds that he argued for *too much* improvisatory or compositional freedom on behalf of bards.[53] With regard to the Gesar tradition, it is clear that his theory does not allow for *enough* compositional freedom on behalf of bards and authors, and moreover, he does not allow enough possibility for an oral poet to also be a great literary innovator and individualist.[54]

This assertion about rhetorical variability is largely based on what I have read and heard of eastern Tibetan versions, but it also seems to be true of contemporary western Tibetan traditions. I cannot say for sure what rhetorical and formulaic congruences there are, for instance, across the recent Ladakhi versions recorded and examined by Silke Hermann, since unfortunately she does not give any Tibetan text in her work, but her methodology suggests that such correspondences were not very marked. In her structural comparison of twelve modern oral versions from Ladakh, she choses a Proppian rather than an Oral-Formulaic method: she breaks the stories down not into shared lines (formulas) and descriptive passages (themes), as Lord's method demands, but into broader narrative "events," equivalent to Propp's "functions." For example, she breaks down the prefatory episode, which she calls *Lhayul*, into fourteen *Segmente* or events, and the birth-story, or *Lingyul*, into seven, which the different tellings do or don't include.[55] Her method is explicitly based on Vladimir Propp's influential deconstruction of the Russian fairytale into thirty-one *functions*, where a "function" is defined as an act of a character, defined from the point of view of its significance for the course of the action.[56]

This formalist approach seeks to uncover a broad structural framework for traditional literature rather than the rhetorical or poetic specificity which was Lord's primary focus.

Hermann's use of Proppian rather than oral-formulaic methodology with regard to western Tibetan traditions, and my own sense with regard to eastern Tibetan traditions that verbal congruence across versions is limited to a handful of formulas, suggests that the core of the Gesar narrative tradition — those mnemonic elements that are shared across versions — are by and large *narrative* and *imagistic* features, rather than verbally specific poetic or rhetorical features.

While individual tellers do indeed use their own formulaic and poetic mnemonic devices for remembering and incorporating such imagistic or narrative features (often repetitively) into their songs and recitations, these are not, strictly speaking, entirely "traditional" in the way Lord depicted.

This is of course a drawback to the Oral-Formulaic theory, and certainly should not disqualify Gesar narratives from being regarded as both oral and traditional. While different versions are expressively diverse, they contain a host of specific features and shared motifs that testify to the wealth of a discreet Gesar tradition. Therefore, in my own breakdown of such motifs in the birth of Gesar, I do not try to assert any formalist or structuralist model or to uncover any "grammar" of the narrative, but simply aim to illuminate the "open" nature of those core motifs which are given expression across diverse versions.

Given this core openness of the Gesar oral tradition, it is an epic genre that is subject to many changing influences. Not least among these influences, as I argue elsewhere, is the influence of political and religious patronage on shaping the orientation of the epic, particularly in its textual forms. The politics of patronage and publication is therefore one of the most potentially illuminating avenues of research into the Tibetan epic tradition, which may also furnish insights into the formation of older "classical" epic traditions, which have long since been ossified in text. The Gesar epic has been, and continues to be, many things: an ethnic and cultural charter of identity for the highlanders of eastern Tibet; a validation of traditional Tibetan class society; the vehicle for the dissemination of a particular brand of charismatic Vajrayana Buddhism (particularly of the Nyingmapa); and an entertaining, colorful and diverting expression of Tibet's apolitical folk culture (as, for instance, it is depicted in modern China); or a symbolic assertion of Tibetan nationalism and militarism. In the hands of different tellers working under different patronage regimes, the epic displays an extraordinary malleability in its interpretation, which provides a fertile and fruitful area for further research.

Notes

1 I myself have come across over seventy different volumes of Gesar tales published in China and Tibet since the early 1980s. Gesar researchers in China talk of one hundred and twenty different episodes already available in textual form. The repertoires of individual bards are also still in the process of transcription and publication. For example, bSam grub has recorded over three thousand hours of narration, which constitute forty-three episodes, while Grags pa recorded nine hundred and ninety-eight hours before his death in 1986, and these constituted twenty-five episodes.

2 As Geoffrey Samuel has observed, there are three main regional strands of the Gesar epos which constitute "three relatively independent transmissions of the epic," namely those "in Ladakh, Mongolia, and East Tibet." Geoffrey Samuel, "The Origins and Meaning of the East Tibetan Epic." In *Tibetan Studies: Proceedings of the Fifth IATS Conference, Narita 1989*, ed. Ihara and Yamaguchi (Narita: Naritasan Shinshoji, 1992), 711–21. Central and southern Tibet are not generally regarded as important areas of the epic's transmission, though we do have some texts from these areas which tend to hark back to eastern Tibetan traditions. However, although broadly speaking the division into three regional traditions is valid, it is far from a clear-cut taxonomy, and versions overlap across these divisions in complex ways which defy simple regionalization. A very interesting set of congruences was observed in this regard by Rolf Stein between the text I call the "Amdo manuscript," translated into German by Matthias Hermanns (1965), and the western Tibetan versions recorded by Francke in Ladakh (1905–1941). See Rolf Stein, "L'Épopée de Gesar dans sa Version Écrite de l'Amdo." In *Indo Tibetan Studies: Papers in Honour and Appreciation of David L. Snellgrove's contribution to Indo-Tibetan Studies*, ed. Tadeusz Skorupski (Tring: Institute of Buddhist Studies, 1990), 293–304. For more on the question of regional traditions, see Solomon George FitzHerbert, *The Vagrant Child: Narrative Diversity and Social Resonance in the Tibetan Epic Tradition* (New York: Oxford University Press, forthcoming).

3 For example August Hermann Francke, *A Lower Ladakhi Version of the Kesar Saga* (1905–1941; reprint, New Delhi: Asian Educational Services, 2000), 372; George Roerich "The Epic of King Kesar of Ling," *Journal of the Asiatic Society of Bengal* 8.7 (1942), 277–311; Matthias Hermanns, *Das National-Epos der Tibeter gling König Ge sar* (Regensburg: Habbel, 1965).

4 Huang Wenhuan, a Chinese scholar of ancient Tibet who has worked on the Dunhuang manuscripts since the 1970s, is an influential example of a scholar who has seen the Gesar epic as a depiction of the society of the Tibetan imperial period (known in Chinese as the period of the *Tubo* Kingdom). Huang Wenhuan, "Ge sar sgrung gi lo rgyus nang don gyi gnad don 'ga' zhig la zhib tu dpyad pa" (translated from Chinese). In *Ge sar rig gter*; *Ge sar sgrung gi dpyad rtsom kun bsdus*, vol. 1, ed. lHa mchog rgyal, dKon mchog tshe *brtan* et al. (Gansu Nationalities Publishing House, 2004), 149–68. His arguments are shared by many others, for example Chab 'gag rdo rje tshe ring, "'Dzam gling ge sar rgyal po'i sgrung rtsom de khams phyogs gling ge sar rgyal po'i lo rgyus mtshon byed yin nam." In *Ge sar rig gter*, 316–26.

5 The filial association in the Gesar epic between the god-child/prince (*lha sras*; *lha sras* is also one of the most common titles used in early Tibetan documents for the "heaven-sent" Tibetan kings of the Yarlung/lDe dynasty), and a "great god" (*lha chen* or *lha dbang*) is found in all versions.

However, the identification of this "great god" with Tshangs pa dkar po, the Tibetan rendering of Brahma, is not universal. One often encounters a conflation or interchangeability in Gesar texts between Tshangs pa (Brahma) and brGya byin (Indra). Iconographically, Tshangs pa is depicted in Tibet as a mounted warrior (see René de Nebesky-Wojkowitz, *Oracles and Demons of Tibet: the Cult and Iconography of the Tibetan Protective Deities* (Gravenhage: Mouton, 1956), 145–53. Robin Kornman was certainly right to suggest that Tshangs pa was first an important native pre-Buddhist Tibetan deity later recruited to fill the role of Brahma by Lamaism, which also recruited him as one of the "Eight wrathful protectors" *(drag gshed brgyad)*; Robin Kornman, "A Comparative Study of a Buddhist Version of the Epic of Gesar of Ling" (PhD Dissertation: Princeton University, 1995). Etymologically, it is likely that the name Tshangs pa comes from the same source as the name of the Bonpo creation deity Sangs po 'bum 'khri, otherwise known as Srid pa'i rgyal po ("Lord of Creation"). The latter is in turn identified in Buddhist tradition with the protector-deity Pe har (or Pe dkar), whose legend suggests he was a pre-Buddhist deity associated with the north of Tibet. There are several versions of the story of how Pe har, who, like Tshangs pa dkar po, is depicted as a warrior riding a white horse, came to be adopted as the chief of the "worldly protectors" *('jig rten pa'i srung ma)* in Buddhist tradition. One prominent version is that Pe har resided at Bhata Hor as the Hor deity gNam the dkar po until he was subdued and bound by oath by Padmasambhava, who brought him to Samye, where he was made the protector of the treasures housed there (Nebesky-Wojkowitz, 94–104; also Heather Stoddard, "The Nine Brothers of the White High." In *Les Habitants du Toit du Monde: Études Recueilles en Hommage à Alexander W. Macdonald,* ed. Samten Karmay and Philippe Sagant (Nanterre: Société d'ethnologie, 1997), 75–110. Tshangs pa is also associated with Pe har by means of their shared association with the deity gNam the dkar po. The early significance of Tshangs pa is given weight by the observation that he was the principal guardian deity for the first Buddhist temple in Tibet, Khra 'brug. Hazod also suggests that the name is etymologically connected to that of the great river of central Tibet, the gTsang po which becomes the only 'male' river in India as the 'son of Brahma,' the Brahmaputra. On this see Per K. Sørensen and Guntram Hazod, in cooperation with Tsering Gyalbo, *Thundering Falcon: An Inquiry into the History and Cult of Khra-'brug, Tibet's First Buddhist Temple* (Vienna: Österreichische Akademie der Wissenschaften, 2005), 275, n. 85; also Nebesky-Wojkowitz, 94–133; also R.A. Stein, *Recherches sur l'Épopée et le Barde au Tibet* (Paris: Presses Universitaires de France, 1959), 287–91. gNam the dkar po is also familiar in the Gesar tradition as the principal god of Gesar's main enemies, the Yellow Horpas. Thus the significance of Tshangs pa in pre-Buddhist Tibetan religion is given credence by this matrix of associations found in Tibetan between the names Tshangs pa, gNam the and Pe har, and the web of association between these and the Indian deities Brahma and Indra.

6 Gesar's celestial "aunt" and guardian deity is known under a variety of names in different versions but is a salient figure in all, and is widely known simply as Ne ne or Ma ne ne. She is instrumental in giving the hero regular instructions in the form of prophecies, and protecting him from harm. She is not a figure to be found in the Buddhist pantheon, but one with many resonances in Bon tradition. For example sNam sman dkar mo — which is homophonous with her name in the "Lingtsang woodblock" version of the Gesar epic (R.A. Stein, *L'Épopée Tibetaine de Gesar dans sa Version Lamaïque de Ling* (Paris: Presses Universitaires de France, 1956)), gNam sman dkar mo — is the name of one of the "nine primordial females" and the "eighteen brothers and sisters who are the forebears of mankind" in Bon tradition. These primordial ancestors were born from Srid pa Sang po 'bum khri's union with Chu lcam rgyal mo, a woman miraculously born from "an egg of blue light." Namkhai Norbu, *Drung Deu and Bon: Narrations, Symbolic Languages and the Bon Tradition of Ancient Tibet* (trans. Adriano Clemente) (Dharamsala: LTWA, 1995), 166. According to Namkhai Norbu, sNam sman dkar mo is also the name of one of the nine grid squares used in Bonpo lDe'u sprul divination (Norbu, 27). gNam sman dkar mo

is also described by Samten Karmay as a "Bonpo guardian of the esoteric teachings." Samten Karmay, "A General Introduction to the History and Doctrines of Bon," *Memoirs of the Research Department of the Toyo Bunko* 33, 171–218. Reprinted in Samten Karmay, *The Arrow and the Spindle,* vol. 1 (Kathmandu: Mandala Book Point, 1998), 105–156. In many versions this celestial guardian is depicted riding on a white snow lion, and carries an arrow with five silk ribbons attached to it, or a vase containing ambrosia of immortality or longevity.

7 The "hidden lands" narrative trope is perhaps not of Buddhist origin, and is found as a central feature of many only partially Buddhicized utopian belief traditions in the Himalaya (such as that of the Lepcha). However, the "hidden land" motif is also central to Tibetan Vajrayana Buddhism — expressed, for example, in the Shambhala tradition associated with the Kalachakra Tantra and often alluded to in Buddhist *gnas yig* and *rnam thar* traditions. The hidden land theme does not appear to be central to the Gesar tradition, but is a theme on which many (particularly literate Buddhist) Gesar authors appear to draw.

8 See R.A. Stein, "Une Source Ancienne pour l'Histoire de l'Épopée Tibétaine: Le Rlangs Po-Ti bSe-Ru," *Journal Asiatique* 250 (1962) 99–100.

9 See his 1981 article, written to introduce the thirty-volume edition of the Gesar epic published in Bhutan. R.A. Stein, "Introduction to the Gesar Epic," *Tibet Journal* 6.1 (1981), 3–14.

10 In his *Poetics*, Aristotle considers unity of plot to be as important for epic poetry as it is for tragedy: "it [epic poetry] should have for its subject a single action, whole and complete, with a beginning, a middle and an end" (*Poetics*: XXIII); and "thus the story of the Odyssey can be stated briefly...this is the essence of the plot; the rest is episode" (XVII). Within the singularity of action, an open-ended number of episodes may be admitted which diversify the poem, but without the "single view," the poetry becomes merely or purely "episodic," and "of all plots and actions the episodic are the worst" (Poetics: IX). Robin Kornman argued in his PhD Dissertation that such unity of plot for the Gesar epic is furnished by the heavenly prelude or *lHa gling* which establishes the hero's divine mission.

11 This is a feature of the Gesar tradition shared with the Kyrgyz Manas tradition. It is also of comparative interest with regard to the ancient Greek epics, concerning which the role of the Muses continues to be a lively area of scholarship. For a recent contribution, see for example Elizabeth Minchin, "The Poet Appeals to his Muse: Homeric Invocations in the Context of Epic Performance," *The Classical Journal* 91.1 (1995), 25–33.

12 A self-educated Gesar scholar in 'Bri stod named Wang dra told me in a filmed interview in 2004 that the Gesar epic is like the "bones and marrow (*rkang dang rus*) of the people: since the lineage descent (*rus* lit: bone) of the people is unbroken, so the Gesar tradition is also unbroken." Recorded interview, 'Bri stod July 2004.

13 Grags pa's songs, for example, often end with some variation on the lines: *go na rna ba'i yid la 'ching// ma go glu la skyor rgyu med.*

14 However, some modern "inspired" Tibetan bards do assert the importance of telling the epic "correctly" and not just "making it up." For example, there is a revealing mention in bSam grub's life story by Yang Enhong of the first meeting between bSam grub and Tshe ring dbang 'dus (another celebrated contemporary Gesar bard) at the First International Gesar Conference in Chengdu in 1989. bSam grub was not impressed by his fellow bard, and criticized him for being too concerned with the performance while ignoring the content. bSam grub straightforwardly questioned Tshe ring dbang 'dus on his knowledge of the epic plot, but was later satisfied by Tshe ring dbang 'dus' answers. Yang Enhong, *Min jian shi shen: ge sa er yi ren yan jiu* (Beijing: Chinese Tibetology Publishing House, 1995), Chapter 5. Unpublished English translation of various chapters from this work have been kindly given to me by Geoffrey Samuel.

15 Walther Heissig, *Geser-Studien: Untersuchungen zu der Erzählstoffen in den 'neuen' Kapiteln des mongolischen Geser-Zyklus* (Opladen: Westdeutscher Verlag, 1983).

16 Silke Herrmann, *Kesar-Versionen aus Ladakh* (Wiesbaden: Otto Harrassowitz, 1991).

17 Jack Goody, *The Interface between the Written and the Oral* (Cambridge: Cambridge University Press, 1987), 80; Stuart Blackburn, "Introduction." In *The Oral Epics of India*, ed. Stuart H. Blackburn and Peter J. Claus et al. (Berkeley: University of California Press, 1989), 10; Margaret Beissinger, "Introduction." In *Epic Traditions in the Contemporary World: The Poetics of Community*, ed. Margaret Beissinger and Jane Tylus et al. (Berkeley: University of California Press, 1999), 10–11.

18 For example, John Miles Foley, *Oral-Formulaic Theory and Research: an Introduction and Annotated Bibliography* (New York: Garland, 1985); *The Theory of Oral Composition: History and Methodology* (Bloomington: Indiana University Press, 1988); *Traditional Oral Epic: the Odyssey, Beowulf, and the Serbo-Croatian return song* (Berkeley: University of California Press, 1990); *Immanent Art: From Structure to Meaning in Traditional Oral Epic* (Bloomington: Indiana University Press, 1991); *Homer's Traditional Art* (University Park, PA: Pennsylvania State University Press, 1999); *How to Read an Oral Poem* (Urbana: University of Illinois Press, 2002).

19 For a recent assessment of the state of the debate on the authorship of the Homeric epics, a debate which was as alive in ancient Greece as it has been for the centuries since then, see Barbara Graziosi, *Inventing Homer: The Early Reception of Epic* (Cambridge: Cambridge University Press, 2002).

20 This is largely a supposition on my behalf on the basis of reading the transcriptions of illiterate poets such as Grags pa and bSam grub; the inconsistencies and circularities they display suggest the improvised nature of their recitation. It is also based on the more particular evidence furnished by my recording of the young bard Zla ba grags pa in Jyekundo in 2004. One morning I recorded a short public performance by him at a popular picnic spot outside Jyekundo. Later the same day, Karma lha mo, the Tibetan PhD student working with Zla ba grags pa, transcribed the material he had recited (without the use of a recording device). That evening we met up again and Karma lha mo kindly gave me a copy of her transcription. Then Zla ba grags pa performed a part of the same section again. When I compared the transcription with the morning performance and the evening performance — I found that none of the three were identical. The morning performance was longer than the transcription, while the evening performance followed the transcription very closely, but was not identical — the order of some lines and words were reversed and a few adjectival phrases were different, exactly the kind of variations one would expect according to Lord's theory.

21 For a list of the published episodes narrated by Grags pa, see the bibliography. His narrations have also been taken as the basis of the forty-volume composite edition of the Gesar epic — the *Gling sgrung gces btus* series — currently being compiled in Lhasa and Beijing.

22 Walter Ong, *Orality and Literacy* (New York: Routledge, 1982), 46–56.

23 These invocatory sections in Grags pa's narrations are extremely uniform in their structural features. This was the subject of an article by Yang Enhong in which she looks at some songs from Grags pa's *bDud 'dul*. Yang Enhong, "On the Study of the Narrative Structure of Tibetan Epic: *A Record of King Gesar*," *Oral Tradition* 16.2 (2001), 294–316.

24 The question of bSam grub's illiteracy has long been a moot point for me. His style seems very literary, and a scholar-friend from the Tibetan Academy of Social Sciences (TASS) in Lhasa (where bSam grub also holds a tenured position as the Gesar bard-in-residence) had initially assured me that he could read. However, other scholars in Lhasa who work closely with bSam grub have since confirmed that he is in fact illiterate, and my friend has acknowledged his initial mistake.

25 In his seminal work, based on 25 years of collection, transcription and interpretation in the field of oral literature, *The Singer of Tales*, Lord defines a *formula* as "a group of words which is

regularly employed under the same metrical conditions to express a given essential idea" (this is the definition he adopts from Milman Parry, "Studies in the Epic Technique of Oral Verse-Making I: Homer and Homeric Style," *Harvard Studies in Classical Philology* 41 (1930), 80), and *themes* are "the repeated incidents and descriptive passages in the songs." Albert Lord, *The Singer of Tales* (Cambridge: Harvard University Press, 1960), 4. In fact, throughout his career, and despite his fondness for apparently clear definitions, Lord maintained an ambiguity in his definition of themes. Sometimes his definition was narrow: a *theme* is a "repeated passage with a fair degree of verbal or formula repetition from one occurrence to the next." Albert Lord, *Epic Singers and Oral Tradition* (Ithaca: Cornell University Press, 1991), 26. Elsewhere, however, he also depicts *themes* as being broad narrative motifs. In his 1953 article on "Homer's Orginality" for instance, we can see Lord using both definitions (narrow and broad) within the space of just two pages: first *themes* are defined narrowly as "the repeated narrative or descriptive elements [that] function in building songs in much the same way in which formulas function in building lines," but then on the very next page he uses, as an example of bardic "combination and separation and recombination" of *themes*, the combination in the Odyssey of two stories — of a hero setting out from home in search of his father, and the hero's return after many years of captivity to find his wife on the point of remarrying. These are clearly broad narrative motifs, not narrow, verbally specific descriptive passages. Lord 1991, 41–42.

26 To take just a few examples, the following are lines that find some close correlation in most eastern Tibetan versions (always in the song sections): *sa 'di sa ngo ma shes na; nga dang nga ngo ma shes na; snga bod gna' mi'i gtam dpe la; dpe bzhag na 'dra ma e 'dra gda'*; some sung formulaic refrains are also found across eastern Tibetan *and* Ladakhi versions, such as *de ring nga la dpung rogs mdzod*. There are also formulas in the narrative sections which tend to be specific to particular characters, especially Khro thung. For example, Khro thung's humorously transparent ploys are often marked by the phrase: *thabs gcig byed dgos*; or one of his "calculating" formulas: *bsam blo bzhi gsum bcu gnyis btang/ blo rtse nyi shu rtsa lnga bkug*. There are many more possible examples of rhetorical formulas employed in a wide range of oral and literary versions. However, this stock of shared phrases only accounts for a very small fraction of any given recitation or text.

27 Lord 1991, 42.

28 Lord takes *The Wanderings of Oisin*, a poem by W. B. Yeats, as a point of comparison between oral and literary poetry and says, for example, that the phrase "sooty fingers" has no traditional resonance, and the same can be said for the sentence "many a tree rose out of the warm sea." This, says Lord, "is neither traditional diction nor traditional imagery. It is individualistic in an individualist's milieu. Its particular style, its striking choice of words and ideas and poetic combinations are purely Yeats….These delights are in the tradition of *written* poetry, but are not in an oral *traditional* Hiberno-English poetry." Lord 1991, 18.

29 FitzHerbert forthcoming.

30 For example, the singing and narrating style of the young bard I recorded in 'Bri stod in summer 2004 is very similar (at least in style) to the recorded narrations of an older bard (bSod nams nor bu) from the same area, who was away when I visited; a local scholar gave me a cassette of his recordings. It is certainly conceivable that their songs could match one another at a verbally specific formulaic level.

31 The three-volume text I refer to as the "Lingtsang woodblock" is the most widely published Tibetan version of the birth and youth of Gesar. For modern print editions of this text, see the bibliography.

32 gCod pa don grub, "Gling ge sar rgyal po'i skyes rabs lo rgyus rags tsam brjod pa." In gCod pa don 'grub, *Gling ge sar rgyal po'i shul rten gyi ngag rgyun ngo mtshar me tog phreng mdzes* (Xining: Mtsho sngon mi rigs dpe skrun khang, 1989), 4–7. Samten Karmay also gives

a translation of this summary. Samten Karmay, "The Theoretical Basis of the Tibetan Epic," *Bulletin of the School of Oriental and African Studies* 16.2 (1993), 234–46. Also republished in Karmay 1998, 472–88.

33 Stein (1956, 1959) dated this text in vague terms to the late 19th century. His dating was also adopted by Geoffrey Samuel (1996). However, my research suggests persuasively that it was in fact commissioned by the Lingtsang *rgyal po* dBang chen bstan 'dzin chos rgyal and authored by the abbot of the Nyingmapa rDzong 'go Monastery, which adjoins the old Lingtsang *rgyal po*'s palace, sometime around 1910. For a detailed treatment of this question see FitzHerbert forthcoming.

34 *rim bzhin ci yin 'di yin ma shes par gling rje ge sar rgyal po'i sgrung las "'Khrungs gling me tog ra ba" zhes bshad shes song.* gCod pa don grub and Chab 'gag rDo rje tshe ring, *Ya mtshan che ba'i gling ge sar sgrung pa'i gsang ba* (Beijing: Mi rigs dpe skrun khang, 2001), 77.

35 Paraphrased translation from gCod pa don grub and Chab 'gag rDo rje tshe ring 2001, 76–77.

36 gCod pa don grub and Chab 'gag rDo rje tshe ring 2001, 77.

37 Ruth Finnegan, *Oral Poetry: Its Nature, Significance and Social Context* (Cambridge: Cambridge University Press, 1977); Foley, 1991; Carol Poster, "Review of Homer's Traditional Art by JM Foley," *Rocky Mountain Review of Language and Literature* 54.2 (2000), 95–98.

38 Lord understands the term "literature" in its evaluative use and hence as applicable to oral, non-written forms, despite its etymology. Lord 1991, 16.

39 Lord 1991, 185.

40 Lord 1960, 129. Lord was bent on insisting that literate educated people cannot, of necessity, produce oral epic, and that all texts are either oral or literary and without any transitional category in between. He argued that mature oral style cannot simply transfer to mature literary style with the advent of writing, but that mature oral style gives way to embryonic literary style. Thus Homer could not have been a "transitional poet," because his style is mature. Lord 1960, 124–38.

41 The last ruler of the Yarlung Dynasty in the ninth century CE. He is remembered in Tibetan history as a great oppressor of Buddhism, whose attacks on Buddhism led to the disintegration of the Tibetan Empire. Recent researchers have challenged this traditional portrayal.

42 Sa skya bSod nams rgyal mtshan (1312–1375), *rGyal rabs gsal ba'i me long*, ed. Ngag dbang blo bzang and mGon po rgyal mtshan (Beijing: Mi rigs dpe skrun khang, 1995), 79–82. English translation in McComas Taylor and Lama Choedak Yuthok, *The Clear Mirror: A Traditional Account of Tibet's Golden Age* (Ithaca: Snow Lion, 1996), 112–14.

43 An interesting recent article sets out the issues of oral/aural textual transmission with regard to manuscripts from the Dunhuang collection. Sam van Schaik, "Oral Teachings and Written Texts: Transmission and Transformation in Dunhuang." In *Contributions to the Cultural History of Early Tibet* ed. Matthew T. Kapstein and Brandon Dotson (Leiden: Brill, 2007), 183–208.

44 Finnegan 1977.

45 Jack Goody, *The Interface between the Written and the Oral* (Cambridge: Cambridge University Press, 1987).

46 Jacques Derrida, the hugely influential philosopher of language, also suggested the marginality of the distinction between phonic and graphic "inscription," and argued that meaning in language — language being the durable institution of signs — should not privilege speech over writing. Rather, speech can be understood as a form of writing:

> If "writing" signifies inscription and especially the durable institution of a sign...writing in general covers the entire field of linguistic signs. In that field a certain sort of instituted signifiers may appear, "graphic" in the narrow and derivative sense of the word, ordered by a certain relationship with other instituted — hence "written" even if they are "phonic" — signifiers.

Jacques Derrida, *Of Grammatology* (trans. Gayatri Chakravorty Spivak) (Baltimore: Johns Hopkins University Press, 1976), 44. Cited by Foley 1991, xiii.

47 gCod pa don grub and Chab 'gag rdo rje tshe ring 2001, 56–58.

48 Such as anaphora (the use of the same word at the beginning of each series of lines); epiphora (the use of the same word at the end of each of a series of lines); alliteration, assonance, rhyme, both internal, medial and final, and the sense of balanced structure as typefied by parallelisms in sentences and other forms of parataxis. Lord 1991, 32.

49 Receptionalism is a broad church in literary criticism. On a simple level, in the "semiotic triangle" of author-text-reader, it assigns priority in the generation of meaning by the reader. It has also meant an emphasis (particularly in the field of Classics) on looking not for the objective meaning of texts, but at how they have been interpreted and perceived through history.

50 This idea is found also in his earlier work, in which he describes traditional referentiality as "a kind of metonymy designating a mode of signification wherein the part stands for the whole." Foley 1991, 7.

51 Foley 1999, 18.

52 For references see Solomon George FitzHerbert, "The Birth of Gesar: Narrative Diversity and Social Resonance in the Tibetan Epic Tradition" (DPhil thesis: University of Oxford, 2007), 143–44.

53 This was the basis of John D. Smith's critique of Lord. Smith's criticisms are based on his work on Punjabi epic traditions. John D. Smith, "The Singer or the Song? A Reassessment of Lord's 'Oral Theory,'" *Man* 12 (1977), 141–53.

54 Either way, too much or too little, Smith's critique holds, namely that Lord's theory involves a circularity, as his terms are predicated on each other: "orality" is defined in terms of formulaic improvisation and "formulas" are defined in terms of orality. For example, "one cannot have formulas outside oral or oral traditional verse." (Lord 1975 as cited by Smith 1977, 144.) Lord's theory is modelled on a culturally specific model, that of Balkan heroic rhapsody, and this model is used to define the parameters of oral-traditional poetry. If the poetry of another tradition does not fit the model that works for the Balkan material, then it is simply denied the titles "oral" or "traditional." By this reckoning, Smith's *pabuji* epic would not be properly considered "oral" and Gesar would not be properly considered "traditional." This kind of terminological monopoly is obviously unacceptable.

55 For tables showing the incidence of the various *Segmente* across her twelve different versions of four core episodes of the epic (Divine descent, Birth, the Great Demon and the War with Hor), see Herrmann 1991, 30–36.

56 Vladimir Propp, *Morphology of the Folktale* (trans. Lawrence Scott) (1928; reprint, Austin: University of Texas Press, 1968), 21. Propp regarded these *functions* as operating with regard to the Russian fairytale as grammar operates with regard to language. The main problem with the Proppian method is that it doesn't prove much beyond the observation that "similar tales resemble one another." This was an objection that Propp himself levelled at his colleague Volkov as being "a conclusion which is completely non-committal and leads nowhere" but one which his own work doesn't, to my mind, entirely evade. Propp, 15.

10

བོད་མངའ་མཛོད་བཅུའི་དུས་རབས་ཀྱི་ངོ་སྤྲོད་མདོ་ཙམ་གླེང་བ།

ཟེ་རི་འཇིགས་མེད་དབང་རྒྱལ།

སྔོན་དུ་གླེང་བའི་གཏམ།

བོད་ཀྱི་ལོ་རྒྱུས་བྱུང་རིམ་ཁྲོད། འོ་དེ་པུར་རྒྱལ་གཉའ་ཁྲི་བཙན་པོ་ཚུན་ཆད་ཅུང་ཟད་ཁ་གསལ་བའི་ལུགས་སུ་མཆིས་མོད། དེའི་ཡར་སྔོན་བོད་སྟོད་སིལ་གྱི་བྱུང་རིམ་དང་འབྲེལ་བའི་མངའ་མཛོད་སྐོར་སྔོན་གྱི་ལོ་རྒྱུས་ཁ་ཤས་སུ་རྐང་གྲངས་ཙམ་ངོས་འཛིན་བྱས་པ་དང་། ཡང་ན་ཕྱོགས་སྟོན་ཙམ་གནང་བ་ལས། བོད་མངའ་མཛོད་ཆེན་པོ་བཅུའི་བྱུང་རིམ་རྒྱལ་དུ་བརྗོད་ནས་དཔྱད་རྩོམ་སྤེལ་མཁན་ཞིག་ད་ཕན་ཕལ་ཆེར་བྱུང་མྱོང་མེད་པ་འདྲ།

བོད་ཀྱི་ལོ་རྒྱུས་དང་རྒྱལ་རབས་ཀྱི་སྒྲོམ་གཞིའི་ཆ་ལག་ཡོངས་སུ་ཚང་བ་ཞིག་བསླང་དགོས་ན། བོད་མངའ་མཛོད་ཀྱི་བྱུང་རིམ་གྱི་སྟོང་ཆ་མི་ལུས་པ་ཞིག་དགོས་པ་ཡང་བཤད་མི་དགོས་པ་ཞིག་རེད་སྙམ། ཕྱིར་རྒྱལ་རབས་དང་ལོ་རྒྱུས་ཀྱི་སྒྲོམ་གཞི་བརྟན་པོའི་ཡིག་ཆ་གསོག་འཇོག་གི་ལམ་ལུགས་ཐོག་མར་བྱུང་ས་ནི་བཙན་པོ་ཁྲི་སྲོང་གི་སྐབས་ཡིན་ལ། ཁྲི་སྲོང་རང་གི་མི་རྒྱུད་སྤུ་མའི་བྱུར་རིམ་འབུར་དུ་བརྗོད་ནས་སྐབས་དེའི་ལོ་རྒྱུས་རྩོམ་སྒྲིག་དང་ཡིག་ཆ་བདག་ཉར་གནང་མཁན་ཚོས་གཉའ་ཁྲི་མན་ཆད་ཀྱི་ལོ་རྒྱུས་ཆ་ལས་ཅུང་མཐུས་ཚང་གནང་འདུག་པ་ལས། དེ་མིན་མངའ་མཛོད་ཀྱི་སྐོར་ལ་དེ་ཙམ་ཡིག་འཇོག་དང་དོ་སྣང་གནང་མེད་པ་ཏུན་ཏོང་ཡིག་རྙིང་ལ་བརྟེན་ནས་ཤེས་ཐུབ་པ་ཞིག་རེད་སྙམ། ཁྲི་སྲོང་རང་གི་མི་རྒྱུད་སྤུ་མས་རྒྱལ་སྲིད་བཟུང་མཁན་དང་པོ་གཉའ་ཁྲིའི་མི་ཁོང་རྒྱ་གར་ལ་གཏུགས་པས། དེས་ན་གཉའ་ཁྲི་ཡར་སྔོན་དུ་བྱུང་བའི་བོད་མངའ་མཛོད་ཆེན་པོ་རྣམས་དང་ཁྲི་སྲོང་དབར་ཆོས་དང་མི་རྒྱུད་གཉིས་ཐད་ནས་འབྲེལ་བ་དེ་ཙམ་མི་ཆེ་བས། སྔོན་གྱི་ལོ་རྒྱུས་ཕལ་མོ་ཆེའི་ནང་བོད་མངའ་མཛོད་ཀྱི་ལོ་རྒྱུས་དེ་ཙམ་གྲ་རྒྱུས་མི་ཡོང་བའི་རྒྱུ་མཚན་ཡང་དེ་ཉིད་ཡིན་སྲིད་སྙམ།

དེར་བརྟེན་ད་ཕན་གཉའ་ཁྲིའི་གོང་གི་མངའ་མཛོད་དང་བོད་སྟོད་སིལ་གྱི་ལོ་རྒྱུས་ཆ་ལག་ཡོངས་སུ་རྫོགས་པའམ་འཐུས་ངེས་ཅན་ཚང་བ་ཞིག་ད་ལམ་སུས་ཀྱང་བྲིས་མེད་པ་འདྲ། ལོ་རབས་དགུ་བཅུ་པའི་མཇུག

མཐར་ཕྲན་གྱིས་འཕགས་བོད་ཆོས་འབྱུང་འཛམ་བུའི་གསེར་གྱི་ཁྲི་ཤིང་ཐོག་ཐང་ཡིག་དང་ཆོས་འབྱུང་མཁས་པའི་དགའ་སྟོན་སོགས་ལ་བརྟེན་ནས་མངའ་མཛད་ཀྱི་སྐོར་རགས་ཙམ་བྲིས་ཁུལ་བྱས་མོད། འོན་ཀྱང་འདོད་པ་ཚིམས་པ་ཞིག་འབྲི་ཐུབ་མ་སོང་།

དུས་རབས་ཉེར་གཅིག་པའི་དུས་མགོར་སླར་ཡང་བོད་མངའ་མཛད་ཀྱི་སྐོར་ལ་ཉམས་ཞིབ་བྱེད་འདོད་ཡོད་པའི་མུར། ས་སྐྱའི་གདུང་རབས་ལ་ལྟ་ཞིབ་ནན་པོར་བྱས་པས། བོད་མངའ་མཛད་དང་ས་སྐྱའི་གདུང་རབས་དབར་འབྲེལ་བ་ཆེན་པོ་ཡོད་པའི་ཚོར་སྣང་བྱུང་། དེར་བརྟེན་སྤྱི་ཕྱིར་དཔྱད་གཞི་མང་པོ་ཞིག་ལ་ཞིབ་འཇུག་བྱས་ནས་མངའ་མཛད་བཅུའི་ལོ་རྒྱུས་འབུར་དུ་བཏོན་ནས་དཔྱད་རྩོམ་མདོར་བསྡུས་ཤིག་བྱས་ཏེ། ལྷ་ར་ཆ་སི་བོད་ཀྱི་གཙུག་ལག་སློབ་གཉེར་ཁང་དུ་སྒྲོག་སྦྱངས་དང་བགྲོ་གླེང་བྱས། དེ་རྗེས་ལྷ་ཆའི་དཔེ་མཛོད་ཁང་སོགས་ཀྱི་དཔེ་དེབ་གལ་ཆེར་འགའ་ཞིག་གསར་རྙེད་བྱུང་བ་ལ་བརྟེན་ནས་སྔོན་འཕྲི་གང་ཙམ་གྱིས་སྤྱར་བས་ཅུང་མཐུས་ཚང་བ་བྱས་ནས། ནོར་གླིང་བོད་ཀྱི་མཐོ་སློབ་ཏུ་རྒྱལ་རབས་ཁྲིད་སྐབས་སླར་ཡང་ལུང་རིགས་ཀྱིས་དཔྱད་ཞིབ་ནན་པོའི་ལུགས་སུ་བྱས་ནས་པར་བཞུས་ཁོ་བོའི་གྲོགས་ཀྱི་ཡང་རྗེ་ཨ་མྱེས་རྨ་ཆེན་བོད་ཀྱི་རིག་གཞུང་ཞིབ་འཇུག་ཁང་གི་འགན་འཛིན་མཁས་དབང་བཀྲ་ཤིས་ཚེ་རིང་ལགས་སུ་སྤྲུན་སྦྱར་དང་འབྲེལ་ཁོང་གི་ལམ་སྟོན་བཞིན་ཞིབ་གཞིར་ནན་པོའི་ལུགས་སུ་བྱས་གཏན་ལ་ཕབ་པས། གཅིག་བྱས་བོད་མངའ་མཛད་སྐབས་ཀྱི་ལོ་རྒྱུས་བྱུང་རིམ་ཐད་དཔྱད་རྩོམ་འདི་ཉིད་ཁ་གསལ་ཤོས་དང་ཁུངས་བཙན་བཙན་ཤོས་དེ་ཡིན་སྙིད་སྙམ།

མངའ་མཛད་ཐོག་མ་གང་ལས་བྱུང་བའི་ཁུངས།

རང་རེ་བོད་ཀྱི་ཕ་མེས་དང་ཡང་མེས་སྤྲ་དང་སྤྲེའི་གནས་བབ་རིམ་གྱིས་འགྱུར་བ་ཐེབས་ཏེ། འགྲོ་བ་མིའི་རྣམ་པར་གྱུར་ནས་གདུང་དྲུག་ལས་མཆེད་པའི་མི་རྒྱུད་རིམ་པར་འཕེལ་བ་ལས། སེ་ལས་བྱུས་ལེགས་བུ་བཞི་སྲིད། །རྨུ་ལ་གོད་ལེ་ཕྲ་བརྒྱད་སྲིད། །ལྡོང་ལས་རུས་ཆེན་བཅོ་བརྒྱད་སྲིད། །སྟོང་ལས་རྗེ་བཞི་ཁོལ་བརྒྱད་སྲིད། །[1] ཞེས་པ་ལྟར། སེ་ལས་བྱུས་ལེགས་བུ་བཞི་དང་། རྨུ་ལས་གོད་ལེ་ཕྲ་བརྒྱད། ལྡོང་ལས་རུས་ཆེན་བཅོ་བརྒྱད། སྟོང་ལས་རྗེ་བཞི། ཁོལ་བརྒྱད་སོགས་སུ་གྱེས་པ་ནས། བོད་བཙན་པོ་གཉའ་ཁྲིས་དབང་བསྒྱུར་མ་བྱས་གོང་དུ་མངའ་མཛད་བཅུ་སོགས་ཀྱིས་དབང་བསྒྱུར་བྱས་པ་ཡིན་ཏེ། དང་པོ་གནོད་སྦྱིན་ནག་པོ། གཉིས་པ་རེ་ཏི་མགོང་ཡག གསུམ་པ་སྲིན་པོ་གཉའ་རེངས་ཁྲག་མིག བཞི་པ་དམར་འཛམ་ལྷ། ལྔ་པ་རྨུ་རྒྱལ་ཁོ་རྗེ། དྲུག་པ་གྲོག་གྲོག་འདྲེ་ཧང་སྟེ། བདུན་པ་མ་སངས་སྤུན་དགུ། བརྒྱད་པ་ཀླུ། དགུ་པ་རྒྱལ་འགོང་ངམ་པོ་ཆེའམ་འགོངས་པོ་སྤུན་དགུ། བཅུ་པ་ཟ་རིང་སྐྲེས་དྲུག་སོགས་ཀྱིས་དབང་བསྒྱུར་བར་བཤད་དེ། དེ་དག་གི་ཁུངས་རྣམས་སྟོན་དུ་འགོད་ན། ལྡེའུ་ཆོས་འབྱུང་རྒྱས་པ་ལས།[2] དང་པོ་གནོད་སྦྱིན་ནག་པོ་ཞེས་བྱ་བ་བྱུང་སྟེ།། ཡུལ་གྱི་མིང་ཡང་བཟང་ཡུལ་རྒྱན་མེད་བྱ་བར་བཏགས། །ལག་ཆར་མདའ་གཞུ་འཕེན་པ་དེ་ནས་བྱུང་། །གཉིས་པ་རེ་སྡེ་མགོ་གཡག་བདུད་ཀྱིས་བྱས། །ཡུལ་གྱི་མིང་ཡང་བདུད་ཡུལ་གླིང་དགུ་ཟེར།། སྟ་རེ་དགྲ་སྟ་དུས་དེར་ལག་ཆར་བྱུང་།། གསུམ་པ་གཉའ་རེང་ཕྲག་མེད་སྲིན་གྱིས་བྱས།། ཡུལ་གྱི་མིང་ཡང་ནག་པོ་དགུ་དུལ་ཟེར།། ལག

ཆར་སྲིན་མོ་རྐང་དང་སྒྲོགས་གཉིས་བྱུང་།། བཞི་པ་དམར་འཇམ་ཞེས་བྱ་ལྷ་ཡིས་བྱས།། ཡུལ་གྱི་མིང་ནི་ལྷ་ཡུལ་གུང་ཐང་ཟེར།། ལག་ཆར་ཁ་ཏཾ་རྩེ་གསུམ་དེ་ནས་བྱུང་།། ལྔ་པ་ཀླུས་དབང་བྱས་ངམ་བྲང་ཅང་བྲང་ཟེར།། ལག་ཆ་མདུང་ལ་བྱེད་པ་དེ་ནས་བྱུང་།། དྲུག་པ་འདྲེས་དབང་ལང་ཏང་ལིང་ཏང་ཟེར།། ལག་ཆར་རྒྱུག་པ་ཀྲོག་ཅན་དེ་ནས་བྱུང་།། བདུན་པ་མ་སངས་རྦ་དགུས་དབང་བྱས་ཏེ།། ཡུལ་གྱི་མིང་ནི་བོད་ཁམས་གཡང་དྲུག་ཟེར།། ལག་ཆར་དོང་རལ་ཕུབ་ཆུང་དེ་ནས་བྱུང་།། བརྒྱད་པ་ཀླུས་དབང་བྱས་བོད་ཁམས་གླིང་དགུར་བཏགས།། དགུ་པ་མི་མ་ཡིན་གྱིས་དབང་བྱས་ཏེ།། ཡུལ་གྱི་མིང་ནི་ངམ་ཡུལ་ནག་པོར་བཏགས།། བཅུ་པ་ཟ་རིད་སྤུན་དྲུག་དག་གིས་དབང་བྱས་ཏེ།། ཡུལ་གྱི་མིང་ལ་སྟོང་སྡེ་བཅོ་བརྒྱད་ཟེར།། བཅུ་གཅིག་རྒྱལ་ཕྲན་བཅུ་གཉིས་དབང་བྱས་སྐད།། ཀུན་གྱི་ཐ་མར་སིལ་མ་བཞི་བཅུ་བྱས།། ཡུལ་གྱི་མིང་ནི་བཟང་ཡུལ་གྲུད་དུ་བཏགས།། ཞེས་བཤད། ཆོས་འབྱུང་མཁས་པའི་དགའ་སྟོན་ལས།[3] དང་པོར་གནོད་སྦྱིན་ནག་པོས་དབང་བྱས་ཏེ།། ཡུལ་གྱི་མིང་ཡང་བཟང་ཡུལ་རྒྱན་མེད་ཟེར།། མཚོན་ཆ་མདའ་གཞུ་དེ་ཡི་དུས་སུ་བྱུང་།། དེ་ནས་རེ་ཏི་མགོ་གཡག་བདུད་ཀྱིས་བྱས།། མིང་ཡང་བདུད་ཡུལ་ཁ་རག་རོང་དགུར་བཏགས།། སྟ་རེ་དགྲ་སྟ་དེ་ཡི་དུས་སུ་བྱུང་།། དེ་ནས་སྲིན་པོ་གཉའ་རེངས་ཁྲག་མིག་བྱས།། ཡུལ་མིང་སྲིན་པོ་ནག་པོ་དགུ་ཡུལ་ཟེར།། སྲིན་མོ་རྐང་དང་སྒྲོགས་གཉིས་ལག་ཆ་བྱུང་།། བཞི་པ་དམར་འཇམ་ལྷ་ཡིས་དབང་བྱས་ཏེ།། ལྷ་ཡུལ་གུང་ཐང་ལག་ཆར་ཆུ་གྲི་བྱུང་།། ལྔ་པར་རྨུ་རྒྱལ་ཁོ་རྗེ་ཞེས་བྱས་བཟུངས།། ད་ཕྲང་ཅང་ཕྲང་ལག་ཆར་ཞགས་པ་འཕེན།། དྲུག་པ་ཀྲོག་ཀྲོག་འདྲེ་ཡིས་དབང་བྱས་ཏེ།། ལང་ཏང་ལིང་དང་བར་ཁ་ཅུར་རྡོ་འཕེན།། བདུན་པ་མ་སངས་སྤུན་དགུས་དབང་བྱས་ཏེ།། ཡུལ་གྱི་མིང་ནི་བོད་ཁ་ཉ་དྲུག་ཟེར།། ལག་ཆར་དོང་རལ་གོ་ཆ་ཕུབ་ཆུང་བྱུང་།། བརྒྱད་པ་ཀླུས་བཟུང་བོད་ཁམས་གླིང་དགུ་བཏགས།། དགུ་པ་རྒྱལ་པོས་དབང་བྱས་ངམ་པོ་ཅེ།། བཅུ་པ་འགོང་པོ་སྤུན་དགུས་དབང་བྱས་ཏེ།། ཡུལ་གྱི་མིང་ཡང་སྟོང་སྡེ་བཅོ་བརྒྱད་ཟེར།། ཞེས་དང་། རྒྱལ་པོའི་བཀའི་ཐང་ཡིག་ལས་ཀྱང་།[4] བོད་ཡུལ་གངས་རི་རྩེ་དགུའི་ལྗོངས་འདི་རུ།། སྔར་རྒྱལ་གོང་དུ་མདའ་མཛོད་དྲུག་ཏུ་བྱུང་།། དང་པོར་གནོད་སྦྱིན་ནག་པོས་དབང་བྱས་ཏེ།། ཡུལ་མིང་བདུད་ཡུལ་ཁ་རག་མགོ་དགུར་བཏགས།། སྟ་རྟགས་གཉེན་པོ་བཙན་པོ་དེ་ནས་བྱུང་།། དེ་ནས་བདུད་དང་སྲིན་པོས་དབང་བྱས་ཏེ།། མིང་ཡང་ལྷ་འདྲེ་གཉིས་ཀྱི་ཡུལ་དུ་བཏགས།། སྟ་རྟགས་ཤ་ཟ་གདོང་པ་དམར་བ་བྱུང་།། དེ་ནས་ཀླུ་དང་བཙན་གྱིས་དབང་བྱས་ཏེ།། ཡུལ་གྱི་མིང་ལ་བོད་ཁམས་གླིང་དགུ་བཏགས།། སྟ་རྟགས་དཀར་བུ་ཆུ་ལ་སྤྱོད་པ་བྱུང་།། དེ་ནས་མ་སངས་སྤུན་དགུས་དབང་བྱས་ཏེ།། ཡུལ་མིང་བོད་ཁམས་གཡའ་དྲུག་བྱ་བར་བཏགས།། སྟ་རྟགས་མདའ་མདུང་མཚོན་ཆ་དེ་ནས་བྱུང་།། ཞེས་དང་། གཡུང་དྲུང་བོན་གྱི་གཞུང་གླིང་བཞི་བསྟན་པའི་འབྱུང་ཁུངས་ལས།[5] གཉིས་པ་ས་ཚིགས་དབུས་ནི་བོད་ཡུལ་ན་ཡོད་པས། གངས་ཏི་སེ་དང་མཚོ་མ་ཕམ་གཉིས་ཡིན་པར་ཞི་ཁྲོ་རྩ་འགྲེལ་ལས་གསུངས་སོ།། དེ་ལ་འོ་སྐོར་བོད་ཀྱི་རྒྱལ་ཁམས་འདི་ཡང་། དང་པོ་གནོད་སྦྱིན་གྱིས་དབང་བགྱིས་ཏེ། ཡུལ་གྱི་མིང་ནི། ཁ་རག་སྒོ་དགུ་བཏགས་སོ།། དེའི་དུས་སུ་བདུད་བོན་ཁ་སྡེ་འགྲིང་ཡུག་བྱུང་སྟེ། བདུད་ཀྱི་གོང་ན་གཤེན་གནན་པ་ལགས། བདུད་རོ་རོང་རྩོལ་པ་ལ་སོགས་པས་བཀུར་བསྟི་བོན་ལ་བྱས་པ་ལགས། དེ་ནས་སྲིན་པོས་དབང་བགྱིས་ཏེ། ཡུལ་གྱི་མིང་ཡང་སྲིན་ཡུལ་བྲག་ཚལ་གླིང་དགུ་བཏགས་སོ།། དེའི་དེ་སྲིན་བོན་བདུད་བོན་འདུལ་བོན་གཤེན་པོ་མུས་པའི་རྗེ་ཕུར་བྱུང་བ་ལ། སྲིན་སྐྱ་རེངས་འཕྲུག་མེད་ལ་སོགས་པས་བཀུར་བསྟི་བོན་ལ་བགྱིས་ཏེ། སྲིན་གོང་ན་བོན་གཤན་

པ་ལགས་སོ།། དེ་ནས་ཀླུས་དབང་བགྱིས་ཏེ། ཡུལ་གྱི་མིང་ཡང་ཀླུ་ཡུལ་ན་ར་སེང་སྔོན་དུ་བཏགས་སོ།། དུས་དེར་ཀླུ་བོན་དབྱར་སྣན་གྱིམ་བུ་བྱུང་སྟེ། ཀླུ་གཙུག་ཕུད་དང་དུན་ཙེ་ལ་སོགས་པས་བཀུར་བསྟི་བོན་ལ་བགྱིས་ཏེ། ཀླུའི་གོང་ན་གཤེན་རབ་གཉན་པ་ལགས་སོ།། དེ་ནས་མ་སངས་ཀྱིས་དབང་བགྱིས་ཏེ། ཡུལ་གྱི་མིང་ཡང་བོད་ཀ་གཡག་དྲུག་ཏུ་བཏགས་སོ།། དེའི་དུས་སུ་གཉན་བོན་ཐོག་ལྷ་ཁྲོལ་བ་དང་། གཉན་གསུམ་ཐོད་དེ་རྒྱལ་བ་ལ་སོགས་པ་བྱུང་ནས་མ་སངས་མཆེད་དྲུག་ལ་སོགས་པས་བཀུར་བསྟི་བོན་ལ་བགྱིས་ཏེ། མ་སངས་ཀྱི་གོང་ན་གཤེན་རབ་གཉན་པ་ལགས་སོ།། དེ་ནས་ཟ་རང་གི་བུ་བྲེད་སྐྱེས་དྲུག་གིས་དབང་བགྱིས་ཏེ། ཡུལ་གྱི་མིང་ཡང་བྲེས་ཡུལ་དབྱེ་ཆེན་སྟེ་བརྒྱད་དུ་བཏགས་སོ།། དེའི་དུས་སུ་སྟེ་བོད་བྲེད་མཁས་བཙན་པ་བྱུང་། སྐྱེས་སུ་རྩོལ་བོ་ལེགས་པས་བཀུར་བསྟི་བོན་ལ་བགྱིས་ཏེ། དེའི་གོང་ན་བོན་དང་གཤེན་གཉན་པ་ལགས་སོ།། དེ་ནས་སིལ་མ་བཅུ་གཉིས་ཀྱིས་དབང་གྱིས་བྱས་ཏེ། ཡུལ་གྱི་མིང་ཡང་རྗེས་པོ་ཁ་བརྒྱད་བྱ་བ་ལགས་སོ།། དེའི་དུས་སུ་བོན་ཐོད་དཀར་བྱུང་སྟེ། རྒྱལ་གྱིས་བཀུར་བསྟི་བོན་ལ་བགྱིས་ཏེ། རྒྱལ་གོང་ན་བོན་དང་གཤེན་གཉན་པ་ལགས་སོ།། ཞེས་གསུང་སྟེ། གོང་གསལ་ཡིག་ཆ་དེ་དག་ལས་མངའ་མཛད་བཅུ་དང་དྲུག་གི་ཁྲིད་ཙམ་ལས། བྱུང་རྩལ་གྱི་གོ་རིམ་དང་སྐབས་དེ་དང་དེ་དག་ཏུ་མཆོན་ཆ་གང་ཞིག་སྤྱོད་པ་དང་། ཡུལ་གྱི་མིང་ལ་གང་ཞིག་འདོགས་པ་སོགས་ཀྱང་ཕལ་ཆེར་མཐུན་པར་སྣང་ཞིང་། བོད་ཀྱི་མི་རྒྱུད་རིམ་པར་བྱུང་བ་དེ་དག་གི་ཁྲོད་དུ་རྒྱལ་ཕྲན་བཅུ་གཉིས་དང་། སིལ་མ་བཞི་བཅུ(འགའ་ཞིག་ཏུ་ཞེ་གཉིས་ཞེས་པའང་སྣང་)གྱིས་ཏེ། རུ་སྡེ་སོ་སོས་རང་འཚམས་ས་ཁུལ་བཙད་བཟུང་བྱས་ནས་ཕན་ཚུན་རྣ་ས་ཆུ་རྩོད་ཀྱིས་མཐར་འོ་ལྡེ་སྤུ་རྒྱལ་གྱིས་བོད་ཁམས་གཅིག་གྱུར་མ་བྱས་བར་དུ་རྒྱལ་ཕྲན་ཕན་ཚུན་འཁྲུག་ཅིང་རྩོད་པ་རྒྱུན་མར་བྱུང་བ་ཡིན་ཏེ། ལྡེའུ་ཆོས་འབྱུང་རྒྱས་པ་ལས།[6] དེ་ནས་གློ་བུར་རྒྱལ་པོའི་བྲོན་ལུགས་ནི།། མཚན་ནི་གཉའ་ཁྲི་བཙན་པོ་ཞེས་སུ་གྲགས།། མ་བྱོན་གོང་ནས་དབང་མཛད་བཅུ་གཉིས་རྣམས།། རིམ་པར་བྱུང་བས་ཕྱོགས་བཞིའི་དགྲ་མ་ཐུལ།། ཞེས་དང་། ཏུན་ཧོང་ཡིག་ཆར།[7] གནའ་ཡུལ་ཡུལ་ན་རྒྱལ་ཕྲན་དང་གློན་པོ་འདི་ལྟར་བབ་སྟེ། མི་མང་གི་རྗེ་ཡུལ་ཆེའི་བདག་བྱེད་བྱེད་པ་ལས་རྒྱལ་པོ་བཙན་པ་དང་བློན་པོ་མཛངས་པ་དགུ་ཆེ་བ་རྣམས་ཀྱིས་གཅིག་ཞེས་གཅིག་བརླག་སྟེ་འབངས་སུ་བཀུག་ན། མཐར་འོ་སྡེ་སྤུ་རྒྱལ་གྱི་དབུ་རྨོག་མ་ཐོབ། མར་ནི་ལྷ་ནར་གྱིས་མནརད། ཐུན་ནི་རྗེ་ཐུན་གྱིས་བཐུན་ཏེ་བཐུག་གོ། ཞེས་པ་འདིས་ཞེས་ནུས་སོ།།

མངའ་མཛད་དང་པོ། གནོད་སྦྱིན་ནག་པོས་དབང་བྱས་ཚུལ།

མཁས་པའི་དགའ་སྟོན་ལས། དང་པོར་གནོད་སྦྱིན་ནག་པོས་དབང་བྱས་ཏེ།། ཡུལ་གྱི་མིང་ཡང་བཟང་ཡུལ་རྒྱན་མེད་ཟེར།། མཆོན་ཆ་མདའ་གཞུ་དེ་ཡི་དུས་སུ་བྱུང་།། ཞེས་དང་། ལྡེའུ་ཆོས་འབྱུང་ལས། དང་པོ་གནོད་སྦྱིན་ནག་པོ་ཞེས་བྱ་བ་བྱུང་སྟེ། ཡུལ་གྱི་མིང་ཡང་བཟང་ཡུལ་རྒྱན་མེད་བྱ་བར་བཏགས།། ལག་ཆར་མདའ་གཞུ་འཕེན་པ་དེ་ནས་བྱུང་།། ཞེས་དང་། རྒྱལ་པོ་བཀའ་ཐང་ལས། དང་པོར་གནོད་སྦྱིན་ནག་པོས་དབང་བྱས་ཏེ།། ཡུལ་མིང་བདུད་ཡུལ་ཁ་རག་མགོ་དགུར་བཏགས།། སྔ་རྟགས་གཉེན་པོ་བཙན་པོ་དེ་ནས་བྱུང་།། ཞེས་གསུངས། གླིང་བཞི་བསྟན་པའི་འབྱུང་ཁུངས་ལས། དེ་ལ་འོ་སྐོར་བོད་ཀྱི་རྒྱལ་ཁམས་འདི་ཡང་། དང་པོ་

གནོད་སྦྱིན་གྱིས་དབང་བསྒྱིས་ཏེ། ཡུལ་གྱི་མིང་ནི། ཁ་རག་སྒྲོ་དགུ་བཏགས་སོ།། དེའི་དུས་སུ་བདུད་བོན་ཁ་སྡེ་འགྲིང་ཡུག་བྱུང་སྟེ། བདུད་ཀྱི་གོང་ན་གཤིན་གཉན་པ་ལགས། བདུད་རོ་རོང་རྩོལ་པ་ལ་སོགས་པས་བཀུར་བསྡི་བོན་ལ་བྱས་པ་ལགས། ཞེས་འབྱུང་། བོད་ཀྱི་ལོ་རྒྱུས་དེབ་ཐེར་རྣམས་སུ་གསལ་བ་ལྟར་ན།[8] བོད་ཀྱི་ཡུལ་འདི་ཆེས་སྔ་མོའི་དུས་སུ་མི་མ་ཡིན་རྣམས་ཀྱིས་དབང་སྒྱུར་བྱ་ཡུལ་ལམ་གནས་ཡུལ་ཞིག་ཡིན་པར་བཤད། དེ་ནི་བསྐལ་པ་ཡར་ཐོག་གི་སྐབས་བོད་ཡུལ་འདིར་འཛམ་གླིང་ན་སྣང་གྲགས་ཆེ་ལ་འཇིགས་སྣང་བྱེད་དགོས་པའི་རྒྱལ་ཐོག་འགའ་བྱུང་ཡོད་པ་སྟེ། གནོད་སྦྱིན་ནག་པོ། བདུད་པོ་རེ་ཏི་མགོ་ཡག སྲིན་པོ་གཉའ་རེངས་ཁྲག་མིག །ཀྲོག་ཀྲོག་འདྲེའི་རྒྱལ་པོ་ཟེར་བ་སོགས་རྒྱལ་རབས་མང་པོ་ཞིག་གི་རིང་ཆབ་སྲིད་དང་། དཔལ་འབྱོར། རིག་གནས་སོགས་གང་ཅིར་སྤྱོད་བཙན་གྱི་སྐབས་ལྟར་དར་རྒྱས་ཏ་ཅང་ཆེ་ལ། ལྷག་པར་དམག་དོན་གྱི་ཐད་ཟིལ་ཤུགས་ཆེ་བས་སུས་ཀྱང་འཐབ་པའི་ཡ་བོར་མ་འཕེར་ཏེ། ཐམས་ཅད་དངངས་ཤིང་སྐྲག་ནས་གནོད་སྦྱིན་དང་། བདུད་དང་། སྲིན་པོ་སོགས་སུ་བཏགས་ཏེ་མི་མ་ཡིན་གྱི་གྲས་སུ་བརྩིས། ཚན་རིག་པ་ཁ་ཤས་ཀྱིས་གནོད་སྦྱིན་ནག་པོ་ནི་ཚོ་པ་ཆུང་ཆུང་ཞིག་གི་དཔོན་པོ་འདྲ་ཞེས[9] བཤད་པ་ཡང་མི་བདེན་ཏེ། དེ་ལྟར་ན་གནོད་སྦྱིན་ནི་རྒྱ་གར་བས་མིའི་ཚད་ལས་བརྒལ་བའི་སྟོབས་ཤུགས་ཅན་ཞིག་ཏུ་བརྩི་དགོས་དོན་མེད། དཔེར་ན། ལྷའི་གདོན་རྣམས་དང་། ནས། གནོད་སྦྱིན་གྱི་གདོན་རྣམས་དང་།[10] ཞེས་དང་། ལྷ་ཡི་སྐད་དང་ཀླུ་དང་གནོད་སྦྱིན་སྐད།། གྲུལ་བུམ་དག་དང་མི་ཡི་སྐད་རྣམས་དང་།།[11] ཞེས་པ་ལྟར་གྱི་བང་རིམ་བསྒྲིགས་ནས་འཇིག་རྟེན་ན་སྟོབས་ཆེ་ཤོས་ནི་ལྷ་དང་། དེ་ནས་ཀླུ། དེ་ནས་གནོད་སྦྱིན་བཞག་པར་སྣང་ཞིང་། དེ་འདྲའི་གནོད་སྦྱིན་དེ་ནི་གཞན་སུ་ཡང་མིན་པར་བོད་ཁོ་ན་ཡིན་ཏེ། གནོད་སྦྱིན་ནི་བྱང་ཕྱོགས་སུ་ཡོད་པར་བཤད་ལ་དེ་ཡང་རྒྱ་གར་ནས་རྩིས་པ་དང་། གནོད་སྦྱིན་ཕྱོགས་ནི་བྱང་ཕྱོགས་ཀྱི་མངོན་བརྗོད་ཀྱང་ཡིན།[12] གནོད་སྦྱིན་དེ་དག་ལ་སྒྲོ་ཕྱུགས་གནག་ལུག་མང་པོ་ཡོད་པར་མཐོང་ནས་ནོར་ལྷ་ཡིན་པར་བསམ་སྟེ་མཚམས་རི་རྒྱ་གར་བས་གནོད་སྦྱིན་ནི་ནོར་ལྷའི་གྲལ་དུའང་བཞག་སྲོལ་ཡོད་པ་དང་།[13] ཁྱད་མཚར་བ་ཞིག་ལ་རྒྱ་གར་བས་གནམ་གྱི་དགུ་ཚིགས་ནི་གནོད་སྦྱིན་གྱི་ཁ་ཧླངས་རེད་ཅེས་ཟེར།[14] གྲང་ངར་གྱི་ནང་དུ་ཁ་ཧླངས་ནི་དགུ་ཚིགས་ཀྱི་མདོག་ལྟར་ཡོད་པས་བོད་ས་མཐོའི་གྲང་ངར་གྱི་ནང་ནས་གནོད་སྦྱིན་མང་པོས་དུས་གཅིག་ཏུ་ཁ་ཧླངས་བཏང་བ་དགུ་ཚིགས་སུ་འགྱུར་གྱི་ཡོད་པ་རེད་བསམས་ནས་གནོད་སྦྱིན་གྱི་སྟོབས་ཤུགས་ལ་སྐྲག་སྣང་བྱེད། ཡང་། གནོད་སྦྱིན་ལག་ན་དབྱུག་པ་ཐོགས།། ནོར་སྐྱོང་གདོན་གྱི་བདག་པོ་སྟེ།། བྱང་ཕྱོགས་གདོན་གྱི་ཚོགས་བཅས་ལ།། མཆོད་ཅིང་བསྟོད་དེ་ཕྱག་ཀྱང་འཚལ།།[15] ཞེས་ནོར་སྐྱོང་སྟེ་ཛྫ་བོའི་སྐད་དུའང་འབོད་ལ། མཆོད་པ་དང་བསྟོད་པ་དང་ཕྱག་འཚལ་བ་སོགས་བྱེད་དོ།། གནོད་སྦྱིན་ནག་པོ་ཞེས་པ་ནི་སྦྲ་ནག་པོའི་ནང་བསྡད་པས་སམ། དོམ་ནག་གི་པགས་པའི་ང་ཁོ་གྱོན་པའམ་དེ་སྐབས་རི་ལྡེའི་གོས་ཀྱང་གྱོན་སྲོལ་ཡོད་པས་ནག་པོའི་སྒྲ་སྒྱུར་བ་ཡིན་གྱི། བོད་ཀྱིས་ལས་བརྒལ་ཏེ་སོང་ན་གནོད་སྦྱིན་གྱི་གྲིབ་མ་ཙམ་ཡང་རྙེད་མི་ཐུབ། ད་དུང་གནའ་བོའི་བོད་ལ་རྟ་ཧ་ཅང་འབེལ་པོ་ཡོད་ཅིང་དམག་དཔུང་ཐམས་ཅད་རྟ་དམག་ཡིན་པ་དང་། དེ་བཞིན་གནའ་བོའི་རྒྱ་ནག་པས་ཐོན་སྐྱེད་གཙོ་བོ་གླང་ལ་བརྟེན་པ་དང་། རྒྱ་གར་ལྷོ་ཕྱོགས་སུ་མ་ཧེ་ལ་བརྟེན་པས། ཤར་ཕྱོགས་བརྒྱ་སྦྱིན་གླང་ལ་ཆིབས།། ལྷོ་ཕྱོགས་གཤིན་རྗེ་མ་ཧེར་ཆིབས།། བྱང་ཕྱོགས་གནོད་སྦྱིན་རྟ་ལ་ཆིབས།། ཞེས་ཀྱང་གསུངས་སྣང་། གནོད་སྦྱིན་ནག་པོ་ཞེས་པ་ནི་མིང་འདོགས་ལས་འོས་མེད་པས། མིང་དངོས་ནི་རྣམ་ཐོས་ལྷ་བུ་ཡིན་ཚོད་ལ། དེའི་བུ་ལ་

རྣམ་ཐོས་ཀྱི་བུ་དང་རྣམ་ཐོས་ཀྱི་སྲས་ཞེས་བཤད་དམ་སྙམ་སྟེ། རྣམ་ཐོས་ཀྱི་བུ་ནི་གནོད་སྦྱིན་གྱི་དཔོན་ནམ་རྒྱལ་པོ་ཡིན་པར་བཤད་པའི་ཕྱིར་རོ།།[16] རྒྱལ་རྩེ་རྫོང་ཁོངས་ན་གནོད་སྦྱིན་གངས་བཟང་ཞེས་པའི་གངས་རི་མཐོ་ཚད་ཕི་ཀྲི་༧༡༥༠ ལྷག་ཡོད་པ་དེ་གནོད་སྦྱིན་རྟ་བདག་བརྒྱད་ཀྱི་ནང་ནས་གནོད་སྦྱིན་གངས་བཟང་ཡིན་ཀྱང་ཟེར་སོང་། སྐབས་དེར་རྒྱལ་ས་གངས་རི་དེའི་ཞོལ་ཞིག་ཏུ་ཡོད་དམ་སྙམ་སྟེ། རི་དེའི་མིང་གིས་བྱས་པའི་གནོད་སྦྱིན་དང་། གངས་བཟང་གི་བཟང་གིས་བརྟས་དྭངས་ནས་ཇི་ཙམ་ཁྱབ་པའི་མངའ་ཁོངས་ལ་བཟང་ཡུལ་ཞེས་ཐོགས་སམ་སྙམ་སྟེ་དཔྱད་པར་བྱ་བའི་གནས་སོ།། ཡང་མཁས་པ་འགའ་ཞིག་གིས་སྟོད་མངའ་རིས་ཀྱི་ཟངས་དཀར་ལ་ངོས་འཛིན་བྱེད་པའང་སྣང་ཞིང་། མངའ་མཛད་ཕྱི་མ་འགའ་ཞིག་རྒྱལ་ས་ལྷར་བ་ཕལ་ཆེ་བ་མངའ་རིས་ཕྱོགས་སུ་ཡིན་པར་བལྟས་ན་ཟངས་དཀར་ལ་ངོས་འཛིན་གནང་བ་ཡང་རྒྱུ་མཚན་ཆེ་བ་སྙམ། རྒྱ་གར་གྱི་སླན་ངག་པ་ནག་མོ་ཁོལ་གྱི་སྤྲིན་གྱི་ཕོ་ཉ་ལས། འབངས་མི་ཞིག་གནོད་སྦྱིན་གྱི་བཀའ་ཆད་ཕོག་ནས་བྱང་ཕྱོགས་ནས་ལྷོ་ཕྱོགས་ར་མའི་རི་བོར་རྒྱངས་འབུད་བྱས་ཚུལ་ལས་མགོ་རྩོམ་པའི་གནོད་སྦྱིན་ཡང་རྒྱ་གར་ནས་རྩིས་པའི་བྱང་ཕྱོགས་བོད་ཀྱི་མངའ་མཛད་གནོད་སྦྱིན་ནག་པོ་ལ་གོ་བའི་བབ་ཏ་ཙང་ཉེ་བ་སེམས་ཏེ། དེ་སྔོན་ཕྲན་གྱིས་འདི་ཡང་བོད་ནས་ཡིན་སྙིད་སྙམ་ཚུལ་བྲིས་མོད། འདི་ལྷ་ཊའི་པཎྜི་ཏ་མཁས་པ་འགའ་ཞིག་ལ་གཏུགས་འདྲི་ཞུས་པས། འདིའི་བྱང་ཕྱོགས་ནི་དེང་སང་གི་ཀ་ཤིམྨིར་གྱི་ཡུལ་རེད། ཅེས་གསུངས་ཤིང་། སྙན་ཚིག་དེའི་འགྲེལ་བའི་ནང་དུའང་ཀ་ཤིམྨིར་རང་འབྱུངས་བས། ཅེས་ཀྱང་ཁོ་ཚོ་རྒྱུས་ཆེ་བས་འདིའི་བྱང་ཕྱོགས་ནི་བོད་པ་མིན་པ་འདྲ། གནོད་སྦྱིན་ནག་པོའི་རྒྱལ་རྒྱུད་ཀྱིས་སྲིད་དབང་རིང་མཐར་ཇི་ཙམ་གནས་ཡོད་མེད་ཤོད་པར་དཀའ་ཡང་། ཉུང་མཐར་ལོ་ངོ་བརྒྱ་ཕྲག་ཁ་ཤས་གནས་པར་དཔོག་ཐུབ་སྟེ། ཡུད་ཙམ་ཞིག་གིས་གནོད་སྦྱིན་ཞེས་ཏ་ཙང་སྐད་གྲགས་ཆེན་པོ་དེ་ལྷ་བུར་འབྱུང་བ་དཀའ་བའི་ཕྱིར་རོ།།

མངའ་མཛད་གཉིས་པ། བདུད་རི་ཏི་མགོ་གཡག་གིས་དབང་བྱས་ཚུལ།

མཁས་པའི་དགའ་སྟོན་ལས། དེ་ནས་རི་ཏི་མགོ་གཡག་བདུད་ཀྱིས་བྱས།། མིང་ཡང་བདུད་ཡུལ་ཁ་རག་རོང་དགུར་བཏགས།། སྟ་རེ་དགྲ་སྟ་དེ་ཡི་དུས་སུ་བྱུང་།།ཞེས་དང་། མཁས་པ་ལྡེའུ་ཆོས་འབྱུང་ལས། དེ་ནས་རི་ཏི་མགོ་གཡག་བདུད་ཀྱིས་བྱས།། མིང་ཡང་བདུད་ཡུལ་ཁ་རག་རོང་དགུར་བཏགས།། སྟ་རེ་དགྲ་སྟ་དེ་ཡི་དུས་སུ་བྱུང་།། ཞེས་དང་།

རྒྱལ་པོའི་བཀའ་ཐང་ལས། དེ་ནས་བདུད་དང་སྲིན་པོས་དབང་བྱས་ཏེ། མིང་ཡང་ལྷ་འདྲེ་གཉིས་ཀྱི་ཡུལ་དུ་བཏགས། ཞེས་བདུད་དང་སྲིན་པོ་གཉིས་སྲིབ་སྦྲོར་མཉམ་སྒྲིག་བྱས་ནས་གསུངས་འདུག། གླིང་བཞི་བསྟན་པའི་འབྱུང་ཁུངས་ལས་མངའ་མཛད་འདི་ཉིད་མི་གསལ། དེ་ཡང་། གནོད་སྦྱིན་ནག་པོའི་རྒྱལ་རྒྱུད་ཀྱི་སྲིད་དབང་ཉམས་པ་ན། སླར་ཡང་འཛམ་གླིང་ན་དེ་ལས་ཀྱང་སྙན་གྲགས་ཆེ་བའི་རྒྱལ་ཁབ་ཅིག་བྱུང་བར་རྒྱལ་པོའི་མིང་ལ་རི་ཏི་མགོ་ཡག་དང་། སྲས་མོའི་མིང་ལ་དྲི་ལྡན་མ་ཞེས་ཟེར། རྒྱལ་པོ་དེ་ལ་ལྷག་པར་མཚོན་ཆ་དགྲ་སྟ། ཐོ་རིལ། སྟ་རེ་ཡུ་རིང་སོགས་ཐོགས་པའི་དམག་གི་དཔུང་ཆེན་པོ་ལུས་ལ་རེ་ལྡེའི་གོས་དང་། མགོ་དང་མཆོན་ཆའི་སྐྱེད་པར་བལ་དང་རྔ་མ་ལ་ཙག་བྱུགས་པས་བརྒྱན་ཏེ་རྔམས་ཟིལ་ཆེ་ལ་དམར་ཟིང་ངེ་བ་ཞིག་ཡོད་

དེ།[17] དེང་སང་ཡང་རྒྱ་དཀར་ནག་སོགས་ཀྱིས་བདུད་ཀྱི་ལྷད་མོ་འཁྲབ་དུས་གྱོན་པ་ནག་པོ། དགྲ་སྔ་ཐོགས་པ་དམར་ཟྲིང་ངེ་བ་ཞིག་བྱེད་སྲོལ་ཡོད་པ་ཡང་སྔར་བོད་ཀྱི་བདུད་དམག་དེ་དག་གི་ཆ་ལུགས་ལའང་སྐྲག་ཐག་ཆོད་པའི་བག་ཆགས་ཀྱི་ལྷག་མ་ད་དུང་ལུས་པ་ཞིག་ལོས་ཡིན་སྙམ།

ཡང་ན་རེ་ཧྲི་མགོ་ཡག་ནི། གནོད་སྦྱིན་ནག་པོའི་མངའ་ཁོངས་ཀྱི་ཆོ་པ་ཞིག་གམ་བློན་པོ་ཞིག་ཡིན་ལ། རང་གི་རྒྱལ་པོ་ལ་ངོ་ལོག་བརྒྱབ་ནས་སྲས་མོ་དྲི་ལྡན་མའི་དཔུང་གིས་ཡང་ཡང་དམག་འཁྲུག་བསློངས་པ་ལ་བརྟེན་ནས་སྲིད་དབང་ཐོབ་པ་ཞིག་ཡིན་ནམ་ཡང་སྙམ་སྟེ། འདིའི་སྲས་མོ་དང་གནོད་སྦྱིན་གྱི་རྒྱལ་པོ་གཉིས་དམག་འཁྲུག་བྱས་པའི་ལོ་རྒྱུས་ཤིག་ཀྱང་ཡོད་འདུག་པའི་ཕྱིར་རོ།། འདི་དག་དམག་འཁྲུག་བྱས་པའི་གཏམ་རྒྱུད་རིག་བྱེད་ཀྱི་སྙིང་འདྲ་པོ་ཞིག་བླ་མ་འགའི་ཞལ་ལས་ཐོས་མྱོང་ཡང་མཐོང་མ་མྱོང་། གལ་སྲིད་དེ་འདྲ་ཞིག་མཐོང་ན་བོད་ཀྱི་གནའ་བོའི་ལོ་རྒྱུས་ལ་དཔྱད་གཞིའི་རིན་ཐང་འགངས་ཆེར་ལྡན་ཡོད་པར་ཐེ་ཚོམ་མེད། གང་ལྟར་འཛམ་གླིང་འདིའི་ཐོག་ལྷོ་འདུལ་བྱུང་འཐབ་ཀྱི་དམག་འཁྲུག་ཐམས་ཅད་ནང་སུས་ཀྱང་འགྲན་ཟླ་མེད་པས་ཀུན་གྱིས་ཐད་དེ་བདུད་དུ་རྩིས་ནས་འཐབ་པའི་རེ་བ་ལྷ་བཞག་མིང་ཙམ་ཐོས་པས་སྐྲག་སྣང་བྱེད་དགོས་པ་ཞིག་ཏུ་གྱུར། ལྷག་པར་སྲས་མོ་དྲི་ལྡན་མས་དམག་དཔོན་བྱས་ནས་འཛམ་གླིང་ཤར་ནུབ་ཀུན་ཏུ་དམག་བཀྱེས་ཏེ། འཐབ་ན་མི་རྒྱལ་བ་མེད་པའི་རྒྱལ་ཁ་བསྟུད་མར་བླངས་པས་སྙན་པའི་གྲགས་པ་ཕྱོགས་བཅུར་ཁྱབ་སྟེ་དམག་ཟོར་རྒྱལ་མོ་ཞེས་པའི་མཚན་གསོལ། འཆར་ཡན་གྱི་རྟོག་པའི་བག་ཆགས་ཤུགས་ཆེར་ལྡན་ཞིང་། ལྷ་འདྲེ་གདོན་བགེགས་རྣམས་ནི་འཇིགས་སྐྲག་གི་བསམ་བློས་ཕར་བཏགས་པ་ཞིག་མིན་པར་ཚུགས་ཐུབ་ལེང་ངེ་བ་ཞིག་འཛིན་པ་དག་གིས་དམོད་པ་དང་ཁྲེལ་རྒོད་སོགས་བྱེད་སྲིད་མོད། ལེགས་པར་བསམས་ན་བསླལ་པ་ཡ་ཐོག་གི་བུད་མེད་གྲགས་ཅན་ཐམས་ཅད་ཀྱི་ཆེ་བ་ལྷ་མོ་འདིའི་སྟེང་དུ་བསྡུས་ནས་བཤད་ཡོད་པ་སྟེ། ལྷ་ཡུལ་ན་གྲགས་ཆེ་བ་བརྒྱ་སྦྱིན་གྱི་བུ་མོ་ཡིད་འོང་མ་དང་། གཙུག་ནའི་བུ་མོ་ནོར་འཛིན་མ། གནོད་སྦྱིན་ལ་གྲགས་ཆེ་བ་གནོད་སྦྱིན་གངས་བཟང་གི་བུ་མོ་གཟི་ལེགས་མ་དང་། རྒྱ་གར་ཡུལ་ན་མ་མོ་ཁྲ་ཞམ་ཀུ་རུ་མ། རྒྱ་ནག་ཡུལ་ན་རྒྱ་མོ་སྒྲོན་མོ་མཁྱེན་བཟང་མ། བོད་ཀྱི་ཡུལ་ན་མ་གཅིག་དཔལ་ལྡན་ཨ་ཕྱི་མ་སོགས་སྐྱེ་བ་སྤུ་ཕྱི་དུ་མ་བཞེས་ཚུལ་དང་འབྲེལ་ནས་ཆོས་ལུགས་པ་དག་གིས་བསྔོད་པ་རྩོམ་པའང་མང་མོད།[18]

བདུད་རེ་སྦྲེ་མགོ་གཡག་གི་བུ་མོ་དྲི་ལྡན་མའི་གནས་ཡུལ་ནི། ཇི་སྐད་དུ་ཛེ་དགེ་འདུན་རྒྱ་མཚོས་[19] འདི་ནས་བྱང་ཤར་མཚམས་ཕྱེད་ནས། །རྩྭ་རྒུ་ཤིང་སོགས་མེད་པ་ཡི། །ལུང་མང་བརྒྱལ་བའི་ཕ་རོལ་ན། །བྱང་རི་དམར་པོ་ཧྲམས་ཤིང་འཁྱིངས། །བྱང་ལམ་དམང་པོ་གྲུ་མ་གྲི། །གཙན་གཟན་མང་པོ་མདུར་རྒྱུག་བྱེད། །འདྲི་བྱ་སྣ་ཚོགས་སླད་སྒྲོག་ཅིང་། །གནམ་ལྕགས་སེར་ཆེན་ཤ་ར་ར། །དུང་གི་བུ་ཡུག་ཆིལ་ལི་ལི། །མི་ལེ་དུང་གི་མཚོ་ནང་ན། །ཞེས་པ་འདི་དག་ཀྱང་། རྒྱ་གར་རྡོ་རྗེ་གདན་ནས་རྩིས་པའི་བྱང་ཤར་དུ། ལ་ལུང་རི་བྲག་མང་པོ་བརྒྱལ་བའི་ཕ་རོལ་དབྱར་དུས་ཐོག་སེར་རྒོད་ཅིང་དགུན་དུས་ཁ་བ་བུ་ཡུག་འཚུབ་པའི་ཞིང་ཁམས། ད་ལྟའི་རྒྱལ་དུ་ཡོངས་གྲགས་སུ་ལྷ་མོའི་བླ་མཚོ་ཞེས་པ་འདི་ཉིད་ཁོ་ནར་ངེས་ཤིང་། མི་རོ་རྟ་རོ་བཅལ་དུ་བཀྲམས། །མི་ཁག་རྟ་ཁྲག་མཚོ་རུ་འཁྱིལ། །མ་མོ་འབུམ་དང་ཤ་ཟ་སྟོང་། །ཁྲག་འཐུང་བྱེ་བའི་ཚོགས་འཁོར་རྒྱས།[20] །ཞེས་པའང་ཤ་ཁྲག་ཟོས་སུ་བྱེད་ཅིང་མི་བསད་ཁྲག་སྦྱོར་ལ་འདུ་སྲིན་གསོད་པའི་རྩིས་སུ་མི་གཏོང་པའི་འཁོར་འབངས་འབུམ་ཕྲག་དུ་མ་ཡོད་པ་དང་། དེ་ཡང་སྐྱེས་པ་ཕོ་གཅིག་པོ་མིན་པར་མི་གསོད་ཁྲག་སྦྱོར་གྱི་ལས་ལ་

ཞུགས་མཁན་ནག་དམག་ཀྱང་འབུམ་ཕྲག་དུ་མ་ཡོད་པ་ཤེས་ཐུབ་སླམ། བསེ་མཁར་སྣུག་པོ་གྲུ་བཞི་པ།། ཞེས་པ་ནས། རྨང་གཞི་ནག་པོ་ལྷུགས་ལས་བྱས།། ཞེས་པ་འདིས་སྐབས་དེ་ནས་རྫོ་ནག་གི་རྨང་གཞི་བྱས་པའི་སྟེང་དུ་ཀ་ར་དགུ་ལྡན་གྱི་སྦྲ་ནག་གྲུ་བཞི་པ། ཟུར་བཞི་ལ་ཚལ་གྱི་རྩི་བྱུགས་པ། ཁ་བད་ལ་ས་སེར་གྱི་རྩི་བྱུགས་པའི་ནང་དུ་སྡོད་གནས་བྱས་པ་འདྲ་སྟེ། རྗེ་དགེ་འདུན་རྒྱ་མཚོས།[21] བདུད་ལ་དབང་བསྒྱུར་བདུད་མོ་དཔལ་འབར་མ། །རི་ཏི་མགོ་གཡག་བུ་མི་དྲི་ལྡན་མ། །བདུད་མཁར་རྩེ་དགུའི་གནས་ཀྱི་གཙོ་མོ་སྟེ། །ཞེས་པ་དང་ཡང་འཁོར་བ་སྣང་ངོ་། །རྨང་གཞི་ནག་པོ་ལྷུགས་ཞེས་པའང་རྫོ་ནག་ཙམ་ལ་གོ་དགོས་པ་སླམ། གཞལ་ཡས་དེ་ཡི་ནང་ཚོད་ན། །མ་མོ་ཀུན་གྱི་རྒྱལ་མོ་བཞུགས།། ཞེས་པ་འདིས་བདུད་རྒྱལ་ཡབ་ཡུམ་བཞུགས་ཡུལ་གྱི་རྒྱལ་ས་ལྷེ་བའང་དེ་བ་རང་ལ་ཡིན་སྲིད་སླམ། མདོར་ན་ཡུམ་མོ་འདིའི་དམག་གི་སྟོབས་ཤུགས་ལ་བརྟེན་ནས་གནོད་སྦྱིན་ནག་པོའི་རྒྱལ་སྲིད་ལ་མཆོན་ཆ་དང་དམག་འཁྲུགས་ཀྱིས་བཞི་ཤད་བཏབ་སྟེ། སྲིད་ཀྱི་རྫུས་ཡོངས་རྫོགས་བདུད་རི་ཏི་མགོ་གཡག་གིས་བཟུང་། ས་ཞིང་སོ་ནམ་དང་ཐོན་སྐྱེད་འཛུགས་བསྐྲུན་དམིགས་བསལ་བ་གང་ཡང་མེད་པས། ཟས་སུ་ཤ་ཁྲག་ཁོ་ན་ལ་རོལ། གོས་སུ་རི་སྐྱེས་སྤྱོག་ཆགས་ཀྱི་པགས་རིགས་གོན། ལས་སུ་མི་གསོད་ཁྲག་སྦྱོར་ཁོ་ན་ལ་གོམས་པས། རིགས་ལ་བདུད་ཀྱི་རིགས་དང་། ཡུལ་གྱི་མིང་ཡང་བདུད་ཡུལ་ཁ་རག་རོང་དགུར་བཏགས་པར་སེམས་སོ། །

རི་ཏི་མགོ་གཡག་གི་རྗེས་སུ་མུ་མཐུད་རང་གི་བུ་མོ་དྲི་ལྡན་མས་སྲིད་སྐྱོང་། འདིས་དབང་བསྒྱུར་བྱས་པའི་མཐའ་མཇུག་ཏུ་རང་གི་བློན་པོའི་གྲས་ནས་སྲིན་པོ་མཉའ་རེངས་ཁྲག་མེད་ཀྱིས་གྱེན་ལངས་དམག་འཐབ་བྱས་ཏེ། རྒྱལ་སྲིད་ལ་ཐམ་ཉེས་བཏང་། བདུད་ཀྱི་རྫུས་ཡོངས་སུ་ཤོར་ཏེ་མཐར་རི་ཏི་མགོ་གཡག་གི་སྲས་མོ་དྲི་ལྡན་མ་རང་ཉིད་ཀྱང་སྲིན་པོས་གསོན་བཟུང་ཐོག་བཙོན་འཇུག་བྱས། རྗེ་དགེ་འདུན་རྒྱ་མཚོས།[22] སྲིན་པོའི་གཙོ་མོ་མཛད་ཙན། །ཞབས་ལ་ལྕགས་སྒྲོགས་རྒྱན་དུ་བྱས།། ཞེས་པ་ཡང་དོན་ལ་སྲིན་པོས་བཙོན་དུ་བཟུང་ནས་རྐང་ལག་ལ་ལྕགས་སྒྲོགས་བརྒྱབ་པ་ཞིག་ཡིན་ཡང་། སྲིན་པོའི་གཙོ་མོ་མཛད་ཙན། ཞེས་རབ་བཏགས་ཀྱིས་བསྟོད་པ་ཡིན་ནམ་སླམ།

གསུམ་པ། སྲིན་པོ་མཉའ་རེངས་ཁྲག་མེད་ཀྱིས་དབང་བྱས་ཚུལ།

ཆོས་འབྱུང་མཁས་པའི་དགའ་སྟོན་ལས། དེ་ནས་སྲིན་པོ་མཉའ་རེངས་ཁྲག་མེད་བྱས། །ཡུལ་མིང་སྲིན་པོ་ནག་པོ་དགུ་ཡུལ་ཟེར། །སྲིན་མོ་རྐང་དང་སྒྲོགས་གཉིས་ལག་ཆ་བྱུང་།། ལྡེའུ་ཆོས་འབྱུང་ལས། གསུམ་པ་མཉའ་རེང་ཕྲག་མེད་སྲིན་གྱིས་བྱས། །ཡུལ་གྱི་མིང་ཡང་ནག་པོ་དགུ་དུལ་ཟེར། །ལག་ཆར་སྲིན་མོ་རྐང་དང་སྒྲོགས་གཉིས་བྱུང་།། བོན་གྱི་ཤེལ་བྲག་མའི་གཏེར་བོན་ལས།[23] དེ་ནས་སྲིན་པོས་དབང་བགྱིས་ཏེ། ཡུལ་གྱི་མིང་ཡང་སྲིན་ཡུལ་བྲག་ཚལ་གླིང་དགུ་བཏགས་སོ།། དེའི་དེ་སྲིན་བོན་བདུད་བོན་འདུལ་བོན་གཤེན་པོ་མུས་པའི་རྫི་ཕྱུར་བྱུང་བ་ལ། སྲིན་སྐྲ་རེངས་འཕྲུག་མེད་ལ་སོགས་པས་བཀུར་བསྟི་བོན་ལ་བགྱིས་ཏེ། སྲིན་གོང་ན་བོན་གཉན་པ་ལགས་སོ།། ཞེས་འབྱུང་།

གསུམ་པ་སྲིན་པོ་མཉའ་རེངས་ཁྲག་མེད་ཀྱིས་དབང་བྱས་ཚུལ་ནི། བདུད་རི་སྟེ་མགོ་གཡག་གི་ཆབ་སྲིད་ཀྱི་རྫུས་ཐ་མ་དེ་རང་གི་བློན་པོ་སྲིན་པོ་མཉའ་རེངས་ཁྲག་མེད་ལ་ཤོར། དེ་ཡང་སྲིན་པོ་ནི་ཤ་ཁྲག་ལ་རོལ་བའི་

སྲོག་ཆགས་ཆུང་ངུའི་རིགས་ལ་སྲིན་འབུ་ཟེར་ཞིང་ཆེན་པོའི་རིགས་ལ་སྲིན་པོ་ཞེས་དོན་གྱིས་ཐོབ་པར་སེམས། རང་རེ་ལྷ་འདྲེ་ལ་གོམས་པ་ཆེས་པ་ཕལ་བོ་ཆེས་སྲིན་པོ་ཟེར་དུས་ཁ་གདངས་པ། མཆེ་བ་བཙིགས་པ། མདོག་ནག་པ། མིག་དམར་བ། སྙིང་རྗེ་མེད་པ། མིའི་སྲོག་དབུགས་ལེན་མཁན་གྱི་གཟུགས་མེད་གདོན་འདྲེ་འདྲ་བ་ཞིག་རྟོག་པའི་འཆར་སྣང་ཁྲ་ལམ་མེར་ཤར་སྲིད་མོད། མཆིམས་ནམ་མཁའ་གྲགས་ཀྱི་མཛོད་འགྲེལ་མངོན་པའི་རྒྱན་ལས།[24] སྲིན་པོ་ནི་མིའི་བྱེ་བྲག་ཏུ་གསུངས་ཤིང་། མིའི་བྱེ་བྲག་ཇི་ལྟ་བུ་ཞིག་ལ་གོ་སྙམ་ན། ཟས་སུ་ཤ་རྗེན་ཟ་བ། གོས་སུ་པགས་རིགས་གྱོན་པ། ལས་སུ་སྲོག་གཅོད་ལ་གོམས་པ། གདོང་གི་མདོག་དམར་བ། སྐད་ཀྱི་གདངས་མཛེར་བ། མཚན་མོ་འགྲོ་བ་ལ་མི་མཛེར་པ་བཅས་ཡིན་ལ། ཚིག་འགའ་ཞིག་གི་ནང་དུ།[25] སྲིན་པོ་ཤ་རྗེན་ཟ་བ་དང་།།ལྡོན་ཤིང་གན་པ་སོགས་གནས་དང་།།ཞེས་སྲིན་པོ་ནི་ཟས་སུ་ཤ་རྗེན་པ་ཟ་མཁན་ཞིག་ཡིན་པ་བསྟན་འདུག་པ་ལྟར། རང་རེའི་མེས་པོ་སྔ་མ་དེ་ཚོའི་སྐབས་ས་ཞིང་སོ་ནམ་གྱི་ཐོན་སྐྱེད་མ་དར་བ་དང་རང་བྱུང་ཤིང་འབྲས་སོགས་ཀྱང་དབྱར་དགུན་ལ་ལྟོས་ཤིང་སྤྱོད་མཁན་མང་བས་འདང་ཐབས་མེད་སྐབས། ཤ་ཁྲག་མི་སྤྱོད་ཐབས་མེད་ཡིན་ལ། སྐབས་དེར་མེ་ཡི་བེད་སྤྱོད་ཀྱང་གཏོང་ཤེས་པའི་ལག་རྩལ་མེད་སྐབས་ཤ་རྗེན་ཟ་སྲོལ་བྱུང་བ་ལ་རྒྱུ་མཚན་ཤིན་ཏུ་ལྡན་ཏེ། དེའི་བག་ཆགས་ནི་ད་ལྟའི་བར་རང་རེ་བོད་དུ་དར་སྣང་བ་འདིས་ཀྱང་བདེན་དཔང་བྱེད་དོ་སྙམ། ཤ་ཁྲག་རྗེན་པ་ཟ་འཐུང་བྱས་པ་ལས་གདོང་རིས་དམར་པོ་ཆགས་པ་ཡང་དོན་དང་མཐུན་པ་ཡིན་པས་རང་རེ་ལ་ཐང་ཡིག་སོགས་སུ་སྲིན་པོ་གདོང་དམར་[26]ཞེས་བྲིས་འདུག་པ་འདིས་ཀྱང་གནའ་བོའི་དུས་ནས་བོད་ལ་སྲིན་པོ་ཞེས་འབོད་སྲོལ་བྱུང་ཡོད་པའི་བདེན་དཔང་བྱེད་ནུས་སྙམ། ཡང་སྲིན་པོ་ལ་འབོད་སྒྲོག་[27]ཞེས་སྟོན་གྱི་འཕགས་བོད་མཁས་པའི་གསུང་རྩོམ་དུ་མའི་ནང་གསལ་བ་ལྟར། སྐབས་དེར་རང་རེ་ཡབ་མེས་པོ་ཚོ་འཚོ་སྐྱོད་བྱེད་སའི་རི་བྲག་སྤང་ཐང་གང་སར་སྐབས་འགར་ཇག་ཚོགས་དང་རྐུ་མ་འཇོང་བ་དང་། གཅན་གཟན་རི་དྭགས་འཚེ་བ་ཅན་དུ་མ་ཚོ་བའི་ནང་ཐོལ་བྱུང་གིས་འཛུལ་བ་སོགས་བྱུང་དུས། ཚོ་བ་དེར་གནས་སྡོད་བྱེད་མཁན་ཚོས་ཉེན་ཁ་དེ་ལས་སྐྱོབ་ཆེད་ཉེ་འགྲམ་གྱི་ཚོ་བ་གཞན་དང་གཞན་གྱིས་གོ་བའི་སྐད། ཨ་ཧི་ཧི་དང་ཀི་ཧི་ཧི་ཞེས་འབོད་སྐད་ཆེན་པོ་སྒྲོག་སྲོལ་དར་བས། འབོད་སྒྲོག་ཙམ་ཟེར་སྲོལ་བྱུང་འདུག་པའང་དོན་ལ་ཤིན་ཏུ་འགྲོར། མཁས་པ་དོན་གྲུབ་རྒྱལ་གྱིས་ཀྱང་[28]རང་རེ་ལ་བོད་ཅེས་བཏགས་པའི་རྒྱུ་མཚན་ཐད་འགྲེལ་བཤད་དེ་ག་རང་གསུངས་འདུག་པ་དང་ཡང་མཐུན་པ་སྙམ། ད་དུང་མངོན་བརྗོད་རྣམས་སུ་སྲིན་པོ་ལ་མཚན་མོར་རྒྱུ་བ་ཞེས་སུ་བཏགས་འདུག་པའང་བོད་ལ་མཚན་འགྲུལ་གྱི་ལུགས་སྲོལ་ཤས་ཆེ་བ་དང་། ལྷག་པར་མཚན་མོར་འབོད་སྐད་སྒྲོག་ཚུལ་བཤད་པ་ནི་དེ་བས་ཀྱང་དོན་ལ་འགྲོར་ཏེ། རྐུན་ཇག་དང་གཅན་གཟན་བཙུམ་པོ་དག་མཚན་མོར་ཡོང་པ་ཆོས་ཉིད་ཡིན་ལ། སྐབས་དེ་དང་བསྟུན་ནས་ཉེན་སྐྱོབ་ཀྱི་འབོད་སྐད་ཆེན་པོ་རྒྱག་སྲོལ་ཡོད་པ་ནི་བཤད་ག་ལ་དགོས། དེས་ན་སྔོན་གྱི་མཁས་པ་ཚོས་བྲིས་པའི་སྲིན་པོའི་མཚན་ཉིད་དང་ཁྱད་ཆོས་ཕལ་བོ་ཆེ་རང་རེའི་སྔོན་གྱི་ཡབ་མེས་ཚོར་ལྡན་པས། སྲིན་པོས་དབང་བྱས་ཞེས་པའང་རང་རེའི་ཡབ་མེས་ཀྱི་ཚོ་བ་གཅིག་གིས་ཡུལ་ལུང་དབང་བསྒྱུར་བྱས་པ་རང་ལས་གཞན་དུ་གོ་ས་གང་ཡང་མེད།

སྲིན་པོ་ནག་པོ་དགུ་ཡུལ་གྱི་གནས་ཡུལ་གཙོ་བོ་ནི། འབྲི་གུང་གདན་རབས་སོ་བཞི་པ་ཆུང་ཚང་ཆོས་ཀྱི་བློ་གྲོས་ཀྱིས།[29] གྲོང་ཁྱེར་སུམ་བརྩེགས་སམ་པུ་རི་ཁའི་གྲོང་ཁྱེར་ཞེས། སྟོན་སྲིན་པོ་ལང་ཀའི་རྒྱལ་པོ་མགྲིན་བཅུ་པའི་གནས་ཀྱང་མངའ་རིས་སྐོར་གསུམ་གྱི་ནང་ཚན་པུར་རང་འདི་ཡིན་པར་ལུང་རིགས་གཉིས་ཀྱིས

བསྒྲུབས་འདུག་པར་བལྟས་ན། སྔོན་གྱི་མཁས་པ་མང་པོའི་གསུང་རྩོམ་ནང་སྲིན་པོའི་གནས་ཞེས་ཡང་དང་ཡང་དུ་འབྱུང་བའི་ཁུངས་ནི་བོད་རང་ཡིན་པ་འདྲ་ཞིང་། སྲིན་པོའི་གནས་ལྷོ་ནུབ་ཏུ་ཡིན་པར་བཤད་པ་ཡང་། བོད་ཀྱི་རིག་གཞུང་གི་འབྱུང་ཁུངས་དང་པོ་ཞང་ཞུང་ལྡེ་བར་བྱུས་ནས་རྗེས་པ་ཡིན་ནམ་ཡང་སྙམ་སྟེ། གླིང་བཞི་བསྟན་པའི་འབྱུང་ཁུངས་ལས།[30] ས་ཆོགས་དབུས་ནི་བོད་ཡུལ་ན་ཡོད་པས། གངས་ཏི་སེ་དང་མཚོ་མ་ཕམ་གཉིས་ཡིན་པར་ཞི་ཁྲོ་རྩ་འགྲེལ་ལས་གསུངས་སོ།།[31] ཞེས་གསུངས་པ་འདི་དང་མཐུན་པ་སྣང་ངོ་།། གཞན་རྡོ་རྗེ་གདན་ནས་རྩིས་པའི་ལྷོ་ནུབ་ཨོ་རྒྱན་སོགས་སྲིན་ཡུལ་དུ་ངོས་བཟུང་ཚུལ་ཡང་ཡོད་མོད། དགེ་འདུན་ཆོས་འཕེལ་གྱི་གནས་ཡིག་ཏུ།[32] ཨོ་རྒྱན་ཡུལ་དུ་རིག་སྔགས་གྲུབ་པའི་རྟོགས་ལྡན་ཡོད་རབས་ལས། རི་ཐམས་ཅད་རྣུས་པའི་བསྲི་མཁར་དང་། ཆུ་ཐམས་ཅད་ཁྲག་གི་རླབས་རྒྱུན་འཁྱོ་བའི་སྲིན་ཡུལ་ཞིག་མཐོང་རྒྱུ་མེད་ལུགས་བཤད་འདུག་པ་འདིས་ཀྱང་རྗེ་འབྲི་གུང་ཆུང་ཚང་པའི་གསུང་ལ་བདེན་ཁ་བྱིན་འདུག་སྙམ། ད་དུང་དེ་བས་ཁ་གསལ་བའི་དཔང་རྟགས་ཤིག་ལ། དེང་སང་གི་པུ་རངས་སུ་སྲིན་པོ་གཉའ་རིངས་ཁྲག་མེད་བསད་པའི་དུར་ས་དང་། དེའི་ཉེ་འགྲམ་དུ་སློབ་དཔོན་པདྨ་འབྱུང་གནས་ཀྱི་སྒྲུབ་ཕུག་ཀྱང་ཡོད་འདུག དེའི་སྔོར་ངའི་གྲོགས་པོ་ཨ་ཚོགས་བསྟན་འཛིན་འཇམ་དབྱངས[33] སྔོན་ས་གནས་དེ་ནས་རྒྱ་གར་དུ་ཕེབས་འདུག་པ་ཁོང་གིས་གསུང་དོན། ༡༩༩༠ལོར་ཁོ་བོ་གངས་ཏི་སེ་བརྒྱུད་རྒྱ་གར་ལ་བྲོས་བྱོལ་དུ་ཡོང་བའི་ལམ་ཞོར་དུ། གནས་མཆོག་པྲེ་ཏ་པུ་རི་ལ་གནས་མཇལ་དུ་སོང་བ་ཡིན། དེ་གར་སློབ་དཔོན་པདྨའི་སྒྲུབ་ཁང་དང་རྒྱལ་བ་རྒོད་ཚང་བའི་སྒྲུབ་ཕུག་གཉིས་ལ་མཇལ་ས་འདུག སྒྲུབ་ཕུག་བདག་གཉེར་བས། ལུང་ཁུག་བྱེ་གཞོངས་དེར་ས་དམར་རི་བརྒྱུད་ཆུང་དུ་ཞིག་མར་ལུང་དཀྲུས་སུ་འཐེན་བཞིན་པ་དེར་འཛུབ་བཙུགས་གནང་སྟེ། ཕ་གི་སློབ་དཔོན་པདྨ་འབྱུང་གནས་ཀྱིས་འདུལ་གནང་མཛད་པའི་སྲིན་པོ་གཉའ་རི་ཕྲུག་མེད་ཀྱི་བམ་རོ་སྦྲས་པའི་དུར་ས་རེད་ཅེས་གནས་བཤད་མཛད་ཀྱི་འདུག ཅེས་གསུངས་པ་ནི། སྲིན་པོ་གཉའ་རིངས་ཁྲག་མེད་སློབ་དཔོན་པདྨས་འདུལ་མིན་ཇི་ལྟར་ཡང་ཡུལ་དེར་གནའ་སྔ་མོ་ནས་སྲིན་པོ་གཉའ་རིངས་ཁྲག་མེད་ཀྱི་དུས་ས་ཞེས་པ་ཞིག་ཡོད་པ་དེ་ཉིད་མི་དངོས་པོས་མཐོང་ཞིང་ས་གནས་ས་ཐོག་དེ་ག་རང་གིས་འགྲེལ་བཤད་རྒྱག་པ་ཞིག་ཡིན་པས། དཔྱད་གཞིའི་རིན་ཐང་ངེས་ཅན་ལྡན་པའི་བདེན་དཔང་ཞིག་ཏུ་བརྩི་རུང་ངོ་སྙམ།

དེས་ན་སྲིན་པོས་དབང་བྱས་ཞེས་པ་ནི། རང་རེའི་ཡབ་མེས་ཀྱི་ཚོ་བ་གཅིག་གིས་བོད་ལ་དབང་བསྒྱུར་བྱས་པའི་དོན་དུ་གོ་དགོས་ལ། ཚོ་བ་དེ་ཉིད་ཀྱི་འཚོ་སྡོད་བྱེད་ས་ཡང་འབྲི་གུང་ཆུང་ཚང་པས་གསུང་ལྟར་སྟོད་མངའ་རིས་པུ་རང་དུ་ཡིན་ངེས། ཚོ་བ་དེས་དང་ཐོག་སྟོབས་འགྱུར་ཀྱི་གནས་ཚོད་ངེས་ཅན་ཞིག་འཕེལ་རྒྱས་བྱུང་བ་ན། རང་གི་རྗེ་བོ་བདུད་རེ་ལྡེ་མགོ་གཡག་གི་སྲིད་གཞུང་ལ་གྱེན་ལོག་དམག་འཐབ་བྱས་པའི་མཐའ་མཇུག་གི་རྒྱལ་ཁ་རང་ཉིད་ཀྱིས་ཐོབ་པར་མ་ཟད། བདུད་ཀྱི་སྲིད་འཛིན་དྲི་ལྡན་མ་གསན་བཟུང་གིས་རྐང་ལག་ལ་ལྕགས་སྒྲོག་སྐོན་ནས་བཙོན་འཇུག་བྱས་ཚུལ་གོང་དུ་གསལ་བ་ལྟར་ལགས་སོ། །སྐབས་དེར་རང་རེའི་ཡུལ་ལ་ཡུལ་མིང་སྲིན་པོ་ནག་པོ་དགུ་ཡུལ་ཟེར་ཚུལ་དང་། མཚོན་ཆ་སྲིན་མོ་རྐང་དང་སྒྲིགས་གཉིས་ལག་ཆ་བྱུང་ཚུལ་བཤད་པ་དེ་དག་གང་དང་གང་ཡིན་ཞེ་ན། དབང་མཛད་གོང་མའི་སྐབས་ཀྱི་མདུང་དང་ཁ་ཏཾ་སོགས་ཡོད་པ་སློས་མེད་ཐོག །རྐང་དུང་སོགས་རྣུས་པ་ལ་རྣོ་ཕྱུངས་ནས་མདུང་རྩེར་བསྒར་བ་དང་རྡོ་སྒྲིགས་བཅས་ནས་རི་དྭགས་གསད་ཐབས་དང་ཇག་རྐུན་འགོག་སྲུང་བྱེད་པའི་ལག་རྩལ་ཡང་དར་བ་ཡིན་ནོ་སྙམ།

བཞི་པ། དམར་འཇམ་ལྷ་ཡིས་དབང་བྱས་ཚུལ།

ཆོས་འབྱུང་མཁས་པའི་དགའ་སྟོན་ལས།[34] བཞི་པ་དམར་འཇམ་ལྷ་ཡིས་དབང་བྱས་ཏེ། །ལྷ་ཡུལ་གུང་ཐང་ལག་ཆར་ཆུ་གྲི་བྱུང་།། ལྡེའུ་ཆོས་འབྱུང་ལས། བཞི་པ་དམར་འཇམ་ཞེས་བྱ་ལྷ་ཡིས་བྱས། །ཡུལ་གྱི་མིང་ནི་ལྷ་ཡུལ་གུང་ཐང་ཟེར། །ལག་ཆར་ཁ་ཏཾ་རྡོ་གསུམ་དེ་ནས་བྱུང་།།[35] ཞེས་འབྱུང་། རྒྱལ་པོའི་བཀའ་ཡི་ཐང་ཡིག་ནང་ལྷ་ཡིས་དབང་བསྒྱུར་བྱས་ཚུལ་མི་གསལ་ཡང་བདུད་དང་སྲིན་པོས་དབང་བསྒྱུར་བྱས་པའི་སྐབས་ཡུལ་གྱི་མིང་ལ་ལྷ་འདྲེ་གཉིས་སུ་གྲགས་ཚུལ་གསུངས་འདུག་པ་འདིའི་རྒྱབ་ཏུ་དཔྱོད་པ་རགས་ཙམ་བྱས་ན། ཤུགས་བསྟན་དུ་ལྷས་དབང་བསྒྱུར་བྱས་སྐབས་ལྷ་ཡུལ་དུ་གྲགས་ཚུལ་གོ་བ་ལེན་མི་འོས་པའི་ངེས་པ་མི་འདུག་སྟེ། མཁས་པ་ལྡེའུ་དང་གཙུག་ཕྲེང་གཉིས་ཀས་སྐབས་དེའི་ཡུལ་གྱི་མིང་ལ་ལྷ་ཡུལ་གུང་ཐང་དུ་བཏགས་ཚུལ་བཤད་པ་དང་སྒྲོ་མཐུན་པས་སོ།།

དམར་འཇམ་ལྷས་བོད་དབང་བསྒྱུར་བྱས་པ་འདི་སྲིན་པོ་གནྱའ་རིང་ཁྲག་མིད་ཀྱི་རྗེས་སུ་ཡིན་པ་ལྡེའུ་དང་གཙུག་ཕྲེང་གཉིས་ཀའི་མགྲིན་གཅིག་དབྱངས་གཅིག་གིས་བཤད་པ་དང་། ས་སྐྱའི་གདུང་རབས་ཡ་རབས་ཁ་རྒྱན་མཁས་པའི་དབང་པོ་ངོར་པ་དཀོན་མཆོག་ལྷུན་གྲུབ་ཀྱིས་མཛད་པ་ལས། གདུང་གི་ཐོག་མ་འོད་གསལ་ལྷ་ཡུལ་དུ། ། སྤྱི་རིང་གཡུ་རིང་གཡུ་སེ་མཆེད་གསུམ་བྱོན། །གཡུ་སེས་མི་རྗེ་མཛད་ནས་སྲས་བཞི་བསྐྲུན། །དེ་ཡི་གྲོགས་སུ་གཅེན་པོ་གཡུ་རིང་བྱོན།།[36] ཞེས་དང་། དེའི་ཐད་ཀྱི་བདག་ཆེན་པ་ཨ་མེས་པའི་ས་སྐྱའི་གདུང་རབས་རིན་ཆེན་བང་མཛོད་ལས།[37] ས་སྐྱའི་རུས་ནི་བོད་ཀྱི་རུས་ཆེན་བཞི་དང་། མིའུ་རིགས་དྲུག་ཏུ་གྲགས་པ་སོགས་ལས་ཆད་པ་མ་ཡིན་གྱིས། གདུང་རུས་གཙང་མ་ལྷ་ནས་བབས་པ་ཡིན་ཏེ། དེ་ཡང་ངེས་པའི་དོན་དུ་འཇམ་པའི་དབྱངས་ཉིད་གདུལ་བྱ་གཞན་གྱི་ངོར་འོད་གསལ་གྱི་ལྷ་ཡི་རུས་སུ་སྤྲུལ་པ་ནི། གནམ་ལྷ་སྤྱི་རིང་གཡུ་རིང་གཡུ་སེ་སྤྱི་མཆེད་གསུམ་དུ་གྲགས་པ་མི་ཡུལ་བབས་པ་ལ་མིའི་རྗེ་ཞུས་པས། གནམ་ལྷ་ཆུང་བ་གཡུ་སེས་མི་རྗེ་མཛད་པས། སྲས་སེ་བྱི་ལི་སྤྱུན་བཞིར་གྲགས་པ་བྱུང་། དེ་དག་དང་ལྡོང་གི་རུས་ཆེན་བཅོ་བརྒྱད་འཐབ། དེའི་གྲོགས་ལ་གནམ་ལྷ་བར་བ་གཡུ་རིང་བྱུང་ནས་ལྡོང་རུས་རྣམས་བཏུལ་ནས་བྲན་དུ་བྱས། ཞེས་འབྱུང་བས། དེས་ན་དམར་འཇམ་ལྷ་ཞེས་པ་ནི་འཁོན་རིགས་ཐོག་མ་གང་ལས་ཆད་པ་འོད་གསལ་ལྷ་ཡི་རུས་གནམ་ལྷ་སྤྱི་རིང་དང་། གཡུ་རིང་། གཡུ་སེ་ཟེར་བ་མཆེད་གསུམ་མི་ཡུལ་གྱི་འཇིག་རྟེན་དུ་བབས་པར། གང་དུ་བབས་པའི་མི་ཡུལ་གྱི་ས་ཁུལ་དེ་དག་གིས་རྗེ་བོར་བསྐུར་བས་བུ་སྤྱུན་གསུམ་ལས་ཆུང་བ་གཡུ་སེ་ཡིས་ས་གནས་དེ་ཡི་མི་རྗེ་མཛད།

གནམ་ལྷའི་རུས་ལས་ཆད་པ་དེ་དག་གིས་ཐོག་མ་རང་ཉིད་གང་དུ་འཚོ་སྡོད་བྱེད་ས་ལྷ་ཡུལ་གུང་ཐང་གི་ས་ཁུལ་དབང་བསྒྱུར་བྱས། ལྡོང་གི་རུས་ཆེན་བཅོ་བརྒྱད་དང་འཐབ་ནས་དེ་དག་ཕམ་པར་བྱས། དེའི་ཁེངས་པ་དང་སྟོབས་ལ་བརྟེན་ནས་སྲིན་པོ་གནྱའ་རིང་ཁྲག་མིད་ལ་ཁྲལ་མི་འཇལ་ཁྲིམས་མི་ཁུར་བས་ལྷ་དང་སྲིན་པོ་འཁོན་འཛིན་ཤོར། ཕན་ཚུན་དམག་འཐབ་བྱས་མཐར་སྲིན་པོ་གནྱའ་རིང་ཁྲག་མིད་བསད། དེའི་ཆུང་མ་གཡའ་འབྲུམ་སི་ལི་མ་འཁྲོག་ནས་རང་གི་ཆུང་མར་བསྟེན་པར་བཤད་དེ། ས་སྐྱའི་གདུང་རབས་ཡ་རབས་ཁ་རྒྱན་ལས།[38] གང་དེས་སྲིན་པོ་སྐྱ་རེངས་ཁྲག་མིད་ནི།། བསད་ནས་ཆུང་མ་གཡའ་འབྲུ་སི་ལི་མ།། ཕྲོགས་ཏེ་ཉིད་ཀྱི་ཁབ་ཏུ་བཞེས་པ་ལས།། སྲས་གཅིག་བྱུང་བ་འཁོན་པར་སྐྱེས་ཞེས་གྲགས།། ཞེས་དང་། དེའི་ཐད་ཀྱི

ངོ་མཚར་བང་མཛོད་ལས།[39] གཡའ་སྤྱང་སྐྱེས་ཞེས་གྲགས་པའི་དཔའ་བོ་ཆེན་པོ་དེས། སྲིན་པོ་སྐྲ་རིངས་ཁྲག་མེད་ཅེས་བྱ་བ་ལ་ཆུང་མ་གཡའ་འབྲུ་སི་ལི་མ་ཞེས་བྱ་བ་ཤིན་ཏུ་མཚར་བ་ཞིག་ཡོད་པས། སྲིན་པོ་དང་འཐབ་རེས་བྱས། ཁྲོ་བསད། ཆུང་མ་ཁབ་ཏུ་བཞེས། ལྷ་དང་སྲིན་པོ་འཁོན་པའི་བར་དུ་བྱུང་བས་ལྷ་ཕྱུག་འཁོན་པ་སྐྱེས་སུ་བཏགས་ཞེས་གསུངས།

མཁས་པ་ལྡེའུ་དང་གཙུག་ཕྲེང་གཉིས་མགྲིན་གཅིག་ཏུ་སྲིན་པོ་གཉའ་རེངས་ཁྲག་མེད་ཀྱི་རྗེས་སུ་དམར་འཇམ་ལྷ་ཡིས་བཟུང་ཚུལ་བཤད་པ་དང་། ས་སྐྱའི་གདུང་རབས་ལས་ལྷ་རིགས་ཀྱིས་སྲིན་པོ་སྐྲ་རིངས་ཁྲག་མེད་བསད་ཚུལ་བཤད་པའི་བར་མི་ཐོག་སྒྲིག་གཏང་གི་བང་རིམ་སྔ་ཕྱི་ཙུང་ཟད་མི་འདྲ་བ་འདུག་པ་ལས་གཞན་མིང་དང་བཅས་པ་གཅིག་མཚུངས་སུ་འདུག་པས་གཅིག་བྱས་ན་མངའ་མཛད་སྔ་ཕྱི་སྒྲིག་སྟངས་ཐད་ས་སྐྱའི་གདུང་རབས་ལས་འབྱུང་བ་ལྟར་འཐད་པའང་སྲིད་དོ། །ད་དུང་ཅིས་ཀྱང་དཔྱད་པ་བྱ་དགོས།

དམར་འཇམ་ལྷ་ཡིས་སྲིད་དབང་བཟུང་ས་ལྡེ་བ་ལྷ་ཡུལ་གུང་ཐང་ཞེས་པ་ཡང་ས་སྐྱའི་གདུང་རབས་རིན་ཆེན་བང་མཛོད་ལས།[40] གངས་རིའི་ཕྲེང་བ་ཆེན་པོའི་ནང་ན་ཤིན་ཏུ་མཛེས་ཤིང་མཐོ་བ་ཤེལ་ཆ་རྒྱ་མོའི་གངས་སུ་གྲགས་པ་དང་། གཡའ་སྤྱང་གི་ལྗོ་འགྲམ་ན་ས་སྐྱ་བའི་བླ་མ་མཆོ་ཡང་ཡོད་དོ། ཐོག་མ་འོད་གསལ་གྱི་ལྷ་མི་ཡུལ་དུ་བབ་པའི་ཚེ་ཡང་ཤེལ་ཚ་རྒྱ་མོའི་གངས་དེ་ཉིད་ཀྱི་རྩེ་མོར་བབས་པ་ཡིན་ཅེས། སྔགས་འཆང་ཆོས་ཀྱི་རྒྱལ་པོའི་གསུང་རྒྱུན་བདག་གི་བླ་མ་འཇམ་དབྱངས་སྐུ་མཆེད་ལས་དངོས་སུ་ཐོས་སོ། །ཞེས་རང་ལུགས་བཞག་རྗེས། གདན་རབས་པ་ཁག་ཅིག[41] ཡུལ་མཐོ་ཞིང་གཙང་མ་མངའ་རིས་སྟོད་ཀྱི་ས་ཡི་ཆར་བབས་པར་བཤད་དོ། ཞེས་གཞན་ལུགས་བཤད་པ་དང་། ཆོས་འབྱུང་མཁས་པའི་དགའ་སྟོན་ལས། ཡུལ་གྱི་མིང་ཡང་ལྷ་ཡུལ་གུང་ཐང་ཟེར། །ཞེས་མངའ་རིས་གུང་ཐང་ཡིན་པ་བཤད་པ་གཉིས་ཆུ་ལ་ཆུ་བཞག་པ་ལྟར་གྱུར་འདུག་ལ། མངའ་རིས་ཀྱི་ཡུལ་དུ་སྔར་མ་ཟད་དུས་ཕྱིས་སུའང་གཡུང་དྲུང་བོན་གྱི་རིང་ལུགས་སུ་ལྷ་ཡུལ་རང་དུ་ངོས་འཛིན་བྱས་འདུག་ལ། རྒྱ་གར་བས་ཀྱང་ལྷའི་གཙོ་བོ་དབང་ཕྱུག་གི་ཡུལ་རང་དུ་ངོས་འཛིན་བྱས་འདུག་པ་བཅས་ལ་བརྟེན་ནས། ལྷ་ཡུལ་ནས་ཆད་ཚུལ་བཤད་པ་དང་ཡང་ཐུན་མོང་སྣང་ངོར་སྟོད་མངའ་རིས་ནས་འཆར་བའི་ཕོ་རྒོད་སྤུན་གསུམ་གྱིས་མངའ་རིས་ས་ཁུལ་དབང་བསྒྱུར་བྱས་རྗེས་རིམ་པར་བཞིན་སྲིན་པོ་གཉའ་རེངས་ཁྲག་མེད་ཀྱང་བསད་ནས་མངའ་རིས་དང་དབུས་གཙང་ཁུལ་ཕལ་ཆེར་དབང་བསྒྱུར་བྱས་པ་ཡིན་སྲིད་སྙམ། ད་དུང་འབྲི་གུང་ཆུང་ཚང་པས། མངའ་རིས་པུ་རང་གིས་ཁུལ་སྲིན་ཡུལ་དུ་བཤད་པ་དང་། རྣམ་ཡ་ནས་སྲིན་པོ་ལ་དམག་བྱས་ཚུལ་གྲགས་ཆེ་བ་ཡང་གཡའ་སྤྱང་སྐྱེས་ཀྱིས་མངའ་རིས་གུང་ཐང་ནས་སྲིན་པོ་གཉའ་རེངས་ཁྲག་མེད་ཀྱི་རྒྱལ་ས་པུ་རང་ལ་དམག་བྱས་ནས་བསད་པ་དང་འགྲོར་ཞིང་། དགའ་བྱེད་རྣམ་ན་ཡང་ས་སྐྱའི་མཁས་པ་ངག་ཆོས་ཀྱིས།[42] གྲོང་ཁྱེར་གསུམ་བརྩེགས་འཇིགས་བྱེད་པ། །ཞེས་པའི་ཚིག་ལ་བརྟེན་ནས་དཔལ་མགོན་གུར་དུ་ངོས་འཛིན་གནང་འདུག་པ་དང་། དཔལ་ལྡན་ས་སྐྱ་བས་དགོན་པོ་ཆེན་ཆུང་སྲུང་མའི་གཙོ་བོར་བསྟེན་པ་བཅས་ལ་བརྟགས་ཤིང་དཔྱད་ན། དཔལ་ལྡན་ས་སྐྱ་བའི་གདུང་རུས་གང་ལས་ཆད་པ་ལྷ་རུས་འཁོན་པ་གཡའ་སྤྱང་སྐྱེས་ཉིད་དགའ་བྱེད་རྣམ་ནའམ་དཔལ་ལྡན་གུར་དང་གཅིག་པ་མ་ཡིན་པའི་ངེས་པའང་མི་འདུག་སྙམ། གྲོང་ཁྱེར་སུམ་བརྩེགས་ཞེས་པའང་དེང་སང་གི་པུ་རང་འདི་ཉིད་ཁོ་ན་ངོས་འཛིན་བྱས་ན། འབྲི་གུང་དང་ངག་ཆོས་གཉིས་ཀའི་དགོངས་པ་དང་ཉེ་བར་སྣང་སྟེ་ད་དུང་ཞིབ་ཏུ་དཔྱད་པར་བྱ་འོས་སྙམ།

འདི་དག་ཕན་ཚུན་དམག་འཐབ་བྱེད་པའི་སྐབས་སྔར་ཡོད་དགྲ་སྟ་སོགས་ཀྱི་ཐོག་ཆུ་གྲི་བཟོས་ནས་བོད་སྤྱོད་གཏོང་ཤེས་པ་བྱུང་ཚུལ་མཁས་པའི་དགའ་སྟོན་ལས་འབྱུང་བ་དང་། དཔལ་མགོན་གུར་གྱི་སྐང་གསོ་ལས། ཆུ་གྲི་སྟ་རེ་ལ་སོགས་པས། །མ་ཏྲ་ཀ་ལའི་ཐུགས་དམ་སྐོང་། ཞེས་འབྱུང་བ་འདི་དང་ཤིན་ཏུའང་འགྲོར་ཏེ། ལྷག་པར་མཁས་པ་ལྡེའུ་ལྟར་ན་སྐབས་དེར། ལག་ཆར་ཁ་ཏཾ་རྩེ་གསུམ་དེ་ནས་བྱུང་།། ཞེས་མཚོན་ཆ་ཁ་ཏཾ་བོད་སྤྱོད་བྱེད་ཚུལ་བཤད་པ་དང་རྒྱ་གར་བས་སྤྱོད་གདངས་རི་དབང་ཕྱུག་གི་བཞུགས་གནས་ལྷ་ཡུལ་རྩེ་བར་མ་ཟད་ཁ་ཏཾ་ནི་དབང་ཕྱུག་གི་ལག་ཆར་འཛིན་པ་འདིས་ཀྱང་ལྷ་ཡུལ་གྱང་ཐང་ནི་མངའ་རིས་རང་དུ་ངོས་འཛིན་ཆོག་པའི་དཔང་རྟགས་སུ་རུང་ངོ་སྙམ། ད་དུང་རིག་བྱེད་ཀྱི་གཞུང་ལས[43] རཱ་མ་ཡ་ན་ཡིས་སྲིན་རྒྱལ་བསད་ནས། སི་ཏཱ་འཕྲོག་ཚུལ་དང་འདིས་སྲིན་པོ་གཉའ་རེངས་ཁྲག་མེད་བསད་ནས་དེའི་ཆུང་མ་གཡའ་འབྲུམ་སི་ལི་མ་འཕྲོག་ཚུལ་ཀུན་ཆུ་ལ་ཆུ་བཞག་པ་ནང་བཞིན་གཅིག་མཚུངས་སུ་འདུག་པས། ལོ་རྒྱུས་སྨྲ་བ་ཚོའི་དཔྱད་གཞི་གལ་ཆེ་ཞིག་ཏུ་མཐོང་མོད། ཁོ་བོས་ཞིབ་ཏུ་དཔྱོད་པའི་དུས་མ་བྱུང་བས་འཇུབ་མོས་རི་བསྟན་ཙམ་ཞུས་པ་ལགས་སོ།།

མངའ་མཛད་ལྔ་པ། སྒྱུ་རྒྱལ་ཁོ་རྗེས་དབང་བྱས་ཚུལ།

ཆོས་འབྱུང་མཁས་པའི་དགའ་སྟོན་ལས། ལྔ་པར་སྒྱུ་རྒྱལ་ཁོ་རྗེ་ཞེས་བྱས་བཟུངས། །ད་ཕྲང་ཅང་ཕྲང་ལག་ཆར་ཞགས་པ་འཕེན།། ཞེས་དང་། ལྡེའུ་ཆོས་འབྱུང་ལས། ལྔ་པ་སྐྱུས་དབང་བྱས་ངམ་བྲང་ཅང་བྲང་ཟེར། །ལག་ཆ་མདུང་ལ་བྱེད་པ་དེ་ནས་བྱུང་།། ཞེས་པས། མངའ་མཛད་ལྔ་པ། སྒྱུ་རྒྱ་ཁོ་རྗེས་དབང་བྱས་ཚུལ་ནི། སྒྱུ་རྒྱ་ཁོ་རྗེ་ཞེས་པ་ཡང་ས་སྐྱའི་གདུང་རབས་རིན་ཆེན་བང་མཛོད་ལས།[44] བར་བ་གཡུ་རིང་འདྲིས་དམུ་(སྨི)[45] ཡི་བུ་མོ་དམུ་བཟའ་ལྡེམ་བུ་ཁབ་ཏུ་བཞེས་པས་སྲས་མ་བཟང་སྤྱུན་བདུན་བྱུང་ཚུལ་གསུང་པ་དང་། ལྡེའུ་དང་གཙུག་ཕྲེང་ལས་བཤད་པའི་དམར་འཛམ་ལྷ་ཡི་རྗེས་སུ་སྒྱུ་ཡིས་བཟུང་ཚུལ་ཇི་ལྟར་ཡིན་ཞེ་ན། དེ་ཡང་ས་སྐྱའི་གདུང་རབས་ལས་འབྱུང་བ་ལྟར། གཡུ་རིང་གིས་སྒྱུ་ཡི་བུ་མོ་སྒྱུ་བཟའ་ལྡེ་བུ་ཞེས་པ་ཁབ་ཏུ་བླངས་པ་ལས་སྲས་སྒྱུ་རྒྱལ་ཁོ་རྗེ་བྱུང་། འདི་ཉིད་ཕ་ཡི་རུས་ལྷ་དང་ཚ་འབྲངས་མ་ནི་སྨི་ཡི་རིགས་ཡིན་ལ། མིང་ཟུར་དང་པོ་སྨི་ཞེས་པ་མ་ཡི་མིང་ནས་དྲས་ཏེ་བཏགས་པ་ཞིག་ཡིན་སྙམ། དུས་ཕྱིས་བོད་ཀྱི་བཙན་པོ་རིམ་བྱོན་སྐབས་ཀྱང་མ་ཡི་མིང་ནས་དྲས་ཏེ་བཏགས་པའི་མིང་མང་སྟེ་དཔེར་ན། ཡབ་གཉའ་ཁྲི་དང་ཡུམ་གནམ་མུག་གི་བུ་ལ་མུ་ཁྲི་བཙན་པོ་བཏགས་པ་སོགས་ཀྱིས་མཚོན་ནུས།[46]

འདི་ལྟར་ན་སྒྱུ་ཡིས་སྲིད་དབང་བཟུང་བའི་སྐབས་དམར་འཛམ་ལྷ་ཡི་སྲིད་དབང་གཏོར་ནས་སྲིད་གཞུང་གསར་པ་ཞིག་ཟུར་འཛུགས་བྱས་པ་མ་ཡིན་པ་སྲིད་དབང་བཟུང་མཁན་གྱི་མ་ཕྱོགས་གཉེན་ཉེའི་སྟོབས་འབྱོར་དབང་ཆས་ཤན་ཤུགས་ཆེན་པོ་ཐེབས་པས། དེ་སྔོན་ཡབ་ཐོག་ལྷ་ཡིས་བཟུང་བ་དང་བུ་ཐོག་སྒྱུ་ཚ་ཡིས་བཟུང་བའི་དབར་ཁྱད་པར་ཆེན་པོ་བྱུང་བས་མངའ་མཛད་ཀྱི་དབྱེ་མཚམས་ཤིག་ཏུ་བགྲངས་པ་ཡིན་འདྲ། ས་སྐྱའི་གདུང་རབས་ལས།[47] གཡུ་རིང་གིས་དམུ་བཟའ་བསུས་བའི་བུ་མ་སངས་(བསངས)སྤྱུན་བདུན་བྱུང་ཚུལ་གསུངས་པ་ཡང་། གཡུ་རིང་དང་སྒྱུ་བཟའི་བུ་དང་ཚ་བོ་ཡང་ཚ་བཅས་ཀྱི་བར་རིམ་ཞིབ་ཆ་མ་བྱུང་བ་མཁས་པ་ལྡེའུ་དང་གཙུག་ཕྲེང་གཉིས་ཀྱིས་བདེན་དཔང་བྱེད་ནུས་སྙམ། འོན་ཀྱང་རྒྱལ་པོའི་བཀའ་ཡི་ཐང་ཡིག་ལས།[48]

བདུད་དང་སྲིན་པོས་དབང་བསྒྱུར་བྱས་པའི་རྗེས་ཀླུ་དང་བཙན་གྱིས་དབང་བསྒྱུར་བྱས་ཚུལ་ལས། དེའི་བར་དུ་ཛྨི་ཡིས་དབང་བསྒྱུར་བྱས་ཚུལ་མི་གསལ་བས། དེའི་རྒྱུ་མཚན་གང་ཡིན་ཡང་དཔྱོད་དགོས་པར་སེམས། རྣམ་པར་གཅིག་ཏུ་ན་ཛྨི་ཞེས་ཟུར་དུ་འདྲེན་པ་ཙམ་མ་གཏོགས་ལྷའི་སྲིད་གཞུང་གཏོར་ནས་གཞུང་གསར་པ་བཙུགས་པ་མིན་པར་དོན་ལ་མ་རིགས་ནས་དྲས་པའི་ཛྨི་ཞེས་འདོགས་པ་ལྷ་ཡི་རིགས་རྒྱུད་ཀྱིས་སྲིད་དབང་བཟུང་པས་ཛྨི་ཞེས་ཟུར་དུ་མི་འདྲེན་པ་ཡིན་ཀྱང་སྲིད་སྙམ། མངའ་མཛད་འདིས་རྒྱལ་ས་ལྟེ་བ་ད་ཕྱང་ཙང་ཕྱང་དུ་ཡིན་པར་བཤད་མོད། ས་གནས་འདི་ཆོད་དཔག་བྱས་ན་སྟོད་མངའ་རིས་བསྐོར་གང་རུང་ཞིག་གི་ས་ཁུལ་ཡིན་ནམ་སྙམ་སྟེ། མངའ་མཛད་སྤྱི་ཕྱིར་ཕན་ཚུན་ཐོབ་ཤོར་རྩོད་ས་དང་རྩོད་མཁན་ཕལ་ཆེར་མངའ་རིས་ཕྱོགས་འདིར་འཁེལ་བ་མངའ་མཛད་གོང་འོག་ལས་ཤེས་ནུས་སྙམ་སྟེ། གཞན་དུ་ངོས་འཛིན་གསལ་བ་བྱས་པའི་ལོ་རྒྱུས་ཀྱི་ཁུངས་མ་རྙེད།

སྐབས་དེར་སྔར་ཡོད་ལག་ཆ་དགྲ་སྟ་དང་ཆུ་གྲི་སོགས་ཀྱི་སྟེང་དུ་ཞགས་པ་བཟོས་ནས་རི་སྐྱེས་སྲོག་ཆགས་ཁག་གཅིག་སྒོ་ཐོག་ཏུ་ཕབ་པ་དང་། ཐག་སྐྱི་བཞག་ནས་གཅན་གཟན་གདུམ་པོའི་རིགས་བཟུང་བ། དེ་དག་གི་ལྤགས་པ་གདན་དུ་གཏིང་བ་དང་གོས་སུ་གོན་པ་སོགས་བྱེད་པའི་ལུགས་སྲོལ་དར། དེ་ཡང་རྒྱལ་པོ་སྟག་པགས་ཀྱི་གདན་དང་གོས། ཞང་བློན་ཆོས་གཅན་གཟན་གཞན་དང་གཞན་གྱི་པགས་པ་ལ་ལོངས་སུ་སྤྱོད། ད་དུང་རྩྭ་གཟན་རི་དྭགས་རིགས་མང་པོ་ཕ་མེས་ཡང་མེས་ཚོའི་སྐབས་བཞིན། རྗོ་དང་སྟ་རེ་མདུང་སོགས་ཁུར་ནས་རྗེས་འདེད་གཏོང་བའི་ངལ་བ་ལ་བརྟེན་མི་དགོས་པར། ཕྱོགས་གང་སར་ཐག་པས་སྐྱི་བཞག་པའི་ཐབས་ལམ་ལ་བརྟེན་ནས་རི་དྭགས་མང་པོ་བཟུང་ནས་ཤ་ཁྲག་ལ་སྤྱོད་ཐུབ་པ་བྱུང་བ་བཅས་ནི་མི་རབས་སྔ་མ་ཚོ་ལས་ཡར་ཐོན་ཕྱིན་པ་ཡིན་སྙམ།

མངའ་མཛད་དྲུག་པ། གྲོག་གྲོག་འདྲེ་ཡིས་དབང་བྱས་ཚུལ།

ཆོས་འབྱུང་མཁས་པའི་དགའ་སྟོན་ལས། དྲུག་པ་གྲོག་གྲོག་འདྲེ་ཡིས་དབང་བྱས་ཏེ།། ལང་ཏང་ལིང་དང་བར་ཁ་ཅུར་རྗེ་འཕེན།། ཞེས་དང་། ལྡེའུ་ཆོས་འབྱུང་ལས། དྲུག་པ་འདྲེས་དབང་ལང་ཏང་ལིང་ཏང་ཟེར།། ལག་ཆར་རྒྱུག་པ་གྲོག་ཅན་དེ་ནས་བྱུང་།། ཞེས་པས། མངའ་མཛད་དྲུག་པ་གྲོག་གྲོག་འདྲེ་ཡིས་དབང་ཚུལ་ནི། ཛྨི་ཡིས་དབང་བྱས་པའི་མཐའ་མཇུག་གྲོག་གྲོག་འདྲེ་ཡི་རིགས་ཀྱི་ཚོ་བ་ཁག་གཅིག་གིས་འབངས་གྱེན་ལོག་གི་ལས་འགུལ་བསྐྱོད་མར་སྤེལ་ཏེ་སྲིད་དབང་འདྲེ་ཡིས་ཕྲོགས་པ་སྙམ་ལ། འདྲེ་ཞེས་པའང་རང་རེས་རྟོག་པས་བཟོས་པའི་ལྷ་འདྲེ་གནོད་པ་འདྲ་མིན་གཏོང་མཁན་གྱི་གཟུགས་མེད་འཇིགས་སུ་རུང་བ་དེ་འདྲ་ཞིག་མིན་པར། མིའི་རིགས་ལ་སྤྱི་བཏང་གི་མི་ལས་དཔའ་མཛངས་བློ་གྲོས་དང་། ཐབས་འཕྲུལ་གཡོ་རྫུས་མཁས་པའི་ཚོ་བ་ཞིག་ཡིན་ངེས་སྙམ། རྒྱལ་པོའི་བཀའ་ཐང་དང་ས་སྐྱའི་གདུང་རབས་རིན་ཆེན་བང་མཛོད་གཉིས་ཀའི་ནང་དུ་གྲོག་གྲོག་འདྲེ་ཞེས་པ་འདི་མི་གསལ་བས་དེ་རྒྱུ་མཚན་གང་ཡིན་ལ་བརྟག་དགོས། གཅིག་བྱས་ན་དཔལ་ལྡན་ས་སྐྱའི་གདུང་རབས་རིན་པོ་ཆེ་གང་ལས་བྱུང་བའི་ཁུངས་ལྷ་རིགས་མངའ་མཛད་ཀྱི་རྒྱུད་པ་མིན་པས་གྲོག་གྲོག་འདྲེ་ཟུར་དུ་མ་བཀྲངས་པ་ཡིན་སྲིད་སྙམ། དཔེར་ན་བོད་ཀྱི་རྒྱལ་རབས་རྣམས་སུ་སྟོད་ཀྱི་སྟེང་གཉིས་བཤད་པའི་

སྐབས། ཁྲི་གུམ་བཙན་པོའི་རྗེས་སུ་བློན་པོ་ལོ་ངམ་གྱིས་སྲིད་དབང་ལོ་ཤས་བཟུང་ཡང་། བོད་བཙན་པོའི་རྒྱལ་རབས་བགྲང་པའི་སྐབས་གྲི་གུམ་གྱི་རྗེས་སུ་པུར་དེ་གུང་རྒྱལ་བགྲང་པ་མ་གཏོགས་ལོ་ངམ་མི་བགྲང་པ་བཞིན་ནོ།། ཀྲོག་ཀྲོག་འདྲི་ཡང་མ་སངས་ཀྱི་གདུང་རབས་སྤུ་མ་མིན་པས་ས་སྐྱའི་གདུང་རབས་སུ་བགྲང་པར་འབྲེལ་བ་གང་ཡང་མེད་པས་ཡིན་ནམ་སྙམ་སྟེ་ད་དུང་ཡང་དཔྱད་པར་བྱ་དགོས་སོ།། ལྡེའུ་དང་གཙུག་ཕྲེང་གཉིས་ཀྱིས་ཁྲུ་སྟོན་གྱི་ལོ་རྒྱུས་ཆེན་པོར་བལྟས་པས། དེའི་ནང་དུ་གསལ་བ་ཡིན་ཡང་སྙམ་མོད། ཡིག་རྙིང་དེ་ཉིད་ད་ལྟར་ལག་ཏུ་སོན་ཐབས་དཀའ་བས་དཔྱད་པར་བྱ་བའི་ཐབས་གཞན་མ་རྙེད།

ཀྲོག་ཀྲོག་འདྲི་ཡི་རིགས་འཚོ་སྐྱོང་བྱེད་ས་ལང་ཏང་ལིང་ཏང་ནི། དེང་སང་གི་སྟོད་མངའ་རིས་པུ་རང་བ་ཁ་ཞེས་པ་དེར་ཡིན་ཚུལ་ལོ་རྒྱུས་སླ་བའི་མཁས་པ་འགས་བྲིས་འདུག་པ[49] བདེན་ཆ་ཆེན་ཏེ། དེ་སྟོན་སྲིན་པོས་བཟུང་སྐབས་ཀྱི་མངའ་རིས་པུ་རང་དང་། དམར་འཛམ་ལྷ་ཡིས་བཟུང་སྐབས་ཀྱི་མངའ་རིས་གུང་ཐང་རྣམས་ཕན་ཚུན་ཁ་ཐག་ཉེ་བས། དེ་དག་ལ་འཚོ་སྐྱོང་བྱེད་མཁན་ཚོ་རྟ་ས་ཀུ་རྟོད་ཀྱི་ཐོབ་ཤོར་ཡང་ཡང་ཡོང་གི་ཡོད་པ་ཆོས་ཉིད་ཡིན་པས་སོ། །ད་དུང་འདྲི་དང་སྲིན་པོ་གཉིས་གདུག་རྩུབ་ཆེ་བ་དང་། གཞན་ལ་འཚེ་བ། ཤ་ཁྲག་པ་རྫམས་པ་སོགས་ཀྱི་འདྲ་ཆོས་མང་བས། མངའ་རིས་སྟོད་སྨད་ཀྱི་ས་གནས་འདི་དག་མི་རྒྱུད་དེ་དག་གིས་རིམ་པར་བེད་སྤྱོད་དང་འཚོ་སྐྱོད་བྱས་པས་འདྲི་ཡུལ་དང་སརིན་ཡུལ་དུ་ངོས་འཛིན་བྱས་ན་རྒྱུ་མཚན་ཆེ་བ་སྙམ་མོད། འོན་ཀྱང་དཔྱད་གཞི་གཞན་དག་ལག་སོན་བྱུང་ན་སླར་ཡང་བསྐྱར་ནས་དཔྱད་དགོས།

མི་ཐོག་དེའི་སྐབས་སྔར་ཡོད་མཆོན་ཆའི་ཐོག་གང་དུ་རྐོལ་ལན་སློག་པ་དང་འཐབ་འཁྲུགས་བྱེད་སྐབས་དགྲ་བོའི་གོམ་དུ་བཅར་ནས་གྲི་དང་སྟ་རེས་ཁྱེད་ཤིང་གསོན་གྱི་དམར་འཛིངས་མི་དགོས་པར། རྒྱང་དུ་ཀྱེད་ནས་རྡོ་ལོག་འཕེན་པའི་ལག་ཆ་ཐེངས་དང་པོ་ཁུར་རྡོ་བཟོ་རྒྱུའི་ལག་རྩལ་གསར་པའང་འདི་ནས་རྙེད། ལག་ཆ་འདི་ལ་བརྟེན་ནས་དགྲ་རྐུན་ཛག་གསུམ་དང་། གཅན་གཟན་གདུག་པོའི་རིགས་རྣམས། རྟ་སྤྲེའམ་ཚོ་བའི་ནང་ཐོལ་བྱུང་དུ་འཛུལ་བ་ལ་རྐོལ་ལན་སློག་ཐབས་སྟབས་བདེ་བྱུང་བ་སེམས། ད་དུང་རྒྱུག་པ་ཀྲོག་ཅན་ནམ་བར་ཁ་སྟེ། རྒྱུག་པ་རྣ་གཉིས་ཅན་སྤྱད་ནས་དགྲ་བོ་དང་གཅན་གཟན་ལ་རྐོལ་ཞིང་རང་ཕྱོགས་འགེབས་སྲུང་གི་ལག་ཆར་སྤྱད་ཤེས་པར་བྱུང་ཡང་ཤེས་ནུས་སོ།།[50]

མངའ་མཛད་བདུན་པ། མ་སངས་སྤྱུན་དགུས་དབང་བྱས་ཚུལ།

ཆོས་འབྱུང་མཁས་པའི་དགའ་སྟོན་ལས། བདུན་པ་མ་སངས་སྤྱུན་དགུས་དབང་བྱས་ཏེ། །ཡུལ་གྱི་མིང་ནི་བོད་ཁ་ཉ་དྲུག་ཟེར། །ལག་ཆར་དོང་རལ་གོ་ཆ་ཕུབ་ཆུང་བྱུང་།། ལྡེའུ་ཆོས་འབྱུང་ལས། བདུན་པ་མ་སངས་རུ་དགུས་དབང་བྱས་ཏེ། །ཡུལ་གྱི་མིང་ནི་བོད་ཁམས་གཡང་དྲུག་ཟེར།། ལག་ཆར་དོང་རལ་ཕུབ་ཆུང་དེ་ནས་བྱུང་།། མ་སངས་སྤྱུན་དགུ་ནི་ཆོས་འབྱུང་མཁས་པའི་དགའ་སྟོན་ལས།[51] ༡ གཉན་མ་སངས་གཡའ་སྤང་སྐྱེས་གཅིག ༢ གར་མ་སངས་གཙོ་གར་སྐྱེས་ཀྱི་སྡིག་ནམ་ཚ། ༣ གླི་མ་སངས་ངན་ལམ་རྩང་སྐྱེས། ༤ རྟ་མ་སངས་ཐོ་གར་སྐྱེས། ༥ ཤེ་མ་སངས་ཐོད་དཀར་ནམ་ཚ། ༦ མེ་མ་སངས་པད་མ་སྐྱེས་ཀྱི་སྙིང་ནམ་ཚ། ༧ མི་མ་སངས་རྒྱ་མཚོ་སྐྱེས་ཀྱི་དྲ་ང་འགྱུར། ༨ ཨོད་མ་མ་སངས་སྟོན་ནམ་ཚ། ༩ གཡའ་གྲུམ་སི་

ཡི་མ། བཅས་ཡིན་ཚུལ་གསུང་འདུག ས་སྐྱའི་གདུང་རབས་རིན་ཆེན་བང་མཛོད་ལས།[52] གཡུ་རིང་དང་རྨུ་བཟའི་སྲས་མ་བཟང་བུ་སྤྱུན་བདུན་བྱུང་ཚུལ་དང་། སྤྱུན་གྱི་ཐ་ཆུང་མ་བཟང་སྤྱི་རྗེ་ཡིན་ཚུལ། དེ་དང་ཐོག་ལྷུམ་ཙུར་མོ་འདུས་པ་ལས་སྲས་དཔའ་བོ་སྟག་ཅེས་བྱ་བ་བྱུང་ཚུལ་གསུངས་སྣང་སྟེ། དེ་ཉིད་དུ་ཡ་རབས་ཁ་རྒྱན་བགྲངས་པར། གཡུ་རིང་དང་ནི་དམུ་བཟའ་ལྡེམ་བུའི་སྲས།། བཟང་བུ་བདུན་གྲོན་པའི་གཅེན་པོ་དྲུག། ཡབ་དང་བཅས་པ་ལྷ་ཡི་ཡུལ་དུ་གཤེགས།། བདུན་པ་ཐ་ཆུང་མ་བཟང་སྤྱི་རྗེ་དང་།། ཐོག་ལྷུམ་ཙུ་མོའི་སྲས་ནི་དཔའ་བོ་སྟག། ཞེས་དང་། དེའི་ཐད་ཀྱི་འགྲེལ་བཤད་ལས། བར་བ་གཡུ་རིང་འདིས་དམུ་ཡི་བུ་མོ་དམུ་བཟའ་ལྡེ་བུ་ཁབ་ཏུ་བཞེས་པས་མ་བཟང་བུ་བདུན་དུ་གྲགས་པ་བྱུང་ཞིང་། དེ་ལྟར་བདུན་གྱི་གཅེན་ཡབ་དང་བཅས་པ་ལྷ་ཡུལ་དུ་གཤེགས། བདུན་པ་མ་བཟང་སྤྱི་རྗེ་བྱ་བ་དེས། མི་ཡུལ་དུ་བཞུགས་ནས་ཐོག་ལྷ་འོད་འབར་ཅན་གྱི་བུ་མོ་ཐོག་ལྷུམ་ཙུར་མོ་ཆེ་ཁབ་ཏུ་གཞེས་པ་ལ་སྲས་ཐོག་ཚ་དཔའ་བོ་སྟག་ཏུ་གྲགས་པ་འཁྲུངས། ཞེས་གསུངས། མཁས་པའི་དགའ་སྟོན་དང་ས་སྐྱའི་གདུང་རབས་བར་མ་སངས་སྤྱུན་བདུན་དང་དགུའི་བཤད་པ་མི་འདྲ་བ་མ་ཟད། བདུན་པའམ་ཡང་ན་ཐ་ཆུང་དགུ་པ་གང་ལ་བྱས་ནའང་། ས་སྐྱའི་གདུང་རབས་ལས་བྱུང་བའི་མ་སངས་སྤྱི་རྗེ་བྱ་བ་ཞིག་མཁས་པའི་དགའ་སྟོན་ནང་མི་འབྱུང་མོད། འོན་ཀྱང་མི་གཅིག་ལ་མིང་གི་རྣམ་གྲངས་དུ་མ་ཡོད་ཚོག་པས་འགལ་བ་མི་སེམས་ལ། རྣམ་པ་གཅིག་ཏུ་ན། མ་སངས་བུ་ཐ་ཆུང་གིས་ཡུལ་གྱི་རྗེ་བོ་མཛད་པའི་རྗེས་སུ་རུས་མ་སངས་དང་བོད་སྤྱིའི་རྗེ་བོ་གྱུར་པས། མ་སངས་སྤྱི་རྗེ་ཞེས་པ་འདི་རྗེས་སུ་གྲུབ་པའི་མིང་ཡིན་ཚོག་པའང་སེམས་མོད། ད་དུང་དཔྱད་པར་བྱ་བའི་གནས་སོ།། ས་སྐྱའི་གདུང་རབས་རིན་ཆེན་བང་མཛོད་ལས་གཡུ་རིང་དང་དམུ་བཟའ་ལས་མ་སངས་སྤྱུན་བདུན་བྱུང་ཚུལ་གསུང་པའི་ཐད། གོང་འོག་ལོ་རྒྱུས་མང་པོ་ཞིག་གྱུང་བསྒྲིགས་ན། གཡུ་རིང་དང་དམུ་བཟའི་སྲས་དམུ་རྒྱལ་ཁོལ་རྗེ་འཁྲུངས། དེས་ཁྲིམ་བཟུང་བའི་རྒྱུན་འཛིན་མ་སངས་སྤྱུན་བདུན་ནམ་དགུ་བྱུང་ན་འབྲེལ་ཆགས་པར་སྣང་བས་དཔྱད་པར་བྱ་དགོས།

མ་སངས་ཀྱིས་བོད་ཀྱི་དབང་བྱས་ཚུལ་ཐད། ས་སྐྱའི་གདུང་རབས་ལས[53] མ་སངས་ཀྱི་ཕ་རིགས་ལྷ་དང་མ་རིགས་རྨི་ཡིན་ཚུལ་བཤད་པ་གཞིར་བཅོལ་ནས་དཔྱོད་པ་རགས་ཙམ་གཏོང་ན། མ་སངས་ཀྱི་མེས་པོ་རྨི་རིགས་ཀྱི་ལག་ནས་མངའ་རིས་ཀྱི་ལང་ཧྲང་ལེང་ཧྲང་པ་གྲོག་གྲོག་འདྲེ་མགོ་ཚོ་བས་སྲིད་དབང་ཕྲོགས་པའི་ཞེན་ནད་འཁོན་འཛིན་ཡོད་ནའང་དཔའ་དང་དཔུང་པས་གཞན་སྡེ་གནོན་པའི་ནུས་པ་མི་འདང་བར། གྲོ་གྲོག་འདྲེ་ཡི་ཚོ་བའི་འོག་བསྡད་དགོས་བྱུང་བའི་མཐའ་མཇུག་ཡབ་རྨི་ཡི་རྒྱལ་རྒྱུད་ལས་བུ་སྤྱུན་དགུ་བྱུང་བ་དེ་དག་དཔའ་དང་བློ་ཁོག ཐབས་དང་གཡོ་རྒྱུས། ཕ་རུས་མ་ཞེན་ཤེན་ཏུ་ཆེ་སྟབས་ཡབ་མེས་ཀྱི་སྲིད་དབང་འཕྲོག་མཁན་གྲོག་གྲོག་འདྲེ་ཡི་ཚོ་བ་ལ་ཕ་རུས་མ་ཞེན་གྱི་འཁོན་འཛིན་བཅངས་ནས་ཤི་འཛིངས་རོ་འཐབ་བྱས་པས་ཐ་མའི་རྒྱལ་ཁ་དེ་མ་སངས་སྤྱུན་དགུས་ཐོབ་པར་སེམས་ཏེ། ས་སྐྱའི་གདུང་རབས་ལས། མ་སངས་ཀྱི་ཡབ་དང་ཕུ་བོ་རྣམས་ལྷ་ཡུལ་ལ་གཤེགས་ཚུལ་གསུངས་པ་འདིས་དེ་རྣམས་གྲོག་གྲོག་འདྲེ་དང་དམག་འཐབ་བྱས་པའི་གཡུལ་སར་རང་སྲོག་གཏོང་པ་ཡིན་སྲིད་སྙམ།

འདིའི་དུས་ནས་རང་རེའི་ཡུལ་ལྗོངས་ལ་བོད་ཅེས་པའི་མིང་འདི་བྱུང་འདུག་པ་ལོ་རྒྱུས་ཐོག་མཐོང་རྒྱ་ཆེ་བ་དུ་མས་ངོས་འཛིན་གནང་བ་དོན་ལ་གནས་པ་སེམས་ཏེ། བཀའ་ཐང་ལས། བོད་ཁམས་གཡའ་དྲུག་དང་།[54] ཁུ་སྟོན་གྱི་ལོ་རྒྱུས་ཆེན་པོར་བོད་ཁ་ཉ་དྲུག་ཅེས་དང་།[55] ལྡེའུ་ཆོས་འབྱུང་ལས། བོད་ཁ་གཡང་དྲུག་ཅེས།[56]

སྐབས་དེ་དག་ཏུ་དག་ཆ་གཅིག་གྱུར་མེད་སྟབས་སྒྲ་གདངས་ཉེ་བའི་ཡི་གེ་འདྲ་མིན་བྲིས་འདུག་ནའང་། བོད་ཅེས་པ་འདི་གཅིག་མཐུན་དུ་བྱུང་འདུག་པས་སོ།།

མ་སངས་ཀྱི་ཕ་དང་ཕུ་བོ་རྣམས་ཀྱོག་ཀྱོག་འདྲི་དང་འཐབ་ནས་གཡུལ་སར་གཤེགས་པའི་རྗེས། མ་སངས་ཀྱི་བུ་ཆུང་བ་བཀོད་སྟོར་ནམ་ཆས་སྲིད་དབང་བཟུང་བ་ནས་མ་སངས་སྤྱི་རྗེར་འབོད་པ་འདིའི་སྐབས་སྔོན་གྱི་མི་རབས་ཚོས། གཞན་ཕྱོགས་ལ་རྒོལ་བྱེད་ཀྱི་ལག་ཆ་དེ་དག་གི་སྟེང་དུ་རང་ཉིད་ཀྱི་ངོ་གདོང་སྲུང་སྐྱོབ་བྱེད་པའི་གདོང་རལ་དང་། གཟུགས་པོ་འགེབས་པའི་གོ་ཁྲབ་དང་ཕུབ་ཆུང་ཡང་གསར་དུ་བཟོ་ཤེས་པ་བྱུང་བས། གཡུལ་སར་ཕ་རོལ་པོ་གསོད་རྨས་མང་དུ་གཏོང་བ་དང་། རང་ཕྱོགས་ལ་ཤི་རྨས་ཀྱི་གནད་ཆགས་ཆེན་པོ་མི་ཡོང་བའི་ཐབས་ཤེས་ཀྱང་འདི་ནས་དར་བས། གཡུལ་སར་གདོང་མཆོང་བྱེད་པར་སྟ་བས་གློ་ཁོག་དང་གདེང་སྤོབས་ཆེ་རུ་འགྲོ་བའང་བཤད་མི་དགོས་པ་ཞིག་རེད་སྙམ།

ཡང་རང་རེའི་གནའ་མི་ཚོའི་ངག་སྒྲོས་སུ། མ་སངས་ནི་མི་མ་ཡིན་པ་དང་། ཐེའུ་རང་ཡིན་ལུགས། ཐེའུ་རང་ཞེས་པ་འང་མི་དངོས་མིན་ཡང་མི་མ་ཡིན་གྱི་ཁྲོད་ནས་མི་དང་འབྲེལ་བ་ཉེ་ཕྱོགས་དེ་ཡིན་པ་དང་། དེ་ཡང་མི་ལས་སྟོབས་དང་རྫུ་འཕྲུལ་དཔའ་རྩལ་སོགས་ཆེ་བ་ཡོད་ཚུལ་ཡང་གྲགས་ཆེ་སྟེ། མཁས་དབང་ནམ་མཁའི་ནོར་བུའི་སྒྲུང་ལྡེའུ་བོན་གསུམ་གྱི་གཏམ་ཨེ་མ་ཧོ་ཞེས་བྱ་བ་ལས།[57] །མ་སངས་གི་སྒྲུང་ནི་གནའ་བོའི་དུས་ཀྱི་བྱུང་རབས་བཤད་པའི་སྒྲུང་རྣམས་ཏེ། སྒྲུང་དེ་མ་སངས་ཙམ་དུ་མ་ཟད་མི་མ་ཡིན་གཞན་དག་གི་སྒྲུང་མང་པོ་ཞིག་ཀྱང་དེའི་ཁོངས་སུ་འདུས་ཡོད། གང་ལ་ཟེར་ན། སྤྱི་བཏང་མིའི་འགྲོ་བ་རྣམས་མི་མ་ཡིན་པའི་རིགས་གཞན་དག་དང་འབྲེལ་བ་ཅི་རིགས་ཤིག་ཡོད་ནའང་། མི་ཕལ་བོ་ཆེར་དེ་དག་མངོན་གསལ་འབྱུང་བ་དཀའ་ཞིང་། ཐེའུ་རང་ནི་མི་མ་ཡིན་པའི་གྲས་ཤིག་ཡིན་རུང་། མིའི་རིགས་དང་ཤིན་ཏུ་འབྲེལ་བ་ཆེ་བ་ཞིག་ཡིན་སྟབས་མིའི་རིགས་ཀུན་ལ་མངོན་གསལ་ཆེ་ཙམ་བྱུང་བ་དེའི་རྐྱེན་གྱིས། གནའ་མི་ཚོས་མི་མ་ཡིན་པའི་ཁྱད་མཚར་གྱི་ཅི་སྲིད་པ་དེ་ཀུན་མ་སངས་གི་ཆོ་འཕྲུལ་དུ་བསམས་ནས། མ་སངས་གི་སྒྲུང་མང་ཞིག་བཤད་སྲོལ་བྱུང་བ་ཡིན།

མ་སངས་གི་སྒྲུང་སྐོར་དཔེར་མཚོན་ན། བོད་ཀྱི་ཡུལ་འདིར་སྔོན་ཐོག་མར་མིའི་འགྲོ་བ་མེད་སྐབས་དེར་བོད་ཀྱི་སྣོད་བཅུད་ཐམས་ཅད་མ་སངས་སྤུན་དགུས་དབང་བྱས་ཚུལ་གྱི་སྒྲུང་དང་། བོད་ཀྱི་མི་རྒྱུད་བྱུང་ནས་ཀྱང་། འགྲོ་བ་མིའི་ཚོགས་དང་མ་སངས་གི་འབྲེལ་བ་རྣམ་པར་སྣ་ཚོགས་པ་བྱུང་མྱོང་བའི་སྒྲུང་དང་། མིའི་འགྲོ་བ་འགའ་ཞིག་མ་སངས་དང་གཉེན་སྦྲེལ་བྱས་པ་ལས་རིགས་རྒྱུད་མཆེད་ཚུལ་གྱི་སྒྲུང་དང་། མ་སངས་གི་འཕྲུལ་གྱིས་བཟོས་པའི་གོ་མཚོན་ནམ། ཡོ་བྱད་ཅི་རྒྱགས་པ་རྣམས་མིའི་ལག་ཏུ་བྱུང་བའི་སྒྲུང་དང་། མ་སངས་གི་རྗེ་བོས་སྐྱེས་བུ་མཐུ་ཆེན་པོ་དང་། སྟོབས་ཆེན་པོ་དང་། འབྱོར་པ་ཆེན་པོ་རྣམས་ལ་རྒོལ་བ་བྱས་པའི་སྒྲུང་། མཐུ་ཆེན་པདྨ་སཾ་བྷ་ཝས་མ་སངས་གི་རྗེ་བོ་དམ་ལ་བཏགས་པས་དམ་ཅན་རྡོ་རྗེ་ལེགས་པར་གྱུར་པ་དེ་ལྷ་བུའི་སྒྲུང་དང་། ཐག་རིང་གི་མགྲོན་པོ་དང་། ཚོང་པ་ཁ་ཤས་མ་སངས་གི་གྲོགས་པོ་ཆགས་ནས་དེ་རྣམས་ལ་མ་སངས་གི་རོགས་རམ་ཐོབ་ཚུལ་གྱི་སྒྲུང་དང་། ཞྭ་པ་འགའ་ཞིག་གིས་མ་སངས་བསྒྲུབས་པས་དངོས་སུ་གྲུབ་སྟེ་མ་སངས་གིས་རྒྱན་པོའི་གྲོགས་བྱས་པའི་སྒྲུང་དང་། ཐ་ནའང་བོད་ཀྱི་ཞྭ་པ་ཚོས་ཞྭ་རྟ་བའི་སྐབས་སུ་ཞོ་འབོད་སྐད་ཤུགས་ཆེན་པོས་བྱེད་སྲོལ་ཡོད་པ་དེའི་རྒྱུ་མཚན་ཇི་ལྟར་བྱུང་བའི་ཚུལ་ཡང་། གནའ་དུས་སུ་མ་སངས་ལ་རྒྱུས་ཆེ་བའི་ཞྭ་པ་འགས་མ་སངས་ཞྭ་ལ་དགྱེས་པར་ཤེས་ན། ཞྭ་རྟེ་སྐབས་སུ་སྐད་ཤུགས་ཏ་ཙང་ཆེན་པོས་ཞྭ་འབོད་བྱས་པས། མ་སངས་དངོས་སུ་འོངས་

ནས་ཤོ་པ་དེ་ལ་རིགས་པ་བྱས་པ་དང་། ཤོ་འབོད་བྱེད་པའི་སྐབས་སུའང་ཤོའི་གྲངས་རྩིས་ནམ་རྒྱུན་དང་མི་འདྲ་བའི་སྐད་ལུགས་ཤིག་ཡོད་པ་སྟེ། ཞེས་གསུངས་པས་ཀྱང་ཤེས་ནུས།

མ་སང་ཐེའུ་རང་ཡིན་རབས་དང་ཐེའུ་རང་ལ་རྐང་པ་ཡ་གཅིག་ལས་མེད་པའི་བཤད་སྲོལ་གྱིས་ཤན་ཞུགས་ཐེབས་ཏེ་གླིང་སྒྲུང་[58] རྣམས་སུ། ཐེའུ་རང་བླ་མ་རྐང་གཅིག་ཟེར་བ་བས་མཐུ་དང་རྫུ་འཕྲུལ་ངོམས་རབས་དང་། ཡང་མ་སང་རྩལ་ཆོད་པ་དང་མཐུ་ཆེ་བའི་བཤད་སྲོལ་ལ་བརྟེན་ནས་གླིང་གེ་སར་ལ་ཡང་། མ་སང་སྐྱེས་བུ་དོན་འགྲུབ་ཅེས་འབོད་པ་གླིང་རྣམས་ལས་ཡང་ཡང་འབྱུང་། བསད་སྲོལ་དེ་དག་ནི་མ་སང་ལ་སྐབས་དེའི་མི་སྤྱི་སྤྱང་ས་པ་ཆོས་དཔའ་དང་བློ་ཁོག ཐབས་དང་བཀོད་ཇུས། མཐུ་དང་རྫུ་འཕྲུལ། ཐ་ན་རྒྱུན་དང་རྩེད་མོ་སོགས་གང་ས་ཅི་ཐད་ནས་འགྲན་པ་མི་ནུས་པས། མ་སང་ནི་མིའི་གནས་ཚད་ལས་བརྒལ་བའི་འགྲོ་བ་གཞན་ནམ་མི་མ་ཡིན་པ་ཞིག་ཏུ་ངོས་འཛིན་བྱས་པ་ལས། དོན་དངོས་ཐོག་མི་ཡི་བྱེ་བྲག་ལས་འདའ་བ་ཞིག་མིན་པ་སེམས་སོ།།

གཞན་བོན་གྱི་ཡིག་ཆར་མ་སངས་ཀྱི་སྒྲུང་མང་དུ་ཡོད་ཚུལ་གོ་བ་ཙམ་ལས་ཡིག་ཆ་མཇལ་སྐྱོད་མེད། མཁས་དབང་ནམ་མཁའི་ནོར་བུས། [59] མ་སང་གི་སྒྲུང་སྐོར་དཔེར་འཕོད་པ་ནི། བན་བོན་གྱི་ཡིག་རྙིང་ཁ་ཤས་སུ་མ་སང་སྤུན་དགུའི་སྐོར་ཐར་ཐོར་ཙམ་རེ་འབྱུང་བ་ལས་གཞན་དམིགས་བསལ་གྱི་དཔེ་གང་ཞིག་ཀྱང་མ་མཐོང་། ཞེས་དང་། དེ་དག་གི་དཔེ་འགའ་ཞིག་ཡོད་ཀྱང་སྲིད་ལ། གལ་ཏེ་མེད་དུ་ཆུག་ཀྱང་། བོད་ཀྱི་ཤེས་རིག་ལ་གཅེས་སྤྲས་གནང་མཁན་མཁྱེན་ཡོན་དང་ལྡན་པ་རྣམས་ནས་བོད་མི་རྐན་གྲས་དངོས་བཞུགས་རྣམས་ཀྱི་ཞལ་ཐོག་ནས་མ་སང་སྐོར་གྱི་སྒྲུང་དེ་རིགས་ཡི་གེར་འགོད་ཐུབ་ན་དེ་སྐོར་གྱི་སྒྲུང་མི་ཉུང་བ་ཞིག་འགོད་དུ་ཡོད་ངེས། ཞེས་པ་འདིར་བལྟས་ན་མཐོང་རྒྱ་ཆེ་བའི་མཁས་པ་ཁོང་གིས་ཀྱང་མ་སང་སྐོར་གྱི་སྒྲུང་ཡིག་ཐོག་ཏུ་ཡོད་རབས་ཙམ་ལས་མཐོང་ཐོས་བྱུང་བ་མང་པོ་རང་མིན་པས། གཅིག་བྱས་ན་འདི་རིགས་དཔེ་རྒྱུན་ཧ་ཅང་དཀོན་པའམ། ཡང་ན་ཡིག་ཐོག་ཏུ་འཕོད་པ་ཉུང་ཉུང་ཡིན་ངེས་ཀྱང་སྙམ་སྟེ། གང་ལྟར་ཡང་ཐུགས་ཞིབ་གནང་འོས་པ་ཞིག་རེད་སྙམ།

བོད་ཀྱི་སྤྱི་ཚོགས་ཁྲོད་གནའ་ནས་ད་བར་ཤོ་རྩེད་ཀྱི་ལུགས་སྲོལ་རྒྱ་ཆེར་ཡོད་པ་འདི་དག་ཀྱང་གཅིག་བྱས་ན། མ་སང་གི་སྐབས་སུ་གསར་དུ་དར་བ་ཞིག་ཡིན་ཡང་སྙམ་ལ། ད་དུང་ཤོ་རྩེད་ཀྱི་སྐབས་གྲངས་གནས་ཀྱི་མིང་ཡང་དེང་སང་བོད་ཡོངས་གྲགས་ཀྱི་ཐ་སྙད་དང་མི་འདྲ་བར། གཉིས་ལ་པ་ར། གསུམ་ལ་སུག བཞི་ལ་ཛིག ལྔ་ལ་ཁ། དྲུག་ལ་འབྲུག བདུན་ལ་རི། བརྒྱད་ལ་ཤ། དགུ་ལ་དགུ། བཅུ་ལ་ཀུ། བཅུ་གཅིག་ལ་ཐོག བཅུ་གཉིས་ལ་ཅ་ལོའམ་ཡང་ན་འཛམ། ཞེས་འབོད་པ་འདིའི་ཐོག་ནས། སྐབས་དེའི་བོད་ཀྱི་གྲངས་གནས་བགྲང་སྟངས་དེ་ག་རང་ཡིན་པ་ལ། དུས་ཕྱིས་རིམ་གྱིས་འགྱུར་བ་སོང་ནས་དགུ་མ་གཏོགས་གཞན་རྣམས་སྒྲ་ཟུར་ཉམས་ནས་དེང་སང་གི་གྲངས་གནས་བགྲང་སྟངས་འདི་བྱུང་པའང་ཡིན་སྲིད་སྙམ་སྟེ། ད་དུང་ཡང་དཔྱད་པར་བྱ་དགོས།

འདིའི་རྒྱལ་ས་ལྡེ་བ་ནི། ད་ལྟའི་མོན་རྟ་དབང་གི་ས་ཁུལ་དུ་ཡིན་པ་སེམས་ཏེ། རྒྱུ་མཚན་གང་གིས་ན། ལོ་རྒྱུས་ཀྱི་ཡིག་ཆར་འཕོད་མིན་ཇི་ལྟར་ཡང་། ལྷོ་མོན་གྱི་ཕྱོགས་སུ་མ་སངས་ཀྱི་སྐོར་བཤད་སྲོལ་མང་པོ་གོ་རྒྱུ་དང་མཐོང་རྒྱུ་འདུག་པ་དཔེར་ན། ལྷོ་མོན་གྱི་རི་སུལ་འགར་རྫོ་ཕ་བོང་ཆེན་པོ་གཅིག་ཐོག་གཅིག་བརྩེགས་ཅན་དུ

མ་ཡོད་པར་ཡུལ་མི་ཚོས། དེ་དག་ལ་མ་སངས་ཀྱི་རྫོ་བརྩིགས་དང་། ཡང་རྫོ་རིང་གྲིབ་དུ་ཀ་བ་ལྟར་བསྒྲེངས་པ་དུ་མ་ཡོད་པ་དེ་དག་ལ་མ་སངས་ཀྱི་ཀ་བ་དང་། ཡང་རྫོ་རིལ་ཆེན་པོ་ཁག་གཅིག་ལ་མ་སངས་ཀྱི་སོར་རྫོ་ཡིན་ཚུལ་དེང་སང་གི་བར་དུ་གྲགས་ཆེ་བ་ཤེས་གསལ་ཡིན། དེ་བཞིན་ཟེར་མའི་བྱང་རྒྱུད་དུ་བྱང་ཟེར་བའི་གྲོང་པའི་ཕར་ཕྱོགས་སུ་བྲ་མཐའ་ཟེར་བའི་གཡང་གཟའི་ལྷོ་ངོས་ནས་འབབ་པའི་ཆུ་ཞིག་ལ། མ་སངས་ཀྱི་གཙུན་རྒྱངས་སུ་འབོད་པ་དང་། ས་ཁུལ་དེར་སྐྱེས་པའི་སྔ་ཆུང་གསེར་མགོ་ཟེར་བའི་སྨན་ལྷུམ་ལ་མ་སངས་ཚོད་མ་འབོད་སྲོལ་ཡོད་པ་ཡོངས་གྲགས་ཡིན་པས། རྒྱུ་མཚན་དེ་དག་ལ་བལྟས་ན་ཕལ་ཆེར་མ་སངས་ཀྱི་རྒྱལ་ས་ལྡེ་བ་དེ། དེང་སང་མོན་རྟ་དབང་ཕྱོགས་འདིར་ཡིན་ཚོད་པར་སེམས།[60]

མངའ་མཛད་བརྒྱད་པ་གླུས་དབང་བྱས་ཚུལ།

ཆོས་འབྱུང་མཁས་པའི་དགའ་སྟོན་ལས། དེ་ནས་གླུ་དང་བཙན་གྱིས་དབང་བྱས་ཏེ།། བརྒྱད་པ་གླུས་དབང་བྱས་བོད་ཁམས་གླིང་དགུར་བཏགས།། ལྡེའུ་ཆོས་འབྱུང་ལས། བརྒྱད་པ་གླུས་བཟུང་བོད་ཁམས་གླིང་དགུ་བཏགས།། རྒྱལ་པོ་བཀའ་ཐང་ལས། དེ་ནས་གླུ་དང་བཙན་གྱིས་དབང་བྱས་ཏེ།། ཡུལ་གྱི་མིང་ལ་བོད་ཁམས་གླིང་དགུ་བཏགས།། ཐུ་རྟགས་དཀར་བུ་ཆུ་ལ་སྤྱོད་པ་བྱུང་།། མངའ་མཛད་བརྒྱད་པ་གླུས་དབང་བྱས་ཚུལ་ནི། མ་སངས་སྤྲེ་རྗེའི་བུ་དཔའ་བོ་སྟག་གིས་སྲིད་བཟུང་མཐར་གླུ་ལྷམ་བྲ་མ་ཞེས་པ་ཆུང་མར་བསུས་པའི་སྲས་གླུ་ཚ་སྟག་པོ་འོད་ཅེས་པ་འཁྲུངས། དེའི་ཚུལ་ཡང་། ཡ་རབས་ཁ་རྒྱན་ལས།[61] བདུན་གྱི་ཐ་ཆུང་མ་བཟང་སྤྲེ་རྗེ་དང་།། ཐོག་ལྷམ་འུར་མོའི་སྲས་ནི་དཔའ་བོ་སྟག། དེ་དང་གླུ་ལྷམ་བྲ་མ་གཉིས་ཀྱི་སྲས།། གླུ་ཚ་སྟག་པོ་འོད་ཅན་ཞེས་བྱ་བྱུང་།། ཞེས་དང་། དེའི་ཐད་ཀྱི་རིན་ཆེན་བང་མཛོད་ལས།[62] བདུན་པ་མ་སངས་སྤྲེ་རྗེ་བྱ་བ་དེ་མི་ཡུལ་ལ་བཞུགས་ནས་ཐོག་ལྷ་འོད་ཅན་གྱི་བུ་མི་ཐོག་ལྷམ་འུར་མོ་ཁབ་ཏུ་བཞེས་པ་ལ་སྲས་ཐོག་ཚ་དཔའ་བོ་སྟག་ཏུ་གྲགས་པ་འཁྲུངས་ཏེ། དེས་གླུའི་བུ་མོ་གླུ་ལྷམ་བྲ་མ་ཁབ་ཏུ་བཞེས་པས་གླུ་ཚ་སྟག་པོ་འོད་ཅན་བྱ་བ་སྲས་སུ་བྱུང་། ཞེས་མ་སངས་ཀྱི་རྒྱུད་ལས་གླུ་ཚ་བྱུང་ཚུལ་གསུངས་པ་དང་། མཁས་པ་ལྡེའུ་དང་གཙུག་ཕྲེང་ཀུན་གྱི་བཞེད་པ་ཀུན་ཤིན་ཏུ་མཐུན་པས། གླུས་བཟུང་ཞེས་པ་ནི། གླུ་ཚ་སྟག་པོ་འོད་ཅན་འདི་ཉིད་ཁོ་ན་ངེས་པར་སེམས་སོ།།

དེས་ན། བོད་ཡུལ་གླུ་ཚས་བཟུང་ཚུལ་ཡང་ཕ་རྒྱུད་མ་སངས་ཀྱི་རུས་ནས་མི་འབོད་པར། མ་རྒྱུད་གླུའི་ཚོ་རིགས་ནས་དྲས་ཏེ་གླུས་བཟུང་ཞེས་པ་ཙམ་ལས་མ་སངས་གཏོར་ཕམ་བཏང་ནས་གླུས་སྲིད་གཞུང་གསར་དུ་བཙུགས་པ་མ་ཡིན་པ་འདྲ། སྐབས་དེར་རང་རེའི་ཡུལ་ལ་བོད་ཁམས་གླིང་དགུ་ཞེས་བཏགས་ཤིང་། དེ་ཡང་བོད་ཀྱི་མིང་ཐོར་ཡོད་ཐོག་ནང་ཁུལ་སྡེ་ཚན་ནམ་གླིང་དགུར་གྱེས་པ་ཡིན་ནམ་ཡང་སྙམ། རྒྱལ་པོའི་དཀའ་ཐང་ལས། ལྷ་དང་འདྲེས་དབང་བྱས་པའི་རྗེས་སུ་གླུ་དང་། དེ་རྗེས་མ་སངས་སྤྱུན་དགུས་དབང་བྱས་བཀོད་དེ། གཙུག་ཕྲེང་དང་ལྡེའུ། ཡ་རབས་ཁ་རྒྱན་སོགས་དང་གཞེད་པ་མི་འདྲ་བ་འདུག་པས་དཔྱད་དགོས། གཅིག་བྱས་ན་འདི་ཉིད་འགོང་པོ་སྤྱུན་དགུ་དང་མིང་ཚིག་ནོར་བ་ཡིན་ཡང་སྲིད་སྙམ་སྟེ། ཚད་ལྡན་ལོ་རྒྱུས་གཞན་དང་གཞན་[63]དུ་མའི་ནང་དུ་གླུའི་རྗེས་སུ་རྒྱལ་འགོང་ངམ་འགོང་པོ་སྤྱུན་དགུས་བཟུང་ཚུལ་གསལ་བར་གསུངས་པས་སོ།།

མངའ་མཛད་དགུ་པ་རྒྱལ་འགོང་གིས་དབང་བྱས་ཚུལ།

ཆོས་འབྱུང་མཁས་པའི་དགའ་སྟོན་ལས། དགུ་པ་རྒྱལ་པོས་དབང་བྱས་རམ་པོ་ཅེ། །བཅུ་པ་འགོང་པོ་སྤུན་དགུས་དབང་བྱས་ཏེ། །ཡུལ་གྱི་མིང་ཡང་སྟོང་སྡེ་བཅོ་བརྒྱད་ཟེར།། ཞེས་དང་། ལྡེའུ་ཆོས་འབྱུང་ལས།དགུ་པ་མི་མ་ཡིན་གྱིས་དབང་བྱས་ཏེ། །ཡུལ་གྱི་མིང་ནི་ངམ་ཡུལ་ནག་པོར་བཏགས།། རྒྱལ་པོ་བཀའ་ཐང་ལས། དེ་ནས་མ་སངས་སྤུན་དགུས་དབང་བྱས་ཏེ། །ཡུལ་མིང་བོད་ཁམས་གཡའ་དྲུག་བྱ་བར་བཏགས། །སྤྱི་རྟགས་མདའ་མདུང་མཚོན་ཆ་དེ་ནས་བྱུང་།།ཞེས་དང་། གླིང་བཞི་བསྟན་པའི་འབྱུང་ཁུངས་ལས། དེ་ནས་མ་སངས་ཀྱིས་དབང་བགྱིས་ཏེ། ཡུལ་གྱི་མིང་ཡང་བོད་ཀ་གཡག་དྲུག་ཏུ་བཏགས་སོ།། དེའི་དུས་སུ་གཉན་བོན་ཐོག་ལྷ་ཁྲོལ་བ་དང་། གཉན་གསུམ་ཐོད་དེ་རྒྱལ་བ་ལ་སོགས་པ་བྱུང་ནས་མ་སངས་མཆེད་དྲུག་ལ་སོགས་པས་བཀུར་བསྟི་བོན་ལ་བགྱིས་ཏེ། མ་སངས་ཀྱི་གོང་ན་གཞི་ཤེན་རབ་གཉན་པ་ལགས་སོ། །ཞེས་གསུངས། མཁས་པའི་དགའ་སྟོན་དུ།[64] དགུ་པ་རྒྱལ་པོ་དང་བཅུ་པ་འགོང་པོ་ཞེས་སོ་སོར་འཆད་ཀྱང་། གཙུག་ཕྲེང་རང་ཉིད་ཀྱིས་ཁུངས་གང་ལ་གཏུགས་སའི་མཁས་པ་ལྡེའུའི་གསུང་དུ།[65] དགུ་པ་མི་མ་ཡིན་ཞེས་གཅིག་ཏུ་འཆད་འདུག་པ་ཁུངས་དག་པའི་ལུགས་སུ་བྱས་ནས་འཆད་ན། འགོང་པོ་སྤུན་དགུ་ནི་སྐབས་དེར་མིའི་བསམ་བློའི་ནང་མི་འདུ་བའི་ཐབས་འཕྲུལ་དང་སྙིང་སྟོབས་ཆེས་ཤིན་ཏུ་ཆེ་བའི་བུ་སྤུན་དགུ་བྱུང་ཞིང་། དེ་དག་གི་མིང་ཡང་། ༡ གཉའ་གཡའ་སྤུངས་སྐྱེས། ༢ གར་ཏིང་ནམ་ཚོ། ༣ གླི་ངན་ནམ་ཙང་སྐྱེས། ༤ རུ་ཐོ་གར་སྐྱེས། ཤེ་ཏོ་གོར་ཏིང་ནས། ༦ མི་པད་སྐྱེས། ༧ གསང་གི་འཕྲུལ་པོ་ཆེ། ༨ དྲང་པ་དྲང་མ་མགུར། ༩ བགོད་སྟོར་ནམ་ཚ་ཞེས་འབྱུང་བ་ལྟར་ལགས་སོ།། བཀའ་ཐང་དང་གླིང་བཞི་བསྟན་པའི་འབྱུང་ཁུངས་ལས།[66] འགོང་པོ་སྤུན་དགུ་དང་མ་སངས་སྤུན་དགུ་གཅིག་པ་ལྟར་བྱས་ནས་འཆད་འདུག་ལ། ད་དུང་བོད་ཀ་གཡག་དྲུག་ཅེས་པའི་མིང་ཡང་འགོང་པོ་སྤུན་དགུའི་སྐབས་བྱུང་ཚུལ་འཆད་འདུག་པ་ལའང་དཔྱད་པར་བྱ་དགོས་སོ།། འདི་དག་གི་དཔའ་འཛངས་རྟུལ་ཕོད་ལ་བརྟེན་ནས་ཀླུ་ཚའི་རིགས་རྒྱུད་ཀྱི་སྲིད་དབང་ལ་གྲིབ་ལོག་བྱས། དཔའ་དང་དཔུང་པ། ཐབས་དང་གཡོ་འཕྲུལ་ཅི་རིགས་སྣ་ཚོགས་ཀྱིས་རང་ཕྱོགས་གཅིག་སྒྲིལ་ཡོང་ཐབས་ཐོག དེ་སྔོན་ཀླུ་ཚའི་སྲིད་གཞུང་དང་འཁོན་འཛིན་ཡོད་པའི་ཕྱོགས་གཏོགས་ལ་ཉེ་ཕྱོགས་བཟུང་ནས། ཀླུ་ཚའི་ཚོ་བ་དང་རུ་སྡེ་ཀུན་རིམ་པར་བཞིན་བཅོམ། མཐར་རྒྱལ་ཁའི་གྲུབ་འབྲས་རང་ལག་ཏུ་ལྷུང་བ་ན། ད་བཟོད་སྲིད་གཞུང་གསར་པ་བཙུགས་པའི་མིང་ལ་ལོ་རྒྱུས་ཐོག་འགོངས་པོ་སྤུན་དགུ་ཞེས་གྲགས་པ་འདི་ཉིད་བཙུགས་པས། མི་རྣམས་ཀྱིས་འདི་དག་མི་རང་ག་ཞིག་མིན་པར་ལྷ་འདྲེའི་ཆོ་འཕྲུལ་འདྲ་བར་མཐོང་ནས་འགོངས་པོ་ཞེས་བཏགས་པ་ཡིན་སྙམ། སྲིད་འཛིན་ལྟེ་བ་ནི། ངོམ་ཡུལལ་ནག་པོ་ཞེས་བྱ་བའི་ཡུལ་དུ་ཡིན་ལ། དེ་ནི་དེང་སང་གི་མཁས་པ་འགས་[67] གཙང་གི་ངོམ་རིའི་ཡུལ་དུ་ཡིན་ཚུལ་བྲིས་འདུག་པར་ཁུངས་ཇི་ཡིན་བརྟག་དགོས།

བཅུ་པ། ཟ་རིད་སྤུན་དྲུག་གིས་དབང་བྱས་ཚུལ།

ལྡེའུ་ཆོས་འབྱུང་ལས། བཅུ་པ་ཟ་རིད་སྤུན་དྲུག་དག་གིས་དབང་བྱས་ཏེ། །ཡུལ་གྱི་མིང་ལ་སྟོང་སྡེ་བཅོ་བརྒྱད་ཟེར།། གླིང་བཞི་བསྟན་པའི་འབྱུང་ཁུངས་ལས། དེ་ནས་ཟ་རང་གི་བུ་བྱེད་སྐྱེས་དྲུག་གིས་དབང་བགྱིས་ཏེ།

ཡུལ་གྱི་མིང་ཡང་བྲིས་ཡུལ་དབྱེ་ཆེན་སྡེ་བརྒྱད་དུ་བཏགས་སོ།། དེའི་དུས་སུ་སྡེ་བོད་བྲེད་མཁས་བཙན་པ་བྱུང་། སྐྱེས་སུ་རྩོལ་བོ་ལེགས་པས་བཀུར་བསྟི་བོན་ལ་བགྱིས་ཏེ། དེའི་གོང་ན་བོན་དང་གཤེན་གཉན་པ་ལགས་སོ།། ཞེས་འབྱུང་། བཅུ་པ་ཟ་རིད་སྐྱེས་དྲུག་གིས་དབང་ཚུལ་ནི། ཆོས་འབྱུང་མཁས་པའི་དགའ་སྟོན་ལས་ནི།[68] དགུ་པ་རྒྱལ་འགོང་དང་བཅུ་པ་འགོང་པོ་སྤྱུན་དགུས་དབང་བྱས་ཚུལ་འཁོད་འདུག་མོད། གཞན་རྣམས་ཀྱི་དཔེ་ལྟ་སའི་ཁུངས་ལྡེའུ་ཆོས་འབྱུང་འདི་ཉིད་ཁོ་ན་ཡིན་པ་ཚིག་སྒྲོས་ཀྱི་ཐོག་ནས་ཀྱང་ཤེས་ཐུབ་ཀྱང་བཅུ་པ་འདི་ཉིད་བཤད་སྲོལ་མི་འདྲ་བ་གཞན་དུ་ངོས་འཛིན་བྱས་འདུག་པ་དེའི་ཁུངས་གང་ཞིག་ལ་བརྟེན་པ་ཡིན་པའི་སྐོར་དཔྱད་པར་བྱ་དགོས་སོ།། རྒྱལ་པོ་བཀའ་ཐང་ལས་ཀྱང་འདི་ཉིད་མི་འབྱུང་། གཡུང་དྲུང་བོན་གྱི་བསྟན་འབྱུང་རྣམས་སུ་[69] ཟ་རང་གི་བྲེད་སྐྱེས་དྲུག་ཅེས་གསལ་བར་འབྱུང་བ་གོང་དུ་དྲངས་པ་ལྟར་ལ། ཁུ་སྟོན་གྱི་ལོ་རྒྱུས་ཆེན་མོའི་ནང་ཇི་ལྟར་འཁོད་ཡོད་མེད་མ་མཐོང་། ཟ་རིད་སྤྱུན་དྲུག་གིས་འགོང་པོའི་སྲིད་དབང་འཕྲོག་པའམ་སྲིད་དབང་ཟུར་འཛུགས་གང་ཞིག་བྱས་པའི་ལོ་རྒྱུས་ཡིག་ཆ་ཁ་གསལ་ད་ཕན་མ་མཐོང་། ཟ་རིད་སྐྱེས་དྲུག་གིས་དབང་བསྒྱུར་བྱས་པའི་སྐབས་བོད་ཀྱི་ཡུལ་ལ་སྟོང་སྡེ་བཅོ་བརྒྱད་ཟེར་ཚུལ་ལྡེའུ་ཆོས་འབྱུང་དང་། མཁས་པའི་དགའ་སྟོན་[70] དུའང་མངའ་མཛད་བཅུ་པའི་སྐབས་ཡུལ་ལ་སྟོང་སྡེ་བཅོ་བརྒྱད་བཏགས་ཚུལ་འཁོད་འདུག པདྨ་ཀྲ་གའི་ལྡེ་མིག་ལས།[71] སྟོང་སྡེ་བཅོ་བརྒྱད་ནི་དེང་སང་མདོ་ཁམས་ཕྱོགས་ཀྱི་ཆབ་མདོ་ཡན་མན་ཞིག་གི་ཡུལ་གྲུ་ཞིག་ལ་ངོས་འཛིན་བྱས་འདུག་པའི་ཁུངས་གང་ཡིན་ནི་མ་ཤེས། གླིང་བཞི་བསྟན་པའི་འབྱུང་ཁུངས་ལས།[72] སྐབས་དེའི་ཡུལ་གྱི་མིང་ལ་བྲིས་ཡུལ་དབྱེ་ཆེན་སྡེ་བརྒྱད་འདོགས་ཚུལ་དང་། གཙོ་སྐྱོང་སྐྱེས་སུ་རྩོལ་བོ་ལེགས་སྐྱོང་ཟེར་ཚུལ་འཁོད་སྣང་མོད། ལོ་རྒྱུས་གཞན་མ་མཐོང་། མངའ་མཛད་བཅུ་པོ་དེ་དག་གི་སྐབས་ནས་བོན་གྱི་སྟོན་པ་བྱུང་ཚར་བའི་ཚུལ་བོན་གྱི་བསྟན་འབྱུང་ལས་གསལ་བ་དེ་དག་ཕལ་ཆེན་གདོན་མའི་བོན་གྱི་ཆོས་ལུགས་ཡིན་འཆི་སླམ་མེད་ད་དུང་དཔྱད་པར་བྱ་དགོས་སོ།།

རྒྱལ་ཕྲན་བཅུ་གཉིས་དང་སིལ་མ་བཞི་བཅུར་འཐོར་ཚུལ།

ལྡེའུ་ཆོས་འབྱུང་ལས། བཅུ་གཅིག་རྒྱལ་ཕྲན་བཅུ་གཉིས་དབང་བྱས་སྐད། །ཀུན་གྱི་ཐ་མར་སིལ་མ་བཞི་བཅུ་བྱས། །ཡུལ་གྱི་མིང་ནི་བཟང་ཡུལ་གྲུད་དུ་བཏགས།།[73] གླིང་བཞི་བསྟན་པའི་འབྱུང་ཁུངས་ལས། དེ་ནས་སིལ་མ་བཅུ་གཉིས་ཀྱིས་དབང་བྱིས་བྱས་ཏེ། ཡུལ་གྱི་མིང་ཡང་རྟིས་པོ་ཁ་བརྒྱད་བྱ་བ་ལགས་སོ།། དེའི་དུས་སུ་བོན་ཐོད་དཀར་བྱུང་སྟེ། རྒྱལ་གྱིས་བཀུར་བསྟི་བོན་ལ་བགྱིས་ཏེ། རྒྱལ་གོང་ན་བོན་དང་གཤེན་གཉན་པ་ལགས་སོ།།[74] དེ་ནས་རྒྱལ་ཕྲན་བཅུ་གཉིས་དང་སིལ་མ་བཞི་བཅུ་ལྷག་གྱིས་ནས་བོད་སིལ་བུར་ཐེངས་དང་པོ་དེ་འཐོར་བ་ཡིན་ནོ།།

དེ་ལ་སིལ་མ་བཞི་བཅུ་ནི་ལོ་རྒྱུས་རྣམས་སུ་བགྲང་ཚུལ་མི་འདྲ་བ་འགའ་མཆིས་ཀྱང་། འདིར་ཁུན་རྫོང་ཡིག་ཆ་ནང་བཀོད་པ་ལྟར་བགྲང་ན།[75] རྒྱལ་ཕྲན་ཕྲན་ཡུལ་ཡུལ་ན། མཁར་བུ་རེ་རེ་ན་གནས་སྟེ། རྒྱལ་ཕྲན་ཕྲན་བགྱིད་པ་དང་། རྒྱལ་ཕྲན་གྱི་བློན་པོ་བགྱིད་པའི་རང་རབས་ལ། ཞང་ཞུང་དར་པའི་ཇོ་ཇོ། བོ་ལེགས་སླ་ཤུར།

བློན་པོ་ཁྲུང་པོར་སངས་རྗེ་དང་། སྟོང་ལོམ་མ་ཙེ་གཉིས། མྱང་རོའི་ཕྱིན་ཕྱེད་ཀར་ན། རྗེ་རྨང་རྗེའི་ཐོད་ཀར། བློན་པོ་སུ་རུ་དང་གནང་གཉིས། ཡུལ་གནུབས་ཀྱི་གླིང་དྲུག་ན། རྗེ་གནུབས་རྗེའི་སྲིས་པ། བློན་པོ་རྨེའུ་དང་གྲོ་གཉིས། ཡུལ་མྱང་རོའི་ཤམས་པོ་ནི། རྗེ་ལོ་ངམ་གྱི་བྲོམ་ཚ། བློན་པོ་མྱ་དང་བྲེ་གཉིས། ཡུལ་སྐྱི་རོའི་ལྗང་སྔོན་ན། རྗེ་ཀྱི་རྗེའི་མང་པོ། བློན་པོ་ཞེའུ་དང་སུག་གཉིས། ཡུལ་ངས་པོའི་ཁྲ་གསུམ་ན། རྗེ་དགུག་གྱི་འི་ཟིང་པོ་རྗེ། བློན་པོ་མགར་དང་གཉན་གཉིས། ཡུལ་དབྱེ་རོ་ཡུལ་བཞི་ན། རྗེ་དབྱེ་རྗེ་འི་མཁར་པ། བློན་པོ་དབོ་དང་རྡུག་གཉིས། ཡུལ་འོ་ཡུལ་གཡི་སྦྱང་ཀར་ན། རྗེ་འོ་རྗེའི་ཟིན་བྲང་ཚ། བློན་པོ་རྫོ་དང་དབའས་གཉིས། ཡུལ་རྫིགས་ཡུལ་གྱི་གྲུ་བཞི་ན། རྗེ་རྫོག་རྗེའི་ལ་བྲང་། བློན་པོ་སས་པ་དང་མྱང་ནད་གཉིས། ཡུལ་ཀླུམ་རོའི་ཡ་སུམ་ན། རྗེ་ནམ་པའི་བུ་གསེང་ཏེ། བློན་པོ་མྱང་དང་སྦྲང་གཉིས། ཡུལ་སྲིབས་ཡུལ་གྱི་རལ་མོ་གོང་ན། རྗེ་དྲང་རྗེའི་རྔོལ་ནམ། བློན་པོ་ཞུག་ཚམས་དང་དབྲད་གཉིས། ཡུལ་ཀོང་ལ་བྲེ་སྣར་ན། རྗེ་ཀོང་རྗེའི་དཀར་པོ། བློན་པོ་མཁར་པ་དང་ཕ་དྲུག་གཉིས། ཡུལ་མྱང་ཡུལ་གྱི་ཧྲ་གསུམ་ན། རྗེ་མྱང་ཙུང་སླང་རྒྱལ། བློན་པོ་འོ་རུ་དང་སྦྲགས་གཉིས། ཡུལ་དྭགས་ཀྱི་གྲུ་བཞི་ན། རྗེ་དྭགས་རྒྱལ་གྱི་སྤྲོག་ཟིན། བློན་པོ་ཕོ་གྱུ་དང་པོག་རོལ་གཉིས། ཡུལ་མཆིམས་ཡུལ་གྱི་དགྱུའ་ཡུལ་ནའ། རྗེ་མཆིམས་རྗེའི་ནེ་འུ། བློན་པོ་དང་དང་དིང་དི་གཉིས། ཡུལ་སུམ་ཡུལ་གྱི་ཡ་སུམ་ནའ། རྗེ་འབས་ལྤྱི་མང་རུ་ཏེ། བློན་པོ་ཧླང་དང་ཀམ་གཉིས། ཡུལ་འབྲོག་མོ་རྣམ་གསུམ་ནའ། རྗེ་སེ་རི་ཁྲི། བློན་པོ་སྐྱང་རེ་གནག ཞེས་གསལ་བ་ལྟར་རོ།།

དེ་ལྟ་ན་བོད་ཀྱི་ལོ་རྒྱུས་ལ་ཞིབ་འཇུག་གནང་མཁན་ཚོས། སྤྱིར་རྒྱལ་གཉའ་ཁྲི་མན་ཆད་ཀྱི་ལོ་རྒྱུས་ཙམ་གྱིས་ཆོག་པར་མ་གནང་བར། དེའི་གོང་གི་བོད་ཀྱི་བྱུང་རིམ་ལའང་ཞིབ་ཏུ་གཟིགས་ཏེ། ཆོས་མགོ་སངས་རྒྱས་དང་། ཆུ་མགོ་གངས་ཀྱི་དཔེ་ལྟར། བོད་རང་གི་མི་རྒྱུད་གང་ལ་ཐུག་པའི་སྔོར་རྩུན་ཆད་ནས་ཞིབ་ཏུ་དཔྱད་པར་མཛོད་ཅིག་ཅེས་ཀྱང་བསྐུལ་ལོ།།

Notes

1 རྗེ་འབངས་རྣམས་ཀྱི་རིགས་རུས་གསལ་བའི་སྒྲོན་མེ་》ཆ་སྤེལ་ཆེ་བརྟན་ཕུན་ཚོགས་དང་ནོར་འབྲངས་ཨོ་རྒྱན་སོགས་ཀྱིས་བསྒྲིགས་པའི་《རྒྱལ་རབས་གཡུ་ཡི་ཕྲེང་བ། སྟོད་ཆ་》ལས་དྲངས་པ། བོད་ལྗོངས་སྤྱི་ཚོགས་ཚན་རིག་ཁང་གི་དཔར་མ། ཤ ༨༧

2 ལྡེའུ་ཇོ་སྲས་ཀྱིས་མཛད་པའི་《ལྡེའུ་ཆོས་འབྱུང་རྒྱས་པ་》གངས་ཅན་རིག་མཛོད། པོད་གསུམ་པ། བོད་ལྗོངས་སྤྱི་ཚོགས་ཚན་རིག་བོད་ཡིག་དཔེ་རྙིང་དཔེ་སྐྲུན་ཁང་ནས་བསྒྲིགས། བོད་ལྗོངས་མི་དམངས་དཔེ་སྐྲུན་ཁང་གི་དཔར་མ། ཤ ༢༢༨

3 དཔའ་བོ་གཙུག་ལག་ཕྲེང་བས་བརྩམས་པའི་《ཆོས་འབྱུང་མཁས་པའི་དགའ་སྟོན་》སྟོད་ཆ། ཝཱ་ཎ་བཛྲ་བིདྱཱ་དཔེ་མཛོད་ཁང་གི་དཔར་མ། ཤ ༡༥༡

4 གུ་རུ་ཨོ་རྒྱན་གླིང་པས་ཡར་ཀླུང་ཤེལ་གྱི་བྲག་ཕུག་ནས་བཏོན་པའི་《རྒྱལ་པོ་བཀའ་ཐང་》མི་རིགས་དཔེ་སྐྲུན་ཁང་། སྤྱི་ལོ་༡༩༨༥ ལོའི་དཔར་མ། ཤ ༡༡༢

5 ཁྲུང་པོ་བློ་གྲོས་རྒྱལ་མཚན་གྱིས་བརྩམས་པའི་《གླིང་བཞི་བསྟན་པའི་འབྱུང་ཁུངས་》སྤྱི་ལོ་༡༩༣༨ལོར་ཁྲུང་པོ་རྒྱལ་བ་ཐོད་དཀར་གྱི་རི་ཁྲོད་དུ་སྦྲར། རྒྱ་གར་སྨན་རི་དགོན་གྱི་བླ་བྲང་ཕྱག་དཔེ་ཡིག་ནག་བྲིས་མ། ཤ ༨། བོད་ཀྱི་གཙུག་ལག་གཅེས་བཏུས་པོད་ཕྲེང་སུམ་ཅུ་པའི་པར་གཞིར་བཀོད་ཀྱང་ད་ལྟར་པར་སྐྲུན་ཞུ་ཐུབ་མི་འདུག།

6 《མཁས་པ་ལྡེའུའི་ཆོས་འབྱུང་》ཤ ༢༢༨

7 《ཏུན་ཧོང་ནས་ཐོན་པའི་བོད་ཀྱི་ལོ་རྒྱུས་ཡིག་ཆ་》མི་རིགས་དཔེ་སྐྲུན་ཁང་། ༡༩༩༢ ལོའི་དཔར་མ། ཤ ༦༧

8 《ཆོས་འབྱུང་མཁས་པའི་དགའ་སྟོན་》 ཤ ༡༠༦

9 དེབ་ཐེར་དཔྱིད་ཀྱི་རྒྱལ་མོའི་གླུ་དབྱངས་ཀྱི་མཆན་འགྲེལ། 《དོན་གྲུབ་རྒྱལ་གྱི་གསུང་འབུམ་》པོད་དྲུག་པ། མི་རིགས་དཔེ་སྐྲུན་ཁང་། ༡༩༩༢ལོའི་དཔར་མ། ཤ ༡༦༥

10 མདོ་གཙུག་ཏོར་གདུགས་དཀར།

11 མདོ་ཕལ་པོ་ཆེ།

12 རི་སྤྱངས་ངག་དབང་འཇིག་གྲགས་ཀྱིས་བརྩམས་པའི་ 《མངོན་བརྗོད་མཁས་པའི་རྣ་རྒྱན་》བོད་ལྗོངས་མི་དམངས་དཔེ་སྐྲུན་ཁང་། ༡༩༨༣ལོའི་དཔར་མ། ཤ ༥༠ ལས། ཕྱོགས་ཀྱི་མིང་མིང་འཆད་པའི་སྐབས། ཕྱོགས་ཉིད་སྟོན་གསལ་གན་དང་། །ཀུན་ཁྱབ་དང་ནི་འཕྲོག་བྱེད་དེ། །སྔ་དྲོ་ཤར་དང་གུང་ལྷོ་ཕྱོགས། །ཕྱི་དྲོ་ནུབ་དང་བྱང་ཕྱོགས་སྟེང་། །དབང་པོ་མེ་ལྷ་གཤིན་རྗེ་དང་། །བདེན་བྲལ་མཆི་བདག་རླུང་གི་ལྷ། །གནོད་སྦྱིན་དབང་ལྡན་གོ་རིམ་བཞིན།། ཞེས་གསུངས།

13 པཎྜི་ཏ་མཆི་མེད་སི་ཀྐིམ་མཛད་པའི་ 《མངོན་བརྗོད་མཆི་མེད་མཛོད་》 Palale monastery Sikkim: བླ་མ་ཤེས་རབ་རྒྱལ་མཚན། ༡༩༨༩ལོའི་དཔར་མ། ཤ ༩

14 གྲང་དབྱི་སུན་གྱིས་གཙོ་འགན་བཞེས་ནས་རྩོམ་སྒྲིག་མཛད་པའི་ 《བོད་རྒྱ་ཚིག་མཛོད་ཆེན་མོ་》སྟོད་ཆ། མི་རིགས་དཔེ་སྐྲུན་ཁང་། ༡༩༩༦ ལོའི་དཔར་མ། ཤ ༡༥༥༩

15 《ཆ་བཞི་》

16 སློ་ལུང་གཞེད་པའི་རྡོ་རྗེས་ཞིང་སྨག་ལོར་མཛད་པའི་ 《དམ་ཅན་བསྟན་སྲུང་རྒྱ་མཚོའི་རྣམ་པར་ཐར་པ་སྟོན་མེད་ལེགས་བཤད་》ལྡི་ལི་པར་མ། ལས་དྲངས་པ་ 《རྒྱལ་པོ་ཆེན་པོ་རྣམ་ཐོས་སྲས་ཀྱི་རྒྱུད་སྣ་ཚོགས་རབ་ཏུ་གྲུབ་པ་》ཤ ༢༠༨ ལས། དེའི་མཚན་ཡང་གནོད་སྦྱིན་གྱི་མཚན་འཆང་བས་རྣམ་སྲས་ཞེས་བཏགས་སོ།། ཞེས་དང་། ཡང་རྣམ་ཐར་དེ་ཉིད་ལས་དྲངས་པ《གནོད་སྦྱིན་དབྱུག་པ་ཅན་གྱི་རྒྱུད་》ཤ ༢༡༡ ལས། ནམ་ཞིག་ལྕང་ལོ་ཅན་གྱི་ཕོ་བྲང་ན། གནོད་སྦྱིན་ཐམས་ཅད་ཀྱི་རྗེ་དྲང་སྲོང་རྣམ་ཐོས་སྲས་ཞེས་བྱ་བ་དང་། གནོད་སྦྱིན་ཆེན་པོ་བརྒྱད་ཀྱིས་ཀྱང་བཅོམ་ལྡན་འདས་ཀྱི་སྤྱན་སྔར་རྣམ་ཐོས་ཀྱི་བུའི་འཁོར་དུ་ཁས་བླངས་ཤིང་དམ་བཅས་སོ།།

17 ཆོས་སྐྱོང་ཁག་གི་གསོལ་ཁ་བསྐོང་པ་དང་བཅས་པ། 《རྒྱལ་བ་དགེ་འདུན་རྒྱ་མཚོའི་གསུང་འབུམ། པོད་གསུམ་པ་》ཆོས་ཚན་རི་པ། ལས་དྲངས།

18 ཆོས་སྐྱོང་ཁག་གི་གསོལ་ཁ་བསྐོང་པ་དང་བཅས་པ། ལས་དྲངས། སློ་ལུང་གཞེད་པའི་རྡོ་རྗེས་མཛད་པའི་ 《བསྟན་སྲུང་རྒྱ་མཚོའི་རྣམ་ཐར་》ལས་དྲངས་པ་ 《མེ་ལྕེ་འབར་བའི་རྒྱུད་》ལས།

19 བསྟན་སྲུང་རྒྱ་མཚོའི་རྣམ་ཐར་ལས་དྲངས་པ་ 《དཔལ་ལྡན་ལྷ་མོའི་རྒྱུད་》ལས།

20 བསྟན་སྲུང་རྒྱ་མཚོའི་རྣམ་ཐར།

21 《རྗེ་དགེ་འདུན་རྒྱ་མཚོའི་དམག་ཟོར་མའི་བསྐོང་པ་》པོད་གསུམ་པ། ཆོས་ཚན་རི་པ། ཆོས་སྐྱོང་ཁག་གི་གསོལ་ཁ་བསྐོང་པ་དང་བཅས་པ། ལས་དྲངས།

22 ཆོས་སྐྱོང་ཁག་གི་གསོལ་ཁ་བསྐོང་པ་དང་བཅས་པ་ལས་དྲངས།

23 《བོན་གྱི་ཞལ་གདག་མའི་གཏེར་བོན་》གླིང་བཞི་བསྟན་པའི་འབྱུང་ཁུངས།

24 མཆིམས་ནམ་མཁའ་གྲགས་སམ་མཚན་གཞན་མཆིམས་འཇམ་པའི་དབྱངས་ཀྱིས་དུས་རབས་བཅུ་གསུམ་པའི་ནང་སོག་ཡུལ་ཅ་ཏི་ཁ་ཞེས་པར་མཛད་པའི་ 《མཛོད་འགྲེལ་མངོན་པའི་རྒྱན་》དེའི་གནས་གསུམ་པའི་ཐད་ཀྱི་འགྲེལ་བ་ལས། སྲིན་པོ་ཡང་མིའི་བྱེ་བྲག་ཡིན་པའི་ཕྱིར། ཞེས་གསུངས། འཕགས་བོད་གཉིས་སུ་མཛོད་འགྲེལ་རྒྱས་ཤོས་དེ་ཡིན།

25 ཆ་བཞི།

26 བཀའ་ཆེམས་ཀ་ཁོལ་མ་སོགས་སུ་གདོང་དམར་བོད་ཞེས་ཡང་ཡང་བྱུང་།

27 《མངོན་བརྗོད་མཁས་པའི་རྣ་རྒྱན་》ཤ ༩༢ ལས། སྲིན་པོ་སྤྱིའི་མིང་འཆད་པའི་སྐབས། སྲུ་སྲོག་འཕོད་སྲོག་མཁའ་འགྲོ་སྐྱེས། །མཚན་རྒྱུ་མཚན་སྤྱོད་ཐུན་མཚམས་སྤོབས། །ཤ་ཟ་ཁྲག་འཐུང་མགྲིན་པ་ཅན། །ཀུན་གསོད་རོ་ཟན་མི་ལ་འཚེ། །མིག་དམར་བསོད་མའི་སྐྱེ་བོ་དང་། །ཤ་རྗེན་ཟ་སོགས་སྲིན་པོའི་མིང་། །ཞེས་འབྱུང་ངོ་། །

28 《དོན་གྲུབ་རྒྱལ་གྱི་གསུང་འབུམ་》པོད་དྲུག་པ།

29 ཆབ་མདོ་བློ་བཟང་ཤེས་རབ་ཀྱིས་བརྩམས་པའི་《ཆབ་མདོའི་ཡིག་ཚང་རིན་ཆེན་སྤུངས་པ་》སྟོད་ཆ། ཛ་ས་ཆབ་མདོ་སྐྱིད་སྡུག། ༢༠༠༥ལོའི་དཔར་མར། འབྲི་གུང་ཆུང་ཚང་ཆོས་ཀྱི་བློ་གྲོས་ཀྱི་གསུང་འབུམ་དྲངས་པ་ལས་དཔེ་དངོས་མཇལ་མ་བྱུང་།

30 《གླིང་བཞི་བསྟན་པའི་འབྱུང་ཁུངས་》

31 ཞི་ཁྲོ་རྩ་འགྲེལ་འདི་ཉིད་《གླིང་བཞི་བསྟན་པའི་འབྱུང་ཁུངས་》སུ་བགྲངས་པ་ལས་ད་ལྟར་དཔེ་དངོས་ལག་སོན་མ་བྱུང་། འོན་ཀྱང་གངས་ཏི་སེ་དང་མཚོ་མ་ཕམ་འཛམ་གླིང་གི་དབུས་དཀྱིལ་དུ་ངོས་འཛིན་མཛད་པ་ནི། མཉམ་མེད་ཤེས་རབ་རྒྱལ་མཚན་གྱིས་མཛད་པའི་《སྲིད་པའི་མཛོད་ཕུགས་ཀྱི་གཞུང་དང་འགྲེལ་བ་འཕྲུལ་གྱི་སྒྲོན་མེ་》གཡུང་དྲུང་བོན་གྱི་བཤད་སྒྲུབ་འདུས་སྡེ་ནས་༢༠༠༩ལོའི་དཔར་མ། ཤ ༧༥ རྟའང་སྣང་སྡེ། དྲན་པ་ནམ་མཁས་མཛད་པའི་《སྲིད་པའི་མཛོད་ཕུགས་རྩ་འགྲེལ་》ལྷ་ཀྲ་མཐོ་སློབ་གཡུང་དྲུང་བོན་སྒྲི་ལས་ཁྲུངས་ནས་༡༩༩༣ལོའི་དཔར་མ་དེ་ཉིད་ལས། འཛམ་བུ་གླིང་གི་དབུས་ཀྱི་གནས་ལུགས་ལ། །ཏི་བྱང་ནི་ཏི་སེའི་བྱང་ཕྱོགས། །ཁ་རོང་ལ་སོགས་ནི་རི་ནག་པོ་དགུ་སྟེ་གཡུང་དྲུང་དགུ་སེལ་ཞེས་ཀྱང་བྱའོ།།

32 《དགེ་ཆོས་གནས་ཡིག་》གངས་ཅན་རིག་མཛོད་པོད་བཅུ་གཉིས་པ། བོད་ལྗོངས་སྤྱི་ཚོགས་ཚན་རིག་བོད་ཡིག་དཔེ་རྙིང་དཔེ་སྐྲུན་ཁང་ནས་བསྒྲིགས། བོད་ལྗོངས་མི་དམངས་དཔེ་སྐྲུན་ཁང་། ༡༩༩༠ལོའི་དཔར་མ། ཤ ༢༢༩

33 ཨ་ཆོགས་བསྟན་འཛིན་འཇམ་དབྱངས་ནི་འབྲས་སྤུངས་ནས་ཕར་ཕྱིན་རབ་འབྱམས་པ་ཐོན་ཞིང་ད་ལྟ་ནོར་གླིང་བོད་ཀྱི་མཐོ་སློབ་དགེ་རྒན་ཡིན།

34 《ཆོས་འབྱུང་མཁས་པའི་དགའ་སྟོན་》སྟོད་ཆ། ཤ ༢༢༥

35 《ལྡེའུ་ཆོས་འབྱུང་རྒྱས་པ་》ཤ ༢༢༥

36 མཁས་པའི་དབང་པོ་ངོར་པ་དཀོན་མཆོག་ལྷུན་གྲུབ་ཀྱིས་མཛད་པའི་《ས་སྐྱའི་གདུང་རབས་ཡ་རབས་ཁ་རྒྱན་》《ས་སྐྱའི་གདུང་རབས་རིན་ཆེན་བང་མཛོད་》ལས་དྲངས་པ། ཤ ༨

37 བདག་ཆེན་ཨ་མེས་ངག་དབང་ཀུན་དགའ་བསོད་ནམས་ཀྱིས་བརྩམས་པའི་《ས་སྐྱའི་གདུང་རབས་རིན་ཆེན་བང་མཛོད་》ལྡི་ལི་པར་སློག་པར་མ། ཤ ༧

38 《ས་སྐྱའི་གདུང་རབས་ཡ་རབས་ཁ་རྒྱན་》ཤ ༨

39 《ས་སྐྱའི་གདུང་རབས་རིན་ཆེན་བང་མཛོད་》ཤ ༨

40 《ས་སྐྱའི་གདུང་རབས་རིན་ཆེན་བང་མཛོད་》ཤ ༨

41 གདན་རབས་ཁ་ཅིག ཅེས་《ས་སྐྱའི་གདུང་རབས་རིན་ཆེན་བང་མཛོད་》དུ་གསུངས་པའི་ཕྱོགས་སྔ་མ་དེ་སུ་ཡིན་ཤེས་མ་བྱུང་།

42 《ས་སྐྱ་ངག་ཆོས་ཀྱི་མགོན་པོའི་ཆོས་འབྱུང་》ཇ་ས་དཔེ་མཛོད་ཁང་དུ་འདུག་ཀྱང་ད་ལྟར་ཤོག་གྲངས་མི་རེས།

43 《ཁྱད་པར་འཕགས་བསྟོད་》དང་《དཀའ་ཆེམས་ཀ་ཁོལ་མ། ཤ ༩༨》གཉིས་ཀའི་ནས་རིག་བྱེད་ཀྱི་གཏམ་བརྒྱུད་ལས་དྲངས་ནས་རྒྱས་པར་བཤད་ཡོད།

44 《ས་སྐྱའི་གདུང་རབས་རིན་ཆེན་བང་མཛོད་》ཤ ༨

45 《ལྡེའུ་ཆོས་འབྱུང་རྒྱས་པ་》དང་《མཁས་པའི་དགའ་སྟོན་》རྣམས་སུ་རྨུ་ཞེས་བྲིས་སྣང་ཞིང་《ས་སྐྱའི་གདུང་རབས་རིན་ཆེན་བང་མཛོད་》དུ་དམུ་ཞེས་བྲིས་འདུག་ཀྱང་དོན་ལ་ཁྱད་པར་མི་སེམས་ཏེ། གཞའ་སྨུ་མོར་དེང་སང་ནང་བཞིན་བརྡ་དག་གཅིག་གྱུར་མེད་པ་འདི་འདྲ་ཤིན་ཏུ་མང་བས་སོ། །

46 སྤྱི་རྨི་ཡི་སྐོར་བོན་གྱི་ཡིག་ཆ་ཁ་ཤས་ནས་མཐོང་མྱོང་ཡང་ད་ལྟར་མི་དྲན།

47 《ས་སྐྱའི་གདུང་རབས་རིན་ཆེན་བང་མཛོད་》ཤ ༨

48 《རྒྱལ་པོ་བཀའ་ཐང་》ཤ ༡༡༢

49 སྡེ་དགེ་ཐུབ་བསྟན་ཕུན་ཚོགས་ཀྱིས་བརྩམས། 《བོད་ཀྱི་ལོ་རྒྱུས་སྤྱི་དོན་པདྨ་རཱ་གའི་ལྡེ་མིག》 མི་རིགས་དཔེ་སྐྲུན་ཁང་གི་དཔར་མ། ཤ ༥༣

50 《ཆོས་འབྱུང་མཁས་པའི་དགའ་སྟོན》 ལས། ཡང་ཏང་ཡིང་དང་བར་ཁ་འུར་རྡོ་འཕེན།། ཞེས་དང་། 《མཁས་པ་ལྡེའུའི་ཆོས་འབྱུང》 ལག་ཆར་རྒྱུག་པ་ཀྱོག་ཅན་དེ་ནས་བྱུང་།། ཞེས་པའི་བར་ཁ་དང་རྒྱུགས་པ་ཀྱོག་ཅན་ནི། རྒྱུགས་པ་རྣ་གཉིས་ཅན་ལ་ཟེར།

51 《ཆོས་འབྱུང་མཁས་པའི་དགའ་སྟོན》 ཤ ༡༥༢

52 《ས་སྐྱའི་གདུང་རབས་རིན་ཆེན་བང་མཛོད》 ཤ ༥

53 《ས་སྐྱའི་གདུང་རབས་རིན་ཆེན་བང་མཛོད》 ཤ ༧

54 《རྒྱལ་པོ་བཀའ་ཐང》 ཤ ༡༡༢

55 《བུ་སྟོན་གྱི་ལོ་རྒྱུས་ཆེན་མོ》 མཁས་པ་ལྡེའུས་རང་གི་ཆོས་འབྱུང་དུ་ལུང་དྲངས་པ་དེ་ཉིད་མཇལ་བ་ཙམ་ལས་ཕྱག་དཔེ་ཁ་ཚང་མཇལ་སྐྱོང་མེད།

56 《ལྡེའུ་ཆོས་འབྱུང་རྒྱས་པ》 ཤ ༢༢༥

57 ཆོས་རྒྱལ་ནམ་མཁའི་ནོར་བུས་བརྩམས་པའི 《སྲུང་ལྡེའུ་བོན་གསུམ་གྱི་གཏམ་ཨེ་མ་ཧོ》 བོད་ཀྱིས་དཔེ་མཛོད་ཁང་། ༡༩༨༨ལོའི་དཔར་མ། ཤ ༨༩

58 《གླིང་གེ་སར་རྒྱལ་པོའི་སྒྲུང་མོན་གླིང་གཡུལ་འགྱེད》 བོད་ལྗོངས་མི་དམངས་དཔེ་སྐྲུན་ཁང་ནས་པར་དུ་བསྐྲུན་པ། ༣༩༨ ...༣༨༢

59 《སྒྲུང་ལྡེའུ་བོན་གསུམ་གྱི་གཏམ་ཨེ་མ་ཧོ》 ཤ ༨༧

60 མཁས་དབང་རག་རྡོ་སྤྲུལ་སྐུ། ཕྱ་ཆ་ཆེས་མཐོའི་གཙུག་ལག་སློབ་གཉེར་ཁང་གི་སྔགས་སྡེ་ཚན་གྱི་སློབ་དཔོན་ཆེན་པོ་ཡིན།

61 《ས་སྐྱའི་གདུང་རབས་ཡ་རབས་ཁ་རྒྱན》 ཤ ༥

62 《ས་སྐྱའི་གདུང་རབས་རིན་ཆེན་བང་མཛོད》 ཤ ༧

63 《ཆོས་འབྱུང་མཁས་པའི་དགའ་སྟོན》 སྟོད་ཆ། ཤ ༡༥༡

64 《ཆོས་འབྱུང་མཁས་པའི་དགའ་སྟོན》 སྟོད་ཆ། ཤ ༡༥༡

65 《ལྡེའུ་ཆོས་འབྱུང་རྒྱས་པ》 ཤ ༢༢༥

66 《རྒྱལ་པོ་བཀའ་ཐང》 ཤ ༡༡༢ དང་ 《གླིང་བཞི་བསྟན་པའི་འབྱུང་ཁུངས》

67 སྡེ་དགེ་ཐུབ་བསྟན་ཕུན་ཚོགས་ཀྱིས་བརྩམས་པའི 《བོད་ཀྱི་ལོ་རྒྱུས་སྤྱི་དོན་པདྨ་རཱ་གའི་ལྡེ་མིག》 མི་རིགས་དཔེ་སྐྲུན་ཁང་གི་དཔར་མ། ཤ ༥༣

68 《ཆོས་འབྱུང་མཁས་པའི་དགའ་སྟོན》 སྟོད་ཆ། ཤ ༡༥༡

69 《གླིང་བཞི་བསྟན་པའི་འབྱུང་ཁུངས》 ཤ ༡༠

70 《ལྡེའུ་ཆོས་འབྱུང་རྒྱས་པ》 ཤ ༢༢༥། 《ཆོས་འབྱུང་མཁས་པའི་དགའ་སྟོན》 སྟོད་ཆ། ཤ ༡༥༡

71 《བོད་ཀྱི་ལོ་རྒྱུས་སྤྱི་དོན་པདྨ་རཱ་གའི་ལྡེ་མིག》 ཤ ༥༣

72 《གླིང་བཞི་བསྟན་པའི་འབྱུང་ཁུངས》 ཤ ༡༠

73 《ལྡེའུ་ཆོས་འབྱུང་རྒྱས་པ》 ཤ ༢༢༥།

74 《གླིང་བཞི་བསྟན་པའི་འབྱུང་ཁུངས》 ཤ ༡༠

75 《ཏུན་ཧོང་ནས་ཐོན་པའི་བོད་ཀྱི་ལོ་རྒྱུས་ཡིག་ཆ》 ཤ ༨༧

བེ་རི་འཇིགས་མེད་དབང་རྒྱལ།

Abstract

A Brief Introduction to the Era of the Ten Overlords

BERI JIGME WANGYAL

Although the period from the appearance of the first Tibetan emperor is generally well known, it seems that up until now few scholarly works have paid attention to the period prior to this, during which time tradition holds that Tibet was ruled in turn by ten different classes of daemonic overlords. The present chapter examines this tradition with recourse to its various written sources, and considers each of the ten classes of non-humans who held sway over Tibet. This era comes to an end with the advent of human rule in the form of the twelve minor kingdoms, which were then united under the first Tibetan emperor.

11

The "Nephew–Uncle" Relationship in the International Diplomacy of the Tibetan Empire (7th–9th Centuries)

BRANDON DOTSON

Introduction

Tibet's foreign relations during the imperial period were driven forward by dynastic marriages between the Tibetan royal family and the ruling houses of its neighbors. Princesses became cultural and political ambassadors in their new environs and played key political roles as links between their husbands' kingdoms and those of their fathers. These marriages were by definition contracted between culturally disparate peoples, each with their own assumptions about dynastic marriage, and this created a climate in which this key element of political alliance and diplomacy could be interpreted differently by each party. Here, as is perhaps the case in most premodern kingdoms or empires, we find a type of fluidity that allows *de-facto* eventualities to confound *de-jure* arguments, a situation that will be familiar to those aware of the problematic nature of Tibet's subsequent international relations contracted in the language of patronage (*mchod yon*), suzerainty and, more recently, autonomy.

This union of matrimony and politics is a common, probably universal feature of premodern diplomacy, and one can imagine its origins in the earliest and most fundamental exchanges between one group and another. There are a number of points at issue when considering dynastic marriage in a given setting. What are the assumptions concerning the status of bride-givers and bride-receivers? What is the role of the out-marrying princess, be she an aunt, sister, daughter or otherwise, in her new environs following a marriage? How are collateral lineages

— the king's brothers and cousins — kept from usurping royal power? What is the role of the king's maternal relatives? What sort of power do unmarried princesses exercise? More generally, we can also ask whether or not the rules governing dynastic marriage reflect those operating on a more general level in the marriages of aristocrats and commoners.

The practice of dynastic marriage in Central Eurasia has a very long history of accommodation between Chinese and steppe peoples, who borrowed from each other various ideas about marriage and status. While this history has been well documented, less has been written about the Tibetan approach to dynastic marriage and how this relates to the diplomatic language found, for example, in the bilingual 823 Lhasa Treaty Inscription that describes Tibet and China respectively as "nephew" (*dbon*) and "uncle" (*zhang*).[1] This chapter will investigate the nature of the so-called "nephew–uncle relationship" (*dbon zhang*) during the period of the Tibetan Empire (ca 600–850 CE), and consider how it served as a model for Tibet's international relations during this period.

The Nature of the *dBon Zhang* Relationship

In a Tibetan cultural setting, the "nephew–uncle relationship" (*dbon zhang*) describes simultaneously the relationship between uterine nephew and maternal uncle, son-in-law and father-in-law and bride-receiver and bride-giver, all of which can, and often do overlap in a single pair. While it refers fundamentally to individuals, who may be of any social stratum, the terms *dbon* and *zhang* also can extend to include these individuals' families, their clans and, in the case of dynastic marriage between ruling houses, to their countries. In the case of the famous *dbon zhang* relationship between Tibet and China, for example, the terms *dbon* and *zhang* referred initially to Emperor Srong btsan sgam po (ca 605–649) and Emperor Taizong (626–649) respectively, but the terms extended to include all subsequent Tibetan and Tang emperors, and were used metonymically to refer to Tibet and China. It is for this reason that we find the phrase "Uncle China" (*zhang po rgya*) used in later Tibetan histories.[2]

One possible reason for the ability of the term *dbon zhang* to expand sufficiently to describe the relationship between two countries is its already expansive use as a kinship term. *dBon* designates not only son-in-law and bride-receiver, but can also extend to his descendants.[3] Similarly, *zhang* can be applied not only to an individual father-in-law or bride-giver, but to his descendants as well. An *dbon zhang* relationship created between individuals through marriage thus comes to pervade their lineages, sometimes for generations. This practice is informed by traditional patterns of exchange in Tibet, in particular matrilateral cross-cousin marriage. A by-product of this pattern of exchange is that *zhang* means not only father-in-law and bride-giver, but also maternal uncle (mother's brother), while *dbon*, besides meaning son-in-law and bride-receiver, also means uterine nephew (sister's son).

This inquiry is concerned primarily with dynastic marriage. The vocabulary of such marriages is necessarily based on those found in society at large, but dynastic marriage tends to be governed by unique, or at least extreme sets of circumstances. The most obvious of these would be inheritance: during the period of the Tibetan Empire, only one son could inherit the Tibetan throne. By comparison, an aristocrat might inherit his father's land, might have to share it with his brother(s) or might indeed strike off on his own and set up his own household.[4] Another obvious circumstance peculiar to the royal line is that of hypergamy: if everyone is "marrying up" in the status hierarchy, then this leaves those at the top with few marital options. So while we might investigate the nature of the *dbon zhang* relationship between Tibet and China, for example, with recourse to the relationship between nephew and uncle / bride-receiver and bride-giver / son-in-law and father-in-law as it operates on a more general level in Tibetan societies, we cannot assume a one-to-one correspondence between the rules and circumstances governing dynastic marriage and those obtaining in the marriages of aristocrats and commoners. On the other hand, the one informs the other, or rather, they interpenetrate and borrow from each other, as we see, for instance, in the many wedding songs existing up to the present day that refer back to the marriage of Srong btsan sgam po and the Chinese princess, Wencheng.

The dBon Zhang Relationship and Dynastic Marriage in Old Tibetan Sources

Not all of Tibet's dynastic marriages were referred to as creating an *dbon zhang* relationship. Limiting ourselves to select Old Tibetan sources, the term *dbon zhang* is found in the *Old Tibetan Annals*, where it refers to the relationship between 'A zha and Tibet, and in the Lhasa Treaty Inscription and *The Religious Annals of Khotan*, where *dbon zhang* refers to Tibet and China. It is certain that there were others such relationships. The king of Dags po, a vassal minor kingdom in southern Tibet to the west of Kong po, was referred to as *dbon* in the *Old Tibetan Annals* because of the *dbon zhang* relationship between Dags po and Tibet that existed in the late 7th century.[5] Similarly, the *Old Tibetan Annals* records other cases of dynastic marriage where Tibetan princesses depart to foreign countries, and we might assume that these unions also created *dbon zhang* relationships.

Other Old Tibetan sources, such as the *Old Tibetan Chronicle*, record further dynastic marriages, some of them even prior to the Yarlung Kingdom's expansion to become the Tibetan Empire in the late 6th century.

Rather than providing a narrative blow-by-blow account of Tibet's dynastic marriages as recounted in Old Tibetan sources, it will be sufficient here to examine in some detail those two relationships explicitly referred to as *dbon zhang* in Old Tibetan sources, that between Tibet and China, and that between 'A zha and Tibet. Besides attending to the all-important power dynamics at play and the issue of status, I will also consider a question at the heart of the ambiguity (or elasticity) of *dbon zhang* as a relationship that can span generations: does it begin with marriage or with the birth of an heir? Put differently, must the "nephew–uncle" relationship even involve a nephew and an uncle?

Tibet's *Zhang*: "Uncle China?"

The *Jiu Tangshu,* or *Old Tang Annals,* briefly describes the marriage of the Chinese princess and the Tibetan emperor in the following terms:

> The 15th year of Chenkuan (641) the Emperor gave Princess Wencheng, of the imperial house, in marriage. He appointed the President of the Board of Rites, Daozong, Prince of Jiangxia, to preside over the ceremony, and he was given special credentials, and escorted the princess to Tufan. Lungtsan led his warriors to await her arrival at Pohai, and went himself to receive her at Heyuan. He received Daozong most respectfully, with the rites due from a son-in-law.[6]

Here the marriage has only just begun, but there is already mention of ritual duties of the son-in-law vis-à-vis his father-in-law. This tells us more about the Chinese perception of this relationship than anything else.

Almost two hundred years after this marriage, the bilingual text of the Lhasa Treaty Inscription of 823 (commemorating the treaty of 821–822) refers to the *dbon zhang* relationship between the Tibetans and Chinese as follows:

> Twenty-three years of the Tang era having passed from when the first lord of China, Li, assumed the throne. After one generation, the divine emperor, Khri Srong brtsan, and the Lord of China The'i tsong BUn bU Sheng Hwang te [Taizong] both agreed to unite their kingdoms. In the Ceng kwan year Mun sheng Kong co was married to the bTsan po. Later, the divine emperor Khri lDe gtsug brtsan and the Chinese lord Sam Lang kha'e 'gwan sheng bUn shIn bU Hwang te [Xuanzong], agreed to unite their

> kingdoms, and building on their relationship (*gnyen*), Kim shing Kong co was wed to the bTsan po in the keng lung year. Having become *dbon* [and] *zhang*, they rejoiced ... in this way, as neighbors and relatives (*gnyen*), and acting precisely in the manner of *dbon* [and] *zhang* ..."[7]

The inscription refers first to the marriage mentioned above in the *Jiu Tangshu*, then to the second and final marriage between a Tibetan emperor and a Chinese princess. This second marriage took place in 710, when the young Khri lDe gtsug brtsan (704-ca 754), who would not be enthroned for another two years, married the Princess of Jincheng. The text of the inscription describes the *dbon zhang* relationship in terms of uniting polities (*chab srid*) and in terms of relation / affinity (*gnyen*). The inscription's statement that Tibet and China act "precisely in the manner of *dbon* and *zhang*" again emphasizes that rights and duties are attached to the relationship and that there is a proper "manner" (*tshul*) in which the relationship ought to be conducted.

The first term used to qualify the *dbon zhang* relationship, *chab srid*, is usually translated with "politics," and demonstrates the primary function of such dynastic marriages. In fact, the term's use in Old Tibetan sources, particularly the *Old Tibetan Annals*, has a wider range of meaning. *Chab srid* refers to political alliance in the treaty pillar quoted above when the rulers of China and Tibet agree to unite their polities (*chab srid gcig du mol*). Similarly, in the *Old Tibetan Annals* entry for 762–764, the political alliance is destroyed (*chab srid zhig*) preceding the Tibetan invasion of the Chinese capital.[8] In the context of dynastic marriage, we find several references in the *Old Tibetan Annals* to Tibetan princesses who are sent as brides to foreign lands, where they "go to [conduct] politics" (*chab srid la gshegs*). Stein compares this phrase, which he translates with "va comme épouse," with a similar phrase in the *Old Tibetan Annals* in the same context, "va comme fiancée" (*bag mar gshegs*). Stein's translation of *chab srid la gshegs* is contextual, but is also based on an analysis of the term *chab srid* that focuses on *srid* and its meaning "to create, to procreate."[9] While this is certainly relevant, a more formal translation as "politics" highlights the important diplomatic role these princesses played as agents of statecraft.

The second term that qualifies the Tibet–China *dbon zhang* relationship in the above passage is *gnyen*, meaning "relatives." This is the same term that is used in the celebrated fragment at the beginning of the *Royal Genealogy* (PT 1286), the "tale of the ancient relatives of the four borders" (*gna' gnyen mtha' bzhi'i rabs*). The short, fragmentary list mentions ladies of four districts who were taken into the royal line as queens.[10] This might suggest a narrowing of the definition of *gnyen* to "affinal relatives." This meaning is supported by such phrases as "to ask for one's hand in marriage" (*gnyen slong*); "to divorce" (*gnyen slog*); "the in-marrying bride (*mna' ma*) or groom (*mag pa*) visiting their natal family for the first time after getting married" (*gnyen log*); "to establish marriage relations" (*gnyen lam 'dzugs*), "to marry" (*gnyen byed*) and "marriage by sale" (*gynen tshongs*).[11] On the other hand, the term *gnyen*, misspelled *gnyan*, unequivocally refers to patrilineal relatives in the Old Tibetan legal document PT 1071. In a clause treating a case in which one clansman shoots another with an arrow during the hunt, a *gnyen* [*gnyan*] is qualified as a clansman (*phu nu po*), and is subject to the law governing fratricide (*dmer brtsi khrims*).[12] This constitutes rather incontrovertible evidence that *gnyen* cannot be refined to indicate solely affines, and indicates relatives more generally.

The Tibet–China *dbon zhang* relationship is also mentioned in an Old Tibetan Dunhuang document, *The Religious Annals of Khotan*. "At about that time [during the events in Khotan described earlier in the text] the divine Tsenpo of Tibet and the lord of China formed [the relationship of] nephew and uncle, at which the Chinese princess, too, became the divine Tsenpo's bride."[13] The text is here referring to the marriage of the second Chinese princess in 710, and essentially echoes the information found in the Lhasa Treaty Inscription.

The above quotations demonstrate that the *dbon zhang* relationship between Tibet and China began with the first marriage in 641, was renewed with a second and final marriage in 710, and was still characterized Tibet–China relations in the treaty of 821–822. It is also evident from the above quotation from the *Jiu Tangshu* that the Chinese equivalent of the *dbon zhang* relationship began with marriage. The Chinese kinship terms — *sheng* and *jiu* — overlap, however, in precisely the same manner as Tibetan *dbon* and *zhang*, so the later passage from the bilingual Lhasa Treaty Inscription could also conceivably refer to a blood relationship.[14] Uebach has demonstrated rather conclusively, however, that the first Chinese princess did not give birth to a Tibetan emperor.[15] Likewise, the *Old Tibetan Annals* clearly shows that the second Chinese princess was not the mother of Khri Srong lde btsan (742–ca 800) or any other Tibetan emperor, so we can conclude with some certainty that the *dbon zhang* relationship between Tibet and China was an affinal relationship only and not a blood relationship.[16] That a relationship of Tibetan son-in-law to Chinese father-in-law would in fact be fictive because neither Chinese princess was a daughter of the Chinese emperor is beside the point; while princesses closely related to the emperor were deemed more prestigious, they were not required to establish the *dbon zhang* relationship, or indeed any other such treaty marriage with a foreign power. This again emphasizes that the bond created is not simply between two royal families, but between two kingdoms or empires.

The Tibet–China *dbon zhang* relationship demonstrates that *dbon zhang* was a lasting relationship that could be based on little more than marriage. Here it describes Tibet and the Tibetan emperor as the son-in-law or bride-receiver in relation to China and the Tang emperor, who stands as father-in-law and bride-giver. It is also evident that this relationship was classificatory, and that it persisted for almost two hundred years from the initial marriage in 641, with dynastic marital relations being renewed only once, in 710. In so far as neither Chinese princess gave birth to an heir to the Tibetan throne, one cannot accurately refer to the Tibet–China *dbon zhang* relationship as "nephew–uncle."

Tibet's *dBon*: "Nephew 'A zha"

While the Tibet–China example is obviously the most famous of Tibet's *dbon zhang* relationships, it is not the only one, and is not even the best documented in Old Tibetan sources. This honor belongs to the *dbon zhang* relationship between 'A zha and Tibet, where, in the inverse of the Chinese example, Tibet stood as *zhang* in relation to 'A zha, a once-independent Turkic kingdom incorporated into the Tibetan Empire as one of its vassal "minor kingdoms" (*rgyal phran*) after its conquest in 663. The 'A zha people, referred to as Tuyuhun in Chinese, occupied the area around Lake Kokonor, and in particular the areas to the west, probably stretching into the Qaidam Basin.

The *Old Tibetan Annals* records a marriage in the ox year 689–690 that appears to have inaugurated this *dbon zhang* relationship between 'A zha and Tibet: "Princess (bTsan mo) Khri bangs went as a bride to the lord of the 'A zha."[17] In the *Annals of the 'A zha Principality*, an official court record of 'A zha modelled on the annals kept by the Tibetan court, and which covers the years from 706–707 to 714–715, the ruler of the 'A zha, who is referred to by the title Ma ga tho gon Kha gan, is most certainly the son of this Tibetan princess, who is called "the mother, Princess Khri bangs" (*yum btsan mo khri bangs*).[18] The Tibetans seem to have referred to the rulers of 'A zha only by their titles, and the *Old Tibetan Annals* uses the term "lord of the 'A zha" ('A zha rje) to refer to successive rulers.

The ruler of the 'A zha does not appear again in the *Old Tibetan Annals* until the entry for the hare year 727–728 — nearly forty years after the last such reference — where it states that the bTsan po "met with 'Bon 'A zha rje [as] bride-giver and bride-receiver" (*zhang dbon gdan tshom*).[19] This relates to a new ruler of the 'A zha who is referred to by the same title. The passage most likely indicates the renewal of the Tibet – 'A zha matrimonial relationship, and here *'bon* is a variant for *dbon*. dBon 'A zha rje is mentioned once again in the *Old Tibetan Annals*' entry for 745–746,[20] so we see that *dbon* as a kinship term-cum title persisted over time and continued to be attached to the ruler of the 'A zha. This point is further demonstrated by two other references to the lord of the 'A zha as *dbon* in Old Tibetan edicts preserved in the 16th-century *mKhas pa'i dga' ston* of dPa' bo gtsug lag phreng ba. In the edict (*bka' tshigs*) of Khri Srong lde btsan accompanying the *bSam yas Inscription*, dating to ca 779, the monarch pledges to uphold the Buddhist religion. The edict gives a list of all those who swore an oath to this effect, beginning with "dBon 'A zha rje."[21] Over thirty years later, in ca 812, the son of Khri Srong lde btsan, Khri lDe srong btsan (reigned ca 798–815), renewed his father's oath to promote the Buddhist religion with his *sKar cung Inscription*, again accompanied by an edict preserved in the *mKhas pa'i dga' ston*. After listing the names of three queens who swore to the oath, the edict lists three minor kings, the first of whom is "dBon 'A zha rje Dud kyi bul zhi khud par Ma ga tho yo gon Kha gan."[22]

It cannot be known for certain whether or not another marriage was contracted between an 'A zha ruler and a Tibetan princess following the marriage with Khri bangs in 689–690. Nonetheless, the appellation *dbon* applied to the lord of 'A zha at least from 727–728 to approximately 812, which is to say over several generations. The apparent longevity of the term's application to the hereditary rulers of the 'A zha is mirrored also by the use of the term *dbon zhang* in Tibet's relations with China. Khri lDe gtsug btsan's marriage with the Princess of Jincheng in 710 was contracted three generations after the marriage of Princess Wencheng to a Tibetan emperor in 641. Khri gTsug lde btsan (reigned 815–841), in proclaiming a treaty with China in 821–822 three generations after Khri lDe gtsug btsan's marriage with the Princess of Jincheng, defines the relationship between Tibet and China as *dbon zhang*.

The main difference between the two examples of an *dbon zhang* relationship with Tibet is that while the arrangement with China was based solely on marriage, the relationship with 'A zha was based also on the birth of an 'A zha ruler to a Tibetan princess. In the Tibet–China *dbon zhang* relationship, the term refers to bride-receivers and their descendants and bride-givers and their descendants. This is also true of the relationship between 'A zha and Tibet, but here *dbon zhang* additionally refers to a relationship that is based on descent, where the rulers of the 'A zha are classificatory nephews in relation to their classificatory maternal uncles, the Tibetan emperors. The precise relationship between the two rulers who met in 727–728, assuming that Princess Khri bangs was a sister of Khri 'Dus srong (676–704), is in fact between cross-cousins: the lord of the 'A zha is Khri lDe gtsug btsan's father's sister's son, and from the latter's perspective Khri lDe gtsug btsan is his mother's brother's son. Along with the continued use of the term *dbon* to refer to the hereditary rulers of the 'A zha until at least ca 812, this demonstrates that *dbon zhang* applies to the descendants of those who undertook the initial pact as bride-receiver and bride-giver, and in as much as this is not a generational relationship, it cannot be accurately termed "nephew–uncle."

Status and Hierarchy in Tibet's Dynastic Marriages

We have seen above that "nephew–uncle" can be a misleading translation for *dbon zhang*. We might more accurately revise this to "the relationship between bride-receivers and their descendants and bride-givers and their descendants." Something, however, would be lost in translation. This is because the point that is most inexact in the phrase *dbon zhang*, namely its generational aspect, is the very point that reveals the explicit hierarchy in this relationship. The *zhang* are the classificatory elders of their *dbon*, and the *zhang* stand in a position of superiority vis-à-vis their *dbon*.

We see this principle at work in Tibet's dynastic marriages not as a categorical marker of status in every marriage, but only in those where an heir is produced. The essential point at issue in these dynastic marriages is the birth of the heir to the throne: an heir born to a foreign princess can jeopardize a kingdom because the heir may fall under the power of his mother and her brother, a foreign king (in other words, the heir's *zhang*). This accounts for the king of Zhang zhung's sexual avoidance of his Tibetan bride Sad mar kar in the early 7th century,[23] for the minor kingdom of Dags po's loss of its semi-autonomous status in the early 8th century[24] and for the incorporation of 'A zha as a vassal kingdom within the Tibetan Empire. The power of the heir-bearing queen in subordinating her son to her father or brother and his kingdom informs the power dynamics of Tibet's dynastic marriages. In marrying off his sisters and daughters, the Tibetan emperor's imperative was that they be chief queens (that is to say, heir-bearing queens) in their new countries. Reciprocally, no foreign princess accepted as a bride of the Tibetan emperor enjoyed heir-bearing privileges.[25] This practice is not quite as inflexible as that of the Chinese, who in their "peaceful marriage arrangements," known as *heqin*, famously always gave brides and never received, but at the same time it ensures that Tibet's princesses "went to [conduct] politics" (*chab srid la gshegs*) in foreign lands as chief, heir-bearing queens while in-marrying foreign princesses were never allowed to gain the upper hand for their countries by giving birth to heirs to the Tibetan throne.

Matthew Kapstein writes insightfully that "the uncle–nephew relationship may have had very different cultural connotations in Tibet and China, and that this, unfortunately, has contributed to the long history of Sino-Tibetan misunderstanding."[26] It is interesting to observe how in the negotiation of the symbolism and ritual to solemnize peace treaties, each side attempted to subordinate the other, often according to cultural codes poorly understood by the other side. So it is in the treaty of 783 performed in Gansu, for example, that the original (presumably Chinese) arrangement, whereby the Tibetans would sacrifice a horse and the Chinese would sacrifice an ox, was swiftly abandoned when one of the Chinese officials realized that this could be seen as placing Tibet above China both in Chinese terms (the *Yijing* associates the horse with the sun and the ox with the moon) and in Tibetan terms (the Tibetans raid Chinese towns on horseback and the ox is a beast of burden).[27]

What is most striking is the relative absence of a marital or diplomatic *lingua franca* in Sino-Tibetan relations at this time, and the way in which treaties were celebrated in a double ceremony. In solemnizing a treaty, there were extensive negotiations on the form and protocol of the ceremony itself, which often had both a Chinese and a Tibetan component.[28] In an additional double movement, the agreed-upon ceremony took place once on Chinese soil and once on Tibetan soil, a protocol that has been seen as an indicator of the equality of the two parties.[29]

This sense of diplomatic fluidity or give-and-take is evident in the case of the Tibet–China *dbon zhang* relationship. The principal Chinese imperatives — that they give brides but never receive, and that brides very seldom be actual daughters of the emperor — were met, while the chief concern from the Tibetan side, namely, that no foreign bride received be allowed to bear an heir, was also achieved. In this context, one cannot say that Tibet, as *dbon*, stood in a structurally inferior relationship to its *zhang*, China, for the simple reason that no Chinese princess gave birth to a Tibetan emperor. In other words, China was never "uncle." As a consequence of this fluidity and the tolerance of divergent interpretations of their status vis-à-vis one another, one might argue that the *dbon zhang* relationship, beginning in 641 and cited by both Chinese and Tibetans in their treaties and their official correspondence, is far less important as a signifier of status than the blunt instruments of incursions and military victories.[30] In this sense, the *dbon zhang* relationship can be seen as one of the few constant elements in the relationship between two empires whose balance of power changed several times.

In the other *dbon zhang* relationship examined here, by contrast, Tibet was indeed "uncle" to 'A zha, whose rulers were of Tibetan blood after the Tibetan princess, Khri bangs, bore an heir to the 'A zha throne. Both structurally (as classificatory nephew) and practically (as a vassal minor kingdom or *rgyal phran* within the Tibetan Empire), 'A zha was subordinate to Tibet.

The Legacy of the *dBon zhang* Relationship

In the political arena, the *dbon zhang* relationship was predicated on marriage between the royal family of Tibet and the royal houses of neighboring countries. Its legacy as a model for Tibet's international relations waned therefore with the collapse of the Tibetan royal line from the mid-9th century. With the absence of a centralized monarchy, and with the renaissance of Tibetan culture through tantric Buddhism and the development of incarnation lineages, new models for Tibet's international relations, such as the so-called "priest–patron" (*mchod yon*) relationship, came to the fore.[31]

While *dbon zhang* ceased to have great relevance in international relations, it remained and remains a fundamental concept in Tibetan culture that informs basic patterns of exchange.[32] The sort of alliance created by the *dbon zhang* relationship also operated sometimes on a local level between Tibetan principalities. This is evident in the case of Tshal Gung thang and Grib, two neighboring districts in the Lhasa Valley. Here the *dbon zhang* relationship is a symbolic union between the male protector deity of Grib, rDzong btsan, and the female goddess Gung thang lHa mo of Tshal Gung thang. This creates a fictive kin relationship between the two areas that is re-enacted annually during the Gung thang flower-offering festival (*me tog mchod pa*), when a statue of Grib rDzong btsan is carried in procession to visit his bride in Tshal Gung thang.[33] Here we also see an interesting coexistence of *dbon zhang* and *mchod yon*, with the latter relationship between the two areas said to go back to Bla ma Zhang (1123–1193) of Tshal gung thang and his donor (*yon bdag*), an official of the mGar clan in Grib.[34]

A similar *dbon zhang* relationship between neighboring principalities is immortalized in the epic of Gesar, where one of the principal characters, 'Dan ma spyang khra (sometimes spelled mDan ma or lDan ma), is known as *tsha zhang* 'Dan ma. This epithet refers to the *dbon zhang* (or *tsha zhang* in its non-honorific form) relationship between the region of 'Dan ma, from which 'Dan ma spyang khra takes his name, and Gesar's kingdom of Gling. In this case 'Dan ma were bride-givers (*zhang*) and Gling were bride-receivers (*dbon*), but 'Dan ma had a tributary status towards Gling. While this is largely based on oral tradition, it seems to have persisted up until modern times.[35]

Conclusions

The *dbon zhang* relationship, as a model for Tibet's international relations during the imperial period, was based on uniting polities (*chab srid*) and on kinship (*gnyen*). It began with a dynastic marriage between the Tibetan royal line and a foreign royal house, and could continue for several generations. The term *zhang* refers to the bride-giver and his descendants, and *dbon* to the bride-receiver and his descendants. The same is true regardless of whether or not the bride, usually a "treaty princess," gave birth to an heir to the throne. In such cases where an heir is produced, the explicit hierarchy of the *dbon zhang* relationship becomes evident: the bride-receiver and his descendants are now also classificatory nephews, and are by this point usually the vassal of the bride-givers / classificatory maternal uncles. It is for this reason that the power dynamics of Tibet's dynastic marriages are most apparent by examining the status of the princesses. During the period of the Tibetan Empire, Tibet accepted foreign princesses from the Chinese, the Turks and possibly many others. None, however, was permitted to give birth to a Tibetan emperor. As a result we cannot say that the Tibet–China *dbon zhang* relationship subordinated Tibet to China. Reciprocally, those kingdoms who accepted Tibetan princesses as chief, heir-bearing queens were in most cases vassal kingdoms on their way to becoming consolidated within the Tibetan Empire. This is true of Zhang zhung in the early-to-mid-7th century, and both 'A zha and Dags po in the late 7th century.

With the collapse of a centralized monarchy ruling over all of Tibet and with the rise of new models of political alliance less dependent on the ties of kinship, and usually predicated on religious lineages, *dbon zhang* ceased to be as relevant on a dynastic or "international" level. It continued to serve as a model for alliance within the Tibetan cultural area, where neighboring principalities were often linked through marriage, either between their ruling houses or their local deities. Alongside this, the basic and fundamental context of the *dbon zhang* relationship as uniting two groups through marriage, and describing their rights and duties, remains relevant up to the present day.

Notes

1 For a summary of China's dynastic marriage arrangements, see Pan Yihong, "Marriage Alliance and Chinese Princesses in International Politics from Han through T'ang," *Asia Major* 10.1–2 (1997), 95–131; and Jennifer Holmgren, "Imperial Marriage in the Native Chinese and Non-Han State, Han to Ming." In *Marriage and Inequality in Chinese Society*, ed. Rubie S. Watson and Patricia Buckley Ebrey (Berkeley: University of California Press, 1991), 58–96. I wish to thank Georgios Halkias for his comments to earlier drafts of this chapter, and to Per Sørensen for pointing out to me some valuable sources on Chinese dynastic marriage.

2 dPa' bo gtsug lag phreng ba (1504–1566), *Dam pa'i chos kyi 'khor lo bsgyur ba rnams kyi byung ba gsal bar byed pa mKhas pa'i dga' ston* (Beijing: Mi rigs dpe skrun khang, 1985), 334.

3 In fact *dbon*, like its non-honorific equivalent *tsha*, can indicate not only uterine nephews, but parallel cousins and cross-cousins, as well as grandsons. For a discussion of this term, see Helga Uebach, "Notes on the Tibetan Kinship Term *dbon*." In *Tibetan Studies in Honour of Hugh Richardson*, ed. Michael Aris and Aung San Suu kyi (Warminster: Aris and Phillips, 1980).

4 For a discussion of inheritance and related issues in early Tibet, including royal succession dynastic marriage, see Brandon Dotson, *The Old Tibetan Annals: An Annotated Translation of Tibet's First History* (Vienna: Verlag der Österreichischen Akademie der Wissenschaften, 2009), 25–37.

5 Helga Uebach, "Eminent Ladies of the Tibetan Empire According to Old Tibetan Texts." In *Les Habitants du Toit du Monde*, ed. Samten Karmay and Phillipe Sagant (Nanterre: Société d'Ethnologie, 1997), 61.

6 Stephen W. Bushell, "The Early History of Tibet. From Chinese Sources," *Journal of the Royal Asiatic Society* 12 (1880), 444–45; Paul Pelliot, *Histoire Ancienne du Tibet* (Paris: Adrien-Maisonneuve, 1961), 4–5; D.Y. Lee, *The History of the Early Relations between China and Tibet. From the Chiu t'ang-shu, a Documentary Survey* (Bloomington, Indiana: Eastern Press, 1991), 9–10.

7 Lines 21–33 (with some elisions) of the east inscription: *dang po rgya rje // rgyal sar zhugs nas// de'i tang gi srId lo nyi shu rtsa gsum lon// rgyal rabs gcIg gi 'og du// 'phrul gyi lha btsan po khri srong brtsan dang// rgya rje the'e tsong bUn BU zheng hwang te gnyIs// chab srid gcIg du mol nas// ceng kwan gyI lo la/ mun sheng kong co// btsan po'i khab du blangs// phyis 'phrul gyI lha btsan po khri lde gtsug brtsan dang// rgya rje sam lang kha'e 'gwan sheng bUn shIn bU hwang te [gnyIs]// chab srid gcIg du mol te// gnyen brtsegs nas// keng lung gI lo la kIm shang kong co// btsan po'I khab du blangs nas// dbon zhang du 'gyur te dgyes pa las// ... 'di ltar nye zhIng gnyen pa yIn na// dbon zhang gI tshul kho na ltar//.* (Capital 'I' indicates the reverse *gi gu*, otherwise the transliteration follows extended Wylie.) For alternate translations, transcription and transliteration, see Hugh E. Richardson, *A Corpus of Early Tibetan Inscriptions* (London: Royal Asiatic Society, 1985), 110–13; and Fang Kuei Li and W. South Coblin, *A Study of the Old Tibetan Inscriptions* (Taipei: ROC, 1987), 48–49, 96–97.

8 Jacques Bacot, Frederick W. Thomas and Charles Toussaint, *Documents de Touen-Houang relatifs a l'histoire du Tibet* (Paris: Libraire Orientaliste Paul Geuthner, 1940–1946), 59, 65; Dotson 2009, 132–33. A single entry in the *Old Tibetan Annals* covers one year according to the Tibetan calendar followed at that time. The year began in March or April, so the entry for the ox year 689–690, for example, begins in the spring of 689 and ends in the spring of 690, hence I have rendered it "689–690," with the two years separated by a hyphen to indicate not a range of dates but a single Tibetan year. In the case of 762–764, this entry in fact covers two years; for further details see Géza Uray, "The Location of Khar-can and Leng-chu of the Old Tibetan Sources." In *Varia Eurasiatica: Festschrift Fur Professor Andras Rọna-Tas* (Szeged, 1991), 203–05.

9 Rolf A. Stein, "Un ensemble sémantique Tibétain: créer et procréer, etre et devenir, vivre, nourrir et guérir," *Bulletin of the School of Oriental and African Studies* 36.2 (1973), 414–17. Stein is doubtful of the translation of *chab srid la gshegs* as indicating going to battle, though one can easily see that a "political campaign" could be a prelude to a military campaign.

10 On this fragment see Hugh E. Richardson, "Further Fragments from Dunhuang." In *High Peaks Pure Earth: Collected Writings on Tibetan History and Culture, Hugh Richardson*, ed. Michael Aris (London: Serindia, 1998), 28–29.

11 On this last term, see Tsuguhito Takeuchi, *Old Tibetan Contracts from Central Asia* (Tokyo: Daizo Shuppan, 1995), 162–64.

12 PT 1071, ll. 325–28; Hugh E. Richardson, "Hunting Accidents in Early Tibet." In *High Peaks Pure Earth: Collected Writings on Tibetan History and Culture, Hugh Richardson*, ed. Michael Aris (London: Serindia, 1998), 155.

13 *dus de sham na / bod kyi lha btsan po dang / rgya rjer yang dbon zhang du mdzad / nas // kong co yang lha btsan po'i khab tu bzhes ste //* (PT 960, ll. 57–58). Translation from Matthew T. Kapstein, *The Tibetan Assimilation of Buddhism. Conversion, Contestation, and Memory* (Oxford: Oxford University Press, 2000), 41; transliteration following Ronald E. Emmerick, *Tibetan Texts Concerning Khotan* (London: Oxford University Press, 1967), 85. The document was first translated in Frederick W. Thomas, *Tibetan Literary Texts and Documents Concerning Chinese Turkestan. Part I: Literary Texts* (London: Royal Asiatic Society, 1935), 303–23.

14 Paul K. Benedict, "Tibetan and Chinese Kinship Terms," *Harvard Journal of Asiatic Studies* 6.3–4 (1942), 337.

15 Uebach 1997, 66.

16 For an analysis of the episode in later Tibetan histories that makes Khri Srong lde btsan the son of the Chinese Princess of Jincheng, see Kapstein, 23–30. It may in fact be the case that the Princess of Jincheng had a son, lHas bon, but he died in 739–740, in the same year of the princess' death, and it is not clear that he would have been crown prince.

17 Bacot et al., 17, 37; Dotson 2009, 96.

18 Zuiho Yamaguchi, "Matrimonial Relationship Between the T'u-Fan and the T'ang Dynasties (Part 2)," *Memoirs of the Research Department of the Toyo Bunko* 28 (1970), 63. On the *Annals of the 'A zha Principality* (PT 1368), see Géza Uray, "The Annals of the 'A zha Principality: the Problems of Chronology and Genre of the Stein Document, Tun-Huang, vol. 69, fol. 84." In *Proceedings of the Csoma De Kőrös Symposium*, ed. Louis Ligeti (Budapest, 1978), 541–78.

19 Bacot et al., 24, 47; Dotson 2009, 116.

20 Bacot et al., 55, 62; Dotson 2009, 126.

21 *mKhas pa'i dga' ston,* 372.

22 *mKhas pa'i dga' ston,* 411–12. Kha gan indicates a Turkic ruler, in this case the lord of the 'A zha. Ma ga tho gon is not a name, but an epithet, and is also found to indicate the 'A zha ruler during the early 8th century in the *Annals of the 'A zha Principality.*

23 Géza Uray, "Queen Sad-mar-kar's Songs in the *Old Tibetan Chronicle*," *Acta Orientalia Academiae Scientiarum Hungaricae* 25 (1972), 36.

24 Uebach 1997, 61.

25 Heirs to the Tibetan throne were provided by wives taken from Tibetan aristocratic clans, notably four clans – 'Bro, mChims, Tshes pong and sNa nam – whose members were known as *zhang*. These heir-producing unions followed certain rules that created a sort of "*zhang* rotation" such that no single *zhang* clan could gain a monopoly on mothering Tibetan emperors; see Brandon Dotson, "A Note on *źaṅ*: Maternal Relatives of the Tibetan Royal Line and Marriage into the Royal Family," *Journal Asiatique* 292.1–2 (2004), 94–96. That "international *zhang*" in the context of dynastic marriage were thought of differently than "domestic *zhang*" who provided heirs is evident in a famous couplet from the *sBa bzhed*, cited by Matthew Kapstein in the context of a conflict between the Princess of Jincheng and a lady of the sNa nam clan over which was the mother of the young heir, Khri Srong lde btsan. To resolve the conflict the young prince exclaims, "Khri Srong lde btsan is China's nephew. Pray what's for the sNa nam uncles to do?" (*khri srong lde btsan rgya tsha lags/ sna nam zhang gi ci gyi 'tshal*); Kapstein, 28. Here the prince pits the domestic *zhang*, the sNa nam clan, against the international *zhang*, China, spotlighting the incongruity of the pretensions of the former. This is of course a literary episode, and has no basis in the historical record (Khri Srong lde btsan was in fact the son of a sNa nam princess, *contra* the claim put into his mouth here); its value, rather, is in its illustration of a principle, namely that dynastic marriage operates on a different level than "domestic" marriages involving the royal line.

26 Kapstein, 221, n. 77. Kapstein goes on to argue that in the process of becoming bride-givers (*zhang*) of the Tibetan emperor, and being granted titles such as "ministers" (*zhang blon*),

Tibetan clans participated in a "symbolic code" in which "a familial designation of seniority was in effect exchanged for a subsidiary political position; real power was alienated for a gain in political prestige." I am less sure that the rights and duties of the *dbon zhang* relationship were dispelled or replaced by a lord-and-vassal-type arrangement. One could argue more persuasively, I think, that the conflict between these two models of power accounts for several of the Tibetan Empire's crises, and played a large role in the events leading up to and following its collapse.

27 Rolf A. Stein, "Les serments des traités sino-tibétains (8ᵉ–9ᵉ siècles)," *T'oung Pao* 74 (1988), 132–33; Pan Yihong, "The Sino-Tibetan Treaties in the Tang Dynasty," *T'oung Pao* 78 (1992), 140–42.

28 It is for this reason, in fact, argues Stein, that Tibetans performed blood sacrifices to solemnize treaties; they were enacting the Chinese custom after having performed their own, presumably bloodless, rites; Stein 1988, 129–30, 136. Imaeda disputes Stein's interpretation of the Chinese sources on this point, and argues that both sides simply performed the ritual that had been agreed upon, and that sacrifice was relevant to both Chinese and Tibetan traditions; Yoshiro Imaeda, "Rituel des traités de paix sino-tibétains du VIIIᵉ au IXᵉ siècle." In *La Sérinde, Terre d'échanges*, ed. Monique Cohen, Jean-Pierre Drège and Jacques Giès (Paris: La Documentations Française, 2001), 89–91.

29 Stein 1988, 127–28; Pan 1992, 152; Imaeda 90.

30 This point comes across clearly in the tone of official diplomatic correspondence from the Tang court to the Tibetan emperor, where the form of address opening the letter, though theoretically determined simply by the legal status of the addressee as either vassal or rival, in fact was influenced more often than not by recent political events and whether the Tang emperor was pleased or displeased with the Tibetans at the time of writing. See Kaneko Shuichi, "T'ang International Relations and Diplomatic Correspondence," *Acta Asiatica* 55 (1988), 96–100. In these letters the Tibetan emperor is addressed as "son-in-law."

31 The so-called "priest–patron" (*mchod yon*) relationship characterized Tibet's political relations with the Mongols and the Manchus, and can be viewed as the forerunner to later terms such as suzerainty, which was equally problematic from a legal perspective. On *mchod yon*, a contraction of "officiant-donee" (*mchod gnas*) and "donor" (*yon bdag*), see David Seyfort Ruegg, *Ordre spirituel et ordre temporel dans la pensée Bouddhique de l'Inde et du Tibet. Quatre conférences au Collège de France* (Paris: *Collège de France*, 1995). The term *mchod yon*, like *dbon zhang*, not only designates the two sides of the pair, but also implies the rights and duties attached to their relationship.

32 There is a danger of being too categorical on the matter of the superiority of bride-givers to bride-receivers across the Tibetan cultural area. One can certainly point to instances where the opposite appears to be the case, such as Corlin's description of exchange in rGyal thang; Claes Corlin, "A Tibetan Enclave in Yunnan: Land, Kinship, and Inheritance in Gyethang." In *Tibetan Studies: Presented at the Seminar of Young Tibetologists, Zurich, June 26–July 1, 1977*, ed. Martin Brauen and Per Kvaerne (Zürich: Völkerkundemuseum der Universität Zürich, 1978), 75–89. On the variability of alliance systems and kin classification over the Tibetan cultural area (mostly the Himalayas), see Michael Oppitz, "Close-Up and Wide-Angle. On Comparative Ethnography in the Himalayas – and Beyond. The Mahesh Chandra Regmi Lecture, Dec. 15th 2006," *European Bulletin of Himalayan Research* 31 (2007), 155–71.

33 Guntram Hazod, "In the Garden of the White Mare: Encounters with History and Cult in Tshal Gung-thang." In *Rulers on the Celestial Plain: Ecclesiastical and Secular Hegemony in Medieval Tibet. A Study of Tshal Gung-thang*, Per Sørensen and Guntram Hazod in cooperation with Tsering Gyalbo (Vienna: Verlag der Österreichischen Akademie der Wissenschaften, 2007), 585–93.

34 Ibid., 583–84. In other words, Tshal Gung thang stood as "officiant-donees" (*mchod gnas*) and bride-givers (*zhang*) in relation to Grib, who were the donors (*yon bdag*) and bride-receivers (*dbon*). Incidentally, it can be observed that the very name "Bla ma Zhang" demonstrates the persistence of *zhang* as a kinship term-cum-title, since it refers to his membership to the sNa nam clan, one of the four *zhang* clans of the imperial period. The relevance of these clans that mothered the Tibetan emperors would have ceased to be applicable in a formal sense with the collapse of the royal line in the 9th century, but whose symbolic historical resonance continued to link them to the glory of the imperial period well into the 12th century and beyond; Per Sørensen and Guntram Hazod in cooperation with Tsering Gyalbo, *Rulers on the Celestial Plain: Ecclesiastical and Secular Hegemony in Medieval Tibet. A Study of Tshal Gung-thang* (Vienna: Verlag der Österreichischen Akademie der Wissenschaften, 2007), 75, n. 11.

35 Solomon George FitzHerbert, "The Birth of Gesar: Narrative Diversity and Social Resonance in the Tibetan Epic Tradition" (DPhil Dissertation: University of Oxford, 2007), 263–64.

12

གནའ་རབས་བོད་དང་པར་ཟིག་དབར་གྱི་འབྲེལ་བ་ལས་ཧ་ཐོག་ཕོ་ལོང་གི་འབྱུང་ཁུངས་ལ་དཔྱད་པ།

ཤར་གཞོན་ཚེ་རིང་ཟླ་བ།

གླེང་གཞི།

ཨོ་ཤི་ཡ་དཀྱིལ་མའི་ས་ཁུལ་དུ་གནས་པའི་གནའ་རབས་ཀྱི་བོད་དང་པར་ཟིག[1] གཉིས་པོར་རང་རང་གི་ལོ་རྒྱུས་དང་ཤེས་རིག་ཧ་ཅང་ཡུན་རིང་ལྡན་ཞིང་། གནའ་བོའི་ལོ་རྒྱུས་ཡིག་ཚང་ཁག་དང་ས་འོག་ནས་ཐོན་པའི་རིག་དངོས་སོགས་མང་པོའི་ཐོག་ནས་གནའ་རབས་ས་ཁུལ་དེ་གཉིས་དབར་གྱི་མཛའ་འབྲེལ་འགྲོ་འོངས་ཤིན་ཏུ་ཟབ་པ་མ་ཟད། ཤེས་རིག་བརྗེ་རེས་བྱས་པའི་བརྒྱུད་རིམ་ཁྲོད་ཕན་ཚུན་ཤུགས་རྐྱེན་ཡང་ངེས་ཅན་ཞིག་ཐེབས་ཡོད་པ་ར་སྒྲོད་ཐུབ་ཀྱི་ཡོད། དཔེར་ན། པར་ཟིག་ས་ཁུལ་དུ་དར་ཁྱབ་ཆེ་བའི་གནའ་བོའི་ཆོས་ལུགས་ཛོ་རོ་ཨ་སི་ཏི (Zoroastrianism) ཞེས་པ་དེས་བོད་ཀྱི་གཡུང་དྲུང་བོན་པོའི་ཆོས་ལུགས་དར་སྤེལ་ཡོང་བར་སྐུལ་འདེད་དང་ཤུགས་རྐྱེན་ངེས་ཅན་ཐེབས་ཡོད་ལ། བོད་ཀྱི་གླུ་རྩེ་ནི་པར་ཟིག་ཁུལ་དུ་བྲིན་ཁ་སྐྱེན་པའི་ཐོན་རྫས་ཤིག་ཡིན་པ་མ་ཟད། སྤྱི་ལོའི་དུས་རབས་བཞི་པའི་སྐབས་སུ་ཐོན་པའི་ལོ་རྒྱུས་དེབ་ཐེར་ཁག་ནང་གསལ་བར་གཞིགས་ན་གནའ་རབས་རོ་མ་བཙན་རྒྱལ་(Roman Empire) དུའང་ནང་འདྲེན་བྱེད་བཞིན་ཡོད་པ་སོགས་བརྗོད་ཀྱིས་མི་ལང་བས་རྒྱས་པར་མི་སྤྲོ། འདིར་བརྗོད་པར་བྱ་བའི་ཧ་ཐོག་ཕོ་ལོང་དེ་ཡང་བོད་དང་པར་ཟིག་གཉིས་དབར་རིག་གནས་བརྗེ་རེས་བྱས་པའི་བརྒྱུད་རིམ་ཁྲོད་ས་ཁུལ་གཉིས་པོར་ཧ་ཅང་དར་ཁྱབ་ཆེན་པོ་བྱུང་བའི་གནའ་རབས་ཀྱི་རྩེད་རིགས་རྣམ་གྲངས་ཤིག་ཡིན་ལ། ཡར་ཀླུང་བོད་བཙན་པོའི་རྒྱལ་རབས[2] ཀྱིས་བོད་ཁམས་ཡོངས་ལ་དབང་བསྒྱུར་བའི་སྐབས་སུ་བོད་པ་ཚོའི་ཧ་ཐོག་ཕོ་ལོང་རྩེན་པའི་ལག་རྩལ་རྩེར་སོན་ཡོད་པ་ནི་ཐང་དེབ་གསར་རྙིང་སོགས་ལས་གསལ། དེས་ན། དེང་སྐབས་རྒྱལ་ཕྱི་རྒྱལ་ནང་དུ་ཧ་ཐོག་ཕོ་ལོང་ལ་ཞིབ་འཇུག་བྱེད་མཁན་མང་དག་ཅིག་གསར་དུ་ཐོན་ཡོད་རུང་། བོད་ཀྱི་གཏམ་དཔེར། བླ་མ་རེ་ལ་ཆོས་ལུགས་རེ། །ལུང་པ་རེ་ལ་སྐད་ལུགས་རེ། །ཞེས་ཟེར་བ་ལྟར་མཁས་པ་རེ་རེས་དགོངས་ཚུལ་མི་གཅིག་པ་རེ་གསུངས་སྟབས་ངོས་འཛིན་གཅིག་གྱུར་ཡོང་བར་དཀའ། དེའི་རྒྱུ་མཚན་གཙོ་བོ་ནི་རྩེད་རིགས་དེའི་འབྱུང་ཁུངས་སྐོར་གྱི་གནའ་རབས་

ཀྱི་ཡིག་ཆ་ཁུངས་བཙན་ཤིན་ཏུ་དཀོན་པའི་རྐྱེན་གྱིས་རེད། ཁོ་བོས་རྟ་ཐོག་ཕོ་ལོང་གི་འབྱུང་ཁུངས་སྐོར་གྱི་དཔྱད་གཞིའི་ཡིག་ཆ་སྣ་ཚོགས་དུས་ཡུན་གང་མང་རིང་འཚོལ་བསྡུ་གང་ཐུབ་བྱས་ཤིང་། དེའི་རྨང་གཞིའི་ཐོག་གནའ་རབས་བོད་དང་པར་ཟིག་གཉིས་དབར་གྱི་ཆོས་ལུགས་དང་། རིག་གནས། ཚོང་ལས་དཔལ་འབྱོར་སོགས་ཀྱི་འབྲེལ་བར་སྨྱུང་ཞིབ་རྟག་དཔྱད་ལན་མང་བྱས་པ་བརྒྱུད། ད་ལྟ་འདིར་གནའ་རབས་རྟ་ཐོག་ཕོ་ལོང་གི་འབྱུང་འཕེལ་སྐོར་ལ་རང་ཉིད་ཀྱི་འདོད་ཚུལ་རགས་ཙམ་ཞིག་འཆད་པར་བྱ་སྟེ། འདི་འཆད་པ་ལ་གནའ་རབས་བོད་དང་པར་ཟིག་དབར་གྱི་འབྲེལ་བའི་སྐོར་དང་། གནའ་རབས་རྟ་ཐོག་ཕོ་ལོང་གི་འབྱུང་ཁུངས་སྐོར། མཐའ་དཔྱད་པ། རྟ་ཐོག་ཕོ་ལོང་གི་དར་འཕེལ་བཅས་ཁག་བཞིར་དབྱེའོ། །

དང་པོ། གནའ་རབས་བོད་དང་པར་ཟིག་དབར་གྱི་འབྲེལ་བའི་སྐོར།[3]

གཅིག གནའ་རབས་བོད་དང་པར་ཟིག་དབར་ཆོས་ལུགས་དང་རིག་གནས་ཀྱི་འབྲེལ་བ།

བོད་དང་པར་ཟིག་དབར་གྱི་འབྲེལ་བ་ལས་ཆེས་གཙོ་བོ་ནི་ཆོས་ལུགས་དང་རིག་གནས་ཀྱི་འབྲེལ་བ་དེ་ཡིན་གཤིས། གནའ་རབས་བོད་དང་པར་ཟིག་དབར་གྱི་མཇལ་འབྲེལ་འགྲོ་འོངས་ཁྲོད་དུ་གལ་ཆེའི་གནས་བབས་ཀྱང་བཟུང་ཡོད།

༼ དེའང་གནའ་རབས་ཨེ་ཤི་ཡ་དཀྱིལ་མའི་ས་ཁུལ་དུ་གངས་ཏི་སེས་ལྟེ་བ་བྱས་པའི་བོན་ཆོས་ཀྱི་ཤེས་རིག་གམ་ཞང་ཞུང་གི་ཤེས་རིག་ཅིག་དང་། ཡང་པར་ཟིག་མཐོ་སྒང་སྟེང་དུ་ཛོ་རོ་ཨཱ་སེ་ཏེ་ཞེས་པའི་ཆོས་ལུགས་དེས་གཙོ་བྱས་པའི་གནའ་རབས་ཀྱི་ཤེས་རིག་ཅིག་དར་ཡོད་ཅིང་། ཤེས་རིག་དེ་གཉིས་ཀྱི་འབྲེལ་འདྲིས་ན་ཅང་ཟབ་མོ་ཡིན་ཏེ། དེའང་པར་ཟིག་ཏུ་ན་ལམ་སྤྱི་ལོའི་སྔོན་གྱི་དུས་རབས་བཅུ་དྲུག་ནས་བཅོ་ལྔའི་བར་དུ་འབྱུང་གཉིས་སྨྲ་བའི་(Dualism) འདོད་ཚུལ་གཙོ་བོར་འཛིན་ཞིང་། མེ་ཡི་མཆོད་པ་བྱེད་པའི་ཆོས་ལུགས་ཛོ་རོ་ཨཱ་སེ་ཏེ་བྱ་བ་ཞིག་དར་འགོ་ཚུགས་པ་དང་། སྤྱི་ལོའི་སྔོན་གྱི་དུས་རབས་དྲུག་པའི་དུས་མཇུག་ཏུ་པར་ཟིག་གི་བཙན་ཕྱུག་རྒྱལ་ལྡན་རྒྱལ་རབས་སྔ་མ་ཨ་ཆས་མན་ཏེའི་(Achaemendids, 558–330BCE) སྐབས་རྒྱལ་ཡོངས་ནས་དད་མོས་བྱ་དགོས་པའི་ཆོས་ལུགས་སུ་གཏན་འཁེལ་བྱས་སྐབས་ཆོས་ལུགས་དེ་པར་ཟིག་ཏུ་དར་ཁྱབ་ཆེན་པོ་བྱུང་བ་རེད། ཁོང་ཚོས་ཨ་ཧུ་ར་མ་ཛ་ཟ་(Ahura Mazda) སྟོན་པར་བཀུར་ཞིང་། ཨ་ཝེ་སི་ཏ་(Avesta) ཞེས་པ་ནི་སྐོ་གསུམ་གྱུས་བཏུད་ཞུ་བའི་གསུང་རབ་བཀའ་བསྟན་དུ་ངོས་འཛིན།[4] པར་ཟིག་གི་ཛོ་རོ་ཨཱ་སེ་ཏེའི་ཆོས་ལུགས་དེ་ཞང་ཞུང་གི་བོན་ཆོས་དང་ག་དུས་འབྲེལ་འདྲིས་བྱུང་མིན་ཐད་ཞིབ་འཇུག་པ་ཚོའི་ཁྲོད་དགོངས་ཚུལ་མི་གཅིག་པ་མང་པོ་མཆིས། འགའ་རེས་ཆོས་ལུགས་དེ་གཉིས་དབར་གྱི་འབྲེལ་བ་དེ་ན་ལམ་སྤྱི་ལོའི་སྔོན་གྱི་དུས་རབས་དྲུག་པ་ནས་སྤྱི་ལོའི་དུས་རབས་གསུམ་པའི་བར་དུ་བྱུང་ཡོད་ཚུལ་བཤད་ཅིང་།[5] པར་ཟིག་གི་ཛོ་རོ་ཨཱ་སེ་ཏེའི་ཆོས་ལུགས་དེས་དུས་ཕྱིས་ཞང་ཞུང་དང་བོད་ཁམས་ རྫིལ་པོར་དར་ཁྱབ་ཆེ་བའི་གཡུང་དྲུང་བོན་པོའི་ཆོས་ལུགས་ཀྱི་ལྟ་སྒོམ་སྤྱོད་གསུམ་དང་གཞི་ལམ་འབྲས་གསུམ་སོགས་ལ་ཤུགས་རྐྱེན་ངེས་ཅན་

ཞིག་ཐེབས་ཡོད། ཕྲན་ལ་དེའི་ཐད་ཀྱི་ཐོས་བསམ་ཅུང་ཕྲ་བས་ཆོས་ལུགས་དེ་གཉིས་ཀྱི་འབྲེལ་འདྲིས་ཐོག་མ་ག་དུས་བྱུང་མིན་ཐད་ཐོལ་བྱུང་གི་གཏམ་སྨྲ་བའི་སྤོབས་པ་མེད་ཀྱང་། མ་མཐར་ཡང་བོད་རྒྱལ་གྲི་གུམ་བཙན་པོའི་དུས་(སྤྱི་ལོའི་དུས་རབས་དང་པོའི་སྐབས་)ཆོས་ལུགས་དེ་གཉིས་དབར་ཏ་ལམ་འབྲེལ་འདྲིས་བྱུང་ཡོད་པར་འདོད་དེ། དེའང་། བན་དེའི་ཆོས་འབྱུང་ཁག་གི་ནང་དུ་བོན་པོར་བརྗོལ་བོན་དང་། འཁྱར་བོན། བསྒྱུར་བོན་བཅས་རིགས་གསུམ་དུ་དབྱེ་བ་ལས། འཁྱར་བོན་ནི་བྲུ་ཞའི་ཡུལ་ནས་བོད་དུ་དར་ཚུལ་གསུངས་ལ།[6] བོན་གྱི་ལོ་རྒྱུས་ཡིག་ཆ་མང་པོས་ཀྱང་བོན་ཁུངས་སྟག་གཟིག་ལ་གཏུགས་བཞིན་མཆིས་པར་རྒྱུ་མཚན་མེད་པ་མ་ཡིན། སྤྱིར་ན་བོན་ཁུངས་སྟག་གཟིག་གམ་པར་ཐིག་ལ་གཏུགས་པ་དེ་ཅུང་ཟད་ལོ་རྒྱུས་ཀྱི་དོན་དངོས་དང་མི་འཚམས་ཀྱང་། དེའི་ཐོག་ནས་མ་མཐར་ཡང་སྐབས་དེ་དུས་ས་ཁུལ་གཉིས་པོའི་དབར་ཆོས་ལུགས་ཀྱི་འབྲེལ་འདྲིས་ཆེ་ཙམ་ཡོད་པ་ཤུགས་ཀྱིས་མཚོན་ནོ། །

༄ ཡང་རིག་གནས་ཐད་ཀྱི་འབྲེལ་བའི་སྐོར་དཔེ་མཚོན་ཙམ་ཞུས་ན། ཞང་ཞུང་རྒྱལ་རབས་སྐབས་དང་ལྷག་དོན་བོད་བཙན་པོའི་རྒྱལ་རབས་སྐབས་པར་ཐིག་གི་སྲོལ་རྒྱུན་གྱོན་ཆས་དང་ཡུལ་སྲོལ་གོམས་གཤིས་ཀྱིས་བོད་ལ་ཤུགས་རྐྱེན་ཆེན་པོ་ཐེབས་ཡོད་དེ། མཁས་དབང་དགེ་འདུན་ཆོས་འཕེལ་གྱིས་མཛད་པའི་《དེབ་ཐེར་དཀར་པོ》ལས། དེ་དུས་ཕྱིའི་རྒྱལ་ཁབ་ཀྱི་ཁྲོད་ན་བོད་དང་མཛའ་འབྲེལ་ཆེ་བ་ནི་ཏ་ཟིག་པ་རྣམས་ཡིན་ལ། ཏ་ཟིག་ཡུལ་དུ་ནི་སྐབས་དེར་ནང་པའི་བསྟན་པ་དར་བར་མ་ཟད། ཤེས་རིག་ཡོན་ཏན་གྱི་ཆ་ལ་ཡང་ཁོང་རྣམས་འགྲན་ཟླ་དང་བྲལ་བ་ཤིས། བོད་ཀྱི་རྗེ་བློན་རྣམས་ཀྱང་ཕལ་ཆེར་ཏ་ཟིག་པའི་སྲོལ་ལུགས་གནང་བ་ཡིན་ནམ་སྙམ་སྟེ། སྲོང་བཙན་གྱིས་དར་དམར་པོའི་ཐོད་བཞེས་པ་སོགས་ཀྱང་བཤད་ལ། ཟ་འོག་གི་བེར་དང་། ཕྲུགས་ལྷམ་སྣེ་འཁྱིལ་གྱོན་པ་སོགས་ཀྱང་ཏ་ཟིག་གི་སྲོལ་དང་འདྲ། ལར་ཟ་འོག་ནི་སྔོན་དུས་རྒྱ་གར་ནག་གཉིས་གར་ཡང་གྱོན་སྲོལ་མེད་པར་འདུག[7] ཅེས་འཁོད་ཡོད་པ་དང་། དེ་མིན་ད་དུང་《དེབ་དཀར》ལས། མངའ་རིས་ཀྱི་ བླ་དྭགས་སུ་ཆོས་རྒྱལ་གྱི་གདུང་རྒྱུད་དུ་གྲགས་པ་ད་ལྟའི་བར་དུ་ཡོད་པ་རྣམས་ནས། ལོ་གསར་སོགས་ཀྱི་ཚེ་སྟོན་གྱི་ཆས་ཡིན་ཟེར་ནས་ཞྭ་དམར་བཙན་ཞྭའི་དབྱིབས་ཅན་རྩེ་མོ་མཐོ་ཞིང་ཕྲ་བའི་ཡས་ཟུར་དུ་ཚེ་དཔག་མེད་ཀྱི་སྐུ་བརྐོན་ཞིག་དང་དམར་གྱིས་བཅིངས་པའི་ལྷག་མ་མདུན་ནས་བསྣོལ་བསྒྲིགས་ཏེ་གྱོན་པ་སོགས་ཡིན་འདུག[8] ཅེས་འཁོད་པར་དཔྱད་ན། བོད་ཀྱི་སྲོལ་རྒྱུན་གྱོན་གོས་ལ་པར་ཐིག་གི་ཤན་ཞུགས་ཆེན་པོ་ཐེབས་ཡོད་པ་མངོན་ཐུབ་ལ། ཐང་རྒྱལ་རབས་ཀྱི་དུས་སུ་རི་མོ་བ་ཡན་ལི་སྦྲན(阎立本) གྱིས་བོད་ཀྱི་བློན་པོ་མགར་སྟོང་བཙན་གཉེན་སློང་བར་ཐང་རྒྱལ་རབས་སུ་ཕེབས་པའི་རྣམ་པའི་རི་མོ་ཞིག་བྲིས་ཡོད་པ་དེའི་ནང་བློན་པོ་མགར་སྟོང་བཙན་གྱི་ལྭ་བའི་སྟེང་མཛེས་སྤྲུག་ལྡན་པའི་པར་ཐིག་སྣ་སན་རྒྱལ་རབས་ཀྱི་རི་མོ་དང་བྲ་བྲིའུ་སོགས་རྒྱན་ཡོད་པའི་ཆ་ལུགས་ལ་བལྟས་ན་གྱོན་གོས་སྟེང་གི་ཤུགས་རྐྱེན་ཇི་འདྲ་ཐེབས་ཡོད་པ་རང་བཞིན་གྱིས་རྟོགས་ནུས་སོ། །

༄ གཞན་ཡང་། སྐད་ཡིག་གི་ཐོག་ནས་བལྟས་ན། རང་རེའི་བོད་སྐད་ནང་དུ་པར་ཐིག་གི་གཡར་ཚིག་མང་པོ་མཐོང་རྒྱུ་ཡོད། སྤྱིར་གཡར་ཚིག་ནི་སྤྱི་ཚོགས་ཀྱི་སྐད་བརྡའི་སྣང་ཚུལ་གལ་ཆེན་ཞིག་ཡིན་ཞིང་། དེ་ནི་མི་རིགས་ཕན་ཚུན་ནམ་རྒྱལ་ཁབ་ཕན་ཚུན་དབར་འབྲེལ་གཏུགས་བྱས་པའི་བརྒྱུད་རིམ་ཁྲོད་རིམ་པས་གསར་དུ་ཐོན་པ་ཞིག་ཡིན་ལ། གོམས་པ་ལུགས་སྲོལ་མི་གཅིག་པའི་ས་ཁུལ་གཉིས་པོའི་དབར་རིག་གནས་ཐད་ཕན་ཚུན་ཤུགས་རྐྱེན་ཇི་འདྲ་ཐེབས་ཡོད་པའི་དན་རྟགས་ལྟ་བུའང་ཡིན་ནོ། །དཔེར་ན། བོད་སྐད་ཁྲོད་ཀྱི་པད་མ་དང་

ཡོ་ག་སོགས་ནི་ལེགས་སྦྱར་སྐད་ཀྱི་གཡར་ཚིག་ཡིན་པ་དང་། མོ་ཊ་(motor) དང་ཀོག་ཧྥི་(coffee) ཧྥ་ཧྥ་(sofa) སོགས་ནི་དབྱིན་སྐད་ཀྱི་གཡར་ཚིག་ཡིན། དེ་དང་འདྲ་བར་གུར་གུམ་ཟེར་བའི་མིང་བརྡ་དེ་ནི་པར་ཟིག་སྐད་ཀྱི་གཡར་ཚིག་ཡིན་ལ། དེ་པར་ཟིག་སྐད་དུ་ཀུར་ཀུམ་(kurkum) ཡང་ན་ཀར་ཀམ་(karkam) ཞེས་འབོད།[9] དེའང་གུར་གུམ་ནི་གནའ་བོའི་པར་ཟིག་དང་ཁ་ཆེའི་ཡུལ་དུ་འདེབས་བཞིན་ཡོད་པའི་སྐྱེ་དངོས་ཤིག་དང་ཕྱིས་བོད་དུ་དར་ཁྱབ་བྱུང་བ་ཞིག་ཡིན། ད་དུང་བོད་སྐད་ཁྲོད་ཀྱི་ཟི་ར་ནི་པར་ཟིག་སྐད་ལས་བྱུང་བ་དང་། དེབ་ཐེར་ནི་པར་ཟིག་གི་སྐད་དབ་ཏེར་(dābtĕr) སྒྲ་བསྒྱུར་བྱས་[10] ཚུལ་སོགས་ཤིན་ཏུ་མང་བས་རེ་རེ་བཞིན་བརྗོད་པར་མི་དཔོག་ཀྱང་དོན་གཅིག་ཏུ་དྲིལ་ན་བོད་སྐད་ཁྲོད་པར་ཟིག་གི་མིང་བརྡ་མང་པོ་དེ་འདྲ་ཡོད་པས་གནའ་སྔ་མོ་ནས་བཟུང་ས་ཁུལ་གཉིས་དབར་ཆོས་ལུགས་དང་། རིག་གནས། དཔལ་འབྱོར། སྒྱུ་རྩལ་སོགས་ཀྱི་ཐད་འབྲེལ་འདྲིས་ཟབ་མོ་བྱུང་ཡོད་པ་ཤུགས་ཀྱིས་མཚོན་ནོ། །

གཉིས། གནའ་རབས་བོད་དང་པར་ཟིག་དབར་ཚོང་ལས་དཔལ་འབྱོར་གྱི་འབྲེལ་བ།

ཏ་ཟིག་རྒྱལ་པོ་བོད་ལ་ཁྲ་ལྟར་གདུག །ཐབས་མི་འདྲ་བ་བཞི་བཙུ་ཐམ་པས་བཏུལ། །གཟི་མཚོང་གསེར་སོགས་རིན་པོ་ཆེ་རྣམས་མཚོན་བརྗོལ། །འདེབས་རལ་གྱི་ཏ་ཟིག་འོག་ཏུ་འདུ། །ཞེས་《བཀའ་ཐང་སྡེ་ལྔའི་བློན་པོ་བཀའ་ཐང་》དུ་འཁོད་ཡོད་པ་དང་།[11] བོད་ཀྱི་ལོ་རྒྱུས་སྔན་རྩོམ་རིང་མོ་《གླིང་རྗེ་གེ་སར་རྒྱལ་པོའི་སྒྲུང་》ནང་དུའང་སྟག་གཟིག་ནོར་རྫོང་བྱ་བ་ཞིག་འཁོད་ཡོད་པ། དེ་བཞིན་བོད་མི་རྣམས་ཀྱི་ཁ་རྒྱུན་དུའང་ཏ་ཟིག་ནོར་གྱི་རྒྱལ་པོ་ཞེས་འཆད་སྲོལ་ཡོད་པ་ལས་ཤུགས་སུ་དཔོག་ཐུབ་པར། གནའ་སྔ་མོ་ནས་བཟུང་བོད་མིའི་བསམ་བློའི་འདུ་ཤེས་ནང་ཏ་ཟིག་གམ་པར་ཟིག་ནི་གསེར་དངུལ་གཡུ་བྱུར་དང་རྒྱུ་ནོར་ལོངས་སྤྱོད་ཟད་མཐའ་མེད་པ་ལྟར་གྱི་ཡུལ་ཞིག་ཡིན་པར་ངོས་འཛིན་བྱེད། དོན་དུའང་གནའ་རབས་ཀྱི་པར་ཟིག་གམ་ཏ་ཟིག་ནི་རང་བྱུང་ཐོན་ཁུངས་ཕུན་སུམ་ཚོགས་ལ། རྒྱུ་ནོར་གྱི་བང་མཛོད་ལྟ་བུ་ཡིན་ཞིང་། དེང་གི་དུས་སུའང་པར་ཟིག་སྟེ་དབྱི་རན་(Iran) ནི་འཛམ་གླིང་སྟེང་རྡོ་སྣུམ་གྱི་ཐོན་ཁུངས་གཙོ་གྲས་སུ་གྲུབ་ཡོད་དོ། །

གནའ་རབས་ཀྱི་པར་ཟིག་པ་རྣམས་ཚོང་ལས་དཔལ་འབྱོར་སྐྱུབ་པར་ཤིན་ཏུ་བརྩོན། དེའང་ཁོང་ཚོའི་ཡུལ་གྱི་གཡུ་དང་བྱུ་རུ་སོགས་ཨེ་ཤེ་ཡས་གཙོས་པའི་འཛམ་གླིང་ས་ཕྱོགས་ཀུན་ན་ཁྱབ་བརྡལ་དུ་སོང་ཡོད་པ་དང་། བྱེ་བྲག་བོད་དང་པར་ཟིག་དབར་གཡུ་དང་། བྱུ་རུ། མུ་ཏིག གཟི་སོགས་ཀྱི་ཚོང་ལས་ལ་འབྲུག་ཆ་ཧ་ཅང་དོད།[12] དེང་སྐབས་བོད་ཀྱི་ཞིང་འབྲོག་ཁུལ་གྱི་གྲོང་སྡེ་རེ་འགར་གཟི་མིག་དགུ་པ་ཡོད་པའི་ཁྱིམ་ཚང་ནི་གྲོང་སྡེ་དེའི་ཕྱུག་པོའི་ཁྱིམ་དུ་བརྩིས་སྲོལ་ཡོད། ཁྱད་པར་དུ་ལི་ཡུལ་བརྒྱུད་ནས་ཞང་ཞུང་དུ་སྐྱེལ་འདྲེན་བྱས་པའི་པར་ཟིག་གི་ཟ་འོག་དང་དར་གོས་རྣམས་རྒྱུ་སྤུས་དག་ལ་ཆུ་རིས་བཟང་པོ་དང་ལྡན་པས་ཞང་ཞུང་སོགས་བོད་ཀྱི་ས་ཆ་གཞན་ན་དགའ་བསུ་ཆེན་པོ་ཐོབ་ཀྱི་ཡོད་དོ། །ཡང་གནའ་དུས་མདོ་དབུས་མཐོ་སྒང་སྟེང་གི་གཡག་དང་རི་དྭགས་ཀྱི་པགས་ཤ་སོགས་ནི་བོད་ནས་ནུབ་ངོས་སུ་འདྲེན་པའི་ཚོང་ཟོག་གཙོ་བོའི་གྲས་ཤིག་ཡིན་ལ། པར་ཟིག་ཏུ་བོད་ཀྱི་གླ་རྩི་དགའ་པོ་བྱེད་ཅིང་ཁྲོམ་ར་ཡང་རྒྱ་ཆེན་པོ་ཡོད། གླ་རྩི་གཉན་ཁ་འཛོག་པ་དང་དུག་སེལ་བ་སོགས་སྨན་བཅོས་ཀྱི་ནུས་པ་ཆེས་ཆེར་ལྡན་པ་མ་ཟད། དྲི་མ་ཞིམ་པས་མཁའ་དབུགས་གཙང་མ་བཟོ་བའི་ཁྱད་

ནུས་ལྡན། དེ་བས་ཀྱང་བླ་རྡོ་ནི་པར་ཐིག་པ་རྣམས་ཆོས་ལུགས་ཀྱི་ཆོ་ག་སྒྲུབ་སྐབས་མེད་དུ་མི་རུང་བའི་རྫས་སྣ་ཞིག་ཀྱང་ཡིན། པར་ཐིག་པ་ཆོས་མདོ་དབུས་མཐོ་སྒང་དང་། རྒྱ་ནག ཀ་ཤི་མྀ་ར(Kashmir) སོགས་ས་ཁུལ་ནས་བླ་རྡོ་ནང་འདྲེན་བྱས་ཡོད་རུང་ས་ཁུལ་དེ་དག་གི་བླ་རྡོའི་ཁྲོད་རྒྱ་སྲུས་དག་ཤོས་ནི་བོད་ཀྱི་བླ་རྡོ་ཡིན[13] པས་བོད་དང་པར་ཐིག་དབར་གྱི་བླ་རྡོའི་ཚོང་ལས་ལ་འབྲུག་ཆ་ཏ་ཅང་དོད་པོ་ཡོད་དོ། །

གཉིས་པ། གནའ་རབས་ཧྲ་ཐོག་ཕོ་ལོང་གི་འབྱུང་ཁུངས་སྐོར།

གཅིག ཕོ་ལོང་ཟེར་བའི་མིང་བརྡ་ལ་དཔྱད་པ།

ཕོ་ལོང་ཞེས་པའི་མིང་བརྡ་དེ་ནི་བོད་དུ་གནའ་སྔ་མོ་ནས་དར་ཡོད་དེ། དུས་རབས་བརྒྱད་པ་ནས་དགུ་པའི་བར་དུ་ཕྱོགས་བསྒྲིགས་མཛད་པའི་བོད་ཀྱི་གནའ་རབས་མིང་མཛོད་《བྱེ་བྲག་རྟོགས་བྱེད་ཆེན་མོའི་》ནང་དུ་ཕོ་ལོང་ཞེས་པའི་མིང་བརྡ་དེ་འཁོད་ཡོད་པ་དང་། བོད་སྐད་ཡིག་ནང་གི་ཕོ་ལོང་ཟེར་བའི་མིང་བརྡ་དེ་ནི་པོ་ལོའམ་གྱུ་གུའི་བརྡ་རྙིང་ཡིན་ཏེ། 《ལི་ཤིའི་གུར་ཁང་》ལས། ཕོ་ལོང་ནི་གྱུ་གུ། ཞེས་གསུངས་ཡོད་ལ།[14] 《བོད་རྒྱ་ཚིག་མཛོད་ཆེན་མོ་》[15] སོགས་དེང་རབས་ཀྱི་ཚིག་མཛོད་ཁག་གི་ནང་དུའང་འདི་ལྟར་འགྲེལ་བཤད་གནང་ཡོད། འོ་ན། ཕོ་ལོང་ཟེར་བའི་མིང་བརྡ་དེ་སྔར་བེད་སྤྱོད་ཡོད་པ་ནས་དེང་སྐབས་བེད་སྤྱོད་མེད་པར་གྱུར་བ་དང་། དེང་སྐབས་ཕོ་ལོང་ལ་པོ་ལོ་ཡང་ན་གྱུ་གུ་ཞེས་བརྗོད་དོན་གང་ཡིན་ཞེ་ན། ང་ཚོས་དེང་སྐབས་བེད་སྤྱོད་པའི་པོ་ལོ་ནི་ཕོ་ལོང་ལས་གཟུགས་གྱུར་བ་ཙམ་མ་གཏོགས་བརྡ་ཆད་འདི་ཉིད་ཕྱིས་གསར་དུ་བཟོས་པ་ཞིག་མིན་པར་འདོད་དེ། ཕོ་ལོང་གི་ཕོ་ཟེར་བའི་མིང་གཞི་ཕ་དེ་རིམ་པས་པ་རུ་གྱུར་ནས་པོ་ཆགས་པ་དང་། ལོང་ཟེར་བའི་རྗེས་འཇུག་ང་དེ་ཡིག་ཟོར་ཡང་བའི་ཆེད་དུ་སྐྱུར་ནས་ལོ་རུ་བྲིས་སྲོལ་བྱུང་སྟབས། མཐར་མིང་བརྡ་ཕོ་ལོང་ཟེར་བ་དེ་པོ་ལོར་གྱུར་བ་ཡིན་ངེས་སྙམ།[16] དེ་ལྟའི་ཆོད་ཉིད་ནི་བོད་ཀྱི་ཡིག་རྙིང་ཁག་ལས་མིང་གཞི་ཕ་དེ་པ་རུ་གྱུར་བ་དང་། ཕ་དང་པ་གཉིས་ཕན་ཚུན་བརྗེ་རེས་བྱས་པ་མང་པོ་རིག་རྒྱུ་ཡོད་པ་ལས་ར་འཕྲོད། དཔེ་མཚོན་ཙམ་ཞུས་ན། དམག་དཔོན་ཞེས་པར་དམག་ཕོན་དང་། བཙན་པོ་ཞེས་པར་བཙན་ཕོ། ཆེན་པོ་ཞེས་པར་ཆེན་ཕོ་ཞེས་བྲིས་པ་སོགས་མང་དུ་བྱུང་སྟེ། དེའང་ཏུན་ཧོང་ཡིག་རྙིང་ལས། སྟོང་རྩན་གཡུའི་ཡིགེ། སྐལ་ཏེ། སོ་མཐའ་བ་[ཞི]། དམག་ཕོན་དུ་བཀའ་སྩལད། །ཞེས་དང་།[17] ཡང་། སྟགི་ལོ་ལ་བབ་སྟེ། བཙན་ཕོ་མེར་ཁེ་ནའ་བཞུགས་×××ཞེས་དང་།[18] དབྱརད་བློན་ཆེན་ཕོ་བཙན་སླས་འདུན་མ××× ཞེས་སོགས་བྱུང་ངོ་།།[19] དེ་མིན་ད་དུང་། དཔང་པོ་ནི་དཔང་པོའམ་བར་མིའི་དོན་དང་། དཕུང་ནི་དཔུང་གི་དོན། དཕྱད་པ་ནི་བརྟག་དཔྱད་བྱས་པའི་དོན། དཕྱིད་སླ་ནི་དཔྱིད་ཟླའི་དོན་ཡིན་ཚུལ་སོགས་《བོད་ཡིག་བརྡ་རྙིང་ཚིག་མཛོད་》ཅེས་པར་འཁོད་འདུག[20] ཡིག་ཐོབ་ལ་འཛེག་ནས་འདིར་དཔེ་མཚོན་ཙམ་ལས་རྒྱས་པར་མི་སྤྲོའོ། །མདོར་ན། ཕོ་ལོང་ནི་པོ་ལོ་དང་གྱུ་གུའི་བརྡ་རྙིང་ཡིན་ལ། མིང་བརྡ་དེ་གསུམ་པོ་དོན་གཅིག་མིང་གི་རྣམ་གྲངས་ཡིན་པར་ངེས་སོ། །

ཡང་དེང་སྐབས་རྟ་ཐོག་པོ་ལོ་ང་ལ་དབྱིན་སྐད་གཙོས་པའི་ནུབ་གླིང་གི་སྐད་རིགས་མང་པོའི་ནང་དུ་པོ་ལོ་(polo) ཞེས་བརྗོད་བཞིན་ཡོད་པ་དེ་བོད་སྐད་ཀྱི་གཡར་ཚིག་ཡིན་པ་རྩོད་མེད་ཉི་མ་སྤྲིན་བྲལ་ལྟར་བློ་གཟུ་བོར་གནས་པ་ཀུན་ནས་ཁས་ལེན་བྱེད་ལ། དེའི་ཐད་དུ་ལའོ་ཧྥེར་ (Berthold Laufer 1874–1934) ནས། ང་ཚོའི་དབྱིན་སྐད་ཁྲོད་ཆེས་ངོ་མཚར་ཅན་གྱི་བོད་སྐད་ནས་གཡར་བའི་མིང་བརྡ་ནི་པོ་ལོ་(polo) ཡིན། ཞེས་གསུངས་ཡོད་པ་དང་།[21] 《ཁེམ་བྲི་རི་ཅིའི་ཤེས་བྱ་ཀུན་ཁྱབ་》(The Cambridge Encyclopedia) སོགས་ཀྱི་ནང་དུའང་དེ་ལྟར་ཁས་ལེན་བྱས་ཡོད།[22] དེ་མིན་ནུབ་གླིང་གི་དཔེ་དེབ་ཁ་ཤས་ནང་དབྱིན་སྐད་ཀྱི་མིང་བརྡ་པོ་ལོ་(polo) ནི་སྦལ་ཏིའི་སྐད་ཡིན་ཞེས་བརྗོད་ཀྱི་ཡོད་ཀྱང་།[23] གནའ་རབས་བྱུ་ཤའི་ཡུལ་དུ་ཨེ་སི་ཡམ་རིག་གནས་ཀྱི་ཤུགས་རྐྱེན་ཆེན་པོ་མ་ཐེབས་གོང་ཡུལ་དེའི་སྐད་ཡིག་ནི་བོད་སྐད་ཡིག་ཡིན་པས་མ་ཚད། ལ་དྭགས་ཀྱི་ཡུལ་གྲུ་འདི་བཞིན་ཆོས་དང་རིག་གཞུང་གང་གི་ཆ་ནས་ཀྱང་གནའ་རབས་ནས་བཟུང་བོད་གངས་ཅན་ལྗོངས་དང་ཆ་འགོ་གངས་ཐུག་ལྟ་བུའི་འབྲེལ་ལམ་ཤིན་ཏུ་ཟབ་མོ་ཡོད་པས། ཁོང་ཚོས་མིང་བརྡ་དེ་སྦལ་ཏིའི་སྐད་རེད་ཅེས་བརྗོད་འདུག་མོད་དོན་དམ་དུ་བོད་སྐད་ཡིན་པར་གདོན་མི་ཟའོ། །

གཉིས། གནའ་རབས་རྟ་ཐོག་པོ་ལོ་ང་གི་འབྱུང་ཁུངས་སྐོར་གྱི་ལྟ་ཚུལ་ཁག་ལ་དཔྱད་པ།

གནའ་རབས་རྟ་ཐོག་པོ་ལོ་ང་གི་འབྱུང་ཁུངས་སྐོར་ལ་རྒྱལ་ཁབ་ཕྱི་ནང་གི་མཁས་པ་ཚོས་དཔྱད་པ་མང་པོ་གནང་ཡོད་ཅིང་། ཞིབ་འཇུག་གི་གྲུབ་འབྲས་ཀྱང་གང་འཚམས་ཐོབ་ཡོད་མོད། རྟ་ཐོག་པོ་ལོ་ང་ནི་ཆེས་གནའ་རབས་ཀྱི་རྩེད་རིགས་ཤིག་ཡིན་ལ། ད་ལྟའི་ཆར་དེའི་ཐོག་མའི་འབྱུང་ཁུངས་སྐོར་གྱི་ཁུངས་བཙན་ཡིག་ཆ་ཏ་ལམ་རེག་རྒྱུ་མེད་པས། ཞིབ་འཇུག་པ་ཚོར་ལྟ་ཚུལ་ཡང་མི་གཅིག་མང་པོ་བྱུང་ཡོད། དེ་དག་ལས་ཆེས་གཙོ་བོའི་ལྟ་ཚུལ་གསུམ་ཡིན་ཏེ། རྟ་ཐོག་པོ་ལོ་ང་གི་འབྱུང་ཁུངས་རྒྱ་ནག་ས་ཁུལ་ནས་ཡིན་པར་སྨྲ་བ་དང་། པར་ཟིག་ནས་ཡིན་པར་སྨྲ་བ། ཡར་ཀླུང་བོད་བཙན་པོའི་རྒྱལ་རབས་ནས་ཡིན་པར་སྨྲ་བ་བཅས་སོ། །ད་ནི་ལྟ་ཚུལ་ཁག་ལ་རིམ་པས་དཔྱད་པར་བྱ་སྟེ།

༡༽ རྒྱ་ནག་ས་ཁུལ་ནས་ཡིན་པར་སྨྲ་བ་ལ་དཔྱད་པ།

གནའ་རབས་རྟ་ཐོག་པོ་ལོ་ང་གི་འབྱུང་ཁུངས་རྒྱ་ནག་ས་ཁུལ་ནས་ཡིན་པར་སྨྲ་བའི་འདོད་ཚུལ་འཛིན་མཁན་ཐོག་མ་ནི་རྒྱ་རིགས་མཁས་པ་ཐང་ཧའོ་(唐豪)ཡིན་པ་དང་། དེ་རྗེས་ལི་སུང་ཧྥུ་(李松福)དང་ཙུའུ་ལི་ཆོན་(崔乐泉) སོགས་ཀྱིས་འདོད་ཚུལ་དེར་མོས་མཐུན་གནང་ཡོད། ཁོང་ཚོས་རང་ཉིད་ཀྱི་ལྟ་བ་དེ་འཐད་ལྡན་དུ་སྒྲུབ་ཆེད་གཙོ་བོ་གཤམ་གསལ་གྱི་རྒྱུ་མཚན་དག་ལུང་འདྲེན་གནང་ཡོད་དེ། ༡༽དུས་རབས་གསུམ་པའི་དུས་འགོར། ཧན་ལུའི་སྐབས་ཀྱི་རྩོམ་རིག་མཁས་ཅན་ཚའོ་ཀྲིས་(曹植) བྲིས་པའི་སྙན་ངག 《གནས་མཆོག་མིང་ཅན་གྱི་ལེའུ་》 《名都篇》ཞེས་པ་དང་། སྙན་ངག 《ཅིང་ཁྲུའུ་ལོ་ཟླའི་ཟིན་བྲིས་》《荆楚岁时记》 དེ་བཞིན་ཐང་རྒྱལ་རབས་ཀྱི་སྙན་ངག་པ་ཚའོ་ཧྥུས་(曹浮) བྲིས་པའི་སྙན་ངག 《པོ་ལོ་རྩེན་པའི་ལེའུ་》 《打毬篇》 ཞེས་པ་བཅས་ཀྱི་ནང་དུ་ཅི་ཙུའི་(击鞠)[24] དང་ཏྭ་ཆེའུ་(打毬)[25] སོགས་

ཀྱི་མིང་བརྡ་མང་པོ་མཐོང་རྒྱུ་ཡོད་ཅིང་། དེ་ཡང་ཐང་རྒྱལ་རབས་ཀྱི་རྗེས་སུ་བྱུང་བའི་རྒྱ་ནག་གི་ལོ་རྒྱུས་ཡིག་ཆ་ཁག་ནང་རྟ་རྡོག་པོ་ལོ་ལ་པོ་ལོ་ཆིའུ་(波罗毬) ཞེས་འབོད་པ་ཕུད། གཞན་ཡང་ཅི་ཙུའི་(击鞠) དང་ཏྲ་ཆིའུ་(打毬) ཡང་སྨྲ་བས། དེའི་ཐོག་ནས་རྟ་རྡོག་པོ་ལོ་དེ་ཐང་རྒྱལ་རབས་ཤར་མའི་དུས་སུ་ཆེས་ཐོག་མར་དར་ཡོད་པ་ར་སྤྲོད་ཐུབ་ཅིས་དང་། ༢༽ ཚའོ་ཧྲུའི་སྐྱན་ངག་《པོ་ལོ་རྩེན་པ་》ཞེས་པའི་ནང་དུ་ཐང་རྒྱལ་རབས་ཤར་མའི་གོང་མའི་ཕོ་བྲང་བདེ་ཡངས་ཀྱི་སྐྱིད་ཚལ་ལྷུམ་ར་བྱང་མར་(德阳宫北苑) པོ་ལོ་རྩེད་སའི་ཐང་ཆེན་ཞིག་ཡོད་པའི་སྐོར་བྲིས་ཡོད།[26] ཁོང་ཚོས་གཙོ་བོ་རྒྱུ་མཚན་དེ་གཉིས་ལ་བརྟེན་ནས་རྟ་རྡོག་པོ་ལོ་དེ་ཐང་རྒྱལ་རབས་ཤར་མའི་དུས་རྒྱ་ནག་ས་ཁུལ་དུ་ཐོག་མར་དར་ཡོད་པར་བཤད་ཅིང་། བོད་བཙན་པོའི་རྒྱལ་རབས་སྐབས་བོད་པ་རྣམས་རྟ་རྡོག་པོ་ལོ་རྩེན་པར་ཧ་ཅང་དགའ་བ་དེ་ནི་ཐང་རྒྱལ་རབས་ཀྱི་དུས་མཇུག་དང་རྒྱལ་ཁབ་གསུམ་གྱི་རིང་མདོ་ཁམས་དཀར་མཛེས་ཁུལ་བརྒྱུད་དེ་བོད་དབུས་གཙང་ས་ཁུལ་དུ་དར་ཚུལ་གསུངས་སོ། །

རྒྱ་ནག་ཏུ་ཆིན་རྒྱལ་རབས་(སྤྱི་ལོའི་སྔོན་གྱི་ལོ་༢༢༡ནས་སྤྱི་ལོའི་སྔོན་གྱི་ལོ་༢༠༦བར་)སྐབས་ནས་བཟུང་གནའ་རབས་ཀྱི་རྐང་རྩེད་པོ་ལོའི་རིགས་ཚུའུ་ཙུའུ་(蹴鞠) ཟེར་བ་ཞིག་དར་བ་དང་། ཧན་རྒྱལ་རབས་(སྤྱི་ལོའི་སྔོན་གྱི་ལོ་༢༠༦ནས་སྤྱི་ལོ་༢༢༠བར་)དུས་སུ་དེ་དམངས་ཁྲོད་དུ་དར་ཁྱབ་ལྷག་པར་ཆེ། ཐང་རྒྱལ་རབས་(སྤྱི་ལོ་༦༡༨ནས་སྤྱི་ལོ་༩༠༧བར་)རྗེས་ཀྱི་ལོ་རྒྱུས་ཡིག་ཆ་ཁག་ནང་ཚུའུ་ཙུའུ་(蹴鞠) ཟེར་བའི་ཙུའུ་(鞠) དང་ཏྲ་ཆིའུ་(打毬) ཟེར་བའི་ཆིའུ་(毬) གཉིས་སྐབས་རེ་གོ་ལྡོག་པ་དང་། སྐབས་རེ་ཕན་ཚུན་བརྗེས་པ་སོགས་མིང་བརྡ་བརྗེ་རེས་བྱས་པའི་གནས་ཚུལ་མང་པོ་མཐོང་ཆོས་སུ་གྱུར་བས། ཧན་རྒྱལ་རབས་དུས་ཀྱི་སྐྱན་ངག་ནང་ཐོན་པའི་མིང་བརྡ་ཅི་ཙུའི་ (击鞠) དང་ཏྲ་ཆིའུ་(打毬) གཉིས་པོ་ཡང་སྙིང་རྟ་རྡོག་པོ་ལོ་ལ་གོ་བ་ཡིན་ནམ། ཡང་ན་ཆིན་རྒྱལ་རབས་ནས་དར་བའི་པོ་ལོའི་རིགས་ཚུའུ་ཙུའུ་(蹴鞠) ལ་གོ་བ་ཡིན་ད་དུང་ཁ་ཚོན་གཅོད་པར་དཀའ། གཞན་ཡང་། ཅི་སྟེ་རྟ་རྡོག་པོ་ལོ་ཆེས་ཐོག་མར་རྒྱ་ནག་ས་ཁུལ་དུ་ཐང་རྒྱལ་རབས་ཤར་མའི་དུས་སུ་དར་བར་ཆ་བཞག་ན། ཧན་རྒྱལ་རབས་ནས་ཐང་རྒྱལ་རབས་བར་ལོ་ངོ་བརྒྱད་བརྒྱ་ལྷག་ཙམ་རིང་གི་ལོ་རྒྱུས་ཡིག་ཆའི་ནང་ཟུར་ཙམ་ཡང་འཁོད་མེད་ལ། རྟ་རྡོག་པོ་ལོ་དེ་རྒྱ་ནག་གི་ལོ་རྒྱུས་དེབ་ཐེར་ནང་དུ་འཁོད་པའི་དུས་ཚོད་སྔ་ཤོས་ནི་ཐང་རྒྱལ་རབས་ཡིན། རྒྱ་ནག་གི་ལོ་རྒྱུས་སྨྲ་བའི་མཁན་པོ་སི་མ་ཀོང་(司马光)གིས་རྩོམ་སྒྲིག་གནང་བའི་གྲགས་རྩོམ་《རྒྱལ་སྲིད་སྐྱོང་བྱེད་མེ་ལོང་》《资治通鉴》[27] ཞེས་བྱ་བའི་ནང་དུའང་ཐང་རྒྱལ་རབས་སྐབས་རྟ་རྡོག་པོ་ལོ་རྩེན་པའི་ལོ་རྒྱུས་མུ་ཏིག་ཕྲེང་བར་བརྒྱུད་པ་ཇི་བཞིན་མངོན་སུམ་གསོན་རྗེན་དུ་བཀོད་འདྲི་མཛད་ཡོད་རུང་། ཧན་རྒྱལ་རབས་སྐབས་སུ་རྟ་རྡོག་པོ་ལོ་དར་ཡོད་པའི་སྐོར་ཡིག་འབྲུ་གཅིག་ཀྱང་བྲིས་མེད་པས། རྟ་རྡོག་པོ་ལོ་དེ་ཆེས་ཐོག་མར་ཧན་རྒྱལ་རབས་ཀྱི་དུས་སུ་རྒྱ་ནག་ས་ཁུལ་ནས་དར་བའི་འདོད་ཚུལ་དེ་ལ་སྐྱེར་འདོད་མོས་ཡོད་དཀའོ། །

༢༽ པར་ཐྱིག་ནས་དར་ཚུལ་སྐྱ་བར་དཔྱད་པ།

རྟ་རྡོག་པོ་ལོ་དེ་བཞིན་ཆེས་ཐོག་མར་པར་ཐྱིག་ནས་དར་ཚུལ་སྨྲ་བ་ལ་དེང་སྐབས་ནུབ་གླིང་གི་མཁས་དབང་ཕལ་མོ་ཆེས་ཁས་ལེན་བྱེད་ལ། རྒྱ་རིགས་མཁས་པ་ཧེ་གེང་ཧྲེང་(郝更生) དང་། ཞང་ཏྲ།(向达) ལོ་

ཞང་ལིང་(罗向林) སོགས་ཀྱིས་ཀྱང་མོས་མཐུན་གནང་ཡོད། བོད་ཀྱི་ལོ་རྒྱུས་ཞིབ་འཇུག་བྱེད་མཁན་སྐུ་ཞབས་ཀྲང་ཡུན་(张云) གྱིས་ཀྱང་། ང་ཚོས་རྡ་ཐོག་ཕོ་ལོང་གི་རྩེད་མོ་དེ་ཆེས་ཐོག་མར་པར་ཟིག་ནས་བྱུང་བའི་ཕྱོད་སྟངས་ལ་སྒྲུབ་བྱེད་དེ་བས་ཀྱང་ཕུན་སུམ་ཚོགས་པ་དང་། དོན་དངོས་ཀྱི་ངེས་གཏན་རང་བཞིན་ཡོད་པའི་ངོས་འཛིན་བྱེད་ཀྱི་ཡོད།[28] ཅེས་བརྗོད་འདུག རྩེད་རིགས་དེའི་འབྱུང་ཁུངས་པར་ཟིག་ནས་ཡིན་པར་འདོད་མཁན་ཕལ་མོ་ཆེས་ཕྱོགས་གཅིག་ནས་རྡ་ཐོག་ཕོ་ལོང་ལ་མ་མཐར་ཡང་ལོ་ངོ་ཉིས་སྟོང་ལྔ་བརྒྱ་ལྷག་ཙམ་གྱི་ལོ་རྒྱུས་ཡོད་པ་དང་། རྩེད་རིགས་དེ་ཆེས་ཐོག་མར་པར་ཟིག་མཐོ་སྒང་སྟེང་འཚོ་སྡོད་བྱས་པའི་མི་རིགས་ཚོའི་ཁྲོད་དུ་དར་ཡོད་པར་ཁས་ལེན་ལ། ཡང་ཕྱོགས་གཞན་ཞིག་ནས་དེང་དུས་དབྱིན་སྐད་ཁྲོད་ཀྱི་མིང་བརྡ་པོ་ལོ་(polo) ནི་བོད་སྐད་ཡིན་པ་ཁས་ལེན་བྱེད་དོ། ། ཁོང་ཚོས་རྡ་ཐོག་ཕོ་ལོང་གི་འབྱུང་ཁུངས་པར་ཟིག་ནས་ཡིན་པར་གཞུམ་གསལ་གྱི་སྒྲུབ་བྱེད་འདི་དག་བཀོད་ཡོད་དེ། ༡༽ རྡ་ཐོག་ཕོ་ལོང་ལ་པར་ཟིག་སྐད་དུ་རྒུ་ཡི་(gui) ཞེས་ཟེར་བ་དང་། ཐང་རྒྱལ་རབས་སྐབས་རྩེད་རིགས་དེར་ཏྭ་ཆིའུ་(打毬) ཞེས་འབོད་པ་ལགས། མིང་བརྡ་དེའི་ཆིའུ་(毬) ནི་རྒྱ་ཡིག་ཏུ་སྦྱར་ཡོད་པའི་ཡིག་འབྲུ་ཞིག་མ་ཡིན་པར་པར་ཟིག་གི་སྐད་རྒུ་ཡི་(gui) ཞེས་པའི་སྒྲ་ཟུར་དུ་ཆགས་ནས་བཟོས་པ་ཞིག་ཡིན་པས། རྡ་ཐོག་ཕོ་ལོང་ནི་ཐང་རྒྱལ་རབས་སྐབས་སུ་དར་གོས་གནའ་ལམ་བརྒྱུད་དེ་པར་ཟིག་ནས་རྒྱ་ནག་དབུས་ཁུལ་དུ་དར་བར་འདོད། ༢༽ ཏ་ལམ་སྤྱི་ལོ་༦༠༠ གཡས་གཡོན་དུ་པར་ཟིག་སཱ་སན་རྒྱལ་རབས་ཀྱི་རྒྱལ་པོ་ཕར་ཕྲེ་སི་(Khosrow Parviz, reigned 590–628) ཡི་གཉེན་སྒྲོན་མཛད་སྒོའི་ཐོག་པར་ཟིག་པ་རྣམས་ནས་རྡ་ཐོག་ཕོ་ལོང་རྩེན་པའི་འགྲན་བསྡུར་གཟབ་རྒྱས་ཤིག་བྱས་སྐོར་དུས་རབས་བཅུ་གཉིས་པའི་ནང་གི་པར་ཟིག་གི་རྩོམ་རིག་མཁས་ཅན་ནེ་ཙཱ་མི་(Nezāmi نظامی گنجوی; 1141–1209) ཡིས་བྲིས་ཡོད་[29] པ་སོགས་མདོར་ན་སྤྱི་ལོའི་དུས་རབས་བདུན་པའི་རྗེས་སུ་བྱུང་བའི་པར་ཟིག་གི་རྩོམ་རིག་མཁས་ཅན་ཚོའི་སྙན་རྩོམ་ལས་པར་ཟིག་གི་སྐྱ་དྲག་དང་གོང་མའི་ཕོ་བྲང་ནང་གནའ་སྔ་མོ་ནས་རྡ་ཐོག་ཕོ་ལོང་རྩེན་བཞིན་པའི་རྣམ་པ་བཀོད་འབྲི་བྱས་ཡོད་པས། དེའི་ཐོག་ནས་རྡ་ཐོག་ཕོ་ལོང་གི་འབྱུང་ཁུངས་པར་ཟིག་ནས་ཡིན་ཚུལ་བརྗོད་པའོ། །

རྡ་ཐོག་ཕོ་ལོང་གི་འབྱུང་ཁུངས་པར་ཟིག་ལ་བཙོལ་མཁན་ཚོའི་སྒྲུབ་བྱེད་ལ་ང་ཚོས་དབྱེ་ཞིབ་བྱས་ན་ངེས་ཤེས་འདི་ལྟ་བུ་ཞིག་རྙེད་ཐུབ། དེའང་ནུབ་གླིང་བས་དབྱིན་སྐད་ཁྲོད་ཀྱི་མིང་བརྡ་པོ་ལོ་(polo) ནི་བོད་སྐད་ཡིན་པ་ཁས་ལེན་བྱེད་བཞིན་ཡོད་ལ། བརྡ་སྤྲོད་རིག་པ་དང་ལོ་རྒྱུས་རིག་པ་སོགས་གང་གི་ཆ་ནས་བལྟས་རུང་དེ་ནི་བསྙོན་མེད་སྐྱོན་བྲལ་རང་ཡིན། ཡིན་ནའང་། རྡ་ཐོག་ཕོ་ལོང་ལ་མ་མཐར་ཡང་ལོ་ངོ་ཉིས་སྟོང་ལྔ་བརྒྱ་ལྷག་ཙམ་གྱི་ལོ་རྒྱུས་ཡོད་ཟེར་བར་སྒྲུབ་བྱེད་ཁུངས་བཙན་དེ་ཙམ་འདྲེན་རྒྱུ་མེད་པར་འདོད། དེའང་《དབྱིན་ཇིའི་ཤེས་བྱ་ཀུན་ཁྱབ་གསར་མ་》ཞེས་པ་ལས། རྩེད་རིགས་དེ་ནི་ཆེས་ཐོག་མར་པར་ཟིག་ནས་བྱུང་བ་དང་། དེ་རྗེས་རིམ་པས་ཨ་རབ་དང་། བོད། རྒྱ་ནག ལྗར་པན་བཅས་ལ་དར་ཡོད་ཚུལ་འགྲེལ་བརྗོད་བྱས་ཡོད་མོད།[30] གོང་བཀོད་སྒྲུབ་བྱེད་དེ་ལྟ་བུར་བརྟེན་ནས་རྡ་ཐོག་ཕོ་ལོང་གི་འབྱུང་ཁུངས་པར་ཟིག་ལ་བཙོལ་བར་ཡིད་རྟོན་རུང་བའི་ཆ་དེ་ཙམ་མེད་པར་སྣང་། དེ་མིན་ཐང་རྒྱལ་རབས་སྐབས་སུ་རྡ་ཐོག་ཕོ་ལོང་ལ་ཏྭ་ཆིའུ་(打毬) ཟེར་བཞིན་ཡོད་པ་དེ་ཐང་དེབ་གསར་རྙིང་སོགས་ལོ་རྒྱུས་ཀྱི་ཡིག་ཆ་ཁག་ནས་ཤེས་ཐུབ་ཀྱང་། ཆིའུ་(毬) ཟེར་བའི་མིང་བརྡ་དེ་པར་ཟིག་སྐད་སྒྲ་བསྒྱུར་བྱས་ནས་གསར་དུ་བཟོས་པ་ཞིག་རེད་ཅེས་ཟེར་བ་ནི་དོན

དངོས་དང་ཡོངས་སུ་བཀྲལ་བའི་བཤད་སྟངས་ཤིག་ཡིན། དེའང་ཧན་རྒྱལ་རབས་དུས་སུ་རྒྱའི་ཡིག་རིགས་མཁས་ཅན་ཤུའི་ཧྲེང་(许慎) གིས་བརྩམས་པའི་《ཡིག་བཤད་འབྲུ་འགྲེལ་》《说文解字》ཞེས་བྱ་བའི་ནང་དུ་ཆིའུ་(毬) ཟེར་བའི་མིང་བརྡ་དེ་དངོས་སུ་མཐོང་རྒྱུ་ཡོད་པས། མིང་བརྡ་དེ་མ་མཐར་ཡང་ཐང་རྒྱལ་རབས་གོང་གི་ལོ་ངོ་དྲུག་བརྒྱ་ལྷག་གི་ཡ་སྔོན་ན་རྒྱ་ཡིག་ནང་དུ་ཡོད་པ་ར་སྤྲོད་ཐུབ། དེར་བརྟེན། ཆིའུ་(毬) ནི་པར་ཟེག་སྐད་སྒྲ་བསྒྱུར་བྱས་པ་ཞིག་མིན་པ་ཤེས་གསལ་ལགས། དེ་ལས་ལྡོག་ཏེ་པར་ཟེག་སྐད་དུ་རྟ་ཐོག་པོ་ལོང་ལ་ཆོའོ་གན་(Chogân or Chaugan) ཞེས་འབོད་པ་པོ་ལོང་ཞིབ་འཇུག་མཁན་མང་པོས་ཁས་ལེན་བྱས་ཡོད་ལ། འགའ་རེས་དེའི་གོ་དོན་ནི་རྩེད་རྒྱུགས་ཡིན་པའི་འགྲེལ་བརྗོད་ཀྱང་གནང་གི་འདུག[31] ཧ་ཅང་ཡ་མཚན་སྐྱེ་དགོས་པ་ཞིག་ལ་རྒྱ་ནག་གི་སྐད་དུ་རྩེད་རྒྱུགས་ལ་ཆིའུ་གན་(球杆) ཟེར་ཞིང་། དེ་པར་ཟེག་སྐད་ཆོའོ་གན་དང་སྒྲ་འདོན་སྟངས་ཧ་ཅང་འདྲ་བས་ན། ཁོ་བོའི་འདོད་ཚུལ་ལ་གཅིག་ན་པར་ཟེག་སྐད་ཆོའོ་གན་ཞེས་པ་དེ་རྒྱ་སྐད་ཆིའུ་གན་གྱི་གཡར་ཚིག་མིན་ནམ་སྙམ་རྒྱུང་། འདི་ལྟར་མཐའ་གཅིག་ཏུ་ངེས་པའི་ཁ་ཚོན་གཅོད་མི་ནུས། དེས་ན་རྟ་ཐོག་པོ་ལོང་གི་འབྱུང་ཁུངས་པར་ཟེག་ནས་ཡིན་ཚུལ་སྨྲ་བ་རྣམས་ལའང་དེ་ཙམ་ཡིད་ཆེས་ཡོང་དཀའོ། །

༣༽ བོད་བཙན་པོའི་རྒྱལ་རབས་ནས་བྱུང་ཚུལ་སྨྲ་བ་ལ་དཔྱད་པ།

འདོད་ཚུལ་འདི་འཛིན་མཁན་གཙོ་བོ་ནི་སྐུ་ཞབས་ལའོ་ཧྥེར་དང་རྒྱ་ནག་གི་ལོ་རྒྱུས་མཁས་ཅན་དབྱིན་ཧྥ་ལུའུ་(阴法鲁) ཡིན་པ་དང་། ཕྱིས་སུ་ཁོང་གི་རྗེས་འབྲངས་པ་ཝང་ཡའོ་(王尧) སོགས་ནས་བཞེད་པ་དེར་མོས་མཐུན་གནང་ཞིང་། སྐུ་ཞབས་མ་གྲོང་མི་འགྱུར་རྡོ་རྗེས 《བོད་ལྗོངས་ཞིབ་འཇུག》ཅེས་པའི་དུས་དེབ་ནང་《བོད་ཀྱི་སྲོལ་རྒྱུན་ལུས་རྩལ་དང་བོད་ཀྱི་གནའ་བོའི་རྩེད་རྩལ་རྟ་ཐོག་པོ་ལོའི་སྐོར་ཅུང་ཟད་གླེང་བ》ཞེས་པའི་དཔྱད་རྩོམ་ཞིག་སྤེལ་འདུག རྩོམ་ཡིག་དེའི་ནང་དུའང་རྩེད་རིགས་དེའི་འབྱུང་ཁུངས་བོད་ནས་ཡིན་ཚུལ་སྐོར་རྒྱས་བཤད་མཛད་ཡོད།[32] གཞན་ཡང་།《བོད་ཀྱི་ལོ་རྒྱུས་སྤྱི་དོན་པདྨ་རཱ་གའི་ལྡེ་མིག》སོགས་ཀྱི་ནང་དུའང་དེ་དང་འདྲ་བའི་བཞེད་ཚུལ་གསུངས་ཡོད་པ་རེད།[33] ཁོང་ཚོས་རྟ་ཐོག་པོ་ལོང་དེ་བཞིན་འབྱུང་ཁུངས་བོད་ལ་གཏུགས་པར་གཙོ་བོ་གཤམ་གསལ་གྱི་རྒྱུ་མཚན་འདི་དག་དྲངས་རྒྱུ་ཡོད་དེ། དབྱིན་སྐད་ཁྲོད་ཀྱི་མིང་བརྡ་པོ་ལོ་(polo) ནི་བོད་སྐད་པོ་ལོང་ངམ་ཡང་ན་པོ་ལོ་སྒྲ་བསྒྱུར་བྱས་པ་ཡིན་ཚུལ་གསུངས་པ་དང་གཅིག རྒྱའི་ལོ་རྒྱུས་ཡིག་ཚང་ལས། ཞན་ཆིན་ཁྲི་ལོ་གསུམ་པའི་ཟླ་བཅུ་པར། བོད་ནས་བློན་མངགས་ཏེ་གཉེན་བསླངས། གསེར་གྱི་པོ་ལོང་སོགས་སྐྱེས་སུ་ཕུལ།[34] ཅེས་འཁོད་ཡོད་པ་དང་གཉིས། བོད་རྗེ་ཁྲི་ལྡེ་གཙུག་བརྟན་མེས་ཨག་ཚོམ་དང་ཐང་གོང་མ་ཀྲུང་ཙུང་སྐུ་རིང་ལ། བོད་ཀྱི་བློན་པོ་ཞང་བཙན་ཧོ་སོགས་ཁྲང་ཨན་དུ་གྲིམ་ཤིང་གོང་ཇོ་བསུ་བར་ཕེབས་པ་དང་། གོང་མ་ཀྲུང་ཙུང་གིས་སྐྱེས་མོས་ཚལ་གྱི་པོ་ལོང་རྩེད་རར་གསོལ་སྟོན་བཤམས་ཐོག གོང་མའི་པོ་བྲང་རྟ་ཁག་དང་བོད་ཀྱི་རྟ་ཁག་གཉིས་ནས་རྟ་ཐོག་པོ་ལོང་གི་འགྲན་བསྡུར་ངོ་མཚར་ཅན་ཞིག་བྱས་ཡོད་པའི་སྐོར[35] ལོ་རྒྱུས་ཀྱི་དེབ་ཐེར་ཁག་ལས་གསལ་བ་མ་ཟད། འགྲན་བསྡུར་དེའི་གནས་ཚུལ་དངོས་ཇི་མ་ཇི་བཞིན་ཐང་རྒྱལ་རབས་ཀྱི་རི་མོ་བ་ཡན་ལི་སྤུན་(阎立本) གྱིས་རི་མོའི་ལམ་དུ་བཀོད་པ 《ཐང་མིང་ཧྭང་གིས་མཚན་མོར་རྟ་ཐོག་པོ་ལོང་འགྲན་པ》ཞེས་པ་ཞིག་ཡོད་ཅིང་། དཔེ་རིས་དེ་ད་ལྟའི་རྒྱལ་ས་པེ་ཅིང་

གྱི་གནའ་བོའི་ཕོ་བྲང་ནང་ཉར་ཚགས་ཞུས[36] ཡོད་པ་དང་གསུམ། 《རྒྱུང་རྗེའི་མཐོང་ཐོས་ཟིན་ཐོའི་》《封氏闻见记》 ནང་དུ་ཐང་ཐེ་ཙུང་གིས། ནུབ་ཕྱོགས་ཀྱི་བོད་མི་(西蕃人) རྣམས་ཏྲ་ཐོག་ཕོ་ལོང་རྩེན་པར་དགའ་པོ་ཡོད་ཚུལ་གོ་ཐོས་བྱུང་།[37] ཞེས་གསུངས་པའི་ནང་གི་ནུབ་ཕྱོགས་ཀྱི་བོད་མི་(西蕃人) ཞེས་པ་ནི་སྐབས་དེ་དུས་ཀྱི་བོད་པ་རྣམས་ལ་གོ་དགོས་པ་དང་བཞི་བཅས་སོ། །

གོང་གསལ་ལུང་འདྲེན་དག་ལས་ང་ཚོས་གཞམ་གསལ་གྱི་གནད་དོན་དེ་དག་རྟོགས་ཐུབ་པ་སྟེ། ཐང་དེབ་གསར་རྙིང་སོགས་ལས་བྱུང་བའི་བོད་པས་གསེར་གྱི་གཞོང་པ་དང་གསེར་གྱི་ཕོ་ལོང་སྐྱེས་སུ་ཕུལ་བ་དང་། ཁྲིང་ཨན་དུ་ཏྲ་ཐོག་ཕོ་ལོང་གི་འགྲན་བསྡུར་བྱས་པ་སོགས་ནི་ལོ་རྒྱུས་ཀྱི་དོན་དངོས་ཡིན་ལ། དེའི་ཐོག་ནས་སྐབས་དེ་དུས་བོད་པ་རྣམས་ཏྲ་ཐོག་ཕོ་ལོང་རྩེན་པར་ཧ་ཅང་དགའ་བ་མ་ཟད། 《རྒྱུང་རྗེའི་མཐོང་ཐོས་ཟིན་ཐོ》 ཡི་ནང་དུ་བཀོད་པའི་ནུབ་ཕྱོགས་ཀྱི་བོད་མི་རྣམས་ནི་སྤྱིར་བོད་པ་ཡིན་པ་སྤྱི་ལོ༧༡༠ལོར་གྱིམ་ཤིང་ཀོང་ཇོ་བོད་དུ་ཕེབས་སྐྱོང་སྐབས་ཐང་རྒྱལ་རབས་ཀྱི་ཞོལ་རྗེ་རྗེན་ཆོན་ཆིས་(学士沈佺期) དང་ཝུའུ་ཕིང་(武平) སོགས་ཀྱིས 《གྱིམ་ཤིང་ཀོང་ཇོ་ནུབ་ཕྱོགས་བོད་དུ་ཕེབས་པར་ཆེད་དུ་ཕུལ་བའི་སྙན་ཚིག》《送金成公主适西蕃诗》 ཅེས་པ་སོགས་བྲིས་པ་ལས་ར་སྤྲོད་ཐུབ་ཀྱི་ཡོད། ཡིན་ནའང་། གོང་གསལ་གྱི་སྒྲུབ་བྱེད་ཁག་གིས་བོད་བཙན་པོའི་རྒྱལ་རབས་སྐབས་བོད་པ་ཚོ་ཏྲ་ཐོག་ཕོ་ལོང་རྩེན་པར་ཤིན་ཏུ་མཁས་པོ་ཡོད་པ་མཚོན་ཐུབ་པ་ལས། རྩེད་རིགས་དེའི་འབྱུང་རྩ་ས་ཁུལ་དེ་ནས་ཡིན་པའི་གསལ་བཤད་དེ་ཙམ་མི་ཐུབ་བོ། །གཞན་ཡང་། ཏུན་ཧོང་ནས་ཐོན་པའི་གནའ་བོའི་ཤོག་དྲིལ་ཁག་གི་ནང་གནའ་རབས་ས་ཁུལ་དེར་ཏྲ་ཐོག་ཕོ་ལོང་ཤིན་ཏུ་དར་ཁྱབ་ཆེན་པོ་ཡོད་པའི་ལོ་རྒྱུས་ཀྱི་ཡིག་ཆ་མང་པོ་རིག་རྒྱུ་ཡོད་ཅིང་། ཡིག་ཆ་དེ་དག་གིས་སྐབས་དེ་དུས་ཏུན་ཧོང་གཙོས་པའི་བོད་ཀྱི་མཐའ་མཚམས་ཁུལ་མང་པོར་དམག་དོན་གྱི་དགོས་དབང་དང་བསྟུན་ནས་རྩེད་རིགས་དེ་དར་ཁྱབ་ཆེ་ཙམ་བྱུང་ཡོད་ངེས་སྙམ་མོ། །

གསུམ་པ། མཐའ་དཔྱད་པ།

གོང་དུ་ཏྲ་ཐོག་ཕོ་ལོང་འབྱུང་ཁུངས་སྐོར་གྱི་ལྟ་ཚུལ་ཁག་ལ་དཔྱད་པ་བྱས་ཟིན་ཞིང་། རྩེད་རིགས་དེ་ནི་ཆེས་གནའ་རབས་ཀྱི་ལུས་རྩལ་རྣམ་གྲངས་ཤིག་ཡིན་པ་གང་ཞིག་ལ། དེའི་འབྱུང་ཁུངས་དང་ལོ་རྒྱུས་འཁོད་པའི་ཁུངས་བཙན་གྱི་ཡིག་ཆ་ཤིན་ཏུ་དཀོན་སྟབས། ཞིབ་འཇུག་གི་ལས་ཀར་དཀའ་ངལ་མི་ཉུང་བ་ཞིག་འཕྲད་བཞིན་མཆིས་མོད། ཁོ་བོའི་བསམ་པར་ང་ཚོས་རྩོད་སྒྲུབ་དངོས་གཙོའི་ཐབས་ལམ་ལ་བརྟེན་ནས་ད་ཡོད་ཀྱི་དཔྱད་གཞིར་དབྱེ་ཞིབ་ལེགས་པོ་བྱས་ཐོག གནའ་རབས་བོད་དང་པར་ཟིག་དབར་གྱི་འབྲེལ་བར་བསམ་གཞིགས་བྱས་ཚེ། སྤྱིར་བཏང་ལོ་རྒྱུས་ཀྱི་དོན་དངོས་དང་ཅུང་ཟད་ཆ་འདྲ་བའི་ལྟ་ཚུལ་ཞིག་ཡོང་ངེས་སེམས། དེའང་ཁོ་བོའི་འདོད་ཚུལ་ལ་ཏྲ་ཐོག་ཕོ་ལོང་དེ་གངས་ཏི་སེས་ལྟེ་བ་བྱས་པའི་ཞང་ཞུང་ཤེས་རིག་ཁུལ་དང་ཨེ་ཤེ་ཡ་དཀྱིལ་མའི་འབྲོག་ལས་གཙོ་བོར་གཉེར་བའི་མི་རིགས་ཚོའི་ཁྲོད་དུ་མ་མཐར་ཡང་སྤྱི་ལོའི་སྔོན་དུ་དར་བར་འདོད། གང་ལགས་ཤེ་ན།

སྤྱིར་ན་ལོ་རྒྱུས་ཀྱི་ཡིག་རིགས་ཁག་ཏུ་གསལ་བ་བཞིན། གནའ་རབས་ཧ་ཐོག་ཕོ་ལོང་ཆེས་དར་ཁྱབ་ཆེ་བའི་ས་ཁུལ་གང་དུ་ཡིན་པ་དང་། དེར་རིག་གནས་གང་གི་ཤན་ཞུགས་ཆེ་བ་ཐེབས་ཡོད་མེད་ལ་བལྟས་ན། ཞང་ཞུང་དང་། བྲུ་ཤ་ཆེ་ཆུང་གཉིས། ལ་དྭགས། ཨེ་ཤེ་ཡ་དཀྱིལ་མའི་པར་ཟིག་སོགས་ནི་གནའ་རབས་ཧ་ཐོག་ཕོ་ལོང་དར་ཁྱབ་ཆེན་པོ་བྱུང་བའི་ས་ཁུལ་ཤ་སྟག་ཡིན་ལ། ས་ཁུལ་དེ་དག་ལས་ཀྱང་བྲུ་ཤ་ཆེ་ཆུང་གཉིས་དང་པར་ཟིག་ཏུ་ཧ་ཐོག་ཕོ་ལོང་ཤིན་ཏུ་དར་ཁྱབ་ཆེའོ། །ས་ཁུལ་དེ་དག་ལ་བོན་ཆོས་གཙོ་བོ་བྱས་པའི་ཞང་ཞུང་ཤེས་རིག་དང་། ཛོ་རོ་ཨཱ་སི་ཏེར་གཙོར་བྱས་པའི་གནའ་རབས་ཀྱི་པར་ཟིག་ཤེས་རིག་གི་ཤུགས་རྐྱེན་ཆེན་པོ་ཐེབས་ཡོད་པ་མ་ཟད། ཤེས་རིག་བརྗེ་རེས་བྱས་པའི་བརྒྱུད་རིམ་ཁྲོད་དུ་ཕན་ཚུན་སྐྱལ་འདེད་ཀྱང་ངེས་ཅན་ཞིག་ཐེབས་ཡོད། ལར་ཡར་ཀླུང་བོད་བཙན་པོའི་རྒྱལ་རབས་ཀྱི་དབང་ཤུགས་ས་ཁུལ་དེ་དག་ལ་མ་བསྐྱེད་གོང་ས་ཁུལ་དེ་དག་དང་རྒྱ་ནག་ས་ཁུལ་གྱི་རིག་གནས། དེ་བཞིན་ཡར་ཀླུང་རིག་གནས་དབར་གྱི་འབྲེལ་འདྲིས་ཙུང་ཟད་ཙུང་བ་ཡིན། དེ་མིན་ཧ་ཐོག་ཕོ་ལོང་རྟེན་པ་ནི་གནའ་སྔ་མོ་ནས་བཟུང་ལ་དྭགས་དང་བྲུ་ཤ་སོགས་ཀྱི་སྲོལ་རྒྱུན་ཞིག་ཆགས་ཡོད་པས། ཡུལ་གྲུ་དེ་དག་ལ་དེང་དུས་ཀྱང་ཧ་ཐོག་ཕོ་ལོང་རྟེན་པའི་ལུགས་སྲོལ་མ་ཉམས་སོར་གནས་ཐུབ་ཡོད། དེར་བརྟེན། གནའ་རབས་ཧ་ཐོག་ཕོ་ལོང་དེ་ས་ཁུལ་དེ་དག་ལ་དར་འཕེལ་ཡོང་བར་ཕྱི་དངོས་པོའི་མཐུན་རྐྱེན་ཚང་ཡོད་པ་མ་ཟད་རིག་གནས་ཀྱི་རྒྱབ་ལྗོངས་ཀྱང་ལེགས་པོ་ཞིག་ཡོད་དོ། །

དུས་ཀྱི་དབང་དུ་བྱས་ན། གནའ་རབས་མདོ་དབུས་མཐོ་སྒང་དང་པར་ཟིག་དབར་གྱི་མཛའ་འབྲེལ་འགྲོ་འོངས་དེ་ཧ་ལམ་སྤྱི་ལོའི་སྔོན་གྱི་དུས་རབས་དྲུག་པ་ནས་བྱུང་ཟིན་ཡོད་ཅིང་།[38] ས་ཁུལ་གཉིས་དབར་ཚོང་ལས་དང་། དཔལ་འབྱོར། ཆོས་ལུགས། རིག་གནས། སྒྲ་རྩལ་སོགས་གང་ཅིའི་ཐད་དུ་འབྲེལ་ལམ་ཟམ་མི་ཆད་པ་ཚུགས་ཡོད་ལ། རིག་གནས་སྟེང་ཕན་ཚུན་ཤན་ཞུགས་ཀྱང་ཆེས་ཆེར་སྣང་། ཁ་ཆེའི་ལོ་རྒྱུས་ཞིབ་འཇུག་པ་ཧ་སན་དྷ་ནིའི་ (Ahmad Hasan Dani) བརྩམས་ཆོས་ནང་དུ་པ་ཀི་སི་ཐན་བྱང་ཕྱོགས་ས་ཁུལ་ཅིའི་ལ་སི་(Chilas) ཞེས་པ་ནས་རྙེད་པའི་སྤྱི་ལོའི་སྔོན་གྱི་བྲག་བརྐོས་རི་མོའི་སྐོར་གྱི་འདྲ་པར་ཞིག་འཁོད། བྲག་བརྐོས་རི་མོའི་འདྲ་པར་དེའི་ནང་དུ་རྟ་བཞོན་ཅིང་ལག་ཏུ་རྟེད་རྒྱུག་བཟུང་བའི་མི་གསུམ་ཡོད་པ་དང་། ས་ངོས་སུ་པོ་ལོ་ཞིག་ཀྱང་ཡོད་པ་མངོན། ཁོང་གིས་རི་མོ་དེར་དབྱེ་ཞིབ་བྱས་པ་བརྒྱུད་དེ་ནི་ཕལ་ཆེར་ཧ་ཐོག་ཕོ་ལོང་རྟེན་པའི་རྣམ་པ་ཡིན་ཞེས་གསུངས།[39] བྲག་བརྐོས་རི་མོ་དེ་སྤྱི་ལོའི་སྔོན་གྱི་སྐབས་རེས་ཡིན་མིན་ཐད་དུ་ང་ཚོས་ད་དུང་དཔྱད་པ་བྱེད་དགོས་མོད། དེས་མ་མཐར་ཡང་ས་ཁུལ་དེ་དག་ལ་གནའ་རབས་ནས་བཟུང་སྔེ་ཧ་ཐོག་ཕོ་ལོང་དར་འཕེལ་བྱུང་ཡོད་པ་གསལ་བཤད་བྱེད་ཐུབ་བོ། །

དེར་བརྟེན་ཁོ་བོའི་བསམ་པར་རིག་གནས་དང་། ལོ་རྒྱུས། ས་ཁམས་སོགས་གང་གི་ཆ་ནས་བལྟས་ཀྱང་གནའ་སྔ་མོ་ནས་བཟུང་སྔེ་ཧ་ཐོག་ཕོ་ལོང་ཆེས་དར་ཁྱབ་ཆེ་བའི་ས་ཆ་ནི་ཞང་ཞུང་རིག་གནས་དང་པར་ཟིག་རིག་གནས་གཉིས་ཀྱི་ཤུགས་རྐྱེན་ཆེན་པོ་ཐེབས་ཡོད་པའི་ཨེ་ཤེ་ཡ་དཀྱིལ་མའི་འབྲོག་ལས་གཙོ་བོ་གཉེར་བའི་ས་ཁུལ་དག་ཏུ་ཡིན་པས། རྟེད་རིགས་དེ་ཡང་ཆེས་ཐོག་མར་ས་ཁུལ་དེ་དག་ནས་དར་བར་འདོད་ཅིང་། འགའ་རེས་རྟེད་རིགས་དེའི་འབྱུང་ཁུངས་ཡར་ཀླུང་བོད་བཙན་པོའི་རྒྱལ་རབས་དང་། རྒྱ་ནག་ས་ཁུལ་ལ་གཏུགས་པར་དེ་ཙམ་འདོད་མོས་ཡོང་དཀའ་བའི་ངོས་འཛིན་བྱེད་ཀྱི་ཡོད་དོ། །

བཞི་པ། རྟ་ཐོག་ཕོ་ལོང་གི་དར་འཕེལ་སྐོར།

གཅིག ལ་དྭགས་དང་བོད་སོགས་ལ་དར་ཚུལ།

ད་ནི་སྐབས་བབས་སུ་རྟ་ཐོག་ཕོ་ལོང་གི་དར་འཕེལ་སྐོར་ཆེ་ལོང་ཙམ་འཆད་པར་བྱ་སྟེ། རྩེད་རིགས་དེ་མ་མཐར་ཡང་སྤྱི་ལོའི་སྔོན་དུ་གངས་ཏི་སེས་ལྷོ་བ་བྱས་པའི་ཞང་ཞུང་ཤེས་རིག་ཁུལ་དང་། ཨེ་ཤེ་ཡ་དཀྱིལ་མའི་འབྲོག་ལས་གཙོ་བོར་གཉེར་བའི་མི་རིགས་ཚོའི་ཁྲོད་དུ་ཐོག་མར་བྱུང་བ་དང་། ལོ་རྒྱ་བརྒྱ་ཕྲག་དུ་མའི་རིང་ཞང་ཞུང་དང་། པར་ཐེག མཐའ་འཁོར་གྱི་ལ་དྭགས། བྲུ་ཤ་སོགས་སུ་དར་ཁྱབ་ཆེན་པོ་བྱུང་ཡོད། རྩེད་རིགས་དེ་ཧ་ལམ་སྤྱི་ལོའི་དུས་རབས་ལྔ་པ་དང་དྲུག་པའི་གཡས་གཡོན་དུ་དམག་དོན་གྱི་དགོས་དབང་དང་ཡར་ཀླུང་བཙན་པོའི་རྒྱལ་རབས་ཀྱི་སྟོབས་ཤུགས་ཇེ་ཆེར་སོང་བ་དང་བསྟུན་ཏེ་ཞང་ཞུང་ནས་ཡར་ཀླུང་གཙོས་པའི་བོད་ཀྱི་དབུས་གཙང་ཁུལ་དུ་དར་བ་དང་། སྐབས་དེ་དུས་གཙོ་བོ་རྒྱལ་བློན་སྐུ་དྲག་གི་ཁྲོད་དང་དམག་དོན་གྱི་རྩལ་སྦྱོང་ཐད་ཤིན་ཏུ་མགོ་བ་མ་གཏོགས་དམངས་ཁྲོད་དུ་དེ་ཙམ་དར་མེད་དོ། །སྤྱི་ལོའི་དུས་རབས་དགུ་པའི་དུས་དཀྱིལ་ནང་། བོད་དུ་སྟོར་བྱུང་མ་སྨོང་བའི་ཆོས་ལུགས་ཀྱི་འགལ་ཟླ་རྙོ་ངར་ཅན་ཞིག་བྱུང་བ་དང་། ལྷ་སྲས་དར་མ་འུ་དུམ་བཙན་པོའང་བཀྲོངས་པའི་མཐའ་འབྲས་སུ་གཅིག་གྱུར་གྱི་བོད་བཙན་པོའི་རྒྱལ་རབས་དེ་སིལ་བུར་ཐོར་བ་རེད། དེ་རྗེས་རྟ་ཐོག་ཕོ་ལོང་གི་རྩེད་རིགས་དེ་ཡང་ནམ་མཁའི་འཇའ་ཚོན་ཡལ་བ་ཇི་བཞིན་བོད་ནས་རྒྱུན་ཆད། འོན་ཀྱང་བོད་ཀྱི་མཐའ་མཚམས་ས་ཁུལ་ལ་དྭགས་དང་བྲུ་ཤ་སོགས་བོད་པའི་ཆོས་དང་རིག་གཞུང་གིས་ཤན་ཞུགས་ཆེན་པོ་ཐེབས་པའི་བོད་རིགས་གནས་སྡོད་ཁུལ་དེ་དག་ལ་དུས་ད་ལྟའང་རྩེད་རིགས་འདི་མ་ཉམས་པར་གནས་ཡོད་པ་མ་ཟད། དེ་ཁུལ་སྲོལ་རྒྱུན་གྱི་རྩེད་རིགས་ཤིག་ཏུ་གྱུར་ཡོད། དེང་སྐབས་རྟ་ཐོག་ཕོ་ལོང་ལ་རྩེད་མོའི་རྒྱལ་པོ་(King of Game) དང་། རྒྱལ་པོའི་རྩེད་མོ་ (Game of King) ཞེས་བསྔགས་པ་ལྟར་སྤྱིར་རྩེད་རིགས་འདི་ནི་འབྱོར་པ་ཅན་ཆོས་སྤྲོ་སྐྱིད་གཏོང་བའི་ལུས་རྩལ་རྣམ་གྲངས་ཤིག་ཡིན་མོད། ལ་དྭགས་ཁུལ་དུ་རྟ་ཐོག་ཕོ་ལོང་ནི་འབྱོར་པ་ཅན་ཚོའི་རྒྱས་སྤྲོས་ཙམ་མ་ཡིན་པར་སྲོལ་རྒྱུན་གྱི་རོལ་རྩེད་ཅིག་ཏུའང་གྱུར་ཡོད། དེང་སང་ལ་དྭགས་ཀྱི་གྲོང་ཚོ་ཕལ་མོ་ཆེར་རྟ་ཐོག་ཕོ་ལོང་རྩེན་པའི་ཐང་ཆེན་ཡོད་ལ། ཕོ་ལོང་གི་འགྲན་བསྡུར་བྱེད་སྐབས་གླིང་རྗེ་གེ་སར་རྒྱལ་པོའི་སྒྲུང་གི་ནང་གསེས་དུམ་བུ་འགའ་ཡང་མགུར་དུ་ལེན་སྲོལ་མཆིས།[40] གཞན་ཡང་། ལ་དྭགས་ཀྱི་བོད་སྐད་ནང་དུའང་རྟ་ཐོག་ཕོ་ལོང་ལ་ཕོ་ལོང་ངམ་པོ་ལོ་ཞེས་འབོད་པའོ། །

གཉིས། རྒྱ་ནག་ས་ཁུལ་དུ་དར་ཚུལ།

རྩེད་རིགས་དེ་རྒྱ་ནག་ས་ཁུལ་དུ་ག་དུས་དར་རམ་ཞེ་ན། ཤིང་ཕོ་རྟ་ཡི་ལོ་སྟེ་སྤྱི་ལོ་༦༣༤ལོར་ཐང་བོད་ཀྱི་འབྲེལ་བ་དངོས་སུ་ཚུགས་པའི་རྗེས་སུ་ཐང་བོད་གཉིས་དབར་ཕན་ཚུན་སྐྱེས་བསྐུར་རེས་ལན་མང་བྱས་ལ། ལྷག་དོན་དུ་རྒྱ་བཟའ་ལྷུན་ཤིང་བོད་བཙན་པོའི་བཙུན་མོར་བཞེས་རྗེས་ཐང་བོད་འབྲེལ་བ་ཇེ་ཟབ་ཏུ་ཕྱིན་ཡོད། དེ་དུས་བོད་ནས་བློ་རིག་རྩོ་བའི་བོད་ཕྲུག་མང་དག་གཅིག་ཁྲང་ཨན་གྱི་གོའོ་ཞོའི་ (国学) ཞེས་བྱ་བའི་སློབ་གྲྭར་སློབ་གཉེར

ལ་བརྫངས་པ་དང་། ཁོང་ཚོ་སློབ་གསེང་སྐབས་རྟ་རྒོག་པོ་ལོང་རྩེན་པར་ཞེན་ཏུ་སྤྲོ་བས།[41] རྩེད་རིགས་དེའང་སྐབས་དེ་དུས་ཆེས་ཐོག་མར་བོད་ནས་ཐང་རྒྱལ་རབས་སུ་དར་བར་འདོད། ཐང་རྒྱལ་རབས་ཀྱི་དུས་འགོར་རྟ་རྒོག་པོ་ལོང་དེ་རྒྱ་ནག་གི་བྱང་ཕྱོགས་ས་ཁུལ་དུ་དར་ཁྱབ་ཆེན་ཙམ་བྱུང་ཞིང་། ཐང་རྒྱལ་རབས་ཀྱི་དུས་དཀྱིལ་དུ་སླེབས་སྐབས་དར་བའི་རྩེ་མོར་སོན་པ་དང་། སྐབས་དེ་དུས་རྩེད་རིགས་དེ་ད་དུང་ཀུ་རི་ཡ་དང་ལྗར་པན་སོགས་མཐའ་འཁོར་རྒྱལ་ཁབ་ཁག་ཏུའང་དར་ཁྱབ་བྱུང་ཡོད། དེ་རྗེས་སུང་རྒྱལ་རབས་སྐབས་(སྤྱི་ལོ་༩༦༠ནས་སྤྱི་ལོ་༡༡༢༧བར་)རིམ་པས་དམངས་ཁྲོད་དུ་དར་བ་དང་། ལོ་ངོ་ཉིས་བརྒྱ་ལྷག་ཙམ་སོང་བའི་རྗེས་ཀྱི་མིང་རྒྱལ་རབས་(སྤྱི་ལོ་༡༣༦༨ནས་སྤྱི་ལོ་༡༦༤༤ བར་) ནས་བཟུང་རྩེད་རིགས་དེ་ཉམས་རྒུད་འགྲོ་འགོ་ཚུགས་ཏེ་མཐར་ཆིང་རྒྱལ་རབས་(སྤྱི་ལོ་༡༦༡༦ནས་སྤྱི་ལོ་༡༩༡༡ བར་)ཀྱི་དུས་སུ་རྒྱ་ནག་ནས་རྒྱུན་ཆད་དོ། །[42]

གསུམ། རྒྱ་གར་དང་ནུབ་གླིང་དུ་དར་ཚུལ།

རྒྱ་གར་དུ་རྟ་རྒོག་པོ་ལོང་ནམ་དར་བ་དང་། དེང་སྐབས་ནུབ་གླིང་དུ་དར་ཁྱབ་ཆེ་བའི་རྟ་རྒོག་པོ་ལོང་དེ་ཇི་ལྟར་བྱུང་བ་ཡིན་ནམ་ཞེ་ན། དེའང་རྒྱ་གར་དུ་མ་མཐར་ཡང་ཇི་ལི་སུལ་ཏན་ (Delhi Sultanate, 1206–1525) རྒྱལ་ཁབ་སྟེ་སུལ་ཏན་རྒྱལ་རབས་ཀྱིས་རྒྱ་གར་གྱི་རྒྱལ་སྲིད་སྐྱོང་སྐབས་རྟ་རྒོག་པོ་ལོང་ཆེས་ཐོག་མར་བྱུ་ཤ་ཆེ་ཆུང་གཉིས་སོགས་བརྒྱུད་དེ་དར་བ་དང་། དེ་རྗེས་འཕེལ་རྒྱས་སྨུར་པོ་བྱུང་སྟེ་སྤྱི་ལོའི་དུས་རབས་བཅུ་དྲུག་པར་སོག་པོའི་རྒྱལ་རྒྱུད་མོར་གན་(Mughal Empire, 1525–1857) གྱིས་རྒྱ་གར་ཁ་ལོ་བསྒྱུར་བའི་སྐབས་རྩེད་རིགས་དེ་དར་བའི་རྩེ་མོར་སོན། རྒྱལ་པོ་ཨཀྐ་ཁ་པ་(Akbar, 1565–1605) ཡི་དུས་སུ་རྩེད་རིགས་དེར་བརྩི་མཐོང་ཆེན་པོ་བྱས་པར་གྲགས་ཤིང་། རྒྱ་གར་གྱི་ས་གནས་ཨག་ར་(Agra) ཞེས་པར་སྐབས་དེ་དུས་རྟ་རྒོག་པོ་ལོང་རྩེན་པར་ཆེད་དུ་སྐྲུན་པའི་རྟ་ར་ཞིག་ད་ལྟའང་དངོས་སུ་མཇལ་རྒྱུ་ཡོད། དུས་རབས་བཅུ་བདུན་པ་དང་ལྷག་པར་དུ་དུས་རབས་བཅོ་བརྒྱད་པའི་ནང་རྒྱ་གར་དུ་ཕྱིའི་བཙན་འཛུལ་པ་འབོར་ཆེན་ལྷགས་རྗེས་རྙིན་ཏུ་ཕྱེད་གླིང་གི་རྟ་རྒོག་པོ་ལོང་ཡང་རིམ་བཞིན་ཉམས་རྒུད་ཕྱིན། འོན་ཀྱང་རྒྱ་གར་བྱང་ཤར་བླང་ག་ལའི་ས་མཚམས་ཀྱི་མངའ་སྡེ་མཎི་ཕུར་(Manipur) དང་ནུབ་བྱང་བརྒྱུད་ཀྱི་ལ་དྭགས་སོགས་ལ་སྔར་བཞིན་མ་ཉམས་སོར་གནས་ཐུབ་པ་བྱུང་ཡོད། དེའང་མཎི་ཕུར་ས་ཁུལ་གྱི་རྟ་རྒོག་པོ་ལོང་ལ་པོ་ལོ་(polo) ཞེས་འབོད་ཀྱི་ཡོད། སྤྱི་ལོ་༡༨༥༧ལོར་རྒྱ་གར་ལ་དབྱིན་ཇིས་དབང་བསྒྱུར་བྱས་ཏེ་རྒྱ་གར་དབྱིན་ཇིའི་མི་སེར་སྒྲིལ་ཡུལ་དུ་གྱུར་བ་དང་། དབྱིན་ཇིས་མཎི་ཕུར་ས་ཁུལ་དུ་རྟ་རྒོག་པོ་ལོང་ཡོད་པ་ཤེས་རྗེས་ལོ་དེ་རང་ལ་རྒྱ་གར་བའི་རྟ་རྒོག་པོ་ལོང་གི་རྩེད་རིགས་ལ་སློབ་སྦྱོང་དང་བྱས་ཤིང་འགྲན་བསྡུར་ཡང་ལན་མང་བྱས། སྤྱི་ལོ་༡༨༦༩ལོར་རྟ་རྒོག་པོ་ལོང་དེ་རྒྱ་གར་ནས་མཚོ་ལམ་བརྒྱུད་དབྱིན་ཇིར་དར་བ་དང་། རྩེད་རིགས་དེའི་འབོད་སྟངས་ཀྱང་བོད་སྐད་པོ་ལོང་ཟེར་བ་དེ་རང་སོར་བེད་སྤྱོད་བཏང་བ་དང་ཆབས་ཅིག་རྩེད་སྒྲོལ་གསར་པ་མང་པོ་གཏན་འཁེལ་བྱུང་། དེ་རྗེས་དུས་ཐུང་ལོ་ངོ་བཅུའི་ནང་རྩེད་རིགས་དེ་ནུབ་ཕྱོགས་ཀྱི་རྒྱལ་ཁབ་མང་པོར་ཁྱབ་བརྡལ་ཤུགས་ཆེན་བྱུང་ཞིང་། སྤྱི་ལོ་༡༩༠༠ནས་བཟུང་སྟེ་ལོ་ངོ་སུམ་བཅུ་ལྷག་ཙམ་རིང་རྩེད་རིགས་དེ་འཛམ་གླིང་ཨོ་ལིམ་ཕིག་ལུས་རྩལ་འགྲན་ཚོགས་(The Olympic Games) ནང་དུའང་ཚུད་ཐུབ་པ་བྱུང་ཡོད། གོང་གི་རྒྱུ་མཚན་ཁག་ལ་

བརྟེན་ནས་མཆི་ཕུར་ས་ཁུལ་ནི་རྟ་རྒོག་པོ་ལོང་གི་འབྱུང་ཁུངས་ལྟ་བུར་གྱུར་ཏེ་ས་གནས་དེའི་མི་ཚོས་ཀྱང་རང་ཡུལ་ནི་རྟ་རྒོག་པོ་ལོང་གི་ཕ་ཡུལ་(Home of Polo) དུ་བསྔོམས་ཀྱང་། དོན་དམ་གང་འདྲ་ཡིན་མིན་ལོ་རྒྱུས་སྨྲ་བ་རྣམས་ཀྱིས་དགོངས་བཞེས་གནང་དགོས་སོ།། །།

Notes

1 པར་ཟིག་ནི་མདོ་དབུས་མཐོ་སྒང་གི་ནུབ་ངོས་སུ་གནས་ཡོད་ཅིང་། གནའ་རབས་ཨེ་ཤི་ཡའི་ས་ཁུལ་ན་འབྱོར་ཕྱུག་ལྡན་ལ་ཤེས་རིག་གི་རྒྱུ་ཚད་མཐོན་པོར་སླེབས་ཡོད་པའི་མི་རིགས་ཤིག་ཡིན། པར་ཟིག་ལ་ནུབ་གླིང་བས་ཕར་ཞི་ཡ་(Persia) དང་། རྒྱ་ནག་པས་པོ་སི་(波斯)ཞེས་འབོད། བོད་ཀྱི་ཆོས་འབྱུང་ཁག་ནང་སྟག་གཟིག་གམ་ཏ་ཟིག་ཅེས་འབོད་པ་ཤས་ཆེའོ། །ཁ་ཅིག་ན་རེ། བོད་ཡུལ་དུ་གྲགས་པའི་ཏ་ཟིག་གམ་སྟག་གཟིག་ནི་ཁ་ཆེའི་ཆོས་ཨི་སི་ལམ་དད་མཁན་གྱི་ཨ་རབ་(Arab, 阿拉伯) སྤྱིར་གོ་དགོས་ཟེར་བ་ཡིན་ཀྱང་དེ་ནི་ཁུངས་ལུང་མེད་པ་ཡིན་ཏེ། མཁས་དབང་ནམ་མཁའི་ནོར་བུ་དང་རྗེ་དུང་དཀར་བློ་བཟང་འཕྲིན་ལས་སོགས་མཁས་པ་མང་པོས་བསྟན་པ་ཕྱི་དར་སྐབས་སུ་བྱུང་བའི་བར་དེའི་ཆོས་འབྱུང་ལོ་རྒྱུས་ཁག་ཏུ་འཁོད་པའི་ཏ་ཟིག་གམ་སྟག་གཟིག་ནི་དོན་དམ་དུ་དེང་གི་པར་ཟིག་དབྱི་རན་ལ་གོ་དགོས་ཚུལ་གསུངས་པ་དོན་དངོས་དང་མཐུན་ནོ། །

2 འདིར་ཡར་ཀླུང་བོད་བཙན་པོའི་རྒྱལ་རབས་ཞེས་པ་ནི་རྒྱལ་པོ་གཉའ་ཁྲི་བཙན་པོ་ནས་དར་མ་འུ་དུམ་བཙན་གྱི་དབང་བསྒྱུར་མཇུག་མ་རྫོགས་པའི་བར་ལ་གོ་དགོས་སོ། །

3 འདིར་བརྗོད་པར་བྱ་བའི་གནའ་རབས་བོད་དང་པར་ཟིག་གི་འབྲེལ་བའི་སྐོར་འདི་ནི་དུས་ཀྱི་དབང་དུ་བྱས་ན་ཡ་རྒོག་གི་དུས་ནས་ཧ་ལམ་སྤྱི་ལོའི་དུས་རབས་བདུན་པའི་བར་ཡིན་ཏེ། བོད་དུ་ཡ་རྒོག་གི་དུས་ནས་ཡར་ཀླུང་བཙན་པོའི་རྒྱལ་རབས་ཀྱིས་བོད་ཁམས་ཡོངས་ལ་གཅིག་གྱུར་གྱི་དབང་བསྒྱུར་བྱེད་འགོ་ཚུགས་པའི་བར་དང་། པར་ཟིག་དུ་ཡ་རྒོག་གི་དུས་ནས་པར་ཟིག་གི་བཙན་ཕྱུག་རྒྱལ་ལྡན་རྒྱལ་རབས་ཕྱི་མ་སྣ་སན་རྒྱལ་རབས་ (Sassanian Dynasty, 224–642CE) ཀྱི་དབང་བསྒྱུར་མཇུག་མ་རྫོགས་གོང་བར་ངོས་འཛིན་གནང་དགོས་སོ། །

4 James Thrower, *The Religious History of Central Asia From The Earliest Times To The Present Day* (New York: The Edwin Mellen Press, 2004), 63.

5 张云:《上古西藏与波斯文明》. 中国藏学出版社， 2005年版本， 第233页

6 ཐུའུ་བཀྭན་བློ་བཟང་ཆོས་ཀྱི་ཉི་མས་བརྩམས་པའི་《ཐུའུ་བཀྭན་གྲུབ་མཐའ་》ཀན་སུའུ་མི་རིགས་དཔེ་སྐྲུན་ཁང་། སྤྱི་ལོ་༡༩༨༩ལོའི་དཔར་མ། ཤ ༣༨༠ ནང་གསལ།

7 དགེ་འདུན་ཆོས་འཕེལ་གྱིས་བརྩམས་པའི་《དེབ་ཐེར་དཀར་པོ་》མི་རིགས་དཔེ་སྐྲུན་ཁང་། སྤྱི་ལོ་༢༠༠༠ ལོའི་དཔར་མ། ཤ ༡༥ ནང་གསལ།

8 《དེབ་ཐེར་དཀར་པོ་》ཤ ༡༦ ནང་གསལ།

9 张云:《上古西藏与波斯文明》. 中国藏学出版社, 2005年版, 第298页

10 བསོད་ནམས་དོན་གྲུབ་ཀྱིས་བརྩམས་པའི་《སྟག་གཟིག་དང་གནའ་རབས་བོད་ཀྱི་འབྲེལ་བའི་སྐོར་ལ་དཔྱད་པ་》བོད་ལྗོངས་ཞིབ་འཇུག སྤྱི་ལོ་༡༩༩༢ ལོའི་དུས་དེབ་གསུམ་པ། ཤ ༣༢ ནང་གསལ།

11 གུ་རུ་ཨུ་རྒྱན་གླིང་པས་ཡར་ཀླུངས་ཤེལ་གྱི་བྲག་ཕུག་ནས་བཏོན་པའི་《བཀའ་ཐང་སྡེ་ལྔ་》མི་རིགས་དཔེ་སྐྲུན་ཁང་། སྤྱི་ལོ་༡༩༨༦ ལོའི་དཔར་མ། ཤ ༩༩༥ ནང་གསལ།

12 《སྟག་གཟིག་དང་གནའ་རབས་བོད་ཀྱི་འབྲེལ་བའི་སྐོར་ལ་དཔྱད་པ་》ཤ ༢༧ ནང་གསལ།

13 张云:《上古西藏与波斯文明》. 中国藏学出版社, 2005年版, 第291页

14 སྐྱོགས་སྟོན་རིན་ཆེན་བཀྲ་ཤིས་ཀྱིས་མཛད་པའི་《བོད་ཀྱི་སྐད་ལས་གསར་རྙིང་གི་བརྡའི་ཁྱད་པར་སྟོན་པ་ལེགས་པར་བཤད་པ་ལི་ཤིའི་གུར་ཁང་》ཞེས་པར་གསལ། ཁྲི་བསམ་གཏན་དང་ཚེ་དབང་ཐར་གཉིས་ཀྱིས་གཙོ་སྒྲིག་བྱས་པའི་《སྐད་གཉིས་སྨྲ་བའི་སྒྲོན་མེ་》ལས་བཏུས། ཀན་སུའུ་མི་རིགས་དཔེ་སྐྲུན་ཁང་། སྤྱི་ལོ་༢༠༠༠ ལོའི་དཔར་མ། ཤ ༡༥༦ ནང་གསལ།

15 ཀྲང་དབྱི་སུན་གྱིས་གཙོ་འགན་བཞེས་ནས་རྩོམ་སྒྲིག་བྱས་པའི་《བོད་རྒྱ་ཚིག་མཛོད་ཆེན་མོ་》མི་རིགས་དཔེ་སྐྲུན་ཁང་། སྤྱི་ལོ་༢༠༠༣ ལོའི་དཔར་མ། ཤ ༡༧༢༨ ནང་གསལ།

16 པོ་ལོང་ཞེས་པའི་མིང་ཚིག་འདི་བོད་ཡིག་གི་བརྡ་རྙིང་ཡིན་པའི་སྐོར་ལ་རིག་གཞུང་བགྲོ་གླེང་སྐབས་ཕྲན་གྱི་རིག་པའི་གྲོགས་པོ་ཞིག་གིས། པོ་ནི་པོ་བའི་དོན་དང་། ལོང་ནི་ལུག་སོགས་ཀྱི་ལོང་ཀ་སྟེ་དབྱིབས་གཟུགས་རིལ་མོ་ཡིན་སྟབས་མིང་བརྡ་དེས་པོ་ལོའི་གོ་དོན་མཚོན་གྱི་ཡོད་པ་རེད། ཅེས་གསུངས་བྱུང་བར་མུ་མཐུད་ཞིབ་དཔྱད་གནང་དགོས་པ་འདུག་གོ །

17 བོད་མིང་དབང་རྒྱལ་དང་བསོད་ནམས་སྐྱིད་ཀྱིས་བསྒྱུར་བའི་《ཏུན་ཧོང་ནས་ཐོན་པའི་བོད་ཀྱི་ལོ་རྒྱུས་ཡིག་ཆ་》མི་རིགས་དཔེ་སྐྲུན་ཁང་། ཤ ༩༡ ནང་གསལ།

18 《ཏུན་ཧོང་ནས་ཐོན་པའི་བོད་ཀྱི་ལོ་རྒྱུས་ཡིག་ཆ་》ཤ ༡༦ ནང་གསལ།

19 《ཏུན་ཧོང་ནས་ཐོན་པའི་བོད་ཀྱི་ལོ་རྒྱུས་ཡིག་ཆ་》ཤ ༡༨ ནང་གསལ།

20 རྣམ་རྒྱལ་ཚེ་རིང་གིས་བསྒྲིགས་པའི་《བོད་ཡིག་བརྡ་རྙིང་ཚིག་མཛོད་》 ཀྲུང་གོའི་བོད་རིག་པ་དཔེ་སྐྲུན་ཁང་། སྤྱི་ལོ་༢༠༠༡ལོའི་དཔར་མ། ཤ ༣༢༩ ནས་ ཤ ༣༩༥ བར་གསལ།

21 《马球(POLO)新证》载: "'在（英语中）我们最有意思的藏语借词是polo，马球戏……'" 王尧:《马球(POLO)新证》载:《中国马球史研究》, 李金梅编, 甘肃人民出版社, 2002年版, 第41页

22 David Crystal, ed., *The Cambridge Encyclopedia* (Cambridge: Cambridge University Press, 1990), 959.

23 Encyclopædia Britannica, Inc., *The New Encyclopædia Britannica*, vol. 14 (1768; reprint, USA, 1980), 760.

24 ཅི་ཏུའི་(击鞠)ཞེས་པའི་ཅི་(击)ནི་བཞུས་པའམ་བརྒྱབ་པའི་དོན་དང་། ཏུའི་(鞠)ནི་གནའ་རབས་ཀྱི་པོ་ལོའི་རིགས་ཤིག་ལ་གོ་བས། ཅི་ཏུའི་ཞེས་པའི་གོ་དོན་ནི་གནའ་རབས་ཀྱི་པོ་ལོ་དེ་རིགས་རྩེད་པའི་དོན་ནོ། །

25 རྡ་ཆིའུ་(打毬)ཞེས་པའི་རྡ་ (打)ནི་བཞུས་པའམ་རྩེད་པའི་དོན་དང་། ཆིའུ་ (毬)ནི་པོ་ལོའི་དོན་ཡིན་པས། མིང་བརྡ་རྡ་ཆིའུ་ནི་པོ་ལོ་རྩེད་པར་གོ་དགོས་སོ། །

26 崔乐泉: 《古代马球起源及发展研究的历史回顾 —兼及有关问题的考古资料分析》. 载:《中国马球史研究》, 李金梅编, 甘肃人民出版社, 2002年版, 第85页

27 《རྒྱལ་སྲིད་སྐྱོང་བྱེད་མེ་ལོང་》《资治通鉴》དམ་《ཙི་ཀྲི་ཐུང་ཅན་》ཞེས་པ་ནི་རྒྱ་ནག་གི་ལོ་རྒྱུས་སྨྲ་བའི་མཁན་པོ་སི་མ་ཀོང་(司马光, 1019–1086)གིས་གཙོ་འགན་བཞེས་ཏེ་རྩོམ་སྒྲིག་གནང་བའི་གྲགས་རྩོམ་ཞིག་ཡིན། དེའི་ནང་དོན་གཙོ་བོ་ནི་རྒྱ་ནག་གི་ཆབ་སྲིད་དང་། དམག་དོན། མི་རིགས་སོགས་ཀྱི་འབྲེལ་བའི་སྐོར་སོགས་ཡིན་ཞིང་། ད་ཕན་ཀུན་ནས་ཚད་མར་འཛིན་པའི་ལོ་རྒྱུས་དེབ་ཐེར་རྨད་དུ་བྱུང་བ་ཞིག་ཡིན།

28 张云:《上古西藏与波斯文明》. 中国藏学出版社, 2005年版, 第307页

29 崔乐泉:《古代马球起源及发展研究的历史回顾 —兼及有关问题的考古资料分析》.载:《中国马球史研究》, 李金梅编, 甘肃人民出版社, 2002年版, 第84页

30 Encyclopædia Britannica, 760.

31 Encyclopædia Britannica, 760.

32 མི་འགྱུར་རྡོ་རྗེས་བརྩམས་པའི་《བོད་ཀྱི་སྲོལ་རྒྱུན་ལུས་རྩལ་དང་བོད་ཀྱི་གནའ་བོའི་རྩེད་རྩལ་རྟ་ཐོག་པོ་ལོའི་སྐོར་ཅུང་ཟད་གླེང་བ་》བོད་ལྗོངས་ཞིབ་འཇུག སྤྱི་ལོ་༡༩༨༩ལོའི་དུས་དེབ་གཉིས་པ། ཤ ༡༨ ནས་ ཤ ༢༦ བར་གསལ།

33 དེའང་《པདྨ་རཱ་ག》ལས། ལོ་རྒྱུས་ཐོག་ཏུ་སྔོན་གྲགས་ཅན་གྱི་རྟ་ཐོག་པོ་ལོ་རྒྱག་རྒྱུའི་ལུས་རྩལ་དེ་ནི་ཐོག་མར་བོད་ནས་དར་ཡོད་པ་གཟུར་གནས་ཀྱི་(ཀྱི་)ལོ་རྒྱུས་སློབ་ཀུན་གྱིས་ངོས་འཛིན་གཅིག་མཐུན་དུ་བྱེད་ཅིང་། དབྱིན་ཇི་ལ་སོགས་པ་ཕྱི་རྒྱལ་གྱི་སྐད་དུ་དེང་དུས་ཀྱང་པོ་ལོ་ཞེས་བོད་སྐད་ཀྱི་སྒྲ་རང་སོར་བཞག་ནས་བེད་སྤྱོད་བྱེད། ཅེས་འཁོད་འདུག ཐུབ་བསྟན་ཕུན་ཚོགས་ཀྱིས་བརྩམས་པའི་《བོད་ཀྱི་ལོ་རྒྱུས་སྤྱི་དོན་པདྨ་རཱ་གའི་ལྡེ་མིག》སྟོད་ཆ། སི་ཁྲོན་མི་རིགས་དཔེ་སྐྲུན་ཁང་། སྤྱི་ལོ་༡༩༩༦ ལོའི་དཔར་མ། ཤ ༣༣༢ ནང་གསལ།

34 《<册府元龟>吐蕃史料校正》, 苏晋仁、萧鍊子 校正, 四川人民出版社, 第360页

35 《册府元龟》载:“正月，宴吐蕃使者于院内，驸马都尉杨慎交与之打球。”《<册府元龟>吐蕃史料校正》, 苏晋仁、萧鍊子 校正, 四川人民出版社, 第361页

36 ཆབ་སྤེལ་ཚེ་བརྟན་ཕུན་ཚོགས་དང་ནོར་བྲང་ཨོ་རྒྱན་གྱིས་་རྩོམ་སྒྲིག་མཛད་པའི་《བོད་ཀྱི་ལོ་རྒྱུས་རགས་རིམ་གཡུ་ཡི་ཕྲེང་བ་》སྟོད་ཆ། བོད་ལྗོངས་དཔེ་རྙིང་དཔེ་སྐྲུན་ཁང་། སྤྱི་ལོ་༡༩༨༩ལོའི་དཔར་མ། ཤ ༢༦༦ ནང་འཁོད།

37 唐封演《封氏闻见记》卷六载: 太宗常御安福门, 谓侍臣曰:“闻西蕃人好打毬，比亦令习, 会一度观之。昨升仙楼有群蕃街里打毬, 欲令朕见, 此蕃疑朕爱此, 聘为之。以此思量, 帝王举动, 岂宜容易, 朕以焚此毬以自诫。”

38 张云:《上古西藏与波斯文明》. 中国藏学出版社, 2005年版, 第233页

39 《巴基斯坦北部地区的马球》, 陆水林选译 载: 《国外藏学研究译文集》第十六集, 王尧、王启主编, 西藏人民出版社, 2002年版, 第195–209页

40 《巴基斯坦北部地区的马球》陆水林选译, 载:《国外藏学研究译文集》, 第十六集, 王尧、王启主编, 西藏人民出版社, 2002年版, 第195–201页

41 《བོད་ཀྱི་ལོ་རྒྱུས་རགས་རིམ་གཡུ་ཡི་ཕྲེང་བ་》ཤ ༢༦༥ ནང་གསལ།

42 崔乐泉:《古代马球起源及发展研究的历史回顾 — 兼及有关问题的考古资料分析》, 载:《中国马球史研究》, 李金梅编, 甘肃人民出版社, 2002年版, 第86–88页

Abstract

An Analysis of the Origin of Polo through the Ancient Relationship between Tibet and Persia

TSERING DAWA

This chapter examines the origin of polo through the analysis of the multifaceted relationship between Tibet and Persia before the Yarlung Dynasty. As we all know, polo is one of the world's oldest sports and was very popular in Gilgit, Baltistan, Persia, Tibet, and China during the 7th century. However, after several centuries, it disappeared from those areas. In recent years, many scholars from all parts of the world have become concerned about the origin of polo. Meanwhile, different people hold different ideas as ancient documents have not noted much about polo. Three main opinions about the origin of polo have therefore flourished. This theoretical thesis challenges the argument that polo originates from China, Tibet, and Persia, and comes to the conclusion that polo originated from Zhang zhung and pastoral areas of Central Asia.

The argument is supported in the following ways. First, it concerns the religious, cultural, commercial, and economical relationship between Tibet and Persia. Second, it concerns the origin of polo, which explains the word '*pho long*' (polo), and analyzes the three different ideas about its origin. Third, it presents a theory based on original research. Fourth, it gives a brief introduction to the development and dispersion of this game.

13

The Role of Confucius in Bon Sources

Kong tse and his Attribution in the Ritual of Three-Headed Black Man

KALSANG NORBU GURUNG

Kong tse is a well-known figure in a number of Bonpo ritual, biographical and astrological texts. My interest in this particular subject has been stimulated by my ongoing research on a myth of Shenrab Miwo (gShen rab mi bo), the founder of Bon. A relationship between Kong tse and the founder is described in many early Bon sources. The name Kong tse is written in the sources variously as *kong tse*, *kong rtse*, *kong tshe*, *gong tse*, *rkong tse*, *skong rtse,* and sometimes with the epithet *'phrul gyi rgyal po* (or in abbreviation *'phrul rgyal*). The Tibetan spelling *kong tse* is a phonetic transcription of the Chinese original *kongzi*, used by early Tibetan authors in a manner similar to the way Confucius was adopted from *kongfuzi* in the West. Kongzi / Kongfuzi was a sage / philosopher / thinker who was born in an ancient city called Zhou in the east of China and lived from 551–479 BCE.[1]

Kong tse was introduced in Tibet evidently from the 11th century CE in the earliest known hagiography of Shenrab, titled *mDo 'dus*.[2] He was depicted in several different ways in Bon sources and sometime even worshiped for the sake of well being and prosperity. The role of Kong tse (Confucius) in Tibet and its great influence on Tibetan religion, culture, and particularly to the "indigenous" ritual of Tibet, is still untouched by academic Confucian scholars. This gap may be for several reasons, such as Buddhism's strong influence with regard to the study of religion and culture of Tibet, the great distance of the ritual attributed to Kong tse in Tibetan sources from Confucian teaching preserved in other parts of Asia and the limited Bon and Buddhist sources for the study of Kong tse. The role of Confucius in Tibet, particularly in Bon ritual, has not received adequate attention in Western academia.

In this chapter, I shall focus on the role of Kong tse in Bon sources. Several Bonpo texts on Kong tse exist, some of which can be dated before the earliest reference from Buddhist sources; thus Kong tse was most likely adopted first by Bonpos. The sources available in Bonpo collections can be classified into two groups based on the cohesive data from the sources. One group of texts consists of the biographies of Shenrab and those related to the biography datable from 11th century CE, in which Kong tse is portrayed more as an earthly being, such as a king, who later became a patron and father-in-law of the founder of Bon. The other group of texts focus on ritual aspects of Kong tse, which may be a few centuries later. Having agreed with previous scholars on the theme of Kong tse being none other than Kongzi from China, I will illustrate how Confucius was portrayed in the early Bonpo sources and how he was associated with Bonpo rituals. I hope this study will shed light on the development of Bon tradition in Tibet. Before pursuing his role in detail, I will briefly discuss an overview of previous studies on Kong tse.

Previous Studies on Kong Tse

Since the Kong tse described in Bon sources is a Tibetan form of the Chinese sage Kongzi, there is no reason to view him as a Tibetan. Norbu indicated in his book that the word "*rgya*" connected to name Kong tse is not to be taken as the land of "China," as in the Tibetan lexicon, but is one of the six royal clans (dMu, Shag, Hos, dPo, rGya, and gNyan) of 'Ol mo lung ring; thus Kong tse was born in one of the royal clans of 'Ol mo lung ring.[3] As the existence of 'Ol mo lung ring itself is ambiguous, rather a myth than a historical place, this theory of six clans belonging to that place seems vague. In addition, I should like to speculate on further details in regard to the origin of this theory, which may clarify its reliability. Since Norbu refers to the history by Shar rdza[4] as his source, I shall first present here the list actually found in the history and then speculate on his interpretation of the names in the list. Shar rdza listed six royal lineages (*gdung rgyud 'dzin pa'i rgyal po drug*) as follows: 1) *dmu rigs gshen lha'i gdung rgyud*; 2) *shāg rigs gar gsas kyi gdung rgyud*; 3) *hos rigs gnam gsas kyi gdung rgyud*; 4) *dpo rigs gsas rje'i gdung rgyud*; 5) *rgya ha shang rgod gsas kyi gdung rgyud;* and 6) *gnyen rigs mkha' 'gying gi gdung rgyud*. As presented here, Shar rdza listed "rGya" among the six royal lineages, but he does not mention that the rGya is a race or a clan of 'Ol mo lung ring. On the contrary, he explicitly mentioned rGya and Ha shang together. The latter name (Ha / Hwa shang) can also be found in many other Tibetan histories as a monk from China,[5] who went to Tibet in the

8th century. This may suggest that Shar rdza was indeed referring to China by the rGya in his list.

Looking carefully at these six lineages, it can be understood that Shar rdza was reconstructing the six lineages by consulting important names and their family backgrounds given in the early biographies of Shenrab, the *mDo 'dus* and the *gZer mig*.[6] In particular, the list of six lineages is clearly mentioned in the *gZi brjid*,[7] which seems to be a source for Shar rdza's interpretation. For instance, three names — *dmu rigs*, *hos rig* and *dpo rigs* — are respectively from Shenrab's own lineage, called *dmu'i rigs*, from the Hos king named Dang ba yid ring and from the *dpo* king 'Bar ba'i sgron ma can. The two kings are said to be Shenrab's fathers-in-law, because, according to the biographies, they offered their daughters to the Bon founder. The last two lineages, *rgya ha shang* (or *rgya rigs*) and *gnyen rigs*, could possibly be derived from the story of Kong tse and his wife, who also offered their daughter to Shenrab. Kong tse was said to be born in the family of a Chinese king and his wife, 'Od ma gsal, was a daughter of the *gnyen* family. The third lineage, *shāg rigs*, does not appear in the two early biographies, but is found in a third biography, the *gZi brjid*, and in another early Bonpo text.[8] Beyond any doubt, it is referring to the Śākya clan of Śākyamuni Buddha, which in Tibetan is written as *shag gi rigs* or *shāg rigs*.

An 18th-century Tibetan historian, Thu'u bkwan Blo bzang chos kyi nyi ma (1732–1802), is the earliest to identify *kong tse* to be a Tibetan reading of *kongzi* from Chinese sources.[9] Interestingly, he further commented with his critical view on those romantic images of Kong tse in the Tibetan sources. He writes:

> Some Tibetan portrayed Kong tse as a magical king and called him Kong tse 'phrul gyi rgyal po. He was visualized as a deity in meditation of some *gto* rituals in astrology (*nag rtsis*). Some scholars described him as skilled in architecture work and thus called him the architect Kong tse. These [theories] are comparable to [the understanding of] a person who holds an [unknown] thing in his hand in a totally dark room.[10]

In the West, Prof. Ferdinand D. Lessing seems to be the first scholar who connected Kong tse and Kongzi. He explored a Tibetan ritual text dated from the mid-18th century that he acquired from Yonghe Gong (the Tibetan "Lama Temple" in Beijing) during his research in 1930–32. According to this ritual text, Kong tse is described as *bodhisattva* or future Buddha. Lessing identified this Kong tse as the Chinese sage he called "Bodhisattva Confucius," whom he listed among the non-Buddhist divine beings found in Tibetan religion, worshipped by Chinese.[11] We can also see the similar depiction in Bon sources, presented later in this paper.

Other pioneering scholars like Soymié and Karmay also related the name Kong tse to the Chinese sage Kongzi / Kongfuzi. They dealt with the story of Confucius from Tibetan Dunhuang manuscripts and from the *gZer mig*. Karmay believes that Confucius is the prototype of Kong tse 'phrul gyi rgyal po in Bon sources.[12] He also points out that the epithet *'phrul gyi rgyal po* in a Tibetan Buddhist source by Padma gling pa (1450–1521) to refer to Kong tse[13] maintains a similar connotation to that of *rlung nam 'phrul gyi rgyal po*, the epithet belonging to an early Tibetan king, and in turn derived from *'phrul gyi lha btsan po*, a title used for early Tibetan kings.[14] Recently, Shen-yu Lin presented some more interesting issues and references regarding the names of Kong tse found in both Buddhist and Bonpo sources. Lin believes that the labels of "*kong tse*" in Tibetan literature do not necessarily refer to Confucius. Her conclusion is based on the reference to Kong tse 'phrul chung, who, according to *sBa bzhed*[15] and the History by the Fifth Dalai Lama (1617–1682), was the father of the Chinese princess Kong jo who married Srong btsan sgam po. Thus, this Kong tse 'phrul chung must, Lin suggests, refer to Tang Taizong, not to Confucius.[16] However, this may be the case with Kong tse 'phrul chung, who, according to Bon sources, is not the same as Kong tse 'phrul rgyal (cf. Kong tsha 'phrul bu chung, son of Shenrab, and Kong za 'phrul bsgyur in the *mDo 'dus* and the *gZer mig*). In addition, when we consult other sources preserved in the Bon collection and look at the origin of the name of Kong tse, it is more plausible to say that the label of "Kong tse" originally referred to the Chinese sage Confucius, as Lin also suggests in her conclusion.[17]

Kong Tse in the Early Bon Sources

There are two early biographical sources of the founder of Bon, the 11th-century *mDo 'dus* and the *gZer mig*, probably sometime later. In these sources, Kong tse (here with epithet *'phrul rgyal*) is recorded on many occasions and is depicted as a king and Chinese by birth, who later became a patron as well as follower of Shenrab.[18] His most important contribution, according to these sources, is building a castle in the middle of the sea, which became a holy object of veneration for Bonpos. The story of Kong tse began with his previous life in the *mDo 'dus* (chapter xi). A king named Sai Nyingpo (*sa'i snying po*, essence of earth) in the south of Jambudvīpa had three princes. The youngest of them was called Salchog (*gsal mchog*, supreme radiance) as he was a noble, kind hearted and virtuous man. Because of these qualities, the youngest prince was reborn as Kong tse in the next life. Kong tse was born in the palace Khri sgo rtse brgya (ten thousands doors with hundred peaks) in the city 'Phrul bsgyur bkod pa on the island rGyal lag 'od ma, located to the west of 'Ol mo gling. His father was Ka 'da ma gser 'od and his mother was Mu tri gsas 'od ma. In the sea called Mu khyud bdal pa, he built a castle, dKar nag bkra gsal (black white vividly clear castle).[19] The first half of the castle was built with the help of a *nāga* and a demon, and the second half was completed with An tse (Keng tse in the *gZer mig*), a god who descended from the land of Phya. According to the *mDo 'dus*, the *nāga* and the demon were the other two princes of King Sai Nyingpo, thus they were two brothers of Kong tse in his past life. They committed crimes (one chopped off his father's head, the other sliced off his mother's breasts), which were inexcusable.[20] Despite this, by the power of their prayer to help the youngest one (i.e. Kong tse), they were able to be born in their next life as a black *nāga* and a demonic spirit.

For further details in this regard, I should like to consult the *gZer mig*, in which the reason for building the castle is explained at length; the *mDo 'dus* also presents a brief account. Kong tse was born with many special qualities and features all over his body. In particular, both his palms were filled with thirty magic letters called *kong rtse* (*gab tse* in another edition of *gZer mig*), therefore he was named Kong tse 'phrul gyi rgyal po.[21] At the age of nine, he prayed to the four primary *sugatas* to fulfill his wishes: to marry the daughter of *gnyan*, dKar mo 'od ma gsal; to have three sons and two daughters; to earn five hundreds sacks of rice from his fields as the fortune of foods; and to obtain thousands of livestock when he reached his age of twenty-five. All his wishes were fulfilled at the age of twenty-five by the effect of that prayer. Thus he became the luckiest man. Yet his mother covetously asked him to pray for more wealth, animals, beautiful wives and hundreds of children. Kong tse replied to his mother, saying that all those are illusionary properties and cause only *samsaric* suffering and have no meaning for the next life. Instead, he must do something unusual which can give pleasure not only in this life, but also be useful for the life after death. He therefore promised his mother that he would build a huge and extraordinary castle for worship and veneration in the middle of the sea. Since the task was abnormal, he had to summon inhuman forces to carry out that work by using magic power.

Kong tse managed to summon demonic forces to build the castle, but he was bound to keep this activity secret from his family as a contract agreement. The demonic forces manifested one hundred figures looking identical to Kong tse and carried out the construction work. Nevertheless, Kong tse could not keep the project secret from his parents, as he worried for his aged parents' anxiety and even feared of their death by his long absence. Indeed, his long absence from the palace, in order to carry out the construction work, eventually made his wife and children anxious. This circumstance forced Kong tse's mother to reveal the secret regarding the whereabouts of Kong tse to his wife. When the wife and children showed up unexpectedly at the construction site, all the demonic forces ran away and blamed Kong tse for breaking his promise. The construction project was stopped only half finished.

By this interference, Kong tse became very disappointed and decided to leave and to wander his entire kingdom without a specific destination. At the end of his journey, he met a little boy name Phya Keng tse (An tse in the *mDo 'dus*) who came down from the land of mGon btsun phya,[22] and he requested the boy to be his instructor to rebuild the unfinished castle. The boy thereupon helped Kong tse to complete the task together with the help of gods, *nāga*s, demi-gods, a son of gods and a son of *nāgas*.[23]

To build the castle dKar nag bkra gsal and to sponsor its opening ceremony are the most popular activities of Kong tse described in the biographical sources. The meeting of Kong tse and the little boy who helped to complete the unfinished castle is particularly interesting in regard to a link between Kongzi in China and Kong tse in Tibet. This story of the meeting, which is given with lengthy detail in the *gZer mig*, is very much similar to the pattern of the story in the dialogue between Confucius and the boy Xiang Tou preserved in Dunhuang documents.[24] As Karmay believes, the story in the *gZer mig* was adapted from Dunhuang documents. However, in the whole process before finishing the castle's construction, Shenrab Miwo is mentioned nowhere in the biographical sources. Shenrab was invited only after the construction to carry out the inauguration and consecration ritual of the castle. The meeting of Kong tse and the Bon founder could not have been possible if not for the consecration ritual. It is clear that the story of the construction and the consecration ritual became a significant thread to connect the two figures.

Apart from Kong tse becoming the sponsor of all activities for the construction of the castle, he was also depicted as a follower or a disciple of the founder Shenrab. According to the *mDo 'dus*, he requested Shenrab to teach him five great miracles (*cho phrul*), which are the supreme methods to pacify evil and to help others.[25] In exchange, he offered his royal authority (*rgyal srid*) and also his daughter, the princess 'Phrul bsgyur, to be Shenrab's wife. Kong tse became a father-in-law of Shenrab. The union of Kong tse's daughter 'Phrul bsgyur and Shenrab produced a son named 'Phrul bu chungs, who studied astro-science (*gtsug lag rtsis*) with his father Shenrab and became expert at this science.[26]

Although this family relationship of Kong tse and Shenrab is unlikely to be a historical fact, it opens up a possibility for a Bonpo author to weave the following story. It has become significant in the development of Bon, because it not only helps to understand the history of Bon literature, but also reveals a fact of religious interpretation, which has been largely based on those writings. Through the relation of Kong tse and Shenrab, the Chinese master Kongzi was imported into Bon history, and has expanded the territory of Bon teaching by authenticating astro-science and divination. In other words, Bonpo claims through this story that astro-science, which has been attributed to Kong tse in a number of Tibetan Buddhist and Bon sources, originated from Bon.

Kong Tse in Funerary and Ritual Offering Texts

Several ritual texts also contain similar depictions of Kong tse as a king, patron, follower and father-in-law of Shenrab, as discussed above. They are mainly composed for ritual purposes although the texts are strongly related to the biographical sources. One of them, a ritual text known as *Klong rgyas*,[27] is considered to be excerpted from the *gZer mig*, chapter xiv. This ritual has been actively performed by Bonpos from at least the early 12th century. It is confirmed by the commentary of the ritual written by Me ston Shes rab 'od zer (1058–1132).[28] However, the function of this ritual has been not only for offerings made to Buddhas and to accumulate good merit for oneself, it has also been performed as a funerary ritual; we know this from Me ston's biography composed by gShen ston Nam mkha' rgyal mtshan (1088–1163).[29]

This ritual text consists of eighteen acts (*phrin las bco brgyad*), which I shall summarize in the following. The first few acts deal with the preparation of altars and the drawing of mandala, an imaginative abode of the *sugata*. Then the *sugata* are to be invited and other activities, such as prostration, reading praises, offering, confession, prayer, dedication, receiving blessing and initiation, are performed. To end the ritual, the invited guests are to be escorted out and the entire creations of altars including *mandala* are to be demolished as a sign of dissolving into their natural state.

This sort of ritual system can be found in other Bon rituals, and also in Tibetan Buddhist rituals. There is no doubt that this ritual system has been influenced by developed Buddhist ritual systems. In the *gZer mig*, the chapter dealing with this ritual is placed immediately after the section regarding the building of the castle. According to that chapter in the *gZer mig*, this ritual was performed at the behest of Kong tse on an auspicious day after the successful completion of the castle construction. One purpose of the ritual is to earn merit for the life after death, as understood by later Bonpo followers. Because the ritual concerns, among other things, life after death, this may have led to its adoption as part of funeral rites.

As for Kong tse, his name is mentioned several times in the ritual text as the principal patron (*yon bdag*) of the ceremony. Furthermore, he is even designated on one occasion as the head of the world of men, and listed next to the other two: Indra, the king of gods (brGya byin) (*śakra*); and 'Jog po, the king of *nāgas*. As can be understood from this list, Kong tse is placed among the three world rulers (rulers of the god world, of humans and of *nāgas*). The relevant chapter in the *gZer mig* further adds that Kong tse achieved liberation after he received initiation from the priest who performs the *Klong rgyas* ritual.[30]

Another collection of texts related to the above theme is the *rNam rgyal sgrub pa* (Bonpo Katen, vol. 104), which is said to be a discovery of Go lde 'phags pa (b. 1215).[31] This concerns a ritual offering and worship of ten primary victorious deities (*rnam rgyal*).[32] Although Kong tse is mentioned only in a few pages (236–38), these references are crucial because they change the depiction of Kong tse from the above sources. In this text, he is portrayed as a *gshen* deity (*gshen gsas*) surrounded by a retinue of the enlightened beings and those to be enlightened. He is also described as a resident of the pure land of merit and an object of veneration to accumulate merit. These depictions place him as a primary god or deity of worship, because even the enlightened beings surrounded him as his followers. On another occasion, he is worshiped as a protector as well as a *bodhisattva*. There is also a passage that briefly refers to the meeting of Kong tse and Phya Keng tse, discussed above. Nevertheless, the passage regarding Kong tse's wandering and his meeting with Keng tse of Phya, which mentions the four wrathful deities (the nine-headed *zo bo,* the nine-headed *gze ma,* the ninth class *ru co* and the nine-pronged *rom po*) in connection with Kong tse, confirms that the text was partly derived from the *Klong rgyas* and the *gZer mig*.[33]

We have seen so far from the presented sources that Kong tse was first depicted as a king, a wealthy patron, a follower and the father-in-law of Shenrab Miwo. He was said to have achieved enlightenment after he received initiation from gTo bu 'bum sangs and he was even presented as a *bodhisattva* and a deity followed by Buddhas and *bodhisattvas*. These views possibly have influenced the depiction of Kong tse as a god or a deity for worship in later Bonpo *gto* ritual texts. However, none of the above texts presents Kong tse as the initiator of Chinese astrology in Tibet and author of *gto* rituals.[34] The particular details of the astrology will not be discussed. Part of that subject, though, may frequently be referenced in relation to the *gto* rituals, which will be the focus of the following discussion.

Kong Tse in *gto* Ritual Texts

In the collection of the *Nye lam sde bzhi* (Bonpo Katen, vol. 253), seven texts (texts fourteen to twenty) also shed light on the role of Kong tse. This collection may possibly be dated from the late 12th to 13th century, as it is said to be a discovery of Khyung rgod rtsal (b. 1175). The collection consists of healing rituals that deal with local spirits, animals and natural environments, and the first two texts in the collection are even attributed to Kong tse. The first text concerns a healing rite to cure illness by applying eight kinds of medicinal plants and trees (*shing ris*). The plants and trees are described as possessed by eight living spirits, such as gods, *gnyan*,[35] *nāga*, *sa bdag* (local landowner deities), *gtod*,[36] *gza'* (planets), stars and *btsan* spirits for their pleasure. These plants are used to heal any illness caused by these eight spirits. Although Kong tse is mentioned only in the colophon as the author of this text, this may be taken together with the above-mentioned biographical works as an indication that he was involved in a healing ritual.

The second text in the collection concerns the cures for an illness caused by a turtle (*rus sbal*), and belongs to the *nāga* group. This text is also attributed to Kong tse. In this text, Kong tse 'phrul rgyal is placed in a very important position; he is said to have been blessed by the compassion of Shenlha Ökar (gShen lha 'od dkar, the *gshen* deity of white light), who is one of the four supreme *sugata*s given in *Klong rgyas* ritual. To be blessed by compassion could also be interpreted as receiving initiation or teaching, thus this statement seems to indicate that Kong tse is a student of Shenlha Ökar, who is also considered by Bonpos as the teacher of their founder, Shenrab Miwo. Moreover, Kong tse, Shenlha Ökar and *nāgas* were given offerings of desirable wealth, food (such as three white dairy products), three sweets (food products), milk, soup, butter and medicines, and supplicated in order to get relief from the illness caused by a turtle.

The third text is about a healing rite of the bird king Garuda to cure an illness caused by *nāga* and *gnyan* spirits, in which Kong tse is listed among *bodhisattvas* to whom homage should be paid as part of that ritual. Although his name does not appear frequently in this ritual text, Kong tse's function is maintained similar to that of the *Klong rgyas* and the *rNam par rgyal ba* rituals.

The fourth text in which Kong tse's name appears is titled *Ba yi nad sel*, a sacrifice ritual of a white cow to cure illness. His name is clearly written as rGya Kong tse 'phrul gyi rgyal po, which explicitly confirms him as belong to rGya, China. According to the text, Kong tse is the narrator and the priest of this particular ritual. He is also mentioned in connection to a divine Bonpo (*lha bon*) named Yongs su dag pa, who is listed in many Bonpo texts as one among the three divine figures of Bon.[37] Besides the above references, Kong tse is depicted as a universal king (*'khor lo bsgyur ba*) of three thousands worlds, and a patron (*yon bdag*) of a ritual in the fifth text, and he is worshiped as a deity in order to remove obstacles caused by four groups of spirits (*gnyan*, *nāga*, *sa bdag* and *gtod*) in the other two texts. In the last text, it is also stated that Kong tse's command shall not be disobeyed. It clearly indicates that his power is comparable to that of a powerful deity and the *sugata*, whose words are generally considered as undeniable in ritual procedure.

Similarly, there are two small texts (texts twenty-one and twenty-two) in another collection titled *sTong gsum 'khrug pa yo bcos*.[38] In the first text, Kong tse is again worshipped as a deity in order to settle the conflicts between gods and *nāgas*; he also performs a purification rite with water, thus indicating that in the second text he may be a priest.

Kong Tse in the Collected Liturgies of *gto* Ritual

In regard to Kong tse's involvement in *gto* ritual, the largest Bonpo work I have found so far is the collected liturgies of these *gto* rituals (*gto phyogs bsdus*, Bonpo Katen vol. 157). The collection consists of seventy-nine different works containing various *gto* rituals, and Kong tse is mentioned in twenty-seven texts (texts twenty-three to forty-nine), including those attributed to him as the author and those explicitly depicting Kong tse as a spirit mediator or priest of exorcisms and ransom rituals. The accurate date of these texts is unknown because, apart from attribution to Kong tse, other works are also attributed to gTo bu 'bum sangs (said to be the eldest son of Shenrab), lHa bdag sngags grol (one of six foremost translators of Bon; according to *mDo 'dus*, he was originally from India) and gShen gSang ba 'dus pa (a master of Bonpo tantric transmission).[39] Since no dates exist for these Bonpo masters, the available colophons do not shed light on dating these works. However, estimating from one of the texts in the collection, which was discovered by sPrul sku dbyil ston (also known as dPon gsas khyung rgod rtsal, b. 1175), the collection (or at least part of it) possibly existed from the late 12th to 13th century. This is merely a generalization and will be left for further study. Moreover, some texts in the collection are also related to Shenrab's biographical sources, as they contain a passage describing Kong tse as a king and the building of the magnificent castle. This also indicates that the collection may have been influenced by those biographical sources dating from the 11th century.

Many texts in the collection deal with exorcism, that is, the expelling of evil forces or harmful influences with the help of powerful demonic forces. For instance, text 23 (also text twenty-four), attributed to Kong tse, is a ritual to invoke a demonic force, a black man with a dog's head (*khyi nag lcags mgo*), to defeat evil spirits and harmful attacks from enemies. In this ritual, Kong tse 'phrul rgyal, also called *gto mkhan 'phrul rgyal* (the priest / performer of *gto* ritual), communicates with the black man with a dog's head. This man was said to be born from a black iron egg that emerged out of a stirring of the five elements (space, wind, fire, water, earth) at the beginning of the universe. This story seems to have derived from the myth of the cosmic egg, the origin of all living beings according to Bon cosmogony.[40] Kong tse summons the black man and pleases him with various wish-fulfilling offerings (*'dod pa'i yas*); he then commands the man to destroy the power of the enemy and all harmful obstacles. This text shows a very different character of Kong tse compared to the above-mentioned sources. According to many Bonpo ritual texts, this kind of work can be carried out only by transforming oneself into a powerful deity. Therefore, one can clearly see that Kong tse is depicted here as a powerful priest, which may have consequently resulted in his presentation as a powerful deity among later Bonpo ritual authors.

In terms of the obstacles to be exorcized, the collection also contains a text related to divination and astrological content, such as *ba gua* (eight trigrams, spelled in Tibetan as *par kha*), which originated from the Chinese *Yijing* (*I-ching*). In particular, this text (text twenty-five) is also known as the great thread-cross ritual of existence (*srid pa'i mdos chen*), which dispels obstacles and misfortunes caused by the eight trigrams,[41] the seventh edge (*bdun zur*),[42] obstacles regarding the animals of one's birth year,[43] the month, the day, the week and the hour of one's birth. It also contains a cosmological account of the origin of the outer existences from the five elements, such as the wishful-filling tree, seven mountains and seven oceans, and eight continents. In regard to the origin of living beings, first there originated a god, a demon and a human being, and thereafter *khen* (the sky) and *khon* (the earth). From the meeting of *khen* the father and *khon* the mother, a yellow turtle arose. This yellow turtle gave birth to the eight trigrams, and from the latter arose the sixty-year cycle. This process came together to form an existence that never existed before (Tib. *ma srid srid pa*), and which caused the origin of obstacles. This ritual, also mentioned in the title, is believed to have been performed by Kong tse, and he received the instructions from gTo bu 'bum sangs in the castle dKar nag bkra gsal. As can be seen, the source relates not only to the *gto* ritual expert gTo bu 'bum sangs (eldest son of Shenrab, who compiled the *gto* rituals performed by his father Shenrab after his death), but also to the castle that Kong tse built, according to the biographical sources.[44]

Kong Tse and *gto nag* Ritual

Apart from Kong tse's involvement in the *gto* ritual discussed above, he is also mentioned as a crucial figure in another *gto* ritual of a black man with three animal heads (*gto nag po mgo gsum*). This ritual, sometimes known as the black *gto* ritual (*gto nag*), is mainly performed in the lay community.[45] According to text twenty-six, the three-headed black man is regarded as the lord of death (*gshin rje*) and his three heads are as follows: on the right a tiger, which is the form of hatred or anger; in the middle a *glang* (ox or elephant),[46] the form of desire; and on the left a pig, the form of ignorance. This order of three heads appears in many other sources and seems to be the most common arrangement. However, other variations of the three heads exist; for instance, text thirty-three describes nine different kinds of three-headed black men.

	Right	Middle	Left
1	mottled tiger	yellow ox	black pig
2	pig	lion	buffalo/ox
3	bird	red pig	bird
4	pig	dragon	tiger/horse
5	pig	bear (*dred*)	tiger
6	pig	owl	black water bird
7	pig	crocodile	snake
8	pig	deer	yak
9	pig	*garuda* (bird king)	*mamo* (?)

In the same collection as above (the collected liturgies of *gto* rituals), many other texts also contain a ritual of *gto nag*, such as texts twenty-seven to twenty-nine, thirty-three, thirty-five, thirty-seven, thirty-nine, and forty-seven to forty-nine. Texts twenty-seven and twenty-eight contain a conversation between a king of tantric practitioners (*sngags 'chang rgyal po*) and Kong tse regarding the three-headed black man. In these texts, Kong tse is addressed with many epithets, such as the priest of *gto* ritual (*gto mkhan*), the king of *gto* (*gto rgyal*), the primordial omniscient (*ye mkhyen*), the omniscient (*kun mkhyen*), a god (*lha*) and a king (*rgyal po*). Similarly, in text thirty-two, Kong tse is depicted as a god (*lha*) and a ritual priest (*gto mkhan*). These sorts of depictions are also found in manuscripts that recently became available for study from Gansu province.[47]

I should like to elaborate further by discussing the origin of the three-headed man according to the above ritual texts. It is interesting and worth mentioning here because Kong tse is also involved in this process. The origin of the three-headed man is given in two different sources from the same collection, which I shall paraphrase.

First, according to the historical part of text twenty-nine, when the world was empty, three living beings (god, human, demon) were born together due to their collective karmic power. Because of their different behaviors, they were involved in different activities: the god became savior, the human became creator of the world and base of existence, and the demon became destroyer. There occurred 360 various kinds of obstacles in the human world, which caused humans to suffer. The god sNang ba 'od ldan understood that painful situation and manifested as the king of *gto* ritual, the primordial omniscient (gTo rgyal ye mkhyen). He left a drop of saliva and prayed for the origin of the elements to begin on this base of existence. By the power of that prayer, there arose an ocean with outer and inner existence. The ocean was churned and there emerged a big turtle in gold from the essence of that churned ocean. Thereupon, the elements, eight trigrams (*ba gua*), *sme ba* (nine numbers), year (twelve animals), stars and land-owners were originated respectively from that turtle, and thus began existing as the base of the science of elements. A child with dark skin having three animal heads was born from the meeting of *khen* and *khon*, the first two of the eight trigrams. The child was so powerful that no one could challenge him. The king of the Phya, Ye mkhyen, managed to bind him under oath and appointed him to be the lord of obstacle-removal and *byo zor* (an enchanted weapon hurled towards the enemy). When the son of elements (this black man) was conquering people, Kong tse from China demonstrated astrology (*gtsug lag*) in his palm and exorcized the obstacles.

However, text twenty-nine does not give details on why it was necessary for Phya Ye mkhyen to subdue this child of dark skin. In this regard, I should relate a story from the second text (text thirty-five), which adds interesting points. The text contains a longer story, but I shall only relate here the essential part.

As the child was found to be a sinful and embodied form of three poisons (hatred, ignorance and desire), his parents put him in a black pan and threw him towards the main crossroads. He killed and ate up all the people he encountered on his way. When gTo rgyal Ye mkhen (king of ritual, the primordial omniscient) saw such a demonic act by the three-headed black man, he manifested as the son of Phya bar srid pa (cf. Phyi rab srid pa), summoned Phya Ye mkhyen 'phrul gyi rgyal po and departed to subdue that three-headed black man. This Phya Ye mkhyen 'phrul gyi rgyal po and the son of Phyi rab srid pa are identified as different forms of Kong tse in other texts.

In the ritual part of text twenty-nine, Kong tse is regarded as the main deity to be visualized. In the visualization, one is to imagine oneself as Kong tse 'phrul gyi rgyal po having white as his body color — like a snow mountain — with one face and two hands. In his right hand he holds a *mda' dar* that belongs to *skos*,[48] and in the palm of the left hand, rotating self-emerged letters of the sky, the earth and *gab tse*. On his head he wears a turban the length of an arrow,[49] and on his body a brocade (*za 'og*) cloak with a decoration of the sun and moon. Such a magnificent body must be visualized while sitting crossed-legged on a throne decorated with gold and turquoise and covered with a mattress made from brocade. A similar description of Kong tse as a visualized deity is also found in text thirty-four.[50]

In addition, Kong tse's position as a deity for worship is represented by ritual cakes. In Tibetan ritual, one can find that the ritual deities are sometime represented by cakes of various sizes and shapes, which are placed on the main altar. Likewise, according to ritual text thirty-four, a cake (*bshos bu*) with five peaks and square in shape is made to represent Kong tse. The four sides of the cake are surrounded by the effigies of four animals, yak, sheep, goat and chicken (or bird). The cake is placed on top of a four-level altar and the offerings are prepared: *bshos gsang* (clean cake), the first pouring of wine (*chang phud*), clean meat and various grains. The offerings to Kong tse also contain the effigy of a yak and sheep made from white rice flour, clean cake, the first pouring of wine, gold, turquoise and other precious treasure.

These pieces of evidence demonstrate that Kong tse was depicted as highly as other Bonpo deities such as *dbal gsas*, *gtso mchog*, *stag la* and *ge khod*,[51] and was worshipped as a primary deity. There is also a reference in text thirty-four to building the castle dKar nag bkra gsal on lake Mu khyud bdal pa, and Kong tse's summoning of the chief demon to carry out the labor for the construction. This part of the story confirms its relation to the biographical sources. However, the role of Kong tse according to these texts is much more developed than that given in the hagiographies and the other related sources.

Furthermore, in text thirty-six, a passage briefly reports the origin of *gto* ritual. According to the passage, the *gto* ritual is indicated to have originated from the east where the Chinese king was in power, and which belonged to Kong tse. This passage connects Kong tse to China.

Kong Tse and His Different Forms

In connection with the different epithets of Kong tse discussed above, he is also depicted as having many different forms in some of the ritual texts. This may be comparable to other Bonpo deities found in Bonpo rituals texts, who have many different forms. Kong tse's depiction, similar to those deities, could possibly mean that he was worshipped either as a very important figure equivalent to those deities or as the principal deity of the *gto nag* ritual. I shall specify the relevant texts in the following.

In text thirty-three, Kong tse invoked the black man with three heads and ordered him to destroy the magic weapons of (spiritual) enemies. In order to frighten the black man and to make him listen to his order, Kong tse pronounced his different forms. He pronounced himself as a manifestation of the son of Phyi rab srid pa (cf. Phya bar srid pa, above), the supreme wrathful deity, the lord of the universe and the king of blood drinkers (*khrag 'thung*). Similarly, in text thirty-four, he is presented as the son of gTsug lag srid pa, the king of Phya Ye mkhyen (the primordial omniscient), the son of god Shenrab, the protector of all beings, and the owner of the four truths.[52] In text forty-five his different forms are Ye mkhyen sgam po, the son of the Phya king Srid pa, and he is even depicted as an all-knowing Buddha.[53]

Conclusion

As is the case in most Bonpo texts, many of the sources presented here either have no colophon or are of uncertain date. Therefore, the arrangement of the sources here is simply based on those containing approximate dates. According to this tentative arrangement, the two early biographies of the Bon founder seem to be the earliest among the Bonpo sources listed in the appendix.

In the early sources, Kong tse was known first as a king from China who built a magnificent castle in the middle of the sea; this castle became a holy object of veneration for Bonpos. To carry out that abnormal task, he had to summon demonic forces by using magic power. These early sources already describe his possession of inhuman power, which became an important quality in later sources. This construction of a castle not only made the meeting of Kong tse and the Bon founder possible, but also brought them even closer into a family relationship as a father-in-law and son-in-law and disciple and teacher. Through an invitation to Shenrab to perform the consecration ritual of the castle, Kong tse was able to meet the Bon founder, and that story became a significant thread to connect these two figures. Apart from sponsoring the construction of the castle, he also became a follower and a disciple of Shenrab, as he learnt five great miracles from him. Kong tse's offering of his daughter to Shenrab in exchange for the teaching made him a father-in-law of Shenrab. Furthermore, this relation also indicates an association of the teaching attributed to Kong tse with Bon teaching. Particularly, the importing of the Chinese master could possibly expand the territory of Bon literature by authenticating astro-science and divination as part of Bon property.

Astro-science and divination have been attributed to Kong tse in many Bon sources as well as in many Tibetan Buddhist sources. The claim clarifies how early Bonpo authors were active to adopt important figures like Confucius in their literatures and to relate them to their founder. This may be taken as a traditional method to strengthen their hold on the religious territory and, particularly for Bon, to be recognized as a source of other tradition. On the contrary, these resulted in a larger confusion on the reliability of those stories in the sources. Although those stories may not be taken as historical fact, it is important to study carefully to understand the historiography of Bon literature, and to reveal a fact behind the religious interpretation that has been largely based upon those writings.

In several ritual texts, Kong tse was designated as the head of the world of men and listed next to the king of gods and the king of *nāgas*, which suggests that he is one of the rulers of the spiritual world. The depiction of Kong tse as a deity surrounded by the Buddha and *bodhisattvas* and a resident of the pure land makes him even higher as a supreme god, and an object of veneration to accumulate merit, like the Bonpo adherent still do with their supreme Buddhas. This can be also seen in other sources regarding the Bonpo *gto* ritual texts, in which he was placed next to a Bonpo deity, Shenlha Ökar, and propitiated and supplicated in order to get relief from illness. These texts present Kong tse as an author or a priest of ritual to expel evil forces or harmful influences with the help of powerful demonic forces, which suggest that Kong tse was a powerful priest. Similarly, the ritual texts regarding the three-headed black man (*gto nag po mgo gsum*) is also particularly interesting, because this combines the *gto* ritual with astro-science and divination, for which he is well known in Tibetan astrology.

Like many other Bonpo deities, Kong tse has many epithets in those texts, and is regarded as the main deity to be visualized. This demonstrates that Kong tse's position in Bon sources has been as highly esteemed as other Bonpo deities. Kong tse's achieving enlightenment in the early biography has possibly influenced his role as a heavenly figure in later Bonpo sources. Such a role is also reflected in the sources dealing with exorcism, which also include astrological content.

As seen from the above sources, the role of Kong tse in the Bon sources is not limited to the *gto* ritual or the Chinese king who built an extraordinary Bon castle, but can be compared to the role of Shenrab, the Bon founder. In two areas, however, Kong tse falls short of Shenrab: no philosophical teaching has been attributed to Kong tse, and Bonpos never wrote a detailed biography of him, as they did for Shenrab. Although the image of Kong tse in Tibetan sources may not be historic, its influence over Tibetan culture, society and history is evident, and this research illustrates a distinct character of Confucius known by Tibetan people. Such research in the future needs further connection with the study of classical Confucianism interpreted in other Asian countries.

Appendix

Bonpo sources[54]

1. *mDo 'dus pa rin po che'i rgyud thams cad mkhyen pa'i bka' tshad ma* (abbr. title *mDo 'dus*). Translated by sNya li shu stag ring; relevant chapters: vi, xi, xxi.[55]
2. *Dus gsum gshen rab kyi byung khungs dang mdzad pa'i rgyud 'dus pa rin po che gzer mig gi mdo* (abbr. title *gZer mig*). Excavated by Drang rje btsun pa gSer mig (ca 12th century). Relevant chapters: xiii, xiv.
3. *'Dus pa rin po che'i rgyud dri ma med pa gzi brjid rab tu 'bar ba'i mdo* (abbr. title *gZi brjid*), Blo ldan snying po (b. 1360). Relevant chapter: 50, vol. Da, pp. 182–392.
4. *gShen rab kyis phrin las bco brgyad kyi don bstan pa'i mdo g.yung drung klong rgyas cho ga*, (abbr. title *Klong rgyas,* datable to 11th–12th century), Bonpo Katen vol. 265/10, pp. 125–353 (actual text pp. 269–316).
5. *'Khor ba dong sprug skye sgo gcod pa* (this manuscript is kept in the library of Bonpo temple in Jomsom, Nepal), 48 fols.
6. *rNam rgyal stong mchod sogs kyi lag len dwangs shel me long,* Nyi ma bstan 'dzin (b. 1813), pp. 1–85 (see only historical part from pp. 3–10).[56]
7. Prayer by *rgya kong rtse*, Drung mu nyi wer (uncle of Nyi ma bstan 'dzin), pp. 120–21.
8. *gShen rab rnam par rgyal ba'i mngon rtogs 'dod 'byung nor bu'i 'phreng ba,* rNam dag 'od zer (19th century), pp. 189–219.
9. *gShen rab rnam par rgyal ba'i mchod gzhung nges pa'i thig le,* discovered by Go lde 'phags pa (b. 1215), pp. 231–425.
10. *rNam par rgyal ba'i mchod bskangs*, by Kong tse 'phrul rgyal, discovered by Go lde 'phags pa (b. 1215), pp. 427–47. [Another version under the title *gShen rab rnam par rgyal ba'i mchod skong chen mo,* published in Bonpo Katen, vol. 88: 32].
11. *Dam chu (glud mdos cha lag),* Nyi ri shel zhin (Nyi ma bstan 'dzin, b. 1813), pp. 557–61.
12. *'Dod 'gyur cha lag gyi rjes bya*, no author, pp. 563–66.
13. *gShen rab rnam par rgyal ba'i dbang khrid dang rjes gnang lung gi rim pa dgos 'dod kun 'byung yid bzhin nor bu,* rNam dag 'od zer (19th century), pp. 637–71.
14. *Shing ris nad sel bzhugs pa'i dbu yi khangs pa bde zhing yang pa,* Kong tse, pp. 447–55.[57]

15. *Da ni sbal pa'i nad sel gyi dbus phyogs bzhugs pa (rus sbal nad sel)*, Kong tse 'phrul gyi rgyal po, pp. 923–34.
16. *Ye shes khyung gi nad sel bzhugs pa'i dbus phyogs,* gShen rab, pp. 957 –69.
17. *Ba yi nad sel*, no author, pp. 971–84.
18. (*bKra shis*), no author, pp. 1011–13.
19. *Nye lam sde bzhi'i klu gnyan sa bdag gtod gzhi'i dal bkyag bzhugs pa'i dbus phyogs*, no author, pp. 1021–36.
20. *Nye lam sde bzhi'i spar khams lo bdud bkar ba*, no author, pp. 1057–67.
21. *Yo bcos kyi bca' thab* (Preparatory guide book for *lha klu'i 'khrugs pa yo bcos*), no author, pp. 7–10.[58]
22. *Kong tse'i bsang khrus,* Kong tse, pp. 31–34.
23. *sGra bzlog khyi nag lcags mgo'i mdos gtor cho ga,* Kong tse 'phrul rgyal, pp. 51–62.[59]
24. *Kong tse'i gto bsgyur mi kha [dgra] bzlog bsgyur,* Kong tse, pp. 63–91.
25. *Kong tse pas keg bsgyur,* gTo bu 'bum sangs, pp. 117–35.
26. *Bon lug mgo gsrum gyi bskyed chog gsal ba'i me long,* Kong tse 'phrul gyi rgyal po, pp. 331–41.
27. *sNgags 'chang bdag gi kong tse 'phrul rgyal*, no author, pp. 343–50.
28. *mGo 3 (gsum) zhu 'bul lan 2 (gnyis)*, no author, pp. 351–61.
29. *mGo gsum mtshan ma'i dgra zor*, no author, pp. 363–76.
30. *sPyan 'dren gyi le'u*, no author, pp. 377–96.
31. *dKar po lha gsum bzhugs pa'i dbus phyog*, no author, pp. 397–418.
32. *Khye'u gsang ba*, no author, pp. 419–23.
33. *mGo gsum khro bo dgu skor bzhugs pa'i dbus phyog*, no author, pp. 425–52.
34. *Kong tse gsang ba,* Kong tse, pp. 453–61.
35. *gTo nag po sgyur gto dang cho 'brang*, no author, pp. 463–78.
36. *Mi dmar mgo gsum bzhugs pa'i dbus*, no author, pp. 485–98.
37. *Bar gyi rus 'dren*, no author, pp. 521–28.
38. *Drug bcu lo'i bsgyur gto*, no author, pp. 529–42.
39. *sPyan 'dren gsang ba*, no author, pp. 543–54.
40. *gZa' dang rgyun skar lo zla dus tshod sa bdag gi bsgyur gto,* no author, pp. 555–636.
41. *Bar mi 'kha'i gto,* no author, pp. 661–66.
42. *Bar kha'i bsgyur gto bzhugs pa'i dbus phyogs*, no author, pp. 667–79.
43. *Bu pa gsang ba*, no author, pp. 695–97.
44. *gTo skor gsang ba yod*, no author, pp. 721–24.
45. *gSer skyem dang sgo dbye*, no author, pp. 729–40.

46. *gNyan chen bzhi yi srung bzhi*, no author, pp. 741–46.
47. *mGo 3 (gsum) lam bstan,* no author, pp. 747–56.
48. *mGo 3 (gsum) gto nag gi bhyo bsgyur dang dgra zor,* no author, pp. 769–87.
49. *mGo gsum gyi smon rdzong*, no author, pp. 813–18.
50. *Man ngag gto sgro dkar nag khra gsum rin chen kun 'dus,* Kong tse 'phrul rgyal. In *Khro bo'i dbang byangs*, Bonpo Katen volume 230, pp. 967–1011.
51. *Dag pa gser gyi mdo thig mdo sde pad ma spungs pa* (In *gZungs 'dus* Vol. II), no author, pp. 169–72.[60]
52. *Kong tse 'phrul gyi rgyal po'i[pos] mdzad pa'i rgya nag keg zlog* (In *gZungs 'dus Vol. II*), Kong tse 'phrul gyi rgyal po, pp. 439–48.
53. *Dag pa gser gyi mdo thig* (In *mDo mang* Vol. II), Kong tse, pp. 413–66.
54. *Kong tse 'phrul rgyal gyis mdzad pa'i rgya nag kag bzlog gi gzungs* (In *mDo mang* Vol. II), Kong tse 'phrul rgyal, pp. 467–75.
55. *dGu mig gi lto,* Tshe dbang 'byor rgyas, 6 fols.[61]
56. *sKong rtse 'phrul rgyal gyis mdzad pa'i sri gnan gyi cho ga,* sKong rtse 'phrul rgyal, 10 fols.
57. *Gong tse gdon skyur dbu*, 9 fols.[62]
58. *Gong rtse gto' mkhan dbu*, 4 fols.
59. *'Phrugs pa lo bcos dbu*, 13 fols.
60. *Phyi'i pa kha rgyad kyis 'bru sna dbu*, 4 fols.
61. *Pham 'ang*, 7 fols.
62. *Gong rtse dbus lags so*, 6 fols.

Notes

1 Thomas A. Wilson ed., *On Sacred Grounds: Culture, Society, Politics, and the Formation of the Cult of Confucius* (Cambridge: Harvard University Asia Center, 2002).

2 *mDo 'dus pa rin po che'i rgyud thams cad mkhyen pa'i bka' tshad ma*, Bonpo bKa' 'gyur vol. 30 (third edition, Chengdu: Mongyal Lhasey Rinpoche and Shense Namkha Wangden, 1995–1999). For date of the source, see my forthcoming paper, "History and Antiquity of the *mDo 'dus* in Relation to *mDo chen po bzhi*." In *Proceedings of the Eleventh Seminar of the International Association for Tibetan Studies, Königswinter 2006* (Halle: International Institute for Tibetan and Buddhist Studies).

3 Namkhai Norbu, *Drung, Deu and Bön, Narrations, Symbolic Languages and the Bön Tradition in Ancient Tibet*, tr. A. Lukianowitcz (Dharamsala: Library of Tibetan Works and Archives, 1997), 271, n. 36.

4 Shar rdza bKra shis rgyal mtshan (1859–1935), *Legs bshad rin po che'i gter mdzod* (Beijing: Mi rigs dpe skrun khang 1985), 17.

5 As "*ha shang*" or "*hwa shang*" are similar to the correct Chinese word for Buddhist monk (*he shang*), Tibetan authors used these forms to refer to monks from China. There are two main references found in Tibetan sources. One is for the famous Hashang Mahāyāna, who is said to have came to Tibet and led the dispute in the Samye debate; for details about this Hashang, see Penpa Dorjee, "bSam yas rtsod pa: An Analytical Study on Samye Debate" (PhD Dissertation, Varanasi: Central Institute of Higher Tibetan Studies, 2005), 175. The other Hashang is listed among a group of eight monks who attended the ordination of dGongs pa rab gsal. See *bTsan po khri srong lde btsan dang mkhan po slob dpon padma'i dus mdo sngags so sor mdzad pa'i sba bzhed zhabs btags ma* (known as *sBa bzhed zhabs btags ma*), R.A. Stein, ed., *Une chronique ancienne de bSam-yas: sBa-bzed* (Paris: Publications de L'institut des Hautes Etudes Chinoises, 1961), 83–84; Ne'u pan di ta Grags pa smon lam blo gros (late 13th century), *sNgon gyi gtam me tog phreng ba*. Rare Tibetan Historical and Literary Texts from the Library of Tsepon W. D. Shakabpa Series I (New Delhi, 1974), 123–24; and Tshal pa Kun dga' rdo rje (1309–1364), *Deb ther dmar po* (Peking: Mi rigs dpe skrun khang, 1993), 40–41.

6 Drang rje btsun pa gSer mig, revealer, *Dus gsum gshen rab kyi byung khyungs dang mdzad pa'i rgyud 'dus pa rin po che gzer mig gi mdo*, ed. Tsering Thar (Qinghai: Krung go'i bod kyi shes rig dpe skrun khang, 1991).

7 Blo ldan snying po (14th century), *'Dus pa rin po che'i rgyud dri ma med pa gzi brjid rab tu 'bar ba'i mdo* (Dolanji, 1964–1967), vol. Ja, chapter 30, p. 129. A passage can be read as follows, "*gdung rgyud rgyal po sde drug ste/ shag dang hos dang dpo' dang rgya/ gnyen dang dmu rigs 'phrul dang drug/.*"

8 *g.Yung drung bon gyi sgra bsgrags pa rin po che'i gling grags* (ca 14th century), Bonpo Katen vol. 72: 1 (Lhasa: Sog sde bstan pa'i nyi ma, 1998), 19.

9 Thu'u bkwan Blo bzang chos kyi nyi ma (1732–1802), *Grub mtha' thams cad kyi khungs dang 'dod tshul ston pa legs bshad shel gyi me long* (Gansu: Mi rigs dpe skrun khang, 1985), 394. Thu'u bkvan follows rather closely the Chinese spellings such as *khung tse* and *khung phu'u tsi*.

10 Thu'u bkwan, 395.

11 Ferdinand. D. Lessing, "Bodhisattva Confucius." In *Ritual and Symbol: Collected Essays on Lamaism and Chinese Symbolism*, ed. Professor Lou Tsu-K'uang (Taipei: The Chinese Association for Folklore, 1976), 91–94.

12 Samten G. Karmay, "The Interview between Phyva Keng-tse lan-med and Confucius." In *The Arrow and the Spindle: Studies in History, Myths, Rituals and Beliefs in Tibet* (Kathmandu: Mandala Book Point, 1998), 171, n. 6.

13 Idem, "The Soul and the Turquoise: a Ritual for Recalling the bla." In *The Arrow and the Spindle: Studies in History, Myths, Rituals and Beliefs in Tibet* (Kathmandu: Mandala Book Point, 1998), 324.

14 Idem, "An Open letter by Pho-brang Zhi-ba-'od." In *The Arrow and the Spindle: Studies in History, Myths, Rituals and Beliefs in Tibet* (Kathmandu: Mandala Book Point, 1998), 23, n. 38. For an extensive discussion on *'phrul gyi rgyal po, 'phrul gyi bu,* see Shen-yu Lin, "The Tibetan Image of Confucius," *Revue d'Etudes Tibetaines*, 12 (2007), 106 ff.

15 There are three different versions: 1. *dBa' bzhed: the Royal narrative concerning the bringing of the Buddha's doctrine to Tibet*, tr. and ed. by Pasang Wangdu and Hildegard Diemberger (Wien: Verlag der Österreichischen Akademie der Wissenschaften, 2000); 2. *sBa bzhed ces bya ba las sba gsal snang gi bzhed pa*, ed. mGon po rgyal mtshan (Beijing: Mi rigs dpe skrun khang, 1982); and 3. *sBa bzhed zhabs btags ma* (Stein 1961). The reference to Kong tse 'phrul chung appears only in the Stein version (see p. 2), whereas version two mentions Kong 'phrul in a similar episode (see p. 2). The episode is not given in *dBa' bzhed.* An interesting reference on Kong tse 'phrul chung or Kong 'phrul can be found also in a Bon source, which is associated

with Kong tse and his son 'Phrul bu chung. Like Kong 'phrul in the second version, who was from the city of ten thousand doors (*khri sgo*) called Kem shing (Gyim shang or Gyim shing in other versions) and was a master of 360 *gab tse*, Kong tse and his son 'Phrul bu chung are also associated with ten thousand doors and 360 *gab tse*.

16 Lin, 112 and 114.

17 Lin, 129.

18 In Chinese sources, Confucius is also regarded as a king without a throne and Laozi is said to have met Confucius (Wilson 2002, 223–24). Similarly, in Bon sources, Shenrab is said to have met Kong tse, and Shenrab is sometimes identified as Laozi; cf. Zeff Bjerken, "Exorcising the Illusion of Bon 'Shamans': A Critical Genealogy of Shamanism in Tibetan Religions," *Revue d'Etudes Tibétaines 6* (2004), 18; William W. Rockhill, *The Land of the Lamas: Notes of a Journey through China, Mongolia and Tibet* (New Delhi: Asian Publication Services, 1975), 217–18, n. 2; and Tsung-lien Shen, *Tibet and the Tibetans* (California: Stanford University Press, 1973), 37.

19 Black refers to the demon and white to the god, the two labor groups who helped Kong tse to build the castle.

20 *mDo 'dus,* ch. xi.

21 On a similar narrative about Confucius being born with a five-character inscription on his chest, see Wilson 2002, 173.

22 According to the *mDo 'dus,* 85, Phya An tse len med felt compassionate and came down from the city of mGon btsun phya to fulfill the virtuous will of Kong tse 'Phrul gyi rgyal po. He came down in the form of a little boy wearing a woolen cloak (*tsi ber*) and holding a conch shell rosary (a crystal rosary according to *gZer mig,* 552). He acts as a witness of disputes over constructions between gods and demons, and also declares the truth between virtue and non-virtue. The supporter of virtuous acts, gods and humans, won the debate, upon which the King Kong tse became extremely happy. For *tsi ber*, see Karmay 1998, 172, n. 10. mGon btsun phya is probably to be understood either as a deity or merely a mythical figure, as given in the Dunhuang documents: mGon tshun phywa' and mGon tshun gtings na rje' as father and son in PT 1134 and ITJ 731 (also spelled mGon chun phva and mGon phyva), mGon tsun in PT 1043 and mGon btsun ni phya in ITJ 739. However, it needs further investigation to draw a concrete conclusion.

23 According to the *mDo 'dus*, ch. xi, the temple features are as follows: "the base of the temple is very solid as it is built by demons; the middle part is glorious as it is built by the powerful god; the interior is beautiful as it is painted with magic by *nagas*; the design is wonderful as its architect is the wise Phya; the construction is successfully completed as it is carried out by a fortunate human being; and the temple is outstanding (*byin brlabs rgyas*) as it is blessed by the enlightened ones."

24 Karmay 1998, 169–89; see Michel Soymié, "L'entrevue de Confucius et de Hiang T'o," *Journal Asiatique* 242 (1954), 311–92 for different versions of the story.

25 Five great miracles according to the *mDo 'dus*, ch. xxi, are: miracle of nature (*rang bzhin*), blessing (*byin gyis brlabs pa*), magic power (*rdzu 'phrul*), miraculous display (*rjes su bstan pa*) and preserving teaching for the future (*bstan pa rjes bzhag*).

26 See *mDo 'dus,* ch. vi, xi.

27 *gShen rab kyis phrin las bco brgyad kyi don bstan pa'i mdo g.yung drung klong rgyas cho ga*, Bonpo Katen, volume 265–10, 125–353.

28 *g.Yung drung klong rgyas gsal byed kyi go don*, Bonpo Katen vol. 156–1.

29 Karmay 1998, 169.

30 *gZer mig*, 674.

31 Go lde 'phags pa is also known as dBang ldan gshen gsas lha rje or gNyos nyi ma shes rab; see Samten G. Karmay, *The Treasury of Good Sayings: A Tibetan History of Bon* (1972; reprint,

Delhi: Motilal Banarsidass, 2001), 175. His name also appeared in *Srid pa rgyud kyi kha byang chen mo*, discovered by Khod spo Blo gros thogs med (b. 1292), f. 95b/7. For his dates, see also Dan Martin, *Unearthing Bon Treasures: Life and Contested Legacy of a Tibetan Scripture revealer with a general Bibliography of Bon* (Leiden: Brill 2001), 46.

32 The ten victorious deities are: the nine-headed great wrathful Zo bo in the east, the nine-headed wrathful king gZe ma in the north, the ninth-class wrathful king Ru co in the west, the nine-pronged wrathful king Rom po in the south, the king of gods Seng gsas in the south-east, the king of men Seng gsas in the north-east, 'Brug gsas lde bo gsung chen in the north-west, 'Brug gsas gnam grags ngar chen in the south-west, Khyung gsas sangs rgyas klu bdud 'dul in the sky and gShen rab, the victorious one over obstructers on the earth.

33 These texts seem to have influenced another ritual text titled *'Khor ba dong sprug skye sgo gcod pa* which also contains few references on Kong tse.

34 On Bonpo *gto* ritual, see David L. Snellgrove, *The Nine Ways of Bon* (London: Oxford University Press, 1967), 24 ff.

35 Cf. Snellgrove, 297 in which he translates the term as "Gods of vengeance," and see Karmay 1998, 253 ff. and 443 ff. for a detailed discussion on the various meanings of this term.

36 Snellgrove, 297 translates this as "Local divinities living in rocks."

37 Karmay 1972, 15, n. 3 and 58.

38 This collection may be dated from the 13th century, as the last volume of the collection is said to be discovered by Go lde 'phags pa.

39 See Karmay 1972, xxi for a brief account of *gSang ba 'dus pa*.

40 See Norbu, 165–66.

41 The misfortune is said to occur because of the wrong combination of two trigrams: one of the current year and the other of the individual's birth year. For details about eight trigrams, see Philippe Cornu, *L'Astrologie Tibétaine* (Millau: Les Djinns, 1990), 114–18.

42 In the Tibetan lunar calendar, twelve animals are used for counting one's age and this cycle repeats in the same order every twelve years. When one's birth year (animal) happens to be seven years away in the future, counting from and including the current animal year, this encounter is called *bdun zur*; for instances, one matches with seven, two with eight, and so on. It is believed that the individual will face misfortune that year.

43 Such an obstacle is believed to return every twelve years with the animal of one's birth-year. Therefore, at the ages of thirteen, twenty-five and so on, everybody is advised to take extra precautions according to Tibetan astrology.

44 See texts thirty to thirty-one, thirty-eight, forty to forty-two and forty-six in the collection regarding similar ritual contexts.

45 I have witnessed this ritual carried out in a Bonpo village in Nepal, and to my surprise this remains a rituals that is still conducted in the old fashion.

46 The term *glang* refers to two animals: in text thirty-five (466), he is described as having a long fleshy nose (*sha sna ring*), thus this *glang* must be referring to an elephant; in text thirty-three (430), he is attached to the family of buffalo (*ma he*), thus this seems to refer to ox or bull.

47 In texts fifty-seven, fifty-nine, sixty and sixty-two, Kong tse is worshiped as divine (*lha*), while in text fifty-seven, fifty-eight and sixty-one, Kong tse is presented as a ritual priest who performs rituals to exorcize obstacles, negative omens, evil forces, curses, illnesses and epidemic diseases, and who has power to control other spirits to do such exorcisms. In these manuscripts, the name is spelled as *gong tse / rtse*.

48 The term *mda' dar* is an arrow that has fabrics of different colors fastened to it; the arrow is used in rituals. The term *skos* may be referring to sKos rje, the lord who according to Bon myth was assigned to control the course of existence. See Norbu, 147 ff. and Karmay 1998, 128 for sKos rje.

49 A length of an arrow is approximately one meter.

50 Text thirty-four, 455–56, "Kong tse 'phrul gyi rgyal po from China was residing in the palace, his body color white and clear like glass (mirror), and thousands of followers surrounded him. He lived for ten thousand and a hundred thousand years (*khri dang 'bum*)." (These numbers should not be taken literally; they may just an indication that he lived a very long life.) "He wears a turban the length of an arrow (*thod dkar mda' gang*) on his head, and his body is filled with ornaments of noble marks. He holds *mda' dar* and belongs to *skos*, and eighty thousands (spelled *stong phrag brgya bcu*, but must be read as *stong phrag brgyad bcu*) *gab tse* letters of the sky, the earth and the space rotate in his palm. He displays *gtsug lag* (fortune) of the past, the future and the present on his palm by emanating the *'phrul yig* letter in his hand."

51 For *dbal gsas*, see Anne-Marie Blondeau, "The mKha' klong gsang mdos: Some Questions on Ritual Structure and Cosmology." In *New Horizons in Bon Studies*, ed. Yasuhiko Nagano and Samten G. Karmay (Osaka: National Museum of Ethnology, 2000), 257; Masahide Mori, "The Bon Deities Depicted in the Wall Paintings in the Bon-brgya Monastery." In *New Horizons in Bon Studies*, ed. Yasuhiko Nagano and Samten G. Karmay (Osaka: National Museum of Ethnology, 2000), 512 and 530. For the myth of Ge khod, see Karmay 1998, 394. There is also a short description for each of these Bonpo deities (see *dbal gsas* at Walse Ngampa, *gtso mchog* at Trowo Tsochog Kagying, *stag la* at Tagla Membar and *ge khod* at Walchen Geko) in Samten G Karmay and Jeff Watt, eds., *Bon: The Magic Word. The Indigenous Religion of Tibet* (New York and London: Rubin Museum of Arts and Philip Wilson Publishers, 2007) 217.

52 The four truths listed here are the truth of the teacher, the truth of the Buddha, the truth of Bon and the truth of *bodhisattva*.

53 In text fifty-five, another of Kong tse's forms is 'Phags pa 'jam dpal (*ārya mañjusrī*). He is also described as the lord of *srid pa lto* (*gto*) and king of existence (*srid pa'i rgyal po*). A king named Li mkhyen then rtse, who resided in the east at Ri bo rtse lnga (five peaked mountain; 五台山 Wu tai shan) in the land of China, invited Kong tse to perform a ritual to remove obstacles caused by *dgu mig*. Text fifty-six presents Kong tse as ritual specialist who performs exorcism rituals.

54 The following texts are listed in the order I have accessed them, but not necessarily studied in detail for this paper. I believe there are still more to be found.

55 Texts one to three are hagiographies of the Bon founder, Shenrab Miwo.

56 Texts six through thirteen are published in *rNam rgyal sgrub pa*, Bonpo Katen vol. 104, discovered by Go lde 'phags pa (b. 1215).

57 Texts fourteen through twenty are published in *Nye lam sde bzhi*, Bonpo Katen vol. 253, discovered by Khyung rgod rtsal (b.1175).

58 Texts twenty-one and twenty-two are published in *sTong gsum 'khrug pa yo bcos*, Bonpo Katen vol. 84, possibly discovered by Go sde 'phags pa (b. 1215).

59 Texts twenty-three through forty-nine are published in *gTo phyogs bsdus*, Bonpo Katen vol. 157.

60 Texts fifty-one through fifty-four are published in *gZungs 'dus* and the *mDo mang* Collection, Dolanji, 1974.

61 Texts 55–56 are preserved in the Van Manen Collection, Kern Institute Library, Leiden.

62 Texts 57–62 are preserved in Gansu Manuscripts and have no author. These manuscripts (in two volumes) were obtained from sTag ra and rGya nag of 'Phan chu region in Gansu province in recent years by a good friend, Awang Jiatsho. The accessed materials are only photocopies of the original, but have not yet been published or edited. Many folios are missing in these texts. The number of folios given here only shows the number of the last folio in the volume, and is not necessarily complete.

14

Dating and Authorship Problems in the *sNgags log sun 'byin* Attributed to Chag lo tsā ba Chos rje dpal

KADRI RAUDSEPP

Polemical Writings, Different Appellations and their Consistency

From the 11th century onwards, the beginning of the *gsar 'gyur* ("new translations"), there was a proliferation of historical accounts of lineage transmissions in Tibet.[1] Reconstructing the history of lineages and attaching their origins to foreign Buddhist countries (mostly India) was prevalent in all emerging Tibetan Buddhist schools. This gave rise to different kinds of polemics about what constitutes authentic Dharma. Polemical traditions, while having their roots in India, have become an essential part of Tibetan Buddhism, allowing the generation and formulation of new ideas and ways of thinking. These various kinds of polemical writings could be classified under the heading of *dgag lan* (*dgag* "to refute" and *lan* "to answer," "to reply"), normally described as "polemical literature" in Western sources,[2] even if this designation doesn't cover the multi-faceted aspects of the term in Tibetan. In Tibetan, many synonyms are used for polemical literature with slight nuances to their meaning. For example, when introducing a polemical question, terms like *rtsod gleng, rtsod pa, dgag pa* or *dgag yig* may be used; while for refuting, *dgag lan* ("refute" and "answer"), *brgal lan* ("objection" and "reply"), *rtsod zlog* ("debate" and "reverse," "expel"), *btsod gleng* ("debate" and "discuss"), simply *lan*, and so forth, are employed.

Throughout Tibetan history the representatives of all Buddhist schools have been engaged, in some way, with polemics, sometimes arising between different Buddhist schools and other times between masters from the same school. Generally speaking, it is said that polemics contribute to the purification of the teachings and stimulate religious activities because they create an exchange of diverse and varied views. In most cases, this is true. Polemics do contribute to the diversification of the polemicist's outlook and in some cases to probable rectification of his views. However, this is not always the case in polemics about authenticity, and we find that polemicists commonly become constrained by entrenched sectarian views and their arguments tend to be devoid of objectivity.

Polemics can be very specific, aimed at a certain opponent, or can be intended for the public in general. When tracing texts with polemical features in the beginning of the *gsar 'gyur*, a variety of names were in use for designating a polemical text. We also notice that the terms used in such texts often lack internal coherence. This lack of precision continues later on when we observe that the same text was named differently by different authors. For example, the earliest polemical writings in the beginning of *phyi dar*, those of lHa Bla ma Ye shes 'od and Pho brang Zhi ba 'od, were known as "open letters" or "edicts" (*bka' shog*). In later sources, these *bka' shog* are sometimes called *'byams yig, springs yig,* or even *sngags log sun 'byin.*[3] The *bka' shog* of Pho brang Zhi ba 'od was called *springs yig* in the *NgL* attributed to Chag lo, while Bu ston Rin chen grub (1290–1364) and Sa paṇ (1182–1251) referred to it as *ngl*; later Sum pa mkhan po (1704–1788) called it *bka' shog.*

These different appellations, even if inconsistent, should distinguish between different forms of polemical texts. *bKa' shog* has a connotation of being a kind of royal edict, a letter issued by superior authorities, while *springs yig* is used for a letter that is sent (this often implies the act of sending a letter by a messenger) and is not necessarily polemical in nature.[4] *'Byams yig* denotes a scholastic letter which implies the intention of being distributed. One type of polemic appears under the name of *ngl*. The appellation *ngl* is the only designation that makes direct reference to the subject matter of an edict or a letter that directly deals with the "refutation of false mantras." From these few examples, we see that the variations of names were connected more to the form of the text, which could be a royal edict, scholastic letter, just a letter, etc. There is no direct reference in the name about the subject matter of the text. When classifying these early polemics by their subject matter, they could be indexed under the name of *ngl* as they all were somehow dealing with the refutation of false mantras.

When trying to summarize the main characteristics of polemics in the beginning of the *phyi dar*, these mainly concern refutations between the rNying ma and the gSar ma.[5] In the commencement of the *phyi dar*, polemics between Buddhists and Bon po were vivacious as well.[6] Controversial themes such as the authenticity of texts and practices and the correct transmission of lineages from India into Tibet were the main focus. It seems that while polemics were more fervent in central Tibet (dBus and gTsang) and western Tibet, a mutual tolerance reigned in southern (lHo brag, lHo kha) and eastern (Khams, A mdo) Tibet. For example, almost all the early well-known polemicists, such as lHa bla ma Ye shes 'od, Pho brang Zhi ba 'od, lHa btsun Byang chub 'od, Lo chen Rin chen bzang po, 'Gos khug pa lhas btsas, 'Bri gung sKyob pa, and so forth, originated from gTsang or mNga' ris. That could be explained by the fact that central power started to re-establish itself in these regions. There seems to be a correlation between the formation of small state-like entities and the patronage of Buddhist activities in western and central Tibet.[7] In A mdo and Khams, far from the eyes of monastic and political rulers, polemics never attained the fervor that they did in dBus and gTsang.

According to the remarks of Andreas Doctor, in the early debates about authenticity the authors did not develop their arguments and offered little historical, philosophical or philological deduction to support their critiques.[8] If we read these early polemics, this statement seems to be true. At the same time, we cannot ignore the multiple ideological and political mechanisms that contributed to systematize the Tibetan canon according to the idea of the Chinese "closed canon" model (though at the same time the promoters of the "closed canon" were claiming that it was something particular to the Indian canon), followed generally by gSar ma pa in opposition to rNying ma pa, who followed the idea of an Indian "open canon" model.[9] Although not explicitly expressed, these mechanisms are surely present also in early polemics. Even if the *NgL* attributed to Chag lo also remains ambiguous about the reasons why certain texts should be considered false, there is one salient feature which recurs throughout the text. This is pointed out by Ronald Davidson as one of the characteristics of early polemics – it seems that the question became understood as an issue of geography or ethnicity: if the texts (tantric texts and their supplementaries) were produced in India or by Indians, then they were considered authentic; if by Tibetans or in Tibet, then they were inauthentic, even if it was often difficult to decide where a text came into existence and who was its author.[10] Early polemics often concentrated on the search for the Indian origins of texts, as well as on setting boundaries to a variety of ritual, doctrinal and meditative instructions which contributed to the development of indigenous tantras.[11] This implied also that tantric practices or the misunderstanding of tantric practices was considered a threat to Buddhist teachings, as we see from the polemics of lHa Bla ma Ye shes 'od.[12]

Early Well-known Authors of *sngags log sun 'byin*

Very often we cannot be sure about the authorship of historical writings which have come down to us. Attribution of authorship is open to a variety of interpretations: sometimes we simply lack sufficient data for determining the authorship or the time of composition of a text, while often a disciple of a well-known teacher or scholar is the real author of the text. It is evident that during the beginning of the *phyi dar*, issues of authorship and problems of dating arose frequently. The first famous authors of *ngl* – called *bka' shog* – were lHa Bla ma Ye shes 'od,[13] the king of Pu rangs (written ca 985) and Pho brang Zhi ba 'od (written ca 1092).[14] Among early *sngags log sun 'byin pa* figured lHa btsun Byang chub 'od, the younger brother of Pho brang Zhi ba 'od, who was himself also vigorous in the activities of "purification." He is particularly well known for inviting Atiśa (982–1054) to western Tibet. Even if he is described by the Fifth Dalai Lama as a *lo tsā ba* of great renown, we find no translations under his name in the *bKa' 'gyur* or *bsTan 'gyur*.

The first scripture known under the name of *NgL* is attributed to Rin chen bzang po (958–1055)[15] and is often cited by later authors.[16] Although little is known about the text, we are familiar with Rin chen bZang po's position towards ancient tantras, which he considered non-authentic (*yang dag ma yin pa*).[17] We do know much more about the well-known *NgL*, which has been handed down from the 11th century and was written by 'Gos khug pa lhas btsas, the translator. The precise years of his life are unclear, but he was contemporary to Zur chen Shākya 'byung gnas (1002–1062), Zur chung Shes rab grags pa (1014–1074)[18] and Rong zom chos kyi bzang po (11th century), all of whom he met personally. We know that he was notorious as a promoter of the *Secret Assembly* (*gSang ba 'dus pa'i rgyud*) and as a fierce adversary of the old school (which only later became known as the rNying ma school), setting up conflict with Zur Junior (1014–1074).[19] Sa paṇ makes references to 'Gos lHas btsas and his *NgL*. Bu ston mentions him in his *Chos 'byung* as one of the rNying ma detractors, but at the same time he remains silent about his oeuvre. Bu ston adds that he had gone to India three times and studied with seventy-two *paṇḍita* with mystic powers, having been the disciple of Shāntibhadra and Rāhulabhadra. He also enumerates his translations.[20]

A khu chin mentions one certain *springs yig*, four folios long, written by lHas btsas.[21] Sog bzlog pa Blo gros rgyal mtshan (1552–1624), a famous rNying ma scholar, attributes three *'byams yig* to lHas btsas: a vast *'byams yig* (*rgyas*), a middle (*'bring*) and a short (*bsdus*) one. At the time of writing his *Nges don 'brug sgra* he had access only to two texts,[22] concluding that the third *'byams yig* never existed. Sog bzlog pa finally ends up by analyzing the stylistic elements and the contents of the text, concluding that these letters were probably not written by lHas btsas. Nevertheless, he refutes him anyway.[23]

'Gos lHas btsas refutes the *Tantra of Secret Essence*: *Definitive Suchness* (*gSang ba snying po de kho na nyid nges pa,* skt. *Guhyagarbhatantra*),[24] which, according to him, was composed by rMa rin chen mchog.[25] Other works that he refutes include later commentaries about *Guhyagarbhatantra* made by Zur chen and Zur chung;[26] commentaries of Aro yi 'byung gnas; compositions of Spa gor ba'i ro tsa na;[27] compositions of rDo rje dpal gyi grags pa;[28] innumerable cycles of *mamo* composed by Tibetans; the *Mighty Lotus Tantra* (*Pad ma dbang chen*), which is mixed with non-Buddhist tantras;[29] Five Instructive Tantras for Practice[30] (*sGrub lung rgyud lnga*), which are included among eighteen tantras of Mahāyoga, and its supplementary texts.

Generally, 'Gos lHa btsas calls all this "false contaminated dharma."[31] Sometimes he claims that it is contaminated because it is "mixed with non-Buddhist traditions," sometimes because it is a "Tibetan composition."[32] He demonstrates that the composition of texts by Tibetans themselves may lead to severe consequences; for example, rMa Rin chen mchog, for having composed the *gSang ba snying po* and its supplementary text, was "severely punished."[33] Nevertheless, as in the case of the *bka' shog* of Pho brang Zhi ba 'od, the *NgL* attributed to 'Gos lHas btsas is a mere list of texts. At the end of the text, while enumerating "non-contaminated" texts, he reveals his criteria of authenticity: texts are authentic if commentaries, *sādhana* or *maṇḍala* rituals written by Indians exist about the text.[34] He concludes his refutation by declaring that his *NgL* was composed "in order to distinguish between false and infallible dharma"[35] and "for the well-being of all the *māntrika* and monks who have taken the wrong path."[36]

The *NgL* Attributed to Chag lo tsā ba Chos rje dpal

With this short introduction about polemical literature and the early *ngl*, it is time to introduce the *NgL* attributed to Chag lo tsā ba Chos rje dpal (1197–1264), known under his Indian name Dharmasvāmin. His hagiography (*rnam thar*),[37] written by his disciple Chos dpal dar dpyang,[38] is rather autobiographical and in the main dictated by Chag lo himself. It was translated by G.N. Roerich, providing details about his activities and travels. It is known that he was born in the village of Chag in 1197, the female fire serpent year (*me mo sbrul*). Under the direction of his uncle, Chag dgra bcom (1153–1216), he undertook the study of Sanskrit at an early age. After the death of his uncle in 1216, he spent ten years in gTsang, visiting famous scholars. After that, Chag lo traveled to Nepal and

India. He spent eight years in Nepal and probably started his journey towards India in 1234 (staying there for two years); in so doing, his fame increased even more.[39] Even though there are some imprecisions in his narrative, he provides us with valuable geographical and historical details about the actual situation in the large Buddhist centers in India. After staying for about four years in Nepal, he returned to Tibet in 1240–1241. During the rest of his life he sojourned in lTe'u ra Monastery, making short journeys to other monasteries, such as Yang tog in Mang yul, Thang po che, 'Ju' phu and 'Phyos in Yar klungs. He also stayed some years in the Sa skya Monastery in gTsang. He is known for having participated in the translation of an important number of shorts texts, such as *sādhana*, *vidhi* etc., which were later included in the *bsTan 'gyur*.[40] Bu ston also mentions that he went to India and, assisted by Devendra, Ratnarakśita and other tantrists, he completed the translation of nine Uṣṇīṣa tantras (*gTsug dgu'i rgyud*) and made many corrections to already translated texts.[41] During the last years of his life, he spent most of his time preaching in different monasteries, also meditating, translating and writing commentaries on the texts. There is no mention about *NgL* in his *rnam thar*.

In his *rnam thar* he expresses his concern about the purity of dharma, saying that it was no longer pure in Tibet. He explains that during the *dharmarāja* era, the doctrine of Ha shang Mahāyāna spread. He claims that dharma had become similar to this, and there was a need to perform some purificatory practices.[42] This idea is in accordance with the general tone of *NgL* attributed to Chag lo. Being a gSar ma pa, only authentic Indian scriptures offered authority for him, and not the personal experience or the cult of the saints as in the case of the "accomplishment tantras" (*sgrub rgyud*). But before starting to discuss problems concerning the authorship of this text, it would be pertinent to give a short introduction about the text by pointing out the main position of the author and the refuted texts.

Although the structure of the *NgL* attributed to Chag lo is very repetitive, it is more than a simple directory of texts.[43] In some cases the author is giving justifications about his considerations why a certain text or practice was erroneous or why certain teachers should be regarded as false. His use of metaphors and other stylistic elements present considerable advances over the style of his predecessors. We find expressions that compare Tibetan compositions to good food (because a "good name" is attached to texts) mixed with poison.[44] Wrong views are compared to an obscure veil.[45] It seems that the authors, who were refuting false texts and practices, knew exactly what these "wrong dharma composers" had in mind while composing these texts: La stod mar po was driven by the desire for gold, Ras chung pa by the desire to deprecate others,[46] etc.

In the opening lines of the text, the author expresses his concern about the purity of the teachings, like lHa Bla ma Ye shes 'od had done earlier. He says that the decline of the teaching is due to the lack of a royal code (in other words, centralized power).[47] For this reason the dharma law is nonexistent, too, leading the Buddhist doctrine to decline.

In the *NgL* introduction and conclusion, we read of Chag lo's high erudition, as one who is "versed in logic, scriptures, reasoning, *Piṭaka*, tantras, treatises, and philosophical systems," and composed this "excellent sword of discernment."[48] The concluding part is very similar to the conclusion of *NgL* attributed to 'Gos lHas btsas. In *NgL* of 'Gos lHas btsas we read: "This [work] was not composed with the motivation of anger, pride, or envy,"[49] and in Chag lo: "I haven't written it because of envy, pride, or the wish to oppress others."[50] In the introductory and concluding lines, the authors are also referred to in the third person, which make it plausible that these could be later insertions. It may also support the hypothesis that the entire text has been written by somebody else.

The author is critical towards rNying ma and gSar ma teachers. Among others, he is particularly dismissive of sPa gor Ba'i ro tsa na, Guru Chos kyi dbang-phyug (1212–1270),[51] Pha dam pa Sangs rgyas (d. 1117),[52] La stod mar po (second part of the 11th century–beginning of the 12th century)[53] and Ras chung pa (1083–1161).[54]

sPa gor Ba'i ro tsa na is accused of having been possessed by a demon (we can assume that the author finds this a destiny of most rNying ma teachers). He is the author of five sūtras of *rdzogs chen* view, *Tantra of Equal Union* (*mNyam sbyor*), *Heruka Gal po Tantra*, *sNga* Tantra, *rTog pa'i Dum bu* Tantra, twenty-one texts altogether.[55] These texts have been said to be false because of their origins, giving birth to other texts and impure transmissions. The author mentions that Ba'i ro tsa na composed the *Golden Cycle of rDzogs chen, Rin po che* Teachings and *Liberation through Wearing Tantra* (*bTags grol*), which were all innumerable. He declares that "all this is mixed up with nihilist and heretical views of Jain doctrines and 'the six unions' (*sbyor drug*) of Buddhist *Kālacakra*. As the Bon view is mixed with the views of *bal nag*, so it is evident that it leads to the erroneous path."[56]

Apart from sPa gor Ba'i ro tsa na, almost all the other teachers refuted by the author of *NgL* were the principal masters or founders of certain new lineages with gSar ma background. They belonged to lay religious movements from the 11th to the 12th centuries, which were opposing new emerging monastic institutions.[57] According to the author of the polemic, the fact that the practices were propagated by teachers who did not want to be part of the monastic system and who declared direct visionary contact with religious authority – receiving benedictions without the intermediary of monastic or scholastic chiefs – was sufficient to classify their teachings as false dharma. In the same way, the compositions of Guru Chos kyi dbang phyug (1212–1270) are all false; the author mentions his *Hayagriva Who Subjugates All the Demons* (*rTa mgrin dregs pa kun 'dul*), according to which seven tantras of *The Jewel which Accomplishes Wishes and Subjugates All the Demons* (*Dregs pa zil gnon yid bzhin nor bu*) were composed.[58] Pha dam pa sangs rgyas, here called Dam pa nag chung, was the author of *Declaration from Afar of Simultaneous Pure Awareness* (*gCig char rig pa rgyang 'dod*), the White Pacification (*Zhi byed dkar po*) cycle, and the practice of Cutting (*gcod*).[59] La stod dmar po (second half of 11th century–first half of the 12th century) is also accused of having interpolated and modified texts:

> Furthermore, someone called La stod dmar po, who was driven by the desire for gold, changed the sound of six syllables of Avalokiteśvara in erroneous dharma, pronouncing the syllable "am" instead of "om." Furthermore, he took deities of the Kriya and Caryā classes and attached to them the channels and the four-channel wheels of Supreme Mother Tantras and mixed together with Levels of Emptiness of Pacifying (*Zhi byed stong rim*), thus composing the wrong dharma which was called "Great Compassion according to the A ma system."[60]

Ras chung pa was accused of having composed the twenty-one chapters of tantra named *The Tantra which Reveals the Secret of Vajrapāni* (*Phyag na rdo rje gsang ba bstan pa*); and twenty different texts on the Inner heat practice cycle (*gTum mo'i sgrub skor*).[61] He had interpolated the esoteric oral transmission of Cakrasamvara (*bDe mchog snyan rgyud*),[62] composing a large number of various completion stage texts (*rdzogs rim*).

According to the author of *NgL*, the principal reasons for the above-mentioned texts (and others) representing the wrong dharma is that they are Tibetan fabrications, which do not exist in India, and are mixed with non-Buddhist traditions of Brahmins or Bon po and depict heretical gods. For example, he mentions that *Mighty Lotus Tantra* (*Pad ma dbang chen*) and the *Supreme Steed Play Tantra* (*rTa mchog rol pa*) are not authentic because the divinities of these tantras are drawn on the walls of heretic temples in India and Nepal.[63] That argument was later criticized by Thu'u bkwan Chos kyi nyi ma (1732–1802). In his *Nor bu ke ta ka'i byi dor* he says that the mere fact that those divinities are found in the heretic temples does not prove that the divinities themselves are heretical.[64]

The author also accuses the elders of Tibet, evidently the rNying ma pa, who have fabricated the *sādhana* of the Pig-Headed Divinity (*pha mgo ma*) in order to perform the heretical convocation, and saying later that it was the ḍākinī of *Abhidhāna* tantra.[65] He states that the elders of Tibet have promoted the status of the lion-headed female spirit (*mu stegs khri 'bum dmar po seng mgo ma*) into a Wisdom divinity.[66]

The author reveals the problem with the initiations. He laments that during the time of his arrival to Tibet, the initiations were given by the elders who themselves had not received initiations from a qualified person. We can read on folio 16:

> Without having received initiation from their personal *vajrācārya*, they give initiations and, as they don't know the five certainties, they are not able to understand the production of the Awakened Mind [but] they pretend to be Mahāyāna followers, and without observing the vows or knowing the *vinaya*, they have taken the functions of abbots. These are the religious habits of the elders of Tibet.[67]

The author of the text expresses his worry about the authenticity of the transmission lineages of the texts, saying that "among all the heretics, false emanations (*gar log*) and Bon po, there are also innumerable black powers and ordinary signs which lead to heaven."[68] He says that all this has become possible because the elders of Tibet have attributed good names to heretical practices and people are not able to distinguish right from wrong. On certain occasions, the author mentions also *gter ma*,[69] but there is no direct and detailed criticism as is the case in *Chos log sun 'byin* attributed to Bu ston.[70]

To conclude the main arguments of this *NgL*, we see that its criticisms extend both to rNying ma pa and gSar ma pa. On several occasions the author is underlining the fact that rNying ma teachings are contaminated in a more extensive way, having been polluted already by their roots (when refuting gSar ma masters, he always points to one particular master and does not attack the whole group of gSar ma pa). One example that confirms this is the story of Ka ka ru 'dzin, incarnation of Pe kar spirit, who, according to *NgL*, immediately after the departure of Padmasambhava started under his name to spread the wrong teachings.[71] Even if the author dares not attack Padmasambhava directly, it seems like his aim is to demonstrate that his lineage was already polluted from the very beginnings. His main "argument" against the elders of Tibet remains the fact that they were all possessed by demons.

In making an attempt to deal with the authorship problems of this *NgL*, we notice that modern scholars attribute its authorship to Chag lo.[72] Andreas Doctor[73] mentions that this *NgL* is the earliest known critique of treasure revelation. Dan Martin gives 1260 as the date of its composition.[74] This *NgL* has become quite popular in Tibet, too. It has been cited by Sum pa mkhan po, Thu'u bkwan,[75] and later refuted by Dudjom Rinpoche.[76]

If looking for arguments regarding the authorship of this text from the Tibetan side, we immediately notice that Sog bzlog pa does not mention this particular text in his *Nges don 'brug sgra*. This is significant because all the other early polemics are present in his oeuvre and he also refutes them in defense of the rNying ma. The main argument against the attribution of this text to Chag lo comes from Thu'u bkwan. After refuting some of the arguments present in this *NgL* in his *Norbu ketaka*, he concludes "that this text cannot have been composed by such an erudite like Chag lo, but composed by someone crazy, full of attachment and hatred and it looks like he has taken the name of Chag lo."[77]

When trying to draw some conclusions about the writing style of the text, in the first place we should be alerted by the note from the publishers, according to which "the spellings in the master copy of the letters by Chag lo and 'Gos are not satisfactory, they are set to print in order to enable further investigation."[78] Also, if comparing the writing style of this *NgL* with the other writings of Chag lo, for example his questions to Sa skya Paṇḍita when he was inquiring about the *Clear Differentiation of the Three Codes*,[79] the style and the centers of interest are very different. According to Jared Douglas Rothon, this letter to Sa paṇ was written somewhere between 1236 and 1241.[80] Chag lo's *Zhu ba* are presented in a sophisticated style, his interests are clearly connected to philosophical issues; he doesn't look like somebody who could be fascinated by banal refutations of different Buddhist schools. One of his questions to Sa paṇ concerns the composition of tantras by Tibetans, and there he does not call them openly false or erroneous.[81] From a humble position, he is asking advice from someone who has more knowledge about these subjects. The answer of Sa paṇ is diplomatic.[82] He simply says that a large number of texts has been composed by Tibetans, but he only mention a few texts such as *lHa mo skye rgyud* and *Bum ril thod mkhar* from the rNying ma side, and *Dus 'byung, Phyag na rdo rje mkha' 'gro* and *Ra li nyi shu rtsa bzhi* from gSar ma side. He adds that "as feelings would be hurt a little if I were to point out all of them clearly, you should investigate this yourself."[83] Knowing from this example and from the autobiography of Chag lo that Sa paṇ was highly respected by him, he should have taken into account his statements when writing this *NgL* – if written by him, as none of the texts mentioned by Sa paṇ appear in *NgL*.

Sa paṇ's concern about the purity of the teachings should be understood in light of the political situation of Tibet in the 13th century. As Chag lo himself also witnessed, Buddhism in India had practically disappeared. The Buddhist Tangut Empire was conquered by the Mongols in 1227, while inside Tibet the constant fight for power was seen as a threat to the Buddhist teachings. The formation of the Buddhist canon during the climax of political instability was not haphazard:

according to Paul Harrison, those involved in political efforts for power also engaged in the struggle for religious prestige.[84] Ideological calculations in the process of compilation of the Buddhist canon by those close to power contributed surely to determining the final form of the canon.

The formation of the canon in the first half of the 14th century under the direction of Bu ston in Zhwa lu Monastery[85] used such selection criteria that only the texts of proven Indian origin were accepted, the position shared by other influential representatives of gSar ma schools. This incited all kinds of polemics to emerge.

All these points tend to support the hypothesis that Chag lo may not have been the author of this polemic. The text could have been written later, possibly around the end of the 13th or beginning of the 14th century, when *ngl* were very helpful in supporting the selection criteria for the canon, and to justify the reasons why certain texts were left out. This *NgL* could be one of the examples of these compositions that worked as ideological tools and were written according to the interests of those in power. And as it has been done many times before in history, the authorship of these texts was often attributed to famous scholars, as may have been the case here – to Chag lo tsā ba Chos rje dpal. At the same time we see that this *NgL* cannot be in any way considered a masterpiece from the learned scholar who has been nonetheless accepted as its author. It would be interesting to research the processes through which some mediocre texts became well known after having been attributed to famous scholars. The next similar example – *Chos log sun 'byin* attributed to Bu ston – falls almost into the same period.

Due to the limits of space, this chapter does not deal with the analysis of the texts refuted in *ngl*. Although some research has already been done on these matters, it would be fruitful to investigate further how much objective basis there was in considering some texts spurious,[86] or how much the issues of open and closed canon influenced the authors.

The composition date of this *NgL* still needs further investigation. As this *NgL* is still considered the first polemical writing in which *gter ma* are refuted, it is also the first polemical writing where the terms "rNying ma" and "gSar ma" appear, indicating distinct Buddhist schools.[87] As the gSar ma schools were homogenizing their theoretical systems during the 13th century,[88] the identities of the rNying ma and gSar ma schools were becoming stronger in opposition to one another. These identities are starting to be seen in the use of vocabulary of polemical writings, where the opposition *snga/phyi* is ceding place to the opposition rNying ma/gSar ma.

Notes

1 This article presents some elements from my Master's thesis, called "Les origines de la distinction entre rNying ma et gSar ma à travers certains textes de 'réfutations des faux mantras'" (*sNgags log sun 'byin*), which I completed under the direction of Matthew Kapstein at the École Pratique des Hautes Études in Paris in 2005.

2 The transfer of occidental vocabulary into Buddhist context very often lacks precision. Donald Lopez, Jr., "Polemical Literature *(dgag lan)*." In *Tibetan Literature: Studies in Genre*, ed. José Ignacio Cabezón and Roger R. Jackson (Ithaca: Snow Lion, 1995), 222–23, argues whether the term *dgag lan* should be rendered by "polemical" or rather by "apologetic literature." As a Tibetan term, it includes the notion of an answer (*lan*), and it suggests that the more appropriate term may be "apology," from the Greek *apologia*, meaning "answer" or "speech in defense." The Tibetan term includes also the notion of refutation (*dgag*) to which the answer is followed. Therefore, two positions are included here: refuter and defender. The problem is also that apologetics are usually concerned with fundamental questions of religious practice and directed to an audience outside of the Christian faith. In a Tibetan context, the refutations were mainly concerned with the subtleties of Buddhist philosophy and practice and took place among members of the same religion. Lopez is citing Schleiermacher, who, in his *Brief Outline on the Study of Theology*, claims that apologetics are directed outward in an effort to ward off hostility toward the community through seeking to make truth recognizable, while polemics take place exclusively within the community, seeking to expose error, what he calls "diseased deviations within the community." In this paper, I consider it more appropriate to use the term "polemical literature" for rendering the term *dgag lan*.

3 Henceforward abbreviated *NgL* or *ngl*: when referring to a text or the title of a text, the abbreviation *NgL* is used; when referring to the genre or the term, *ngl* is used.

4 *Bod rgya tshig mdzod chen mo* (Beijing: Mi rigs dpe skrun khang, 1996) gives also *bskur yig*.

5 In the context of refutations about authenticity we can observe how the appellations rNying ma and gSar ma started to be applied.

6 For example, for disputes between Lo chen Rin chen bzang po and Klu sKar gyal, see Dan Martin, "Lay Religious Movements in 11th and 12th Century Tibet: A Survey of Sources," *Kailash* 18 (1996), 30–31. For disputes between Mi la ras pa and Na ro bon chung, see E. Gene Smith, *Among Tibetan Texts: History and Literature of the Himalayan Plateau*, ed. Kurtis Schaeffer (Boston: Wisdom Publications, 2001), 237, 329. With the passage of time, attacks against the rNying ma pa were multiplying, probably because the rNying ma school, which was opposed to the emerging gSar ma schools, became stronger, and the Bon po in central Tibet were disappearing from the main focus.

7 The continuity of the old royal line and its patronage of Buddhism is related by bSod nams rtse mo in 1167 in his *Chos la 'jug pa'i sgo* (*Sa skya bka' 'bum*, 2. part), 318.3.1–345.3.6.

8 Andreas Doctor, *Tibetan Treasure Literature: Revelation, Tradition and Accomplishment in Visionary Buddhism* (Ithaca: Snow Lion, 2005), 31.

9 Robert Mayer, "Were The gSar ma pa Polemicists Justified in Rejecting Some rNying ma pa Tantras?" In *Proceedings of the 7th Seminar of the International Association for Tibetan Studies, volume II,* ed. Ernst Steinkellner (Vienna: Verlag der Österreichischen Akademie der Wissenschaften, 1997), 627.

10 Ronald Davidson, "gSar ma pa Apocrypha: The Creation of Orthodoxy, Gray Texts, and the New Revelation." In *The Many Canons of Tibetan Buddhism*, ed. Helmut Eimer and David Germano (Leiden: E.J. Brill, 2002), 203; see also idem, *Tibetan Renaissance: Tantric Buddhism in the Rebirth of Tibetan Culture* (New York: Columbia University Press, 2005), 148–154; and idem,

"An Introduction to the Standards of Scriptural Authenticity in Indian Buddhism." In *Chinese Buddhist Apocrypha*, ed. Robert E. Buswell, (Honolulu: University of Hawaii Press, 1990), 291–325.

11 Many refuted teachers belonged to various lay religious movements. Nyang ral nyi ma 'od zer refers to these religious movements as to different practice lineages or *sgrub brgyud* without any polemical tone; *Chos 'byung me rtog snying po brang rtsis bcud*. In *Gangs can rig mdzod*, vol. 5 (Lhasa: Bod ljongs mi dmangs dpe skrun khang, 1988), 492–94.

12 See Samten Karmay, "The Ordinance of lHa bla ma Ye shes 'od." In *The Arrow and the Spindle. Studies in History, Myths, Rituals and Beliefs in Tibet* (Kathmandu: Mandala Book Point, 1998), 3–17.

13 The first indications about this *bka' shog* are available in *Bu ston chos 'byung* (Beijing: Krung go bod kyi shes rig dpe skrun khang, 1988), 313. Bu ston calls them "refutation of false mantras" (*sngags log sun 'byin*). It is also mentioned in the list of A khu chin's *Tho yig* and it is called "letter" (*springs yig*). See Dorji Wangchuk, "An Eleventh Century Defense of the Authenticity of the *Guhyagarbha* Tantra." In *The Many Canons of Tibetan Buddhism*, ed. Helmut Eimer and David Germano (Leiden: E.J. Brill, 2002) 265–91. Sog bzlog pa Blo gros rgyal mtshan in his *Nges don 'brug sgra, Collected writings of Sog bzlog pa* (New Delhi: Sanje Dorji, 1975), 435–44, gives the integral version of the text with commentaries and names it *bka' shog*.

14 Karmay gives a thorough overview of these texts in the article cited above and in "An Open Letter by Pho-brang Zhi ba 'od." In *The Arrow and the Spindle. Studies in History, Myths, Rituals and Beliefs in Tibet* (Kathmandu: Mandala Book Point, 1998), 17–40.

15 David Seyfort Ruegg, "Deux problèmes d'exégèse et de pratique tantriques." In *Tantric and Taoist Studies in Honor of R. A. Stein*, ed. Michel Strickmann (*Mélanges chinois et Bouddhiques* 20, 1981), 224.

16 *Bu ston chos 'byung*, 313: *bdag nyid chen po rin chen bzang pos mdzad pa'i rab gnas kyi sdom dang sngags log sun 'byin pa rgyas pa dang/*. For more references see Wangchuk, 273.

17 *Bu ston chos 'byung*, 266.

18 The Zur clan started to codify for the first time the collection of oral transmission (*bka' ma*). This process was completed in Ka' thog, the first rNying ma monastery constructed during the *phyi dar* period. According to tradition, there were three ancestors in the lineage of Zur: Zur po che, Zur chung ba and sGro phug pa. For more details, see Dudjom Rinpoche, *The Nyingma School of Tibetan Buddhism. Its Fundamentals and History*, trans. Gyurme Dorje and Matthew Kapstein (Boston: Wisdom Publications, 1991), 617–50; and Nathaniel Dewitt-Garson, "Penetrating the Secret Essence Tantra: Context and Philosophy in the Mahāyoga System of rNying ma Tantra" (PhD Dissertation: University of Virginia, 2004), 209–39.

19 See George N. Roerich, *The Blue Annals* (1949; reprint, Delhi: Motilal Banarsidass, 1996), 360; Dewitt-Garson, 154–55; Davidson 2005, 152–53.

20 *Bu ston Chos 'byung*, 266.

21 Wangchuk, 275, gives a reference: *Tho yig*, 673, no 15805, vol. *kha*: *rta nag 'gos khug pa lhas btsas kyi springs yig la bzhi*.

22 According to Wangchuk, 275, we don't know exactly which two of the texts were available to him.

23 One of them is edited by dPal ldan 'brug gzhung, *NgL* of 'Gos lHas btsas (Thimpu: Kunsang Tobgyal and Mani Dorji, 1979),18–25; this text is also fully cited by Sog bzlog pa in *Nges don 'brug sgra* together with commentaries, 475–88. Opening and concluding lines seem to be later insertions, as the author of the text is referred in the third person. A large number of orthographical mistakes are present as well.

24 About *Guhyagarbhatantra*, see Dewitt-Garson, 275–365; also Dan Martin, "Illusion Web. Locating the Guhyagarbha Tantra in Buddhist Intellectual History." In *Silver on Lapis: Tibetan*

Literary Culture and History, ed. Christopher I. Beckwith (Bloomington: The Tibet Society, 1987), 175–220.

25 'Gos lHas btsas, *NgL*, 20–21: *dus phyis rin chen mchog gis gsang ba snying po brtsams*. About rMa rin chen mchog, see Wangchuk, 276–77 and Dewitt-Garson, 203. This refutation was later refuted by Dudjom, 914 –17.

26 For example, the composition of commentaries about *Guhyagarbhatantra* and the composition of many *sādhanas* and maṇḍala rituals by the Zur family, 'Gos lHas btsas, *NgL*, 21: *phyis la rten nas zur chen zur chung gis gsang ba snying po'i grel pa dkyil 'khor gyi cho ga sgrub thabs mang du brtsams*.

27 'Gos lHas btsas, *NgL*, 21; for example, he refutes his compositions that belong to *sems sde*, *Nam mkha' che, Kun las 'jug pa rtsal chen, rDzogs pa sphyi, Rigs pa'i khu byugs, and Chos lnga*. According to Sog bzlog pa, eighteen texts of *sems sde* are five older translations (*snga 'gyur*) of Vairocana and thirteen later translations (*phyi 'gyur*) of Vimalamitra; see Karmay, 34. The rNying ma pa could never arrive at a conclusion as to which texts should be considered as *snga 'gyur* and which *sems sde* texts should be classified as *phyi 'gyur*.

28 Ibid., 22: here called Dar chen dpal gyi grags pa. His compositions: *dGongs 'dus, bKa' 'du,s* and *rGyal po'i chos lnga* (these texts have also been mentioned by Pho brang Zhi ba'od). According to Sog bzlog pa (*Nges don 'brug sgra*, 468), he was a disciple of gNyags Jñānakumāra and rMa rin chen mchog. Jacob D. Dalton, "The Uses of *dGongs pa 'dus pa'i mdo* in the Development of the rNying ma School of Tibetan Buddhism" (PhD Dissertation: University of Michigan, 2002), 288, proposes that the intention of 'Gos lHas btsas by attacking rDo rje dpal gyi sgrags pa was rather to refute sNubs Sangs rgyas ye shes, who was his disciple.

29 Ibid., 22: *yang padma dbang chen bya ba gcig brtsams so/ phyi rol pa'i rgyud bsres pa dang.*

30 Ibid., 23: *ran tra mi rgyud dang/ yon tan rin chen skul ba'i rgyud dang/ 'phrin las kyi rgyud karma khra le dang/ phur pa ki la ya bcu gnyis kyis rgyud dang ma mo 'dus pa'i rgyud dang/ bdud rtsi nag po brgyad pa'i rgyud dang/ de rnams sgrub lung rgyud lnga zer ro.*

31 Ibid.,, 24: *de thams cad chos log dri ma can yin no.*

32 Ibid., 21: *de rnams bod kyis byas pa'i chos log dri ma can yin no.*

33 Ibid., 21: *bka' bcad dam po byas/* (based on the translation by Wangchuk, 277).

34 Ibid., 24: *de la rgya gar mkhas pas byas pa'i 'grel pa mang ngo [po]/sgrubs [sgrub] thabs mang po/dkyil 'khor gyi cho ga mang po/de thams cad ma nor ba dri ma med pas sha stags yin no.*

35 Ibid., 20, 24. He also enumerates texts that belong to the authentic dharma, like the *Secret Assembly* (*gSang ba 'dus pa*), the *Secret Moon Drop* (*Zla gsang thig le*), *the Union of All the Buddhas* (*Sangs rgyas mnyam sbyor*), *the Net of Magical Emanation* (*sGyu 'phrul dra ba*), and so forth.

36 Ibid., 25: *'gos khug pa lhas btsas kyis sngags pa dang rab byung chos nor ba la zhugs pa rnams la phan pa'i phyir du 'di bsgyur* [sic] *ba yin no.*

37 Roerich 1996, 1056–59, gives a brief account.

38 http://www.tbrc.org, P8422.

39 Despite Muslim incursions, India has always been a privileged, ideal place in Tibetan mythology, as the birthplace of Buddhism, "noble country" (*'phags yul*). Each Tibetan Buddhist school retraces the origins of its doctrines to the period of transmission of Buddhism from India into Tibet and assigns its lineage back to an Indian teacher. Establishing a direct historical connection with an Indian teacher was essential for claiming the authenticity of the teaching. Only in the dGe lugs pa school is the connection with an Indian teacher not established through direct contact (as in a journey to India), but through the visionary experiences of Tsong kha pa (1357–1419); see Lopez, 220.

40 The list of the texts is given in the introduction of his *rnam thar* translated by George N. Roerich: *Biography of Dharmasvāmin* (Patna: K.P. Jayaswal Reseach Institut, 1959), 501–3.

41 Ernst Obermiller, *The History of Buddhism in India and Tibet by Bu ston* (1932; reprint, Delhi: Sri Satguru Publications, 1999), 223.

42 Roerich, 1959, 566: for example, one of the purificatory practices could be reciting of the *Mādhyamaka-Ratnavālī*.

43 It is different from the letters of Zhi ba 'od and 'Gos lHas btsas. lHa Bla ma's *Open letter* is written for didactic aims, centering on the description of wrong practices and not giving precise names of Tibetan compositions. According to Samten Karmay, his text can be divided into three parts. In the first part, the king gives a summary of Buddhism as he understood it, in the second part, various tantric practices are criticized by means of colorful comparisons, and the third part is clearly didactic, calling for the abandoning all the wrong practices mentioned in the text and for the practice of virtues, love, compassion, etc. Karmay 1998, 8–16.

44 *NgL*, attributed to Chag lo, ed. dPal ldan 'brug gzhung (Thimpu: Kunsang Tobgyal and Mani Dorji, 1979), 11–12: *de yang dug dngos su byin na sus mi bza'/kha zas bzang po bsres na kun gyi bza'.*

45 Ibid., 17: *log rtog byed kyi sgrib g.yogs bsal ba'i phyir dang...*

46 Ibid., 14–15, *yang la stod dmar po bya ba gcig gis/gser 'dod pa'i phyir du (...);* and: *yang bla ma ras chung pas gzhan khyad gsod dang (...) 'dod nas...*

47 Ibid., 5: *khyod bod mtha' 'khob yin pas chos khrims dang rgyal khrims gnyis ka med par 'dug/ nged rgya gar du 'di 'dra'i rang bzo'i chos log dang gzhung lugs byas na/ chos khrims dang rgyal khrims gnyis ka phog nas/ de byed mkhan gyi rigs rgyud bcas brlag 'gro'o/.* In this passage, through the sayings of Indian paṇḍitas (among whom were Rāhulaśrībhadra, Mahāsthavira, Ratnarakṣita etc.) the author expresses also his opinion that there was no dharma law or state law in Tibet and this was the main reason why Tibetans started to compose texts.

48 Chag lo, *NgL*, 1: *sngags log sun 'byin shes rab ral gri 'di/ bla ma chen po chag lo tshes rje/ sgra tshad lung rigs sde snod rgyud sde bstan bcos grub mtha' dag la mkhas pa.*

49 'Gos lHas btsas, *NgL*, 25: *zhes sdang nga rgyal dang phrag dog dbang gis 'di byas pa ma yin no.*

50 Chag lo, *NgL*, 17: *phrag dog dang nga rgyal dang gzhan zil gyis gnon pa'i phyir ma byas shing* (...).

51 For further details about this personality see Dudjom, 760–70.

52 This Indian master had visited Ding ri Glang 'khor, where he had stayed for almost twenty years before his death in 1117; see Martin 1996, 32; and Roerich 1996, 435. For more details about this personality, see Roerich 1996, 867–979 (chapter about the later *Zhi byed* lineage); see also Barbara N. Aziz, "Indian Philosopher as Tibetan Folk Hero," *Central Asiatic Journal* 23.1/2, (1979), 19–37.

53 See Roerich 1996, 1025–30; also Martin 1996, 35–39.

54 See Martin 1996, 33–35; Roerich 1996, 434–36.

55 Chag lo, *NgL*, 10: *yang spa gor be'e ro tsa na bya ba la lha'i bu'i bdud zhugs nas rdzogs chen lta ba'i mdo lnga bya ba brtsams de dang cha mthun par [m]snyam sbyor bya ba sogs te rgyud gal nga rtog pa'i dum bu sogs nyi shu rtsa gcig brtsams//.*

56 Chag lo, *NgL*, 10: *'di rnams mu stegs chad lta ba dang/ mchod 'os pa dang nang pa'i dus 'khor gyi sbyor drug bsres/ bon po'i lta ba bal nag bsres par 'dug 'dis lam log par 'gro des te/.*

57 See Martin 1996, 23–55.

58 Chag lo, *NgL*, 10: *yang gru gu dbang phyug bya bas rta mgrin dregs pa kun 'dul bya ba'i rgyud dang/ de'i rjes su dregs pa zil gnon yid bzhin nor bu bya ba sogs bdun brtsams/* According to the *rNying ma rgyud 'bum*, sDe dge edition, they could be tantras enumerated in the volume 18 (*tsha*).

59 Ibid., 14.

60 Ibid., 14–15: *yang la stod dmar po bya ba gcig gis/ gser 'dod pa'i phyir du thugs rje chen po'i yi ge drug pa sgra log par bsgyur nas/ om la am du bos pas dang/ bya spyod kyi lha la bla med rgyud kyi rtsa 'khor bzhi btags pa la zhi byed stong rim brses nas/ thugs rje chen po a ma lugs yin zer ba'i chos log brtsams so.*

61 Ibid., 15.

62 *bDe mchog snyan brgyud* is the general term for designating esoteric oral transmissions of Cakrasaṃvara, which have come down through three disciples of Milarepa: Ngam rdzong ston pa, Dwags po lha rje (sGam po pa) and Ras chung pa, and who were respectively called *Ngam rdzong snyan brgyud, Dwags po snyan brgyud* and *Ras chung snyan brgyud.*

63 Ibid., 8: *'di'i lha tshogs rnams kyang rgya gar dang bal po na mu stegs lha khang rnams na bris 'dug.*

64 Thu'u bkwan blo bzang chos kyi nyi ma, *gSung rab rnam dag chu'i sel byed nor bu ke ta ka'i tshig don la dogs dpyod snyan sgron du gsol ba nor bu ke ta ka'i byi dor* (Varanasi: Tarthang Tulku, 1967), 34–35: */gal te mu stegs kyi lha khang na yod srid kyang de na yod pas mu stegs kyi lha yin mi dgos te.*

65 Chag lo, *NgL,* 16: *bod rgan 'gas mu stegs kyi 'gugs byed phag mgo ma'i sgrub thabs byas nas sngon byung rgyud kyi mkha' 'gro ma bya ba yin no/.* Martin 1996, 34 also adds that the expression *sngon byung rgyud* should be read as *mngon byung*, which, according to the text, is the tantra of Vajravārāhī-Abhidhāna.

66 Ibid., 16: *yang mu stegs khri 'bum gyi dmar po seng mgo ma bya ba'i mo 'gugs bsgrub nas/ ma rgyud kyi rdzogs rim bstan te dam pa rgya gar gyis mdzad pa'i ye shes mkha 'gro ma senge'i gdong pa yin zer la/ gzhan yang mkha' 'gro ma dang ming legs po btags nas ye shes kyi lha yin zer lo.*

67 Ibid., 16: *rang gi rdo rje slob dpon gyi dbang ma thob par phar bskur ba dang/ nges pa lnga ldan mi shes pas sems skyed mgo bar/ theg chen par khas len pa dang/ sdom pa mi brsungs zhing 'dul ba mi shes par mkhan po byed pa rnams bod rgan rnams kyi chos lugs yin.*

68 Ibid., 12: *de ltar yin na mu stegs dang/ gar log dang bon po rnams la yang mthu dang thun mong gi rtags nam mkha' la 'gro ba sogs dpag med yod.*

69 Ibid., 13–14.

70 For example, *Chos log sun 'byin* attributed to Bu ston Rin chen grub, ed. dPal ldan 'brug gzhung, (Thimpu: Kunsang Tobgyal & Mani Dorji, 1979, 25–36), 27: */gal te gter nas bton gyur kyang/ dbang dang lung sogs med pa'i phyir/ de dag spyad bya ma yin te/.* The authorship of this text is controversial. The text is not mentioned by Sog bzlog pa, and it does not appear in the catalogues of *Bu ston gsung 'bum.* Thu'u bkwan Chos kyi nyi ma also says openly that this text cannot have been written by Bu ston. See Matthew Kapstein, *The Tibetan Assimilation of Buddhism: Conversion, Contestation and Memory* (New York: Oxford University Press, 2000), 253–54.

71 Chag lo, *NgL,* 13: *yang bsam yas bzhengs dus rgya gar nas gu ru padma 'byung gnas byon nas chos log tshar bcad/ rjes su bzung ba'i rten 'brel 'ga' brtsams nas slar rgya gar du gshegs so/ de rjes su rgyal po pe kar bal po ka ka ru 'dzin bya ba'i spangs su zhugs nas [...] bsam yas su padma yin zhes bsgrags nas/.*

72 For example, this text is mentioned by Davidson 2005, 291 and idem 2002, 211; Wangchuk, 277; Martin 1996, 27; Doctor, 31, etc.

73 Doctor, 31.

74 Martin 1996, 27.

75 About these two masters, see Kapstein 2000, 121–37. Even if these two masters are dGe lugs pa, Thu'u bkwan is also a sympathizer of rNying ma pa.

76 Dudjom, 891, refutes the argument of Chag lo, according to which the tantras of the rNying ma pa are said not to have Indian origins. He indicates that the sojourn of Chag lo in India was too

brief to draw any conclusions about what texts were present in India at that time. It looks like the arguments stay rather vague from both sides.

77 Thu'u bkwan, 35: *Chag lo tsā ba mkhas pa chen po yin pas de lta bu'i blun gdams ga la gsungs/ des na 'di yang blun po chags sdang tshan zhig gis brtsams nas chag lo la kha gyar ba 'dra'o.*

78 'Gos lHas btsas, *NgL*, 25: *Chag lo dang 'gos kyi springs yig 'di gnyis ma dpe dag cha thon pa mi 'dug kyang dpyod pa 'jug phyir par du bkod pa lags.*

79 *Sa paṇ kun dga' rgyal mtshan gyi gsung 'bum*, Glegs bam gsum pa, (Lhasa: ed. Bod ljong bod yig dpe rnying dpe skrung khang 1992), 531–34. As there are not many texts from Chag lo that have come down to us, this was the only text of Chag lo available to me.

80 Jared Douglas Rhoton, *A Clear Differentiation of the Three Codes: Essential Distinctions Among the Individual Liberation, Great Vehicle, and Tantric Systems: The sDom gsum rab dbye and Six Letters of Sa skya Paṇ ḍi ta Kun dga' rGyal mtshan,* (Albany: State University of New York Press, 2002), 206.

81 *Sa paṇ gsung 'bum*, 533–34: *gsang sngags gsar rnying gnyis la bod kyis ni/ sbyar ba'i rgyud sde mang ste gang dag lags.*

82 About Sa paṇ's motivations, see Robert Mayer, "The Sa skya Paṇḍita, the White Panacea, and Clerical Buddhism's Current Credibilty Crisis," *Tibet Journal*, 21.1 (1994), 79–105.

83 *Sa paṇ gsung 'bum*, 545–46: *dri ba bcu gcig pa gsang sngags gsar rnying la bod kyis sbyar ba'i rgyud sde gang lags gsungs pa'ang/ sngags rnying ma la lha mo skye rgyud dang/ bum ril thod mkhar la sogs pa shin tu mang bar gda'/ gsar ma la bod kyis sbyar ba'i rgyud dus 'byung dang/ phyag na rdo rje mkha' 'gro dang/ ra li nyi shu rtsa bzhi la sogs pa shin tu mang po brjod kyis mi lang ba cig gda' ste/ thams cad gsal kha ston na phog thug bag tsam yong bar gda' bas khyed nyid kyis dpyod mdzod.*

84 Robert Mayer, *A Scripture of the Ancient Tantra Collection: The Phur pa bcu gnyis* (Oxford: Kiscadale Publications, 1996), 17–18.

85 1334 is a date of redaction of the *bsTan 'gyur* by Bu ston. Exact dates of compilation of the *bKa' 'gyur* are not known but there is firm evidence that in the first half of the 14th century the Zhwa lu *bKa' 'gyur* came into existence. For further details about the formation of the *bKa' 'gyur* and the *bsTan 'gyur*, see Paul Harrison, "A Brief History of the Tibetan bKa' 'gyur." In *Tibetan Literature: Studies in Genre*, ed. José Ignacio Cabezón and Roger R. Jackson (Ithaca: Snow Lion, 1995), 70–94.

86 Mayer 1997, 619–31, has analyzed thoroughly the points that were "wrong" with *vajrakīlaya* tantras, such as the problem of transcription of some mantras.

87 The terms "rNying ma" and "gSar ma" are also mentioned in the mKhas pa lDe'u's *Chos 'byung*, 142–43; and by Nyang ral Nyi ma 'Od zer in his *Chos'byung me tog snying po sbrang rtsi'i bcud*. In *Gangs can rig mdzod*, vol. 5, (Lhasa: Bod ljongs mi dmangs dpe skrun khang, 1988), 482; according to David Germano, "Architecture and Absence in the Secret Tantric History of the Great Perfection (rdzogs chen)," JIABS, 17.2 (1994), 237, the final part (where these terms actually appear) may have not been written by Nyang ral himself, but could be a later amplification either by his son or another direct disciple.

88 Matthew Kapstein, "*gDams ngag*: Tibetan technologies of the Self." In *Tibetan Literature: Studies in Genre*, ed. José Ignacio Cabezón and Roger R.. Jackson (Ithaca: Snow Lion, 1995), 275–89.

15

Elevating Tsongkhapa's Disciples: Khedrup Jey and the *Jey Yabsey Süm*

ELIJAH ARY

Within the Gelugpa (*dge lugs pa*) tradition, three figures have come to collectively represent the highest position of doctrinal authority: the school's founder, Tsongkhapa Lobsang Dragpa (Tsong kha pa Blo bzang grags pa, 1357–1419), and his disciples Gyaltsab Darma Rinchen (rGyal tshab Dar ma rin chen, 1364–1432) and Khedrup Geleg Pelzang (mKhas grub dGe legs dpal bzang, 1385–1438), hereafter referred to simply as Tsongkhapa, Gyaltsab and Khedrup. Often referred to collectively as the *Jey Yabsey Süm* (*rje yab sras gsum*), or "lordly trio of the [spiritual] father and [his two] sons," these three figures form a sort of Gelugpa triumvirate — a group of three individuals in a joint, yet not necessarily equal, position of power or authority. Their respective philosophical and commentarial works, jointly arranged in the monumental *rJe yab sras gsung 'bum* (*The Collected Works of the Lordly Trio of the Father [and his] Two Sons*), help constitute the basis for study in larger Gelugpa monastic institutions such as Sera (Se ra), Drepung ('Bras spungs) and Ganden (dGa' ldan).[1]

The *Jey Yabsey Süm* is fundamental to the staunch conservatism that has come to characterize the Gelugpa tradition.[2] In fact, for a Gelugpa scholar to disagree with philosophical statements made by a member of the triumvirate is considered to be an outright denial of their validity and thus a refusal of the very tenets that are fundamental to one's identity as a member of the Gelugpa tradition. There are records of authors and their works receiving strong criticism for disagreeing, even slightly, with the teachings of "Tsongkhapa and his two chief disciples."

One such case is the founder of the Jey (*byas*) college of Sera Monastery, Lodrö Rinchen Sengey (Blo gros rin chen seng ge, 14th–15th century), whose works were criticized by one of his later successors, Jetsun Chökyi Gyaltsen (rJe btsun Chos kyi rgyal mtshan, 1469–1544, hereafter simply Jetsunpa), for this very reason.[3] Eventually, Lodrö Rinchen Sengey's works were supplanted by Jetsunpa's own philosophical commentaries, which have remained in use at Sera Jey right up to the present day.

Another similar case is Sera's third abbot, Gungru Gyaltsen Zangpo (Gung ru rGyal mtshan bzang po, 1383–1450), who is said to have been publicly upbraided by Khedrup himself for espousing and propagating theories on emptiness that were purportedly inconsistent with Tsongkhapa's teachings.[4] Whether this event in fact took place is debatable, as it is absent from all of Khedrup's own early biographical accounts, as well as from the earliest extant history of the Gelugpa tradition, the *bKa' gdams chos 'byung gsal ba'i sgron me* (*The Lamp Illuminating the Ecclesiastic History of the Kadampas*), by Lechen Kunga Gyaltsen (Las chen Kun dga' rgyal mtshan, 1432–1506).[5] Nevertheless, it would seem to clearly indicate how disagreement with, or rejection of the seemingly absolute authority of Tsongkhapa and his "two chief spiritual heirs" (*sras kyi thu bo gnyis*) is considered a grave offense for any Gelugpa to commit.[6]

This is not to say, however, that the three figures that comprise the *Jey Yabsey Süm* triumvirate are in perfect agreement with one another themselves; there are multiple cases where we find authors, such as the well-known historian and scholar Panchen Sonam Dragpa (Paṇ chen bSod nams grags pa, 1478–1554) and even Jetsunpa himself, taking great pains to reconcile seemingly contradictory statements made by both Gyaltsab and Khedrup with Tsongkhapa's own doctrines.[7] Nor are the works of these figures relied on for the same topics. Indeed, Gyaltsab's works on *prajñāpāramitā* and *pramāṇa* are given precedence over Khedrup's own works on these topics, while the latter's major Madhyamaka work, the *sTong thun chen mo*, is more heavily relied on than his counterpart's.

But whatever their apparent dissonances, both Gyaltsab and Khedrup are today considered to be inalienable members of the rather momentous *Jey Yabsey Süm*, and their position as Tsongkhapa's closest spiritual heirs and interpreters is rarely, if ever, questioned. In the course of my doctoral research, however, I came across indices that pointed to an important shift in just who was to be considered one of the master's "chief disciples." It is this very shift that I will discuss here. I will focus primarily on Khedrup's hierarchical status, given the lack of space and the odd paucity of early historical sources concerning Gyaltsab.[8]

Khedrup Geleg Pelzang: A Brief Introduction

As I have already said, Khedrup Geleg Pelzang (1385–1438), commonly known as Khedrup Jey, or here simply Khedrup, occupies an exalted position as one of Tsongkhapa's two most important and authoritative disciples and interpreters. As such, he is cast by the Gelugpa tradition as an integral member of the *Jey Yabsey Süm* triumvirate, along with Gyaltsab. Chosen as Tsongkhapa's second successor to the Ganden abbacy by Gyaltsab in 1432, he is often said to have been one of the most important figures for the growth and development of the Gelugpa tradition. Indeed, Khedrup was responsible for establishing the monastery's first college devoted specifically to the study of Buddhist philosophy.[9]

Khedrup's illustrious position as Tsongkhapa's chief spiritual heir alongside Gyaltsab, and the authority it entails, is universally accepted within the Gelugpa school today and constitutes a fundamental part of that tradition's infamous orthodoxy and conservatism. His exalted status is not only stressed by biographers, but is also reaffirmed by historians, and can be found exemplified in traditional Tibetan *thang kha* paintings, where Khedrup is most often depicted seated on Tsongkhapa's left opposite Gyaltsab.

Most Western scholars of Tibet tend to agree with the Gelugpa tradition's opinion that Khedrup occupies the illustrious position as one of Tsongkhapa's two most important disciples and authoritative interpreters, and is an integral member of the *Jey Yabsey Süm*. Tucci, Snellgrove, Richardson, Thurman and Cabezón all describe Khedrup in this way.[10] Cabezón reports that Khedrup was one of Tsongkhapa's *sras kyi thu bo*, or "chief spiritual heirs," which, as we shall see shortly, was not necessarily the case. Similarly, J.C. Kutcher, in her doctoral work focusing on the life of the First Dalai Lama Gendün Drüp (dGe 'dun grub, 1391–1474), dubs Khedrup as one of the founder's "two chief disciples."[11] Furthermore, according to Ngawang Samten and Jay Garfield's recent translation of Tsongkhapa's commentary on the *Mūlamadhyamakakārikā*, upon his death Tsongkhapa left behind numerous followers including his "two principle disciples," who Samten and Garfield readily identify as Gyaltsab and Khedrup.[12]

However, if we look at early Gelugpa historical sources, such as the *bKa' gdams chos 'byung gsal ba'i sgron me* by Lechen Kunga Gyaltsen and Gö Lotsawa Shönupel's ('Gos lo tsa ba gZhon nu dpal, 1392–1481) *Deb ther sngon po* (*Blue Annals*), our vision of Khedrup's position becomes more nuanced. Khedrup is not always portrayed as having been one of Tsongkhapa's two chief disciples. In fact, the current classification of disciples according to which Khedrup holds a prominent and prized position as one of the teacher's chief spiritual heirs seems to occur only around the 15th–16th centuries with Panchen Sonam Dragpa's *bKa' gdams gsar rnying gi chos 'byung yid kyi mdzes rgyan* (*The Mind's Ornament: A History of the Old and New Kadampa Schools*).

Looking back at the aforementioned earliest histories that discuss the Gelugpa school, it first becomes clear that the strong doctrinal conservatism — the strong emphasis on maintaining, respecting and conforming to the existing or traditionally accepted doctrinal norms as defined by the works of Tsongkhapa and interpreted by his "chief disciples" Gyaltsab and Khedrup — which seems to characterize the Gelugpa tradition today, did not necessarily exist during the school's early stages of development. Indeed, according to the *bKa' gdams chos 'byung gsal ba'i sgron me* — (composed ca 1494), one of the earliest, most extensive and richest historical accounts of the Gelugpa school — it would appear that Tsongkhapa's followers often established their own monasteries, had their own disciples and taught his doctrines not only through the use of Tsongkhapa's own works, but especially based on their own understanding and interpretations of his teachings. Students were therefore learning Tsongkhapa's teachings through the interpretive lenses of their own teachers, many of whom had studied with Tsongkhapa directly; they did not learn the founder's theories exclusively through the interpretational lenses of Gyaltsab and Khedrup, as eventually was to become the case.[13] There seems to have been no established orthodoxy of views, especially one that included the teachings of Khedrup. In fact, as we will see, according to Lechen Kunga Gyaltsen's account, Khedrup did not necessarily enjoy the status of a chief spiritual heir at all. Who, then, were considered Tsongkhapa's closest disciples?

Classifying Tsongkhapa's Disciples

From relatively early on in Gelugpa historiography, there seems to have been an attempt to establish a classification of the founder's followers. These classifications often vary from one another depending on the particular criteria privileged by each specific author. Most early historians tend to classify Tsongkhapa's disciples according to their place of origin. Others do so according to each disciple's function with regard to the teacher, such as who attended him during illness, who he sent out as representatives and who accompanied him during his retreats. Later on, however, there is a shift in these classifications marked by an attempt to establish just who constituted his closest and most important disciples. This latter effort seems to take on a more concrete formulation in Gelugpa histories composed by important historians such as Panchen Sonam Dragpa, the Fifth Dalai Lama's regent Desi Sangye Gyatso (sDe srid Sangs rgyas rgya mtsho, 1653–1705) and the

Second Jamyang Sheypa Konchog Jigmey Wangpo ('Jam dbyangs bzhad pa dKon mchog 'jigs med dbang po, 1728–1792). However, the categorization of who was and was not a close disciple of Tsongkhapa had already begun by the time that these authors flourished.

Of the various ways that Tsongkhapa's closer disciples are referred to, one term has become the most prominent in the Gelugpa tradition today. As described briefly above, the term *rje yab sras gsum* today refers to Tsongkhapa, Gyaltsab and Khedrup. Implicitly expressed with this term is the notion that he had *only* two chief disciples. Had there been three disciples, then the term *gsum* (three) would be replaced by the term *bzhi* (four), indicating that together with the "father" (i.e. Tsongkhapa), the total number of people being referred to is four. In Panchen Sonam Dragpa's *bKa' gdams gsar rnying gi chos 'byung*, which I will discuss in more detail shortly, there is one case where the expression *rje yab sras bzhi* (the lordly quartet: the [spiritual] father and [his three] sons) is indeed used to refer to Tsongkhapa, Gyaltsab, Dulwadzinpa Dragpa Gyaltsen ('Dul ba 'dzin pa Grags pa rgyal mtshan, 1374–1434/36) and Khedrup.[14] In any event, the expression *rje yab sras gsum* (lordly trio of the [spiritual] father and [his two] sons) as it is understood today serves to describe a distinct triumvirate within the Gelugpa tradition, excluding from its ranks any figures other than Tsongkhapa, Gyaltsab and Khedrup. The writings of these three figures serve as the defining limits of what is and is not an acceptable view for the school; to deny the absolute authority of the writings of the members of the *Jey Yabsey Süm* is an outright betrayal of Tsongkhapa's teachings as a whole and, in some sense, to renege one's identity as a Gelugpa.[15] A Gelugpa is therefore defined today not merely by his adherence to the views and teachings of Tsongkhapa, but also by his adherence to his views as interpreted and presented by Gyaltsab and Khedrup.

The earliest occurrence I have encountered of the expression *rje yab sras gsum* in reference to Tsongkhapa, Gyaltsab and Khedrup appears to be in the colophon of a text composed by Jetsunpa in defense of one of Khedrup's commentaries on the *Kālacakra* cycle, the *Dus kyi 'khor lo'i sku gsung thugs yongs su rdzogs pa'i sgrub thabs pad ma dkar po'i zhal lung*.[16] This is not to say that Jetsunpa invented the expression; he could very well have been following someone else's lead. However, the term is absent from other early classifications of Tsongkhapa's disciples. For example, Chöden Rabjor (Chos ldan rab 'byor, 15th century), Khedrup's disciple and earliest biographer, does not use the term *rje yab sras gsum* at all in his account of his teacher's life, and it is even missing from Jetsunpa's own secret biography of Khedrup, which leads me to wonder how much in currency it was at this early stage.[17] The expression is more explicitly and intentionally used to refer to Tsongkhapa, Gyaltsab and Khedrup in the colophon of a later Khedrup biography, this time written by Jetsunpa's disciple and main biographer, Deleg Nyima (bDe legs nyi ma, 16th century).[18] The relevant passage states that Khedrup was succeeded on the Ganden throne in 1438 by his disciple Shalupa Legpa Gyaltsen (Zhwa lu pa Legs pa rgyal mtshan,1375–1450), and that the latter, along with Yagdewa Lodrö Chökyong (g.Yag sde ba Blo gros chos skyong, 1389–1463) and Khedrup's other followers, ensured and promoted the tradition of the *Jey Yabsey Süm*.[19] Although this would appear to be the earliest biographical work to explicitly include Khedrup in the *Jey Yabsey Süm*, the aforementioned passage in Jetsunpa's *Kālacakra* text is the earliest use of the expression that I have so far found.[20]

Early Gelugpa histories in fact use a variety of locutions to refer to Tsongkhapa's closer disciples. The term *rje yab sras* ("lordly father and son[s]"), a variation of which we have just discussed, is most often used to designate Tsongkhapa and his group of followers in general. In the earliest sources, it does not designate any particular members of Tsongkhapa's entourage, and is not necessarily limited to a specific number of members.[21] It is also a term often used by Jetsunpa in his undated biographical work on Khedrup, and in this case refers to both the general assembly of Tsongkhapa's disciples but also to Khedrup in particular when the latter is discussed in conjunction with Tsongkhapa.[22] The term *dngos slob*, meaning "direct disciple," is also encountered in such works, though it is used in a very general sense to designate direct disciples as opposed to those who did not receive teachings from him but are nevertheless considered his followers. Of the terms that appear the most, however, the expression *sras kyi thu bo* (chief spiritual heir), sometimes accompanied by the numeral two (*gnyis*), seems to be the most important and frequently employed. Indeed, this expression, used mainly to refer to Tsongkhapa's closest or chief disciples, has been at the center of Gelugpa classification efforts from the very start.

In Lechen Kunga Gyaltsen's *bKa' gdams chos 'byung gsal ba'i sgron me*, for example, we find this expression used frequently to speak of the two disciples closest to Tsongkhapa. Contrary to later classifications, however, which put forth Gyaltsab and Khedrup as the founder's "*sras kyi thu bo gnyis*" (two chief spiritual heirs), this text uses the expression to refer instead to Gyaltsab and Dulwadzinpa Dragpa Gyaltsen (hereafter simply Duldzin), another major Gelugpa figure who is said to have been responsible for teaching all of Tsongkhapa's followers about monastic ethics (*vinaya*), something that Tsongkhapa is said to have regarded as being of the utmost importance.[23] According to Lechen Kunga Gyaltsen's history, Tsongkhapa had no disciples who had not received teachings from both Gyaltsab and Duldzin, dubbed Tsongkhapa's "two chief [spiritual] heirs."[24] It seems, moreover, that Duldzin was already a member of Tsongkhapa's entourage even before

Gyaltsab appeared on the scene around 1396, giving him seniority even vis-à-vis Gyaltsab.[25] Although the author of the *bKa' gdams chos 'byung gsal ba'i sgron me* does give Khedrup the epithet "Dharma king" (*chos kyi rgyal po*), and enumerates him among Tsongkhapa's disciples, Khedrup is invariably mentioned apart from Tsongkhapa's two chief spiritual heirs.[26]

In short, according to Kunga Gyaltsen's account, Khedrup was not originally one of Tsongkhapa's two chief spiritual heirs. This alternate definition of the latter's chief disciples is in fact supported by Khedrup's own *Great Biography of Tsongkhapa* and his *Miscellaneous Writings*, in which Khedrup never once insinuates that he himself enjoyed the exalted status the later Gelugpa tradition claims he did. Instead, he continually refers to Duldzin and Gyaltsab as Tsongkhapa's "spiritual heirs" (*rgyal sras*), portraying them as two of the teacher's closest followers.[27] Khedrup even makes it clear that it was both Gyaltsab and Duldzin, referred to as "the spiritual masters" or "preceptors" (*slob dpon*), that were entrusted with establishing and building Ganden Monastery between 1409 and 1410.[28] So, according to both the *bKa' gdams chos 'byung gsal ba'i sgron me* and Khedrup himself, Tsongkhapa's two chief disciples were not Gyaltsab and Khedrup, as the Gelugpa tradition would now have us believe, but rather Gyaltsab and Duldzin.[29]

Even more interesting, however, is the fact that Khedrup himself did not seem to consider Tsongkhapa to be his most important teacher. In a response to a letter from his disciple Sangye Rinchen (Sangs rgyas rin chen; dates unknown), he clearly states that although he had studied under approximately fifty different masters, his three most important, his root teachers (*rtsa ba'i bla ma*), were Jampel Dorjey Nyingpo ('Jam dpal rdo rje snying po; dates unknown), Lamdreypa Yeshey Pel (Lam 'bras pa Ye shes dpal; dates unknown) and Tsongkhapa's teacher, Rendawa Zhönu Lodrö (Red mda' ba gZhon nu blo gros, 1349–1412).[30] Tsongkhapa's absence from this declaration is striking, especially coming from one of his allegedly closest disciples. Although Khedrup did receive instruction directly from Tsongkhapa, as is clearly apparent throughout his *gSan yig*, it would appear that he saw himself primarily as the disciple of other figures, such as Kunkhyen Sherab Zangpo (Kun mkhyen Shes rab bzang po, 14th–15th century) and Kunga Gyaltsen (Kun dga' rgyal mtshan, 1382–1446),[31] but also of both Duldzin and Gyaltsab, who are also mentioned among his teachers.[32] It seems, therefore, that even Khedrup did not consider himself to be one of Tsongkhapa's two chief disciples.

That Khedrup was Gyaltsab's disciple also helps to explain how the latter could name him as successor to the Ganden throne. Indeed, when we look at abbatial succession practices in the early Gelugpa school, we find that the position of abbot seems to have been handed down from teacher to disciple rather than from peer to peer.[33] The exception to this rule occurs when the benefactors of a monastery or monastic college, usually members of the Tibetan aristocracy, would intervene to entreat a particular religious figure to ascend the throne of the monastery or college of which they were patrons. This custom usually occurs, at least within the Gelugpa tradition, when an abbot dies before naming a successor, or else has no chief students left to fill the position. This was apparently the case with Lodrö Rinchen Sengey's successor to the abbacy of Sera Jey College, Paljor Lhundrup (dPal 'byor lhun grub, 1427–1514). Indeed, when Lodrö Rinchen Sengey passed away, his two main disciples, Jamyang Dragpa ('Jam dbyangs grags pa, 13th–14th century) and Chöjor Zangpo (Chos 'byor bzang po, 13th–14th century), were away teaching in Chamdo and passed away themselves before they could return to Lhasa to assume the position. The throne of Sera Jey therefore remained empty until the college's sponsors, the aristocrat Paljor Gyalpo (dPal 'byor rgyal po, 14th–15th century) and his lady Butri Paldzom (Bu 'khrid dpal 'dzoms, 14th–15th century), asked Paljor Lhundrup, who had studied briefly under Lodrö Rinchen Sengey, to ascend the throne. Eventually, Paljor Lhundrup passed on the abbacy to his own disciple, Dönyo Palden (Don yod dpal ldan,1445–1524), who then passed it on to Jetsunpa, who had briefly studied under both of these masters.[34] Another such account is given in the *bKa' gdams chos 'byung gsal ba'i sgron me*, according to which Paljor Gyalpo asked Tsongkhapa's nephew, Lobsang Nyima (Blo bzang nyi ma, 1439–1492), also a disciple of Lodrö Rinchen Sengey, to take over the abbacy of Drepung, of which Paljor Gyalpo was also a patron. Unfortunately, the text does not mention what motivated Paljor's request.[35]

According to the *bKa' gdams chos 'byung gsal ba'i sgron me*, Khedrup was asked to ascend the throne by Gyaltsab during the latter's last journey to his homeland monastery in Nyangtö (*myang stod*). Lechen Kunga Gyaltsen paints a picture of a nostalgic Gyaltsab who, looking back at his old monastery, realized that his life was almost at an end and that he would not be returning there. He therefore decided to hand over the Ganden abbacy to Khedrup, who had traveled to Nyangtö from his monastery in Tsang (*gtsang*).[36] Following his decision to appoint Khedrup as Ganden's new abbot, Gyaltsab took him on a tour of Drepung and Sera. Khedrup's arrival alongside Gyaltsab seems to have caused unrest at Drepung, where, Lechen Kunga Gyaltsen tells us, a group of monks approached the founder and abbot, Jamyang Chöjey, and asked him if they were obliged to bow down to Khedrup. Jamyang Chöjey answered, "You may do as you will. As for myself, I will touch my head to [Khedrup's] feet."[37] The disciples followed the example of their teacher and paid homage to the new abbot of Ganden.[38]

The hesitation shown by Jamyang Chöjey's followers to show respect for Khedrup is indicative of Khedrup's status in the Gelugpa school ca 1494, when the *bKa' gdams chos 'byung gsal ba'i sgron me* was most likely composed. Indeed, had he been considered one of Tsongkhapa's two chief spiritual heirs and an uncontestable authority for the Gelugpa school, it is unlikely that Lechen Kunga Gyaltsen would portray other Gelugpas as questioning the need to pay him respect. In fact, their hesitation in the episode is an indication that Khedrup's status among Drepung's inmates was an issue, and the story suggests that they did not consider themselves followers of Khedrup, but primarily of Jamyang Chöjey.[39] The episode provides further evidence that Khedrup's status was in flux: he was not yet an established member of an all-powerful Gelugpa triumvirate, and his authority was not yet accepted by all members of the still-young school.[40]

One of the earliest sources after Chöden Rabjor's biography of Khedrup that depicts Khedrup as one of Tsongkhapa's more important followers is Chimey Rabgye's *rJe rin po che'i rnam thar gser gyi mchod sdong*. This work, actually meant as Tsongkhapa's biography, gives multiple lists of his followers, sorting them by their function or by some other characteristic, and could very well be the earliest work to do so. The work gives a number of categories, such as those who accompanied Tsongkhapa on retreats, or those who attended him during his illness, and figures can sometimes be included in multiple categories.[41] Khedrup, for instance, is counted among the "three precious [disciples]" (*rin po che gsum*) — along with Gyaltsab and Duldzin — who make up part of the "seven prophesied sons,"[42] the "seven disciples who attended Tsongkhapa during his illness"[43] and also the "eight great heirs who helped the growth of the two doctrines of the monastic seats."[44] The author does not, however, use the expression "chief spiritual heirs" when referring to Khedrup. Instead, he uses another term, *thugs sras bu chen*, or "great spiritual sons."[45]

It is interesting to note that despite the fact that Chimey Rabgye awards Khedrup the status of one of Tsongkhapa's closer disciples, he is merely one among many others, characterized not simply by their degree of intimacy with the master, as becomes the case in later classifications, but primarily by the particular function they had (and sometimes in relation to him), or by a specific quality or character trait they manifested throughout their life. Furthermore, Rabgye's classification also underscores the lack of any definitive Gelugpa triumvirate composed exlusively of Tsongkhapa, Gyaltsab and Khedrup. On the contrary, the author makes no mention or use of the expression "chief spiritual heirs," let alone of the expression *rje yab sras gsum*.

Still, Rabgye does portray Khedrup as having been an important and close disciple of Tsongkhapa, which is evident from his inclusion along with Gyaltsab and Duldzin in the "three precious disciples," although it is unclear as to exactly why these three are to be considered precious.[46] Rabgye makes reference to a biography of Khedrup by the latter's disciple, Chöden Rabjor, saying that according to Rabjor, Khedrup received the Guhyasāmaja empowerment and other teachings from Tsongkhapa just prior to the latter's death.[47] This is an important element not only for dating Rabgye himself, but also with regards to the way he portrays Khedrup throughout his works.[48] Indeed, Rabjor's work, which we are unfortunately unable to discuss at any length here, paints a very particular picture of his master as an important and close disciple of Tsongkhapa-*qua*-Mañjuśrī. Because Rabgye's own portrayal of Khedrup as an important disciple is based in part on Rabjor's particular vision of Khedrup, we must consider the possibility that these views are to some extent repeated by Rabgye.

The elevation of Khedrup continues in subsequent Gelugpa historiography. In some ways similar to the *bKa' gdams chos 'byung gsal ba'i sgron me*, Panchen Sonam Dragpa's *bKa' gdams gsar rnying gi chos 'byung yid kyi mdzes rgyan*, composed in 1529, also uses the expression "two chief spiritual heirs" when referring to Gyaltsab and Duldzin. In this way, Sonam Dragpa follows in the footsteps of his teacher and fellow historian, Lechen Kunga Gyaltsen. However, Sonam Dragpa's work differs significantly from his teacher's portrayal of Khedrup by taking pains to add that although Gyaltsab and Duldzin were indeed Tsongkhapa's two chief spiritual heirs, Khedrup was actually Tsongkhapa's "only inner-heart son."[49] Here Sonam Dragpa seems to be deliberately entering the fray about the status of Khedrup, elevating him to an entirely new status as the one disciple closest to the master's heart. Sonam Dragpa thereby establishes a stronger connection between Tsongkhapa and Khedrup than what had been previously described, and paves the way for future writers who insist that Khedrup was one of the founder's most important disciples.

Sonam Dragpa provides the earliest specific mention I have found of Khedrup refered to as an "inner-heart disciple," which is a clear elevation of status in comparison to accounts provided by the *bKa' gdams chos 'byung gsal ba'i sgron me*, the *Blue Annals* and the *rJe rin po che'i rnam thar gser gyi mchod sdong*. Indeed, instead of being either another one of Tsongkhapa's direct disciples, or else one of the latter's three precious disciples, Khedrup becomes the disciple dearest to Tsongkhapa. In this way, he is elevated to a privileged and exalted level above all other followers, including both Gyaltsab and Duldzin who, as I already pointed out, were also Khedrup's teachers. Although Panchen Sonam Dragpa also mentions the other disciples, such as Jamyang Chöjey, Jamchen Chöjey Shakya Yeshe (Byams chen chos rje ShAkya ye shes, 1352–1435), Jey Sherab Sengey (rJe Shes rab seng ge, 1383–1445), Gungru Gyaltsen Zangpo and Gendün Drup (dGe 'dun grub,1391–1474), they are only awarded the status of "disciples whose enlightened activities are as vast as the sky," not as chief or even close disciples.[50]

Sonam Dragpa's statements concerning the identification of Tsongkhapa's most important disciples seem at one point to have become a point of contention. In his *dGa' ldan chos 'byung vaidurya ser po*, the regent to the Fifth Dalai Lama, Desi Sangye Gyatso, takes Dragpa to task for his ranking of Tsongkhapa's disciples in the *bKa' gdams gsar rnying gi chos 'byung yid kyi mdzes rgyan*. The Desi argues that Sonam Dragpa's classification is incorrect, saying that there are multiple ways in which Tsongkhapa's followers can be ranked, depending on those qualities that are deemed more important. Thus, he says, although Sonam Dragpa considers both Gyaltsab and Duldzin to be Tsongkhapa's chief spiritual sons, if one were to rank the latter's disciples according to who was of greatest benefit to the growth and glorification of his doctrine, then there are three chief disciples: the First Dalai Lama Gendün Drup, Gyaltsab, "who was an attendant to Tsongkhapa and a philosopher [in his own right]," and finally Khedrup, "who was of the utmost intelligence and expanded activity."[51] We can see from this critique that, first, Desi Sangye Gyatso is quite aware of a dispute concerning the classification of Tsongkhapa's disciples, and second, that even during his time there was no fixed and generally accepted classification of who were the master's main disciples.

It is not entirely surprising that Desi Sangye Gyatso should take issue with Sonam Dragpa's views. The Fifth Dalai Lama Ngawang Lobsang Gyatso (Ngag dbang blo bzang rgya mtsho, 1617–1682), the Desi's teacher and a historian in his own right, also seems to have disliked this scholar's work. He makes this clear in his *History of Tibet*, where he repeatedly comments on the incorrectness of the information given by Sonam Dragpa in his *Tibetan Chronicles*, going so far as to accuse him of being an idiot who "shows his lack of erudition" by misrepresenting events related to the construction of Tashi Lhunpo.[52]

There are, however, later authors who do in fact agree with Panchen Sonam Dragpa's classification of Tsongkhapa's students and use it in their own classification attempts, though they sometimes add supplementary information concerning who ranks where. In his *Byang chub lam gyi rim pa'i bla ma brgyud pa'i rnam par thar pa rgyal bstan mdzes pa'i rgyan mchog phul byung nor bu'i phreng ba*, Tsechogling Yeshe Gyaltsen (Tshe mchog gling Ye shes rgyal mtshan, 1713–1793), for example, follows Sonam Dragpa's classification of Tsongkhapa's followers, adding that Kenchen Ngawang Dragpa (mKhan chen Ngag dbang grags pa, 14th century) was Tsongkhapa's "heart-son," while Khedrup is awarded the status of Tsongkhapa's "inner heart-son" (*nang thugs sras*). This implies that while both of these figures were dear to Tsongkhapa, Khedrup occupied an even dearer place in the master's heart.[53]

Furthermore, in the *dGa' ldan chos 'byung nor bu'i phreng ba*, the Second Jamyang Sheypa Könchog Jigme Wangpo ('Jam dbyangs bzhad pa Kon mchog 'jigs med dbang po, 1728–1791) specifies that Khedrup's elevated status among Tsongkhapa's followers is due to the fact that he was very beneficial to Tsongkhapa's doctrine.[54]

Another later author to use Sonam Dragpa's classification is Tuken Lobsang Chökyi Nyima (Thu'u bkwan Blo bzang chos kyi nyi ma, 1737–1802), who, in his work on Buddhist philosophy, reiterates Sonam Dragpa's claims that Tsongkhapa's two chief heirs were Gyaltsab and Duldzin, while Khedrup was Tsongkhapa's only inner-heart son.[55] Interestingly, Panchen Sonam Dragpa's classification is not the only one used by these authors. Both Tsechogling and Jamyang Shepa also make use of Chimey Rabgye's classification, and Jamyang Sheypa even goes so far as to state that Tsongkhapa actually had three "precious uncontested regent-sons who upheld [the master's] doctrine" — Gyaltsab, Duldzin and Khedrup.[56]

So the question of precisely who got to sit alongside Tsongkhapa as his most important disciples was still an issue even by the end of the 18th century. However, we can also see that by then Khedrup had already come to occupy a relatively secure place among the master's chief spiritual heirs.[57] A little later, in the 19th century, Khedrup is awarded an even more prestigious ranking among Tsongkhapa's disciples. In Sermey Dragpa Khedrup's history of Ganden's Shartse College, he is given the status of Tsongkhapa's chief interpreter and commentator.[58] Dragpa Khedrup's work describes a meeting between Tsongkhapa and Khedrup during which the teacher personally asks him to compose commentaries on his works, especially regarding his theories on Madhyamaka philosophy, thereby appointing him as his chief and official interpreter.[59] This passage thus makes Khedrup the heir chosen by Tsongkhapa himself to comment on and propound his teachings on the middle way. It is important to note here that although there is mention of Tsongkhapa telling Khedrup to compose commentaries on his works in Deleg Nyima's biographical account of Khedrup, this story is absent from most other historical and biographical works depicting Khedrup's interaction with Tsongkhapa.[60] Furthermore, according to Deleg Nyima, although the request to compose commentaries on his works also concerned his exoteric teachings, Tsongkhapa's instruction was that he propound his tantric works in particular.[61] In contrast, in Dragpa Khedrup's story, Khedrup is made the chosen authority concerning Tsongkhapa's Madhyamaka tenets.[62] It must be noted, too, that according to the wording of Deleg Nyima's account, when Tsongkhapa instructed that Khedrup should compose commentaries, Tsongkhapa is shown as intending that Khedrup should do so for the students he would later amass in his own monastic community; not necessarily for the entire Gelugpa community, as is suggested by Sermey Dragpa Khedrup.[63] Deleg Nyima's version of this story is further indication that Tsongkhapa's disciples were not considered to be teaching his thought to their own followers based on a predetermined set of commentaries composed by Gyaltsab and Khedrup, as has become the assumption since. Instead, the passage supports my earlier contention that the early disciples learned Tsongkhapa's thought based on their individual teachers' own commentarial works.

Concluding Remarks

In light of the information given to us by early historical and biographical sources, it would seem that we must view with a grain of salt the contentions of the modern Gelugpa tradition that Khedrup is the integral and inalienable third member of the momentous *Jey Yabsey Süm* triumvirate. Indeed, although he is awarded such an exalted status now, early evidence points out that this was not necessarily always the case. We can see that not only was there an attempt made to identify and classify Tsongkhapa's closest disciples from a relatively early point in the Gelugpa tradition's history, but that these classifications varied widely, indicating a fair amount of dispute and disagreement on how to construe them and who to classify in what kind of position. Exactly who were Tsongkhapa's closest and most important heirs and interpreters seems to have been still undecided even by the late 18th century. What is rather clear is that Khedrup did not necessarily always enjoy the privileged position he does now. Throughout the classifications discussed, we see that his status undergoes a series of gradual, though clear shifts. Starting off as simply one of Tsongkhapa's disciples, he soon becomes exhalted as one of three or seven precious disciples. His status then changes again, and he becomes the teacher's only inner heart son, only to be once again glorified, this time as one of his three foremost spiritual heirs. Finally, he is elevated to his current and most illustrious status as one of only two chief spiritual heirs, and the appointed chief interpreter of the latter's Madhyamaka doctrine. His ascension through the echelons to the very top of the Gelugpa hierarchy therefore appears to have taken place gradually over time, and through the concerted efforts — whether conscious or not — of a number of key Gelugpa historians and biographers.

The relatively late appearance of the expression *rje yab sras gsum* — and subsequently of the *Jey Yabsey Süm* triumvirate as referring specifically to Tsongkhapa, Gyaltsab and Khedrup — would seem to offset even further traditional Gelugpa portrayals of Khedrup as an original and incontestable representative of Tsongkhapa's teachings — an idea that is at the very heart of the staunch conservatism that has now come to characterize the Gelugpa tradition as a whole. Indeed, it would seem to be that even if the number of Tsongkhapa's closest disciples was indeed limited to two, which is far from certain, Khedrup was not originally one of them. As he ascended the hierarchical ladder, he came to occupy the position once held by another very important Gelugpa figure, Duldzin Dragpa Gyaltsen, who according to multiple early sources (and even according to Khedrup himself) appears to have been one of Tsongkhapa's closest disciples.[64] Both Khedrup's ascension, and Duldzin's simultaneous near fading out of Gelugpa memory (only to be replaced with a new version of Khedrup's memory), points out clearly to us that a figure's status within a tradition or a lineage is not at all static, but can change, or rather can be changed, over time.

Notes

1 This is not to say that the entirety of the *Collected Works* of each of these figures is used for philosophical study in the Gelugpa curriculum, or that all three are considered to carry the same authority on different topics such as Madhyamaka and *pramāṇa*. As I will discuss shortly, specific works by one individual or another are used depending on the topic in question.

2 By conservatism, I am referring to the Gelugpa's strong emphasis on maintaining, respecting and conforming to existing or traditionally accepted doctrinal norms, particularly as defined by the works of Tsongkhapa and interpreted by his "chief disciples," Gyaltsab and Khedrup.

3 Paṇ chen bDe legs nyi ma, *rJe btsun chos kyi rgyal mtshan dpal bzang po'i rnam par thar pa dngos grub kyi char 'bebs* – hereafter *JNT* (Lhasa, Tibet: Ser byes mkhas snyen grwa tshang, [n.d.]), 22a.

4 See Paṇ chen bSod nams grags pa. *bKa' gdams gsar rnying gi chos 'byung yid kyi mdzes rgyan* (In *Two Histories of the bKa' gdams pa tradition from the Library of Burmiok Athing*. Gangtok: Gonpo Tseten, 1977), 138, and Thu'u bkwan Blo bzang chos kyi nyi ma, *Thu'u bkwan grub mtha'* (Lanzhou: Kan su'u mi rigs dpe skrun khang, 1989), 323. It should be noted that Gungru's philosophical works also disappeared and have only very recently resurfaced.

5 This event is first reported in an ecclesiastic history (*chos 'byung*) by the latter's disciple, Paṇ chen bSod nams grags pa (1478–1554). See Paṇ chen bSod nams grags pa, 38.

6 These two are by no means the only figures said to have been chastised by Gelugpa scholars for alleged misrepresentations or criticisms of Tsongkhapa's views. Indeed, similar stories are told of Drepung Monastery's founder, Jamyang Chöjey Tashi Palden ('Jam dbyangs chos rje bkra shis dpal ldan, 1379–1449). Another more recent case is that of the scholar Gendün Chöpel (dGe 'dun chos 'phel, 1903–1951). Educated at Drepung, Gendün Chöpel composed the *dBu ma'i zab gnad snying por dril ba'i legs bshad klu sgrub dgongs rgyan*, a Madhyamaka commentary strongly critical of a number of Tsongkhapa's key philosophical positions. Gendün Chöpel's actions drew a large amount of public contempt from within the Gelugpa school, spawning scathing rejoinders by multiple figures including his own teacher, Sherab Gyatso (Shes rab rgya mtsho, 1884–1968). See Donald Lopez, "Tibetan Polemical Literature (*dGag lan*)." In *Tibetan Literature: Studies in Genre*, ed. José Ignacio Cabezón and Roger R. Jackson (Ithaca, N.Y.: Snow Lion, 1996), 225, n.10. For a more detailed discussion of Gendün Chöpel's life and activities, see Lopez, *The Madman's Middle Way* (Chicago and London: University of Chicago Press, 2006), and Heather Stoddard, *Le Mendiant de l'Amdo* (Paris: Société d'Ethnographie, 1985).

7 Guy Newland has remarked that the three major authors of the dGe lugs pa Madhyamaka *yig cha* – Jetsunpa, Panchen Sonam Dragpa and the first Jamyang Sheypa ('Jam dbyangs bzhad pa Ngag dbang brtson grus, 1648–1721/22) – all seem to share the common goals of confirming the

"fundamental coherence" of Tsongkhapa's views. In the course of their efforts, all three authors are faced with the challenge of reconciling or rebutting the views of Gyaltsab and Khedrup that are inconsistent with their own understanding of Tsongkhapa's teachings. As a result, Newland remarks that Panchen Sonam Dragpa "boldly overthrows the assertions of Khedrup and Gyaltsab when they conflict with his own conclusions," while the first Jamyang Sheypa attempts instead to show the inherent consistency by reconciling "apparent contradictions among Tsong kha pa, Khedrup, and Gyaltsab." Guy Newland, "Debate Manuals in dGe lugs Monastic Colleges." In *Tibetan Literature: Studies in Genre*, ed. José Ignacio Cabezón and Roger R. Jackson (Ithaca, N.Y.: Snow Lion, 1996), 208–9.

8 Although there are biographical sketches found in various ecclesiastic histories, there seem to be no available early full-length biographies for Gyaltsab.

9 Las chen Kun dga' rgyal mtshan. *bKa' gdams chos 'byung gsal ba'i sgron me* (manuscript in author's possession), 370b.

10 Giuseppe Tucci, *The Religions of Tibet* (Berkeley: University of California Press, 1980), 37; David Snellgrove and Hugh Richardson, *A Cultural History of Tibet* (1968; reprint, Boston: Shambhala Publications, 1995), 183; Robert Thurman, *The Life and Teachings of Tsong Khapa* (Dharamsala: Library of Tibetan Works and Archives, 1982), 16; José Ignacio Cabezón, *A Dose of Emptiness: an Annotated Translation of the Stong thun chen mo of mKhas grub dge legs dpal bzang* (New York: State University of New York Press, 1992), 14.

11 J.C. Kutcher, "The Biography of the First Dalai Lama, Entitled 'Rje thams cad mkhyen pa dge 'dun grub dpal bzang po'i rnam thar ngo mtshar rmad byung nor bu'i phreng ba': a Translation and Analysis" (PhD Dissertation: University of Pennsylvania, 1979), 24.

12 Ngawang Samten and Jay Garfield, *Ocean of Reasoning: a great commentary on Nagārjuna's Mūlamadhyamakakārikā* (Oxford: Oxford University Press, 2006), xi.

13 Today, a monastic inmate's knowledge of Tsongkhapa's teachings is derived primarily from commentaries by influential figures from within the monasteries, themselves largely based on the interpretations of works by Gyaltsab and Khedrup. To deny the authority either of these authors, or of Gyaltsab's and Khedrup's interpretations, is considered a grave offense; Georges Dreyfus, *The Sound of Two Hands Clapping: The Education of a Tibetan Buddhist Monk* (Berkeley: University of California Press, 2003), 319–20.

14 Paṇ chen bSod nams grags pa, 164.

15 See Dreyfus, 319–20.

16 The passage using the expression *rje yab sras gsum* reads as follows: "The omniscient Khedrup set down clearly in his teachings the unmistaken intended meaning of the trilogy of commentaries [and of] the tantra, the *sādhana* of the lord Kālacakra, in accordance with the [enlightened] speech of the Dharma-lord Tsongkhapa, [who is] an emanation of the lord Mañjuśrī. By composing the *Kālacakra Sādhana: The Oral Instructions of Puṇḍarīka*, [he] accomplished an act of kindness for the fortunate ones who pursue the correct path. This coarse [work entitled] *Means for Eliminating Wrong Views* was undertaken by the learned monk Chos kyi rgyal mtshan, with the crown [of my head] bent towards the immaculate lotus-feet of the Lordly trio of the Father and [two] sons (*rje yab sras gsum*). It was compiled at the supreme place of accomplishments, Ri bo dga' ldan rnam par rgyal ba'i gling. May the teachings endure!" rJe btsun chos kyi rgyal mtshan, *Dus kyi 'khor lo'i sku gsung thugs yongs su rdzogs pa'i sgrub thabs pad ma dkar po'i zhal lung*. In *The Collected Works of mKhas grub dge legs dpal* (vol. *cha*, Delhi: Ngawang Gelek Demo, 1983), 83a.

17 See Chos ldan rab 'byor, *mKhas grub thams cad mkhyen pa'i rnam thar bsdus pa*. In *The Collected Works of mKhas grub dge legs dpal* (vol. 12. New Delhi: Ngawang Gelek Demo, 1983), 470–93; and rJe btsun Chos kyi rgyal mtshan, *mKhas grub thams cad mkhyen pa'i gsang ba'i rnam thar*. In *The Collected Works of mKhas grub dge legs dpal*, vol. 12., 421–70.

18 The text is entitled *The Biography of the Omniscient Khedrup that is Delightful to the Scholar's Mind* (*mKhas grub thams cad mkhyen pa'i rnam thar mkhas pa'i yid 'phrog* – hereafter *KYP*). The authorship of this biography is not entirely certain, as the author given in the colophon (Paṇ chen bDe legs nyi ma, *mKhas grub thams cad mkhyen pa'i rnam thar mkhas pa'i yid 'phrog*, 14a) is simply "Svasti," the Sanskrit equivalent of the Tibetan "Deleg" (*bde legs*, "happiness" or "well-being"). According to Cabezón 1992, 13, this text was composed by Kunga Deleg Rinchen (Kun dga' bde legs rin chen, 1446–1496), a disciple of Khedrup's younger brother Baso Chökyi Gyaltsen (Ba so Chos kyi rgyal mtshan, 1402–1473) and teacher of Jetsunpa. However, according to the *Dungkar Tibetological Great Dictionary*, it would seem instead that it was composed by Deleg Nyima, Jetsunpa's disciple; Dung dkar Blo bzang 'phrin las, *mKhas dbang dung dkar Blo bzan phrin las mchog gis mdzad pa'i bod rig pa'i tshig mdzod chen mo ses bya rab gsal zhes bya ba* (Beijing: China Tibetology Publishing House, 2002), 436. As there is no record of Kunga Deleg Rinchen composing a biography of Khedrup – he did write one of Tsongkhapa that is unfortunately no longer extant – I tend to agree with Dungkar.

19 *khri rin po ches thogs drangs gyag sde ba blo gros chos skyong sogs bu slob thams cad kyis rje btsun thams cad mkhyen pa tsong kha pa blo bzang grags pa // rgyal tshab dar ma rin chen // mkhas shing grub pa mchog brnyes dge legs dpal bzang po ste // rje yab sras gsum gyi mdzad pa'i rgyun rnams mi nyams par gong 'phel du mdzad pa 'di ga lags so //* (*KYP*, 13b–14a).

20 Leonard van der Kuijp has pointed out that Shakya Chogden's (ShAkya mchog ldan, 1428–1507) *Chos kyi 'khor lo bskor ba'i rnam gzhag ji ltar grub pa'i yi ge gzu bor gnas pa'i mdzangs pa dga' byed* (In *The Complete Works of gSer mdog paN chen ShAkya mchog ldan*. vol. *Ma*. Thimpu: Kunzang Topgey, 1975), fol. 472–73, composed in 1495, contains a passage using the expression *tsong kha pa yab sras gsum* in reference to Tsongkhapa, Gyaltsab and Khedrup; Leonard van der Kuijp, "Studies in Mkhas-Grub-Rje I: Mkhas-Grug-Rje's Epistemological Oeuvre and His Philological Remarks on Dignaga's Pramanasamuccaya," *Berliner Indologische Studien* 1 (1985), 98, n. 15. Although this is indeed another early use of the phrase, Jetsunpa's *Kālacakra* work appears to have been composed slightly earlier, during the latter's time at Ganden between 1492 and 1495 (See *JNT*, 12b).

21 The term is used, for example, by Chimey Rabgye (Zang zang ne rings pa 'Chi med rab rgyas, ca 14th century) in his list of Tsongkhapa's disciples, *rJe rin po che'i rnam thar gser gyi mchod sdong* (Delhi: Rakra Tethong, 2001), 18, hereafter *SCD,* which I will discuss below.

22 rJe btsun Chos kyi rgyal mtshan, 7b.

23 Paṇ chen bSod nams grags pa, 63.

24 *Lar na de dus kyi rje'i bu slob thams cad kyis sras kyi thu bo gnyis la chos mi gsan pa med pa yin skad* (Las chen Kun dga' rgyal mtshan, 366b).

25 mKhas grub rje dGe legs dpal bzang po, *rJe btsun bla ma tsong kha pa chen po'i ngo mtshar rmad du 'byung ba'i rnam par thar pad ad pa'i 'jug ngogs*. In *The Collected Works of Rje Tsoṅ Kha Pa Blo bzaṅ grags pa, reproduced from an example of the old Bkra-śis-lhun-po redaction from the library of Klu-'khyil Monastery of Ladakh*, ed. Ngawang Gelek Demo (New Delhi: Ngawang Gelek Demo, 1979), 23b – hereafter *NTC*. Furthermore, Duldzin was among Tsongkhapa's elder disciples who, following the latter's death in 1419, entreated Gyaltsab to take his place on the Ganden throne; see Phur bu lcog Ngag dbang byams pa, *Grwa sa chen po bzhi dang rgyad pa stod smad chags tshul pad dkar 'phreng ba*. In *Three dKar chag's*, Gedan Sungrab Minyam Gyunphel Series, vol. 13 (New Delhi: Ngawang Gelek Demo, 1970), 60. The date of Gyaltsab's initial meeting with Tsongkhapa is taken from Thurman, 21.

26 Las chen Kun dga' rgyal mtshan, 369a.

27 Khedrup (*NTC*, 32b) also lists eight other close disciples, all of whom accompanied Tsongkhapa during one of his important retreats at Ölka Chölung (*'ol kha chos lung*). They are classified according to their places of origin: four disciples from Ü (*dbus*), namely, Jamkarwa Dragpa Palden

Zangpo ('Jam dkar ba Grags pa dpal ldan bzang po, 14th century), Togden Jangseng (rTogs ldan Byang seng, 14th century), Neyten Rinchen Gyaltsen (gNas brtan Rin chen rgyal mtshan, 14th century) and Neyten Zangkyong (gNas brtan bzang skyong, 14th century); four from Domey (*mdo smad*): Jampel Gyatso ('Jam dpal rgya mtsho, 1356–1428), Sherab Drak (Shes rab grags, 14th century), Jampel Tashi ('Jam dpal bkra shis, 14th century) and Palkyong (dPal skyong, 14th century).

28 *NTC*, 50b. Khedrup also refers to both of these figures as his teachers in his *gSan yig*, and extols them in separate eulogies found in his own *Miscellaneous Writings*; see mKhas grub rje dGe legs dpal bzang, *mKhas grub rin po che'i gsung 'bum thor bu*. In *mKhas grub dge legs dpal bzang gi sung 'bum*. vol. *Ba*. CD-ROM (New York: Tibetan Buddhist Resource Center, 2003), 9a–11a and 14b–15b.

29 In contrast to the *bKa' gdams chos 'byung gsal ba'i sgron me*, the *Blue Annals* also places Khedrup as Gyaltsab's successor, but mentions him only once, stating that the latter took over the office of Ganden throne holder in 1431. The text does not give him an epithet, however, and Duldzin, oddly, is not mentioned at all. Another difference between these works is that while the *Blue Annals* merely mentions that Khedrup took over from Gyaltsab, who is said to have passed away the same year, the *bKa' gdams chos 'byung gsal ba'i sgron me* goes into more detail of the handing over of the Ganden abbacy to Khedrup; George Roerich, *The Blue Annals* (1949–1953; reprint, Delhi: Motilal Banarsidass, 1976), 1079; Las chen Kun dga' rgyal mtshan, 365b–366a.

30 mKhas grub rje dGe legs dpal bzang, *mKhas grub rin po che'i gsung 'bum thor bu*, 174a–175a.

31 The *gSan yig* lists these teachers frequently throughout the text.

32 The *bKa' gdams chos 'byung gsal ba'i sgron me* names Gyaltsab as one of Khedrup's main teachers, along with Duldzin and Jamkarwa Jampel Chözang ('Jam dkar ba 'Jam dpal chos bzang, 14th century), 369a. This is further supported by Kharnag Lotsawa Paljor Gyatso (mKhar nag Lo tsā ba dPal 'byor rgya mtsho), who reports that although Gyaltsab had many learned disciples, he chose Khedrub to be his successor on the throne of Ganden; mKhar nag Lo tsā ba dPal 'byor rgya mtsho, *dGdGa' ldan chos 'byung dpag bsam sdong po mkhas pa dgyes byed* (n.d., n.p.), 10b.

33 It was possible for a fellow student to entreat a particular figure to ascend a monastery's throne, as is in some senses the case with Tsongkhapa's first successor, Gyaltsab, who is said to have been requested by a committee of Tsongkhapa's disciples, headed by Duldzin, to take over the Ganden abbacy in their master's stead. However, in this particular situation, Duldzin was not already Ganden's outgoing abbot, and he was in part responsible for finding the monastery's first representative after Tsongkhapa. As Gyaltsab had apparently taught most of Tsongkhapa's disciples, including Duldzin himself, he seems to have been a natural choice for the position. This does not exclude the possibility that he was also selected for political alliances he may have had, but this can only be proven through a closer, more in-depth study of both Gyaltsab's life and of Gelugpa abbatial succession practices in general.

34 Zongtse Champa Thupten, *History of the Sera Monastery of Tibet, 1418–1959* (Delhi: International Academy of Indian Culture and Aditya Prakashan, 1995), 238. Deleg Nyima's account of Donyö Palden's descision to name Jetsunpa as his successor also reflects the importance placed on the candidate's status as a disciple of the outgoing abbot. In this rather interesting passage, Donyö Palden expresses regret at the fact that Jetsunpa had not spent a long time as his student, but saying that given the latter's reputation throughout gTsang as an excellent scholar, he would nevertheless choose this particular candidate as his successor to the Sera Jey abbacy (*JNT*, 14b–15a).

35 Las chen Kun dga' rgyal mtshan, 373a.

36 Las chen Kun dga' rgyal mtshan, 365b.

37 At first glance, Jamyang Chöjey's willingness to bow down to Khedrup could be seen as an indication that he readily accepted Khedrup's authority as one of Tsongkhapa's chief disciples. However, when we consider the fact that he was leading a monastic community whose patronage came from the same source as that of Ganden monastery – namely, the local Phagmodru ruler – and that Gyaltsab, Jamyang Chöjey's own teacher, was present to introduce Khedrup as his successor, then Jamyang Chöjey's actions could be seen as a political move.

38 Las chen Kun dga' rgyal mtshan, 366a.

39 There seems to have been a competition between Jamyang Chöjey and Khedrup. In Jamyang Chöjey's biography by Tsangtön Kunga Gyaltsen, it is said that the two often debated one another, and that upon being asked who was the more astute disciple, Tsongkhapa said that Jamyang Chöjey was the more apt at understanding and commenting texts that he had never seen before. According to this biography, Jamyang Chöjey would often joke about this answer, saying that Tsongkhapa had said that he was the more intelligent of the two (gTsang ston Kun dga' rgyal mtshan, *Thams cad mkhyen pa 'jam dbyangs chos rje bkra shis dpal ldan pa'i zhal snga nas kyi rnam par thar pa ngo mtshar rmad du byung ba'i gtam rab tu gsal ba'i sgron sme* (n.d., n.p.), 17b).

40 It is possible that Gyaltsab brought Khedrup to Drepung and Sera so as to present him officially as his successor to the Ganden throne. Indeed, Gyaltsab's status and authority as Tsongkhapa's successor was already established throughout the Gelugpa school by 1431, and by accompanying Khedrup on a tour of the major Gelugpa institutions, Gyaltsab was officially endorsing his successor, thereby making it difficult for others to refuse or question his decision to name Khedrup to the Ganden abbacy.

41 Chimey Rabgye's classification lists seven prophesied heart-sons; eight retreat-time renunciants; seven great sons who attended [Tsongkhapa] during illness; eight great son-scholars responsible for the propagation of the two traditions in the monastic seats; three sons who ensured the writings; three great sons whose deeds are uncontested; four sons endowed with the characteristics of realized persons who focused mainly on meditative practice; two mountain hermits; two utmost scholars of the highest tradition; two upper and lower Sherab Zangpos; two bodhisattvas; two *sattvas*; two Dragpas; six great sons of the oral transmission lineage; three great uncontested sons who were yogi-rulers; three scholars of true family descent; three great regent sons, holders of the teachings; one ruler who was competent in liberation; and one renunciant-yogi. *SCD*, 14–15.

42 *SCD*, 15.

43 The *bsnyung g.yog mdzad pa'i bu chen bdun* are given as Gyaltsab, Khedrup, Jangtse Chöjey Namkha Pel (Byang rtse chos rje Nam mkha' dpal, 14th–15th century), Shartse Chöjey Rinchen Gyaltsen (Rin chen rgyal mtshan, 14th–15th century), [Jamchen Chöjey] Shakya Yeshe, Shenyen Legzang (bShes gnyen Legs bzang, 14th–15th century), and Chöjey Shönu Gyalchog (Chos rje gzhon nu rgyal mchog, 14th–15th century) (*SCD*, 16.)

44 The *gdan sa'i lugs gnyis spel ba'i bu chen mkhas grub brgyed* are given as follows (Rabgye's list is incomplete): Gyaltsab Jey, Khedrup Jey, Shalu Chöjey Legpa Gyaltsen (Zhwa lu chos rje Legs pa rgyal mtshan, 1375–1450) and Jangtse Chöjey Namkha Pel (*SCD*, 16.)

45 *SCD*, 14.

46 Chimey Rabgye does not explain what he means by this term.

47 *SCD*, 15.

48 Chimey Rabgye's exact dates are uncertain. Judging by one of his statements, it would seem that he was a disciple of Jamyang Chöjey (*SCD*, 35). Rakra Rimpoche, who recently rediscovered and published the text, indicates in his preface to the work that the author must have been a contemporary of Khedrup (Zang zang ne rings pa 'Chi med rab rgyas, *rJe rin po che la mkhas btsun bzang gsum gyi yon tan mnga' tshul rnam thar nor bu'i bang mdzod* (Delhi: Rakra Tethong, ca 2001), iv. However, Chimey Rabgye makes use of Chöden Rabjor's biography of Khedrup

– which could not have been composed prior to 1438 – and also mentions Khedrup's successor's tenure on the throne at Ganden. Furthermore, in another seemingly earlier work, the *rJe rin po che la mkhas btsun bzang gsum gyi yon tan mnga' tshul rnam thar nor bu'i bang mdzod*, he also mentions Tashi Lhunpo (*bkra shis lhun po*) Monastery, founded in 1447. In *sNga 'gyur gsang chen rnying ma'i bstan 'dzin chen mo zang zang ne rings pa 'chi med rab rgyas kyi mdzad pa rJe rin po che'i rnam thar nor bu'i bang mdzod dang bu chen sbyon tshul gser gyi mchod sdong zhes bya ba gnyis dang gzhan yang ne rings pa'i gsung thor bu nang rnyed phyogs gcig tu bsdus pa* (Delhi: Rakra Tethong, ca 2001), 1–13, the work also mentions Mönlam Pel (sMon lam dpal, 1414–1491) who was abbot of Ganden's Shartse College until 1474 and of Ganden from 1480–1489. The *SCD*'s colophon itself gives the tiger year for its composition, which could thus only correspond to 1474.

49 *mkhas grub chos rje ni nang thugs kyi sras gcig bu*; Paṇ chen bSod nams grags pa, 57.

50 Paṇ chen bSod nams grags pa, 57. Panchen Sonam Dragpa's work is not the earliest overt elevation of Khedrup, nor is it the strongest. This honor is reserved for the *Secret Biography of Khedrup*, by a slightly earlier contemporary, Jetsunpa. Unfortunately, space does not permit an in-depth discussion of this work in the present context, nor of the connection and interaction that existed between Jetsunpa and Panchen Sonam Dragpa, particularly with regards to the dGe lugs pa tradition's post-Rinpung resurgence in the early-to-mid 16th century.

51 sDe srid Sangs rgyas rgya mtsho, *dGa' ldan chos 'byung vaidurya ser po* (Gangs ljongs shes rig gi nying bcud. Zi ling: Krung go bod kyi shes rig dpe skrun khang, 1989), 71.

52 Zahiruddin Ahmad, *The History of Tibet, by Ngag dbang blo bzang rgya mtsho, Fifth Dalai Lama of Tibet* (Bloomington, Indiana: Indiana University, Research Institute for Inner Asian Studies, 1995), 212. The Fifth Dalai Lama's overt animosity towards Panchen Sonam Dragpa might also result in part from the fact that the latter represented a rival lineage, and that his third reincarnation, Dragpa Gyaltsen (Grags pa rgyal mtshan, 1619–1656), was originally also a candidate for the position of Fifth Dalai Lama; see Dreyfus, "The Shuk-den Affair: Origins of a Controversy," *Journal of the International Association of Buddhist Studies* 21.2 (1998), 230. According to van der Kuijp, it would seem that the Desi also disliked Khedrup, and his animosity towards the latter led to the Desi's falling out with one of his teachers, the first Jamyang Sheypa Ngawang Tsöndru ('Jam dbyangs bshad pa Ngag dbang brtson 'grus, 1648–1722) over the latter's reliance upon Khedrup's interpretations in his *Pramāṇavārttika* commentary (see van der Kuijp, 79). Eventually, the tension between the Desi and the first Jamyang Sheypa led to the latter's departure from central Tibet (van der Kuijp, personal communication, September 2004). However, Desi's inclusion of Khedrup among Tsongkhapa's three foremost disciples would seem to go against the notion that the Desi felt such an enmity toward Khedrup.

53 Tshe mchog gling Ye shes rgyal mtshan, *Biographies of the Eminent Gurus in the Transmission Lineages of the Teachings of the Graduated Path: Being the Text of Byang chub lam gyi rim pa'i bla ma brgyud pa'i rnam par thar pa rgyal bstan mdzes pa'i rgyan mchog phul byung nor bu'i phreng ba* (Gedan Sungrab Minyam Gyunphel Series; Vols. 18–19. New Delhi: Ngawang Gelek Demo, 1970), 830; 877. Part of this text has been skillfully translated by Jan Willis in her work entitled *Enlightened Beings: Life Stories from the Ganden Oral Tradition* (Boston: Wisdom Publications, 1995).

54 'Jam dbyangs bzhad pa Kon mchog 'jigs med dbang po, *dGa' ldan chos 'byung nor bu'i phreng ba* (New Delhi: Demo, 1971), 647.

55 Thu'u bkwan Blo bzang chos kyi nyi ma, 307.

56 'Jam dbyangs bzhad pa Kon mchog 'jigs med dbang po, 655; *rgyal tshab bstan 'dzin gyi bu chen rtsod med rin po che.*

57 A more nuanced picture of Khedrup's ascension as Tsongkhapa's chief spiritual heir and interpreter would also seem to suggest that Jetsunpa himself operated in a somewhat more tenuous

relationship to authority than would have been the case had Khedrup been well established as one of the constitutive members of the *Jey Yabsey Süm* triumvirate. This is not to say that the expression did not exist during Jetsunpa's time; only that it did not necessarily refer to Tsongkhapa, Gyaltsab and Khedrup as the three members representing the utmost authority for the dGe lugs pa school.

58 Se ra smad pa Grags pa mkhas grub, *mKhas grub bye ba'i btsi gnas 'brog ri bo dge ldan rnam par rgyal ba'i gling gi ya gyal shar rtse nor bu gling gi chos 'byung lo rgyus 'jam dpal snying po'i dgongs rgyan* (New Delhi: Nawang Sopa, 1975).

59 *rje rin po ches nga'i mdo sngags kyi bstan bcos rnams kyi dgongs pa 'grel ba'i bstan bcos rnam par dag pa rtsoms / khyed par du dbu ma'i lta ba dang sngags kyi bstan pa 'di rnams rgyas par gyis shig ces thub bstan yongs rdzogs kyi bdag por mnga' gsol //* (Se ra smad pa Grags pa mkhas grub, 57–58).

60 Sermey Dragpa Khedrup does not say if he used Deleg Nyima's account for his own work.

61 *KYP*, 15.

62 This seemingly minor detail is a pivotal issue for Jetsunpa, who uses Khedrup's work as his main source of inspiration for his own Madhyamaka commentary. This commentary stands at the center of the suppression of the works of Jetsunpa's predecessors from the Sera Jey canon. See Elijah Ary, "Logic, Lives, and Lineage: Jetsun Chokyi Gyaltsen's Ascension and the Secret Biography of Khedrup Geleg Pelzang" (PhD Dissertation: Harvard University, 2007), 128–91.

63 Se ra smad pa Grags pa mkhas grub, 57–58. According to Deleg Nyima, Tsongkhapa is recorded telling Khedrup: *da khyed la man ngag rnams rdzogs par bshad yod pas nga'i sngags kyi yig cha 'di rnams kyi dka' gnad rnams la zin bris thob la / rang yang nyams su long / snod ldan gyi 'dul by are gnyis tsam byung na de rnams la shod / nga'i mdo sngags kyi yig cha'i dgongs pa 'grel ba'i bstan bcos rnam par dag pa rtsom la khyad par du nga'i sngags kyi bstan pa 'di rnams rgyas par gyis shig // KYP*, 15.

64 Despite his importance for the Gelugpa tradition, this figure, oddly, has no extant full-length biography.

16

'Phreng po gter ston Shes rab 'od zer (1518–1584) on the Eight Lineages of Attainment

Research on a Ris med *Paradigm*

MARC-HENRI DEROCHE

Introduction

The so-called *ris med* movement in Khams during the 19th century was probably the last development of Tibetan Buddhism before the turmoil of the 20th century. Its importance could be expressed as a revival or a "cultural renaissance"[1] that refreshed the essential approach to Buddhism in Tibet late in its history and became a major factor in preserving the living traditions without regard to sectarian labels. In its vast activity of transmissions and compilations, the model of the "eight lineages that are vehicles of attainment" (*sgrub brgyud shing rta chen po brgyad*) played a central and paradigmatic role. I will discuss in this chapter[2] why this model was given such importance by the *ris med* movement for both doctrinal and historical reasons. In that regard I will try to shed light on the author to whom this model is generally attributed: 'Phreng po gter ston Shes rab 'od zer (1518–1584). I will give here a translation of his original work on the eight main lineages, which conveyed the highest esoteric Buddhist teachings from India to Tibet.

1. The Model of the Eight Lineages of Attainment

1-1. A paradigm for the ris med *movement*

The *ris med* movement occurred during the 19th century in Khams under the leading inspiration of 'Jam dbyangs mKhyen brtse'i dbang po (1820–1899), 'Jam mgon Kong sprul blo gros mtha' yas (1813–1899) and mChog 'gyur bDe chen gling pa (1829–1870).[3] Ariane Macdonald had already noted the importance of these three figures in later Tibetan Buddhist history, who were connected respectively to the Sa skya pa, bKa' brgyud pa and rNying ma pa schools or orders.[4] *Ris med* means "without bias," "impartial," "non-sectarian," and by extension "eclectic" or "universalist." Accordingly, we could roughly describe the *ris med* movement as a vast activity of collecting, preserving, compiling, practicing and transmitting the different Buddhist teachings of the various lineages without regard to sectarian labels and emphasizing their inner unity. As E. Gene Smith remarked, all the major historical figures of Tibetan Buddhism were *ris med* since their education included the study of various approaches with many masters. One could even consider that their eclectism was an active factor in their excellence, because by combining different complementary views and methods, they were able to gain a greater and deeper understanding. If the Dharma is one in the *ris med* perspective, as shown in Aris's translation of 'Jam dbyangs mKhyen brtse'i chos kyi blo gros' *Brief Discourse on The Essence of All the Ways*,[5] there are different teachings and means of salvation provided by the Buddha, in response to the different needs and capacities of various beings.[6] By collecting teachings from many lineages, the *ris med* masters tried to overcome the limitation of the adherence to one's own school and identity, and at the same time preserve the richness and depth of the diverse traditions, some of which were on the verge of disappearing.

There may be no single doctrinal unification of the *ris med* movement, but Kong sprul's *Five Great Treasuries* (*mDzod chen lnga*) offer a large compilation of the vision and legacy of these masters.[7] In the *Treasury of Knowledge,* Kong sprul, as a "Tibetan Leonardo," condensed the vast Buddhist traditions that were assimilated and practiced in Tibet for centuries in an encyclopaedic form, providing some of the major sources and doctrinal framework for the *ris med* movement.[8] As E. Gene Smith observed, the *Treasury of Spiritual Instructions,* a unified collection of direct spiritual instructions from various traditions, showing their ultimate goal and identity, is particularly important to understand the intention of the *ris med* masters.[9] Following this, Matthew T. Kapstein has demonstrated the special value of the *gdams ngag*, spiritual and heartfelt instructions on the path of realization, and has pointed out the organizational paradigm of the *Treasury of Spiritual Instructions*: the classification of the "eight great conveyances that are lineages of attainment" (*sgrub brgyud shing rta chen po brgyad*).[10] They are the main *Vajrayāna* lineages of meditation and yoga that were propagated from India to Tibet: the rNying ma pa, bKa' gdams pa, Shangs pa bKa' brgyud, Lam 'bras, Marpa bKa' brgyud, Zhi byed, sByor drug and rDo rje gsum gyi bsnyen sgrub. Both mKhyen brste and Kong sprul received the transmissions of these eight lineages[11] and intended to pass them on, totally or partly, to their disciples according to their specific conditions.

Thus, in this sense the model of the eight lineages of practice as used by Kong sprul could be understood as an important paradigm of the *ris med* movement, which made it widely known and used. We may see two aspects within this "*ris med* paradigm": an emphasis on spiritual realization or attainment through the most esoteric and practical instructions, and a non-sectarian spiritual genealogy encompassing all orders of Tibetan Buddhism.

1-2. Tibet's most esoteric systems

Tibet was the full inheritor of the whole corpus of Buddhism that developed in India until the 13th century. It received from the later Indian masters the conception of the three *yāna* or vehicles: *Hīnayāna*, the lesser or fundamental vehicle, *Mahāyāna* the great vehicle and *Vajrayāna*, the adamantine vehicle. This provides a hierarchical and coherent structure of the complex set of Buddhist teachings adapted soteriologically to different beings. *Vajrayāna* is said to be the vehicle of the most inner or esoteric teachings dedicated to those of higher capacities. The eight lineages of attainment all belong to *Vajrayāna*. The rNying ma pa lineage developed in Tibet during the first promulgation of Buddhism in Tibet, principally during the reign of Khri Srong lde btsan (reign 755–ca 800),[12] and received retrospectively this name meaning "the Ancients." The other seven lineages appeared at the time, or even later, of the second promulgation of Buddhism during the 10th and 11th centuries, and are known as the gSar ma pa, the new orders, in explicit contrast to the rNying ma pa, the ancient order.

As Professor Katsumi Mimaki has shown, according to the authoritative traditional texts in their clearest expression, the hierarchical and doctrinal presentation of Tibetan Buddhism is expressible in both rNying ma pa and gSar ma pa systems through a distinction between the exoteric (or lower) teachings and the esoteric (or higher) ones.[13] Professor Mimaki also included in his work the presentation of the Bon po tradition, but since the eight lineages of practice are only concerned with Buddhism we will not take it into consideration in this present work. According to the classification of the teachings of the rNying ma pa, there are nine vehicles that form a progression from the exoteric teachings to the most esoteric ones.[14] The highest of all is the *Atiyoga* or *rDzogs chen*, the "Great Perfection." In the model of the eight lineages of attainment, the main teaching of the rNying ma lineage is the *Atiyoga*. If we follow the progressive classification of the gSar ma pa, the exoteric teachings are the four main *grub mtha'* or philosophical systems.[15] Concerning the esoteric systems, Bu ston Rin chen grub (1290–1364), following Indian classifications, distinguished a hierarchy of four systems of *tantra*.[16] Among them, the highest class is the *Anuttarayogatantra*, which explicitly means the "tantra of unsurpassable union." The seven other lineages of attainment belonging to the gSar ma pa adhere to systems based on this class of *tantra*.[17]

Thus, the eight lineages of practice are in both rNying ma pa and gSa mar pa traditions, the *esotericism of the esotericism*, the highest teachings. The expression itself of s*grub brgyud*, "lineage of attainment or practice," also emphasizes that they are transmitting the effective means and practical guidance of the innermost sacred teachings of Buddhism in Tibet. Since all these lineages belong to the highest systems within both rNying ma pa and gSar ma pa classifications, they are all equal in hierarchy, only differing in their distinct and various ways to obtain the supreme attainment.

Moreover, if the model of the eight lineages of attainment is a non-sectarian paradigm, at the same time it provides the roots of the very identity – spirituality and genealogy – of all the main different Tibetan Buddhist orders. As Professor David Snellgove observed: "Tibetan religious orders developed [...] based upon the transmission of particular late Indian Buddhist tantric traditions, which happened to have been favoured by certain renowned teachers, who in retrospect may be regarded as their 'founders.'"[18] The systems of esoteric instructions of the eight lineages of attainment constituted respectively the highest part of the different main Tibetan orders' curricula.

2. Origins of the Model

2-1. Attribution to 'Phreng po gter ston Shes rab 'od zer (1518–1584)

The classification of the eight lineages of attainment is generally attributed, and particularly by Kong sprul in the *Treasury of Spiritual Instructions*, to the 16th-century master 'Phreng po gter ston Shes rab 'od zer (1518–1584).[19] The introductory verses used by Kong sprul are now well known,[20] but the author himself and his exact contribution still remain unknown. The present paper is precisely a first attempt to shed light on this important but unknown figure. The main mention of him made by Tibetologists was given by Guiseppe Tucci in *Tibetan Painted Scrolls*,[21] one of the best historical surveys of 16th-century central Tibet, a period that is not very well known in Tibetan studies. Tucci observed that all the *Padma thang yig* versions that have reached us derived from one original version revised by Shes rab 'od zer. It is mentioned in these colophons and in the Fifth Dalai Lama's chronicles. The original was printed in 'Phyongs rgyas with the patronage of Hor bSod nams stobs rgyal. For this reason, Gustave-Charles Toussaint paid a special homage to Shes rab 'od zer in his French translation of the *Padma thang yig*.[22]

Until now, as far as I know from the different Tibetan lamas and Tibetologists I have consulted, and as the great scholar Kong sprul himself stated, Shes rab 'od zer seems to be the first master to propose this specific classification of the eight lineages of attainment, which was then given then such importance in the *ris med* movement. All the materials were mainly established a little earlier in the *Blue Annals* (*Deb ther sngon po*), written by 'Gos lo tsā ba gZhon nu dpal (1392–1481), but Shes rab 'od zer was probably the first to organize the esoteric or *gdams ngag* lineages in eight major lineages as a unifying and *ris med* scheme.[23] Shes rab 'od zer was also the founder of dPal ris Monastery, where 'Jigs med gling pa was trained. The latter's tradition has been very influential in the rNying ma pa renaissance and an antecedent of the *ris med* movement, since the mKhyen brtse incarnations are said to be his emanations. This constitutes a major link between Shes rab 'od zer and the *ris med* movement, which will be developed through further research.

As a first step we give here our translation of Shes rab 'od zer's *rnam thar*, written by Kong sprul, to which Tucci and others have generally referred. This is to establish the memories of Kong sprul's tradition about Shes rab 'od zer's life and activity, and to fill a gap in Tibetan studies where only brief references have been given about him. The authorship of the eight lineages' model is not mentioned in this *rnam thar* by Kong sprul. Shes rab 'od zer is, however, called therein both a *dges shes* and a *gter ston*, which is in itself particularly noteworthy as a *ris med* example. Although Shes rab 'od zer lived in a period of intense sectarian rivalries and civil wars of the "Reds against the Yellows" (particularly between the Karma bKa' brgyud pa order and the new ascending dGe lugs pa order), and "dBus against gTsang"[24] (their respective patrons' fiefs), the account of his spiritual training includes high representatives of all the main religious orders. This illustrates very well the paradox noted by Smith: "the roots of eclectism and tolerance are sunk as deep into the soil of Tibetan tradition as those of sectarianism and bigotry."[25] As it has been generally observed, the *ris med* movement was partly a reaction from the rNying ma pa, bKa' brgyud pa and Sa skya pa orders against dGe lugs pa's hegemony. And the transmission model of the eight lineages of attainment can be a way to reconcile the various orders in the awareness of common origins, principles and aims. So it is interesting to note that this model emerged with Shes rab 'od zer at the time when sectarian tensions between these orders were at their height. It must have been from Shes rab 'od zer a devoted *ris med* response and reunifying scheme while he was following his own Buddhist path with different personal teachers.

2-2. *Shes rab 'od zer's* rnam thar *by Kong sprul*

As it is said in Kong sprul's *Root Accounts of Complete Liberation of the Hundred Treasure Discoverers* (*gTer ston brgya rtsa'i rnam thar*):[26]

> The emanation of the great translator Vairocana, 'Phreng po 'Gro 'dul gling pa Shes rab 'od zer[27] was born on the tenth day of the sixth month of the earth male tiger year (1518) from the two households of Khri and bSam in the place of Byang ngom chen, manifesting excellent and auspicious signs. From a very young age, he awakened the potential of *Mahāyanā* through sincere renunciation, great and powerful compassion and wisdom. At the age of eight, he took the vows of a Buddhist layman[28] from the master Tshul khrims 'od zer[29] and was called Shes rab 'od zer. Then, he obtained full ordination from rDo rgyal ba, a disciple of gSer mdog paṇ chen.[30] He studied the treatises of logic (*mtshan nyid*) and *Guhyasamājatantra* under the guidance of dGa' ldan khri chen bstan dar ba[31] for six years. He received from rDo rgyal ba the *tantra* collections of the Sa [skya pa] tradition, the *Kālacakratantra*, etc. His thought reached the highest perfection. When he beat the drum of scriptures and reasoning with the monks [studying] logic, nobody could refute him. So he was known by the name of a great *dge bshes*. At the age of eighteen, he met 'Bri gung Rin chen phun tshogs[32] and a strong faith irresistibly arose. The teacher and the disciple mutually exchanged discourses on the Dharma, so confidence increased. He received limitlessly the deep 'Bri gung and Karma bKa' brgyud teachings; the hundred thousand new and ancient *tantra*, the trilogy of the *mDo sgyu sems*[33] with explanations; the ancient orally transmitted teachings, the revealed treasures teachings with their practices and mainly the *Heart Essence of Ḍākinī* (*mKha' 'gro snying tig*). Following the guru's instructions, in the middle of an assembly's ocean, he made a root text in five points and he categorized in sections the teachings of the *One Hundred and Fifty Vajra Statements* (*rDo rje'i gsung brgya lnga bcu pa*). Having understood the pith of the *Single Intention* (*dGongs cig*)'s philosophical tenet, he explained completely the teachings of the *sūtra*

and *tantra* cycles. Thus he accomplished the guru's intention and composed collections as wonderful supports, which did not exist before. Abiding in ascetic virtues, he lived during eight years as a hermit who had abandoned distractions and diversions. He practiced in the meditation caves of the excellent place of Grogs ri rin chen spungs pa during three years. Inconceivable signs of realization appeared. He mastered the door of meditative absorption. On the tenth day of the sixth month of the fire female sheep year (1546), a *ḍākinī* dressed like a Mon woman offered him a cranial cup of beer; in the midst of a white light he saw the face of the King Guru Pad ma.[34] According to the instructions he was conferred, he revealed in that very place of treasure, the cycle of the teachings of the *Point of Liberation, Natural Liberation of Intention* (*Grol tig dgongs pa rang grol*)[35] and supports of the [enlightened] body, speech and mind. Later, in Lhasa, he revealed relics of the *tathāgata*, diagrams sealed with "A," supports and special sacred substances which he declared to be treasures. During that time, he revealed all kinds of profound treasures from the six places of treasures. With 'Bri gung rin po che, he established the yellow scrolls. While he was practicing the treasure at Sing pa stag mo, in pure vision he came to Padma 'od.[36] In the aspect of the guru of great bliss, the master [Padmasambhava] in union with his consort bestowed upon him empowerments and oral instructions. The vision lasted for one month. At 'Phreng po, he received with 'Bri gung pa [Rin chen phun tshogs] the teachings of the *Summary of the Guru's Intention* (*dGongs 'dus*)[37] from the Lord of the *Summary of the Guru's Intention*, Nyi ma rgyal mtshan. The people of 'Phreng po praising him, he established his seat in this place. He remained three years in retreat at rDo rje brag and had a vision of O rgyan Rin po che,[38] who said: "Nowadays, besides you, there is no one who has the knowledge to distinguish the view without illusions. Teach in order to clarify that point!" Thus he composed a treatise in few words on the profound meaning, called the *Lamp Clarifying the Oral Instructions* (*Zhal lung gsal sgron*). After this, he was renowned to be a scholar and an accomplished being. Everybody received the ambrosia of [his] profound teachings. He transmitted the practices, initiations and instructions of the *Heart Essence of* Ḍākinī (*mKha' 'gro snying tig*), the *Intention, Father and Son* (*dGongs pa yab sras*) and the *Point of Liberation* (*Grol tig*). At the initiation of the *Point of Liberation* (*Grol tig*), each time there was no less than an assembly of seven thousand people. They [saw] rainbows, rains of flowers, etc., and many miraculous signs. Hor bSod nams stobs rgyal,[39] who was endowed with the eye of the Dharma and whose clarity was pure from desires and obstructions, offered [his] patronage and restored 'Phyong dpal ri theg chen gling,[40] the temple with its sacred supports. The Dharma activity [of Shes rab 'od zer] spread in dBus, gTsang and Khams. At the age of sixty-seven, the tenth day of the sixth Mongol month, the water monkey year (1584), he passed into peace. His son, Karma kun bzang and [Karma kun bzang's] mother prayed in [Shes rab 'od zer's] presence during three days. The morning of the

> thirteenth day, miraculous signs appeared. [Shes rab 'od zer] gathered in the miraculous arrangement of the spirit of dPa' bo chen po thod pa'i dum bu rtsal in the city of Śāntapurī. There is a full biography with the history of the treasure-discoveries written by the Lord of Dharma [Kar ma] kun bzang and called the *Ten Chapters of Miraculous Discourses* (*Ngo mtshar ba'i gtam skabs bcu pa*).[41] I ['Jam mgon kong sprul blo gro mtha' yas] had the good fortune to obtain the remaining uninterrupted [initiations that] mature and the [instructions that] liberate in [the tradition of] the *Point of Liberation* (*Grol tig*).

The *rnam thar* of Shes rab 'od zer, also given in *Guru bKra shis chos byung*[42] and the *Zhe chen chos 'byung*,[43] gives some more details on what is here summarized by Kong sprul. It is notably stated that he was praised by the Ninth Karmapa dBang phyug rdo rje, the Fifth Zhwa dmar pa dKon mchog yan lag rnams, and that Pad ma dkar po also became the holder of the *Grol tig*. It is in association with this *gter ma* that he was mainly remembered by the tradition as a *gter ston*. But as we can read, his life included all the major sources of spiritual learning and training of his time.

3. The Original Work of Shes rab 'od zer on the Eight Lineages of Attainment

3-1. Localization

A *gsung 'bum* of Shes rab 'od zer, only one volume in full, has been found in Bhutan in the collection of Lama bSod nams bzang po, published in Gangtok and then digitized by TBRC. We find here his most renowned *gter ma* cycle of the *Grol tig*, included in the *Rin chen gter mdzod*, and his work on the final -s (*sa mtha'*) in Tibetan grammar.

Moreover, there are two treatises of great interest for our present purpose: *Study and Reflection's Ambrosia of Immortality* (*Thos bsam 'chi med kyi bdud rtsi*);[44] and *Meditation's Ambrosia of Immortality* (*sGom pa 'chi med kyi bdud rtsi*).[45]

The two treatises deal with the trilogy of study, reflection and meditation (*śruta cintā bhāvanā, thos bsam sgom*) which form the three steps in the development of wisdom (*prajñā, shes rab*) along with the soteriological path of Buddhism, and treat respectively the exegesis (*bshad*) and the practice or attainment (*sgrub*) of the teachings. Shes rab 'od zer offers in these works a remarkable synthesis of the different fields of Buddhism in Tibet, presenting the great expounders, holders and lineages of transmission coming from India. The first deals with the "ten great pillars who supported the exegetical lineages" (*bshad brgyud 'degs pa'i ka chen bcu*);[46] and the second specifically with the "eight great chariots that are lineages of attainment" (*sgrub brgyud shing rta chen po brgyad*). If the eclectic approach is clear and manifest in these texts, Shes rab 'od zer insists also on what makes the authentic and complete Buddhist path. Thus, at the same time, the identity and specificity of each tradition or aspect is defined and precise, the universal Buddhist approach is developed, and the authenticity of its origin and completion is emphasized. In this sense, we find that the eight lineages of attainment are presented here in a non-hierarchical exposition as valid, authentic and complete traditions, all said to descend from the primordial Buddha Vajradhara.

These two texts were in large part quoted and annotated by 'Jam dbyangs mKhyen brste'i dbang po and then by 'Jam mgon Kong sprul blo gros mtha' yas in his *gDams ngag mdzod*. The complete text of *Study and Reflection's Ambrosia of Immortality* and one third of *Meditation's Ambrosia of Immortality*, with substantial annotations, are included in mKhyen brtse's collected works.[47] The *gDams ngag mdzod*'s *dkar chag* [48] opens with the now well-known first verses of Shes rab 'od zer's *Meditation's Ambrosia of Immortality*.

This text may be considered as an (if not the) original source of the "*ris med* paradigm" of the eight lineages of attainment. For this reason I offer here a translation of its first part. The section here translated, located in Shes rab 'od zer's *gsung 'bum* (243–51), is the original text used and quoted by both mKhyen brtse and Kong sprul. In mKhyen brtse's writings, it forms the root text to which mKhyen brtse added his commentary. Therefore the notes written by mKhyen brste on the first part of this text seem to have been integrated and developed by Kong sprul when writing the *dkar chag* of the *gDams ngag mdzod*. The original text is accompanied with a few allusive notes that I only use here in my comments when necessary. At the end of the full text (266), the colophon indicates that Shes rab 'od zer (Prajñāraśmi) was in 'Phying ba stag rtse at the time of its redaction.

Beginning with a general introduction, which established the model of the eight lineages of attainment, the text treats equally the eight lineages of practice in eight sections of parallel construction with two parts: first a summary of the esoteric instructions' system, and second the origin of the lineage, introduction to Tibet, main masters and diffusion into its various ramifications.

3-2. *Translation of Meditation's* Ambrosia of Immortality

Meditation's Ambrosia of Immortality

Transmitted to the ears of the renunciant meditators
from the hermitages of the snowy mountains

Homage to the Glorious Vajradhara.[49]
Those who aspire to receive the sacred teaching of the realization
Should meditate upon the guru endowed with the three [vows][50] as really being a Buddha,
And practice with intensive and one-pointed attention and aspiration,
The oral lineages' instructions of the former accomplished ones.
If one were to practice continuously, day and night, erroneous instructions,
That would be only pain without benefit.
So these are the instructions of the great accomplished ones.[51]
Listen, great meditators everywhere!
The lord of sentient beings in the Land of Snow[52] prophesied by the Victorious
Was the sole intention of the unique teaching
Of the ancient King of the Dharma, the single divine monarch,[53]
Who was here in the hermitages of the snowy mountains, the Second Teacher.
The definitive translator Pa gor Bai ro,[54]
The descendant of the Victorious' line, 'Brom ston the layman,[55]
The great learned and accomplished, 'Khyung po rnal 'byor pa,[56]
The great guru who spoke the two languages, 'Brog mi,[57]
The almighty yogin, venerable Mar pa,[58]
Dam pa rgya gar[59] who resided in the state of attainment,
The translator Gyi co,[60] the learned and accomplished O rgyan pa.[61]
These eight great pillars established in the north the lineages of attainment
Which perfectly came from the glorious Vajradhara.
Here in the hermitages of the snowy mountains, these eight great traditions of the lineages of attainment,
Are the legacy of the former great accomplished ones.
Those aspiring to liberation should follow their paths.

1. rNying ma pa, "The Ancients' School"

Whatever appearances arise in the field of the six consciousnesses[62]
Are the primordial wisdom of the natural state, perfect since the beginning.

Contemplating one's own face without being distracted from non-meditation,[63]
Abiding in the experience of the four visions,[64]
Are the main practices of the Great Perfection (*rDzogs chen*) teachings.
The three main supports are the *tantra* (*Mahāyoga*), the precepts (*Anuyoga*) and the spiritual instructions (*Atiyoga*).
The sublime and special instructions of Śrī Siṃha[65]
Were initially transmitted to the *mantra* adept Vairocana,
Who having realized them, spread them here in the hermitages of the snowy mountains.
Through [the traditions of] sGyus, Nyang, rMa, 'Khon, Zur, gNubs and gNyos,
Srid, Rags, dPyal, sKyo, sTon and g.Yung, etc,
An infinity of ancient oral transmissions of the initial translation appeared.
The glorious Zur pa[66] are the ornaments of the Great Perfection teachings.

2. bKa' gdams pa, "The Transmitted Precepts and Instructions School"

Meditating assiduously upon the precious human life difficult to obtain, impermanence and death,
The deeds and their ineluctable results, the imperfection of *saṃsāra,*
And the two *bodhicitta*,
Are the main practices of the bKa' gdams pa teachings.
The main supports are the Treatises of the Vast Conduct (*rGya chen spyod pa'i gzhung*).
The sublime and special instructions of the divine lord [Atiśa]
Were initially transmitted to the son of the Victorious 'Brom ston pa,
Who having realized them, spread them here in the hermitages of the snowy mountains.
There are those following the treatises (*gzhung pa*), the study and explanation of the six bKa' gdams pa texts,[67]
Those following the instructions (*gdams ngag pa*) condensing the practice of the Four Noble Truths,[68]
And those following the instructions of Gung thang and Nag tsho's oral transmission,
Sublime followers of the treatises endowed with the two streams of explanation and practice.

3. Shangs pa bKa' brgyud, "The oral lineage of Shangs"

The trunk [is] the six yogas; the branches [are] the reliquary;

The leaves [are] the methods of integration; the flowers [are] the two *Khecharī*;
The fruit is the progressive meditation of the immortality of body and mind:[69]
These are the main Shangs pa bKa' brgyud practices.
The main support is the *tantra* of Cakrasaṃvara.
The sublime and special instructions of the primordial wisdom *ḍākinī* [Niguma],
Were initially transmitted to the learned and accomplished Khyung po rnal 'byor
Who having realized them, spread them here in the hermitages of the snowy mountains.
The unique transmission was kept under the seal of secrecy in a lineage of seven generations.
Sangs rgyas ston pa spread [these teachings] to all the fortunate ones.
The oral transmission branched out in many ways in dBus, Shang and Nyang.
Those who entered the stream of its practice were particularly noble and excellent.

4. Lam 'bras, "the Path and Fruition"

Empowerment conferred on as cause, the external and internal creation phases,
The meditation in four sessions and the profound empowerment as path,
Training in the three paths and inviting primordial wisdom:
These are the main practices of the Path and Fruition (*Lam 'bras*) teachings.
The main support is the *tantra* of Hevajra.
The sublime and special instructions of Gayadhāra
Were initially transmitted to the great guru 'Brog mi,
Who having realized them, spread them here in the hermitages of the snowy mountains.
[There were] the traditions of Gyi co, 'Brom, Zhang ston, Zhwa ma
The traditions of Ko brag, Mang lam, Cha gan, Jo nang,
The traditions of dBang rgyal, Sa [skya]; the traditions of lCe sgom and mTha' rtsa.
The Sa skya pa having accomplished the ocean of the *Dharma* traditions
Are the crown ornaments of all the lineages of attainment.

5. Mar pa bKa' brgyud, "the Oral lineage of Mar pa"

Recognizing one's own face in the phase of the Great Seal (*Mahāmudrā*), pure knowledge,

Remembering it through an attention without distraction,
And meditating upon the path of methods,[70] unifying view and conduct,
These are the main Dwags po bKa' brgyud practices.
The main support is the mother *tantra* of Cakrasaṃvara.
The sublime and special instructions of Nāropa
Were initially transmitted to the venerable Marpa[71]
Who having realized them, spread them here in the hermitages of the snowy mountains.
The Khro phu pa and the glorious 'Brug pa,
The Tshal pa bKa' brgyud, the Kar ma pa emanations,
The 'Bri [gung], Stag [lung], g.Ya' [bzang] and Phag [gru] bka' brgyud,
Adorn most of the snowy mountains and valleys
With the practices of the incomparable Dwags po's[72] oral lineages.
The holders of the glorious 'Brug pa lineage are the treasures of their stream

6. Zhi byed, "Pacification"

All the phenomena apprehended [are] empty in essence,
The mind which apprehends them [is] also non-conceptual emptiness,
In the state of non-conception, immobile in clarity-emptiness,
These are the main practices of the Pacification (*Zhi byed*) teachings.
The main supports are the *Prajñāpāramitāsūtra* and the *River Sūtra*.[73]
The sublime and special instructions of [Pha] Dam pa sangs rgyas,
Instructing others through symbols and words,
[Were transmitted] here in the hermitages of the snowy mountains in three successive lineages:
The first is the lineage of the venerable Ong po lo tsā ba,
The following are the lineages of rMa, So and Kam,
And the last is the lineage of the two great sons' traditions.
Dam pa kun dga' was the foremost spiritual son.

7. sByor drug, "the Six Yogas"

Through withdrawal[74] and meditation[75] the form of emptiness appears;
Through energy control[76] and retention[77] one abides in cessation.
Through consummation[78] and absorption[79] great bliss is generated;
These are the main practices of the Six Yogas (*sByor drug*) teachings.
The main support is the root and condensed *tantra* [of Kālacakra].
The sublime and special instructions of the great Kālacakrapāda[80]

Were initially transmitted to the translator Gyi co,
Who having realized them, spread them here in the hermitages of the snowy mountains.
The profound path of [the traditions of] Gyi co, Rwa, 'Bro, rTsa, gNyos, Chag, dPyal, Rong,
rGwa, Tshal, Ko, 'Gos, master Orgyan pa,
Sa, Jo, Zhang and kLog, Lung, and dBang rgya,
Appeared on the earth of the Land of Snow.
The Jo nang pa are endowed with the continuity of its practice river.

8. rDo rje gsum gyi bsnyen sgrub, "the Service and Attainment of the Three Indestructible Realities"

The service of body controls its energetic centres,
The attainment of speech is the *vajra* recitation and yoga of vital energy.
The great attainment of the mind maintains the essence without effusion.
These are the main practices of the Service and Attainment (*bsnyen sgrub*) teachings.
The main supports are the *tantra* of Cakrasaṃvara and Kālacakra.
The sublime and special instructions of the Indestructible Yoga (*Vajrayoga*)
Were initially transmitted to the learned and accomplished O rgyan pa,
Who having realized them, spread them here in the hermitages of the snowy mountains [to]
mKhar chu rin po che who obtained a prophecy from [his] divinity,
[To] the realized Seng ge, the glorious sBu tra ba,
[And to] the incomparable analyst, venerable Zur phug pa.
Because he had obtained the prophecy, the first lineage holder [was] the sublime [mKhar chu rin po che].

Separated from the *gter ma* and *tantra* or supposedly revealed by divinities,
The oral fabricated lineages
Do not conform to the traditions of the former accomplished and learned ones.
They are not the oral lineages of Vajradhara.[81]

3-3. Tibetan transliterated text[82]

[243] *//Sgom pa 'chi med kyi bdud rtsi zhes bya ba bzhugs so//*

[244] / /gangs ri'i khrod kyi spong ba bsam gtan pa rnams kyi snyan tu bsrings

pa/ sgom pa 'chi med kyi bdud rtsi zhes bya ba/ /dpal rdo rje 'chang la phyag 'tshal lo/ /rtogs pa'i dam chos su len 'dod na/ /gsum ldan bla ma sangs rgyas dngos su bsgoms/ /grub thob gong ma'i snyan rgyud gdams pa la/ /dran 'dun drag pos rtse gcig nyams su long/ /log pa'i gdams pa nyan[83] mtshan khor yug tu/ /nyams su blangs kyangs ngal ba don med pas/ / de phyir grub chen gdams pa 'di yin zhes/ /phyogs kyi sgom chen kun la 'di bsrings so/ /rgyal bas lung bstan [245] /gangs can 'gro ba'i mgon /gcig tu bstan pa 'ba' zhig nyer dgongs pa'i/ /sngon gyi chos rgyal lha gcig khri brtsan de/ /gangs ri'i khrod kyi ston pa gnyis pa yin /zhu chen lo tsā pa gor bai ro dang / /rgyal ba'i gdung tshob 'brom ston u pa si/ /mkhas grub chen po khyung po rnal 'byor pa/ /skad gnyis smra ba'i bla chen 'brog mi dang // rnal 'byor dbang phyug rje btsun mar pa'i zhabs/ /grub pa'i sar bzhugs dam pa rgya gar dang/ /gyi co lo tsa mkhas grub o rgyan pa /byang phyogs bsgrub rgyud[84] 'degs pa'i ka chen brgyad/ /dpal ldan rdo rje 'chang nas legs 'ongs pa'i/ /gangs ri'i khrod 'dir bsgrub rgyud srol chen brgyad/ / de dag grub thob gong ma'i gshegs shul yin /thar 'dod rnams kyang lam de'i [246] rjes su zhugs/

[1. rNying ma pa]

/tshogs drug yul du snang ba gang shar yang / /gdod nas grub pa'i gnyug ma'i ye shes de/ /rang zhal blta zhing bsgom med ma yengs pa/ /snang bzhi'i don la mnyam par 'jog pa nyid/ /rdzogs chen chos kyi nyams len gtso bo yin/ /brten gzhi'i gtso bo rgyud lung man ngag gsum/ /dpal gyi seng ge'i khyad par gdams pa mchog /dang por bka' babs sngags 'chang bai ro yis/ /thugs nyams bzhes nas gangs ri'i khrod 'dir spel/ /sgyus nyang rma dang 'khon zur gnubs gnyos dang/ /srid rags dpyal dang skyong ston g.yung la sogs/ /snga 'gyur rnying ma'i bka' rgyud bgrang yas byon/ dpal ldan zur pa rdzogs chen bstan pa'i rgyan//

[2. bKa' gdams pa]

/[247] dal 'byor brnyed dka' mi rtag 'chi ba dang / /las 'bras bslu med 'khor ba'i nyas[85] dmigs dang / /byang chub sems gnyis nan gyi bsgom byed pa// bka' gdams chos kyi nyams len gtso bo yin/ /rten gzhi'i gtso bo rgya chen spyod pa'i gzhung / /lha gcig jo bo'i khyad par gdams pa mchog/ / dang por bka' babs rgyal sras 'brom ston gyis/ /thugs nyams bzhes nas gangs ri'i khrod 'dir spel/ /bka' gdams gzhung drug nyan bshad gzhung pa dang

/ /nyams len bden bzhir khrid bsdus gdam ngag pa/ gung thang nag tsho'i bka' rgyud gdams pa 'og/ /bshad bsgrub chu bo gnyis ldan gzhung pa mchog

[3. Shangs pa bka' brgyud]

sdong po chos drug yal ga ga'u ma/ /lo ma lam khyer me tog mkha' spyod gnyis/ /'bras bu lus sems 'chi med bsgom rim ste/ /bka' rgyud shangs pa'i nyams len gtso bo yin /rten gzhi'i gtso bo 'khor lo sdom pa'i rgyud/ /ye shes mkha' 'gro'i khyad par gdams pa mchog dang por bka' babs mkhas grub khyung po yis/ /thugs nyams bzhes nas gangs ri'i khrod 'dir spel/ / [248] brgyud rim bdun tu chis rgyud bka' rgyas btab/ /sangs rgyas ston pas skal ldan yongs la spel/ /dbus shang nyang sogs bka' rgyud rnam mang gyes/ /nyams len rgyun gyi 'jags legs khyad par 'phags/ /

[4. Lam' bras]

/rgyu dbang bskur nas phyi nang bskyed rim dang/ /lam dbang zab mo thun bzhir bsgom pa dang/ /lam gsum bsgoms pas ye shes 'dren byed pa/ / lam 'bras chos kyi nyams len gtso bo yin/ /rten gzhi'i gtso bo dgyes pa rdo rje'i rgyud/ /ga ya rda ra'i khyad par gdams pa mchog /dang por bka' babs bla chen 'brog mi yis/ /thugs nyams bzhes nas gangs ri'i khrod 'dir 'pel/ /gyi co 'brom dang zhang ston zha ma lugs/ /ko brag mang lam cha gan jo nang [249] /lugs/ /dbang rgyal sa lugs lce sgom mtha' rtsa lugs/ / chos lugs rgya mtsho'i mthar son sa skya pa/ /gang 'dir sgrub rgyud kun gyi gtsug gi rgyan /

[5. Mar pa bka' brgyud]

phyag chen dus su dangs ma'i shes pa ste/ /rang ngo shes nas ma yengs dran 'dun dang/ /thabs lam bsgoms nas lta spyod zung du sbrel/ /bka' rgyud dags po'i nyams len gtso bo yin /rten gzhi'i gtso bo ma rgyud bde mchog ste/ /nā ro ta pa'i khyad par gdams pa mchog /dang por bka' babs rje btsun mar pa yis/ thugs dam gzhes nas gangs ri'i khrod 'dir spel/ khro phu pa dang dpal ldan 'brug pa dang/ /tshal pa bka' rgyud sprul sku karma pa/ /'bri stag rnam gnyis g.ya' phag bka' brgyud de/ /mnyam med dags po'i bka' rgyud nyams len gyis/ /gangs can ri sul phel bar mdzes par byas/ / dpal ldan 'brug pa rgyud 'dzin chu bo'i gter/ /

[6. Zhi byed]

/gzung ba'i chos kun rang rang ngo bos stong / 'dzin pa'i sems kyang spros bral stong pa nyid// /spros med ngang la gsal stong mi g.yo ba/ /zhi byed chos kyi nyams len gtso bo yin /rten gzhi'i gtso bo sher phyin chu klung mdo/ /dam pa sangs rgyas khyad par gdams pa mchog/ /brda' dang gsung gi gzhan la bstan pa las// [250] gangs ri'i khrod 'dir rgyud pa rim pa gsum/ / brgyud pa dang po rje btsun ong lo sogs / brgyud pa bar ba rma so skam gsum dang/ /brgyud pa tha ma bu chen gnyis gyi lugs/ /dam pa kun dga' thugs sras mchog gis 'phags/

[7. sByor drug]

/sor bsdud bsam stan stong gzugs 'char ba dang/ /srog rtsol 'dzin pa srog 'gog gnas par byed/ /rjes dran ting 'dzin bde chen bskyed pa ste/ /sbyor drug chos kyi nyams len gtso bo yin/ /rten gzhi'i gtso bo rtsa ba bsdus pa'i rgyud/ /dus zhabs paṇ cen khyad par gdams pa mchog /dang por bka' babs gyi co lo tsā yis/ /thugs nyams gzhes nas gangs ri'i khrod 'dir spel/ / gyi co ra 'bro rtsa gnyos chag dpyal rong/ /rgwa tshal ko mgos o rgyan yon ston pa dang/ /sa jo zhang gsum lkog lung dbang rgya lugs/ /de sogs zab lam gangs can 'dzin mar shar/ /nyams len chu bo'i rgyun ldan jo nang pa/ /

[8. rDo rje gsum gyi bsnyen sgrub]

/sku'i bsnyen pa lus gnad byed bcings dang/ gsung gi bsgrub pa rdor bzlas srog rtsol dang/ /thugs kyi sgrub chen dangs ma 'dzag med 'ching/ / bsnyen bsgrub chos kyi nyams len gtso bo yin /rten gzhi'i gtso bo [251] /bde mchog dus 'khor rgyud/ /rdo rje rnal 'byor khyad par gdams pa mchog / dang por bka' babs mkhas grub o rgyan pas/ /thugs nyams bzhes nas gangs ri'i khrod 'dir spel/ /yi dam lung thob mkhar chu rin po che/ /rtogs ldan seng ge dpal ldan bu tra ba/ /rnam dpyod mtshungs med rje btsun zur phug pa/ /brgyud 'dzin lung bstan thob phyir dang po mchog /gter rgyud ma 'brel yi dam lung bstan tu/ /khas len smra ba'i bcos ma'i snyan rgyud rnams/ /mkhas grub gong ma'i srol dang mi mthun pas/ de dag rdo rje 'chang gi bka' rgyud min

Conclusion

The model of the eight lineages of attainment encompasses all the highest esoteric teachings of Buddhism in Tibet and the origins of the main religious orders. As a unifying model based on a soteriological approach, it is a response to sectarianism, while at the same time preserving the specificities of each different tradition. If 'Phreng po gter ston Shes rab 'od zer may be considered as the first to have formulated this model, it was through an eclectic education during a time of intense sectarianism. His original work on the eight lineages of attainment, *Meditation's Ambrosia of Immortality*, demonstrates how these eight lineages share a common origin and goal in the state of Vajradhara: it gives their core instructions, affirms their development in Tibet and highlights the authenticity, identity and specificities of Tibetan Buddhist esoteric traditions. For these reasons, this model was adopted centuries later as a structural element of 'Jam mgon Kong sprul's *ris med* compilation of the *Treasury of Spiritual Instructions*.

Notes

1 The expression is from E. Gene Smith's famous article, "'Jam mgon Kong sprul and the Nonsectarian Movement." In *Among Tibetan Texts: History and Literature of the Himalayan Plateau*, ed. Kurtis Schaeffer (Boston: Wisdom Publications, 2001), 235–72. It was first written as the introduction to *Kongtrul's Encyclopedia of Indo-Tibetan Culture*, ed. Lokesh Chandra (New Delhi: International Academy of Indian Culture, 1970).

2 I would like to express my sincere gratitude to my professor, Matthew T. Kapstein, to Brandon Dotson, Ananda Massoubre and Seiji Kumagai for their valuable readings and comments, which significantly improved this chapter.

3 Other important teachers of this movement were rDza dPal sprul (1808–1887), Ju Mi pham rnam rgyal rgya mtsho (1846–1912), whose works had been most influential in the exposition of the rNying ma pa doctrines, Shar dza bKra shis rgyal mthsan (1859–1934) for the Bon tradition and many others.

4 Ariane Macdonald, *Le Maṇḍala du Mañjuśrīmūlakalpa* (Paris: Adrien Maisonneuve, 1962), 91–95.

5 "There are many other different doctrines of the *Mantrayāna* in Tibet. Apart from differences in the names of all those systems [...], there are not in fact many real distinctions between them; the one aim common to them all is the final attainment of enlightenment. [...] Do not cut the Dharma into divisions and sections. Do not cause inconsistencies in any of the teachings. Discard blasphemies against the Dharma. Having understood that all the aspects of the teachings, which are themselves as broad as the ocean, are present in a mind that has been tamed, then practice it." Michael Aris, "Jamyang Khyentse's *Brief Discourse on The Essence of All the Ways*: A Work of the *Ris-med* Movement," *Kailash* 5.3 (1977), 226–27.

6 The recent International Conference on Esoteric Buddhist Studies held in Koyasan University focused on "Identity in Diversity," a central topic for the *ris med* movement and the present chapter. Chishō Namai expressed it as follows: "The Buddhist teachings were widely disseminated

with much local development, yet and when seen in light of mutual respect and understanding, they form an orderly and unified whole. The principle of identity within duality (*citrādvaita*) makes this possible. The diversity of Buddhism is the diversity of skilful means according to conditions (*pratītya*): means that are sensitive to the myriad forms of suffering encountered by each of those who need the teachings." Chishō Namai, "Foreword. Searching for Identity in Diversity." In *Esoteric Buddhist Studies: Identity in Diversity, Proceedings of the International Conference on Esoteric Buddhist Studies, Koyasan University, 5–8 Sep 2006* (Koyasan, Japan: Koyasan University, Executive Committee, ICEBS, 2008).

7 These are the *Treasury of Knowledge* (*Shes bya mdzod*), the *Treasury of Vast Writings* (*rGya chen bka' mdzod*), the *Treasury of Spiritual Instructions* (*gDams ngag mdzod*), the *Treasury of bKa' brgyud Mantras* (*bKa' brgyud sngags mdzod*) and *the Jewel Treasury* (*Rin chen gter mdzod*).

8 This work is being currently translated into English. In the context of the eight lineages of attainment, the section 8–4, which presents their respective systems of instructions, has just been published and provides excellent information. *The Treasury of Knowledge. Book Eight, Part Four: Esoteric Instructions, A Detailed Presentation of the Process of Meditation in Vajrayana*, trans. Sarah Harding (New York: Snow Lion, 2008).

9 Smith, 263–64.

10 Matthew Kapstein, "*gDams ngag*: Tibetan Technologies of the Self." In *Tibetan Literature: Studies in Genre,* ed. José Ignacio Cabezon and Roger R. Jackson (Ithaca: Snow Lion, 1996), 275–89.

11 Blo gros phun tshog, *'Jam dbyangs mkhyen brtse'i sku phreng gong 'og gi rnam thar (Beijing, Mi rigs dpe skrun khang*, 1994). *'Jam mgon Kong sprul blo gros mtha' yas, Phyogs med ris med kyi bstan pa 'dun shing dge sbyong gi gzugs brnyan 'chang ba blo gros mtha' yas kyi sde'i byung ba brjod pa nor bu sna tshogs mdog can* (Bir: Tibetan Khampa Industrial Society, 1973).

12 For the discussion of these dates, see Brandon Dotson, "'Emperor' Mu rug btsan and the *'Phang thang ma Catalogue*," *JIATS* 3 (December 2007), 1–25. www.thdl.org?id=T3105.

13 Kastumi Mimaki, "Doxographie tibétaine et classifications indiennes." In *Bouddhisme et culture locales: quelques cas de réciproques adaptations. Actes du colloque franco-japonais, septembre 1991*, ed. Fukui Fumimasa and Gérard Fussman (Paris: École française d'Extrême-Orient, 1994), 115–36.

14 The nine vehicles of Buddhism according to the rNying ma pa are those of the 1) *Srāvaka;* 2) *Pratyekabuddha* (belonging also to the *Hīnayāna*); 3) *Bodhisattva* (*Mahāyāna*); and then the tantric or esoteric vehicles (*Vajrayāna*): 4) *Kriyātantra;* 5) *Ubhayatantra;* 6) *Yogatantra;* 7) *Mahāyoga;* 8) *Anuyoga;* 9) *Atiyoga.*

15 These are the four main Indian Buddhist philosophical systems for the Tibetan gSar ma pa exegesis: *Vaibhāṣika, Sautrāntika* for the *Hīnayāna* and the *Yogācāra*, and *Mādhyamika* for the *Mahāyāna.*

16 According to the gSar ma pa, the *Vajrayāna* is composed of four sets of *tantra* from the lower to the higher: 1) *Kriyātantra;* 2) *Caryātantra;* 3)*Yogatantra;* 4) *Anuttarayogatantra.*

17 The tantras of *Cakrasaṃvara*, *Hevajra* and *Kālacakra*, belonging to the class of the *Anuttarayogatantra*, are said to be the main supports of the seven gSar ma pa lineages of attainment, according to Shes rab 'od zer's text thereafter translated. In this same text, the bKa' gdams pa and Zhi byed rely strongly on *Mahāyāna* texts. But further investigations in Kong sprul's works, for example, also show their connection with the highest class of gSar ma pa *tantra.*

18 David Snellgrove, *Indo-Tibetan Buddhism: Indian Buddhists and their Tibetan Successors* (Boston: Shambhala, 1987), 486–87.

19 This has been pointed out by Matthew Kapstein in Kapstein 1996, 277.

20 They have been published with the translation of Kong sprul's quotation of Shes rab 'od zer in several publications. See Cyrus Stearns, *Luminous Lives: The Story of the Early Masters of the Lam 'Bras Tradition in Tibet* (Somerville: Wisdom Publications, 2001), 3–4. Ringu Tulku, *The Ri-me Philosophy of Jamgön Kongtrul the Great. A Study of the Buddhist Lineages of Tibet* (Boston and London: Shambhala, 2006). Matthew T. Kapstein, "Tibetan Technologies of the Self, Part II: The Teachings of the Eight Great Conveyances." In *The Pandita and the Siddha. Tibetan Studies in Honour of E. Gene Smith,* ed. Ramon N. Prats (Dharamsala: Amnye Machen Institute, 2007), 110–11. Jamgön Kongtrul Lodrö Thayé, trans. Sarah Harding, *The Treasury of Knowledge. Book Eight, Part Four: Esoteric Instructions. A Detailed Presentation of the Process of Meditation in Vajrayana* (New York: Snow Lion, 2008), 27.

21 Giuseppe Tucci, *Tibetan Painted Scrolls,* vol. 1 (Rome: La Libreria Dello Stato, 1949), 110–15.

22 Gustave-Charles Toussaint, trans., *Le Dict de Padma, Padma thang yig, Ms. de Lithang* (Paris: Bibliothèque de l'Institut des hautes études chinoises, Librairie Ernest Leroux, 1933).

23 As another inspiration for the *ris med* works, the *Jo nang khrid brgya,* a collection of brief instructions on all of the special teachings that appeared in India and Tibet, was also created during the 16th century by Kun dga' grol mchog (1507–1565/1566) and completed by rJe btsun Tāranātha (1575–1634), the successor in his incarnation lineage. It was also included by Kong sprul in the last volume of the *gDams ngag mdzod.*

24 These are Tucci's expressions; see again Tucci, vol. 1, 39–57, for the political history of this period, which witnessed intense conflicts for spiritual authority and temporal power over central Tibet. These sectarian and partisan rivalries were due for the most part to economic and political conditions.

25 Smith, 237.

26 The full name of this work is *Zab mo'i gter dang gter ston grub thob ji ltar byon pa'i lo rgyus mdor bsdus bkod pa rin chen bai ḍū rya'i phreng ba.* In *Rin chen gter mdzod,* vol. 1 (Paro, Buthan: Ngodrup and Sherab Drimay, 1976–80), 291–759. See Shes rab 'od zer's *rnam thar,* 559–63.

27 Kong sprul used the spelling Phreng po instead of 'Phreng po, which is favored by the Tibetan Buddhist Resource Centre (TBRC). I have followed the latter in this chapter and standardized the use of 'Phreng po.

28 *Upāsaka, dge brnyen.*

29 According to the TBRC, a teacher of unknown sectarian affiliation, probably Sa skya pa, connected with the E wam dgon pa of g.Yag sde paṇ chen. According to the *Nor bu'i rdo shal,* it was in this monastery that Shes rab 'od zer took the vows of layman, as we find also in Khetsun Sangpo, *Biographical Dictionary of Tibet and Tibetan Buddhism,* vol. 3 (Dharamsala: LTWA, 1973), 755.

30 gSer mdog paṇ chen Shākya mchog ldan (1428–1507) of the Sa skya pa Monastery of gSer mdog can.

31 dGe 'dun bstan pa dar rgyas (1493–1568), important dGe lugs pa master connected with Se ra and then with dGa' ldan, where he held the throne from 1565 to 1568.

32 Rin chen phun tshogs Chos kyi rgyal po (1509–1557), famous *gter ston* and abbot of 'Bri gung. See 'Bri gung dkon mchog rgya mtsho, *'Bri gung chos 'byung* (Beijing: Mi rigs dpe skrun khang, 2004), 428–32. And Dudjom Rinpoche, *The Nyingma School of Tibetan Buddhism: Its Fundamentals and History,* ed. and trans. Gyurme Dorje and Matthew Kapstein (Boston: Wisdom, 1991), 676–77, 681.

33 The *Sūtra which Gathers all Intentions* (*mDo dgongs pa 'dus pa*) for *Anuyoga*; the *Magical Net* (*sGyu 'phrul drwa ba*) for *Mahāyoga*; and the *Great Perfection Mental Class* (*rDzogs chen sems phyogs*) for *Atiyoga*. These are the main supports of the rNying ma bka' ma tradition; see Dudjom, 599–739.

34 Padmasambhava, the Precious Guru (Gu ru rin po che), the tantric master at the origin of the *gter ma* tradition of the rNying ma pa.

35 This is Shes rab 'od zer's major *gter ma*, included in the *Rin chen gter mdzod*. See the references given in Dudjom, 257.

36 The Pure Land of Padmasambhava.

37 Cycle revealed by gTer ston Sangs rgyas gling pa (1340–1396).

38 Padmasambhava, named thus because he came from the land of Oḍḍiyāna (O rgyan).

39 We write "*stobs rgyal*" instead of "*stobs gyas*," which is found in Kong sprul. Hor bSod nams stobs rgyal was the prince of 'Phyong rgyas in whose lineage the Fifth Dalai Lama Blo bzang rgya mtsho (1617–1682) was later born. Moreover, the Great Fifth used ritually several of Padmasambhava's images rediscovered by Shes rab 'od zer: the images named Padmaguru and Rigs 'dus brda dbang lnga pa, as indicated by Samten Karmay in *Secret Visions of the Fifth Dalai Lama: The Gold Manuscript in the Fournier Collection* (London: Serindia Publications, 1988), 39, 42, 62, according to what Mrs. Anne Chayet has kindly informed us.

40 The monastery where 'Jigs med gling pa (1730–1798) was trained. Some references to 'Jigs med gling pa's connections with Shes rab 'od zer's monastery of dPal ris and *gter ma* of the *Grol tig* are also given by Janet Gyatso, *Apparitions of the Self. The Secret Autobiographies of a Tibetan Visionary* (Woodstock, UK: Princeton University Press, 1998), 77, 81, 132.

41 According to the TBRC, this work written by Shes rab 'od zer's son probably survived to the time of 'Jam mgon Kong sprul, but has not yet surfaced.

42 Gu ru bKra shis, *Gu ru bKra shis chos 'byung* (Beijing: Krung go'i bod kyi shes rig dpe skrun khang, 1990), 544–50.

43 Zhe chen rgyal tshab 'Gyur med pad ma rnam rgyal, *Zhe chen chos 'byung* (Chengdu: Si khron mi rigs dpe skrun khang, 1994), 262–69. I would like to thank very much Lama Tenzin Samphel for the indications of these two other versions of Shes rab 'od zer's *rnam thar* and for his useful advice concerning the present translation.

44 The full title is *Gangs ri'i khrod kyi klog pa nyan bshad pa rnams kyi snyan tu bsrings pa thos bsam 'chi med kyi bdud rtsi*. In 'Phreng po gter ston Shes rab 'od zer, *Gsung 'bum*, 1 vol. (Gangtok: Gonpo Tseten, 1977), 231–42.

45 'Phreng po gter ston Shes rab 'od zer, *Gangs ri'i khrod kyi spong ba bsam gtan pa rnams kyi snyan tu bsrings pa sgom pa 'chi med kyi bdud rtsi,* 243–66.

46 Thon mi sam bho ṭa (early-to-mid 7th century), Vairocana (8th to 9th century), sKa ba dpal brtsegs (8th to 9th century), Cog ro klu'i rgyal mtshan (8th to 9th century), Zhang ye shes sde (8th to 9th century), Lo chen Rin chen bzang po (957–1055), 'Brom ston pa rGyal ba'i 'byung gnas (1005–1064) and rNgog lo tsā ba bLo ldan shes rab (1059–1109), Sa skya paṇḍita Kun dga' rgyal mtshan (1182–1251), and 'Gos Khug pa lhas btsas (early 11th century).

47 *Gangs ri'i khrod kyi klog pa nyan bshad pa rnams dang spong ba bsam gtan pa rnams kyi snyan du bsrings pa thos bsam dang bsgom pa 'chi med bdud rtsi ldeb*. In Jam dbyangs mKhyen brtse'i dbang po, *The Collected Works* (*gsung 'bum*), vol. 6 (Gangtok: Gonpo Tseten, 1977–80), 327–74.

48 Kapstein, 1996, 277, the reference given is: *gDams ngag mdzod*, vol. 12 (Delhi: N. Lungtok and N. Gyaltsen 1971), 645–46. For the translation of this passage of the *gDams ngag mdzod*, see Kapstein 2007, 110–29.

49 The primordial Buddha or *Ādibuddha* in the tantric teachings.

50 The three vows (*trisaṁvara, sdom pa gsum*) are the vows of personal liberation (*prātimokṣa, so sor thar pa*), of the awakened mind (*bodhicitta, byang chub sems dpa'*) and of a tantric practioner (*vidyādhara, rig 'dzin*), corresponding to the three vehicles of the Buddhist teachings in Tibet (*Hīnayāna, Mahāyāna* and *Vajrayāna*).

51 *Mahāsiddha, grub thob chen po*, great realized tantric adept.

52 Avalokiteśvara.

53 According to M. Kapstein (2007), this refers to the *Maṇi bka' bum* traditions associated with King Srong btsan sgam po.

54 Vairocana, at the time of Khri Srong lde btsan and Padmasambhava, source of the rNying ma pa lineage (no. 1 here in *Meditation's Ambrosia of Immortality*) during the first period of Buddhism in Tibet.

55 'Brom ston rGyal ba'i 'byung gnas (1104–1163), disciple of the Indian master Atīśa Dīpaṅkara Śrījñāna (982–1054), at the origin of the bKa' gdams pa lineage (no. 2).

56 Khyung po rnal 'byor Tshul khrims mgon po (ca 1050–ca 1140), from the valley of Shangs, founded the Shangs pa bKa' brgyud lineage (no. 3).

57 'Brog mi lo tsā ba Śākya ye shes (992–1072), who transmitted the Lam 'bras lineage (no. 4), originated from the Indian *mahāsiddha* Virūpa.

58 Mar pa chos kyi blo gros (1012–1097), disciple of the Indian *mahāsiddha* Nāropa, source of the Mar pa bka' brgyud lineage (no. 5) and its different branches.

59 Pha dam pa Sangs rgyas (d. 1117) transmitted the Zhi byed lineage (no. 6) connected to the gCod lineage.

60 Gyi gyo Zla ba'i 'od zer ("Gyi co" in Shes rab 'od zer's text) introduced the *tantra* of Kālacakra with a first translation in 1027, and its system of yoga through the lineage of sByor drug (no. 7).

61 O rgyan pa rin chen dpal (1230–1309) went to Oḍḍiyāna and received from Vajrayoginī a direct revelation, founding the rDo rje gsum gyi bsnyen sgrub instructions lineage (no. 8).

62 The five sensorial consciousnesses and the mental consciousness.

63 Practices of *khregs chod*, "Cutting through resistance."

64 Visionary practices of *thod rgal*, the "all-surpassing realization."

65 Disciple of the first human rDzogs chen master, dGa' rab rdo rje.

66 On the lineage of the Zur family, see Dudjom, 617–49.

67 The notes of the text briefly refer to the *Garland of Birth Stories* (*Jātakamālā, sKyes rabs*) and the *Collection of Purposeful Sayings* (*Udānavarga, Ched du brjod pa'i tshom*) concerning faith; *the Compendium of Lessons* (*Śīkśāsamuccaya, bSlab btus*) and the *Introduction to the Conduct of a Bodhisattva* (*Bodhicaryāvatāra, sPyod 'jug*) concerning right conduct; the *Bodhisattva Level* (*Bodhisattvabhūmi, Byang sa*) and *the Ornament of the Sūtra of the Great Vehicle* (*Mahāyānasūtralaṃkāra, mDo sde rgyan*) concerning meditation.

68 Taught by the Buddha Śākyamuni in the first turning of the wheel of Dharma: the truth of suffering (*duḥkhasatya, sdug bsngal gyi bden pa*), the truth of origin (*duḥkhasamudayasatya, kun 'byung gi bden pa*), the truth of cessation (*nirodhasatya, 'gog pa'i bden pa*), and the truth of the path (*mārgasatya, lam gyi bden pa*).

69 This classification differs from the traditional one repeated by Kong sprul in which the roots are the six yogas (of Niguma, which are closed to those of Nāropa; see next notes on the Mar pa bKa' brgyud); the trunk is the reliquary of the Great Seal (*Mahāmudrā*), the branches are the methods of integration, the flowers are the two *Khecharī* and the fruit is the immortality of body and mind; so that there is normally no mention of the leaves. These are the Five Golden Teachings (*gSer chos lnga*) of the Shangs pa bKa' brgyud.

70 The six yogas of Nāropa: inner heat (*gtu mo*), apparitional body (*sgyu lus*), dreams (*rmi lam*), luminosity (*'od gsal*), the intermediate state (*bar do*) and transference of consciousness (*'pho ba*, or in another body: *grongs 'jug*).

71 Mar pa lo tsā ba chos kyi blo gros (1012–1097).

72 sGam po pa dwags po lha rje (1079–1153) was the disciple of the great ascetic Mi la ras pa (1040–1123), and is said to have joined the two streams of the bKa' gdams pa and the bKa' brgyud pa's *Mahāmudrā*.

73 *Chu klung mdo*?
74 *Pratyāhāra, sor sdud.*
75 *Dhyāna, bsam gtan.*
76 *Prāṇāyāma, srog rtsol.*
77 *Dhāraṇā, 'dzin pa.*
78 *Anusmṛti, rjes dran.*
79 *Samādhi, ting nge 'dzin.*
80 Cilupā (11th century), who went to the sacred kingdom of Śambhala and then introduced the *Kālacakratantra* in India.
81 This is a strong manner in which to emphasize the authenticity and excellence of the eight lineages of attainment coming from Vajradhara.
82 'Phreng po gter ston Shes rab 'od zer, 243–251. This is the root text translated above. Some variations of the spelling can be observed. Here I remain accurate to this Gangtok edition.
83 I read *nyin*, which is found in mKhyen brtse, 348.
84 The different spelling *sgrub brgyud* is to be found in mKhyen brste and in the later tradition, which we have followed in the present chapter.
85 Again I read *nyes dmigs*, according to mKhyen brtse, 351.

17

གཞུང་ས་དགའ་ལྡན་ཕོ་བྲང་ཆེན་པོའི་གཞུང་བསྟེན་ཆོས་སྐྱོང་ཁག་ལ་དཔྱད་པ།

རྡོ་སྲིད་ཚེ་རིང་རྒྱལ།

བོད་བརྒྱུད་ནང་བསྟན་ཆོས་ལུགས་ཀྱི་གྲུབ་མཐའ་ཀུན་མཐུན་གྱི་འདོད་ཚུལ་ལྟར་ན། ཆོས་མདོ་སྔགས་གཉིས་ཆར་རང་རང་སོ་སོའི་ཆོས་སྐྱོང་གི་རྣམ་གྲངས་མང་ཞིང་། སྤྱིར་བཏང་དུ་ནང་བསྟན་གྱི་ལྷ་ཚོགས་དེ་དག་ཀུང་འཇིག་རྟེན་འདི་དང་ཚེ་ཕྱི་མའི་དོན་ཆེན་གང་ཞིག་ལ་དམིགས་པ་གཏད་ནས་ཡུལ་བྱེ་བྲག་སོ་སོའི་བགྱིད་པར་གཞོལ་བའི་ཁྱད་པར་གྱི་སྟེང་ནས་འཇིག་རྟེན་པའི་ལྷ་དང་འཇིག་རྟེན་ལས་འདས་པའི་ལྷ་ཞེས་རིགས་གཉིས་སུ་དགར་ཡོད། བྱེ་བྲག་ཏུ་འཇིག་རྟེན་ལས་འདས་པའི་སྲུང་མ་ནི། འཕགས་ལམ་ཐོབ་ཅིང་བསམ་བཞིན་དུ་སེམས་ཅན་སོ་སོའི་སྣང་ངོར་གཟུགས་ཅི་རིགས་སྟོན་པ་སྟེ། དེ་ཡང་སངས་རྒྱས་དང་བྱང་སེམས་གཉིས་ཡོད། འཇིག་རྟེན་ལས་མ་འདས་པའི་སྲུང་མ་ནི། སོ་སོའི་སྐྱེ་བོ་སྟེ་དེ་ལ་ལམ་དུ་ཞུགས་པ་དང་། མ་ཞུགས་པ་གཉིས། ལམ་དུ་མ་ཞུགས་པ་དེ་ལ་དཀར་ཕྱོགས་སྐྱོང་བའི་སྲུང་མ། སྔོན་སངས་རྒྱས་སོགས་མཐོང་བ། དམ་པའི་ཆོས་ཐོས་ཤིང་། འཁོར་རྣམ་པ་བཞི་སྟེ་དགེ་བསྙེན་ཕ་མ་དགེ་སློང་ཕ་མ་སོགས་སྐྱོང་བར་དམ་བཅས་པ། སངས་རྒྱས་སོགས་མ་མཇལ་ཡང་། འཕགས་བོད་སོགས་ཀྱི་པཎ་གྲུབ་རྣམས་ཀྱི་དྲུང་ནས་ལེགས་སྨོན་དང་འཇིགས་སྐྱོབ་ཀྱི་སྨོམ་པ་བླང་པ་དང་། བཀའ་བསྒོ་དམ་བཞག་མཛད་པའི་སྲུང་མ་དམ་ཅན་དང་། གཞན་འཕྲུལ་དབང་བྱེད་ཀྱི་ལྷ་ཡི་འཁོར་དུ་གཏོགས་པའི་བདུད་རིས་ནག་ཕྱོགས་ལ་སོགས་ཅི་རིགས་ཡོད།[1] གཞུང་ས་དགའ་ལྡན་ཕོ་བྲང་ཆེན་པོའི་སྲིད་དབང་གི་སྐབས་སུ། གཞུང་ནས་ཆེད་དུ་དམིགས་བསལ་གྱི་ཆོས་སྐྱོང་ཞེས་འཇིག་རྟེན་པའི་ལྷ་ལ་གཏོགས་པ་གང་ཞིག་གདན་འདྲེན་གྱིས་མིའི་ཁོག་ཏུ་བཀླུམས་ཏེ་སོ་སོའི་སྐུ་བསྟེན་པར་(སྐུ་རྟེན་པ་ཞེས་ཀྱང་འབྲི)བཀའ་ལུང་སྩོལ་ཞུས་ཀྱིས་ཕྱིའི་རྒྱ་ཁྱབ་རྗོང་གཞིས་ཁག་དང་ནང་གི་ལས་ཁུངས་ཁག་གི་ཆོས་སྲིད་གཉིས་ཀྱི་འགངས་ཆེའི་སྐབས་དོན་གནད་ཀྱི་མདུད་རྒྱ་བཀྲོལ་བར་ལུང་དོན་བཞིན་དོན་དག་དངོས་ལག་ལེན་དུ་བསྟར་བའི་སྲོལ་ཀ་ཐོག་མར་བྱུང་ཞིང་། དེ་བཞིན་དུ་གཞུང་བསྟེན་གྱི་ཆོས་སྐྱོང་ཁག་ཅིག་རིམ་པར་བྱུང་སྟེ་ཆོས་སྲིད་ཟུང་འབྲེལ་གྱི་ལམ་ལུགས་འཕྱུས་ཚང་དུ་འགྱུར་བའི་གོ་རིམ་ཁྲོད་བྱེད་ནུས་མི་དམན་པ་ཐོན་པ་དང་། གཞུང་ས་དགའ་ལྡན་ཕོ་བྲང་ཆེན་པོའི་སྐབས་ཀྱི་བོད་རང་གི་ཐུན་མོང་མ་ཡིན་པའི་སྲིད་ལུགས་དང་འབྲེལ་བའི་རིག་གནས་

ཁྱད་པར་བ་ཞིག་ཏུ་གྱུར་ཡོད། དེས་ན། དཔྱད་རྩོམ་འདིར་གཞུང་ས་དགའ་ལྡན་ཕོ་བྲང་ཆེན་པོའི་གཞུང་བསྟེན་ཆོས་སྐྱོང་ཁག་གི་བྱུང་འཕེལ་ལོ་རྒྱུས་དང་འབྲེལ་ཏེ། ཆོས་སྐྱོང་ཁག་གི་གདན་ས་དགོན་གནས་གང་དག་གི་དཀར་ཆག་གམ་གདན་རབས་ཡིག་ཆ་གཞིར་བཟུང་ཐོག ལོ་རྒྱུས་ཡིག་ཚགས་ཁྲོད་ཀྱི་འབྲེལ་ཡོད་ཡིག་ཆར་གཞི་བཅོལ་ཏེ་གཞུང་ས་དགའ་ལྡན་ཕོ་བྲང་ཆེན་པོའི་གཞུང་བསྟེན་ཆོས་སྐྱོང་ཁག་དང་དེ་དག་གི་སྐུ་བསྟེན་པའི་སྐོར། གཞན་ད་དུང་གཞུང་བསྟེན་ཆོས་སྐྱོང་ཁག་གིས་གཞུང་ས་དགའ་ལྡན་ཕོ་བྲང་གི་ཆོས་སྲིད་ཟུང་འབྲེལ་གྱི་ལམ་ལུགས་ཁྲོད་ཐོན་པའི་སྤྱི་ཚོགས་ཀྱི་ཕན་ནུས་སོགས་ལ་དཔྱད་ཞིབ་ཙམ་བྱ་རྒྱུ་ཡིན།

གཞུང་བསྟེན་ཆོས་སྐྱོང་ཁག་དང་དེ་དག་གི་སྐུ་བསྟེན་པ།

སངས་རྒྱས་ཆོས་ལུགས་འཕེལ་རྒྱས་སུ་ཕྱིན་པ་དང་བསྟུན་རིས་མེད་དགོན་སྡེ་ཁག་གིས་སྤྱིར་སངས་རྒྱས་བསྟན་པ་དང་ནང་སྒོས་སུ་རང་རང་གི་གྲུབ་མཐའ་འམ་དགོན་སྡེའི་ཆོས་འཆད་ཉན་འཛིན་སྐྱོང་སྤེལ་གསུམ་བགྱིད་པར་མི་དང་མི་མ་ཡིན་པའི་དགྲ་བགེགས་གདོན་འདྲེ་སོགས་ཀྱི་བར་ཆད་བཟློག་པར་ཆོས་སྐྱོང་སྲུང་མར་འཕྲིན་བཅོལ་གྱི་མཆོད་གསོལ་ཞུ་བ་སྟེ། གཞུང་ས་དགའ་ལྡན་ཕོ་བྲང་ཆེན་པོའི་དུས་སྐབས་སུ། བོད་དབུས་ཁུལ་གཙོ་བོར་བྱེད་པའི་ཆོས་སྐྱོང་གཙོ་བོ་ཁག་ནི་དཔེར་ན། གནས་ཆུང་ཆོས་སྐྱོང་དང་། བསམ་ཡས་ཙིའུ་དམར་པོ། ལ་མོ་ཚངས་པ་ཆེན་པོ། ཐང་པོ་ཆེ་ཆོས་སྐྱོང་། ཁྲ་འབྲུག་ཆོས་སྐྱོང་། དགའ་བ་གདོང་ཞིང་བྱ་ཅན། གསང་ཕུ་བསེ་ཁྲབ་པ། ཆོས་སྐྱོང་བྱ་ཁྱི་བ། བོད་ཁམས་སྐྱོང་བའི་བསྟན་མ་ལྷ་མོ་ཚེ་རིང་མཆེད་ལྔ་སོགས་རྣམ་གྲངས་མང་ཞིང་། སྤྱིར་བཏང་ཁ་རྒྱུན་དུ་མི་རྣམས་ཀྱིས་དགོན་པའི་མཚན་གྱིས་བཟུང་ནས་ཆོས་སྐྱོང་གི་མཚན་དུ་འབོད། དེ་ལས་ཀྱང་གཞུང་ས་དགའ་ལྡན་ཕོ་བྲང་གི་གཞུང་བསྟེན་ཆོས་སྐྱོང་ནི་གནས་ཆུང་པེ་ཧར་ཆོས་སྐྱོང་ཆེན་པོ་གཙོ་བྱེད་ཀྱི་དགའ་གདོང་གནས་སྲུང་གནོད་སྦྱིན་ཞིང་བྱ་ཅན་དང་། ལ་མོ་ཚངས་པ་དུང་གི་ཐོར་ཚུགས་ཅན། ཆོས་སྐྱོང་གནོད་སྦྱིན་ཙིའུ་དམར་པོ་བཅས་ཏེ་ཁ་རྒྱུན་དུ་ཆོས་སྐྱོང་ཆེན་མོ་བཞི་ཞེས་འབོད། དེ་དག་སོ་སོ་བོད་ཀྱི་ཆོས་ལུགས་ལོ་རྒྱུས་འཕེལ་འགྱུར་གྱི་དུས་རིམ་ཁྱད་པར་བའི་སྐབས་སུ་རིམ་པར་བོད་དབུས་ཁུལ་དུ་གནས་ཆགས་པའི་གནས་ཆུང་རྡོ་རྗེ་སྒྲ་དབྱངས་གླིང་དང་། དགའ་གདོང་དགོན། ལ་མོ་མི་འགྱུར་བྱང་ཆུབ་ལྷུན་གྱིས་གྲུབ་པའི་ལྷོག་དཔལ་བསམ་ཡས་མི་འགྱུར་ལྷུན་གྱིས་གྲུབ་པའི་གཙུག་ལག་ཁང་བཅས་ཀྱི་ཆོས་སྐྱོང་སྲུང་མར་བསྟེན།

དང་པོ། གནས་ཆུང་པེ་ཧར་ཆོས་སྐྱོང་ཆེན་པོ།

གནས་ཆུང་པེ་ཧར་ཆོས་སྐྱོང་ཆེན་པོའི་མཚན་འབོད་སྟངས་གཞན་ལ་གནས་ཆུང་རྡོ་རྗེ་གྲགས་ལྡན་དང་། སྲུང་མ་འོད་ལྡན་དཀར་པོ་ཟེར། གཞུང་ས་དགའ་ལྡན་ཕོ་བྲང་ཆེན་པོའི་ཆོས་སྐྱོང་གི་གཙོ་བོ་སྟེ། ཆོས་རྒྱལ་ཁྲི་སྲོང་ལྡེའུ་བཙན་སྐབས་ནས་དམ་ཚིག་འགྲིག་ཅིང་གཞུང་ས་དགའ་ལྡན་ཕོ་བྲང་གི་སྲུང་མ་དམར་ནག་གཉིས་ཀྱི་ནང་ཚན་སྲུང་མ་དམར་པོ་པེ་ཧར་རྒྱལ་པོ་དང་ངོ་བོ་དབྱེར་མ་མཆིས་པའི་སྐུ་གསུང་ཐུགས་ཡོན་ཏན་འཕྲིན་ལས

བཅས་རྒྱལ་ཆེན་སྐུ་ལྔའི་ནང་གསེས་གསུང་གི་བྱེད་པོ་ཆོས་སྐྱོང་རྡོ་རྗེ་གྲགས་ལྡན་ཞེས་པ་དེ་ཡིན། པདྨ་བཀའ་ཐང་དང་སྦ་བཞེད་སོགས་བོད་ཀྱི་ཆོས་འབྱུང་ལོ་རྒྱུས་ལྟར་ན། སྔར་བོད་ཀྱི་རྒྱལ་པོ་ཁྲི་སྲོང་ལྡེའུ་བཙན་གྱིས་དཔལ་བསམ་ཡས་གཙུག་ལག་ཁང་བཞེངས་དུས་ལྷ་ཁང་འདི་ཉིད་སྲུང་ཐུབ་མཁན་གྱི་སྲུང་མ་གཉན་པོ་ཞིག་དགོས་པར་བསམས་ནས་སློབ་དཔོན་པདྨ་འབྱུང་གནས་ལ་ཞུས་པས་སློབ་དཔོན་གྱིས་བོད་ཀྱི་ལྷ་སྲིན་སྡེ་བརྒྱད་མང་པོ་ཞིག་ལ་བཀའ་ཐབས་ཀྱང་། སྲུང་མ་ནུས་མཁན་ཞིག་མ་བྱུང་པས་རྗེས་སོར་བྱུང་ཕྱོགས་བྷ་ཊ་ཧོར་གྱི་སྒོམ་གྲྭ་ན་དམུའི་རིགས་ལས་བྱུང་བའི་མི་མ་ཡིན་གྱི་རྒྱལ་པོ་པེ་ཧར་ཟེར་བ་ཞིག་ཡོད་པ་ནོར་རྒྱ་ཁབ་ཙམ་གྱི་རྗེས་ལ་བྱ་རྒོད་པོའི་ཉིན་ལམ་བཅོ་བརྒྱད་ཀྱི་བར་རྗེས་འདེད་བྱེད་ཐུབ་པ་ཞིག་ཡོད་པ་ཤེས་ནས། རྒྱལ་པོ་ཁྲི་སྲོང་ལྡེའུ་བཙན་གྱིས་རང་གི་སྲས་མུ་ཏིག་བཙན་པོ་དམག་དཔུང་ཁྲི་ཕྲག་མང་པོའི་དཔུང་དང་བཅས་མངགས་ཏེ་བྷ་ཊ་ཧོར་གྱི་སྒོམ་གྲྭ་བཅོམ་ཏེ་ཟ་ཧོར་གྱི་རྒྱལ་བརྒྱུད་རྣམ་པ་ལ། གཡུའི་ཐུབ་པ། དུང་གི་སེང་གེ་སོགས་རྒྱུ་ནོར་རིན་ཐང་ཆེ་བ་མང་པོ་བོད་དུ་དྲངས། དེ་དང་མཉམ་དུ་རྒྱལ་པོ་པེ་ཧར་ཡང་རྗེས་འབྲངས་བྱས་ཏེ་བོད་དུ་ཐེབས་པ་དང་སློབ་དཔོན་པདྨ་འབྱུང་གནས་ཀྱིས་དམ་ལ་བཏགས་ཏེ་བསམ་ཡས་གཙུག་ལག་ཁང་གི་སྲུང་མར་བཀུག[2] རྒྱལ་དབང་སྐུ་ཕྲེང་གཉིས་པ་དགེ་འདུན་རྒྱ་མཚོ་ནས་བཟུང་གོང་ས་རྒྱལ་དབང་ཐམས་ཅད་མཁྱེན་པ་ཏཱ་ལའི་བླ་མ་སྐུའི་སྐྱེ་བ་ན་རིམ་གྱིས་སྲུང་མར་བསྟེན་པ་དང་། སྤྱི་ལོ་དུས་རབས་བཅུ་བདུན་པའི་དཀྱིལ་ཙམ་དུ་གཞུང་ས་དགའ་ལྡན་ཕོ་བྲང་ཆེན་པོ་བཙུགས་རྗེས། གནས་ཆུང་པེ་ཧར་ཆོས་སྐྱོང་བསམ་ཡས་ནས་གདན་ས་འབྲས་སྤུངས་དགོན་པའི་འདབས་རོལ་གྱི་གནས་ཆུང་པེ་ཧར་ལྕོག་ཏུ་གདན་དྲངས་ཤིང་།[3] སྡེ་བརྒྱད་ཐམས་ཅད་ཀྱི་ཡང་རྗེ། དྲེགས་པ་ཀུན་འདུས་ཀྱི་རྒྱལ་པོ་ཞེས་རྒྱལ་དབང་ཐམས་ཅད་མཁྱེན་པ་ཏཱ་ལའི་བླ་མ་སྐུའི་སྐྱེ་བ་ན་རིམ་གྱི་སྲུང་མ་དང་། རི་བོ་དགེ་ལུགས་པའི་བསྟན་པ་སྤྱི་དང་ལྷག་པར་དུ་གདན་ས་འབྲས་སྤུངས་དགོན་པ་གཙོ་བྱེད་ཀྱི་ལྷོ་ཁའི་དགའ་ལྡན་དོན་གཉིས་གླིང་དང་། མདོ་སྨད་ཀྱི་གདན་ས་ཆེན་པོ་སྐུ་འབུམ་བྱམས་པ་གླིང་། བླ་བྲང་བཀྲ་ཤིས་འཁྱིལ་སོགས་དགེ་ལུགས་པའི་དགོན་པ་ཆེ་ཁག་གིས་ཆོས་སྐྱོང་སྲུང་མར་མཆོད་གསོལ་བགྱིས་ཐོག་འཇིག་རྟེན་དང་འཇིག་རྟེན་ལས་འདས་པའི་སྲུང་མ་བསམ་གྱིས་མི་ཁྱབ་པ་དེ་དག་གི་ནང་ནས་ཀྱང་ཆེས་ཆེར་འཕྲིན་ལས་མྱུར་ཞིང་དྲག་རྩལ་གྱི་མཐུ་དང་ལྡན་པ་ནི་ཆོས་སྐྱོང་པའི་རྒྱལ་པོ་འདི་ཉིད་ཡིན་པར་གྲགས། དེ་ལྟར་འཇིག་རྟེན་པའི་ལྷར་གཏོགས་པའི་ཆོས་སྐྱོང་ཁག་གི་གཙོ་བོར་བཀུར་བ་མ་ཟད། གཞུང་ས་དགའ་ལྡན་ཕོ་བྲང་རང་གི་བསྟན་སྲིད་ལར་རྒྱའི་འཕྲིན་བཅོལ་གྱི་གཞུང་བསྟེན་དགྲ་ལྷའི་གཙོ་བོར་གྱུར།

གནས་ཆུང་ཆོས་སྐྱོང་གི་སྐུ་བསྟེན་པར་གནས་ཆུང་ཆོས་རྒྱལ་དང་ཡང་ན་གནས་ཆུང་ཆོས་རྗེ་ཞེས་གྲགས་ཤིང་། ཆོས་སྐྱོང་གི་སྐུ་བསྟེན་སེར་མོ་བ་གང་ཞིག་ངེས་པར་དུ་ཆེད་མངགས་ཀྱི་སྦྱོང་བརྡར་བྱེད་དགོས་ལ། སྤྱི་ཁྱབ་ལས་ཁུངས་བཀའ་ཤག་གི་འདེམས་བསྐོད་ཆོག་མཆན་འོག་འགན་འཁུར་བཞེས་གནང་དགོས། གསུང་སྒྲོལ་ཞིག་ལྟར་ན། སྐུ་བསྟེན་གང་ཞིག་ད་དུང་རྒྱལ་དབང་ལྔ་པ་མཆོག་གི་གཏན་འཁེལ་མཛད་པའི་དམིགས་བསལ་གྱི་ཡིག་རྒྱུགས་ཕུལ་ཐོག་ད་གཟོད་གཞི་ནས་གཞུང་ས་དགའ་ལྡན་ཕོ་བྲང་ཆེན་པོའི་སྲུང་མའི་གཙོ་བོ་གནས་ཆུང་ཆོས་སྐྱོང་གི་སྐུ་བསྟེན་པའི་ཐུགས་འགན་བཞེས་དགོས། དེ་མིན་གནས་ཆུང་སྤྲེལ་ཟླ་ཞེས་ལོ་འཁོར་བཅུ་གཉིས་ཀྱི་སྤྲེལ་ལོ་སྟེ་སློབ་དཔོན་པདྨ་འབྱུང་གནས་ཀྱི་རང་ལོར་གནས་ཆུང་ཆོས་སྐྱོང་གཙོ་བྱེད་ཀྱི་བསྟན་མ་དང་། དགའ་གདོང་ཆོས་སྐྱོང་དབུ་བཞུགས་ཐོག་ཉེ་འཁོར་གྱི་ཆོས་སྐྱོང་ཁོག་ཞུགས་ཀྱིས་ལྷ་བབས་རྒྱུ་ཡོད་པ

རྣམས་གདན་འདྲེན་གྱིས་ལྷ་ཚོགས་བརྒྱབ་སྟེ་ལྷ་ངོ་མ་མིན་ན་འདུས་ཚོགས་སར་ཕེབས་མི་ཐུབ་ཅེས་ཟེར་ཞིང་། སྤྱར་ལྷ་སའི་ཉེ་འཁོར་གྱི་སྐུ་བསྟེན་པ་བཅུ་གཉིས་ཙམ་དེའི་ཉིན་ལྷན་འཛོམས་ཀྱིས་ལྷ་བསྐྱར་གནང་སྲོལ་ཡོད་པར་གྲགས། སྐུ་བསྟེན་གསར་པ་རྩ་སྒོ་དབྱེ་ལུགས་ཐད་ལ་ཆ་མཚོན་ན། རྒྱལ་བ་སྐུ་ཕྲེང་ན་རིམ་མམ་ཡང་ན་སྲིད་སྐྱོང་གང་གི་དབང་འཛིན་སྐབས་སུ་འཁེལ་ཐོག་དགའ་གདོང་གནས་སྲུང་དང་གསེར་ཞལ་ལྷན་འཛོམས་ཐོག་རྩ་དབྱེའི་བཀའ་དྲིན་བསྐྱངས་དགོས་ཏེ། དཔེར་ན། སྐྱབས་མགོན་སྲིད་སྐྱོང་སྟེ་དྲུག་མཁྱེན་རབ་དབང་ཕྱུག་མཆོག་དང་དགའ་གདོང་གནས་སྲུང་གསེར་ཞལ་ལྷན་འཛོམས་ཀྱིས་ལྷ་ལྡན་དཔལ་ལྷོག་ཏུ་གནས་ཆུང་ཆོས་རྒྱལ་ཆེན་པོའི་སྐུ་བསྟེན་ཤཱཀྱ་ཡར་འཕེལ་ལགས་ཐོག་མའི་རྩ་དབྱེའི་བཀའ་དྲིན་བསྐྱངས་པ་དང་། དེའི་རྗེས་སྐུ་བསྟེན་བློ་བཟང་བསོད་ནམས་ལགས་གོང་ས་སྐྱབས་མགོན་རྒྱལ་དབང་སྐུ་ཕྲེང་བཅུ་གསུམ་པ་ཆེན་པོ་མཆོག་དང་། དགའ་གདོང་གནས་སྲུང་བཅས་གསེར་ཞལ་ལྷན་འཛོམས་ཀྱིས་འབྲས་སྤུངས་ཡི་དམ་འཇམ་དཔལ་གཤིན་རྗེའི་ཞབས་དྲུང་དུ་ཐོག་མའི་རྩ་དབྱེའི་བཀའ་དྲིན་བསྐྱངས། དེའི་རྗེས་སྐུ་བསྟེན་རྒྱལ་མཚན་མཐར་ཕྱིན་ལགས་གོང་ས་སྐྱབས་མགོན་རྒྱལ་དབང་བཅུ་གསུམ་པ་ཆེན་པོ་མཆོག་དང་། དགའ་གདོང་གནས་སྲུང་བཅས་གསེར་ཞལ་ལྷན་འཛོམས་ཐོག་ནོར་གླིང་བསྐལ་བཟང་ཕོ་བྲང་གི་གཟིམ་ཆུང་ཉི་འོད་དུ་རྩ་དབྱེའི་བཀའ་དྲིན་བསྐྱངས། དེ་མིན་ལོ་རེའི་བོད་ཟླ་དང་པོའི་ཚེས་གསུམ་ཉིན་ཚེས་གསུམ་གཟབ་གསོལ་ཞེས་སྡེ་པ་གཞུང་ནས་བཀའ་བློན་གཙོ་བྱེད་ཀྱི་གཞུང་ཞབས་དྲག་རིམ་ཁག་གནས་ཆུང་དགོན་དུ་སྐུ་བཅར་གྱིས་ཆོས་རྒྱལ་ཆེན་པོར་གསོལ་མཆོད་གང་རྒྱས་བསྟབས་ཐོག་གཞུང་ཐོག་གི་ལྷ་གསོལ་ལུང་ཞུ་ཕུལ་ནས་ལོ་གཅིག་རིང་གཞུང་གི་ཕྱི་ནང་གི་འགངས་ཆེའི་དོན་དག་ཁག་ལ་བཀའ་ལུང་དགོངས་དོན་སྤྱི་ཞུས་ཀྱིས་བསྟན་སྲིད་ལར་རྒྱར་འཕུར་བསྐྱེད་ཀྱི་ཞབས་འདེགས་ཞུ་བཞིན་ཡོད་པས། དམངས་ཁྲོད་དུ་བོད་ཟླ་དང་པོའི་ཚེས་པ་གཅིག་ཉིན་ལ་ བླ་མའི་ལོ་གསར་དང་། ཚེས་པ་གཉིས་ཉིན་ལ་རྒྱལ་པོའི་ལོ་གསར་ཟེར་བ་བཞིན་ཚེས་པ་གསུམ་པ་ལ་ཚེས་གསུམ་གཟབ་གསོལ་ཞུ་སྲོལ་ཡོད་པས་གནས་ཆུང་ལོ་གསར་ཞེས་ཀྱང་འབོད། སྤྱིར་བཏང་ཡིན་ན་གནས་ཆུང་ཆོས་སྐྱོང་གིས་གཞུང་བསྟེན་སྲུང་མའི་གཙོ་བོ་ཟིན་པས་གཞུང་གི་རིམ་པ་བཞི་བ་རྩེ་སྐོར་དྲུང་ཡིག་ཆེན་མོ་བྱ་སྤྱི་ཐོབ་ཅིང་། ནམ་རྒྱུན་སེར་ཆས་བཞེས་ཐོག་ལས་གོས་དྲུང་ཡིག་ཆེན་མོའི་དབུ་ཞྭ་གྱོན་ཞིང་། སྐུ་སྒེར་གྱི་རྟགས་ཐམ་རྡོ་རྗེ་རྒྱ་གྲམ་གྱི་ཁ་རིས་ཅན་ཐམ་རྫི་དམར་པོ་དབྱིབས་སྒོར་མོ་ཡིན་པ་བསྣམས་ཤིང་། ཆིབས་བསྒྱུར་གྱི་སྐབས་སུ་འཁྲུགས་ཕྱུང་ལ་བཞུགས་སྲོལ་ཡོད།[4]

གཉིས་པ། དགའ་གདོང་གནས་སྲུང་གནོད་སྦྱིན་ཤིང་བྱ་ཅན།

དགའ་གདོང་གནས་སྲུང་གནོད་སྦྱིན་ཤིང་བྱ་ཅན་ནི་སྔར་བསམ་ཡས་དགོན་པའི་སྲུང་མ་པེ་ཧར་རྒྱལ་པོའི་ལས་ཀྱི་བློན་ཆེན་གནོད་སྦྱིན་ཤིང་བྱ་ཅན་ཞེས་པ་ཡིན་ཞིང་། རྗེས་སོར་བཀའ་གདམས་པའི་དགོན་པ་དགའ་གདོང་དགོན་པས་སྲུང་མ་གཙོ་བོར་བཀུར།[5] དགའ་གདོང་དགོན་པ་ནི་སྤྱི་ལོ་དུས་རབས་བཅུ་གསུམ་པའི་ནང་ཞིག་པོ་ཤེས་རབ་ཀྱིས་ཕྱག་བཏབ། དེ་རྗེས་རིམ་བཞིན་འཕེལ་རྒྱས་སུ་ཕྱིན་ནས་དབུས་ཀྱི་གདན་ས་ཆེན་པོ་དྲུག་གི་གྲས་ཡིན་པ་དང་། སྤྱི་ལོ་དུས་རབས་བཅུ་བཞི་པར་རྗེ་ཙོང་ཁ་པས་བླ་མ་དབུ་མ་པ་དང་ལྷན་ཅིག་ཏུ་གནས་དེར་སྐྱབས་པ་ཉམས་ལེན་མཛད་ནས་འཇམ་པའི་དབྱངས་ཀྱི་ཞལ་གཟིགས་པ་སོགས་གནས་ཁྱད་པར་ཅན་ཡིན། སྒྲིག་གཞིའི་

ཆ་ནས་བཤད་ན། སྔར་འབྲས་སྤུངས་དགོན་པའི་སྒོ་མང་གྲྭ་ཚང་གི་ཁོངས་སུ་གཏོགས་ཤིང་། དགོན་པའི་དཀོན་གཉེར་སོགས་སྒོ་མང་གྲྭ་ཚང་གིས་བསྒོ་བཞག་བྱས་ནས་གཏོང་། དེ་སྔར་བོད་ཁམས་སུ་སོག་པོའི་དམག་དཔུང་ལྷགས་དུས་ཆོས་སྐྱོང་འདི་བཀུར་ན་ཕན་ཐོགས་ཆེ་ཞེས་གྲགས།[6] རྒྱལ་དབང་སྐུ་ཕྲེང་ལྔ་པ་ནས་བཟུང་གཞུང་བསྟེན་གྱི་སྲུང་མར་བཀུར་ཏེ་གཞུང་གི་ཕྱི་ནང་གི་བསྟན་སྲིད་ལས་རྒྱུའི་དོན་དུ་མཛད་རྗེས་མི་དམན་པ་བཞག་གནང་མཛད་ཡོད། ད་ལྟ་དགོན་པའི་གཡོན་ཕྱུག་གི་ཁྲིན་པ་ལྷ་ཁང་དུ་གནས་ཆུང་ཆོས་སྐྱོང་དང་། དགའ་གདོང་། དཔལ་ལྡན་ལྷ་མོའི་སྐུ་བརྙན་བཞེངས་ཡོད་པ་དང་། ཆོས་སྐྱོང་རྣམ་པ་གཉིས་ཀྱི་རྒྱབ་ལོགས་སུ་ཁྲིན་པ་ཁ་བཅད་ཞིག་ཡོད་པ་ནི་དགའ་གདོང་ཆོས་སྐྱོང་གི་བླ་མཚོ་ཡིན་པར་བཤད་ཅིང་། མཚོ་བདག་ཀླུ་མོ་ནི་ཆོས་སྐྱོང་གི་ཨ་མ་བུ་ཁྲིད་ཡིན་པར་གྲགས། བཤད་སྲོལ་ཞིག་ལ་དང་པོར་མཚོ་བདག་ཨ་མ་བུ་ཁྲིད་ཀྱིས་རང་གི་བུ་དགའ་གདོང་དང་མཉམ་དུ་མཚོ་བདག་གི་ལྕེ་མིག་བསྣམས་ཏེ་ཕེབས་ཤིང་རྗེས་སོར་ལྕེ་མིག་རང་གི་བུ་ལ་སྤྲད་དེ་ཆར་འབེབས་ཀྱི་ལས་འགན་རང་གི་བུ་ཆོས་སྐྱོང་ལ་གནང་ཟེར། ཆོས་སྐྱོང་འདིར་ཆར་འབེབས་ཀྱི་ནུས་པ་གཞན་དང་མི་འདྲ་བ་ཞིག་ཡོད་པར་བཤད་པ་དང་། སྔ་མོར་ས་ཐག་རིང་མདོ་སྨད་ཕྱོགས་ནས་ཀྱང་ཡུལ་ལུང་གང་ཞིག་ལ་ཐན་པ་བྱུང་ཆེ་དགོན་པའི་བླ་མ་སོགས་དགོན་འདིར་ཆོས་སྐྱོང་ལ་ཆར་འབེབས་ཀྱི་ལུང་ཞུ་བར་ཕེབས་སྲོལ་ཡོད།[7] དགའ་གདོང་ཆོས་སྐྱོང་གི་སྐུ་བསྟེན་ནི་ཁྲིམ་རྒྱུད་ཀྱིས་བྱེད་དགོས་ལ་མི་ཚང་ལ་དགའ་གདོང་གཟིམ་ཁང་ཞེས་འབོད། གཞུང་གི་ལས་ཚན་རིམ་པ་བཞི་པ་རྩེ་སྒེར་མཁན་ཆུང་གི་གོ་མིང་ཐོབ་ཅིང་ས་ཞིང་མི་སེར་སོགས་བདག་ཐོབ་ཀྱང་གང་ཙམ་ཡོད་འདུག

གསུམ་པ། ལ་མོ་ཚངས་པ་དུང་གི་ཐོར་ཚུགས་ཅན།

ལ་མོ་ཚངས་པ་དུང་གི་ཐོར་ཚུགས་ཅན་ནི་བོད་ཀྱི་ཆོས་སྐྱོང་གི་ཁོངས་ནས་ལོ་རྒྱུས་རྒྱུན་རིང་ལྡན་ཞིང་ལྷ་གནས་མཐོ་བས་གྲགས་ཆེ་བ་ཞིག་ཡིན་སྟེ། ལྷ་དེ་ཐོག་མར་ཁོག་ཞུགས་ག་དུས་བྱེད་པ་ངེས་གསལ་བྱུང་བའི་ཡིག་ཆ་མ་རྙེད། གསུང་སྲོལ་ཞིག་ལྟར་ན། རྗོག་ལོ་ཙྪ་བ་བློ་ལྡན་ཤེས་རབ་རྒྱ་གར་ནས་ཕྱིར་ཕེབས་དུས་རྗེས་འབྲངས་ཀྱིས་བོད་དུ་སླེབས་པ་དམ་དུ་བཏགས་ཏེ་སྲུང་མར་བཀུག་པ་ལ་མོ་ཚངས་པའམ་ལ་མོ་ཆོར་གསེབ་ཡིན་ཟེར། ཡར་ལུང་གི་ཁྲ་འབྲུག་དགོན་པ་དང་། དགའ་ལྡན་ཤར་རྩེ་གྲྭ་ཚང་། གསང་ཕུ་དགོན་པ་བཅས་ཀྱིས་སྲུང་མར་བསྟེན་ཅིང་། གཞུང་ས་དགའ་ལྡན་ཕོ་བྲང་ཆེན་པོའི་དུས་སྐབས་སུ། གཙོ་བོ་ད་ལྟའི་སྟག་རྩེ་རྫོང་ཁོངས་ཀྱི་ལ་མོ་མི་འགྱུར་བྱང་ཆུབ་ལྷུན་གྱིས་གྲུབ་པའི་ལྷོག་ཏུ་སྐུ་ཕེབས་བྱེད་སྲོལ་ཡོད་པ་མ་ཟད།[8] པཎ་ཆེན་རིན་པོ་ཆེ་སྐུའི་སྐྱེ་བ་ན་རིམ་གྱིས་བསྟེན་གསོལ་གནང་གི་ཡོད། ལ་མོ་ཚངས་པའི་སྐུ་བསྟེན་པར་དེ་སྔའི་སྡེ་པ་གཞུང་གི་ཧྭ་བླ་མའི་གོ་གནས་ཡོད། སྐུ་བསྟེན་ནི་ཁྲིམ་རྒྱུད་ཀྱིས་མཛད་བཞིན་ཡོད་ལ་མི་ཚང་ལ་ལ་མོ་གཞུང་རྒྱུད་ཞེས་འབོད། སྐུ་བསྟེན་པའི་རྟགས་ཐམ་དམར་ཐམ་ཁ་རིས་དུང་དཀར་ཅན་ནི་པཎ་ཆེན་རིན་པོ་ཆེའི་རྟགས་ཐམ་དང་འདྲ། དུས་རབས་བཅུ་བདུན་པའི་ནང་གོང་པོ་ཞི་ཁ་བླ་མ་སོགས་ཀྱིས་གོང་དམག་དབུས་སུ་དྲངས་ཏེ་བདེ་གཟར་བསླངས་སྐབས་དབུས་ཕྱོགས་ནས་ཆོས་སྐྱོང་ལ་མོ་ཚངས་པ་གདན་འདྲེན་གྱིས་གང་འགབ་དྲི་གཙོད་ཞུས་པར་ཚངས་པས་དམུ་གབ་གཡོག་རྒྱུའི་ཁས་བླངས་ནས་གོང་དམག་གཉིད་དུ་ཡུར་སྐབས་མཚན་འགེབས་བརྒྱབ་སྟེ་གོང་དམག

ཚར་བཅད་པའི་བྲིས་རྗེས་སུ་སྡེ་པ་གཞུང་ནས་ལ་མོ་གཞུང་རྐྱང་ཚང་ལ་གཞིས་ཆེན་བརྒྱད་དང་གཞིས་ཆུང་བརྒྱད་གཟིགས་བཟོས་སུ་གནང་སྟབས་གཞིས་ཀ་དང་མི་སེར་གྲྭ་ཆེ་ཙམ་ཡོད་པར་ཆགས།[9]

བཞི་པ། བསམ་ཡས་ཆོས་སྐྱོང་ཙེའུ་དམར་པོ།

བསམ་ཡས་ཆོས་སྐྱོང་ཙེའུ་དམར་པོ་ནི་བཙན་པོ་ཁྲི་སྲོང་ལྡེའུ་བཙན་གྱི་དུས་སྐབས་སུ་སློབ་དཔོན་པདྨ་འབྱུང་གནས་ཀྱིས་དམ་དུ་བཏགས་ཏེ་དཔལ་བསམ་ཡས་མི་འགྱུར་ལྷུན་གྱིས་གྲུབ་པའི་གཙུག་ལག་ཁང་གི་བསྟན་པའི་སྲོག་ཤིང་སྲུང་བར་གཉེར་གཏད་པའི་ཆོས་སྐྱོང་ཞིག་ཡིན་ལ། གནས་ཆུང་ཆོས་སྐྱོང་ཆེན་པོའི་འཁོར་ཙམ་གྱི་ཚོད་ནས་གཙུག་ལག་ཁང་གི་ཕྱི་ནང་དུ་དགྲ་བགེགས་གདོན་འདྲེའི་ཚོགས་ཀྱིས་བར་ཆད་སེལ་བའི་འཕྲིན་བཅོལ་སྲུང་མ་ཞིག་ཡིན། སྤྱིར་བཏང་དུ་གནོད་སྦྱིན་གྱི་རྒྱལ་པོ་ཙེའུ་དམར་པོ་ཞེས་འབོད་པ་དང་། རྒྱ་གར་ན་གནོད་སྦྱིན་ཙེའུ་དམར་ཞེས་གྲགས་ཤིང་། བོད་ཡུལ་ན་མཐུ་ལྡན་ལྷ་བཙན་ཞེས་ཟེར་བ་ལགས། སློབ་དཔོན་གྱིས་གསང་མཚན་ཀུན་ཁྱབ་རྡོ་རྗེ་དྲག་པོ་རྩལ་ཞེས་བཏགས།[10] གཞུང་ས་དགའ་ལྡན་ཕོ་བྲང་གི་དུས་སྐབས་སུ་གཞུང་བསྟེན་དགྲ་ལྷར་གྱུར་ཏེ་རྒྱལ་བ་ཐམས་ཅད་མཁྱེན་པ་ཏཱ་ལའི་བླ་མ་དང་། པཎ་ཆེན་རིན་པོ་ཆེ་སྐུའི་སྐྱེ་བ་ན་རིམ་གྱི་སྐུ་ཚེ་མཛད་པ་འཕྲིན་ལས་ཀྱི་བར་ཆད་སེལ་བ་དང་། གཞུང་གི་ཕྱི་ནང་བསྟན་སྲིད་ལས་རྒྱའི་ཞབས་འདེགས་ཀྱི་སྲུང་མར་བཀུར།

གཞུང་བསྟེན་ཆོས་སྐྱོང་ཁག་གིས་ཐོན་པའི་སྤྱི་ཚོགས་ཀྱི་ཕན་ནུས།

ཆོས་སྐྱོང་ཁག་གིས་གཙོ་བོ་དགོན་པ་དང་གཙུག་ལག་ཁང་གང་དག་གི་བསྟན་སྲུང་གི་ལས་བགྱིས་ཐོག རྒྱལ་དབང་སྐུ་ཕྲེང་ལྔ་བ་ངག་དབང་བློ་བཟང་རྒྱ་མཚོའི་དུས་སྐབས་སུ་གཞུང་ས་དགའ་ལྡན་ཕོ་བྲང་བཙུགས་རྗེས་ནས་གཞུང་བསྟེན་གྱི་ཆོས་སྐྱོང་ཁག་ཅིག་བྱུང་སྟེ། གཙོ་བོ་ཏཱ་ལའི་བླ་མ་དང་། པཎ་ཆེན་ཨེར་དེ་ནི། ས་སྐྱ་བདག་ཆེན་སོགས་བོད་ཀྱི་བླ་སྤྲུལ་ཆེ་ཁག་གི་སྐུའི་སྐྱེ་བ་ན་རིམ་གྱི་སྐུ་སྐྱེ་བཙལ་འཚོལ་སྐབས་སུ་གཞུང་ས་ནས་ཆེད་དུ་ཆོས་སྐྱོང་ཁག་ལ་སྐབས་དོན་ལུང་ཞུ་སྤྱི་ཞུས་ཀྱིས་གང་གི་བཀའ་ལུང་དགོངས་དོན་བཞིན་སྐུ་སྐྱེ་བཙལ་འཚོལ་དུ་ཐེབས་པ་དང་། ཁྱིམ་མཚེས་རྒྱལ་ཁབ་བར་དང་ཡུལ་ཁམས་ས་གནས་བར་དུ་བདེ་གཟར་གྱོད་དོན་བསླངས་ནས་ཉེན་ཁར་ཐུག་པའི་གནད་འགག་གི་སྐབས་སུ་གཞུང་ནས་ཆོས་སྐྱོང་ཁག་ལ་ལུང་ཞུ་འབུལ་གནང་གིས་གང་འགབ་དྲི་གཅོད་ལུང་ཞུ། དེ་མིན་ལོ་རེར་ཡིག་ཚང་ལས་ཁུངས་ཀྱིས་གཞུང་བསྟེན་ཆོས་སྐྱོང་ཁག་སྤྱན་འདྲེན་གྱི་སྟེ་ཤན་སུ་འོས་ཀྱི་འཆར་གཞི་སྒྲོན་ཞུ་གཞུང་སར་ཕུལ་ཐོག་དངོས་སུ་གཏན་འཁེལ་གྱིས་གཞུང་བསྟེན་སྲུང་མའི་གཙོ་བོ་གནས་ཆུང་ཆོས་སྐྱོང་གཙོ་བྱེད་ཀྱི་གཞུང་བསྟེན་ཆོས་སྐྱོང་ཁག་འཆར་ཅན་དང་འཕར་མའི་གནམ་ལོ་གསར་ཆོས་ཀྱི་ལོ་གསོལ་གཟིམ་ཆུང་སྤྱན་འདྲེན་དང་། དབྱར་གསོལ་གཟིམ་ཆུང་སྤྱན་འདྲེན། ཟླ་གསོལ་གཟིམ་ཆུང་སྤྱན་འདྲེན། ཏཱ་ལའི་བླ་མའི་ཆིབས་བསྒྱུར་ཆེ་ཁག་གི་འཆར་ཅན་གཟིམ་ཆུང་སྤྱན་འདྲེན་གྱིས་མཆོད་བསྟོད་གཟབ་གསོལ་ཐོག་སྒྲོན་དར་དང་མཐུན་རྫས་བསྟབས་ཏེ་ལུང་ཞུ་བསྐྱངས་པ་མ་ཟད། རྒྱལ་མཆོག་གང་གི

དཀྱུང་ཀིག་སོགས་ཀྱི་སྐབས་སུ་གཞུང་ནས་བོད་ལྗོངས་སེར་སྐྱ་སྤྱི་མགྲིན་གྱི་ལུང་ཞུ་འབུལ་གནང་གིས་སྐུ་ཕྱྭའི་རྐྱེན་སེལ་དུ་རིམ་མེད་དགོན་སྡེ་ཁག་གིས་སྐུ་རིམ་ཞབས་བརྟན་སློ་ཆོས་སུ་མ་སོང་བར་བསྒྲུབ་པ། དེར་མ་ཟད། བོད་ལྗོངས་སུ་འབྲུམ་ནད་སོགས་ནད་ཡམས་འཁྲུར་བ་དང་། ཡུལ་ཁམས་མི་བདེ་བའི་གངས་སྐྱོན། ཆུ་སྐྱོན། སེར་སྐྱོན། ས་ཡོམ་དང་ཐན་པ་སོགས་རང་བྱུང་གནོད་འཚེའི་རིགས་བྱུང་བ། ད་དུང་དབྱར་དགུན་ཉི་ལྡོག་གི་སྐབས་འཁེལ་ཐོག་གཞུང་བསྟེན་ཆོས་སྐྱོང་ཁག་ལ་ལུང་ཞུ་སྙན་འདྲེན་གྱིས་གང་གི་དགོངས་དོན་བཞིན་དེ་མཐུན་གྱི་སྐུ་རིམ་བཙའ་བ་སྒྲུབ་པ་སོགས་ཆོས་སྐྱོང་ཁག་གིས་སྤྱི་ཚོགས་ཀྱི་ཕན་ནུས་རྒྱ་ཆེན་པོ་ཐོན་བཞིན་ཡོད།

མདོར་ན་གཞུང་གི་ཕྱི་ནང་གི་ཆོས་སྲིད་དོན་དག་འགངས་ཆེའི་རིགས་ཐག་གཅོད་བྱེད་དགོས་ཆེ་གཞུང་བསྟེན་ཆོས་སྐྱོང་ཁག་ལ་ལུང་ཞུ་སྙན་འདྲེན་གྱིས་བསྟུན་སྲིད་ལས་རྒྱའི་འཕྲིན་བཅོལ་དང་། བོད་ལྗོངས་འཚོ་ཆོས་བདེ་ཐབས་སུ་ཕན་ནུས་ཆེན་པོ་ཐོན་ཡོད། དེ་བཞིན་དུ་གནས་ཆུང་ཆོས་རྒྱལ་དང་། དགའ་གདོང་ཆོས་རྗེ། ལ་མོ་གཞུང་རྒྱང་། ཆོས་སྐྱོང་ཙེའུ་དམར་པོ་སོགས་གཞུང་བསྟེན་ཆོས་སྐྱོང་ཁག་གི་སྐུ་བསྟེན་པ་གང་དག་གིས་དགའ་ལྡན་ཕོ་བྲང་གཞུང་གི་ཕྱི་ནང་ལས་ཚན་ཁྲོད་དུ་གོ་གནས་གལ་ཆེན་ཟིན་ཡོད་དེ། སྤྱིར་བཏང་དུ་ཆོས་སྐྱོང་ཁག་གི་སྐུ་བསྟེན་ཁག་ལ་དྲུང་ཡིག་མཁར་མཁན་ཆུང་གི་གོ་མིང་ཆེ་ལོ་དང་། རིམ་པ་བཞི་པའི་ཧོག་གནས་གདན་ཐོབ་ཡོད་ཅིང་། སྐུ་སྒེར་གྱི་རྟགས་ཐམ་དམར་ཐམ་བསྟམས་ཡོད་ལ། དུས་མིན་དུ་གཞུང་ནས་ས་རིས་བཀའ་གཏན་འཛུགས་གནས་བསྐྱལ་ཏེ་གཟིགས་བཟོས་བདག་རྐྱེན་མི་དམན་པ་ཐོབ་པས་གཞུང་ས་དགའ་ལྡན་ཕོ་བྲང་སྐབས་བོད་ཀྱི་མི་ཚང་ཆེ་གྲས་སུ་གྱུར་ཡོད།

མཇུག་བསྡུ་བའི་གཏམ།

བོད་ཀྱི་ལོ་རྒྱུས་ཐོག་ཆོས་སྐྱོང་བྱུང་སྟོ་ཞིང་ལོ་རྒྱུས་རིང་ལ། སྤྱི་ཚོགས་ལོ་རྒྱུས་འཕེལ་འགྱུར་གྱི་གོ་རིམ་ཁྲོད་དུ། ཆོས་སྐྱོང་གི་སྤྱི་ཚོགས་ཕན་ནུས་དང་རིག་གནས་ཀྱི་ཁྱད་ཆོས་ཀྱང་དེ་བཞིན་དུ་འགྱུར་བ་བྱུང་དང་བྱུང་བཞིན་ཡོད་པ་སྟེ། དགའ་ལྡན་ཕོ་བྲང་གི་སྐབས་སུ། དམིགས་བསལ་གྱི་གཞུང་བསྟེན་ཆོས་སྐྱོང་ཁག་བྱུང་ནས་གཞུང་གི་ཆོས་སྲིད་གཉིས་ཆའི་དབང་འཛིན་པའི་གྲས་སུ་གྱུར་ཞིང་ཆོས་སྐྱོང་ལ་བརྟེན་ནས་གཞུང་གི་དབང་ཤུགས་ཆེ་བར་བཏང་ནས་ཆོས་སྲིད་ཟུང་འབྲེལ་གྱི་ལམ་ལུགས་ཕྲ་ཚུགས་པར་བསྐྱངས་རྒྱུར་གཞོལ་བ། དེ་དང་མཚུངས་པར། གཞུང་བསྟེན་ཆོས་སྐྱོང་ཁག་གི་སྐུ་བསྟེན་པ་ནི་གཞུང་གི་ལས་ཚན་རང་རྐྱ་ཐུབ་པ་ཞིག་ཏུ་གྱུར་ཡོད་དེ། གཞུང་གི་རྩེ་ཤོད་དྲུང་རིགས་ལས་ཚན་ཁྲོད་དུ་གོ་གནས་མཐོ་ཞིང་། སྲིད་ཕྱོགས་སུ་ཕན་ནུས་ཆེན་པོ་ཐོན་པ་དང་། སྐུ་བསྟེན་པ་འདི་དག་གཙོ་བོ་ཆོས་ཕྱོགས་ནས་ཡིག་རྒྱུགས་ངེས་ཅན་བླངས་ནས་བདམས་ཐོན་བྱུང་བ་དང་། སྐབས་འགར་ཆོས་སྐྱོང་གི་ཁྲིམ་རྒྱུད་འདེད་པ། ཡང་ལ་ལར་སྐུ་བསྟེན་པའི་སྤྲུལ་སྐུ་བཙལ་འཚོལ་གྱིས་མི་རབས་ནས་མི་རབས་པར་གཞུང་ཞབས་པའི་ཆ་ནས་གཞུང་གི་ལས་དོན་ཐད་ཐོད་པ་འདོགས་ཅི་ཐུབ་ཀྱིས་གཞུང་ས་དགའ་ལྡན་ཕོ་བྲང་ཆེན་པོའི་སྐབས་ཀྱི་བོད་རང་གི་ཐུན་མོང་མ་ཡིན་པའི་སྲིད་ལུགས་དང་འབྲེལ་བའི་རིག་གནས་ཁྱད་པར་བ་ཞིག་ཏུ་གྱུར་ཡོད་དོ། །

ཟུར་བཀོད།

མཆོད་བསྟོད་དྲིགས་པའི་ལྷ་ཚོགས་བྲ་གློང་འབྲུག་ཅིང་དམ་ཅན་རྒྱ་མཚོ་དགྱེས་པར་སྤྱོད་པའི་མགྲིན་བཅུའི་ཕོ་བྲང་ས་ལ་འཕོས་པ་སྟོན་མེད་བཟོ་སྣ་བརྒྱད་ཀྱིས་འཕགས་པའི་གནས་ཆུང་པེ་ཧར་ལྷོག་གི་དཀར་ཆག་ས་གསུམ་གཡོ་བའི་ང་རོ།[11]

རྒྱལ་བ་ཀུན་གྱི་ཡབ་ཏུ་གྱུར་ཀྱང་རྒྱལ་སྲས་པདྨ་དཀར་པོའི་ཚུལ། །སྙིང་རྗེའི་གཏེར་རྒྱ་ཅིག་ཅར་གྲོལ་ཡང་འགྲོ་རྣམས་ཐུགས་རྗེས་དམ་དུ་འཛིན། །རྣམ་བཞིའི་སྤྲིན་པ་ལྷུག་པོར་གཏོང་ཡང་སྲིད་ཞིའི་དཔལ་ཀུན་དབང་དུ་སྡུད། །ཀུན་མཁྱེན་བླ་མ་བློ་བཟང་རྒྱ་མཚོས་བྱང་ཆུབ་བར་དུ་རྗེས་སུ་སྐྱོངས། །ཡེ་ཤེས་དག་པའི་མེ་ཤེལ་རང་བཞིན་མཐུ་སྟོབས་ཉིན་བྱེད་འབར་བའི་གཟི། །དྲེགས་པའི་གཙུག་[ ]མངོན་པར་འཕགས་ཤིང་བདུད་སྡེའི་སྨག་རུམ་ཚར་གཅོད་པ། །རིག་སྔགས་འཆང་བའི་འཁོར་ལོས་སྒྱུར་བ་རང་བྱུང་པདྨ་རྒྱལ་པོ་ཞེས། །སྲིད་ཞིའི་སྣང་མཛོད་འབུམ་དུ་འཁྱིལ་ངེས་དགེ་ལེགས་པད་ཚལ་རྒྱས་པར་མཛོད། །ཇི་སྙེད་ཤེས་བྱའི་ཀུན་གསལ་ཡངས་པར་མཁྱེན་རབ་མཁའ་ལྡིང་ཤུགས་གཅིག་གིས། །ཡོངས་སུ་གཞལ་བས་ཇི་ལྟའི་ཆོས་ཀུན་ལག་པའི་མཐིལ་དུ་ཉེར་བཀོད་པའི། །སྐྱུ་རུ་ར་ཡི་འབྲས་བུ་ཇི་བཞིན་བརྟེན་པར་རབ་གཟིགས་རྣམ་དཔྱོད་མཐུ། །ཟུར་ཕུད་ལྔ་ལྡན་ཆོས་ཀྱི་རྒྱལ་པོ་འཇམ་དཔལ་སྙིང་པོར་རྟག་ཏུ་འདུད། །དྲེགས་པའི་དཀྱིལ་འཁོར་ཆེན་པོར་དབང་འབྱེད་པའི། །ཧྲཱ་སྐད་ང་རོས་སྲིད་གསུམ་འགྱུར་པོའི་ཚོགས། །ཐོས་པའི་རང་མདངས་བྱུ་རུའི་ལྷུན་པོ་ལྟར། །རབ་དམར་པདྨ་དབང་ཆེན་དེས་སྐྱོངས་ཤིག །དག་པའི་དབྱིངས་ལས་འགག་མེད་རོལ་པའི་འཕྲུལ། །སྣ་ཚོགས་ཆུ་ཟླའི་ཟློས་གར་ཇི་བཞིན་དུ། །དྲག་པོའི་ཚུལ་གྱིས་བསྟན་པ་རྗེས་སྐྱོང་བ། །ཆོས་སྐྱོང་རྒྱལ་པོ་སྐུ་ལྔ་དགྱེས་པར་རོལ། །ཞེས་ཚིགས་སུ་བཅད་པའི་དབུ་བའི་དོ་ཤལ་རྣམ་པར་དགོད་པའི་སྐབས་ཚིག་ཡན་ལག་བརྒྱད་ཀྱི་ང་རོ་སྔོན་དུ་སྤྲིངས་ཏེ་སྐབས་དོན། གོང་དུ་ལྷ་དང་བཅས་པའི་འགྲོ་བ་ཐམས་ཅད་ཀྱི་སྐྱབས་མགོན་མཚུངས་ཟླ་བྲལ་བའི་བཀའ་རྩོམ་གྱི་དཀར་ཆག་རིན་པོ་ཆེ་ཕེབས་པར་ཞིབ་ཆ་ལྷན་ཐབས་ཀྱི་ཚུལ་ཙུང་ཟད་ཞུ་བ་ནི། རྒྱལ་བའི་བསྟན་པ་རིན་པོ་ཆེ་འཇིག་རྟེན་དུ་དར་ཞིང་རྒྱས་ལ་ཡུན་རིང་དུ་གནས་པ་ནི་བསྟན་འཛིན་གྱི་སྐྱེས་བུ་དམ་པ་རྣམས་ཀྱི་བདག་རྐྱེན་ཁོན་ལ་རག་ལུས་ཤིང་། དེའང་རྒྱལ་བ་སྲས་དང་བཅས་པའི་སྐུ་གསུང་ཐུགས་གསང་བ་བསམ་གྱིས་མི་ཁྱབ་པའི་ཡེ་ཤེས་སྒྱུ་མའི་ཟློས་གར་སྙིང་རྗེའི་རང་གཟུགས་སུ་ཤར་བ་ཕྱག་ན་པདྨ་ཉིད་རྡོ་རྗེ་སློབ་དཔོན་གྱི་ཚུལ་བཟུང་བ་རྒྱལ་བའི་དབང་པོ་ཐམས་ཅད་མཁྱེན་གཟིགས་ཆེན་པོའི་ཐུགས་རྗེ་ལ་བལྟོས་ཤིང་། མགོན་པོ་འདི་ཉིད་ཞབས་ཀྱི་པདྨ་བསྐལ་བརྒྱར་བརྟན་པ་དང་། འཕྲིན་ལས་ཀྱི་བཞེད་པ་མཐའ་དག་ཚུལ་བཞིན་དུ་བསྒྲུབ་པ་ལ་འགལ་རྐྱེན་སེལ་ཞིང་། མཐུན་རྐྱེན་རྣམས་སྤེལ་བར་མཛད་པའི་ལས་ལ་གཡེལ་བ་མེད་པར་བཀའ་རྟགས་རྡོ་རྗེའི་ཅོད་པན་སྤྱི་བོར་འཛིན་པ་ཕྱག་རྒྱ་གཉན་པོ་བཅིངས་པའི་གཡར་དམ་ལས་ནམ་ཡང་མི་འདའ་བའི་རྡོ་རྗེའི་སྲུང་མ་འཇིག་རྟེན་དང་འཇིག་རྟེན་ལས་འདས་པ་བསམ་གྱིས་མི་ཁྱབ་པར་མཆིས་པ་དེ་དག་གི་ནང་ནས་ཀྱང་ཆེས་ཆེར་འཕྲིན་ལས་མྱུར་ཞིང་དྲག་རྩལ་གྱི་མཐུ་དང་ལྡན་པ་ནི་ཆོས་སྐྱོང་བའི་རྒྱལ་པོ་ཆེན་པོ་འདི་ཉིད་ཡིན་ལ། དེའང་གདོད་མའི་སངས་རྒྱས་ཀུན་ཏུ་བཟང་པོ་ཞེས་བྱ་བའི་ཡེ་ཤེས་དང་ཐུགས་རྗེའི་ཡོན་ཏན་ཐམས་ཅད་ཀྱི་ངོ་བོ། འཁོར་འདས་མ་ལུས་པའི་སྤྱི་དཔལ་དུ་གྱུར་བ་དེ་ཉིད་ཀྱི་རང་གདངས་འགག་པ་མེད་པའི་ལོངས་སྤྱོད་རྫོགས་པའི་སྐུ་རིགས་ལྔར་ཤར་

བ་ལས། གདུལ་བྱ་མི་བསྲུན་དྲག་པོས་འདུལ་བར་འོས་པ་རྣམས་ཀྱི་ངོར་ཞེ་སྡང་རྣམ་པར་དག་པ་ཆོས་ཀྱི་དབྱིངས་ཀྱི་ཡེ་ཤེས་ཀྱི་ངོ་བོ་རྣམ་པར་སྣང་མཛད་ཀྱི་རྣམ་སྤྲུལ་དབུས་ཕྱོགས་ཐུགས་ཀྱི་རྒྱལ་པོ། གཏི་མུག་རྣམ་པར་དག་པ་མེ་ལོང་ཡེ་ཤེས་ཀྱི་ངོ་བོ་རྡོ་རྗེ་སེམས་དཔའི་སྤྲུལ་པ་ཤར་ཕྱོགས་སྐུའི་རྒྱལ་པོ། ང་རྒྱལ་རྣམ་པར་དག་པ་མཉམ་ཉིད་ཡེ་ཤེས་ཀྱི་ངོ་བོ་རིན་ཆེན་འབྱུང་ལྡན་གྱི་སྤྲུལ་པ་ལྷོ་ཕྱོགས་ཡོན་ཏན་གྱི་རྒྱལ་པོ། འདོད་ཆགས་རྣམ་པར་དག་པ་སོ་སོར་རྟོག་པའི་ཡེ་ཤེས་ཀྱི་ངོ་བོ་སྣང་བ་མཐའ་ཡས་ཀྱི་སྤྲུལ་བ་ནུབ་ཕྱོགས་གསུང་གི་རྒྱལ་པོ། ཕྲག་དོག་རྣམ་པར་དག་པ་བྱ་གྲུབ་ཡེ་ཤེས་ཀྱི་ངོ་བོ་དོན་ཡོད་གྲུབ་པའི་རྣམ་སྤྲུལ་བྱང་ཕྱོགས་འཕྲིན་ལས་ཀྱི་རྒྱལ་པོ་སྟེ་རིགས་ལྔ། དེ་ལ་ཡེ་ཤེས་ཀྱི་རང་བཞིན་དགྱེས་པ་བསྐྱེད་པའི་ཡུམ་ལྔ། རྣམ་མང་གི་མཛད་པ་སྐྱོང་ཆེད་སྤྲུལ་བ་ལྔ། ལས་བསྒྲུབ་ཀྱི་བློན་པོ་ལྔ། སྐུའི་སྐྱོ་སངས་འབག་སེང་གར་མཁན། གཡས་གཡོན་དང་གླད་རྗེས་སུ་མྱུལ་བའི་རུ་འདྲེན་ཆེན་པོ་སྟེ་བཞི་སོགས་སྤྲུལ་པ་ཡང་སྤྲུལ་ཉིད་སྤྲུལ་དུ་མར་བསྟེན་ནས་དབང་དྲག་ཞི་རྒྱས་ཀྱི་ལས་རྣམས་བསྒྲུབ་པ་ལ་མཐུ་ཆེ་ཞིང་སྙིང་ཉེ་བསྐུལ་བདེ་བས་ན་སྟོན་ཆོས་སྐྱོང་བའི་རྒྱལ་པོ་ཆེན་པོ་ཁྲི་སྲོང་ལྡེའུ་བཙན་གྱིས་ཟན་གཡང་མི་འགྱུར་ལྷུན་གྱིས་གྲུབ་པའི་གཙུག་ལག་ཁང་ཆེན་པོ་རྟེན་དང་བརྟེན་པར་བཅས་པ་བཞེངས་པའི་སྲུང་མ་ཇི་ལྟར་བསྐོ་མཁན་སློབ་ཆོས་གསུམ་བཀའ་བགྲོས་པ་ན། མཁན་པོའི་ཞལ་ནི་བདུད་ནི་སྲོག་གཅོད་པ་ལ་དགའ། གཟའ་ནི་གདུམ། ཀླུ་ནི་གདུག བཙན་གནོད་པ་ཆེ། དམུ་འཇམ་དྲགས། མ་མོ་ནི་འཇིགས་པས་དེ་རྣམས་མ་ཡིན་བ་སུ་འཐད་གསུང་བ་ལ། སངས་རྒྱས་གཉིས་པ་སློབ་དཔོན་ཆེན་པོ་པདྨ་འབྱུང་གནས་ཀྱིས། ཧོར་གྱི་ཕོ་ལྷ་གནམ་ལྷ་བྱང་ཆུབ་ཡིན། །རྒྱལ་པོ་ཤིང་བྱ་ཅན་ནི་གདན་དྲངས་ནས། །དེ་ལ་གཏད་པས་གཙུག་ལག་ཁང་མི་འཇིག །ལྷ་ཏ་ཧོར་གྱི་སྒོམ་གྲྭ་བཅོམས་པ་ན། །པེ་ཀར་ཀ་ཙའི་ཕྱི་ལ་འབྲངས་ཏེ་འོང་། །ང་ཡིས་པེ་ཀར་གླིང་དུ་རྟེན་འཛུགས་གསུངས། །ཞེས་པ་ལྟར། ལྷ་ཏ་ཧོར་གྱི་སྒོམ་གྲྭ་ནས་དཀོར་སྲུང་པེ་ཀར་རྒྱལ་པོ་འོས་བར་གསུངས་པ་བཞིན་ཧོར་གྱི་སྒོམ་གྲྭ་བཅོམས། ཟ་ཧོར་གྱི་རྒྱལ་བརྒྱུད་ཛྫ་པླ་ལ། གཡུའི་ཐུབ་པ། དུང་གི་སེང་གེ་སོགས་ཀ་ཙ་དུ་མ་དང་བཅས་སྤྱན་དྲངས་ནས་ཆོས་འཁོར་ཐམས་ཅད་ཀྱི་སྲུང་མར་མངའ་གསོལ་ཞིང་ཕྱི་ནང་གི་རྟེན་རྣམས་བཙུགས། རྒྱལ་བསྟན་སྲོག་ཤིང་སྲུང་བར་གཉེར་གཏད་དེ་ཞལ་གྱིས་བཞེས་པ་ཡིན་ཅིང་། རིམ་པར་རྒྱལ་ཆེན་སྐུ་ལྔ་ཐམས་ཅད་ཀྱང་གཙུག་ལག་ཁང་སོགས་དུ་མར་གནས་ཤིང་བཞུགས་པ་ལྟར། ཆོས་རྒྱལ་ཆེན་པོ་འདི་ཉིད་ཀྱང་དབུ་རུ་ཡང་དགོན་གྱི་གཙུག་ལག་ཁང་དུ་གནས་བཞིན་པ་དང་། ཐམས་ཅད་མཁྱེན་པ་དགེ་འདུན་རྒྱ་མཚོའི་དུས་གང་ན་བསྟན་པ་ཚུལ་བཞིན་གནས་པ་དེར་མ་བོས་ཀྱང་འདུ་ཞིང་དགྱེས་པ་ནི་རྡོ་རྗེའི་གཡར་དམ་གཉན་པོ་མི་འདའ་བའི་རྟགས་ཡིན་པ་ལྟར་ཞྭ་སེར་ཅོད་པན་འཆང་བའི་བསྟན་པ་སྤེལ་ཞིང་ཆོས་སྡེ་ཆེན་པོ་འདིའི་སྲུང་མ་དང་བཅས་ཡང་དགོན་ནས་ཧྲ་མགོའི་རྣམ་པར་ཐེབས་ཤིང་། གསོལ་མཆོད་འཕྲིན་བཅོལ་གནང་བས་ཐམས་ཅད་མཁྱེན་པའི་འཕྲིན་ལས་ཐོགས་མེད་དུ་བསྒྲུབས། ཞིང་འདིའི་སྐུའི་བཀོད་པ་བསྡུས་ཏེ་སླར་ཡང་འགྲོ་བའི་དོན་དུ་སྟོད་ལུང་རྩེ་དགའི་ཕྱོགས་སུ་སྐྱེ་སྲིད་བཟུང་བར་ཉེ་དུས་བར་ཆད་ཀྱི་མཚན་མས་ཚུང་ཟད་འགྱངས་སྐབས་ཟངས་མདོག་དཔལ་རིར་ཆེད་དུ་འགྲོ་དོན་དཀའ་བའི་རྒྱ་མཚན་གྱིས་ཐེབས་པའི་ཚེ། སློབ་དཔོན་ཆེན་པོ་ཉིད་རིགས་འཛིན་དཔའ་བོ་མཁའ་འགྲོའི་ཚོགས་ལ་ཟབ་མོའི་ཆོས་སྟོན་ཅིང་བཞུགས་པའི་སྐུ་མདུན་ན་སྲུང་མ་ཆེ་ཆུང་གཉིས་འདུག་པ་གཅིག་སྐུ་མདོག་ནག་པོ་རལ་པ་དཀར་པོའི་ཐོར་ཅོག་ཅན་རལ་གྲི་དང་ཐོད་ཁྲག་བཟུང་བ། གཅིག་སྐུ་མདོ་དམར་པོ་བསེ་ཁྲབ་དང་བསེ་རྨོག་གྱོན་པའི་ལྡེམ་ཕྱུ་དར་སྣས་བརྒྱན་པ། ཕྱག་ན་མདུང་

དམར་དང་ཞགས་པ་ཐོགས་པ་སྡིག་རས་གཟིག་ཤུབས་ཅན། བསེ་ལྷམ་དམར་པོ་གྱོན་པའི་སྟེང་ན་ཨན་རྒྱབ་པ་
ལྷ་བུ་ཞིག་བཞུགས་པའི་སྲུང་མ་གཉིས་སློབ་དཔོན་ཆེན་པོ་པདྨ་ར་ཧི་ལྟར་ལགས་དྲི་བ་ཞུ་བ་མཛད་པས། འདི་
གཉིས་ངའི་བཀའ་སྲོད་ཡིན་པས་འདི་གཉིས་གྲོགས་སུ་ཁྱེད་ལ་བོད་ཡུལ་དུ་བསྟན་པ་དང་འགྲོ་བའི་དོན་དུ་སོང་
ཞིག་ཅེས་གསུངས་བ་ལྟར། འཕྲིན་ལས་བསྒྲུབ་པའི་བྲན་དུ་གཉེར་གཏད་དེ་བསྐུལ་བ་བཞིན་སྲུང་མ་གཉིས་དང་
ལྷན་དུ་གདུལ་བྱའི་དོན་དུ་ཞིང་འདིར་ཐེབས། དེ་ནས་སླར་ཐམས་ཅད་མཁྱེན་པ་བསོད་ནམས་རྒྱ་མཚོ་དེ་ཉིད་
དཔལ་ལྡན་འབྲས་སྤུངས་ཆོས་ཀྱི་ཁྲི་ཆེན་པོར་ཞབས་ཟུང་རྣམ་པར་བཀོད་ནས་མི་རིང་བའི་སྐབས། ཆོས་སྐྱོང་
ཆེན་པོ་འདི་ཉིད་མིའི་ཁོག་ཏུ་བཏྲམས་པའི་ཚུལ་གྱིས་གདུལ་བྱའི་དོན་དུ་འཕྲིན་ལས་རྒྱ་ཆེན་པོ་འགོག་པ་མེད་
པའི་རྟེན་འབྱུང་དུ་སྤྲུལ་སྐུ་ང་ལ་གཟིགས་ཞེས་དབྱངས་ཅན་ལྷ་མོས་ཞལ་མངོན་སུམ་དུ་བསྟན་པ་དེ་ཉིད་འདྲེར་
བཙུག་སྟེ་སྐུ་བརྟན་བྲིས་ཐང་གི་ལྟགས་བཀོད་སྣང་བའི་ཚུལ། རས་གཞི་ཅི་ཙམ་ཆེ་བ་ལེགས་ཞེས་སོགས་དང་།
དེ་དག་དབུས་སམ་ཕྱོགས་གཅིག་ཏུ། །ནུབ་ཕྱོགས་གསུང་གི་རྒྱལ་པོའི་སྐུ། །དྲེའུ་ནག་རྟེང་དཀར་བཅིབས་ཤིང་
རྫམས། །ཞེས་སོགས་དང་། ངོ་བོ་དེ་དག་ཀུན་ལས་ཀྱང་། །རང་འདྲའི་སྤྲུལ་བ་གྲངས་མེད་འཕྲོ། །མོག་རོ་རྫ་
ཡི་སྐུ་ལས་ཀྱང་། །པེ་ཀར་རྒྱལ་པོའི་སྤྲུལ་བ་མང་། །དེ་ཡང་བློ་ཆུང་རྣམས་ལ་བཤད། །བློ་ཆེན་སྟོད་ཡངས་
ཁྲོད་འདྲ་ལ། །ཞེས་སོགས་གསུངས་པ་དང་། སྤྱིར་ན་ཆོས་ཐམས་ཅད་བདེན་པར་མེད་པ་ཞིག་ཡིན་ནའང་ཀུན་
རྫོབ་བདེན་པ་དང་སྣང་བའི་ངོར། སངས་རྒྱས་སྟོང་རྩ་གཉིས་ཀྱི་ཐུགས་ཀྱི་པདྨའི་ཟེའུ་འབྲུ་དེ་པདྨ་འབྱུང་གནས་
ཡིན། ཟངས་མདོག་དཔལ་གྱི་རི་བོའི་རྩེ་མོར་པདྨ་འོད་ཀྱི་གཞལ་ཡས་ཁང་ན་ཡོད་དུས། པདྨ་འབྱུང་གནས་ཀྱིས་
བཀའ་བསྒོས་ཏེ་སངས་རྒྱས་ཀྱི་བསྟན་པའི་དགྲ་ཐེར་ལ་བཏང་བ་ཡིན། དེའང་སྤྲུལ་སྐུ་མཐོང་བ་དོན་ལྡན་གྱིས་ཞི་
རྒྱས་ཀྱི་སྒོ་ནས་བསྟན་པ་འཛིན་སྐྱོང་གི་འཕྲིན་ལས་མཛད། ང་པེ་ཀར་རྒྱལ་པོས་དབང་དྲག་གི་སྒོ་ནས་དེའི་
འགལ་རྐྱེན་སེལ་ཞིང་མཐུན་རྐྱེན་འགྲུབ་པའི་འཕྲིན་ལས་བསྒྲུབ། དེ་ལྟར་གཉིས་ཀས་ཀྱང་བསྟན་པའི་དགྲ་
ཐེར་མཛད་དགོས་རྒྱུ་ཡིན་པ་དགོངས་སུ་གསོལ། ཁྱད་པར་དུའང་པདྨ་འབྱུང་གནས་ཀྱིས་ངའི་ལས་སྐལ་དུ་དགྲ
བོའི་ཤ་ཁྲག་སྲོག་དབུགས་ཕོག། ལས་སྐལ་དུ་བསྟན་པ་དང་བསྟན་འཛིན་བསྲུང་བར་བསྒོས་པ་ཡིན་པས། སྔར་
ཡང་པདྨ་འབྱུང་གནས་ཀྱི་བཀའ་ལས་འདའ་མ་མྱོང་། ད་དུང་ཡང་མི་འདའ་བས་མཐོང་བ་དོན་ལྡན་གྱི་སྐུ་ཚེ་
མཛད་པ་འཕྲིན་ལས་རྣམས་ལ་བར་ཆད་འདུག་ན་ངས་སེལ། མཐུན་རྐྱེན་ཐམས་ཅད་ངས་བསྒྲུབ། གལ་ཏེ་
གནོད་བྱེད་གདོན་བགེགས་ཤིག་ཡོད་ན་མི་དང་མི་མ་ཡིན་པར་སྣང་ཞིང་སྲིད་པའི་ལྷ་མ་སྲིན་སྡེ་བརྒྱད་དྲེགས་པ་
ཅན་གྱི་ནང་ཚན་དུ་གཏོགས་པ་ཞིག་འོང་བ་ལས་འོས་མེད། སྡེ་བརྒྱད་ཐམས་ཅད་ཀྱི་ཡང་རྗེ། དྲེགས་པ་ཀུན་
འདུས་ཀྱི་རྒྱལ་པོ། དེ་ང་ཡིན་པས་ངའི་བཀའ་ལས་འདའ་བར་ནུས་པའི་གདོན་བགེགས་སུ་གྱུར་པ་ནི་སུ་ཡོད།
དེ་བས་ན་བསྐུལ་བར་མ་ཟད་ཞིག་ཐུགས་ཆུང་མཛད་མི་དགོས་སོ།། ཞེས་སོགས་བྱུང་བ་ལྟར། རྒྱལ་དབང་
ཐམས་ཅད་མཁྱེན་པ་འདི་ཉིད་ཀྱི་སྐུ་ན་རིམ་གྱི་སྲུང་མ་དང་། མཉམ་མེད་བཙོང་ཁ་པ་ཆེན་པོའི་བསྟན་པ་སྤྱི་དང་།
ཆོས་སྡེ་ཆེན་པོ་དཔལ་ལྡན་འབྲས་སྤུངས་ཀྱི་ལྷགས་རི་ལྷ་བུར་སྲུང་མར་ངེས་པ་དོན་གྱི་ཆོས་སྐྱོང་ཆེན་པོ་འདི་ཉིད་
རང་བཞིན་ལྷུན་གྱིས་གྲུབ་པའི་གནས་ལ་གར་བཞུགས་མ་མཆིས་ཀྱང་། ཧིང་ངེ་འཛིན་གྱིས་བསྐྱེད་ཅིང་སྤྲུལ་པ་
དང་ལྷབ་ཅིག་པར་དངོས་སུ་གྲུབ་པའི་བཞུགས་གནས་གནས་ཆུང་པེ་ཀར་ལྕོག་གསར་བ་འདི་ཉིད་དཔལ་ལྡན་
འབྲས་སྤུངས་སྤྱི་སོས་ཀྱང་བསྐུལ་མ་བྱུང་བས་རྐྱེན་བྱས་གོང་དུའང་སྐན་འབུལ་དང་། རྩོལ་བ་ཆེན་པོའི་སྒོ་ནས་

ལྷུགས་མོ་བྱའི་ལོ་དཔལ་ལྡན་འབྲས་སྤུངས་ཀྱི་མཆོད་རྟེན་ཆེན་པོར་བཅོམ་ལྡན་འདས་དུས་ཀྱི་འཁོར་ལོའི་ཆོས་
འཁོར་བསྐོར་བའི་དུས་ཆེན་ཧོར་ཟླ་གསུམ་པ་ནས་འགོ་བཙུགས་པའི་ཐོག་མར་གྱི་ཞོག་ཁྲ་དང་གང་ཅིའི་བཀོད་པ་
ངེད་རང་ནས་བགྱིས་ཞིང་། སྒྲོམ་གཏའ་དང་ལྷོ་འཕྱེའི་ཐིག་གིས་མཚོན་གཙུག་ལག་ནས་བཤད་པའི་བཅོས་
ཐབས་གཟའ་སྐར་སོགས་འཕྱོངས་རྒྱས་སྤྱུགས་པ་དག་དབང་གིས་བྱས་པར་ས་འདྲ་བའི་ཉིན་ཐལ་རླུང་སོགས་
ནམ་མཁའ་འཚུབ་པ་བྱུང་། དོ་དམ་སྐྱིད་སྡོད་པ་བསྟན་པའི་རྒྱལ་མཚན་དང་ཕུ་ལྕུང་བ་བདུད་བཙན་དཔལ་བཟང་
གཉིས་ཀྱིས་གཙོ་བྱས་ཆུང་ཁ་རབ་ཐང་དམར་མོ་བ། རོང་རང་བྱོན་པ། ས་བགྲུ་པ། གནང་བྱུང་པ། མཁར་ཆེ་
བ། དགའ་གདོང་། བཞི་སྡེ་བ། ཤར་པ་རབ་གསལ་བ། ཆོས་ལུང་གཞུ་དཀར། ཁང་གསར་རབ་བརྟན། ཕོ་
ལྷ་བ། རོང་རིགས་ལྷ་བ། ཕུན་གླིང་བསོད་ནམས་དར་རྒྱས། གཟིམས་ཆུང་པ་ཉི་ཤུ་རྩ་གཉིས། ཞིང་བཟོ་དབུ་
ཆེན་གནས་གསར་བ་འཇམ་དབྱངས་དང་གྲ་ཕྱི་དགོས་དགོས། དབུ་འབྲིང་ལྷ་ས་ལམ་རྟེན། དབུ་ཆུང་སྤུས་བདེ་
སྨོན་གྲུབ་གླིང་པ། བྱིངས་གྲུས་ཟ་དམ་ཚེ་དབང་སོགས་བརྒྱ་དང་ཉེར་བདུན་རྣམས་དང་། རྗེ་བཟོ་དབུ་ཆེན་འབྲི་
གུང་བསམ་གྲུབ་ཚེ་བརྟན་དང་རྒྱ་མོན་དར་རྒྱས། དབུ་ཆུང་ཕྱུག་པོ་བཀྲ་ཤིས། བྱིངས་གྲུས་མལ་གྲོ་དགོན་
མཆོག་སོགས་དགུ་བཅུ་གོ་གསུམ། ཞལ་མཁན་དབུ་མཛད་ཨེ་པ་ཚེ་བརྟན། བྱིངས་གྲུས་འཇམ་དབྱངས་སོགས་
བདུན། ཨར་གཡམ་འདྲེན་མི་ཀོ་བ་སྨོན་གྲོང་ནས་ཁང་པ་སོགས་ཞེ་གཅིག དོ་དམ་བསོད་ནམས་འཕེལ་དང་
བཟང་པོ་གཉིས་ཀྱིས་བགྱིས་་་ཆེ་རྗེ་གསོག་འུ་ལག་གིས་ཆེད་དུ་བསགས་པ་ལས་ཉིན་མཚན་དུ་མ་བལྟོས་པར་
ཀུན་གྱིས་མཐོང་བར་རི་རྗེ་ལྷ་འདྲེས་བསྒྲིལ་བའི་ཞོགས་ཆེ་ཞིང་། འུ་ལག་ལྷ་སྟོང་དུ་ཉེ་བའི་གྲངས་མང་ལ་ཐོག་
མར་རྒྱལ་གཟེར་སོགས་འཚུབ་ལྟོངས་རེ་གཉིས་ལས་ནད་སྐྱ་མེད་པའི་ཨར་ཟུལ་གཞན་ལས་ཁྱད་པར་མཚར་བ་
སོགས་ཆོས་རྒྱལ་ཁྲི་སྲོང་ལྡེའུ་བཙན་གྱིས་ལུགས་གསུམ་མི་འགྱུར་ལྷུན་གྱིས་གྲུབ་པའི་གཙུག་ལག་ཁང་
བཞེངས་པའི་རྣམ་པར་ཐར་པའི་རྗེས་སུ་རྐང་པ་འདེགས་པར་གྱུར། ལྡེབས་རིས་སུ་མཉམ་མེད་བཙོང་ཁ་པ་ཆེན་པོ་
ཡབ་སྲས་གསུམ། འཇམ་དབྱངས་གཙང་པ་བདུན་བརྒྱད། ལྷ་བརྒྱ་པ་རྣམས་ཀྱི་གཙུག་རྒྱན་རྒྱལ་བའི་དབང་པོ་
ཐམས་ཅད་མཁྱེན་ཅིང་གཟིགས་པ་ཆེན་པོ་སྐུ་ན་རིམ་ལྔ། དཔལ་ཨོཾ་ཏེ་ཡ་ནའི་སློབ་དཔོན་ཆེན་པོ། སྒྲུབ་པ་
བཀའ་བརྒྱད། རྒྱལ་ཆེན་སྐུ་ལྔ། ཡུམ་ལྔ། བློན་པོ་ལྔ་དང་བཅས་པ། བཙན་རྒོད་ཡ་བ་སྐུ་བདུན། ཁྱད་པར་
ཆོས་རྒྱལ་ཆེན་པོ་འདི་ཉིད་ཀྱི་སྐུའི་རྣམ་འགྱུར་རྣམ་གཉིས། བདེ་ཡངས་ཀྱི་ལྡེབས་རིས་ལ་འཁོར་དྲིགས་པའི་སྡེ་
དཔོན་སུམ་ཅུ། དཔལ་མགོན་བདུན་ཙུ་རྩ་ལྔ་སྡེ་བརྒྱད་ཀྱི་ཚོགས་དང་། རྒྱུད་ནས་བཤད་པའི་ཆགས་བྱེད་ཀྱི་ཕྱི་
རྟེན་བྱ་རྒོད། སྤྲེའུ། ནེ་ཙོ། ནང་རྟེན་ཕྱི། གསང་རྟེན་ཟ་འོག བཤན་པ་འགུགས་རྟེན་སྟག་སྤྱང་རྣམས་ཀྱི་རྒྱལ་
མཚན། ཞལ་གྱི་བྲིས་པ་ལོ་བརྒྱད་པ་གཡུའི་སྨིན་མ་ཅན་དུང་གི་མཆེ་བ་གཙིགས་ཞིང་ཕྱག་ན་སྤྱུ་གྲི་བསྣམས་པ་
སེང་གེ་དཀར་མོ་བཅིབས་པ། སྦྲུལ་ནག་མིག་གཅིག་པ་ལག་ན་ལྷུགས་ཀྱི་ཐོགས་པ་སྤྲེའུ་ཞོན་པ། དགྲ་ལྷ་དཀར་
པོ་བེར་དགུ་བརྩེགས་གྱོན་ཞིང་སྤྱུ་གྲི་འབར་བ་འཛིན་པ་སེང་གེ་བཅིབས་པ། གཡས་ན་དགྲ་བཅོམ་བརྒྱ། གཡོན་
ན་ཞུབ་ཅན་བརྒྱ། མདུན་ན་བུད་མེད་བརྒྱ། བརྗེ་དྲིལ་ནག་ཞེན་པ་བརྒྱ། རྒྱ་གར་མོན་ནག་གར་མཁན་ལག་ན་
སིག་ཞིང་ཐོགས་པ་བརྒྱ། ནག་མོ་ཐོད་པའི་ཕྲེང་ཅན་བདུན། བཤན་པ་མིག་གཅིག་པུ་སྦྲུལ་ནག་ཐོད་བཅིངས་
ཅན་ཧ་སྟོན་སྐབ་ནག་ཞེན་པ། བུ་ཧ་ནག་པོ་དྲིའུ་ཞོན་པ། དགྲ་བཅོམ་ཞིང་གི་གསག་ཐེབ་ཅན་ཛ་མོ་ཞོན་པ། བྲ་
རྒོད་ཐང་ནག་རྡོ་རྗེ་འཕེན་པ། གླིང་ཆེན་བྲ་རྒོད་ཀྱི་རྒྱལ་མཚན་འཕྱར་བ་བརྒྱ་དང་སེང་གེའི་རྒྱལ་མཚན་འཕྱར་བ

བརྒྱ། སྒྲོག་བདག་དར་ཆེན་མི་འབར་འཕྱུར་བ་བརྒྱ་དང་ཟ་འོག་གི་འཕན་དང་རྒྱལ་མཚན་འཕྱུར་བ་བརྒྱ། སྒྲོག་བདག་གིང་ཆེན་བསེ་ཁྲབ་གྱོན་པ་བརྒྱ། སེང་དཀར་ཁྲབ་མོ་བྱེད་པ་བརྒྱ། རྒྱུག་པའི་སྤྱང་སྔོན་བརྒྱ། བདུད་གཟའ་ནག་མོ་རྨ་བྱའི་ རྒྱལ་མཚན་འཕྱུར་བ་བརྒྱ། རྟ་ནག་དྲིལ་ནག་ཁྲི་ནག་ཁལ་བཀལ་བརྒྱ། ཇ་མོ་བདུད་ཀྱི་ཁྲམ་ཤིང་བཀལ་བ་བརྒྱ། རྟ་དཀར་ཞོན་པའི་གིཏྐ་ར་བརྒྱ། མོན་པ་ནག་པོ་བརྒྱ། སྤྲུལ་པ་མི་སྡུག་པའི་གཟུགས་སྣ་ཚོགས་པས་གསལ་བྱེད་ཟ་འུག་གི་རྒྱལ་མཚན་འཕྱུར་བ་བརྒྱ། ཇམས་བྱེད་སྟག་གི་རྒྱལ་མཚན་འཕྱུར་བ་བརྒྱ། ཟ་བྱེད་སྤྱང་ཀིའི་རྒྱལ་མཚན་འཕྱུར་བ་བརྒྱ། ལྡིང་བྱེད་བྱ་རྒོད་ཀྱི་རྒྱལ་མཚན་འཕྱུར་བ་བརྒྱ། སྲི་མོ་དང་རྨ་བྱའི་རྒྱལ་མཚན་འཕྱུར་བ་བརྒྱ། སྤྲེའུ་དང་བྱི་ལའི་རྒྱལ་མཚན་འཕྱུར་བ་བརྒྱ་ཕྲག་དཔག་ཏུ་མེད་པ་ཕོ་ཉ་སྤྲུན་གཟིགས་ཀྱི་རིགས་སྣ་ཚོགས་པ་དང་བཅས་པ་རྣམས་རི་མོ་བ་དགུ་འབྲིང་འཇམ་དབྱངས་དབང་པོ་དང་སྨན་ཐང་པ་མགོན་པོ་ཚེ་རིང་། བྱིངས་གྲུས་སྨན་ལུགས་པ་ཤར་གླིང་དགོན་མཆོག ། ལགས་པ་རྒྱལ་མཚན། འཇམ་དབྱངས་དོན་གྲུབ། ཤུན་ཤག་ཁྲི་སྐྱུག། ཨ་ལྐུག ། བསོད་ནམས། འབག་ལུག ། གྲགས་པ། བསྙོས་པ། བྱང་སྟེང་བཀྲ་ཤིས། ཞོལ་བློ་བཟང་། བདེ་ཆེན་ཕུན་ཚོགས་རང་བྱུང་། རིན་ཆེན་རྡོ་རྗེ། དཔལ་འབྱོར། བསམ་གྲུབ་ཚེ་རིང་། སྨིན་རྩ་བློ་བཟང་། རྒྱན་ཚང་ཚེ་བརྟན། མཆོ་སྨད་རྡོ་རྗེ། གཞན་དོན་ཀུན་གྲགས། རམ་པ་བྲག་ལོགས་པ། ཟ་དམ་བསོད་ནམས་བཀྲ་ཤིས། ཨ་ཁྲུ་བསམ་གྲུབ། དཀར་དཀར་ཨ་དཀར། པདྨ་རྒྱལ་པོ། ལྷ་སྲུང་། འཇོག་པོ་དགེ་བསྙེན། ཉན་པོ་འཇམ་དབྱངས། པ་ཚབ་མགོན་པོ། དགེ་བསྙེན་རྒྱལ་པོ། ཨ་འཛིན། བསམ་གྲུབ། རྒྱལ་པོ། བློ་བཟང་། བཀྲིས་དོན་གྲུབ། དོན་གྲུབ་ཚེས་དར། འཇམ་དབྱངས་རྒྱལ་མཚན། བསོད་ནམས་བཀྲ་ཤིས། བདེ་མཆོག ། བསྟན་འཛིན། དབང་ཕྱུག། བློ་བཟང་ཡར་འཕེལ། ལྷུག་ལྷུག། རིང་པ་བསོད་ནམས་རྒྱལ་པོ། དབུ་མཛད། པ་ནམ་མགོན་པོ། ཉི་སྟེངས་ཕན་བདེ། ཐུབ་དབང་བསྟན་འཛིན། བཀྲིས་དོན་གྲུབ་རྣམས་དང་། ཤིང་རྩི་བཟོ་ཕྲན་བཅས་པར་མཁྱེན་བརྩེ་བ་དགུ་འབྲིང་གསང་སྔགས་མཁར་བ་ཚེ་འཕེལ། བྱིངས་གྲུས་ངག་དབང་བསོད་ནམས་བསྟན་འཛིན། ཀུན་དགའ་རྡོ་རྗེ། ཀུན་དགའ་བྱང་ཆུབ། དཔལ་ལྡན་བཟང་པོ། རྣམ་སྲས། སངས་རྒྱས་དོན་གྲུབ། ངག་དབང་མདོ་སྡེ། ཀུན་དགའ་རབ་འཕེལ། ཆོར་སྣ་སྐལ་བཟང་། རྣམ་རྒྱལ་ཚུལ་ཁྲིམས། ཀུན་དགའ་རྒྱ་མཚོ། ངེས་དོན་སྙིང་པོ། བློ་བཟང་བསྟན་འཛིན། ངག་དབང་ཆོས་འཕེལ། ངག་དབང་ཡེ་ཤེས། བློ་གྲོས། སངས་རྒྱས་ཀུན་དགའ། སངས་རྒྱས་དོན་ལྡན། སངས་རྒྱས་ནོར་བུ། ལྷག་ཕུ་བཞིས་གཉེན། འབྲི་གུང་ལྷུན་གྲུབ། སོལ་སོལ། གནས་སྲུང་། བསོད་ནམས་ཤེས་རབ། བཀྲིས་ཚེ་རིང་། ཨོྒྱན། དོན་ཡོད། བློ་ལྡན། ཚེ་རྟ་དགའ་འདོལ། ཡོན་ཏན། བཀྲ་ཤིས་ལྷུན་གྲུབ། ཕུན་ཚོགས་ཚེ་རིང་། བློ་བཟང་དོན་གྲུབ། ལྷུངས་ཁྲོན་པ་ཁ་པ། སློ་ཐང་ཕྲིན་ལས་རྒྱ་མཚོ་རྣམས་ཀྱིས་བྱས་ཤིང་། འབུར་སྐུར་གོང་གནོན་དུ་བླ་མ་གསང་འདུས་ལྷར་གྱི་རྟ་མགྲིན་ཡུམ་བཅས། རྒྱལ་པོ་སྐུ་ལྔ་ཡུམ་བློན་དང་བཅས་པ། སྐུ་འདྲ་སྙིང་བའི་འཇིམ་པ་བསྲེས་པའི་ཐམས་ཅད་མཁྱེན་པ་བསོད་ནམས་རྒྱ་མཚོའི་གཟིགས་སྣང་གི་རྡོ་རྗེ་གྲགས་ལྡན་དང་། གོང་ས་མཆུངས་མེད་སྐྱབས་མགོན་མཆོག་གི་གཟིགས་སྣང་རྒྱ་ཅན་མའི་རྡོ་རྗེ་གྲགས་ལྡན་བཙན་ཆས་འཕྱུལ་ལྡན། རྡོ་རྗེ་དྲག་རྒྱལ་མ། སྒྲོ་སྦྱོང་ལྷ་ཁང་གི་གཙོ་བོ་རྗེ་བཙུན་རྒྱལ་བའི་དབང་བོ་ཐམས་ཅད་མཁྱེན་པ་ཆེན་པོ་ངག་གི་དབང་ཕྱུག་བློ་བཟང་རྒྱ་མཚོ། སྐུ་ན་རིམ་གོང་མ་བཞི། རྒྱལ་བ་བཙོང་ཁ་པ་ཆེན་པོ། ཨོྒྱན་ཡབ་ཡུམ་གསུམ། གུ་རུ་མཚན་བརྒྱད། བསྟན་སྲུང་རྡོ་རྗེ་དྲག་རྒྱལ་མ། སྟེང་ཁང་གཡས་ཀྱི་ཀ་བཞི་མར་གཙོ་བོ

རྒྱལ་དབང་ཐམས་ཅད་མཁྱེན་པ་བློ་བཟང་རྒྱ་མཚོ། རྗེ་བཙུན་བཙོང་ཁ་པ་ཆེན་པོ། འཇམ་དབྱངས་ཆོས་རྗེ། སྨན་བླ་བདེ་གཤེགས་བརྒྱད། གླུ་དབང་གི་རྒྱལ་པོ། སྤྱན་རས་གཟིགས་སེང་གེ་སྒྲ། སྒྲོལ་དཀར། སེང་ལྡེང་ནགས་སྒྲོལ། སྒྲོལ་མ་འཇིགས་པ་བརྒྱད་སྐྱབས། རྣམ་འཇོམས་ལྷུང་སྟོན། སོ་སོར་འབྲང་མ། གཡོན་གྱི་ཀ་བཞི་མར། དུས་གསུམ་སངས་རྒྱས། འཕགས་པ་གནས་བརྟན་བཅུ་དྲུག ཧྭ་ཤང་ལ། རྒྱལ་ཆེན་སྡེ་བཞི་ཧྭ་ཤང་དང་བཅས་པའི་སྣང་བརྙན་སོགས་བཞེངས་པར་འཇིམ་བཟོ་ཨེ་པ་དབུ་མཛད་བག་གྲོ་དང་ཆོས་འཕེལ། དབུ་ཆུང་དཔལ་འཛིན། བྱིངས་བྲུས་བཙུན་ཆུང་། བློ་བཟང་བསྟན་སྐྱོང་། ཀྱོན་མགོན་པོ། ཨ་བར་དར་རྒྱས། འཇོམ་ཕྲུག བློ་བཟང་། གཡུ་འབྲུག བསོད་ནམས་ཚེ་རིང་། སུམ་དགའ། བསྟན་འཕེལ། འཇམ་དབྱངས་དར་རྒྱས། ཨ་བར། ནོར་བུ་ཚེ་རིང་། དོན་གྲུབ། རྡོར་རྒྱལ། སུམ་འཕེལ། བློ་བཟང་ནོར་བུ། ནོར་བུ་དར་རྒྱས་རྣམས་ཀྱི་དོ་དམ་ཆེ་ཁ་འབོག་གོང་བཙུན་པ་བློ་གྲོས་རྒྱལ་མཚན། ཆུང་ཁ་སྐྱིད་གྲོང་གྲ་དཔོན་དང་རྒྱལ་རྩེ་ལྷོག་སྤྲུག་པ། འུ་ལག་དོ་དམ་ལྷུང་ར་བསོད་ནམས་དང་ཟ་དམ་ཚེ་རིང་དོན་གྲུབ་ཀྱིས་བགྱིས་ཤིང་། ཐོག་མར་བཟོ་པོ་དང་ལག་ཆ་སྒྲིག་ཤིང་བྱིན་རླབས་ནས་བར་དུ་གནས་ཡིག་རབ་གནས་སྤྱན་འདྲེན་སོགས་དགེ་སློང་འཇམ་དབྱངས་གྲགས་པས་གོང་གི་བཀའ་གནང་སྤྱི་བོར་བླངས་ཏེ་བྱས། བྲིས་འབུར་རྣམས་ཀྱི་ལྷའི་གཙོ་བོ་གོང་ནས་བསླབ་སྟོན་དང་འཁོར་ཤིང་རྩིས་མཚོན་པ་ངེད་རང་ནས་ཟུར་བརྒྱུད་བར་ལྷ་དང་བཅས་པའི་འགྲོ་བ་ཐམས་ཅད་ཀྱི་སྐྱབས་མགོན་དམ་པ་ཆེན་པོས་བསླབ་སྟོན་གནང་པའི་རྒྱལ་པོ་སྐུ་ལྔ་བཙུན་མོ་བློན་པོ་དང་། གཞན་ཡང་བསྟན་སྲུང་ཆེན་པོ་རྡོ་རྗེ་གྲགས་ལྡན་སོགས་དྲེགས་པ་སྣ་ཚོགས་ཀྱི་མདོས་རྣམས་སྟོང་སྐྱུད་དང་། དེ་མཚུངས་གཏོར་མའི་རྒྱུ་ཆ་ཕུན་སུམ་ཚོགས་ཤིང་མཆོད་དཔོན་ངག་དབང་ཞེས་རབ་ཀྱིས་དོ་དམ་བྱས་གྲ་ཚང་གི་གྲ་པ་ཁ་ཡར་གྱིས་རྩོལ་བས་ཁྲིད་དུ་མཚར་བ་བཅས་བཟོས་ཤིང་ཟ་འོག་དིང་ཡོན་ལས་གྲུབ་པའི་རྒྱལ་མཚན་འཕན་གྱིས་གཙོས་པའི་གནམ་རྒྱན་དང་བཅས་པའི་དོ་དམ་བྱ་གོ་བ་བློ་བཟང་དབང་ཕྱུག་དང་དཔལ་རྡོར། བགྲིས་ཁ་པ། གོས་བཟོ་དབུ་མཛད་ར་རྩེ་ཤག་པ་བསོད་ནམས། བྱིངས་བྲུས་གོང་དཀར་ལྷ་ཡགས་སོགས་སུམ་ཅུ་སོ་གཉིས་'''ཀྱིས་བགྱིས་ཤིང་། སྐུ་དང་བཅས་པའི་ནང་གཙོར་སྐུ་རྟེན་གྲགས་ཅན་རིང་བསྲེལ་སྣ་བཞིས་མཚོན་པའི་བྱིན་རླབས་རྟེན་དང་། ཕྱི་ནང་གསང་བ་ཡང་གསང་ཟུར་བཀོལ་དང་བཅས་པའི་སྒྲིག་འཁོར། ཆགས་རྟེན་དུ་རྒྱལ་པོ་ཧེ་ལྷར་སྟོབས་ནུས་ཆེ་རུང་མི་འོང་ཞིང་མི་ཆགས་པའི་རང་དབང་མེད་པར་འདུ་བའི་བྱུ་རུའི་རྒྱལ་ལག་མཐེ་གང་ཙམ་རེ། ལས་རབ་འབྱམས་ཅི་བཙོལ་ཀྱང་ཐོགས་པ་མེད་པར་མི་བྱ་བའི་དབང་མེད་པར་བྱེད་པ་ཤེལ་དཀར་དྲི་མེད་སྣང་སྲིད་འཆར་བ་གྲུ་བཞི་མཛུབ་རེ་རེ། རང་དང་བསྒྲུབ་བྱ་དཔོན་སློབ་འཁོར་དང་བཅས་པར་མི་འཕྲུ་ཞིང་ལུས་དང་གྲིབ་མ་བཞིན་མི་འགྲོགས་པའི་རང་དབང་མེད་པ་ཉ་ཕྱིས་ཁོག་པ་ཚང་བ་གསུམ་པོ་ལ་སྲོག་ཡིག་རྫས་སྲོག་རྒྱུད་ལས་བྱུང་བ། གཞན་ཡང་རྒྱ་ནག་ཏུ་ཆིབས་ཁ་བསྒྱུར་སྐབས་འུར་དུས་སུ་ཆེད་དུ་གཉེར་བས་དགོས་ཚུལ་གནང་བ་འདི་ལོ་རྟེན་འབྲེལ་ལེགས་པར་འགྲིག་སྙེ་དུང་ངང་ཆོས་རྗེས་ཕུལ་བའི་རིན་པོ་ཆེ་ས་ལེ་སྦྲམ་བཟོ་དབྱིབས་མདོག་རྣམས་ལེགས་བརའི་གློ་བ་ཙམ་པ་ཞིག་གིས་གཙོས་བྱ་སྒོང་ཙམ་རེ། དངུལ་རྡ་རྨིག་མས་གཙོས་པ་རེ། བྱུ་རུ་ཁམ་རློན་ཙམ་རེ། བླ་གཡུ་ངང་སྒོང་ཙམ་རེ། མུ་ཏིག་དང་མུ་མེན་ཟངས་ལྕགས་སོགས་ལྷ་ཀླུ་མིའི་རིན་པོ་ཆེའི་རིགས། ནོར་སྣ། གོས་སྣ། དར་སྣ། རས་སྣ། བྲ་བོ་ཡུངས་ཀར་མིན་པའི་འབྲུ་སྣ། ཨམྲ་དང་ཁ་སུར་པ་སོགས་ཤིང་ཏོག་གི་རྣམ་གྲངས་འཛིག་རྟེན་ན་ཡོད་དོ་ཅོག ། དུག་རིགས་དང་དྲི་མི་ཞིམ་པ་མེད་པའི་ཚན་དན་དཀར་དམར་

གྱིས་གཙོས་སྨན་སྔ་རིང་བུ་སྣ་ཚོགས། དཀར་གསུམ་དང་མངར་གསུམ་སོགས་བཟའ་བ་དང་བཅའ་བའི་རིགས་སྣ་ཚོགས་ཀྱིས་མཐའ་བརྟེན་པའི་ཡོ་བྱད་རྣམས་སྐྱ་དང་མདོས་གཏོར་སོ་སོར་ཚང་ཞིང་། འཁོར་ལོ་ལེ་ཚན་སོགས་ལ་གོང་ནས་ཕྱུགནས་དང་རབ་གནས་ཉིན་རེ། གཞན་མ་བསླབ་སྟོན་གཙོ་བོར་བཏོན་དགེ་སློང་འཇམ་དབྱངས་གྲགས་པས་དོ་དམ་བྱས་འདྲི་མི་ངག་དབང་ཕྲིན་ལས། ངག་དབང་རྒྱ་མཚོ། ལེགས་ལྡན་དབང་རྒྱལ། སྔགས་རམས་པ་བློ་བཟང་སྐྱིས་མཆོག་དང་ཆོས་རྗེ་ཟིལ་གནོན་རྡོ་རྗེ་ཅན་གྱིས་བྱས་ཤིང་དགེ་སློང་འཇམ་དབྱངས་གྲགས་པས་ཀུང་བསྒྲུབས་འབུལ་བའི་ཚ་མིག་ལྔ་དང་བཅས་མཆོད་དཔོན་ངག་དབང་ཤེས་རབ། དགེ་སློང་འཇམ་དབྱངས་གྲགས་པ། སྔགས་རམས་པ་བློ་བཟང་སྐྱིས་མཆོག་ཅན་གྱིས་ཁ་བསྐོས་ནས་བྱས། གཟུངས་འབུལ་གྱི་དུས་ཆོས་སྐྱོང་ཆེན་པོ་ཉིད་སྐུ་ཕེབས་པའི་རལ་གྲི་དང་ཤིང་བུང་གཉིས་ཀུང་རྗེ་བསོད་ནམས་རྒྱ་མཚོའི་གཟིགས་སྣང་མར་འཇུག་དགོས་དང་། བན་ཆུང་རྣམས་ཀྱིས་ཞིས་པར་པེ་ཧར་རྒྱལ་པོ་འཁོར་བཅས་དེ་རིང་དངོས་སུ་ཡོང་ཕེབས་ཤིང་། དེ་ཉིན་གཟུངས་འབུལ་བ་རྣམས་བྱིན་ཆགས་པ་ལས་མཚན་མ་ཤེས་པ་མ་བྱུང་ཡང་། དེ་ནུབ་ནས་ཨེ་པའི་འབུར་པ་རྣམས་རྨི་བལྟས་འབྲུགས་ཏེ་འཚུབ་ལྦོངས་ཤིན་ཏུ་ཆེ་བས་བྱིན་རླབས་དང་། ཆོས་སྐྱོང་སྐུ་ཕེབས་ལ་བསླབ་སྟོན་སོགས་ཞུ་དགོས་པའི་ཡ་མཚན་ཞག་ཁ་ཡར་བྱུང་། རྗེ་མོར་གསེར་སྦྲངས་ཉིས་སྟོང་ཞོ་ལས་གྲུབ་པའི་གཏྱི་ར་ནང་དུ་ཡུངས་འབྲུ་ལྔ་བུའི་རིང་བསྲེལ་གྱིས་གཙོས་བྱིན་རྟེན། ཡུལ་ཕྱོགས་བཀྲིས་ཕྱིར་ཞི་རྒྱས་དབང་དྲག་གི་འཁོར་ལོ་ཁྲིད་ཅན། གཡས་སུ་རྡོ་རྗེ་གྲགས་ལྡན་དང་། གཡོན་དུ་དྲག་རྒྱལ་མ། བྱང་ཕྱོགས་སུ་ཐུགས་ཀྱི་རྒྱལ་པོས་དབུས་པའི་ཕྱོགས་བཞིར་སྐུ་ལྔ་སོ་སོའི་རྟེན་ཐུག ། བར་ཐོག་ཏུ་རྟེན་རྫས་ཀྱི་སྲོག་ཆགས་བཞི་དང་། ཟ་འོག་བཅས་པའི་རྒྱལ་མཚན། ཞོལ་དུ་ཡུམ་ལྔའི་ཐུག་བཅས་ལ་སོ་སོའི་མན་ངག་དང་མཐུན་པའི་འཁོར་ལོ་རྟེན་རྫས་ཀྱིས་བརྒྱན་པ་དང་། སྙེར་ཁག་གི་རྒྱལ་མཚན་ཐུག་ཅོད་པན་སྣ་ཚོགས་པ་བཙུགས་ཤིང་གཏྱི་རའི་སྒྲུབ་པ་རབ་གནས་དགེ་སློང་འཇམ་དབྱངས་གྲགས་པ་ཅན་དང་། ཐུག་གི་ཚོ་ག་སྔགས་རམས་པ་བློ་བཟང་སྐྱིས་མཆོག་ཅན་གྱིས་བྱས། སྒོའི་ཤན་རྣམས་ཀུང་རྟེན་རྫས་དང་མཆོད་པའི་གཟུགས་འགྲོས་སྣ་ཚོགས་ཀྱིས་བརྒྱན་པའི་དོ་དམ་གཞིས་ཀ་སྙིང་སྙིང་དང་ལ་འོག་བཀྲིས། ལྷོ་མོས་ཀུན་དགའ་རྡོ་རྗེ་གསུམ་གྱིས་བྱས་ཤིང་། ལྕགས་བཟོའི་དབུ་ཆུང་ཨོ་ཚང་པ། བྱིངས་གྲུས་གསེར་བཞུ་ཁྲེ་སྐྱག་སོགས་སུམ་ཙུ་སོ་གཉིས་རྣམས་དང་། ཚགས་པ་དབུ་མཛད་རྗེ་ཆེན་བསོད་ནམས་དར་རྒྱས། པ་ནམ་མགོན་པོ། བྱིངས་གྲུས་ར་མ་སྣང་ནོར་བུ་སོགས་ལྔ་བཅུ་ང་གཉིས་རྣམས་དང་། དངུལ་མགར་པ་ཀྱོན་སོགས་བཅོ་ལྔ·····བལ་པོ་པུར་ཙ་སོགས་ལྔ་བཅུ་ང་བདུན། དོ་དམ་སྤྱི་རི་བསྟན་འཛིན་དང་གྲ་ཕྱི་ནོར་བུ་དོན་གྲུབ་ཀྱིས་བྱས་པའི་ཆོན་འདུལ་བ་སྐྱེ་མོ་ཀརྨ་དང་སྟོན་པ་ཆེ་དབང་སྲི་ཐར། བསེ་མཁན་ཆེ་དབང་རྡོ་རྗེ། ཛ་ལས་པ་སྤྲ་བ་མགོ་བ་ཅན་བཞི་དང་། སྒོ་ཕན་ཚུན་གྱི་ཀུན་འཁོར་བཞི་འདར་ལོ་ངག་དབང་ཕུན་ཚོགས་ལྷུན་གྲུབ་དང་རྣམ་གླིང་པཎ་ཆེན་དཀོན་མཆོག་ཆོས་གྲགས། རྒྱ་བོད་ཀྱི་ཡི་གེ་འདྲི་མི་རྒྱལ་རྩེ་འཇམ་དབྱངས་དབང་པོ་དང་དཔག་བསམ་ཚེ་རིང་གིས་བྱས། དགོས་ཆེད་ཕོགས་སོགས་སྤྲོད་མི་དཀྲན་བཀའ་བཅུ་བ་དང་སྦྲུས་སྤྱང་པ་ཆེ་དབང་བཀྲིས་ཀྱིས་བྱས། བཟང་རི། སྙེའུ་སྡོང་། གྲ་ཚང་། གྲོང་སྨད། འབྲས་སྤྱུངས་སྤྱི་པ། སྐྱུ་རྟེན་པ། བློ་གསལ་གླིང་པ། སྒོ་མངས་པ། བདེ་ཡངས་པ། སྔགས་པ། དཀྲན་བཀའ་བཅུ་བ། ཤར་སྡོང་པ། སྦྲུས་སྤྱང་པ་རྣམས་ཀྱིས་བྱ་ལོར་ཨར་སྟོན་དང་། འབྲས་སྤྱུངས་སྤྱི་པ། གྲོང་སྨད། བདེ་ཡངས་པ། སྐྱུ་རྟེན་པ། དཀྲན་བཀའ་བཅུ། སྦྲུས་སྤྱང་པ་རྣམས་ཀྱིས་ཁྱི་ལོར་བཟོ་སྟོན་སོགས་བསྟར་བ་ཐ་ཆེན་

ཀྱི་ལོ་ཐ་སྐར་ཟླ་བའི་འགོར་ལེགས་པར་གྲུབ་པའི་སྐུ་ཆས་དང་སྐུ་རྟེན་རྣམས་ཟླ་བ་དེ་གའི་ཚེས་བརྒྱད་ཀྱི་གཟའ་སྐར་བཟང་བར་སྤྱོས་དུས་ཡ་མཚན་པའི་ལྟས་སྣ་ཚོགས་པ་བྱུང་ཞིང་། རབ་གནས་འཕྲུལ་སེལ་དུ་ཚེས་བཅུ་གསུམ་གྱི་ཉིན་སྣ་གོན་དང་བཅུ་བཞི་ལ་དཔལ་ཆེན་རྡོ་རྗེ་གཞོན་ནུ་ཁྲག་འཐུང་ཁྲོ་བོའི་དཀྱིལ་འཁོར་ལ་བརྟེན་གོང་ས་མཆོག་གིས་ཕྱག་ནས་དང་སྤྱན་དམིགས་གནང་བ་དང་། དཔལ་ལྡན་བླ་མ་དམ་པའི་གསུང་གི་བདུད་རྩི་རིམ་པ་མེད་པར་བཀྲུངས་པའི་ཡི་དམ་ཞི་ཁྲོའི་བསྙེན་སྒྲུབ་ལས་གསུམ་ལ་མཐར་སོན་ཅིང་སུམ་ལྡན་རིག་སྔགས་འཆང་བ་དགེ་སློང་འཇམ་དབྱངས་གྲགས་པས་རྡོ་རྗེ་སློབ་དཔོན་བྱས། ཕྱི་འདུལ་བ་དང་བྱང་སེམས་ཀྱི་སྤྱོད་པ་ལས་སྐད་ཅིག་ཀྱང་མི་འགལ་ཞིང་ནང་ལྷ་སྔགས་ཡེ་ཤེས་ཀྱི་རྣལ་འབྱོར་ཟབ་མོ་ལ་གནས་པའི་རྣམ་པར་རྒྱལ་བའི་ཕན་བདེ་ལེགས་བཤད་གླིང་འདུས་ཚོགས་ཀྱིས་དམ་ཚིག་སེམས་དཔར་ཡེ་ཤེས་པ་དངོས་སུ་བཅུག་པའི་རབ་ཏུ་གནས་ཤིང་མི་རྟག་གི་ཆར་བབ་པའི་ཚེ་སྣ་གོན་གྱི་བགེགས་སྐྲོད་སྐབས་དུས་མིན་རླུང་འཚུབ་ཕྱིར་བུད་པ་དང་སྤྱན་འདྲེན་གྱི་དུས་དར་ཕག་ཡས་སྣ་དང་འབྲས་སྤུངས་ཕྱོགས་ནས་རླུང་འཚུབ་ལངས་པ་གནས་ཆུང་གི་ཐད་ཡལ་བ་དང་སྒྲོག་ཤིང་བྱིན་རླབས་ནས་བཟུང་རབ་གནས་གཟུངས་འབུལ་སོགས་ཡིན་རེས་ཀྱིས་ཁ་ཆར་དང་འདི་སྐབས་ཉི་མ་སྤྲ་རྟིང་ནམཁའ་གཡའ་དག་པར་རབ་གནས་རབ་སྟོན་སོགས་ཀྱི་དུས་ཁ་ཆུབ་དང་ཁྱད་པར་སྐྱིད་ཤོད་ཡས་མས་གང་ལ་མེད་ཀྱང་གནས་ཆུང་རྒྱབ་རིར་ཐུལ་ལེ་སྤྲིན་པ་ཀུན་གྱིས་མཐོང་བར་བྱུང་ཞིང་འདི་ཉིན་ནས་སྐུ་གསོལ་འཕྲུལ་མ་དེ་གློ་བུར་བརྟེད་ཆེ་རུ་སོང་བ་འགྲོགས་མིས་རྟོགས་པ་དང་ཨེ་པ་དབུ་མཛད་བག་གྲོའི་རྨི་ལྟས་གཙང་ཁང་དུ་བཙུན་པ་མང་པོ་བལྟ་བར་ཡོངས་པ་སྐུ་རྣམས་ཆག་དོགས་བྱེད་པ་འཚངས། དབུས་ཀྱི་རྒྱལ་པོའི་སྐུར་ཐིམ་པ་དང་གཞན་ཡང་གྲ་ཚང་གྲ་པ་དང་དྲུང་འཁོར་སོགས་ཁ་ཡར་ལ་ཉམས་རྨིས་ཀྱི་འཚུབ་ཆ་ཆེ་བའི་རིགས་པ་དངོས་སུ་བཞུགས་པའི་ལྟས་ཕུན་སུམ་ཚོགས་པ་བྱུང་། ཚེས་བཅོ་ལྔའི་པ་སངས་ནམ་གྲུའི་འགྲུབ་སྦྱོར་ཀྱི་གཟའ་སྐར་ཕུན་སུམ་ཚོགས་པའི་ཉིན་ཆོས་སྐྱོང་ཆེན་པོ་སྐུ་རྟེན་ཆེ་རིང་དཔལ་འབར་གྱི་ཁོག་ཏུ་ཕབ་ཏེ་ཞལ་སྤྱོའི་རྟེན་འབྲེལ་བསྒྲིགས་པ་དགྱེས་པ་བསྐྱེད་ཅིང་གནས་ཁང་དུ་འདུ་འབྲལ་མེད་པར་བཞུགས་པ་དང་། བསྟན་འགྲོའི་སེལ་ཚེ་གཡེལ་བ་མེད་ཅིང་འཕྲིན་ལས་རྣམ་བཞི་ལྷུན་གྱིས་གྲུབ་པར་ཞལ་གྱིས་བཞེས་པའི་ཡ་མཚན་ཕུན་སུམ་ཚོགས་པར་གྲུབ་པ་ནི་གཙུག་ལག་ཁང་དང་གནས་ཁང་གཞན་ལས་བཟོ་སྣ་བརྒྱད་ཀྱིས་ཁྱད་དུ་འཕགས་པ་སྟེ་ཁྱད་འཕགས་དང་པོ་ནི་གོང་སློས་བཞིན་གྱི་བླ་རྡོ་སྒྲོག་འཁོར་གྱིས་མཆོད་གཞན་དུ་མ་གྲགས་པར་མ་ཟད་བྲིས་འབུར་རྣམས་ཀྱང་འཆི་མེད་ཀྱི་བཟོ་བོ་ལས་སྣ་ཚོགས་པ་མིའི་རྣམ་པར་བསྟན་ནས་བགྱིས་ཉམས་ཀྱི་བཟོ་ཁྱད་རྣམ་འགྱུར་གྱིས་ཡིད་དབང་འཕྲོག་ཅིང་། བྱེད་པ་པོ་རྣམས་ཀྱང་ལྷར་བསྐྱེད་དེ་ཚོན་དང་ལག་ཆ་སོགས་ཀྱང་ལྷག་པར་གནས་པ་བྱིན་རླབས་ཀྱིས་ཉེ་བར་གཏམས་པའི་མདོར་ན་ཆུ་ཕྱུར་མིག་ཙམ་རྣམས་ལ་བྲིས་འབུར་གྱི་རྣམ་པ་ཙམ་ལས། དོན་དམ་གདོད་ནས་རང་བཞིན་ལྷུན་གྱིས་གྲུབ་པའི་སྣང་སྲིད་རིགས་པ་དམ་ཅན་རྒྱ་མཚོ་དངོས་སུ་སྤྲིན་ཕུང་གཏིབས་པ་ལྟར་བར་དང་མཚམས་མེད་པ་ནས་ལང་ལོང་དུ་འདུ་ཞིང་ལས་བྱེད་པའི་ཁྱད་ཅན། གཉིས་པ་ཆོས་སྐྱོང་འདི་ཉིད་རྣམ་སྤྲུལ་བགྲང་ཡས་པས་སྐྱེ་འགྲོ་དབུགས་ཀྱིས་ཟིན་ཚད་ཀྱི་ལྷག་པར་གནས་པ་ཞལ་གྱིས་འཆེས་པ་ལྟར་ཡིན་ནའང་གང་འདུལ་གྱི་རོལ་པས་སྐུའི་རྣམ་འགྱུར་གྱི་སྤྲུལ་པ་རྟ་མགོ་གྲུ་དམར་གཡུའི་ནོར་བུས་མཚན་པའི་ཚུལ་གཟི་བྱིན་བཟོད་པར་དཀའ་བ་ཞིག་ཏུ་བསྟན་ཏེ། རྣམ་སྤྲུལ་དགྱེས་པའི་རྟེན་དུ་དྲི་བསུང་ཕུན་སུམ་ཚོགས་པ་དང་ལྡན་ཞིང་། མེ་ཏོག་དང་འབྲས་བུ་རྣམ་པར་རྒྱས་པ་མྱ་ངན་མེད་པའི་ལྗོན་ཤིང་སྒྲོ་བ་འདི་ཉིད་ལ་

ཐིམ་པའི་ཚུལ་གྱིས་གནས་པ་ལྟར་དམ་ཅན་དགྱེས་པའི་ཕོ་བྲང་དུ། བསྐལ་བ་བཟང་པོའི་སངས་རྒྱས་སྟོང་རྩ་གཉིས་སོགས་དུས་གསུམ་གྱི་རྒྱལ་བ་ཐམས་ཅད་ཀྱི་ཐུགས་ཀྱི་པདྨའི་གེ་སར་ལས་མཆོག་ཏུ་སྤྲུལ་བའི་སྐུ་མཐོང་བ་དོན་ལྡན་སྐུའི་སྐྱེ་བ་ན་རིམ་གྱིས་རྡོ་རྗེའི་རྣལ་འབྱོར་ཟབ་མོའི་ལྷ་སྔགས་ཡེ་ཤེས་ཀྱི་རོལ་བའི་མཐུ་ཆེན་པོས་བྱིན་གྱིས་བརླབས་ཤིང་། ཆོས་སྐྱོང་ཆེན་པོས་ཀྱང་སྤྱན་གཟིགས་མཆོས་རྫས་དུ་མས་བཀྲ་བའི་གཞལ་ཡས་ཁང་དུ་མི་འབྲལ་བར་དགྱེས་པ་ཆེན་པོས་ཆགས་པའི་རྟེན་འདི་ཉིད་ཉམས་པ་མེད་པར་གཙང་ཁང་དུ་བཞུགས་པ་ནི་གནས་འདིའི་སྲོག་ཤིང་ལྟ་བུའི་དགྱེས་པའི་རྟེན་མཆོག་ཏུ་གྱུར་པའི་སྙིང་པོ་ཡིན་ལ། སླད་ནས་དགྱེས་པ་བསྐྱེད་ཅིང་བསྟན་པའི་བསྲུང་སྐྱོབ་ཉམས་པ་མེད་པའི་ཕྱིར། དངོས་བཤམས་ཀྱི་གཞལ་ཡས་སྤྱན་གཟིགས་ཀུན་ཏུ་བཟང་པོའི་མཆོད་སྤྲིན་ལྷ་མིའི་འབྱོར་བ་ཐམས་ཅད་གཅིག་ཏུ་སྤེལ་བ་ལྟར་རིམ་པ་བཞིན་སྤྲོ་བར་མཛད་པས་ན། ཕྱི་ནང་གི་རྟེན་དུ་གྱུར་པས་ཁྱད་པར་འཕགས། གསུམ་པ་གཙང་ཁང་དབུས་མའི་མདོ་ཕྱུགས་ཀྱི་ཕྱུམ་དང་དྲལ་མ་རྣམས་མཐོང་བས་ཀྱང་སྙིང་རྩ་འདར་ཞིང་འབྱིན་པར་ནུས་པའི་ཞིང་ཆེན་གྱི་པགས་པ། ལྷོ་འགྲོ་རིགས་ལྔའི་རྣམ་པ་ཅན་སྤུ་གྲི་དང་ཤང་ལང་རལ་གྲི། དབྱར་རྔའི་ཁ་ནས་ཐོག་སེར་བསྐྲུག་པ་བཅས་འཇིགས་ཤིང་སྐྱི་གཡའ་བའི་བཟོ་ཁྱད། བཞི་པ་ནང་གི་སྒོ་ནི་རྣམ་ཐར་སྒོ་གསུམ་གྱི་ངང་ལས་སྐུ་གསུམ་དུ་ཤར་བ་ཕྱི་རོལ་དུ་ཡེ་ཤེས་ལྷའི་རང་གདངས་རྒྱལ་ཆེན་སྐུ་ལྔ་མཚོན་པར་བྱེད་པའི་སྒོ་ལྔ་ནི། རབ་ཏུ་ཡངས་པའི་སྲིད་པ་གསུམ་གྱི་སྐྱེ་དགུ་ཀུན་དུས་གཅིག་ཏུ་ཞུགས་ཀྱང་དོག་པ་མེད་པར་ཤོང་བའི་ཁྱོན་ཆེ་ཞིང་། བབས་གདོང་ཡང་སྲིད་པའི་རྩེ་མོར་བསྙེག་པར་བྱེད་པས་ན་མགྲིན་པ་ལྡ་ཟུང་གི་ཕོ་བྲང་ཁྱམས་བཅས་དྲག་ཤུལ་གྱིས་ས་འདིར་བླངས་པ་ལྟ་བུས་རྔམས་བརྗིད་དང་ལྡན་པའི་ཁྱད་ཅན། ལྔ་པ་སྒོ་འཕར་གྱི་གླེགས་བུ་དབུགས་བྲལ་གྱི་ཡན་ལག་མཆོག་གི་ཁ་ནས་འཕྱུང་བའི་ལྷོ་འགྲོའི་རང་བཞིན་གྱིས་བཟུང་བའི་ཕྱུང་ཕྱུལ་གྱིས་ཤིན་ཏུ་བརྟན་པའི་བློ་ཅན་རྣམས་ཀྱང་དོན་སྙིང་ཀློག་མར་འབྱིན་ནུས་པའི་ཁྱད་མཚར། དྲུག་པ་རྩེ་མོར་གསེར་སྦྲངས་ཀྱི་རང་བཞིན་ཉི་མ་འབུམ་གྱི་གཟི་བྱིན་འགོག་པར་ནུས་པའི་གཉྫི་ར་ཆེན་པོ་དྲིགས་པའི་སྡེ་དཔོན་འཁོར་དང་བཅས་པས་ཕྲིན་ལས་རྣམ་བཞི་ཐོགས་མེད་དུ་བསྒྲུབ་ཕྱིར་སྐུ་གསུང་ཐུགས་རྟེན་ཕྱི་ནང་ཡང་ཟབ་དང་བཅས་པ་ཚང་བར་བཙུགས་པས་དམ་ཅན་རང་བཞིན་གྱིས་འདུ་བ་དང་། གསེར་ཕྱུའི་ལྦ་འཕྲེང་མི་མགོ་སྐམ་པོའི་འཕྲེང་གཟུགས་ཀྱིས་ཚར་དུ་དངར་བས་སྲིན་པོའི་ཕོ་བྲང་གི་ཡང་ཐོག་ལ་ཅོ་འདྲི་བ་ལྟ་བུའི་ཁྱད་བཟོ། བདུན་པ་ཕྱི་རྒྱ་དྲེགས་པའི་བཞུགས་གནས་དཀྱིལ་འཁོར་གྱི་མཚན་ཉིད་མངོན་སུམ་དུ་གྲུབ་པའི་ཤར་ལྷོ་ནུབ་བྱང་སོ་སོར་འཕྲིན་ལས་བཞིའི་ཁ་དོག་དང་མཐུན་པའི་སྒོ་དང་། གདན་ལ་བཞུགས་ཀྱི་འདོད་སྣམ་ཀ་སྤྱུངས་ཀྱིས་བརྟེག་པའི་རྟ་བབས་དང་བཅས་གཞལ་ཡས་ཁང་གི་རྣམ་པ་མ་ཉམས་པར་ཚང་ཞིང་རྩེའི་བ་གམ་གྱི་མཛེས་པ་བསྲུང་བ་པདྨ་རྣ་གའི་མདོག་ལྡན་གྱི་ཁ་བད་ལ་ཐོད་པ་སྐམ་པོའི་འཕྲེང་བ་འོད་ཟེར་ཕྱོགས་བརྒྱར་འགྱེད་པས་ཕྱོགས་ཀྱི་མུན་པའི་གོ་སྐབས་འཕྲོག་ཅིང་སྣ་བརྒྱད་དེ་གཟའ་ཆེན་བརྒྱད་མཚོན་པའི་ཁྱད་ཆོས། བརྒྱད་པ་ཞིང་བཅུ་བསྒྲལ་བའི་ཁྲག་གི་ཞལ་བ་ཞག་དང་ཀླད་པའི་ལྷུ་འཕྲེང་རྣམ་པར་འཕྱུགས་པས་མཐར་བྱེད་ཀྱི་ཁང་པ་མངོན་སུམ་དུ་གྱུར་པས་ཆར་གྱི་རྒྱུན་འབབ་པར་ཉེ་བའི་ནམ་མཁའི་སྤྲིན་པོ་བཞིན་དུ་ལང་ལོང་དུ་གཡོ་ཞིང་ཀ་བ་བཅུ་དྲུག་སྟེ་ཆོས་སྐྱོང་བཅོ་ལྔ་དང་མིའམ་ཅི་སྟེ་བཅུ་དྲུག་མཚོན་པར་བྱེད་པའི་བཟོ་བཀོད་ཁྱད་པར་འཕགས་ལ། ཀྱོབ་གསོང་འཇིགས་པའི་རང་སྒྲ་འབྲུག་སྟོང་དུས་གཅིག་ཏུ་ལྡིར་བ་ལྟར་སྒྲོག་པ་དང་ལྷན་ཅིག་བཏགས་ཆགས་ཀྱི་ལྷ་མ་སྲིན་སྡེ་བརྒྱད་དྲེགས་པ་ཅན་ཐམས་ཅད་ཤིན་ཏུ་དྲི་ང་བའི་ཤ་རུལ་གྱི་ཕུང་པོར་བུང་བ་འདུ་བའམ་

ཤ་ཁྲག་དྲོན་མོའི་དྲི་རླངས་ལ་དུར་ཁྲོད་དུ་གཅན་གཟན་འདུར་ཞིང་བརྒྱུག་པ་ལྟར་ངམ་ངམ་ཤུགས་ཀྱིས་འདུ་བའི་ཕྱི་ནང་གསང་བའི་རྟེན་རྫས་སྤྱན་གཟིགས་མཆོད་པའི་སྤྲིན་གྱི་ཕུང་པོ་གནམ་ས་བར་མེད་དུ་གཏིབས་པ་སྡེ་བརྒྱད་དྲེགས་པའི་ཕོ་བྲང་ཆེན་པོ་འདི་ཉིད་དུ་ཚང་བ་ཡིན་ནོ། །

ཐུབ་བསྟན་དྲི་མེད་འཛམ་མགོན་བླ་མ་ཡི། །རིང་ལུགས་འཛིན་སྐྱོང་སྤེལ་མཁས་དགྲ་བཅོམ་གྱི། །འབྲས་དཀར་ཕུར་བུར་སྤྱངས་འདྲའི་ཁྲིམས་ལྡན་པའི། །འདུས་ཚོགས་བསྟི་བའི་ཆོས་སྡེ་ཆེན་པོའི་འདབས། །སྡེ་བརྒྱད་དྲེགས་པ་དང་གིས་འདུ་བའི་གནས། །མི་ཆུང་སྲིད་པ་ཡངས་པོར་ཤོང་ནུས་པ། །སྤྲུལ་རྒྱལ་པེ་ཀར་ཡུམ་བློན་དགྱེས་པའི་ཚལ། །བཟོ་སྦ་བརྒྱད་ཀྱིས་འཕགས་པའི་ཡ་མཚན་ལྗོག །ལྟགས་ཁམས་གཉིས་སྐྱེས་ལོ་ལ་འགོ་བརྩམས་ཏེ། །བཻཌཱུར་ཞུན་མའི་མདངས་འཛིན་སུམ་ལྡན་ལོར། །ལེགས་པར་གྲུབ་པའི་ངོ་མཚར་གཏྲོ་ལ། །སྒྲོ་གསུམ་རྩོལ་བས་བཞེངས་པ་འདི་རྨད་བྱུང་། །དེ་ལྟར་འབད་དགོས་ཞུ་སེར་འཆང་བའི་བསྟན། །སྲིད་པའི་རྩེ་མོར་ཐོགས་མེད་རབ་བསྒྲེག་ཅིང་། །དགའ་ལྡན་རྣམ་པར་རྒྱལ་བའི་ཕོ་བྲང་གི །ཆོས་སྲིད་ཉི་ཟླའི་འོད་ཀྱིས་ཡོངས་ཁྱབ་མཛོད། །ཀུན་མཁྱེན་རིགས་བརྒྱའི་ཁྱབ་བདག་རྡོ་རྗེའི་འཆང་། །བསྐལ་པ་རྒྱ་མཚོར་ཞབས་པད་རབ་བརྟན་ཅིང་། །བཞེད་དོན་འཕྲིན་ལས་དུས་ལས་མི་ཡོལ་བར། །རྟག་ཏུ་ཆོས་ཀྱི་དགའ་སྟོན་འགྱེད་པར་ཤོག །བྱེད་པོའི་ནད་གདོན་བར་ཆད་ཀུན་ཞི་ཞིང་། །དབང་དྲག་རྒྱས་པའི་འཕྲིན་ལས་ལེགས་བསྒྲུབས་ཏེ། །བདུད་སྡེའི་གཡུལ་རྒྱལ་འཆི་མེད་རྡོ་རྗེ་ལྟར། །བརྟན་ལ་བསམས་དོན་མ་ལུས་མྱུར་དུ་སྒྲུབས། །བཀྲ་ཤིས་སྣང་བ་གསར་པའི་ཉིན་བྱེད་ཀྱིས། །དགེ་ལེགས་པད་ཚལ་འཛུམ་དང་ཆབས་ཅིག་པར། །མི་བསྲུན་འབྱུང་པོའི་སྨག་རུམ་མཐར་བྱེད་དེ། །བདེ་སྐྱིད་ཧ་བདུན་དབང་པོས་ཁྱབ་གྱུར་ཅིག །ཅེས་གོང་ས་མཆོག་གིས་དཀར་ཆག་སྐལ་བར་ཕྲན་ཚོགས་ཀྱི་ཞིབ་ཆ་ཞབས་འདེགས་ཀྱི་ཚུལ་དུ་ཕྱག་མཛོད་ཀྱི་ཁུར་འཛིན་གྲོང་སྨད་པ་སངས་རྒྱས་རྒྱ་མཆོས་ཕལ་ཆེར་སུག་བྲིས་དང་གཞན་མ་ཆང་བསྟན་གཉིས་ཀྱིས་ཡི་གེའི་ལས་བྱས་ཏེ་ཧ་ཆེན་གྱི་ལོར་བྲིས་པ་ཛ་ཡནྟུ། །

Notes

1 ཆབ་སྲིད་ཚེ་བརྟན་ཕུན་ཚོགས་སོགས་ཀྱིས་དཔེ་སྒྲིག་མཛད། 《གྲོང་རྡོལ་ངག་དབང་བློ་བཟང་གི་གསུང་འབུམ།》 གངས་ཅན་རིག་མཛོད་༢༡ གླེགས་བམ་གཉིས་པ། བོད་ལྗོངས་བོད་ཡིག་དཔེ་རྙིང་དཔེ་སྐྲུན་ཁང་། སྤྱི་ལོ་༡༩༩༡ ལོའི་དཔར་མ། ཤ ༤༦༣ Réne de Nebesky-Wojkowitz, *Oracles and Demons of Tibet: The Cult and Iconography of the Tibetan Protective Deities*, (1956; reprint, Kathmandu: Tiwari's Pilgrims Book House, 1993), 3.

2 མཆོད་བསྟོད་དྲེགས་པའི་ལྷ་ཚོགས་ནྲ་གློང་འཁྲུག་ཅིང་དམ་ཅན་རྒྱ་མཚོ་དགྱེས་པར་སྐྱོང་བའི་མགྲིན་བཅུའི་ཕོ་བྲང་ས་ལ་འཕོས་པའི་སྟོན་མེད་བཟོ་སྦ་བརྒྱད་ཀྱིས་འཕགས་པའི་གནས་ཆུང་པེ་ཧར་ལྟོག་གི་དཀར་ཆག་ས་གསུམ་གཡོ་བའི་ང་རོ》ཤིང་པར་མ། བོད་རབ་བྱུང་བཅུ་གཅིག་པའི་ཆུ་ཁྲི་ལོ་སྟེ་༡༦༢༨ ལོར་སྡེ་སྲིད་སངས་རྒྱས་རྒྱ་མཚོས་མཛད། 《པདྨ་བཀའ་ཐང》(མཚན་བྱང་རྒྱས་པར་ཨུ་རྒྱན་གུ་རུ་པདྨ་འབྱུང་གནས་ཀྱི་སྐྱེས་རབས་རྣམ་པར་ཐར་པ་རྒྱས་པར་བཀོད་པ་ཞེས་བྱ་བ་བཞུགས་སོ) སྤྱི་ལོ་༡༢༨༥ (ལོར་ཨོ་རྒྱན་གླིང་པས་བསམ་ཡས་དང་ཤེལ་བྲག་ནས་གཏེར་ནས་བཏོན། སྡེ་དགེ་དཔར་ཁང་གི་ཤིང་པར་མ།

3 གནས་ཆུང་པེ་ཧར་ལྷོག་གམ། མཚན་གཞན་པར་གནས་ཆུང་རྡོ་རྗེ་སྒྲ་དབྱངས་གླིང་དུ་འབོད་པ་ནི་ད་ལྟའི་གྲོང་ཁྱེར་ལྷ་སའི་ནུབ་ཕྱོགས་སུ་ཆགས་པའི་འབྲས་སྤུངས་དགོན་གྱི་འདབས་རོལ་དུ་ཆགས་ཡོད། སྤྱི་ལོ་དུས་རབས་བཅུ་དྲུག་པའི་དཀྱིལ་ཙམ་དུ་འབྲས་སྤུངས་བདེ་ཡངས་གྲྭ་ཚང་གི་མཁན་པོ་ལྷོག་པ་བྱང་ཆུབ་དཔལ་ལྡན་གྱིས་ལྷོག་ཙམ་དུ་ཐོག་མར་ཕྱག་བཏབ་ཅིང་། རྗེས་སོར་རྒྱལ་དབང་ལྔ་པ་ཆེན་པོའི་དུས་སྐབས་སུ་སྡེ་སྲིད་སངས་རྒྱས་རྒྱ་མཚོས་ལྔ་པ་ཆེན་པོའི་དགོངས་བཞེད་ལྟར་ལས་གྲྭའི་ཐོག་མཐའ་བར་གསུམ་གྱི་ཐུགས་འགན་འཁུར་བཞེས་ཀྱིས་རྒྱ་བསྐྱེད་དུ་བཏང་བ་ནི། སྡེ་སྲིད་ཁོང་གིས་ རྟ་ཆེན་གྱི་ལོ་སྟེ་བོད་རབ་བྱུང་བཅུ་གཅིག་པའི་ཆུ་ཁྱི(སྤྱི་ལོ་༡༧༨༢)ལོར་མཛད་པའི་གནས་ཆུང་པེ་ཧར་ལྷོག་གི་དཀར་ཆག་ས་གསུམ་གཡོ་བའི་ང་རོ་ཞེས་པར། ཐུབ་བསྟན་དྲི་མེད་འཛམ་མགོན་བླ་མ་ཡི། །རིང་ལུགས་འཛིན་སྐྱོང་སྤྱིལ་མཁས་དགྲ་བཅོམ་གྱི། །འབྲས་དཀར་ཕུར་བུར་སྤུངས་འདྲའི་ཁྲིམས་ལྡན་པའི། །འདུས་ཚོགས་བསྡི་བའི་ཆོས་སྡེ་ཆེན་པོའི་འདབས། །སྡེ་བརྒྱད་དྲེགས་པ་དང་གིས་འདུ་བའི་གནས། །མི་ཆུང་སྲིད་པ་ཡངས་པོར་ཡོང་ནུས་པ། །སྤྲུལ་རྒྱལ་པེ་ཀར་ཡུམ་བློན་དགྱེས་པའི་ཚལ། །བཟོ་སྦྱ་བརྒྱད་ཀྱིས་འཕགས་པའི་ཡ་མཚན་ལྷོག །ལྕགས་ཁམས་གཉིས་སྐྱེས་ལོ་ལ་འགོ་བརྩམས་ཏེ། །པི་ཧྲུར་ཞུན་མའི་མདངས་འཛིན་སུམ་ལྡན་ལོར། །ལེགས་པར་གྲུབ་པའི་ངོ་མཚར་གཙུག་ལ། །སྒོ་གསུམ་རྩོལ་བས་བཞེངས་པ་འདི་རྨད་བྱུང་། །ཞེས་གསུངས་པ་ལྟར། བོད་རབ་བྱུང་བཅུ་གཅིག་པའི་ལྕགས་མོ་བྱའི་ (སྤྱི་ལོ༡༧༨༠) ལོར་འགོ་བརྩམས་ཏེ་ལོ་འགའི་རིང་རྒྱ་བསྐྱེད་ཀྱིས་ལེགས་པར་གྲུབ།

4 Nebesky-Wojkowitz, 421.

5 དགའ་གདོང་དགོན་ནི་སྔར་གྲོང་ཁྱེར་ལྷ་སའི་ནུབ་ཕྱོགས་སུ་གནས་ཆགས་པའི་གདོང་དཀར་རྫོང་གི་ཁོངས་སུ་གཏོགས་པ་སྟེ་ད་ལྟའི་གྲོང་ཁྱེར་ལྷ་ས་ནས་སྤྱི་ལེ་བཅོ་བརྒྱད་ཙམ་གྱི་ལམ་ཐག་གིས་ཆོད་པའི་སྟོད་ལུང་བདེ་ཆེན་རྫོང་ཁོངས་ཀྱི་དགའ་གདོང་གྲོང་ཚོར་ཆགས་ཡོད། སྤྱི་ལོ་དུས་རབས་བཅུ་གསུམ་པར་ཞིག་པོ་ཤེས་རབ་ཀྱིས་ཕྱག་བཏབ་ཅིང་དང་ཐོག་གྲུབ་མཐའ་རྙིང་མར་གཏོགས། གདན་ས་སེ་འབྲས་དགའ་གསུམ་ཕྱག་མ་བཏབ་པའི་སྔོན་དུ་གསང་ཕུ་དང་། སྐྱོར་མོ་ལུང་བཅས་དབུས་ཁུལ་གྱི་བཀའ་གདམས་པའི་གདན་ས་གཙོ་བོར་གྱུར་ཞིང་། རྗེས་སོར་དགེ་ལུགས་པར་བསྒྱུར་ཏེ་འབྲས་སྤུངས་སྒོ་མང་གྲྭ་ཚང་གི་ཁོངས་སུ་གཏོགས། རིམ་བཞིན་དབུས་ཁུལ་གྱི་དགེ་ལུགས་པའི་དགོན་པ་ཆེན་པོ་དྲུག་གི་ཡ་གྲལ་དུ་འཕེལ་བ་དང་། དགོན་པའི་མཁན་པོ་དགའ་གདོང་ཆོས་རྗེ་ལགས་ཀྱིས་མཛད་བཞིན་ཡོད།

6 པདྨ་བཀའ་ཐང》གཏེར་ཆེན་ཨོ་རྒྱན་གླིང་པས་གཏེར་ནས་བཏོན། སི་ཁྲོན་མི་རིགས་དཔེ་སྐྲུན་ཁང་། སྤྱི་ལོ་༡༩༩༦ ལོའི་དཔར་མ། ཤ ༣༨༥

7 སྤྱི་ལོ་༢༠༠༨ ལོའི་ཟླ་༡ པོའི་ཚེས་༢ ཉིན་དགའ་གདོང་དགོན་པ་ནས་དགོན་དེ་གར་ལོ་ངོ་ཉི་ཤུ་རིང་བཞུགས་པའི་གྲྭ་རྒན་བློ་བཟང་བསྟན་འཛིན་ལགས་ལ་བཅར་འདྲི་ཞུས་པ་ལྟར་བཀོད།

8 ལ་མོ་མི་འགྱུར་བྱང་ཆུབ་ལྷུན་གྱིས་གྲུབ་པའི་ལྷོག་ནི་གྲོང་ཁྱེར་ལྷ་སའི་ཤར་ལྷོ་མཚམས་ཀྱི་ད་ལྟའི་སྟག་རྩེ་རྫོང་གི་ལ་མོ་ཤང་དུ་གནས་ཆགས་ཤིང་། སྟག་རྩེ་རྫོང་

ནི་སྔར་སྤྱི་སྲིད་ཕག་གྲུ་བའི་སྐབས་སུ་གསར་དུ་བཙུགས་པའི་རྫོང་ཆེན་བཅུ་གསུམ་གྲས་ཀྱི་བྱེ་རི་སྟག་རྩེ་རྫོང་ཞེས་པ་ཡིན་ཏེ། དགའ་ལྡན་ཕོ་བྲང་གི་དུས་མཇུག་ཏུ་དེ་སྔའི་རྫོང་ཆེན་བཅུ་གསུམ་གྲས་ཀྱི་བདེ་ཆེན་བྲག་དཀར་རྫོང་དང་ཟླ་བསྒྲིལ་གྱིས་སྤྱི་མིང་དུ་སྟག་རྩེ་རྫོང་ཞེས་འབོད། སྤྱི་ལོ་༡༡༠༩ལོར་གླུ་མེས་ཚུལ་ཁྲིམས་ཤེས་རབས་ཀྱིས་ཕྱག་བཏབ་ཅིང་། རྗེས་སོར་གཞུང་ས་དགའ་ལྡན་ཕོ་བྲང་གི་སྐབས་སུ་གཞུང་བསྟེན་ཆོས་སྐྱོང་ལྷ་ཆེན་ཚངས་པ་དཀར་པོའི་གདན་ས་གཙོ་བོར་གྱུར།

9 དུང་དཀར་བློ་བཟང་འཕྲིན་ལས་ཀྱིས་བརྩམས། 《དུང་དཀར་ཚིག་མཛོད་ཆེན་མོ》ཀྲུང་གོའི་བོད་རིག་པ་དཔེ་སྐྲུན་ཁང་། སྤྱི་ལོ་ ༢༠༠༢ ལོའི་དཔར་མ། ཤ ༡༩༥༧ ནས ༥༨ བར།

10 ས་སྐྱ་པ་ཤཱཀྱའི་དགེ་བསྙེན་སྟགས་འཆང་ངག་དབང་ཀུན་དགའ་བསོད་ནམས་གྲགས་པ་རྒྱལ་མཚན་གྱིས་བོད་ཆུ་མོ་བྱ་ཡི་ལོར་ས་སྐྱ་དགོན་པར་མཛད། 《དཔལ་བསམ་ཡས་མི་འགྱུར་ལྷུན་གྱིས་གྲུབ་པའི་གཙུག་ལག་ཁང་ཆེན་པོ་བཀའ་སྲུང་དང་བཅས་པའི་བྱོན་ཚུལ་ལེགས་པར་བཤད་པ་ཆོས་སྐྱོང་ཡིད་བཞིན་ནོར་བུ་དགྱེས་པར་བྱེད་པའི་ཡིད་འཕྲོག་ལྷའི་རོལ་མོ་དགོས་འདོད་ཀུན་འབྱུང་》ལག་བྲིས་མ།

11 གྲོང་སྨད་པ་སངས་རྒྱས་རྒྱ་མཚོ་འམ་སྡེ་སྲིད་སངས་རྒྱས་རྒྱ་མཚོ་ལགས་ཀྱིས་རྒྱལ་དབང་ལྔ་པ་ཆེན་པོ་ངག་དབང་བློ་བཟང་རྒྱ་མཚོ་མཆོག་གི་ཕྱག་མཛོད་འཁུར་རིང་གོང་ས་མཆོག་གིས་དཀར་ཆག་སྒྲུལ་བར་ཕྲན་ཚེགས་ཀྱི་ཞིབ་ཆ་ཞབས་འདེགས་ཀྱི་ཚུལ་དུ་རྟ་ཆེན་གྱི་ལོ་སྟེ་བོད་རབ་བྱུང་བཅུ་གཅིག་པའི་ཆུ་ཁྱི(སྤྱི་ལོ་༡༧༨༢) ལོར་མཛད་པའི་དཀར་ཆག་འདི་ནི་ད་ལྟ་བོད་རང་སྐྱོང་ལྗོངས་ཡིག་ཚགས་ཁང་

གཞུང་ས་དགའ་ལྡན་ཕོ་བྲང་ཆེན་པོའི་གཞུང་བསྟེན་ཆོས་སྐྱོང་ཁག་ལ་དཔྱད་པ།

དུ་ཤིང་པར་མ་ཞིག་བཞུགས་ཡོད་པ་གང་ཞིག་ཡིག་འབྲུ་གཅིག་ཀྱང་མ་བཅོས་པར་སོར་བཞག་གིས་ལྷུས་པ་ཡིན་ཏེ། གཙོ་བོ་དཀར་ཆག་འདི་ཉིད་མཐོང་དགོན་ཞིང་། ལྷག་པར་དུ་དཀར་ཆག་འདི་རུ་གཞུང་བསྟེན་ཆོས་སྐྱོང་གི་གཙོ་བོ་གནས་ཆུང་པེ་ཧར་ཆོས་སྐྱོང་ཆེན་པོའི་བྱུང་འཕེལ་དང་འབྲེལ་ཏེ་དང་ཐོག་ཇི་ལྟར་གནས་ཆུང་པེ་ཧར་ལྷོག་དང་དམ་ཅིག་འགྲིག་པའི་སྐོར་ཙུང་ཟད་ཁ་གསལ་དུ་བཀོད་ཡོད་པ་ནི་སྤྱིར་བོད་ཀྱི་ཆོས་སྐྱོང་བྱུང་འཕེལ་གྱི་ལོ་རྒྱུས་དང་སྒོས་སུ་གཞུང་བསྟེན་ཆོས་སྐྱོང་གི་གཙོ་བོ་གནས་ཆུང་པེ་ཧར་ཆོས་སྐྱོང་ཆེན་པོའི་ཐད་ལ་ཞིབ་འཇུག་བྱེད་པར་དཔྱད་གཞིའི་ཡིག་ཆ་གལ་ཆེན་ཞིག་ཏུ་མཐོང་ནས་འདིར་ཟུར་དུ་བཀོད་པ་ཡིན་ནོ། །

Abstract

Remarks on the State Oracles and Religious Protectors of the dGa' ldan pho brang Government

DOBIS TSERING GYAL

The state oracle has existed in Tibet for a long time. During the processes of trajectory of social development, its social function and cultural characteristics have been changing over time. During the *dGa' ldan pho brang* period (1642–1959), the local government had officially recognized its own special state oracles. The local Tibetan government made intended and unintended invitation to them for making decisions on religious and political issues. At the same time, the mediums (*sku bsten pa*) became a special figures of high-ranking status in the administrative system of the *dGa' ldan pho brang*. They played an important role in the process of the development of the theocratic system (*chos srid zung 'brel gyi lam lugs*). The purpose of this chapter is to attempt to discuss four major state oracles and their *sku bsten pa* as well as the function of state oracles in the political system during the *dGa' ldan pho brang* period. An appendix includes an invocation text catalogued by De srid Sangs rgyas rgya mtsho that is now kept in the TAR archives, and which is very important for the study of gNas chung and other state oracles.

18

Risk and Social Mobility

*A Study of the Demotion and Dismissal Cases in the Careers of the dGa' ldan pho brang Officials from 1885 to 1952**

ALICE TRAVERS

At the end of the 19th century and beginning of the 20th century, the officials (*zhung zhabs*) of the Lhasa-based Tibetan central government, or dGa' ldan pho brang, were divided into a monastic branch, whose members were called *rtse drung*, and a lay branch, whose members were known as *drung 'khor*. The monastic branch was recruited from all levels of society, whereas the lay branch was recruited almost exclusively from among the aristocracy. The Tibetan aristocracy (*sku drag*) of the dGa' ldan pho brang, which consisted of around 250 families, was mainly a hereditary administrative elite; the possession of hereditary estates was indeed related to the compulsory holding of a charge by at least one member of the family in the government. The lay nobility had government service and the holding of estates in common, but huge disparities existed between families in terms of wealth, number of estates, political role and prestige. The aristocracy consisted of various hierarchically arranged sub-groups, namely the *sde dpon*, four families who claim to date back to the former kings and ministers of the Tibetan Empire (7th to 9th centuries), the *yab gzhis*, the six ennobled families of the previous Dalai Lamas, the *mi drag*, approximately eighteen rich and politically influential families[1] and finally the *sger pa*, a term that refers to all other landowners' families.[2] Several works have emphasized the significant gap between two groups within the aristocracy: the higher-ranking aristocracy, consisting of around twenty-nine families belonging to the *yab gzhis*, *sde dpon* and *mi drag* groups, who held large estates, monopolized the higher positions[3] and mostly intermarried,[4] and all the lower-ranking families.

A few aristocratic families, moreover, had also specialized in producing monk officials, called *rje drung*. Although the number of lay officials and monk officials was in principle 175 each, in reality each group was larger. Not infrequently, however, the careers of the dGa' ldan pho brang officials were interrupted by demotion (*go gnas rim pa phab*) or dismissal (*go gnas gnas dbyung*) from government service.[5] Some observers, like David Macdonald in 1932, have underlined the vulnerability of the government's officials:

> "In Tibet it is fatally easy for an official to lose favour with the Dalai Lama, or with the Government, which consists mainly of the four chief ministers and the Lonchen, or Prime Minister. The slightest friction that arises causes the lesser man to lose his place. Lama officials of high rank, with the influence of their monasteries behind them, are not in so precarious a position as their lay *brethren*. It sometimes happens that loss of position is not the only punishment that befalls a deposed official. He often suffers confiscation of property, and in some cases imprisonment, and even flogging. For more serious offences the whole family of a disgraced official may suffer, women as well as male members being mercilessly flogged if there is the slightest suspicion of their complicity."[6]

Melvyn Goldstein has also stressed in his work the idea that lay aristocrats were very vulnerable, compared with monasteries: "lay officials stood to lose not only their positions but their family estates and hereditary status."[7] On the contrary, monasteries were quite invulnerable. When they rebelled against the government and lost, they would always argue that the fault was not imputable to the monastic institution but to its temporary inhabitants, and consequently, even when they had plotted against the government, which constituted the worst form of crime, they never lost even one estate.[8] But it is not clear from Goldstein's work that lay officials should be considered more vulnerable than monk officials, as monk officials, not being real monks, could not be identified with monasteries.[9] Besides, according to him, the division between the higher-ranking aristocrats and the common noble families was tightly linked to a risk-taking attitude: "The high-status, wealthy families tended to seek positions that had or led to power and influence, while the poorer, common aristocratic families (and monk officials) tended to seek positions that offered potential for making income. [...] [The majority of the bureaucratic officials] were more interested in winning the lower bureaucratic posts and improving their economic situation than in gaining the higher political posts with their attendant dangers. Although it was hard to move up to the favorite/followers' level, it was all too easy to move downwards to the out-group, this downward movement usually being accompanied by loss of the manorial estate."[10] Indeed, common aristocrats had only one estate and if they were deprived of their government charge they could also be directly or indirectly deprived of their property, that is to say their family hereditary estate, and thus lose their status as aristocrats, although this was very rare. On the other hand, the higher-strata aristocrats who often had more than one estate could afford to lose one of them without incurring the risk of losing their social status completely.

In my research, quite surprisingly, I found that officials who had been dismissed and had lost all their rank and charge not infrequently gained back later an even higher rank than the one held before. Is it possible that dismissals and demotions could be considered paradoxically as springboards in the careers of officials? Although the phenomenon of demotion and dismissals of officials has been mentioned in different works,[11] it has never been, to my knowledge, studied in itself and by considering the whole group of officials. This study aims at checking in a systematic way, first, common statements regarding the vulnerability of government's officials, second, Melvyn Goldstein's assertion regarding the disparity of the officials' vulnerability according to their social status, and last, my query regarding the consequences an official could expect by taking risks in his career.

In order to handle the notions of risk and risk-taking in the context of the careers of the dGa' ldan pho brang officials, I draw on particular sociological works. The British anthropologists Mary Douglas and Aaron Wildavsky, for instance, have emphasized the cultural variety of risk's definitions, and of attitudes towards risk.[12] Most sociologists who have worked on risk see it as an event that can only be harmful. By contrast, here the economic approach will be followed, which does not distinguish risk of losing from risk of gaining,[13] and later we will see why.

I have found ninety cases of dismissal or demotion of officials described in the sources, from ca 1885 for the first one to 1952 for the last one. Although officials could be either monks or lay aristocrats, seventy-four out of the ninety cases concern aristocrats, i.e. more than 80 percent of the cases.[14]

The sources that allowed me to reconstruct the careers of officials having been demoted or dismissed comprise secondary literature written by travelers and diplomats, or by scholars such as Luciano Petech and Melvyn Goldstein, as well as primary sources, mainly the many biographies and autobiographies written by Tibetan noblemen and women both in English and Tibetan, British archives from the India Office Records and the Foreign Office in London, and the National Archives of India. The British presence in Tibet was the result of a long policy of expansion of the British Raj towards Tibet.[15] This policy began to take shape with the opening of a British trade agency in Yatung (Gro mo), inside the boundaries of Tibet, near Sikkim ('Bras ljongs) after the signing of the Sino-

British Convention of 1890 and of the Trade regulations of 1893. The next step was taken with the Younghusband Mission to Lhasa in 1904, whose aim was to have this Convention respected and to establish British trade interests in Tibet. The expedition made it possible for the British to open more trade agencies, in Gyantse (*rGyal rtse*) and in Gartok (*sGar thog*), in Western Tibet. Thus, for the period of study, the main posts of British officers in or near Tibet were the British trade agents of Gyantse, Yatung and Gartok and the political officer of Sikkim in Gangtok (*sGang tog*), India. After 1936 and until 1950 a British mission, called the Indian mission after 1947, was also installed in Lhasa. During this period, these officers compiled several lists of officials or *Who's Who* and wrote a regular correspondence including weekly or monthly diaries to their superiors. The letters of the British trade agents and of the head of the British mission in Lhasa were sent to the Political officer in Gangtok in Sikkim, then sent to Delhi, then sent to the India Office in London, and the most important ones again sent to the Foreign office.[16]

I will first recall some useful information regarding the structure of the Tibetan central government, of the administration and of the Tibetan aristocracy, especially regarding ranks, posts and titles, which will help to understand the whole question of risk-taking in the careers of the officials. Most of the officials were given a post either in the government, in the army, in the house of the Dalai Lama or in the territorial administration. The main structure of the government was shaped by the Fifth Dalai Lama in the 17th century and later reformed several times. The main offices that existed until the 1950s, the council of ministers (*bka' shag*), the ecclesiastic office (*yig tshang*), the finance office (*rtsis khang*) and the numerous smaller offices, were already in existence at the beginning of the 18th century. Government officials were given ranks and titles. Ranks were organized according to a scale inherited from the Manchu system, with seven levels, and introduced in 1792.[17] The first rank was for the Dalai Lama and the Panchen Lama (*Pan chen bla ma*), the second rank for the regent (*sde srid*) and the grand minister (*srid blon* or *blon chen*), the third rank for the ministers of state (*bka' blon* or *zhabs pad*) and the chief abbot (*spyi khyab mkhan po*), and the holders of some titles like *gung*, *dza sag* or *tha'i ji*, the fourth for the grand accountants (*rtsis dpon*) and ecclesiastical secretaries (*drung yig chen mo*), and so on.[18] The hierarchy of ranks had direct implications on the daily life of their recipients in terms of rights, precedence and privileges. Most of the time, ranks were obtained by their being attached to particular posts or titles. The titles could be attached to a post or not, and sometimes an official could have a title that bestowed upon him a higher rank than the charge entitled him to.

A precise study of the demotion and dismissal cases will allow us to delve deeper into aspects of the Tibetan central administration and the officials' lives, which have not been studied in detail before. We would like to investigate a set of questions which this phenomenon raises: What types of sanctions or punishment (*khrims chad*) were taken against the officials concerned? What were the reasons expressed for such demotions or dismissals, what faults or crimes (*nyes pa*) were committed? How were these events experienced by the officials concerned and their families? What were the long term consequences of these events on the careers? Were some sub-strata of the lay aristocracy more vulnerable than others? Which types of posts entailed a risk of going through demotion or dismissal? Can we link these events with special periods and events in Tibet's political history?

All these considerations can lead to a better understanding of the relationship between the dGa' ldan pho brang government and its officials. It sheds light on the way the government managed its staff and on the professional strategies resorted to by the officials, whether successful or unsuccessful. The question of the link between demotion or dismissal and social mobility is of great significance for our understanding of the organization of Tibetan aristocracy. We will try to assess the importance of risk-taking and its consequences in the officials' careers, and to investigate if risk-taking in careers can really be a means of constructing social distinction among lay officials and hence a way of creating or reinforcing the internal hierarchy among the aristocracy.

1. Description of the Dismissal and Demotion Cases

1.1. Officials dismissed or demoted

Generally speaking, only officials were punished, but sometimes their families were also affected. When an official was banished or flogged, the whole family could be sentenced to the same punishment. For instance, an official named Khyung rtse ram pa rDo rje rgyal po was demoted in 1940 by the regent, on the grounds that he had plotted against the government; he was banished to Ru thog in Western Tibet. Because of the seriousness of the accusation, his two wives were sent back to their families and his children forbidden to ever serve in the government.[19] However, the opposite could also happen. The lay official Pha lha, for example, was accused of having helped Sarat Chandra Das, an Indian pandit sent to Tibet by the British government of India. He was banished very far from Lhasa and was allowed to return there only two years later, though he was not re-employed in government service. Before he came back, and despite his banishment, one of his sons was allowed to stay in the family house in Lhasa and to start a career in the government.[20]

The study of our corpus allows us to make it clear that lay officials were more vulnerable than monk officials; although there was nearly the same number of lay and monk officials serving the government, there are actually three times more lay officials than monk officials listed among the demoted or dismissed officials.

1.2. Sanctions taken against the officials at fault

When an official happened to fail in his government service, a sanction was decided either by a trial or by direct decision of the Dalai Lama or the regent. Several degrees in the range of sanctions from the mild to the severe can be identified: financial sanction or fine (*dngul chad*); corporal sanction: flogging (*rta lcag gzhus pa*), rarely blinding[21] and amputations (but this was normally not the case for noblemen);[22] spiritual sanctions, like prostrations (*phyag btsal*); seizure of property (*sa khang gzhung bzhes* or *kha dbang gzhung bzhes*);[23] imprisonment (*btson bcug*) with a temporary suspension of the charges (in thirteen cases, i.e. 14 percent of all cases); demotion from one to several ranks (*go gnas rim pa phab*); dismissal without demotion, that is to say without losing the rank in fourteen cases (15 percent of all cases);[24] demotion with dismissal, which was the most frequent case (*go gnas gnas dbyung*); removal from government service for one or many generations (*las zhabs chab cig gnas dbyung*) (in twenty-two cases out of seventy-one cases where this information was known, i.e. 30 percent of all cases);[25] banishment (*rgyang 'bud btang*) in twelve cases, i.e. 13 percent.

All these sanctions could be temporary or permanent, depending on the evolution of the political background. Some officials who had been banished for life were forgiven and recalled to government service, but in most cases they did not have an outstanding career. Very often officials who had been dismissed and subsequently recalled were given a charge or a mission in a far-flung area, either to punish them or to test them. In the biography written by Tsha rong bDud 'dul rnam rgyal of his father, Tsha rong Zla bzang dgra' dul (1888–1959), we read:

> "What Kungo Surkhang was telling his friends in the tea shop that day was how he had been dismissed from his post, and considered himself lucky not to have been sent on service to Kham (eastern Tibet). This was eventually told to His Holiness, and soon Kungo Surkhang was sent to eastern Tibet on service. However, this was, in fact, exactly where he wanted to go."[26]

Sometimes the punishment was increased if the official tried to reduce it, as was the case of lCags sprag pa dBang chen nor bu,[27] who was degraded in 1942 to the rank of common official, the 7th rank:

> "The reason of the degradation was due to his late attendance in the annual New Year ceremony at the Potala. The Regent has contemplated imposing a trifling punishment of bowing down about 200 times a day before the Cathedral for a fortnight (an olden day's honourable punishment given to the officials by the late Dalai Lama). Chang-tak-pa got this timely information and approached the Regent with customary presents to ask his pardon. This annoyed the Regent and reduced him to the lowest rank."[28]

There were notable disparities in the sanctions for the same kind of offences, probably because Tibetan law codes did not have fixed punishment connected to specific offences. It was up to the judge to decide upon the matter, as "the Tibetan system posits the uniqueness of individual cases as an initial principle."[29]

1.3. Reasons given for the punishment of officials

What charges were leveled against the officials, and what kind of excesses, offences or crimes had they committed? Society shapes delinquency according to the image it projects of itself, so even if these charges were not always true, but sometimes forged, it is still interesting and worthwhile to study them.[30]

Over the whole corpus, there are several different charges leveled against the officials, from the most frequent to the least frequent.[31] In twenty-five cases, the officials are said to have committed a dereliction of duty. They have either

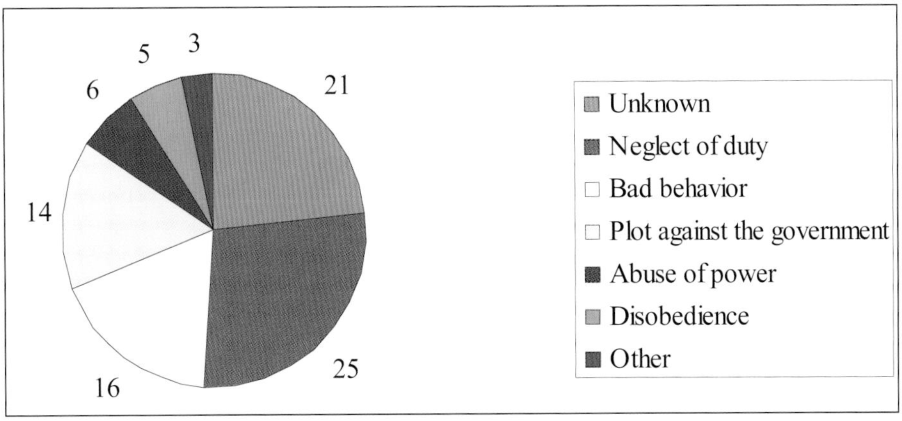

Figure 1: *Charges leveled against the officials (number of cases)*

failed in their mission, been inefficient, failed to transmit orders or failed to transmit orders quickly enough,[32] proven unable to administer such and such things, failed to report a theft,[33] for instance, or in the case of the state oracle, made false prophecies.[34]

In sixteen cases the official was punished for what we could call "inappropriate or bad behavior." This large category encompasses very different offences, such as being late to a ceremony[35] or, for a police officer, arresting monks.[36] Sometimes the charge is so minor that it was obviously only an excuse to get the official concerned removed, such as military officials being dismissed for having cut their hair in a Western fashion,[37] or a monk official who was dismissed for having a picture taken during an official ceremony and hence displaying an "alien body attitude" judged as most inappropriate.[38]

Some officials were also dismissed if they had expressed views not in harmony with what was, at the moment, the "main stream" of ideas regarding external policy. For instance, the ministers who pronounced themselves in favor of negotiating with the British during the Younghusband Mission in 1904 were subsequently dismissed.[39]

An official could be dismissed or demoted not only for a misdeed in his professional life, but in private life as well. A lay official tried to seduce the wife of another lay official and was dismissed;[40] another one was degraded for having used a motorcycle and frightening people.[41]

In fourteen cases, officials were accused of plotting against the government.[42] In six cases, officials were charged with abuses of power: four of them were accusations of corruption, and two were unclear. In five cases, disobedience was the reason invoked: in three cases the officials left their post without permission,[43] and in another case an official was appointed to China as representative of the Tibetan government, but he refused to go there to take up his charge.[44]

The study of the Tibetan nobility raises several questions regarding the importance of careers in the social identity of the aristocrats. More precisely, what were the consequences of their professional advancement or demotion on their global social status? For instance, most families that counted a minister among their ancestors were called *mi drag* and were considered very prestigious and high-ranking aristocrats. The sons of the *sde dpon* and *mi drag* had the privilege of starting their professional career directly with the title of *sras rnam pa*, just beneath the fourth rank, unlike the common new officials who started with the 7th rank. This meant that they had better chances of getting a higher ranking post and of having a better career. In this sense, professional advancement was at the same time the source and the result of a high social status. Therefore, the consequences of career accidents such as demotion or dismissal are worth investigating.

2. Demotion or Dismissal and Careers: the Role of the Event in the Professional and Personal Destiny of Officials

Let us now turn to the relationship between demotion or dismissal and social identity. The key issue here is whether these events could be interpreted as social downward mobility.

2.1. Demotions and dismissals: a ritual and an experience

Demotion and dismissal were quite dramatic events. Except for one case, that of Tsha rong Zla bzang dgra 'dul, who was dismissed through a letter,[45] officials had to undergo a humiliating ritual. In Shud khud pa 'Jam dbyangs mkhas sgrub's account of his case, the whole event is perceived, unsurprisingly, as sad and painful. He recalls how one of the commoners who was working for him when he was a district governor (*rdzong dpon*) placed a complaint against him with the government in Lhasa. Shud khud pa lost the case, and hence his post, and he was forbidden to work for the government ever again:

> "One day a high-ranking accountant named Trogawa arrived from Lhasa to investigate the complaint. Although this official supported my case, my opponents in the Rangpang Pesurva family had secretly sought backing from another high-ranking accounting minister. The case was finally decided against me, using circumstantial evidence of my incompetence and cruelty. I lost my post and was forbidden to work for the government again. I transferred the governorship of the lower dzong to my replacement – a man named Gyimepa who was sympathetic toward me, which only made matters worse. I gave the upper dzong back to the monastery. It was a sorrowful day for my wife and family when I left the (Hray) District in disgrace, returning to my family home on the Shud khud estate."[46]

The same official, who was then reintegrated into government service, later served as a military officer, and was then dismissed again, together with a colleague of his. Apparently, he was informed shortly beforehand and took with him the boots and the hat of his colleague, who was ill and could not come, and went to the morning official's daily assembly in the Potala. These two things, the boots and the hat, were usually confiscated during a dismissal ceremony. In his autobiography, he describes the ritual as follows:

> "At the Shoga, tea was served in the normal fashion; however, they treated me as if I were not there. One of my friends lent me a bowl so that I might drink a cup. Then

the Regent Taktra's number one aide, Thubten Lekmun, signaled me to rise. I got up, took off my hat, and bowed. Then I heard the verdict. They said, 'Your soldiers were responsible for the destruction of the possessions of Reting Monastery; therefore uda [military title meaning 'general of central province'; *dbus kyi mda' dpon or dbus mda'*], the central commander, is to be demoted from the rank of captain to the rank of ordinary staff'. They took away all the signs of my commander's rank: my hat and my brocade robe, my knife and my tea cup container, my rainbow boots, and my hanging gold pendant mounted with a large turquoise. [...] After my demotion, I went to a room nearby to put on civilian boots and a civilian hat. I was instructed to leave from the back door of the Potala.'"[47]

Dismissal was symbolically associated with a kind of social death, as we understand from several accounts. In her autobiography g.Yu thog rDor rje g.yu sgron describes what happened to her father, Zur khang:

"The reading of the demotion order would be followed by the removal of the badges of the former rank together with the official robe of the demoted person. Besides that, other honorary symbols were taken back by the government. Sometimes when the official did not know beforehand that he was to be demoted, he had to return home wearing only the thin robe usually worn underneath the heavy golden robes made from Chinese brocade. This embarrassment happened to careless officials. Our father was once demoted. [...] He happened to know beforehand that his demotion would take place, so on the day he received the summons he brought a servant with him who carried a bag of clothing for my father to wear on the way home. He was made to stand before the monks officials and remove his hat, holding it in both hands before his chest while bowing slightly. The hair ornament which indicated his position, a turquoise and gold amulet box customarily worn on the head by a fourth rank official, was removed. We were surprised when he came home without his beautiful ornaments and naturally felt terrible. It was almost like meeting a person who had died, so everyone in the family started to weep. Even the servants wept. [...] All of us were very worried and upset about the demotion, but father himself was never concerned at all because he was a carefree type of person.'"[48]

The dismissal was usually followed by a period of comfort given by family members and friends. According to custom, people came to pay a consolation visit to the official for a few days after his dismissal with money wrapped in a ceremonial scarf (*kha btags*).[49]

The ritual of banishment was even more dramatic. The culprit, wearing white clothes, was put on a donkey or a mule and sent of.[50] It is interesting to note that this kind of staging, of dramatization, brings to mind another ritual that took place every year at the end of the second month of the lunar calendar, the *glud 'gong rgyal po* (lit. "King-demon-ransom"), as Samten Karmay underlines in his study of this ritual.[51] Two people, the *glud 'gong*, were ritually driven out of Lhasa and banished for a year, one to bSam yas and one to 'Phan po.[52]

The reactions of the concerned officials were various. One committed suicide,[53] two who had only been degraded decided to resign definitely from the government service;[54] they asked permission of the government, which granted it. Sometimes, as in the case of Zur khang, the officials did not seem to be too painfully stricken by the event, and Zur khang even took up the opportunity to indulge more in religious activities. There were, perhaps, good reasons for officials not to worry too much after this kind of incident.

2.2. Demotions and dismissals: a little game without consequences?

From an individual and familial point of view, demotions and dismissals, as we have seen, could be lived as difficult experiences, especially in the rare cases of banishment. But if we look at the group of officials as a whole, dismissals rarely meant a definitive end to an official's career: indeed quite often they did not have serious consequences in the long term. First of all, even when the dismissal was meant as definitive, in most cases the official was later allowed to serve again in the government. So in most cases, sentences were not permanent.[55] Moreover, it is interesting to look at the balance between rank gaining and rank losing for each case. For the seventy-four cases in which the rank is known, the average rank held by officials who were degraded was the fourth rank. The average rank of officials just after the event is sixth, but if we look again some time later, the average rank has again risen to fourth.[56] On average, officials were degraded 2.1 ranks[57] and regained 2.2 ranks.[58] Thus, the majority of the officials who were degraded regained ranks at least as high as those they held before their demotion. In this regard, although lay officials were indeed more vulnerable than monk officials, even they seem to be hardly vulnerable in the long run.

Apparently then, there were few long term consequences when an official was dismissed or removed during his career, but we have to take into account an element which qualifies this claim: regaining one's rank meant that the rank was regained, but not necessarily the charge that went with it. And it should be noted that most of the time, it was the charge itself that gave an official his political influence and prestige.[59]

For instance, a minister who was deprived of his charge and of the fourth rank attached to the post could be later given the title of *dza sag*, which indicates a rank between the third and the fourth, but, in spite of this honorific title, he would never regain the political power and social prestige his previous charge had given him before.

We could now wonder if the fact that the average rank of the demoted officials was the fourth is any indication of the identity of the degraded officials. The work of Mary Douglas and Aaron Wildavsky, *Risk and Culture*, gives us some hints. Indeed, the authors underline this: "The choice of risks and the choice of how to live are taken together. Each form of social life has its own typical risk portfolio. Common values lead to common fears (and, by implication, to a common agreement not to fear other things)."[60] This means that if we consider demotions and dismissals not only as accidents due to bad luck but also as consequences of risk-taking, these events could in fact confirm that the officials concerned belonged to a particular group of the aristocracy which has accepted risk-taking in their careers.

3. Demotions or Dismissals and Hierarchy within the Aristocracy: Risk-Taking as a Criterion of Social Distinction

It is important to establish if these demotions or dismissals are more likely to occur in certain types of careers, and hence if they have something to do with an attitude of risk-taking.

3.1. Professional choices and risk-taking

The first step is to determine more precisely who gets degraded. We can infer from the sources that thirty individuals came from the higher strata of the aristocracy (three *sde dpon*, eleven *yab gzhis*, sixteen *mi drag*), forty-five from the common aristocracy and eleven from commoners – those being monk officials.[61] The higher strata are overrepresented, since they normally represent only 10 percent of the entire aristocracy but over 30 percent of my corpus. This disparity could come from the sources I consulted, since the British were more likely to report what happened to the people they knew best, *i.e.* the higher-ranking aristocrats. This could also confirm Melvyn Goldstein's idea, mentioned above, that the officials who held high ranking posts were more at risk of being deprived of their ranks and functions. The higher you rose, and the more power you wielded, the likelier you were to incur some form of punishment at one time or another.[62] It is a common fact in bureaucracies that some offices carry more risk potential than others, depending on their degree of closeness to political power and their degree of entanglement with political issues.[63] When there are political changes, a purge most often concerns only the higher strata of the pyramid of careers.[64] In Tibet this was also the rule. Officials had more chances of being degraded if they were in charge of certain types of posts. It appears that, among lay officials affected by such unhappy events, we find many municipal officers and many military officers. Reasons accounting for military careers being risky are quite obvious. Indeed, during the first half of the 20th century, the Thirteenth Dalai Lama and other lay officials tried to lead a huge military reform, which was strongly opposed, mainly by monks; and military officers were recruited or demoted depending on the balance of power between the anti-military faction and the military officers with the Dalai Lama and the ministers. Therefore, some fathers did not like the idea of their sons being appointed to a military charge: Tsha rong Zla bzang dgra' dul who, having experienced much hardship in his career, due *inter alia* to his military responsibilities, refused that his son take up a military career.[65] At the same time, we have to admit that if we take the long view, these kinds of posts did offer opportunities for upward mobility as well. The ability of officials to shape to some degree their own careers was dependent on their personal abilities, but also on the material and social capital they enjoyed. This leads us to face the question of the unsteadiness of Tibetan political life during the period under scrutiny, and of subsequent renewal cycles of the political staff.

3.2. Chosen or suffered risk? On the nature of the Tibetan political system

It is important to distinguish between risk that is undergone or suffered during political crises, for instance, and risk that is voluntarily taken when an official embarks upon a military career or high-ranking post. According to our sources, which are not at all exhaustive, there were on average between one and two demotion or dismissal cases each year. But the number of cases per year in fact varied from zero to eleven. The number of demotions or dismissals per year seems to be directly correlated with the fluctuations of political circumstances. These could be linked to the changing of the ruler after the death of the Thirteenth Dalai Lama (1933), and after the changing of the regent. When a dismissal or demotion is not easy to explain, or the ground explained is trivial, very often the event took place in the context of a major political crisis.

If we look at the evolution of the number of dismissal or demotion cases during the period, we can track down three major political crises. The first crisis took place between 1920 and 1925, when there was a huge quarrel on the question of the army, because it was decided to levy a tax to provide for the needs of a new army. The opponents of this policy were convinced that the army represented

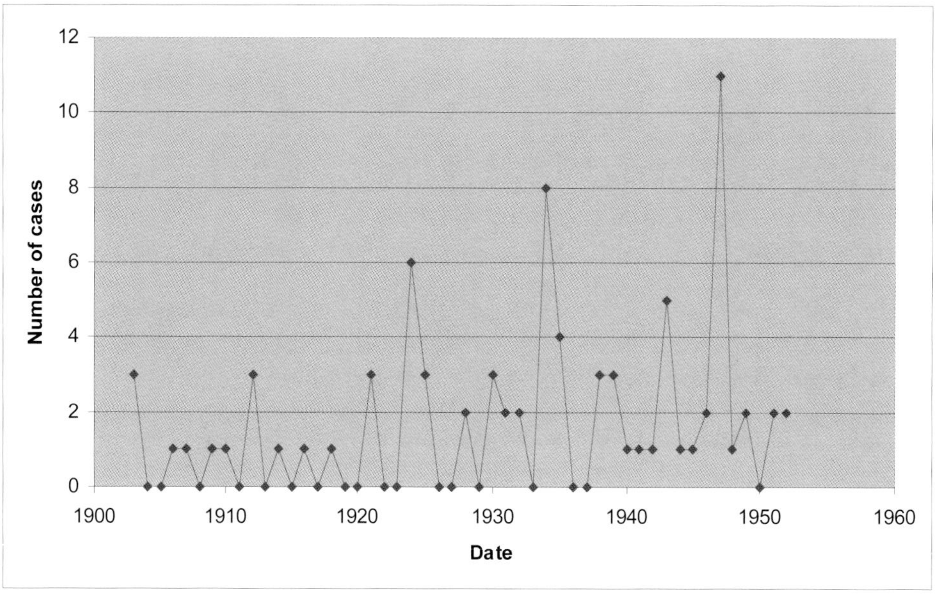

Figure 2: *Chronology of the demotion and dismissal cases*

a danger for the government and used several pretexts to get rid of the military staff.[66] The second crisis happened in 1933, after the death of the Thirteenth Dalai Lama, when Rwa sgreng was chosen as regent. This was to the detriment of other favorites and their political followers who were also demoted. For instance, Lung shar was demoted in 1934 and accused of plotting against the government, because he wanted to reform it. From 1934 to 1940, during Rwa sgreng's rule, "any official who defied him or spoke out against him was demoted, dismissed, or utterly destroyed."[67] In 1940, Rwa sgreng resigned and sTag brag took up the post of regent.[68] The third crisis occurred in 1947, when Rwa sgreng tried to take back the power by force; he was helped by other officials and was arrested with them.[69] Hence, the demotions and dismissals were the result of the combination of chosen and suffered risk. The space for personal initiative in the shaping of careers did exist. It is precisely in this space that the notions of risk and risk-taking are relevant and useful, along with the idea that officials would try to reduce the impact of the diffuse risk caused by unstable political circumstances.

To conclude, the impression that risk-taking might be profitable, because the officials who had fallen the most stood to regain the most, was mistaken. Such an impression is simply the consequence of the fact that in most cases people would regain their former rank, and hence, if they had a high rank or if they belonged to the elite, which was structurally likely to get a high post and a high rank, the demotion or dismissal would only temporarily hinder their career progress. It would then be more correct to say that the whole phenomenon of dismissals and demotions of officials is representative of one interesting aspect of the Tibetan political system, being at the same time very unstable and structurally conservative. It is unstable since the phenomenon of dismissals and demotions was strongly related, as indeed it is in most administrations, to the ups and downs of Tibetan political life and also to the insufficient number of estates available.[70] The Tibetan political system is shown to be conservative because, except for a few spectacular cases, mostly grave crimes, the events in the long term did not have a serious impact on careers or the rank and social status of the once demoted or dismissed officials, mostly aristocrats.

Notes

* I would like to thank the research team EA 1587 of the University of Paris X-Nanterre for their financial assistance, which allowed me to attend the first International Seminar of Young Tibetologists (ISYT). This research is part of a prosopographical study of the dGa' ldan pho brang aristocracy, towards a doctorate in social history under the supervision of Professors Jean Duma (University of Paris X-Nanterre) and Heather Stoddard (INALCO).

1 Their number varies depending on the sources.
2 Although the term *sger pa* technically means all the landowners' families, when speaking of the Tibetan aristocracy, my Tibetan informants often use it to refer to the lesser aristocracy, the ones who do not own any higher title, as opposed to the first three sub-groups, the *sde dpon*, the *yab gzhis* and the *mi drag*. This use can also be found in the literature produced by Tibetan aristocrats, cf. Blo bzang don grub Sreg shing, "De snga'i bod sa gnas srid gzhung gi sku drag shod drung ngam sger pa ngo yod gang dran ming tho." in *Bod kyi lo rgyus rig gnas dpyad gzhi'i rgyu cha bdams bsgrigs*, ed. Bod rang skyong ljongs srid gros lo rgyus rig gnas dpyad gzhi'i rgyu cha u yon lhan khang (Beijing: Mi rigs dpe skrun khang, 2003), vol. 23, 182–185, and Dorje Yudon Yuthok, *The House of the Turquoise Roof* (1990; reprint, Ithaca: Snow Lion Publications, 1995), 31 and 306. So in this paper, this custom will be followed.
3 Melvyn C. Goldstein, *A History of Modern Tibet, 1913–1951: The Demise of the Lamaist State* (1989; reprint, New Delhi: Munshiram Manoharlal Publishers, 1993), 17; Melvyn C. Goldstein, "An Anthropological Study of the Tibetan Political System" (PhD Dissertation, Seattle: University of Washington, 1968), 187; and Luciano Petech, *Aristocracy and Government in Tibet, 1728–1959* (Rome: Serie Orientale Roma, XLV, 1973), 19.
4 Alice Travers, "La noblesse du Tibet central de 1895 à 1959: essai de définition d'un groupe social, stratégies matrimoniales et familiales" (DEA Dissertation: University of Paris X-Nanterre, 2004).
5 By "demotion" I mean the losing of the grade, or degradation, and by "dismissal" I mean the losing of the charge or the position. Both could happen jointly or separately, as we will see later.
6 David Macdonald, *Twenty Years in Tibet* (1932; reprint, New Delhi: Vintage Books, 1995), 209.
7 Goldstein 1989, 820.

8 Ibid. Monasteries were landlords, as were the aristocrats and the government.

9 Ibid., 10. And indeed, according to the same author, for different reasons, the lay segment was superior to the monk segment in the administration, especially because, unlike monk officials, lay officials, having estates and family connections, could afford to be disloyal to the government, cf. Goldstein 1968, 193 and 206.

10 Goldstein 1989, 18. See also Goldstein 1968, 185 and 210.

11 Goldstein 1989 and Petech.

12 Mary Douglas and Aaron Wildavsky, *Risk and Culture, An Essay on the Selection of Technological and Environmental Dangers* (Berkeley: University of California Press, 1982).

13 Patrick Peretti-Watel, *Sociologie du risque* (Paris: Armand Colin, 2000).

14 Sixty-five cases concern lay officials (three *sde dpon*, nine *yab gzhis*, fifteen *mi drag*, thirty-eight *sger pa*), twenty-one concern monk officials, among whom six are noblemen (two *yab gzhis*, one *mi drag*, three *sger pa*), and fifteen are commoners (*mi ser*). Lastly, four cases concern officials whose status, whether monk or lay, is unknown and among whom there are three noblemen and one commoner.

15 See Alastair Lamb's works in the bibliography and Alex McKay, *Tibet and the British Raj. The Frontier Cadre 1904–1947* (London: Curzon, 1997).

16 The British archives I have used to document the cases of demotion and dismissal of Tibetan aristocrats are thus located in three different places: in the National Archives of India in New Delhi, in the India Office Records (British Library) and in the Public Records Office, in London.

17 Petech, 8.

18 Cf. Charles Bell, *Report on the government of Tibet* (Calcutta: Office of the superintendent of government printing, 1906, IOR/L/P&S/10/150); Frederick Williamson, *Note on titles and official ranks in Tibet* (1934, PRO/FO/371/19253), 1–3; "Order of Precedence of Tibetan Government Officials," in *Who's Who in Tibet, Corrected with a few subsequent additions up to 30th September 1948* (Calcutta: Government of India Press, 1949, IOR/L/P&S/20D220/2), 9–12; Petech, 7–14 and Goldstein 1968. This is not the place to enter into details, but it should be noted that the rank system underwent some changes during the period under scrutiny. One of the main changes was that the two first ranks, which were used especially for some titles, were not used during the 1940s; the positions corresponding to these ranks were just said to be "above the system of rank."

19 *Revised Who's Who in Tibet* (1944, PRO/FO/371/46121), 22 and *Lhasa Mission Diary for the month of June 1940* (IOR/L/P&S/12/4193). For a detailed description of the events which are linked to the case, see Goldstein 1989, 347–48; Thub bstan bstan dar lHa'u rta ra, "Tha'i ji Khyung ram Don grub rgyal po las zhabs gnas dbyung gis btson bcug rgyang 'bud btang skor." In *Bod kyi lo rgyus rig gnas dpyad gzhi'i rgyu cha bdams bsgrigs*, ed. Bod rang skyong ljongs srid gros lo rgyus rig gnas dpyad gzhi'i rgyu cha u yon lhan khang (Beijing: Mi rigs dpe skrun khang, 2003), vol. 8, 115–31; Rig 'dzin rnam rgyal Khyung ram, "Nga'i pha Khyung ram Don grub rgyal por khrims chad phog pa'i lo rgyus." In *Bod kyi lo rgyus rig gnas dpyad gzhi'i rgyu cha bdams bsgrigs*, ed. Bod rang skyong ljongs srid gros lo rgyus rig gnas dpyad gzhi'i rgyu cha u yon lhan khang, (Beijing: Mi rigs dpe skrun khang, 2003), vol. 8, 132–38.

20 Petech, 86 and Charles Bell, *The People of Tibet* (1928; reprint, Delhi: Motilal Banarsidass Publishers, 1992), 106. Actually, two of his three sons were employed in the government, the third one being a monk, cf. *Weekly Frontier Confidential Report for the Week ending the 24th January 1903* (IOR/L/P&S/7/151/P347).

21 The only example during the period under scrutiny being that of Lung shar, who was blinded in 1934 after having been charged with conspiracy against the government, cf. Goldstein 1989, 208–209, and *Who's Who in Tibet, Corrected to the Autumn of 1937, with a few subsequent additions up to February 1938* (Calcutta: Government of India Press, 1938, IOR/L/P&S/12/4185A),

44.

22 It was normally forbidden to give this punishment. One example during the period under scrutiny is the amputation inflicted by Tsha rong Zla bzang dgra' dul, for which he himself was punished in 1925, cf. Macdonald, 210.

23 In this study, these four types of sanctions were not taken into account if they occurred alone, without other more serious sentences, because they did not have any direct implication on the official's professional career. Note also that officials could receive a combination of different sanctions at one time.

24 This meant that you could still enjoy the privileges of your rank.

25 An official could be dismissed and lose his post, without losing his status of being an official.

26 Dundul Namgyal Tsarong, *In the Service of His Country. The Biography of Dasang Damdul Tsarong* (Ithaca: Snow Lion Publications, 2000), 82.

27 *Who's Who in Tibet* (1948), 14.

28 *Yatung news for the period ending 15th December 1942* (IOR/L/P&S/12/4208/P1586).

29 See Rebecca Redwood French, *The Golden Yoke: The Legal Cosmology of Buddhist Tibet* (Ithaca: Cornell University Press, 1995), 318.

30 Romain Telliez makes this point in his book *Les officiers devant la justice dans le Royaume de France au XIV*[e] *siècle* (Paris: Honoré Champion, 2005), 12.

31 I have not taken into account the officials who were forced to retire, like the ministers bKras khang *zhabs pad* in 1939, cf. Goldstein 1989, 337, and Khri smon *zhabs pad*, cf, ibid., 314.

32 See for instance IOR/L/P&S/11/75/P1118; IOR/L/P&S/12/4202; *Who's Who in Tibet* (1948), 40, 59, 76.

33 Goldstein 1989, 448 and *Who's Who in Tibet* (1948), 113.

34 Michael E. Hoffman, ed., *Tibet, The Sacred Realm, Photographs 1880–1950*, Chronicle by Lobsang Lhalungpa (1983; reprint, New York: Aperture Foundation, 1997), 21, and Heinrich Harrer, *Seven Years in Tibet* (1953; reprint, New York: Jeremy P. Tarcher/Putnam, 1997), 202.

35 *Yatung news for the period ending 15th December 1942* (IOR/L/P&S/12/4208/P1586).

36 *Annual Report on the British Trade Agency at Gyantse for the year ending 31st March 1925, dated Gangtok the 14th April 1925* (IOR/L/P&S/10/218/P1530).

37 Ibid., and Rinchen Dolma Taring, *Daughter of Tibet* (1970; reprint, London: Wisdom Publications, 1986), 91.

38 Heinrich Harrer, *Return to Tibet* (1984; reprint, London: Phoenix, 2000), 76.

39 *List of leading officials, nobles, and personages in Bhutan, Sikkim, and Tibet, 1908* (Calcutta, Superintendent government printing, India, 1909), 14. I would like to thank Frank Drauschke for having kindly helped me to find this particular document.

40 Yuthok, 41.

41 *Who's Who in Tibet* (1937), 45 and Spencer Chapman, *Lhasa, The Holy City* (Delhi: Bodhi Leaves Corporation, [1940] 1992), 85.

42 For instance Bell 1928, 91; Petech, 27, 62, 215; *Who's Who in Tibet* (1948), 32, 54, 141; *Annual Report on the BTA, Gyantse, Tibet for the year ending 31st March 1930* (IOR/L/P&S/12/4166/P3640).

43 *Who's Who in Tibet* (1948), 73, 79; *Lhasa letter for the week ending 4th July 1943* (IOR/L/P&S/12/4201).

44 *Who's Who in Tibet* (1948), 142.

45 Tsarong, 79.

46 Sumner Carnahan and Lama Kunga Rinpoche, Ngor Thartse Shabtrung, *In the Presence of my Enemies: Memoirs of Tibetan Nobleman Tsipon Shuguba* (New Mexico: Clear Light Publishers, 1995), 38.

47 Ibid., 132.

48 Yuthok, 41. For another official: "His head ornament was taken off and his hair undone; his official silk dress was removed and his official boots. The unfortunate man had to send home for a broadcloth dress." *Lhasa Mission Diary for the month of August 1939* (IOR/L/P&S/12/4193).

49 Ibid., 42. The British agents were involved in these customs. For instance, after Phun khang *zhabs pad* had been degraded to the rank of *gung* on 25 November 1946, Hugh E. Richardson, the then officer in charge of the British mission in Lhasa, paid him a visit of condolence on 30 November, cf. *Lhasa letter for the week ending the 1st December 1946*, IOR/L/P&S/12/4202.

50 An ox is also mentioned in this case, see Samten Karmay, "L'homme et le bœuf: le rituel du *glud* ('rançon')," *Journal asiatique* 279.3–4 (1991), 363.

51 Ibid., 362.

52 See also Rolf A. Stein, *La civilisation tibétaine* (1962; reprint, Paris: L'Asiathèque-Le Sycomore, 1981), 149 and René de Nebesky-Wojkowitz, *Oracles and Demons of Tibet. The Cult and Iconography of the Tibetan Protective Deities* (Kathmandu: Tiwari's Pilgrims Book House, 1993), 507 *sq*. Samten Karmay has shown that, contrary to what many authors thought, the ritual had nothing to do with the idea of a scapegoat. The ritual assumed a protective and therapeutic function: the *glud 'gong* was considered to be the ransom of the body of the Tibetan hierarchs to the divinity Pehar, cf. Karmay, 343.

53 Hor khang, a minister who was degraded in May 1904, cf. *Weekly Frontier Confidential Report for the week ending on Saturday, the 7th May 1904, dated Darjeeling, the 10th May 1904* (NAI/FD/SecE/Nov1905/73-107/P95). See also Petech, 195.

54 *Who's Who in Tibet* (1937), 65 and *Chiefs and Leading Families in Sikkim, Bhutan and Tibet* (Calcutta: Superintendent government Printing, 1915, PRO/F0/371/2318), 21.

55 In sixty cases we know that the sentence was temporary, in only four cases we know it was definitive and twenty-six are undetermined.

56 In the forty-eight cases for which this information is known.

57 In the fifty-two cases where this information is known.

58 In the thirty-six cases where the two pieces of information are known.

59 Goldstein 1989, 12 and Goldstein 1968, 168. Some promotions were in fact disguised demotions, as for instance the bestowing of the honorific title of *mkhan chen* to monk officials who lost their previous charge and no longer had the power they held before, although their title was higher, cf. *Annual Report of the British trade agent, Yatung, for the year ending the 31st March 1944* (IOR/L/P&S/12/4166/P2577).

60 Douglas and Wildavsky, 8.

61 Although my main focus is the lay officials, because some monk officials belong to the aristocracy and because I wanted to get a global view of this phenomenon, I took into account the monk officials in the inventory of the cases of demotion or dismissal.

62 As the Roman saying goes: *Arx tarpeia Capitoli proxima.*

63 "[...] Un contrôle d'autant plus pointilleux que l'on s'élève dans la hiérarchie des offices: les serviteurs du prince font d'autant plus fréquemment l'objet de poursuites qu'ils occupent un rang élevé, bénéficient d'autant plus facilement de la grâce royale qu'ils occupent des postes subalternes," cf. Telliez, 683.

64 Dominique Chagnollaud, *Le premier des ordres. Les hauts fonctionnaires XVIII*[e]*–XX*[e] *siècles* (Paris: Fayard, 1991), 82.

65 Interview with bDud 'dul rnam rgyal Tsha rong (b. 1920), Kalimpong, India, 04 September 2004.

66 For a detailed account of these events, see Goldstein 1989, 89–138.

67 Ibid, 819.

68 For a detailed account of these events, cf. ibid., 139–85.
69 For a detailed account of these events, cf. ibid., 464–521.
70 Melvyn C. Goldstein, "The Circulation of Estates in Tibet: Reincarnation, Land and Politics," *Journal of Asian Studies* 32.3 (May 1973), 445–55.

Bibliography

Tibetan Primary Sources

bKa' thang sde lnga, Gu ru O rgyan gling pa (13th or 14th century), revealer. sDe dge: Wood block print.

bKa' thang sde lnga, Gu ru O rgyan gling pa (13th or 14th century), revealer. Mi rigs dpe skrun khang, 1986.

bKa' gdams chos 'byung gsal ba'i sgron me, Las chen Kun dga' rgyal mtshan (1435–1506). [n.d., n.p.]

bKa' gdams gsar rnying gi chos 'byung yid kyi mdzes rgyan, Pan chen bSod nams grags pa (1478–1554). In *Two Histories of the bKa' gdams pa tradition from the Library of Burmiok Athing*. Gangtok: Gonpo Tseten, 1977, 1–206.

bKa' brgyud sngags mdzod, 'Jam mgon Kong sprul blo gros mtha' yas (1813–1899), 8 vols. Paro, Buthan: Ngodrup and Sherab Drimay, 1982.

mKhas grub bye ba'i bsti gnas 'brog ri bo dge ldan rnam par rgyal ba'i gling gi ya gyal shar rtse nor bu gling gi chos 'byung lo rgyus 'jam dpal snying po'i dgongs rgyan, Se ra smad pa Grags pa mkhas grub (18th–19th century). New Delhi: Nawang Sopa, 1975.

mKhas grub rin po che'i gsung 'bum thor bu, mKhas grub rje dGe legs dpal bzang (1385–1438). In *mKhas grub dge legs dpal bzang gi gsung 'bum*, vol. *Ba*. CD-ROM. New York: Tibetan Buddhist Resource Center, 2003, 345–752.

mKhas grub thams cad mkhyen pa'i rnam thar bsdus pa, Chos ldan rab 'byor (15th century). In *mKhas grub dge legs dpal bzang gi gsung 'bum*, vol. *Ka*. CD-ROM. New York: Tibetan Buddhist Resource Center, 2003, 109–33.

mKhas grub thams cad mkhyen pa'i rnam thar mkhas pa'i yid 'phrog, PaN chen bDe legs nyi ma (16th century). In *mKhas grub dge legs dpal bzang gi gsung 'bum*, vol. *Ka*. CD-ROM. New York: Tibetan Buddhist Resource Center, 2003, 79–108.

mKhas grub thams cad mkhyen pa'i gsang ba'i rnam thar, rJe btsun Chos kyi rgyal mtshan (1469–1544). In *The Collected Works (gsung 'bum) of mKhas grub dge legs dpal bzang*, vol. 12. New Delhi: Ngawang Gelek Demo, 1983, 421–70.

'Khrungs skor. Modern print edition of the "Lingtsang woodblock." Lanzhou: Kan su mi rigs dpe skrun khang, 1981.

'Khrungs gling. Narrated by Bard Grags pa. Beijing: Mi rigs dpe skrun khang, 1996.

'Khrungs gling, vol. 6 of Tibetan Academy of Social Sciences Gesar Series. Bard bSam Grub. Lhasa: Bod rang ljongs spyi tshogs tshan rig khang, 2001.

'Khrungs gling me tog ra ba. Modern print edition of the "Lingtsang woodblock." Chengdu: Si khron mi rigs dpe skrun khang, 1980, 1981, 1999.

Gangs ri'i khrod kyi klog pa nyan bshad pa rnams dang spong ba bsam gtan pa rnams kyi snyan du bsrings pa thos bsam dang bsgom pa 'chi med bdud rtsi ldeb, 'Jam dbyangs mKhyen brtse'i dbang po (1820–1892). In *The Collected Works (gsung 'bum).* Vol. 6. Gangtok: Gonpo Tseten, 1977–80, 327–74.

Gangs ri'i khrod kyi spong ba bsam gtan pa rnams kyi snyan du bsrings pa bsgom pa 'chi med bdud rtsi, 'Jam dbyangs mKhyen brtse'i dbang po (1820–1892). In *'Jam dbyang mkhyen brtse'i dbang po'i gsung rtso gces sgrig.* Beijing: Mi rigs dpe skrun khang, 1989, 337–66.

Gu ru bKra shis chos 'byung, Gu ru bKra shis (b. 18th century). Beijing: Krung go'i bod kyi shes rig dpe skrun khang, 1990.

Ge sar 'khrungs rabs. Modern print edition of the "Lingtsang woodblock." Xining: mTsho sngon ge sar zhib 'jug khang, 1986.

Gling rje'i 'khrungs rabs. 'Jam dpal rgya mtsho, eds. Modern print edition of the "Lingtsang woodblock." Beijing: Mi rigs dpe skrun khang, 2000.

Grwa sa chen po bzhi dang rgyud pa stod smad chags tshul pad dkar 'phreng ba, Phur bu lcog Ngag dbang byams pa (1682–1762). In *Three dKar chag's.* Gedan Sungrab Minyam Gyunphel Series, vol. 13. New Delhi: Ngawang Gelek Demo, 1970, 46–169.

dGa' ldan chos 'byung nor bu'i phreng ba, 'Jam dbyangs bzhad pa II Kon mchog 'jigs med dbang po (1728–1792). In *The Collected Works of Dkon-mchog-'jigs-med-dbang-po, the Second 'Jam-dbyans-bzad-pa of Bla brang bKra-sis-'khyil. Reproduced from prints from the bKra-sis-'khyil blocks by Ngawang Gelek Demo,* vol. 5. New Delhi: Demo, 1971, 655–56.

dGa' ldan chos 'byung vaidurya ser po, sDe srid Sangs rgyas rgya mtsho (1653–1705). Gangs ljongs shes rig gi nying bcud. Zi ling: Krung go bod kyi shes rig dpe skrun khang, 1989.

dGe chos gnas yig. In *Gangs can rig mdzod,* vol. 12. ed. Bod ljongs spyi tshogs tshan rig bod yig dpe rnying dpe skrun khang. Lhasa: Bod ljongs mi dmangs dpe skrun khang, 1990.

rGya gling. Narrated by Bard Grags pa. Beijing: Mi rigs dpe skrun khang, 1999.

rGya chen bka' mdzod, 'Jam mgon Kong sprul blo gros mtha' yas (1813–1899), 20 vols. Paro, Buthan: Ngodrup, 1975–76.

rGya bod kyi chos 'byung rgyas pa, Mkhas pa Lde'u (mid-to-late 13th century). Chab spel tshe brtan phun tshogs, ed., Lhasa: Bod ljongs mi dmangs dpe skrun khang, 1987.

rGya bod yig tshang chen mo, dPal 'byor bzang po (ca 15th c.). Sichuan: Mi dmangs dpe skrun khang, 1985.

rGyal ba dge 'dun rgya mtsho'i gsung 'bum. Chos tshan ri pa. [excerpted from] *Chos skyong khag gi gsol kha bstod pa dang bcas pa.*

rGyal rabs gsal ba'i me long. Sa skya bSod nams rgyal mtshan (1312–1375). rGyal sras ngag dbang blo bzang and mGon po rgyal mtshan, eds. Beijing: Mi rigs dpe skrun khang, 1995.

sGom pa 'chi med kyi bdud rtsi, 'Phreng po gter ston Shes rab 'od zer (1518–1584). In *gSung 'bum.* Gangtok: Gonpo Tseten, 1977, 243–66.

Ngag dbang blo bzang rgya mtsho'i rnam thar, rGyal dbang lnga pa Ngag dbang blo bzang rgya mtsho (1617–1682). 3 vols. Bod ljongs mi dmangs dpe skrun khang, 1989.

Nges don 'brug sgra, Sog bzlog pa Blo gros rgyal mtshan (1552–1624). *Collected writings of Sog bzlog pa.* New Delhi: Sanje Dorji, 1975.

sNgags log sun 'byin, 'Gos khug pa lhas btsas (11th century). dPal ldan 'brug gzhung, ed., Thimpu: Kunsang Tobgyal & Mani Dorji, 1979, folios 18–25.

sNgags log sun 'byin, Chag lo tsā ba Chos rje dpal (1197–1264). dPal ldan 'brug gzhung, ed., Thimpu: Kunsang Tobgyal & Mani Dorji, 1979, folios 1–18.

sNgon gyi gtam me tog phreng ba. Ne'u pan di ta Grags pa smon lam blo gros (late 13th c.). Rare Tibetan Historical and Literary Texts from the Library of Tsepon W. D. Shakabpa Series I (New Delhi, 1974).

Chos kyi 'khor lo bskor ba'i rnam gzhag ji ltar grub pa'i yi ge gzu bor gnas pa'i mdzangs pa dga' byed, gSer mdog paN chen ShAkya mchog ldan (1428–1507). In *The Complete Works (gsung 'bum) of gSer mdog paN chen ShAkya mchog ldan*, vol. *Ma*. Thimpu: Kunzang Topgey, 1975, 457–82.

Chos 'byung mkhas pa'i dga' ston, dPa' bo gtsug lag phreng ba. Varanasi: Vajra Vidhya Library.

Chos 'byung me tog snying po sbrang rtsi'i bcud. Nyang ral nyi ma 'od zer (1124/36-1196/1204). In *Gangs can rig mdzod*, vol. 5. Lhasa: Bod ljongs mi dmangs dpe skrun khang, 1988.

Chos la 'jug pa'i sgo, bSod nams rtse mo (1142–1182). In *Sa skya bka' 'bum*, bSod nams rgya mtsho, ed., *The Complete Works of the Great Masters of the Sa Skya Sect of the Tibetan Buddhism*, 14 vols. 1968, 2. Part, 318.3.1–45.3.6.

Chos log sun 'byin, Bu ston Rin chen grub (1290–1364). dPal ldan 'brug gzhung, ed. Thimpu: Kunsang Tobgyal & Mani Dorji, 1979, folios 25–36.

mChod bstod dregs pa'i lha tshogs rba klong 'khrug cing dam can rgya mtsho dgyes par spyod pa'i mgrin bcu'i pho brang sa la 'phos pa'i sngon med bzo sna brgyad kyis 'phags pa'i gnas chung pe har lcog gi dkar chag sa gsum g.yo ba'i nga ro, sDe srid sangs rgyas rgya mtsho. Written in Water-dog year of 11th *rab 'byung* (1682). Wood block print.

'Jam dbyangs mkhyen brtse'i sku phreng gong 'og gi rnam thar, Blo gros phun tshog. Beijing: Mi rigs dpe skrun khang, 1994.

'Jig rten dbang phyug thams cad mkhyen pa yon tan rgya mtsho dpal bzang po'i rnam par thar pa nor bu'i phreng ba, rGyal dbang lnga pa Ngag dbang blo bzang rgya mtsho (1617–1682). Lhasa: Zhol par khang, Wood block print.

rJe btsun chos kyi rgyal mtshan dpal bzang po'i rnam par thar pa dngos grub kyi char 'bebs, PaN chen bDe legs nyi ma (sixteenth century). Lhasa: Ser byes mkhas snyen grwa tshang, [n.d.], 33 fols.

rJe btsun thams cad mkhyen pa bsod nams rgya mtsho'i rnam thar dngos grub rgya mtsho'i shing rta, rGyal dbang lnga pa Ngag dbang blo bzang rgya mtsho (1617–1682). Lha sa zhol par khang, Wood block print.

rJe bstun bla ma thams chad mkhyen cing gzigs pa 'jam dbyangs mkhyen brtse'i dbangs po kun dga' bstan pa'i rgyal mtshan dpal bzang po'i rnam thar mdor bsdus pa ngo mtshar u dumba ra'i dga' tshal, 'Jam mgon Kong sprul blo gros mtha' yas (1813–1899). In *rGya chen bka' mdzod*, vol. 15. Paro, Buthan: Ngodrup, 1975–76, 343–577.

rJe btsun bla ma tsong kha pa chen po'i ngo mtshar rmad du 'byung ba'i rnam par thar pad dad pa'i 'jug ngogs, mKhas grub rje dGe legs dpal bzang (1385–1438). In *The Collected Works (gsung 'bum) of Tsong kha pa Blo bzang grags pa*. New York: Tibetan Buddhist Resource Center, 2003, vol. 1, 1–147.

rJe rin po che la mkhas btsun bzang gsum gyi yon tan mnga' tshul rnam thar nor bu'i bang mdzod bzhugs, 'Chi med rab rgyas, Zang zang ne rings pa (ca 15th c.). In *sNga 'gyur gsang chen rnying ma'i bstan 'dzin chen mo zang zang ne rings pa 'chi med rab rgyas kyi mdzad pa rJe rin po che'i rnam thar nor bu'i bang mdzod dang bu chen sbyon tshul gser gyi mchod sdong zhes bya ba gnyis dang gzhan yang ne rings pa'i gsung thor bu nang rnyed phyogs gcig tu bsdus pa bzhugs so*, Rakra Tethong, ed. Delhi: Rakra Tethong, ca 2001, 1–13.

rJe rin po che'i rnam thar gser gyi mchod sdong, 'Chi med rab rgyas, Zang zang ne rings pa (ca 15 c.). In *sNga 'gyur gsang chen rnying ma'i bstan 'dzin chen mo zang zang ne rings pa 'chi med rab rgyas kyi mdzad pa rJe rin po che'i rnam thar nor bu'i bang mdzod dang bu chen sbyon tshul gser gyi mchod sdong zhes bya ba gnyis dang gzhan yang ne rings pa'i gsung thor bu nang rnyed phyogs gcig tu bsdus pa bzhugs so*, Rakra Tethong, ed., Delhi: Rakra Tethong, ca 2001, 14–33.

rNying ma'i skyes mchog rim byon gyi rnam thar (Nor bu'i do shal), Kun bzang nges don klong yangs (b. 1814). Dalhousie, H.P.: Damchoe Sangpo, 1976.

rNying ma'i rgyud 'bum, mTshams Brag edition: http://iris.lib.virginia.edu/.

rNying ma'i rgyud 'bum, sDe dge edition: http://iris.lib.virginia.edu/.

Thams cad mkhyen pa 'jam dbyangs chos rje bkra shis dpal ldan pa'i zhal snga nas kyi rnam par thar pa ngo mtshar rmad du byung ba'i gtam rab tu gsal ba'i sgron sme, gTsang ston Kun dga' rgyal mtshan (14th–15th century). [n.d., n.p.]

Thu'u bkwan grub mtha', Thu'u bkwan Blo bzang chos kyi nyi ma (1737–1802). Lanzhou: Kan su mi rigs dpe skrun khang, 1989.

Thu'u bkwan grub mtha', Thu'u bkwan Blo bzang chos kyi nyi ma (1737–1802). Gansu: Mi rigs dpe skrun khang, 1984.

Thob yig gang ga'i chu rgyun, Ngag dbang blo bzang rgya mtsho the Fifth Dalai Lama (1617–1682). In *The Collected Works*, vols. 1–4. Gangtok, Sikkim: Sikkim Research Institute of Tibetology, 1991–95.

Thos bsam 'chi med kyi bdud rtsi, 'Phreng po gter ston Shes rab 'od zer (1518–1584). In *gSung 'bum*. Gangtok: Gonpo Tseten, 1977, 231–42.

Dam pa'i chos kyi 'khor lo bsgyur ba rnams kyi byung ba gsal bar byed pa mkhas pa'i dga' ston, dPa' bo gtsug lag phreng ba (1504–1566). Beijing: Mi rigs dpe skrun khang, 1985.

Dus 'khor gyi sgrub thabs pad ma dkar po'i zhal lung la log rtog sal tshul, rJe btsun Chos kyi rgyal mtshan (1469–1544). In *The Collected Works (gsung 'bum) of mKhas grub dge legs dpal*. Delhi: Ngawang Gelek Demo, 1983, vol. *cha*, 1a–75a.

Deb ther dmar po, Tshal pa Kun dga' rdo rje (1309–1364). Beijing: Mi rigs dpe skrun khang, 1993.

gDams ngag mdzod, 'Jam mgon Kong sprul blo gros mtha' yas (1813–1899). 12 vols. Delhi: N. Lungtok and N. Gyaltsen, 1971.

mDo 'dus. mDo 'dus pa rin po che'i rgyud thams cad mkhyen pa'i bka' tshad ma, Bonpo bKa' 'gyur vol. 30 (3rd edition, Chengdu, 1995–1999).

Pad ma bka' thang, Gu ru O rgyan gling pa (13th or 14th century), revealer. Sichuan: Mi rigs dpe skrun khang, 1996.

Pad ma bka' thang, Gu ru O rgyan gling pa (13th or 14th century), revealer. sDe dge Wood block print.

dPag bsam rin po che'i snye ma, lCang skya rol pa'i rdo rje (1717–1786), 2 vols. Bod ljongs mi dmangs dpe skrun khang, 1990.

dPal bsam yas mi 'gyur lhun gyis grub pa'i gtsug lag khang chen po bka' srungs dang bcas pa'i byon tshul legs par bshad pa chos skyong yid bzhin nor bu dgyes par byed pa'i yid 'phrog lha'i rol mo dgos 'dod kun 'byung, Sa skya pa shākya'i dge bsnyen sngags 'chang Ngag dbang kun dga' bsod nams grags pa rgyal mtshan (1485–1533). Written in Water female bird year at Sa skya monastery (1513), hand-written manuscript.

Phyogs med ris med kyi bstan pa 'dun shing dge sbyong gi gzugs brnyan 'chang ba blo gros mtha' yas kyi sde'i byung ba brjod pa nor bu sna tshogs mdog can, 'Jam mgon kong sprul blo gros mtha' yas (1813–1899). Bir: Tibetan Khampa Industrial Society, 1973.

Bu ston chos 'byung. Bu ston Rin chen grub (1290–1364). Beijing: Krung go bod kyi shes rig dpe skrun khang, 1988.

Bod rgya tshig mdzod chen mo, Zhang Yisun et al., eds. Beijing: 1984; reprint, Mi rigs dpe skrun khang, 2 vols., 1996.

Byang klu btsan rgyal po 'dul ba. Narrated by Bard Grags pa. Beijing: Mi rigs dpe skrun khang, 1997.

Bha ka la 'phrul gyi rgyal po. Narrated by Bard Grags pa. Beijing: Mi rigs dpe skrun khang, 1998.

'Bri gung chos 'byung, 'Bri gung dKon mchog rgya mtsho. Beijing: Mi rigs dpe skrun khang, 2004.

sBa bzhed ces bya ba las sba gsal snang gi bzhed pa. mGon po rgyal mtshan, ed., Beijing: Mi rigs dpe skrun khang, 1982.

Mon gling g.yul 'gyed. Narrated by Bard Grags pa. Lhasa: Bod ljongs mi dmangs dpe skrun khang, 1980.

mDzod 'grel mngon pa'i rgyan, mChims nam mkha' grags alias mChims 'jam pa'i dbyangs. Written in the 13th century at Sog yul ca ti kha.

Zhe chen chos 'byung, Zhe chen rgyal tshab 'Gyur med pad ma rnam rgyal (1871–1926). Chengdu: Si khron mi rigs dpe skrun khang, 1994.

Zab mo'i gter dang gter ston grub thob ji ltar byon pa'i lo rgyus mdor bsdus bkod pa rin chen bai ḍū rya'i phreng ba, 'Jam mgon Kong sprul blo gros mtha' yas (1813–1899). In *Rin chen gter mdzod*, vol. 1. Paro, Bhutan: Ngodrup and Sherab Drimay, 1976–1980, 291–759.

gZer mig. Dus gsum gshen rab kyi byung khyungs dang mdzad pa'i rgyud 'dus pa rin po che gzer mig gi mdo, discovered by Drang rje btsun pa gser mig. Edited by Tsering Thar based on Khro chen block prints, Qinghai, 1991.

g.Yung drung bon gyi sgra bsgrags pa rin po che'i gling grags (ca 14th c.). Bonpo Katen vol. 72:1. Lhasa: Sog sde bstan pa'i nyi ma, 1998.

g.Yung drung bon gyi gzhung gleng gzhi bstan pa'i 'byung khungs, Khyung po Blo gros rgyal mtshan. Written at the hermitage of Khyung po rgyal ba thod dkar in 1439. A manuscript written in *yig nag* kept in the *bla brang* of Menri monastery in India.

Ris med chos kyi 'byung gnas mdo tsam smos pa blo gsal mgrin pa'i mdzes rgyan, 'Jam mgon Kong sprul blo gros mtha' yas (1813–1899). In *rGya chen bka' mdzod*, vol. 9. Paro, Buthan: Ngodrup, 1975–76, 69–99.

Rin chen gter mdzod, 'Jam mgon Kong sprul blo gros mtha' yas (1813–1899), 111 vols. Paro, Buthan: Ngodrup and Sherab Drimay, 1976–1980.

Shes bya mdzod, 'Jam mgon Kong sprul blo gros mtha' yas (1813–1899), 4 vols. Delhi: Shechen Publications, 1997. Also 3 vols. Beijing: Mi rigs dpe skrun khang, 1982.

Sa skya'i gdung rabs ya rabs kha rgyan, mKhas pa'i dbang po Ngor pa dkon mchog lhun grub.

Sa skya'i gdung rabs rin chen bang mdzod, bDag chen a mes Ngag dbang kun dga' bsod nams. Delhi: Par slog par ma.

Sa paṇ kun dga' rgyal mtshan gyi gsung 'bum. Lhasa: Bod ljong bod yig dpe rnying dpe skrung khang. Glegs bam gsum pa, 1992.

Sog po rta rdzong. Narrated by Bard Grags pa. Beijing: Mi rigs dpe skrun khang, 1999.

gSung 'bum, 'Phreng po gter ston Shes rab 'od zer (1518–1584), 1 vol. Gangtok: Gonpo Tseten, 1977.

gSung 'bum (Collected works of the Fifth Dalai Lama), Ngag dbang blo bzang rgya mtsho (1678), vol. 17.

gSung rab rnam dag chu'i sel byed nor bu ke ta ka'i tshig don la dogs dpyod snyan sgron du gsol ba nor bu ke ta ka'i byi dor, Thu'u bkwan Blo bzang chos kyi nyi ma (1732–1802). Varanasi: Tarthang Tulku, 1967.

Srid pa'i mdzod phugs rtsa 'grel, attributed to Dran pa nam mkha' (8th c.). Varanasi: g.Yung drung bon spyi las khungs, 1993.

Hor phyi pa ra rdzong. Narrated by Bard Grags pa. Beijing: Mi rigs dpe skrun khang, 1996.

lHa gling. vol. 1 of Tibetan Academy of Social Sciences Gesar Series. Bard bSam Grub. Lhasa: Bod rang ljongs spyi tshogs tshan rig khang, 2001.

lHa gling gab tse dgu skor. Narrated by Bard Grags pa. Beijing: Mi rigs dpe skrun khang, 1998.

lHa gling gab tse dgu skor. Modern print edition of the "Lingtsang woodblock." Chengdu: Si khron mi rigs dpe skrun khang, 1980, 1999. (LWLL).

lHar bcas srid zhi'i gtsug rgyan gong sa rgyal ba'i dbang po bka' drin mtshungs med sku phreng bcu gsum pa chen po'i rnam par thar pa rgya mtsho lta bu las mdo tsam brjod pa ngo mtshar rin po che'i phreng ba zhes bya ba, Phur lcog yongs 'dzin Thub bstan byams pa tshul khrims, 2 vols. Written in Iron dragon year of 16th *rab 'byung* (1940), Lha sa zhol par khang, Wood block print.

Biographies of the Eminent Gurus in the Transmission Lineages of the Teachings of the Graduated Path: Being the Text of Byang chub lam gyi rim pa'i bla ma brgyud pa'i rnam par thar pa rgyal bstan mdzes pa'i rgyan mchog phul byung nor bu'i phreng ba, Tshe mchog gling Ye shes rgyal mtshan (1713–1793). Gedan Sungrab Minyam Gyunphel Series, vols. 18–19. New Delhi: Ngawang Gelek Demo, 1970.

History of the Sera Monastery of Tibet, 1418–1959, Zongtse Champa Thupten (rDzong rtse Byams pa thub bstan, 12th c.). New Delhi: International Academy of Indian Culture and Aditya Prakashan, 1995.

The Collected Works, 'Jigs med gling pa rang byung rdo rje (1730–1798), 14 vols. Paro, Bhutan: Lama Ngodrup and Sherab Drimay, 1985.

The Epic of Gesar vol. 1. Kunzang Tobgyel and Mani Dorji, eds. Modern print edition of the "Lingtsang woodblock." Bhutan, Thimphu: Kunzang Tobgyel, 1979.

English-Language Primary Sources

Bell, Charles. *Report on the government of Tibet*, Calcutta: Office of the superintendent of government printing, 1906 (IOR/L/P&S/10/150).

Chiefs and Leading Families in Sikkim Bhutan and Tibet. Calcutta: Superintendent government printing, 1915 (PRO/FO/371/2318).

Crystal, David, ed. *The Cambridge Encyclopedia.* Cambridge: Cambridge University Press, 1990.

Encyclopædia Britannica, Inc., *The New Encyclopædia Britannica*, vol. 14. 1968; reprint, Chicago, 1980.

India Office Records, British Library, London: L/P&S, series 7, 10, 11, 12, 20.

List of leading officials, nobles, and personages in Bhutan, Sikkim, and Tibet, 1908. Calcutta: Superintendent government printing, 1909.

National Archives of India, New Delhi: Foreign Department, series ExtlA and SecE.

Public Records Office (National Archives), London: serie 371 (Foreign Office).

Revised Who's Who in Tibet, 1944 (PRO/FO/371/46121).

Who's Who in Tibet, Corrected to the Autumn of 1937, with a few subsequent additions up to February 1938. Calcutta: Government of India Press, 1938 (IOR/L/P&S/12/4185A).

Who's Who in Tibet, Corrected with a few subsequent additions up to 30th September 1948. Calcutta: Government of India Press, 1949 (IOR/L/P&S/20 D 220/2).

Williamson, Frederick. "Note on titles and official ranks in Tibet." 1934 (PRO/FO/371/19253 ex. F271/12/10): 1–3.

Tibetan Secondary Sources

Anon. "Bod kyi skye khams lta ba dang 'brel ba'i bklag deb." In *rMa rgyal gangs thigs*, n.p.: rMa yul skyes khams khor yug srung skyob tsogs pa, n.d., 10–21.

Anon. "mTsho sngon zhing chen skyes dngos brtag dpyad khang dang thun rin zhan rong bo sman bcos khang." In *mDo dbus mtho sgang sman ris gsal ba'i me long*, vol. 1. Zi ling: mTsho sngon mi dmangs dpe skrun khang, 1973, 294–95.

Khri bsam gtan and Tshe dbang thar, eds. *sKad gnyis smra ba'i sgron me.* Gansu: Mi rigs dpe skrun khang, 2000.

dGe 'dun chos 'phel. *Deb ther dkar po.* Beijing: Mi rigs dpe skrun khang, 2000.

Chab mdo blo bzang shes rab. *Chab mdo'i yig tshang rin chen spungs pa*. Dharamsala: Chab mdo skyid sdug, 2005.

Chab spel tshe brtan phun tshogs and Nor brang o rgyan. *Bod kyi lo rgyus rags rim g.yu yi phreng ba*, vol. 1. Bod ljongs: dPe rnying dpe skrun khang, 1989.

Chab spel tshe brtan phun tshogs et al., eds. *Klong rdol ngag dbang blo bzang gi gsung 'bum*. Gangs can rig mdzod vol. 21:2. Bod ljongs: Bod yig dpe rnying dpe skrun khang, 1991.

Chos rgyal nam mkha'i nor bu. *sGrung lde'u bon gsum gyi gtam e ma ho*. Dharamsala: LTWA, 1989.

mNyam med shes rab rgyal mtshan. *Srid pa'i mdzod phugs kyi gzhung dang 'grel ba 'phrul gyi sgron me*. Dolanji: g.Yung drung bon gyi bshad sgrub 'dus sde, 2004.

Thub bstan phun tshogs. *Bod kyi lo rgyus spyi don padma ra ga'i lde mig*. Lhasa: Mi rigs dpe skrun khang, 1996.

Dung dkar blo bzang 'phrin las. *Bod kyi chos srid zung 'brel skor bshad pa*. Mi rigs dpe skrun khang, 1981.

—— *Dung dkar tshig mdzod chen mo*. Beijing: Krung go'i Bod rig pa dpe skrun khang, 2002.

De'u dmar bstan 'dzin phun tshogs. *gSo rig gces btus rin chen phreng ba*. Ziling: mTsho sngon mi rigs dpe skrun khang, 1993.

Don grub rgyal. "Deb ther dpyid kyi rgyal mo'i glu dbyangs kyi mchan 'grel." In *Don grub rgyal gyi gsung 'bum*, vol. 6. Mi rigs dpe skrun khang, 1992.

Don grub rgyal and Khrin chen dbyin, trans. *Thang yig gsar rnying las byung ba'i bod chen po'i srid lugs*. mTsho sngon: Mi dmangs dpe skrun khang, 1983.

Don grub dbang rgyal and Nor sde. "mGo log lo rgyus deb ther." In *mGo log rig gnas lo rgyus*, vol.1. Zi ling: Srid gros mgo khul u rig gnas lo rgyus rgyu cha zhib 'jug u yon ltan khang, 1991.

Pandita mchi med seng ge. *mNgon brjod mchi med mdzod*. Palale monastery, Sikkim: Bla ma shes rab rgyal mtshan, 1984.

dPal chen rDo rje. *Kha char bu yug khrod nas 'tshar long byung ba'i khros po*. (Newspaper article, source and year unknown).

dBang rgyal (Wang Yao) and bSod nams skyid (Chen Jian), eds. *Tun hong nas thon pa'i bod kyi lo rgyus yig cha*. Mi rigs dpe skrun khang.

Mi 'gyur rdo rje. "Bod kyi srol rgyun lus rtsal dang bod kyi gna' bo'i rtsed rtsal rta thog po lo'i skor cung zad gleng ba." *Bod ljongs zhib 'jug* 2 (1984).

g.Yu thog yon tan mgon po. *bDud rtsis snying po yan lag brgyad pa gsang ba mang ngag gi rgyud*. Ziling: mTsho sngon mi rigs dpe skrun khang, 2002.

Rin spungs Ngag dbang 'jig grags. *mNgon brjod mkhas pa'i rna rgyan*. Lhasa: Bod ljongs mi dmangs dpe skrun khang, 1983.

Sle lung bzhad pa'i rdo rje. *Dam can bstan srung rgya mtsho'i rnam par thar pa sngon men legs bshad*. Written in Wood tiger year. Delhi.

bSod nams don grub. "sTag gzig dang gna' rabs bod kyi 'brel ba'i skor la dpyad pa." *Bod ljongs zhib 'jug* 3 (1992).

Secondary Sources

Ahmad, Zahiruddin. *A History of Tibet, by Ngag dbang blo bzang rgya mtsho, Fifth Dalai Lama of Tibet*. Bloomington: Indiana University, Research Institute for Inner Asian Studies, 1995.

Alexander, André. *The Temples of Lhasa: Tibetan Buddhist Architecture from the 7th to the 21st Centuries*. Chicago: Serindia Publications, 2005.

Anand, Dibyesh. "A Contemporary Story of 'Diaspora': The Tibetan Version." *Diaspora* 12.2 (Summer 2003): 211–29.

Anon. "Tibet Rich in Fish." *Tibetan Bulletin* 14.1 (March/April 1983): 19–20.

Anon. *Tibetans, Chinese Battle Over Access to Medicinal Fungus*. http://www.ens-newswire.com/ens/jun2005/2005-06-02-01.asp (accessed 29 August 2007).

Appadurai, Arjun. "Introduction: Commodities and the Politics of Value." In *The Social Life of Things. Commodities in Cultural Perspective*, Arjun Appadurai (ed.). Cambridge: Cambridge University Press, 2001, 3–61.

Aris, Michael, ed. and trans. "'Jamyang Khyentse's *Brief Discourse on The Essence of All the Ways*: A Work of the *Ris-med* Movement." *Kailash* 5.3 (1977): 205–29.

—— *Hidden Treasures and Secret Lives*. London: Kegan Paul, 1989.

Aristotle. *Poetics* (trans. S.H. Butcher). New York: Courier Dover Publications, 1951.

Ary, Elijah. "Logic, Lives, and Lineage: Jetsun Chokyi Gyaltsen's Ascension and the Secret Biography of Khedrup Geleg Pelzang." PhD Dissertation: Harvard University, 2007.

Avedon, John F. *In Exile from the Land of Snows*. London: Michael Joseph, 1984.

Axel, Brian Keith. *The Nation's Tortured Body: Violence, Representation and the Formation of a Sikh "Diaspora."* Durham, NC: Duke University Press, 2001.

Aziz, Barbara N. "Indian Philosopher as Tibetan Folk Hero." *Central Asiatic Journal* 23.1–2 (1979): 19–37.

Bacot, Jacques, Frederick W. Thomas and Charles Toussaint. *Documents de Touen-Houang relatifs a l'histoire du Tibet*. Paris: Libraire Orientaliste Paul Geuthner, 1940–1946.

Barnett, Robert. "Preface." In *Tibetan Modernities: Notes from the Field on Cultural and Social Change. Proceedings of the Tenth Seminar of the International Association for Tibetan Studies, Oxford, 2003*, Robert Barnett and Ronald Schwartz (eds.). Leiden: Brill, 2008, xi–xxi.

Baumann, Martin. "Shangri-La in Exile: Portraying Tibetan Diaspora Studies and Reconsidering Diaspora(s)." *Diaspora* 6.3 (winter 1997): 377–404.

Becker, Jasper. *Hungry Ghosts. Mao's Secret Famine*. New York: Free Press, 1996.

Beissinger, Margaret H. and J. Tylus et al., eds. *Epic Traditions in the Contemporary World: The Poetics of Community*. Berkeley: University of California Press, 1999.

Belcher, B. and K. Schreckenberg. "Commercialisation of Non-Timber Forest Products: A Reality Check." *Development Policy Review* 25.3 (2007): 355–77.

Bell, Charles. *The People of Tibet*. 1928; reprint, Delhi: Motilal Barnasidass Publishers, 1992.

—— *The Religion of Tibet*. 1931; reprint, Delhi: Motilal Banarsidass, 2000.

Benedict, Paul K. "Tibetan and Chinese Kinship Terms." *Harvard Journal of Asiatic Studies* 6.3–4 (1942): 313–37.

Benedict, Ruth. *The Chrysanthemum and the Sword: Patterns of Japanese Culture*. 1946; reprint, New York: Houghton Mifflin, 1989.

Bhattacharjea, Mira Sinha. "1962 Revisited." In *Crossing a Bridge of Dreams: Fifty Years of India China*, G.P. Deshpande and Alka Acharya (eds.). New Delhi: Tulika, 2001, 427–45.

Bjerken, Zeff. "Exorcising the Illusion of Bon 'Shamans:' A Critical Genealogy of Shamanism in Tibetan Religions." *Revue d'Etudes Tibétaines* 6 (2004): 4–59.

Blackburn, Stuart and P.J. Claus et al., eds. *The Oral Epics of India*. Berkeley: University of California Press, 1989.

Blondeau, Anne-Marie. "The *mKha' klong gsang mdos*: Some Questions on Ritual Structure and Cosmology." In *New Horizons in Bon Studies*, Yasuhiko Nagano and Samten G. Karmay (eds). Osaka: National Museum of Ethnology, 2000, 249–87.

Boesi, Alessandro. "The dbyar rtswa dgun 'bu (*Cordyceps sinensis* Berk.): An important trade item for the Tibetan population of the Lithang County, Sichuan Province, China." *Tibet Journal* 28.3 (2003): 29–42.

Buenz, E.J., B.A. Bauer, T.W. Osmundson and T.J. Motley. "The Traditional Chinese Medicine Cordyceps Sinensis and its Effects on Apoptotic Homeostasis." *Journal of Ethnopharmacology* 96.1–2 (2005): 19–29.

Bushell, Stephen W. "The Early History of Tibet. From Chinese Sources." *Journal of the Royal Asiatic Society* 12 (1880): 435–541.

Butler, Kim D. "Defining Diaspora, Refining a Discourse." *Diaspora* 10.2 (Fall 2001): 189–219.

Cabezón, José Ignacio, trans. *A Dose of Emptiness: an Annotated Translation of the Stong thun chen mo of mKhas grub dge legs dpal bzang.* Albany: State University of New York Press, 1992.

Cao, Cheng C. (曹長青) "Tibetan tragedy began with a farce." *Taipei Times*, 25 April, 2001.

Carnahan, Sumner and Lama Kunga Rinpoche, Ngor Thartse Shabtrung. *In the Presence of my Enemies: Memoirs of Tibetan Nobleman Tsipon Shuguba.* New Mexico: Clear Light Publishers, 1995.

Chagnollaud, Dominique. *Le premier des ordres. Les hauts fonctionnaires XVIIIe–XXe siècle.* Paris: Fayard, 1991.

Chang, Jung and Jon Halliday. *Mao, the Untold Story.* London: Jonathan Cape, 2005.

Chapman, F. Spencer. *Lhasa, The Holy City.* 1940; reprint Delhi: Bodhi Leaves Corporation, 1992.

Chen, Peggy. "Tibetans in Taiwan." M.A. Dissertation: National Taiwan University, 2002.

Chen, S.J. and D.H. Yin et al. "Resources and Distribution of Cordyceps Sinensis in Naqu Tibet." *Zhong Yaocai* 23.11 (2000): 673–75.

Chevetzoff, Peter. "L'Architecture Tibétaine en Occident: Mutations et Continuité." DEA Dissertation: Université de Paris X Nanterre, 1991.

Cohen, Robin. "Diasporas and the Nation-State: From Victims to Challengers." *International Affairs* 72.3 (1996): 507–20.

Cohen, Robin. *Global Diasporas: An Introduction.* London: University College London Press, 1997.

Corlin, Claes. "A Tibetan Enclave in Yunnan: Land, Kinship, and Inheritance in Gyethang." In *Tibetan Studies: Presented at the Seminar of Young Tibetologists, Zurich, June 26–July 1, 1977,* Martin Brauen and Per Kvaerne (eds.). Zürich: Völkerkundemuseum der Universität Zürich, 1978, 75–89.

Cornu, Philippe. *L'Astrologie Tibétaine.* Millau: Les Djinns, 1990.

Costello, Susan. "The Flow of Wealth in Golok Pastoralist Society: Toward an Assessment of Local Financial Resources for Economic Development." In *Tibetan Modernities. Notes from the Field on Cultural and Social Change*, Robert Barnett and Ronald Schwartz (eds.). Leiden: Brill, 2008, 73–112.

Czapiński, Janusz and Tomasz Panek, eds. *Diagnoza społeczna 2007. Warunki i jakość życia Polaków.* Warsaw: Rada Monitoringu Społecznego, 2007.

Dalton, Jacob D. "The Uses of *dGongs pa 'dus pa'i mdo* in the Development of the rNying ma School of Tibetan Buddhism." PhD Dissertation: University of Michigan, 2002.

Das, Sarat Chandra. *Tibetan-English Dictionary.* 1902; reprint, Delhi: Book Faith India, 1995.

Davidson, Ronald M. "An Introduction to the Standards of Scriptural Authenticity in Indian Buddhism." In *Chinese Buddhist Apocrypha*, Robert E. Buswell (ed.). Honolulu: University of Hawaii Press, 1990, 291–325.

—— "gSar ma pa apocrypha: The Creation of Orthodoxy, Gray Texts, and the New Revelation." In *The Many Canons of Tibetan Buddhism*, Helmut Eimer and David Germano (eds.). Leiden: E.J. Brill, 2002, 203–24.

—— *Tibetan Renaissance: Tantric Buddhism in the Rebirth of Tibetan Culture.* New York: Columbia University Press, 2005.

Deepak, B.R. *India and China 1904–2004: A Century of Peace and Conflict.* New Delhi: Manak, 2005.

Delog Dawa Drolma. *Delog. Journey to Realms beyond Death.* Varanasi and Kathmandu: Pilgrims Publishing, 2001.

Denwood, Philip. "Uses of Indian Technical Literature in Tibetan Architecture." In *South Asian Studies 6*. London: Society of South Asian Studies, 1990, 95–104.

Derrida, Jacques. *Of Grammatology* (trans. Gayatri Chakravorty Spivak). Baltimore: Johns Hopkins University Press, 1976.

Deshpande, G.P. and Alka Acharya, eds. *Crossing a Bridge of Dreams: Fifty Years of India China.* New Delhi: Tulika, 2001.

Devkota, S. "Yarsagumba [Cordyceps sinensis (Berk.) Sacc.]; Traditional Utilization in Dolpa District, Western Nepal." *Our Nature* 4 (2006): 48–52.

Dewitt Garson, Nathaniel. "Penetrating the Secret Essence Tantra: Context and Philosophy in the Mahāyoga System of rNying ma Tantra." PhD Dissertation: University of Virginia, 2004.

Dideron, Sylvie and Marie-Louise Beerling. "The Socio-economic Situation of the Herders in Guoluo Prefecture. A Review of Research Conducted under the QLDP." In *Living Plateau. Changing Lives of Herders in Qinghai. Concluding Seminar of the Qinghai Livestock Development Project*, Nico van Wageningen and Sa Wenjun (eds.). Kathmandu: ICIMOD, 2001, 25–44.

Dixit, J.N. *Across Borders: Fifty Years of India's Foreign Policy.* New Delhi: Picus Books, 1998.

Doctor, Andreas. *Tibetan Treasure Literature: Revelation, Tradition and Accomplishment in Visionary Buddhism.* Ithaca, New York: Snow Lion, 2005.

Dorjee, Penpa. "bSam yas rtsod pa: An Analytical Study on Samye Debate." PhD Thesis: Central Institute of Higher Tibetan Studies, Varanasi, 2005.

Dotson, Brandon. "A Note on *źaṅ:* Maternal Relatives of the Tibetan Royal Line and Marriage into the Royal Family." *Journal Asiatique* 292.1–2 (2004): 75–99.

—— "'Emperor' Mu rug btsan and the *'Phang thang ma Catalogue.*" *Journal of the International Association for Tibetan Studies* 3 (December 2007): 1–25. www.thdl.org?id=T3105.

—— *The Old Tibetan Annals: An Annotated Translation of Tibet's First History.* Vienna: Verlag der Österreichischen Akademie der Wissenschaften, 2009.

Douglas, Mary and Aaron Wildavsky. *Risk and Culture: An Essay on the Selection of Technological and Environmental Dangers.* Berkeley: University of California Press, 1984.

Dreyfus, Georges B.J. "The Shuk-den Affair: Origins of a Controversy." *Journal of the International Association of Buddhist Studies* 21.2 (1998): 227–70.

—— *The Sound of Two Hands Clapping: The Education of a Tibetan Buddhist Monk.* Berkeley: University of California Press, 2003.

Dudjom Rinpoche, Jigkrel Yeshe Dorje. *The Nyingma School of Tibetan Buddhism: Its Fundamentals and History*, Gyurme Dorje and Matthew Kapstein (eds. and trans.). Boston: Wisdom, 1991.

Duncan, Marion H. *Customs and Superstitions of Tibetans.* 1964; reprint, New Delhi: Book Faith India, 1998.

Earnest, Conrad P., Gina M. Morss, Frank Wyatt et al. "Effects of a Commercial Herbal-Based Formula on Exercise Performance in Cyclists." *Medicine & Science in Sports & Exercise* (2004): 504–09.

Economy, Elisabeth. *The River Runs Black. The Environmental Challenge to China's Future.* London: Cornell University Press, 2007.

Ekvall, Robert B. *Cultural Relations on the Kansu-Tibetan Border.* Chicago: University of Chicago Press, 1977.

Emmerick, Ronald E. *Tibetan Texts Concerning Khotan.* London: Oxford University Press, 1967.

Finnegan, Ruth. *Oral Poetry: Its Nature, Significance and Social Context.* Cambridge: Cambridge University Press, 1977.

Firth, Raymond. *Malay Fishermen. Their Peasant Economy.* London: Routledge & Kegan Paul, 1966.

Fischer, Andrew M. "Close Encounters of an Inner Asian Kind. Tibetan-Muslim Coexistence and Conflict in Tibet, Past and Present." *Crisis State Programme Working Papers*, 68 (2005).

—— *State Growth and Social Exclusion in Tibet. Challenges of Recent Economic Growth.* Copenhagen: NIAS Press, 2005.

FitzHerbert, Solomon George I. "The Birth of Gesar: Narrative Diversity and Social Resonance in the Tibetan Epic Tradition." DPhil Thesis: University of Oxford, 2007.

—— *The Vagrant Child: Narrative Diversity and Social Resonance in the Tibetan Gesar Tradition* (provisional title). New York: Oxford University Press, forthcoming.

Foley, John M. *Oral-Formulaic Theory and Research: an Introduction and Annotated Biography.* New York: Garland, 1985.

—— *The Theory of Oral Composition: History and Methodology.* Bloomington: Indiana University Press, 1988.

—— *Traditional Oral Epic: the Odyssey, Beowulf, and the Serbo-Croatian return song.* Berkeley: University of California Press, 1990.

—— *Immanent Art: From Structure to Meaning in Traditional Oral Epic.* Bloomington: Indiana University Press, 1991.

—— *Homer's Traditional Art.* Pennsylvania: Pennsylvania State University Press, 1999.

—— *How to Read an Oral Poem.* Urbana: University of Illinois Press, 2002.

Francke, A.H. *A History of Western Tibet.* 1907; reprint, Delhi: Pilgrims Books, 1999.

—— *Antiquities of Indian Tibet.* 1914; reprint, Delhi: Low Price Publications, 1999.

—— *A Lower Ladakhi Version of the Kesar Saga.* (1905–1941); reprint, New Delhi: Asian Educational Services, 2000.

Freedman, Maurice. *The Study of Chinese Society: Essays by Maurice Freedman.* Stanford, CA: Stanford University Press, 1979.

French, J.C. *Himalayan Art.* London: Oxford University Press, 1931.

French, Rebecca Redwood. *The Golden Yoke: The Legal Cosmology of Buddhist Tibet.* Ithaca: Cornell University Press, 1995.

Garfield, Jay L. and Ngawang Samten. *Ocean of Reasoning: A Great Commentary on Nāgārjuna's Mūlamadhyamakakārikā.* Oxford: Oxford University Press, 2006.

Gega Lama. *Principles of Tibetan Art vol. 1.* Darjeeling: Jamyang Singe, 1983.

Germano, David. "Architecture and Absence in the Secret Tantric History of the Great Perfection (*rdzogs chen*)." *Journal of the International Association of Buddhist Studies* 17.2 (1994): 203–335.

Gladney, Dru. *Dislocating China. Reflections on Muslims, Minorities, and Other Subaltern Subjects.* London: Hurst, 2004.

Goldstein, Melvyn C. "An Anthropological Study of the Tibetan Political System." PhD Dissertation: University of Washington, 1968.

—— "The Circulation of Estates in Tibet: Reincarnation, Land and Politics." *Journal of Asian Studies* 32.3 (May 1973): 445–55.

—— *A History of Modern Tibet: the Demise of the Lamaist State 1913–1951.* University of California Press, 1989.

—— *Nomads of Golok: a Report* (1996). http://www.cwru.edu/affil/tibet/nomads.htm

—— ed. *The New Tibetan-English Dictionary of Modern Tibetan.* Berkeley: University of California Press, 2001.

—— *A History of Modern Tibet. Vol. 2, The Calm Before the Storm: 1951–1955.* University of California Press, 2007.

Goldstein, Melvyn C. and Cynthia M. Beall. *Die Nomaden Westtibets. Der Überlebenskampf der tibetischen Hirtennomaden.* Nürnberg: DA Verlag, 1991.

Goldstein, Melvyn C. and Matthew T. Kapstein, eds. *Buddhism in Contemporary Tibet. Religious Revival and Cultural Identity.* Berkeley, Los Angeles and London: University of California Press, 1998.

Goodman, David. "The Campaign to 'Open Up the West': National, Provincial-level and Local Perspectives." *The China Quarterly* 178 (2004): 317–34.

Goody, Jack. *The Interface between the Written and the Oral.* Cambridge: Cambridge University Press, 1987.

Gould, Rachelle. "Himalayan Viagra, Himalayan Gold? Cordyceps Sinensis Brings New Forces to the Bhutanese Himalaya." *The Bulletin of the Yale Tropical Resources Institute* 26 (2007): 63–68.

Graziosi, Barbara. *Inventing Homer: The Early Reception of Epic.* Cambridge: Cambridge University Press, 2002.

Guibaut, André. *Tibetan Venture.* Hong Kong: Oxford University Press, 1987.

Gyatsho, Thubten Legshay. *Gateway to the Temple: Manual of Tibetan Monastic Customs, Art, Building and Celebrations.* Kathmandu: Ratna Pustak Bhandar, 1979.

Gyatso, Janet. *Apparitions of the Self. The Secret Autobiographies of a Tibetan Visionary.* Woodstock: Princeton University Press, 1998.

—— "Presidential Address, Tenth Seminar of the International Association for Tibetan Studies, Oxford, 2003." *Journal of the International Association for Tibetan Studies* 1 (2005): 1–5. www.thdl.org?id=T1216.

Gyatso, Tenzin (Fourteenth Dalai Lama). *My Land and My People.* 1977; reprint, New Delhi: Srishti Publishers and Distributors, 1999.

—— *Freedom in Exile: The Autobiography of the Dalai Lama.* London: Hodder & Stoughton, 1990.

Gyurme Dorje. *Tibet Handbook.* Bath: Footprint Handbooks, 1999.

Halkias, Georgios T. "Transferring to the Land of Bliss: Among Texts and Practices of Sukhāvatī in Tibet." DPhil Thesis: University of Oxford, 2006.

—— "Until the Feathers of the Winged Black Raven Will Turn White: Perspectives and Sources for the Tibet-Bashahr treaty of 1679–1684." *Proceedings of the 13th IALS Conference*, (September 2007). Rome: *Rivista degli Studi Orientali*, forthcoming.

Hall, Stuart. "New Ethnicities." In *'Race' Culture and Difference*, D. James and A. Rattansi (eds.). London: Sage, 1989, 252–60.

Handa, O.C. *Buddhist Monasteries of Himachal.* Delhi: Indus Publications, 2004.

Harrer, Heinrich. *Seven Years in Tibet.* 1953; reprint, New York: Jeremy P. Tarcher/Putnam, 1997.

—— *Return to Tibet.* 1984; reprint, London: Phoenix, 2000.

Harris, Clare. *In the Image of Tibet: Tibetan Painting after 1959.* London, Reaktion Books, 1999.

Harrison, Paul. "A Brief History of the Tibetan *bKa' 'gyur.*" In *Tibetan Literature: Studies in Genre*, José Cabezon and Roger Jackson (eds.). Ithaca: Snow Lion, 1996, 70–94.

Hazod, Guntram. "In the Garden of the White Mare: Encounters with History and Cult in Tshal Gung-thang." In *Rulers on the Celestial Plain: Ecclesiastical and Secular Hegemony in Medieval Tibet. A Study of Tshal Gung-thang*, Per Sørensen and Guntram Hazod, in cooperation with Tsering Gyalbo. Vienna: Verlag der Österreichischen Akademie der Wissenschaften, 2007, 571–632.

Heissig, Walther. *Geser-Studien: Untersuchungen zu der Erzählstoffen in den 'neuen' Kapiteln des mongolischen Geser-Zyklus.* Opladen: Westdeutscher Verlag, Abhandlungen der Rheinisch-Westfälischen Akademie der Wissenschaften, 69, 1983.

Herrmann, Silke. *Kesar-Versionen aus Ladakh.* Asiatische Forschungen Band 109. Wiesbaden: Otto Harrassowitz, 1991.

Ho, Peter. *Institutions in Transition. Land Ownership, Property Rights and Social Conflict in China.* Oxford: Oxford University Press, 2005.

Hoffman, Michael E., ed. *Tibet, The Sacred Realm, Photographs 1880–1950*, Chronicle by Lobsang Lhalungpa. 1983; reprint, New York: Aperture Foundation, 1997.
Holliday, John, and Matt Cleaver. "On the Trail of the Yak: Ancient Cordyceps in the Modern World." *Aloha Medicinals Project Report 2004* (2004): 1–63.
Holmgren, Jennifer. "Imperial Marriage in the Native Chinese and Non-Han State, Han to Ming." In *Marriage and Inequality in Chinese Society*, Rubie S. Watson and Patricia Buckley Ebrey (eds.). Berkeley: University of California Press, 1991, 58–96.
Horlemann, Bianca. "Modernization Efforts in Mgo Log: a Chronicle, 1970–2000." In *Amdo Tibetans in Transition: Society and Culture during the Post-Mao Era*, Toni Huber (ed.). Leiden: Brill, 2002, 241–69.
—— "Tibetische Viehzüchter in der VR China: neue Chancen - neue Konflikte." In *Asien heute: Konflikte ohne Ende...*, Stephan Conermann (ed.). Hamburg: EB-Verlag, 2006, 37–52.
—— "The Goloks through Western Eyes: Fascination and Horror." In *Tibet in 1938–1939. Photographs from the Ernst Schäfer Expedition to Tibet*, Isrun Engelhardt (ed.). Chicago: Serindia, 2007, 91–102, 256–57.
Huber, Toni. "Territorial Control by 'Sealing' (*rgya sdom pa*). A Religio-political Practice in Tibet." *Zentralasiatische Studien* 33 (2004): 127–52.
—— "Gewalt in tibetisch-buddhistischen Gesellschaften." *Mitteilungen des Museums für Völkerkunde Hamburg* Neue Folge 36 (2005): 429–61.
Human Rights Watch (HRW). *"No One Has the Liberty to Refuse." Tibetan Herders Forcibly Relocated in Gansu, Qinghai, Sichuan, and the Tibet Autonomous Region. Human Rights Watch* 19.8 (June 2007).
Humphrey, Caroline. "Barter and Economic Disintegration." *Man* 20.1 (1985): 48–72.
Imaeda, Yoshiro. "Rituel des traités de paix sino-tibétains du VIIIe au IXe siècle." In *La Sérinde, Terre d'échanges*, Monique Cohen, Jean-Pierre Drège and Jacques Giès (eds.). (Paris: La Documentations Française, 2001), 87–98.
Jamgön Kongtrul Lodrö Thayé. *The Autobiography of Jamgön Kongtrul. A Gem of Many Colors*, Richard Barron (ed. and trans.). Ithaca: Snow Lion, 2003.
—— *The Treasury of Knowledge: Book One: Myriad Worlds*, Kalu Rinpoche Translation Group (trans.). New York: Snow Lion, 1995; *Book Five: Buddhist Ethics,* Kalu Rinpoche Translation Group (trans.). New York: Snow Lion, 1998; *Book Six, Part Three: Frameworks of Buddhist Philosophy,* Elizabeth M. Callahan (trans.). New York: Snow Lion, 2007; *Book Six, Part Four: Systems of Buddhist Tantra,* Ingrid McLeod and Elio Guarisco (trans.). New York: Snow Lion, 2006; *Book Eight, Part Four: Esoteric Instructions, A Detailed Presentation of the Process of Meditation in Vajrayana,* Sarah Harding (trans.). New York: Snow Lion, 2008.
Jäschke, Heinrich A. *Handwörterbuch der Tibetischen Sprache.* 1871; reprint, Bad Honnef am Rhein: Biblio Verlag, 1971.
Jetly, Nancy. *India China Relations, 1947–1977: A Study of Parliament's Role in the Making of Foreign Policy.* New Delhi: Radiant Publishers, 1979.
Kaneko, Shuichi. "T'ang International Relations and Diplomatic Correspondence." *Acta Asiatica* 55 (1988): 75–101.
Kapstein, Matthew T. "*gDams ngag*: Tibetan technologies of the Self." In *Tibetan Literature: Studies in Genre*, José Cabezón and Roger Jackson (eds.). Ithaca: Snow Lion Publications, 1996, 275–89.
—— "Concluding Remarks." In *Buddhism in Contemporary Tibet – Religious Revival and Cultural Identity*, Melvyn Goldstein and Matthew Kapstein (eds.). Berkeley: University of California, 1998, 139–49.
—— *The Tibetan Assimilation of Buddhism. Conversion, Contestation, and Memory.* Oxford: Oxford University Press, 2000.

—— "The Treaty Temple of De-ga g.yu-tshal: Identification and Iconography." In *Essays on the International Conference on Tibetan Art and Archaeology and Art*. Chengdu: Sichuan ren min chu ban she, 2004, 98–126.

—— "Tibetan Technologies of the Self, Part II: The Teachings of the Eight Great Conveyances." In *The Pandita and the Siddha. Tibetan Studies in Honour of E. Gene Smith*, Ramon N. Prats (ed.). Dharamsala: Amnye Machen Institute, 2007, 110–29.

Karmay, Samten G. *The Treasury of Good Sayings: A Tibetan History of Bon*. London: Oxford University Press (1972; reprint, Delhi: Motilal Banarsidass, 2001).

—— "A General Introduction to the History and Doctrines of Bon." *Memoirs of the Research Department of the Toyo Bunko 33* (1975): 171–218. Also in Karmay 1998, 105–56.

—— "L'homme et le bœuf: le rituel du *glud* ('rançon')." *Journal asiatique* 279.3–4 (1991): 327–81.

—— *Secret Visions of the Fifth Dalai Lama: The Gold Manuscript in the Fournier Collection*. London: Serindia Publications, 1988.

—— "The Theoretical Basis of the Tibetan Epic." *Bulletin of the School of Oriental and African Studies* 16.2 (1993): 234–46. Also in Karmay 1998, 472–88.

—— *The Arrow and the Spindle: Studies in History, Myths, Rituals and Beliefs in Tibet*. Kathmandu: Mandala Book Point, 1998.

—— "An Open Letter by Pho-brang Zhi ba 'od." In *The Arrow and the Spindle. Studies in History, Myths, Rituals and Beliefs in Tibet*. Kathmandu: Mandala Book Point, 1998, 17–40.

—— "The Ordinance of Lha bla ma Ye shes 'od." In *The Arrow and the Spindle. Studies in History, Myths, Rituals and Beliefs in Tibet*. Kathmandu: Mandala Book Point, 1998, 3–17.

Karmay, Samten G. and Jeff Watt, eds. *Bon The Magic Word: The Indigenous Religion of Tibet*. New York and London: Rubin Museum of Arts and Philip Wilson Publishers, 2007.

Kirby, W.C. "China's Internationalization in the Early People's Republic: Dreams of a Socialist World Economy." In *The History of the PRC (1949–1976)*, Julia Strauss (ed.). Cambridge: Cambridge University Press, 2007, 16–36.

Kletter, Christa and Monica Kriechbaum. *Tibetan Medicinal Plants*. Stuttgart: Medpharm Scientific Publishers, 2001.

Klieger, P. Christiaan, ed. *Tibet, Self, and the Tibetan Diaspora: Voices of Difference. Proceedings of the Ninth Seminar of the International Association for Tibetan Studies, Leiden 2000*. Leiden: Brill, 2002.

Knaus, John Kenneth. *Orphans and the Cold War: America and the Tibetan Struggle for Survival*. New York: Public Affairs, 1999.

Kornman, Robin. "A Comparative Study of a Buddhist Version of the Epic of Gesar of Ling." PhD Dissertation: Princeton University, 1995.

Korom, Frank, ed. *Constructing Tibetan Culture: Contemporary Perspective*. St-Hyacinthe, Quebec: World Heritage Press, 1997.

—— "Introduction: Place, Space and Identity: The Cultural, Economic and Aesthetic Politics of Tibetan Diaspora." In *Tibetan Culture in the Diaspora: Papers Presented at a Panel of the 7th Seminar of the International Association for Tibetan Studies, Graz 1995*, Frank J. Korom (ed.). Vienna: Verlag der Österreichischen Akademie der Wissenschaften, 1997, 1–8.

—— ed. *Tibetan Culture in the Diaspora. Proceedings of the Seventh Seminar of the International Association for Tibetan Studies, Graz 1995*. Vienna: Verlag der Österreichischen Akademie der Wissenschaften, 1997.

Kruczkowska, Maria. "Setki aresztowanych po awanturze o Dalajlamę." *Gazeta Wyborcza* 181 (04.08.2007-05.08.2007): 9.

van der Kuijp, Leonard W.J. "Studies in Mkhas-Grub-Rje I: Mkhas-Grug-Rje's Epistemological Oeuvre and his Philological Remarks on Dignaga's *Pramāṇasamuccaya*." *Berliner Indologische Studien* 1 (1985): 75–106.

Kutcher, Joan Carole. "The Biography of the First Dalai Lama, Entitled 'Rje thams cad mkhyen pa dge 'dun grub dpal bzang po'i rnam thar ngo mtshar rmad byung nor bu'i phreng ba': a Translation and Analysis." PhD Dissertation, University of Pennsylvania, 1979.

Lama Zopa Rinpoche, *The Benefits of Building a Monastery*, http://www.lamayeshe.com/lamazopa/build.shtml, accessed 23 July 2008.

Lama, Kunga. "Crowded Mountains, Empty Towns: Commodification and Contestation in Cordyceps Harvesting in Eastern Tibet." MA Thesis: University of Colorado, 2007.

Lamb, Alastair. *British India and Tibet, 1766–1910*. 1960; reprint, London: Routledge & Kegan Paul, 1986.

—— *The McMahon Line. A Study of the Relations between India, China and Tibet, 1904 to 1914*. London: Routledge & Kegan Paul, 1966.

—— *Tibet, China and India, 1914–1950. A History of Imperial Diplomacy*. Hertingfordbury: Roxford Books, 1989.

Lange, Kristina. *Die Werke des Regenten Sans Rgyas Rgya mc'o (1653–1705): eine philologisch-historische Studie zum tibetischsprachigen Schrifttum*. Veröffentlichungen des Museums für Völkerkunde zu Leipzig. Heft 27. Berlin: Akademie Verlag, 1976.

Lee, D.Y. *The History of the Early Relations between China and Tibet. From the Chiu t'ang-shu, a Documentary Survey*. Bloomington, IN: Eastern Press, 1991.

Lessing, Ferdinand D. "Bodhisattva Confucius." In *Ritual and Symbol: Collected Essays on Lamaism and Chinese Symbolism*, Professor Lou Tsu-K'uang (ed.). Taipei: The Chinese Association for Folklore, 1976, 91–94.

Li, Brenda. "A Phyogs med Pilgrimage by a Ris med Bonpo Monk, 1924–1925: as Illustrated in the Biography of Khyung sprul 'Jigs med nam mkha'i rdo rje." MPhil Dissertation: University of Oxford, 2007.

Li, Fang Kuei and W. South Coblin. *A Study of the Old Tibetan Inscriptions*. Taipei: ROC, 1987.

Lin, C. Zhe (林照著). "President Chiang Kai-shek Speech." In *The Lama Killing, the Tragedy of Tibetan 40-year Exile* (喇嘛剎人), Taiwan, 324–40.

Lin, Shen-yu. "The Tibetan Image of Confucius." *Revue d'Etudes Tibetaines* 12 (2007): 105–29.

Lindegger-Stauffer, Peter. "Das Klösterliche Tibet-Institut in Rikon/Zurich." *Asiatische Studien 25* (1971): 377–88.

Liu, Hengwei, Weidou Ni, Zheng Li and Linwei Ma. "Strategic thinking on IGCC development in China." *Energy Policy* 36 (2008): 1–11.

Lopez, Donald, Jr. "Polemical Literature (*dGag lan*)." In *Tibetan Literature: Studies in Genre*, José Ignacio Cabezón and Roger R. Jackson (eds.). Ithaca: Snow Lion, 1996, 217–28.

—— *The Madman's Middle Way: Reflections on Reality of the Tibetan Monk Gendun Chopel*. Chicago: University of Chicago Press, 2006.

Lord, Albert B. *The Singer of Tales*. Cambridge, MA: Harvard University Press, 1960.

—— *Epic Singers and Oral Tradition*. Ithaca: Cornell University Press, 1991.

—— *The Singer Resumes the Tale*. Ithaca: Cornell University Press, 1995.

Macdonald, Ariane. *Le Maṇḍala du Mañjuśrīmūlakalpa*. Paris: Adrien Maisonneuve, 1962.

Macdonald, David. *Twenty Years in Tibet*. 1932; reprint, New Delhi: Vintage Books, 1995.

Malkki, Liisa. "National Geographic: The Rooting of Peoples and the Territorialization of National Identity among Scholars and Refugees." In *Culture, Power, Place: Explorations in Critical Anthropology*, A. Gupta and J. Ferguson (eds.). 1992; reprint, Durham, NC: 1997), 52–74.

Manderscheid, Angela. *Lebens- und Wirtschaftsformen von Nomaden im Osten des tibetischen Hochlandes* (Abhandlungen-Anthropogeographie, Institut für Geographische Wissenschaften, Freie Universität Berlin, Band 61). Berlin: Dietrich Reimer Verlag, 1999.

Marshall, Steven D. and Susette Ternent Cooke. *Tibet outside the TAR. Control, Exploitation and Assimilation. Development with Chinese Characteristics*. CD-Rom, 1997.

Martin, Dan. "Illusion Web. Locating the Guhyagarbha Tantra in Buddhist Intellectual History." In *Silver on Lapis. Tibetan Literary Culture and History*, Christopher I. Beckwith (ed.). Bloomington, IN: The Tibet Society, 1987, 175–220.

—— "Lay Religious Movements in 11th- and 12th-Century Tibet: A Survey of Sources." *Kailash* 18 (1996): 23–55.

—— *Unearthing Bon Treasures: Life and Contested Legacy of a Tibetan Scripture revealer with a general Bibliography of Bon*. Leiden: Brill, 2001.

Mayer, Robert. "The Sa skya Paṇḍita, the White Panacea, and Clerical Buddhism's Current Credibilty Crisis." *Tibet Journal* 19.1 (1994): 79–105.

—— *A Scripture of the Ancient Tantra Collection: The Phur pa bcu gnyis*. Oxford: Kiscadale Publications, 1996.

—— "Were The Gsar ma pa Polemicists Justified in Rejecting Some rNying ma pa Tantras?" In *Proceedings of the 7th Seminar of the International Association for Tibetan Studies, volume II*, Ernst Steinkellner, et al. (eds.). Vienna: Verlag der Österreichischen Akademie der Wissenschaften, 1997, 619–31.

McGovern, William Montgomery. *To Lhasa in Disguise. A Secret Expedition through Mysterious Tibet*. 1924; reprint, New Delhi: Book Faith India, 1992.

McKay, Alex. *Tibet and the British Raj. The Frontier Cadre 1904–1947*. London: Curzon, 1997.

Menzies, Nicholas. *Our Forest, Your Ecosystem, Their Timber: Communities, Conservation, and the State in Community-Based Forest Management*. New York: Columbia University Press, 2007.

Miller, Daniel J. "Tough Times for Tibetan Nomads in Western China: Snowstorms, Settling down, Fences, and the Demise of Traditional Nomadic Pastoralism." *Nomadic Peoples* 4.1 (2000): 83–109.

Miłosz, Czesław. *The Captive Mind*. London: Penguin Books, 2001.

Mimaki, Katsumi. "Doxographie tibétaine et classifications indiennes." In *Bouddhisme et culture locales: quelques cas de réciproques adaptations. Actes du colloque franco-japonais, septembre 1991*, Fukui Fumimasa and Gérard Fussman (eds.). Paris: École française d'Extrême-Orient, 1994, 115–136.

Minchin, Elizabeth. "The Poet Appeals to his Muse: Homeric Invocations in the Context of Epic Performance." *The Classical Journal* 91.1 (1995): 25–33.

Minhas, Poonam. *Traditional Trade and Trading Centres in Himachal Pradesh*. Delhi: Indus Publishing Company, 1998.

Moran, Arik. "From Mountain trade to jungle politics: The transformation of kingship in Bashahr, 1815–1914." *The Indian Economic and Social History Review* 44.2 (2007): 147–77.

Mori, Masahide. "The Bon Deities Depicted in the Wall Paintings in the Bon-brgya Monastery." In *New Horizons in Bon Studies*, Yasuhiko Nagano and Samten G. Karmay (eds). Osaka: National Museum of Ethnology, 2000, 509–49.

MykoTroph Institut für Ernährungs und Pilzheilkunde. *Heilpilze: Cordyceps*. http://www.mykotroph.de/pdf/MykoTroph_Factsheet_Cordyceps.pdf (accessed 25 August 2007).

Namgyal, T. "The twisting saga of Tibet-Taiwan relations." *Asia Times online*, 23 May 2003.

NBS. "Fast Growth on Urban Household Income and Expenditure in Past Half Year." China Statistical Information Network (ed.). National Bureau of Statistics of China, 2006.

Nebesky-Wojkowitz, René de. *Oracles and Demons of Tibet: the Cult and Iconography of the Tibetan Protective Deities*. Gravenhage: Mouton, 1956.

Newland, Guy. "Debate Manuals in dGe lugs Monastic Colleges." In *Tibetan Literature: Studies in Genre*, José Ignacio Cabezón and Roger R. Jackson (eds.). Ithaca: Snow Lion, 1996, 202–16.

Norbu, Dawa. "The Settlements: Participation and Integration." In *Exile as Challenge: The Tibetan Diaspora*, Dagmar Bernstoff and Hebertus Von Welck (eds.). Hyderabad: Orient Longman Private Ltd, 2004, 186–212.

—— "Tibet in Sino-Indian Relations: The Centrality of Marginality." *Asian Survey* 37.11 (November 1997): 1078–95.

Norbu, Namkhai. *Drung Deu and Bon: Narrations, Symbolic Languages and the Bon Tradition of Ancient Tibet* (trans A. Clemente). Dharamsala: Library of Tibetan Works and Archives, 1995.

Noriega, Ernesto. "Tradition and Innovation in the Tibetan Diaspora." In *Managing Change; Sustainable Approaches to the Conservation of the Built Environment*, Jean Marie Teutonico and Frank Matero (eds.). Los Angeles: Getty Trust Publications, Getty Conservation Institute, 2003, 161–79.

Nowak, Margaret. *Tibetan Refugees: Youth and the Generation of Meaning*. New Brunswick, NJ: Rutgers University Press, 1984.

Nyiri, Pál and J. Breidenbach. *China Inside Out: Contemporary Chinese Nationalism and Transnationalism*. Budapest: Central European University Press, 2005.

Obermiller, Ernst. *The History of Buddhism in India and Tibet by Bu ston*. 1932; reprint, Delhi: Sri Satguru Publications, 1999.

Ong, Walter J. *Orality and Literacy*. New York: Routledge, 1982.

Oppitz, Michael. "Close-Up and Wide-Angle. On Comparative Ethnography in the Himalayas – and Beyond. The Mahesh Chandra Regmi Lecture, Dec. 15th 2006." *European Bulletin of Himalayan Research* 31 (2007): 155–71.

Ostrom, Elinor. "Governing the Commons." In *The Political Economy of Institutions and Decision*, James Alt and Douglass North (eds.). Cambridge: Cambridge University Press, 1990.

—— "Revisiting the Commons: Local Lessons, Global Challenges." *Science* 284 (1999): 278–84.

Pabongkapa, Jampa Tenzin Trinley Gyatso. *Liberation in the Palm of Your Hand: A Concise Discourse on the Path to Enlightenment*. Somerville, MA: Wisdom Publications, 1997.

Pan, Yihong. "The Sino-Tibetan Treaties in the Tang Dynasty." *T'oung Pao* 78 (1992): 116–61.

—— "Marriage Alliance and Chinese Princesses in International Politics from Han through T'ang." *Asia Major* 10.1–2 (1997): 95–131.

Panczenlama (10th Panchen Lama, Chos kyi rgyal mtshan). "Wystąpienie na forum Stałego Komitetu TRA Ogólnochińskiego Zgromadzenia Przedstawicieli Ludowych, Pekin 1987." In *Tybet. Zamiast nadziei i błogosławieństw*, Adam Kozieł (ed.). Warszawa: Stowarzyszenie Studenci dla Wolnego Tybetu, 2008, 139–48.

Parry, Milman. "Studies in the Epic Technique of Oral Verse-Making I: Homer and Homeric Style." *Harvard Studies in Classical Philology* 41 (1930): 73–147.

Pelliot, Paul. *Histoire ancienne du Tibet*. Paris: Librairie d'Amérique et d'Orient, 1961.

Peretti-Watel, Patrick. *Sociologie du risque*. Paris: Armand Colin, 2000.

Petech, Luciano. "The Tibet-Ladakhi Moghul War of 1681–83." *The Indian Historical Quarterly* 23.3 (1947): 169–99.

—— *Aristocracy and Government in Tibet, 1728–1959*. Serie Orientale Roma XLV. Rome: IsMEO, 1973.

Petrova, R.D and A.Z. Reznick et al. "Fungal Metabolites Modulating NF-kappa B Activity: An Approach to Cancer Therapy and Chemoprevention (Review)." *Oncology Reports* 19.2 (2008): 299–308.

Phayul, *Bhagat Singh Samithi Asks Tibetans to 'Quit India'*, http://www.phayul.com/News/article.aspx?article=Bhagat+Singh+Samithi+Asks+Tibetans+to+'Quit+India'&id=9771&c=1&t=1.

Phuntsok Takla Tashi interview with *Zla gsar* (new moon), an occasional Tibetan magazine published from Delhi, Issue 3–4 (1991): 120–67.

Pirie, Fernanda. "Feuding, Mediation and the Negotiation of Authority among the Nomads of Eastern Tibet." *Max Planck Institute for Social Anthropology. Working Papers*, 72 (2005).

Poster, Carol. "Review of Homer's Traditional Art by JM Foley." *Rocky Mountain Review of Language and Literature* 54.2 (2000): 95–98.

Powers, Marshall K. "Areas Studies." *The Journal of Higher Education*. 26.2 (1955): 82–89, 113.
Propp, Vladimir. *Morphology of the Folktale* (trans. Lawrence Scott). 1928, reprint Austin: University of Texas Press, 1968.
Rabgey, T. "Normalizing Taiwan-Tibetan Relations." PhD Dissertation: Harvard University, 2003.
Rabinow, Paul. *Anthropos Today: Reflections on Modern Equipment*. Princeton, NJ: Princeton University Press, 2003.
Radio Free Asia (RFA). *Tibetans, Chinese Security Forces Clash in Qinghai*. http://www.rfa.org/english/news/social/2005/06/01/tibetan_clash/ (accessed 29 August 2007).
Rahul, Ram. *The Government and Politics of Tibet*. Delhi: Vikas Publications, 1969.
—— "The System of Administration in the Himalayas," *Asian Survey* 9.9 (Sep. 1969): 694–702.
Rhoton, Jared Douglas. *A Clear Differentiation of the Three Codes: Essential Distinctions Among the Individual Liberation, Great Vehicle, and Tantric Systems: The Sdom Gsum Rab Dbye and Six Letters of Sa skya Paṇ ḍi ta Kun dGa' rgyal mtshan*. Albany: State University of New York Press, 2002.
Richardson, Hugh E. *A Corpus of Early Tibetan Inscriptions*. London: Royal Asiatic Society, 1985.
—— "Further Fragments from Dunhuang." In *High Peaks, Pure Earth: Collected Writings on Tibetan History and Culture, Hugh Richardson*, Michael Aris (ed.). London: Serindia, 1998, 28–36.
—— "Hunting Accidents in Early Tibet." In *High Peaks Pure Earth: Collected Writings on Tibetan History and Culture, Hugh Richardson*, Michael Aris (ed.). London: Serindia, 1998, 149–66.
Ringu Tulku. *The Ri-me Philosophy of Jamgön Kongtrul the Great. A Study of the Buddhist Lineages of Tibet*. Boston and London: Shambhala, 2006.
Rinjing Dorje. *Food in Tibetan Life*. London: Prospect Books Place, 1985.
Rock, Joseph F. "Seeking the Mountains of Mystery. An Expedition on the China-Tibet Frontier to the Unexplored Amnyi Machen Range, One of Whose Peaks Rival Everest." *National Geographic Magazine* 57.2 (1930): 131–85.
—— *The Amnye Ma-chhen Range and Adjacent Regions. A Monographic Study*. Rome: IsMEO, 1956.
Rockhill, William W. *The Land of the Lamas: Notes of a Journey Through China, Mongolia and Tibet*. New Delhi: Asian Publication Services, 1975.
Roerich, George N. *Biography of Dharmasvāmin by 'Ju ba Chos dar*. Historical Researches Series, vol. 2. Patna: K.P. Jayaswal Research Institute, 1959.
—— *The Blue Annals*. 1949–1953; reprint, Delhi: Motilal Banarsidass, 1976.
Ronge, Veronika. *Das tibetische Handwerkertum vor 1959*. Beiträge zur Südasienforschung Bd. 43. Wiesbaden: F. Steiner, 1978.
Rose, H.A. *A Glossary of the Tribes and Castes of the Punjab and North-West Frontier Province: Based on the census report for the Punjab, 1883 / by the late Sir Denzil Ibbetson and the census report for the Punjab, 1892, by Sir Edward Maclagan and compiled by H. A. Rose*. Lahore: Printed by the superintendent, Government printing, Punjab, 1911–19.
Roy, Arundhati. *An Ordinary Person's Guide to Empire*. New Delhi: Penguin Books, 2006.
Roy, H.E., D.C. Steinkraus, J. Eilenberg, A.E. Hajek, and J.K. Pell. "Bizarre Interactions and Endgames: Entomopathogenic Fungi and Their Arthropod Hosts." *Annua. Rev. Entomol.* 51 (2006): 331–57.
Safran, William. "Comparing Diasporas: A Review Essay." *Diaspora* 8.3 (Winter 1999): 255–91.
—— "Diasporas in Modern Societies: Myths of Homeland and Return." *Diaspora* 1.1 (Spring 1991): 83–99.
Samuel, Geoffrey. "The Origins and Meaning of the East Tibetan Epic." In *Proceedings of the Fifth IATS Conference (1989)*, Shoren Ihara and Zuiho Yamaguchi (eds.). Narita: Naritasan Shinshoji, 1992, 711–22.

—— "The Gesar Epic of East Tibet." In *Tibetan Literature. Studies in Genre*, José I. Cabezón and Roger Jackson (eds.). Ithaca: Snow Lion, 1996, 358–67.

Sangpo, Khetsun (mKhas btsun bzang po), ed. *Biographical Dictionary of Tibet and Tibetan Buddhism*. Dharamsala: LTWA. 1973.

Van Schaik, Sam. "Oral Teachings and Written Texts: Transmission and Transformation in Dunhuang." In *Contributions to the Cultural History of Early Tibet*, Matthew Kapstein and Brandon Dotson (eds.). Leiden: Brill, 2007, 183–208.

Semvāl, P. N. "Tibbat aur Buśaihr kī cir-maitrī" (Tibet and Bashahr's Long Lasting Friendship). *Somsī*, 4.2, (April 1978): 37–43.

Sèngué, Tcheuky. *Le Temple Tibétaine et son Symbolisme*. Vernègues: Claire Lumière, 1998

Seyfort Ruegg, David. "Deux problèmes d'exégèse et de pratique tantriques." In *Tantric and Taoist Studies in Honor of R. A. Stein*, M. Strickmann (ed.). *Mélanges chinois et Bouddhiques* 20, 1981, 212–26.

—— *Ordre spirituel et ordre temporel dans la pensée Bouddhique de l'Inde et du Tibet. Quatre conférences au Collège de France*. Paris: Collège de France, 1995.

—— *The Symbiosis of Buddhism/Hinduism in South Asia and of Buddhism with 'local cults' in Tibet and the Himalayan Region*. Vienna: Österreichische Akademie der Wissenschaften, 2007.

Shakabpa, W. D. *Tibet: A Political History*. New York: Potala Publications, 1984.

Shakya, Tsering. *The Dragon in the Land of Snows: A Modern History of Tibet since 1949*. London: Pimlico, 1999.

Sharma, S. "Trade of Cordyceps Sinensis from High Altitudes of the Indian Himalaya: Conservation and Biotechnological Priorities." *Current Science* 86.12 (2004): 1614–19.

Sheffer, Gabriel. *Modern Diasporas in International Politics*. London: Croom Helm, 1986.

—— "Whither the Study of Ethnic Diasporas: Some Theoretical, Definitional, Analytical and Comparative Considerations." In *Les réseaux des diasporas*, Georges Prevelakis (ed.). Paris: L'Harmattan, 1996, 37–46.

—— "Nationalism, Nation-States and Ethno-National Diasporas: Theoretical Aspects," Paper presented at the 2004 World Conference on Nationalities.

Shen, Tsung-lien. *Tibet and the Tibetans*. Stanford, CA: Stanford University Press, 1973.

Sherring, Charles A. *Western Tibet and the British Borderland. The Sacred country of Hindus and Buddhists with an Account of the Government, Religion and Customs of its People*. London: E. Arnold, 1906.

Sidhu, Waheguru Pal Singh and Yuan, Jing-dong, eds. *China and India: Cooperation or Conflict?* Boulder, CO: Lynne Rienner Publishers, 2003.

Smith, E. Gene. "Introduction." In *Kongtrul's Encyclopedia of Indo-Tibetan Culture*, Lokesh Chandra (ed.). New Delhi International Academy of Indian Culture, 1970.

—— *Among Tibetan Texts: History and Literature of the Himalayan Plateau*, Kurtis Schaeffer (ed.). Boston: Wisdom Publications, 2001.

Smith, John D. "The Singer or the Song? A Reassessment of Lord's 'Oral Theory.'" *Man* 12 (1977): 141–53.

Smith, Warren. *Tibetan Nation: A History of Tibetan Nationalism and Sino-Tibetan Relations*. Boulder, CO: Westview Press, 1996.

Snellgrove, David L. *The Nine Ways of Bon*. London Oriental Series vol. 18. London: Oxford University Press, 1967.

—— *Indo-Tibetan Buddhism: Indian Buddhists and Their Tibetan Successors*. 2 vols. Boston: Shambhala, 1987.

Snellgrove, David and Hugh Richardson. *A Cultural History of Tibet*. 1968; reprint, Boston: Shambhala Publications, 1995.

Sood. *Shimla Distric Gazeteer.* Shimla: Goel's Press, 1985.

Sørensen, Per K. and Guntram Hazod, in cooperation with Tsering Gyalbo. *Thundering Falcon: An Inquiry into the History and Cult of Khra-'brug, Tibet's First Buddhist Temple.* Vienna: Österreichische Akademie der Wissenschaften, 2005.

—— *Rulers on the Celestial Plain: Ecclesiastical and Secular Hegemony in Medieval Tibet. A Study of Tshal Gung-thang.* Vienna: Verlag der Österreichischen Akademie der Wissenschaften, 2007.

Soymié, Michel. "L'entrevue de Confucius et de Hiang T'o." *Journal Asiatique* 242 (1954): 311–92.

Stearns, Cyrus. *Luminous Lives. The Story of the Early Masters of the Lam 'Bras Tradition in Tibet.* Somerville, MA: Wisdom Publications, 2001.

Stein, R.A. *L'Épopée Tibetaine de Gesar dans sa Version Lamaïque de Ling.* Paris: Presses Universitaires de France, 1956.

—— *Recherches sur l'Épopée et le Barde au Tibet.* Paris: Presses Universitaires de France, 1959.

—— ed. *Une chronique ancienne de bSam-yas: sBa-bzed.* Paris: Publications de L'institut des Hautes Etudes Chinoises, 1961.

—— "Une Source Ancienne pour l'Histoire de l'Épopée Tibétaine: Le Rlangs Po-Ti bSe-Ru." *Journal Asiatique* 250 (1962): 76–106.

—— *La civilisation tibétaine.* 1962; reprint, Paris: L'Asiathèque-Le Sycomore, 1981.

—— "Les serments des traités sino-tibétains (8è–9è siècles)." *T'oung Pao* 74 (1988): 119–38.

—— "Un ensemble sémantique Tibétain: créer et procréer, etre et devenir, vivre, nourrir et guérir." *Bulletin of the School of Oriental and African Studies* 36.2 (1973): 412–23.

—— "L'Épopée de Gesar dans sa Version Écrite de l'Amdo." In *Indo Tibetan Studies: Papers in Honour and Appreciation of David L. Snellgrove's contribution to Indo-Tibetan Studies*, Tadeusz Skorupski (ed.). Tring: Institute of Buddhist Studies, 1990, 293–304.

Stoddard, Heather. *Le Mendiant de l'Amdo.* Paris: Société d'Ethnographie, 1985.

—— "The Nine Brothers of the White High." In *Les Habitants du Toit du Monde: Études Recueilles en Hommage à Alexander W. Macdonald,* Samten Karmay and Philippe Sagant (eds.). Paris: Nanterre, 1990, 75–110.

Ström, Axel Kristian. "Between Tibet and the West: On Traditionality, Modernity and the Development of Monastic Institutions in the Tibetan Diaspora." In *Tibetan Culture in the Diaspora. Proceedings of the Seventh Seminar of the International Association for Tibetan Studies, Graz 1995*, Frank J. Korom (ed.). Vienna: Verlag der Österreichischen Akademie der Wissenschaften, 1997, 33–50.

Sułek, Emilia. "Tseren's Last Gold Rush. Tales of *yartsa*-hunting in Tibet." *International Institute for Asian Studies Newsletter* 46 (2008): 20–21.

Sun, Shuyun. *The Long March.* London: Harper Perennial, 2007.

Sutherland, Peter. "Travelling Gods and Government by Deity: an Ethnohistory of Power, Representation and Agency in West Himalayan Polity." DPhil Thesis: University of Oxford 1998.

Takeuchi, Tsuguhito. *Old Tibetan Contracts from Central Asia.* Tokyo: Daizo Shuppan, 1995.

Taring, Rinchen Dolma. *Daughter of Tibet.* 1970; reprint, London: Wisdom Publications, 1986.

Taylor, McComas and Lama Choedak Yuthok, trans. *The Clear Mirror: A Traditional Account of Tibet's Golden Age by Sakyapa Sonam Gyaltsen.* Ithaca: Snow Lion, 1996.

Telliez, Romain. *Les officiers devant la justice dans le Royaume de France au XIVe siècle.* Paris: Honoré Champion, 2005.

Tethong, N. Tenzin. "*Tibet and Taiwan: Past History and Future Prospects.*" Paper delivered at Stanford University, 27 December 2005.

Thakur, M.R. *Myths, Rituals and Beliefs in Himachal Pradesh.* Delhi: Indus Publishing Company, 1997.

Thomas, Frederick W. *Tibetan Literary Texts and Documents Concerning Chinese Turkestan. Part I: Literary Texts.* London: Royal Asiatic Society, 1935.

Thrower, James. *The Religious History of Central Asia from the Earliest Times to the Present Day*. New York: The Edwin Mellen Press, 2004.

Thurman, Robert A.F., ed. *The Life and Teachings of Tsong Khapa*. Dharamsala: Library of Tibetan Works and Archives, 1982.

Tibet Information Network (TIN), *Mining Tibet: Mineral Exploitation in Tibetan Areas of the PRC*. London: 2002.

Tibetan Center for Human Rights and Democracy (TCHRD). *Commotion between two Communities lead to Arrest of 30 Tibetans*. July, 2007.

Tölölyan, Khachig. "Rethinking *Diaspora(s)*: Stateless Power in the Transnational Moment." *Diaspora* 5.1 (Spring 1996): 3–36.

—— "The Nation-State and Its Others: In Lieu of a Preface." *Diaspora* 1.1 (Spring 1991): 3–7.

Toussaint, Gustave-Charles. *Le Dict de Padma, Padma thang yig, Ms. de Lithang*. Paris: Bibliothèque des hautes études chinoises, Librairie Ernest Leroux, 1933. [Trans. from the French by Kenneth Douglas and Gwendolyn Bays as *The Life and Liberation of Padmasambhava*, 2 vols. Emeryville, CA: Dharma Publications, 1978.]

Travers, Alice. "La noblesse du Tibet central de 1895 à 1959: essai de définition d'un groupe social, stratégies matrimoniales et familiales." DEA Dissertation: University of Paris X-Nanterre, 2004.

Tsarong, Dundul Namgyal. *In the Service of His Country: The Biography of Dasang Damdul Tsarong*. Ithaca: Snow Lion Publications, 2000.

Tsarong, Tsewang J. *Tibetan Medicinal Plants*. Kalimpong: Tibetan Medical Publications, 1994.

Tucci, Giuseppe. *Tibetan Painted Scrolls*, 3 vols. Rome: La Libreria Dello Stato, 1949.

—— *The Religions of Tibet*. Berkeley: University of California Press, 1980.

Uebach, Helga. "Notes on the Tibetan Kinship Term *dbon*." In *Tibetan Studies in Honour of Hugh Richardson*, Michael Aris and Aung San Suu Kyi (eds.). Warminster: Aris and Phillips, 1980, 301–09.

—— "Eminent Ladies of the Tibetan Empire According to Old Tibetan Texts." In *Les Habitants du Toit du Monde*, Samten Karmay and Phillipe Sagant (eds.). Nanterre: Société d'Ethnologie, 1997, 53–74.

Uray, Géza. "Queen Sad-mar-kar's Songs in the *Old Tibetan Chronicle*." *Acta Orientalia Academiae Scientiarum Hungaricae* 25 (1972): 5–38.

—— "The Annals of the 'A zha Principality: the Problems of Chronology and Genre of the Stein Document, Tun-Huang, vol. 69, fol. 84." In *Proceedings of the Csoma De Kőrös Symposium*, Louis Ligeti (ed.). Budapest, 1978, 541–78.

—— "The Location of Khar-can and Leng-chu of the Old Tibetan Sources. In *Varia Eurasiatica: Festschrift für Professor András Róna-Tas*. Szeged, 1991, 196–227.

Van Dyke, Mary. "Constructing Tradition: Tibetan Architecture in Europe," 2 vols. PhD Dissertation: School of Oriental and African Studies, 1996.

—— "Grids and Serpents: A Tibetan Foundation Ritual in Switzerland." In *Constructing Tibetan Culture: Contemporary Perspectives*, Frank J. Korom (ed.). St-Hyacinthe, Quebec: World Heritage Press, 1997, 178–227.

Vergara, Paola Mortari and Gilles Béguin, eds. *Dimore Umane, Santuari Divini: Origini, sviluppo e diffusione dell'architettura tibetana/Demeures des Hommes, Sanctuaires des Dieux: Sources, développement et rayonnement de l'architecture tibétaine*. Rome: Universita de Roma, 1987.

Vertovec, Steven. "Three Meanings of 'Diaspora', Exemplified among South Asian Religions." *Diaspora* 6.3 (Winter 1997): 277–99.

Waddell, L. Austine. *Lhasa and its Mysteries. With a Record of the Expedition of 1903–1904*. London: John Murray, 1905

Wade, Robert. *Village Republics: Economic Conditions for Collective Action in South India, South Asian Studies*. Cambridge: Cambridge University Press, 1988.

Walker, Keith F. and H. Zhang Yang. *Fish and Fisheries at Higher Altitudes: Asia*, T. Petr (ed.). FAO Fisheries Technical Paper 385. Rome: Food and Agriculture Organization of the United Nations, 1999.

Wangchuk, Dorji. "An Eleventh Century Defense of the Authenticity of the *Guhyagarbha* Tantra." In *The Many Canons of Tibetan Buddhism*, Helmut Eimer and David Germano (eds.). Leiden: E.J. Brill, 2002, 265–91.

Wangdu, Pasang and Hildegard Diemberger (trans. and eds.) *dBa' bzhed: The Royal Narrative concerning the bringing of the Buddha's Doctrine to Tibet*. Vienna: Verlag der Österreichischen Akademie der Wissenschaften, 2000.

Watts, Jonathan. "Doctors Blame Air Pollution for China's Asthma Increases." *The Lancet* (26 August 2006), 719–20.

White, Richard. *The Middle Ground: Indians, Empires, and Republics in the Great Lakes Region, 1650–1815*. Cambridge: Cambridge University.

Williams, Dee Mack. "The Desert Discourse of Modern China." *Modern China* 23.3 (1997): 328–55.

—— *Beyond Great Walls. Environment, Identity, and Development on the Chinese Grasslands of Inner Mongolia*. Stanford, CA: Stanford University Press, 2002.

Williams, Melvin. "Dietary Supplements and Sports Performance: Herbals." *Journal of the International Society of Sports Nutrition* 3.1 (2006): 1–6.

Willis, Janice Dean. *Enlightened Beings: Life Stories from the Ganden Oral Tradition*. Boston: Wisdom Publications, 1995.

Wilson, Thomas A., ed. *On Sacred Grounds: Culture, Society, Politics, and the Formation of the Cult of Confucius*. Cambridge, MA: Harvard University Asia Center, 2002.

Winkler, Daniel. "Yartsa Gunbu – Cordycepts sinensis: Economy, Ecology & Ethno-Mycology of a Fungus Endemic to the Tibetan Plateau." In *Wildlife and Plants in Traditional and Modern Tibet: Conceptions, Exploitation and Conservation*, A. Boesi and F. Cardi (eds.). Milan: Memorie della Società Italiana di Scienze Naturali e del Museo Civico di Storia Naturale di Milano, 2004, 69–85.

—— "Yartsa Gunbu (Cordyceps sinensis) and the Fungal Commodification of the Rural Economy in Tibet AR." *Economic Botany – Special on Fungi*, forthcoming.

World Tibetan Network News (WTNN). *Gun Battle between Rival Tibetan Groups in Kardze leaves 6 Dead*. http://www.tibet.ca/en/wtnarchive/2007/7/20_6.html (accessed 29 August 2007).

Xun, C. and N. Shen et al. "Radiation Mitigation Effect of Cultured Mushroom Fungus Hirsutella Sinensis (CorImmune) Isolated from a Chinese/Tibetan Herbal Preparation – Cordyceps Sinensis." *International Journal of Radiation Biology* 84.2 (2008): 139–49.

Yamaguchi, Zuiho. "Matrimonial Relationship Between the T'u-Fan and the T'ang Dynasties (Part 2)." *Memoirs of the Research Department of the Toyo Bunko* 28 (1970): 59–100.

Yang Enhong. "On the Study of the Narrative Structure of Tibetan Epic: *A Record of King Gesar*." *Oral Tradition* 16.2 (2001): 294–316.

Yang, H. Tung, "*Letter to Bush*." *Taiwan Tati Cultural and Educational Foundation*, October 2000: 2–7.

Yang, Mayfair. "The Resilience of Guanxi and its New Deployments: A Critique of Some New Guanxi Scholarship." *The China Quarterly* (2002): 459–76.

Yeh, Emily T. "Tibetan Range Wars: Spatial Politics and Authority on the Grasslands of Amdo." *Development and Change* 34.3 (2003): 499–523.

—— "Tropes of Indolence and the Cultural Politics of Development in Lhasa, Tibet." *Annals of the Association of American Geographers* 97.3 (2007): 593–612.

Yoshikawa, N. and K. Nakamura et al. "Cordycepin and Cordyceps Sinensis Reduce the Growth of Human Promyelocytic Leukaemia Cells through the Wnt Signalling Pathway." *Clinical and Experimental Pharmacology and Physiology* 34 (2007): S61-S63.

Yoshikawa, N. and K. Nakamura et al. "Cordycepin, an Active Ingredient of Cordyceps Sinensis, Inhibits Tumor Growth by Stimulating Adenosine A3 Receptor." *Acta Pharmacologica Sinica* 27 (2006): 65–69.

Yuthok, Dorje Yudon. *The House of the Turquoise Roof.* Ithaca: Snow Lion Publications, 1990.

Zablocki, Abraham. "Taiwan's Shifting Tibet Policy: The Changing Role of the Mongolian and Tibetan Affairs Commission." Paper delivered at the AAS Annual Meeting, Chicago, March 31–April 3, 2005.

Zhang Chunguang. "Xizang de yulei ziyuan" ("Fish Resources of Tibet"). *Zhongguo Xizang (China's Tibet)*. Beijing (1997), 53–55.

Zhang, W.Y., J.Y. Yang, J.P. Chen, Y.Y. Hou and X.D. Han. "Immunomodulatory and Antitumour Effects of an Exopolysaccharide Fraction from Cultivated Cordyceps Sinensis (Chinese Caterpillar Fungus) on Tumour-Bearing Mice." *Biotechnology and Applied Biochemistry* 42 (2005): 9–15.

Zhu, J.S., G.M. Halpern and K. Jones. "The Scientific Rediscovery of an Ancient Chinese Herbal Medicine: Cordyceps Sinensis Part I." *Journal of Alternative and Complementary Medicine* 4.3 (1998): 289–303.

Chinese Secondary Sources

Duojie Caidan and Jiangcun Luobu. *Xizang jingji jian shi. shang/xia (A Short History of the Economy of Tibet).* Beijing: Zhongguo Xizang chubanshe, 2002.

Guangdong Sheng, ed. *Zhongguo minzu wenhua daguan. Zangzu, Menbazu, Luobazu (The impressive cultures of China's nationalities. Tibetans, Menba, Luoba).* Beijing, 1994.

Yang Enhong. *Min jian shi shen: ge sa er yi ren yan jiu (Popular Divine Poets: A Study on the Ballad Singers of "King Gesar").* Beijing: Chinese Tibetology Publishing House, 1995.

李金梅: 中国马球史研究.甘肃人民出版社, 2002年版。

《<册府元龟>吐蕃史料校正》苏晋仁, 萧銶子 校正.四川人民出版社。

王尧、王启龙: 国外藏学研究译文集 (第十六辑). 西藏人民出版社, 1989年版。

张云: 上古西藏与波斯文明.中国藏学出版社, 2005年版。

催比科夫著, 王献军译《佛教香客在圣地西藏》, 西藏人民出版社, 1993年版。

《一世～四世达赖喇嘛传》(内部资料1), 陈庆英, 马连龙译, 中国藏学研究中心历史所, 2003年版。

Contributors

Diana Altner is a postdoctoral student at the Institute of Asian and African Studies, Humboldt University in Berlin. Her research focuses on infrastructure development and the transformation of everyday life in central Tibet.

Elijah Ary is Lecturer in Politics and Religion at the Ecole Supérieure des Sciences Economiques et Commerciales (ESSEC) in Paris, France, and Lecturer in Buddhism at the Université du Québec à Montréal (UQAM) in Montreal, Canada. His research focuses primarily on the early history of the dDe lugs school, particularly on the early figurations of Tsong kha pa and mKhas grub dGe legs dpal bzang and the use of sacred biography in the school's formation.

Anne-Sophie Bentz is a teaching assistant at the Graduate Institute of International and Development Studies in Geneva. Her research focuses on the politics of the Tibetan diaspora.

Tsering Choekyi completed postgraduate studies in International Relations at the National Chengchi University, Taipei, where her research focused on the role of International NGOs and HR in China. She currently works as an intern at Global Peace Initiative of Women in New York.

Tsering Dawa is a postgraduate student at the College of Tibetan Studies, Nationalities University of China, Beijing. His research focuses on Buddhist rituals and the Bo dong school of Tibetan Buddhism.

Marc-Henri Deroche is a PhD student at the École Pratique des Hautes Études, Paris, currently in a Monbukagakusho scholarship program at the University of Kyôto. His research focuses on the life and works of 'Phreng po gter ston Shes rab 'od zer (1518–1584) in the intellectual history of Indo-Tibetan Buddhism.

BRANDON DOTSON is a British Academy Postdoctoral Fellow at the Oriental Institute, University of Oxford. He is the author of *The Old Tibetan Annals: An Annotated Translation of Tibet's First History* (Vienna: Verlag der Österreichischen Akademie der Wissenchaften, 2009).

SOLOMON GEORGE FITZHERBERT is Departmental Lecturer in Tibetan and Himalayan Studies at the University of Oxford. He is the author of *The Vagrant Child of Tibet*, a study of the early portions of the Tibetan Gesar Epic (forthcoming from Oxford University Press).

KALSANG NORBU GURUNG is a PhD candidate at the University of Leiden. His research focuses on the myth of the founder of Bon, and the formation of Bon religious identity in Tibet at the turn of the first millennium CE.

DOBIS TSERING GYAL works in the Tibet Archives, Lhasa. He received a PhD in Tibetan Cultural Anthropology from Central University for Nationalities, Beijing. His research interests include Tibetan historical archives, the political system of the dGa' ldan pho brang (1642–1959) and Tibetan modern literature.

GEORGIOS T. HALKIAS is a Research Fellow at Ruhr-Universität Bochum. His related work on Tibetan border-lands includes, "Until the Feathers of the Winged Black Raven Turn White: Perspectives and Sources for the Tibet–Bashahr Treaty of 1679–1684." In *Mountains, Monasteries and Mosques*, ed. John Bray (supplement to *Rivista degli Studi Orientali,* forthcoming).

TIM MYATT is a DPhil candidate at the Oriental Institute, University of Oxford. His research focuses on British, Tibetan and Chinese perceptions of the Younghusband Expedition to Tibet of 1903–1904.

KADRI RAUDSEPP is a PhD candidate at Tallinn University, Estonia. Her research focuses on the formation of Buddhist schools, and more specifically on the development of rNying ma — gSar ma divide.

JOONA REPO is a PhD candidate at the School of Oriental and African Studies, University of London. His research focuses on international Tibetan Buddhist art and architecture, specifically the Tibetan Buddhist refugee architecture of South Asia.

Michelle Olsgard Stewart is a PhD student in Geography at the University of Colorado at Boulder. Her research focuses broadly on the politics of natural resource management, with a specific focus on the political ecology of Tibetan harvesting of *yartsa gunbu* (*Cordyceps sinensis*) in NW Yunnan, China.

Emilia Róża Sułek graduated in Social Anthropology and Oriental Studies from the University of Warsaw. She is a doctoral candidate at the Central Asian Seminar, Humboldt University in Berlin.

Alice Travers is a PhD student in modern history at the University of Paris X-Nanterre and INALCO. Her research focuses on the Tibetan aristocracy of the dGa' ldan pho brang from 1895 to 1959.

Chris Vasantkumar is Luce Junior Professor of Asian Studies and Anthropology at Hamilton College. His current research deals with issues of race, nation and indigeneity between China, Tibet and Taiwan.

Beri Jigme Wangyal received his Geshe degree in Buddhist philosophy from Drepung Monastery in India in 2004. He is the author of several books on various subjects ranging from poetry to biography and history.

Index